Colonial Georgia and the Creeks

UNIVERSITY PRESS OF FLORIDA

Florida A&M University, Tallahassee
Florida Atlantic University, Boca Raton
Florida Gulf Coast University, Ft. Myers
Florida International University, Miami
Florida State University, Tallahassee
New College of Florida, Sarasota
University of Central Florida, Orlando
University of Florida, Gainesville
University of North Florida, Jacksonville
University of South Florida, Tampa
University of West Florida, Pensacola

Colonial Georgia and the Creeks

Anglo-Indian Diplomacy on the Southern Frontier, 1733–1763

John T. Juricek

UNIVERSITY PRESS OF FLORIDA
Gainesville / Tallahassee / Tampa / Boca Raton
Pensacola / Orlando / Miami / Jacksonville / Ft. Myers / Sarasota

Printed in the United States of America. This book is printed on Glatfelter Natures Book, a paper certified under the standards of the Forestry Stewardship Council (FSC). It is a recycled stock that contains 30 percent post-consumer waste and is acid-free.

15 14 13 12 11 10 6 5 4 3 2 1

The publication of this book is made possible in part by a grant from Emory College of Arts and Sciences and the Graduate School.

Library of Congress Cataloging-in-Publication Data
Juricek, John T., 1938–
Colonial Georgia and the Creeks : Anglo-Indian diplomacy on the southern frontier, 1733-1763 / John T. Juricek.
p. cm.
Includes bibliographical references and index.
ISBN 978-0-8130-3468-3 (alk. paper)
1. Creek Indians—Georgia—History—18th century. 2. Georgia—History—Colonial period, ca. 1600-1775. 3. Creek Indians—Government relations. I. Title.
E99.C9J87 2010
975.004'97385—dc22 2010004896

The University Press of Florida is the scholarly publishing agency for the State University System of Florida, comprising Florida A&M University, Florida Atlantic University, Florida Gulf Coast University, Florida International University, Florida State University, New College of Florida, University of Central Florida, University of Florida, University of North Florida, University of South Florida, and University of West Florida.

University Press of Florida
15 Northwest 15th Street
Gainesville, FL 32611-2079
http://www.upf.com

In memory of William T. Hutchinson,
inspiring teacher,
distinguished scholar,
exemplary person.

Contents

Maps

Preface

I never expected to do detailed research on colonial Georgia, but about thirty years ago Alden Vaughan of Columbia University asked me to edit several volumes for a new documentary project he was organizing. The general idea was simple and compelling. Although the treaties negotiated between the United States and various Indian nations had long since been published, nothing comparable had been done with the numerous treaties negotiated between English officials and Indian leaders during the colonial era. The series was to be even more ambitious, for it would include related documents, explanatory chapter introductions, and extensive annotation. Entitled *Early American Indian Documents: Treaties and Laws, 1607–1789*, the series was to be published in twenty volumes within five years.

The project proved to be much more difficult than anticipated. It was completed in twenty volumes, but not until twenty-five years had passed. My contribution was two volumes: the first on Georgia, 1733–1763, and the second on Georgia and Florida, 1763–1776. At first I naively expected the story to focus on the Cherokees, for (due to their relative openness to Europeans) sources were relatively abundant and most scholarly works on the Southeastern Indians had been written about them. I soon learned that English diplomacy in early Georgia focused overwhelmingly on the more reticent Creeks. I also found that scholarship on Creeks during the colonial era was surprisingly thin, a situation much amended during the past two decades. Before long it also became apparent that the main issues English and native leaders negotiated about concerned land, a subject I had long been interested in. I found myself making a long-term commitment to tell the story of Anglo-Creek relations during the colonial era. The book before you is the first result.

Along the way I have acquired numerous debts to those who have assisted me. Alden Vaughan provided steady feedback and encouragement, especially during the difficult early stages of research. Many research librarians have helped me locate elusive source materials. I am especially indebted to William L. McDowell Jr., former deputy director of the South Carolina Department of Archives and History; Galen R. Wilson, former manuscript curator at the William L. Clements Library, University of Michigan; Edward Weldon, former director of the Georgia Department of Archives and History; Pat Bryant, former deputy surveyor general of Georgia; J. Larry Gulley, former manuscript librarian, University of Georgia; and Marie M. Nitschke, former reference librarian, Woodruff library at Emory University.

Graduate students I have taught at Emory University—Steve Hahn, Steve Oatis, and the late Doris Fisher—have taught me back in various ways that contributed significantly to this book. Steve Hahn, whose interests are most nearly like my own, has been especially helpful. He has read drafts of every chapter, and his detailed criticism and suggestions have improved each one. Joshua Piker has also read the entire work and has contributed much helpful criticism. Colleagues in the Emory History Department—Thomas Burns, Fraser Harbutt, James Melton, and James Roark—have also read and critiqued various chapters. Errors that remain are mine. Some ideas were developed and refined in a course on "Comparative Frontiers" that I taught jointly with Professor Burns (an authority on Roman frontiers) for many years. Finally, I am indebted to Emory University for various grants from the University Research Fund, the Faculty Travel Fund, and the Completion Grant Fund of Emory College.

Introduction

This book deals with interaction between the English of colonial Georgia and the surrounding Indian nations—most especially the Creeks—from the founding of the colony in 1733 until 1763, the year French and Spanish rivals withdrew from the region. The main focus of the study is Anglo-Creek diplomacy. Attention centers on the more or less continual negotiations between leaders of the two peoples, contacts prompted by their mutual interest in peace—and their more or less continual differences over other matters. The most intractable of these issues concerned how to deal with the French and Spanish, trade and trade abuses, and ownership of territory. As far as the English were concerned, the land question overshadowed all others, and the Creeks would soon agree. Differences over land would lead to dramatic confrontations, disputed agreements, duplicity by both parties, occasional crises, and chronic frustration on both sides. Toward the end of the period, however, the English began to have their way.[1]

The Georgia colonists were overwhelmingly concerned with the Native Americans they called the Creeks. Leaders of the colony paid particular attention to the nearest of these Indians, the "Lower" Creeks. There were two very good reasons for this. First, in 1733 the Lower Creek Indians claimed as their own nearly all of the territory that now constitutes the state of Georgia. Somewhat surprisingly, English officials never disputed these Creek claims, though they were mostly of recent origin and nearly all Creeks lived beyond the Chattahoochee River outside of Georgia. Second, with ample cause the Creeks were feared by all of their neighbors, native or European. The Creeks posed the main potential military threat to nearly all of them, most especially the settlers of colonial Georgia.

In 1760 Governor Henry Ellis ruefully observed that Georgia was not only the weakest of the English colonies, it was "opposed to the most powerful Indian Neighbours of any Province upon this Continent." A few years later, trader-historian James Adair described the Creeks as "certainly the most powerful Indian nation we are acquainted with on this continent." Noting that all other native nations seemed to be "visibly and fast declining," Adair marveled that the Creeks had "increased double in number within the space of thirty years past." Their progress against the demographic tide, he explained, was largely due to "their artful policy of inviting decayed tribes to incorporate with them."[2]

When the first English settlers arrived, the only native people whose settlements were mainly confined to the Georgia area were the Yuchis, who lived on the upper reaches of the Savannah River. Georgia leaders would have little contact with them, for the Yuchis soon became one of the supposedly "decayed tribes" that incorporated with the Creeks. There they maintained their separate identity and flourished, but had little voice in Creek decision making. If the Creeks were far away, the other Indian nations Georgia sometimes had diplomatic dealings with—the Cherokees, Choctaws, and Chickasaws—were remote. There were a few early efforts to establish regular contacts with the Cherokees, then located mainly in the mountain valleys of what is now northwestern South Carolina, southwestern North Carolina, and southeastern Tennessee. These tentative probes came to little, for South Carolina was determined to maintain exclusive control over relations with the Cherokees. Few Georgians cared, for they found trading opportunities with the Creeks much more enticing. Thirty years passed before Georgia would have its first significant dealings with the Cherokees. The Choctaws and Chickasaws were still more remote, in what is now Mississippi and westernmost Tennessee. Diplomatic contacts with both were sparse, though always friendly with the Chickasaws, who were also regular trading partners.

Georgia was the last of the English colonies to be established, and its settlers entered a diplomatic environment that already had a long history and well-established patterns of behavior. South Carolina, founded in 1670, had long since established a far-flung network of relationships with surrounding native societies. There may have been much naïveté in early Georgia, but very little of it concerned Indian relations. Founder James Edward Oglethorpe and the first Georgia colonists promptly adopted attitudes and practices toward the natives developed earlier by the South Carolinians.

For their part, the Southeastern Indians Oglethorpe met were well practiced at dealing not only with Englishmen but with other Europeans as well. The Spaniards had been ensconced at St. Augustine since the 1560s, while the French had been colonizing the Gulf Coast and the lower Mississippi since 1698. It was axiomatic that these imperial rivals would do what they could to thwart British expansion; they could not fail to react against the lunge in their direction that began with the founding of Georgia. The Spaniards would claim the territory of Georgia as their own and incite their remaining native allies, principally the Yamasees, against settlers of the colony. The French would follow suit with their Indian friends, especially the Choctaws and Alabamas. Moreover, the family alliance of Spain and France under the House of Bourbon guaranteed that the two powers would cooperate to some degree in their anti-British efforts.[3]

When Oglethorpe and the first Georgia colonists arrived early in 1733, the area we think of as Georgia was nearly uninhabited. The depopulation of this vast area had begun in the previous century with attacks by natives outside the Spanish orbit, and revolts by others within it. The downward trend continued after 1680 as Carolinians incited their allied Indians into slave-catching wars and raids against Spanish-allied Indians of Apalachee and elsewhere. Then came the Yamasee War of 1715–17, the most momentous conflict ever fought between the English and Southeastern Indians. One result was a general exodus of native peoples from lands around and below the Savannah River.[4]

In 1733 there were probably fewer than ten thousand Creeks, the vast majority of them living in what is now Alabama. These Indians were distributed into about thirty-five autonomous towns, the larger of which had satellite villages. By 1712 Carolinians had begun to distinguish between "Lower Creeks" and "Upper Creeks." This simple geographical distinction soon suggested another with more potent implications: the "Lower Creek Nation" and the "Upper Creek Nation." Carolinians could use such terms because they realized that more than geography separated these two entities. The various town chiefs of these two Creek "nations" met often in separate joint councils but rarely in a conclave that brought together leaders of both divisions. This was still true in 1756, when Carolina Indian agent Daniel Pepper noted that "there is such a great Distance between the Upper and Lower Creek Nations they never come to one another's Talks, but on very extraordinary Occasions."[5]

There were eight Lower Creek towns in 1733. These settlements were strung out along a fifty-mile stretch of the Chattahoochee River. Reflecting the dualistic thinking characteristic of the region, these towns were divided into a moiety system: some were "peace" ("white") towns, others "war" ("red") towns. The northernmost of these towns, Coweta and Cussita, were the most influential. Both were war towns, and apparently relatively recent arrivals from Upper Creek country. Like their Upper Creek cousins, the people of Coweta and Cussita spoke the Muskogean language. The other Lower Creek towns, earlier residents of the Chattahoochee valley, spoke the related Hitchiti language. The most influential of these towns were Apalachicola, a peace town, and Chehaw, a war town.[6]

Cussita was located just below the falls on the eastern bank of the river, roughly at modern Columbus. Coweta was nearby on the other side of the river, while most of the other towns were further downstream on the western side. Down to about 1756 Lower Creek chiefs generally met at Coweta. Afterward, however, they usually gathered at Chehaw or Apalachicola instead.

Although the native communities the English called the Upper Creeks were originally offshoots from Coweta and Cussita, they had grown to include nearly two-thirds of the Creek population. These people were located along the Tallapoosa and Coosa rivers, which join to form the Alabama River. The Upper Creeks divided their towns into two groups, presumably because their wide dispersion usually led two town clusters to hold separate council meetings. The Tallapoosa division, which the English sometimes called the "Middle Creeks," consisted of about eight towns laid out along the great western bend of the Tallapoosa River. The most influential of the Tallapoosa towns were Tuckabatchee, a war town, and Tallassee, a peace town. The dozen or so towns constituting the Abeika division were located farther north on the Tallapoosa and Coosa rivers. The most influential Abeika towns were Okfuskee and Oakchoy. Both were later reckoned peace towns, but their moiety affiliations during the colonial era are uncertain. In addition, the Alabama-Coushattas, distant relations of the Creeks (and Choctaws), lived in four towns near the junction of the Tallapoosa and Coosa rivers. So long as the French remained in the region, they would stand apart as French allies; afterward they were viewed as Upper Creeks.[7]

Today these three aggregations of "Upper Creek" towns might best be described as confederacies. Eighteenth-century Englishmen were unsure what to call them. Most often they simply followed native usage and referred to them in the plural ("the Tallapoosas," "the Abeika towns," etc.). In 1755 Edmond Atkin, soon to become Indian superintendent for the southern colonies, suggested a collective noun. The "Upper [Creek] Nation," he wrote, was composed of "three Tribes," the Tallapoosas, the Abeikas, and the Alabamas. Atkin's use of "tribe" never caught on, but he had not been careless with words. In contemporary usage, a "tribe" was not an autonomous entity but rather a subdivision—any subdivision—of a "nation." When describing the ancient world, eighteenth-century Englishmen said the "Nation of Israel" was composed of twelve tribes, while the Roman nation consisted of three (Latins, Sabines, and Etruscans). During this period the term "tribe" was seldom applied to the natives, but when it was, usually it was as a synonym for an Indian "town" or "clan." On the other hand, "nation" was a general term denoting an extended ethnic and/or political community. Its ordinary synonym was "people" (not nation-state). To minimize confusion, the account that follows will refer often to Indian nations and towns, sometimes to Indian confederacies or clans, but never to Indian tribes.[8]

The principal chief of the Lower Creeks during the early decades of the eighteenth century was a Coweta leader the English knew as Brim. He may have been the *mico* (town chief) of Coweta, but Brim was clearly the preeminent leader of the Lower Creek confederacy (more accurately described as a confederation of confederacies). In 1711 the South Carolina government recognized him as the Creek "Emperor," which the Spanish governor of Florida echoed soon afterward. Brim may have been the mastermind behind native alliances during the Yamasee War; he certainly was the main architect of the strategy for dealing with the three imperial powers that the Creeks would follow for nearly a half century afterward. The war had revealed that, despite Creek acknowledgments of Spanish overlordship, the Spaniards could not be relied upon to support the Creeks in a crisis. It had also shown that without such support it would be nearly impossible to dislodge the English.[9]

Brim concluded that the Creeks should never again commit themselves for or against any of the imperial powers, much less wage war against any of them. Creek interests could best be served by maintaining correct but not close relations with all of them. The Spanish, French, and English would then find it necessary to compete for Creek favor, a reversal that would enable the Creeks to exploit the Europeans. Meeting in Coweta, a council of Lower Creek chiefs headed by Brim endorsed this policy on March 23, 1718. Steven Hahn calls their decision, which proved to be extraordinarily influential in Creek country, "The Coweta Resolution."[10]

All participants in the Yamasee War learned the same lesson: they didn't wish to repeat it. They learned it so well that nearly all of them managed to avoid large-scale warfare with any of the others during the remainder of the colonial era. (The only major exception involved the Cherokees and the English, allies during the Yamasee War, who fought a bitter war in 1760–61.) If the founding of Georgia shielded South Carolina from hostile forces from Florida and the Gulf Coast, Carolinians could easily satisfy themselves that they had earned the favor: their Indian war had spared the Georgians from having one. Conflicts between the English colonists and the native nations did not disappear, but henceforth they usually took the form of diplomatic confrontations. These nonviolent clashes usually led to an oral exchange of complaints and promises.

Occasionally, however, the result was a formal treaty—written, signed, and sealed. The South Carolina government signed at least three such treaties with the Creeks prior to 1733. Leaders of colonial Georgia would sign six treaties with the Creeks (the 1763 treaty also included the other major Indian nations of the Southeast). While the Spanish and French also made oral agreements with southeastern native chiefs, only the English negotiated formal treaties with them during this era.[11]

Different in so many ways, the British and Indians of the Southeast (and elsewhere) were bound to have a somewhat different approach to diplomacy. For Europeans, diplomacy was conceived as an ongoing conversation, a private dialogue between kings or other sovereign authorities about weighty matters of common concern. Such interchange often led to confidential understandings or deals, but occasionally it produced written treaties, with versions in two languages if the parties spoke different ones. While most diplomatic exchange remained private, even secret, formal treaties were more or less public and often published. An agreement frozen in the treaty texts was supposed to last indefinitely, at least until superseded by another or formally repudiated. Thus the 1386 Treaty of Windsor between the kings of England and Portugal supposedly remains in effect today, making it Europe's oldest alliance.[12]

Kings or other sovereigns rarely met each other face-to-face. Normally they delegated the daily business of diplomacy to foreign secretaries, ambassadors, or other specialists (and occasionally even to relatives, friends, or servants). While these patient functionaries from time to time achieved agreements for their masters, most often they were occupied with disagreements, trying to prevent them from becoming something worse. Complex problems often led to multilateral negotiations among parties with dissimilar views and interests.

Negotiation with multiple parties necessarily sometimes meant negotiating with enemies or potential enemies. Thus ordinary diplomatic exchange regularly led to uncomfortable confrontations and heated words, including threats, delivered in private. If blunt and passionate language was obviously potentially dangerous, ordinarily it was considered too useful to forego. Such pointed discourse enabled participants to vent resentments in a relatively safe context, one that allowed both sides to identify their rival's bedrock positions and sensitivities—the better to take advantage of them. Then too, since the actual spokesmen were subordinates, should their performance prove to be too provocative, their sovereigns could always disown them and their "unauthorized" words.

Southeastern Indians understood diplomacy differently. If Europeans saw diplomacy as an indirect linkage between "crowns" or other abstract entities, natives of the region saw it as a direct connection between communities. For them, diplomacy was normally public and positive, and usually involved face-to-face negotiation between top leaders. It often included exchange of symbolic gifts, notably "white wings of peace" (staffs with eagle feathers attached) and wampum belts. For Indians, war and peace were entirely separate, with separate leadership structures and separate codes of behavior. To undertake diplomacy was to engage peace leaders in strictly peaceful activities designed to further the consensus previously reached by the community. Thus when Governor Ellis in 1757 welcomed the leaders of twenty-one Upper and Lower Creek towns for an important treaty conference, he asked whether they were "Authorized" to speak for their people. "To which they answered with one Voice 'We are the Mouth of the Nation.'"[13]

No matter how flawlessly Indian negotiators were authorized, or how carefully they followed their mandate, they were never given final authority to make commitments. Any major agreement they negotiated had to be ratified by the community they represented, failing which there was no agreement. Early in 1756 a high-ranking Upper Creek delegation led by the nation's leading chief, the Gun Merchant, negotiated and signed a treaty with the English in Charles Town. When he took the agreement home for ratification his people refused, thereby reducing the treaty text to worthless paper.[14]

Native peace leaders normally confined negotiation to friends; war leaders would deal with enemies in their own special way. In native cultures, heated words were always proscribed as provocative and dangerous, the kind only "mad young people" or men on the warpath would use. When Indian leaders spoke at diplomatic meetings, their words and manner were seldom angry or threatening; instead, both were almost invariably measured, dignified, and outwardly friendly. Europeans were alternately struck with guilty admiration for the natives' "natural" nobility or dark suspicion of their "savage" duplicity. As the colonial era advanced, English officials increasingly found themselves negotiating with native war leaders, a worrisome trend.

As envisioned by Southeastern Indians, societies at peace with one another were connected by "paths." These linear bonds were both physical and metaphorical. When Choctaws made their first appearance in Savannah in 1734, their leader declared that "we desire a trade very much that a Path may be kept betwixt you and us." Decades would pass before the Choctaws got what they wanted. A "path" was a track beaten into the soil by innumerable human feet and animal hooves, the durable record of a two-way flow of people, animals, and goods between English and Indian towns. At the time of Georgia's founding there was one arterial path leading to Creek country and another leading to Cherokee country. The two paths coincided from Charles Town to Fort Moore on the Savannah River. There they diverged, with the Creek path continuing southwest toward Coweta and Cussita on the Chattahoochee River, while the Cherokee path turned northwest toward Keowee at the headwaters of the Savannah River. From these primary destinations the two paths continued onward and outward into numerous branches.[15]

In 1771 Upper Creek spokesman Emistisiguo described the Creek path as "the Old white Path, which comes from Charlestown to the Cowetas, from thence to the Tuckabatchies, from thence to the Abekas and from thence to the Chickesaws." In other words, the path extended westward from the English settlements around Charles Town through three divisions of the Creek Nation, terminating only when it reached the remote Chickasaws on the Mississippi River. It was a "white" path because it was a route of peaceful commerce and communication. Moreover, the various societies tied together along this route were parts of a larger entity: the "Path" was a network of friends, a kind of alliance.[16]

One of the rare surviving copies of a map made by American aborigines, a Chickasaw map of 1723, provides a graphic illustration of this widespread native conceptualization. The map features five large circles, each representing a nation or major community. Three of these are aligned along the horizontal axis: from right to left they are labeled "English," "Creeks," and "Chickasaw Nation." A straight east-west line, labeled "Creek and English Path," connects the three, implying a trade and diplomatic linkage. The other two large circles, identified as "Charikee" and "Choctau Nation," likewise appear on either side (northeast and southwest, respectively) of the Creeks. Tellingly, no line links either the Cherokees or the Choctaws with the Creeks, or with each other. These voids indicated a lack of friendly relations, accurately representing the actual situation among these three peoples. Elsewhere on this and other native maps, lines suggesting linkage are begun but left incomplete, "signifying a 'broken' path traveled only by war parties and distinguished from the continuous roads of peace."[17]

Another feature of this and other Indian maps is equally striking: none of the circles touches any of the others, or comes close to doing so. Each is clearly separated from all of the others. This implies that Southeastern Indians did not originally conceive of the territory of their society as extending far enough so as to meet the territory of another native group. Instead, these native maps indicate that between any two Indian societies there was a broad interstitial zone that belonged to neither: a buffer zone or no-man's-land. Even the zone between friendly societies linked by a path was represented in this way, suggesting that this "white" path was the only safe route of interaction. The intermediate space between unfriendly societies lacking a connecting path was definitely a danger zone, often a war zone. That was true of the area between the Creeks and the Cherokees to their northeast, and likewise of the territory between the Creeks and the Choctaws to their southwest.

The aboriginal understanding of the latter zone was made clear to Superintendent Edmond Atkin at a meeting with Upper Creek leaders in 1759. Hoping to arrange safe passage for English traders through Creek territory to that of the Choctaws, Atkin posed a question: "What River divides the Creek and Chactaw Country." One of the Upper Creek spokesmen replied: "There is no such thing as a Division." Atkin then asked: "Is there no place between these Towns and the Chactaw Towns, where the Trade may be carried on in safety." Another Upper Creek spokesman promptly answered: "I think not."[18]

When thinking about metaphorical paths, imaginative Indian spokesmen did not always confine themselves to North America. Thus in 1763 the Cherokee leader Oconostota mused that "there have been some of our People over the great Water to King George and have made a clear Path all the Way." Oconostota was not envisioning a latter-day Moses parting the Atlantic; he was offhandedly using a metaphor of linkage that was a staple of native diplomatic rhetoric. When the English leaders of the southern colonies wished to evoke a comparable linear image of their friendship with an Indian people, they often spoke of the "Chain of Friendship" that bound them together. This, as we shall see, was an English adaptation of ideas floated by northern Indians, and first introduced into the Southeast in 1730.[19]

When the southern Indian superintendent, John Stuart, invoked this metallic metaphor at the 1765 Pensacola Congress, Upper Creek spokesman Emistisiguo sought to substitute an organic image familiar to his people:

> I observe that amongst the white people Friendship is Compared to a Chain which links people together. In our Nation friendship is Compared to a Grape Vine, which though Slender and Weak when Young, Grows Stronger as it grows Older.
>
> So it is to be hoped the friendship and Harmony already Commenced between the Great King's White and Red Children, will daily increase and that as they grow up their hearts like the Tendrils of the Vine may be by time more Strongly United and Knit together.

Emistisiguo evidently savored the contrast between the static English view of alliance and the developmental model of the Creeks, the real progressives in the art of diplomacy. He would proudly recall his "vine" speech again and again at later meetings with British leaders.[20]

The Indians' bilateral approach to diplomacy was also graphically represented in their wampum belts. Such belts typically represent a linear connection between two communities, which are often depicted at opposite ends of the belt. A good illustration appears in the first formal meeting between leaders of the Upper Creeks and the government of West Florida in 1765. The Mortar of Oakchoy, declaring that "I am the Voice of my People," presented a "Belt of Whampum" to Governor George Johnstone. Before delivering it, however, he wanted all to understand the meaning of the belt: "one end whereof he desired the Governor to hold and held the other himself as a mark of Unanimity and Friendship." Similarly, five years later a peace belt represented a "Clear" and "Broad Path" between the Choctaws and Upper Creeks, "and for this Strap to Resemble it."[21]

But perhaps the most striking difference between the British and native approaches to diplomacy had to do with time. For Europeans a deal was a deal, in effect until formally repudiated or superseded. Not so for the Indians. Again and again native leaders insisted that the paths which linked them to the English be kept "white" (safe, peaceful), "straight" (direct, honest), and "clear of thorns and

Weeds" (smooth, unobstructed). It was perfectly evident to Indians that chains rusted, vines died, and weeds took root on pathways. Things could be timeless in the world of abstractions, but in the real world everything changed. It was true that a deal was a deal—but only so long as it was properly maintained and regularly renewed. Thus when Governor Ellis in 1757 reminded Creeks of previous treaties, their spokesman replied: "We are Sensible that these treaties are binding. . . . Yet it would be well that they were renewed and confirmed." Ellis, like Oglethorpe before him, readily conceded the point. The first article of the treaty signed later that day provided that "all the former Treaties . . . are hereby ratified and confirmed." Renewal of existing treaties became a routine feature of major meetings, including many that did not lead to new treaties.[22]

As British colonial officials and Southeastern Indian leaders gained experience in negotiating with each other, they learned much about the diplomatic conventions favored by their opposite numbers. Both sides adjusted their own negotiating styles accordingly. Colonial officials learned that decorous public speeches were expected of them; native leaders learned that uninhibited private parleys were often required of them, and became less restrained with their language. Colonial leaders learned to tolerate long-winded speeches without interruption; Indian spokesmen learned to shorten their speeches. Colonial officials learned that normally they had to negotiate with one Indian society at a time; native leaders learned that, nevertheless, sometimes they would be summoned to multilateral meetings. Colonists learned to respect popular ratification of agreements among Indian societies; Indians learned that colonial officials represented a remote king, not a local populace. British officials learned that appropriate gifts were essential not only to seal a new agreement but to maintain the old ones; Indian leaders learned that an agreement the British considered binding had to be committed to writing, with signatures from both parties. Each side borrowed terms, images, and practices from the other, but adapted them to its own purposes. In short, the diplomacy that evolved in the colonial Southeast was a composite diplomacy rooted in both British and native Indian traditions, but significantly different from both. If there was a "middle ground" here, there was also a middle-ground diplomacy.[23]

The most important diplomatic issues between the English and the Creeks in colonial Georgia concerned land. Nevertheless, the two sides differed profoundly over what they thought they were negotiating about. Creek chiefs thought their differences with Georgia leaders involved land ownership; Georgia leaders thought the overriding issue was territorial sovereignty. Historians of colonial Georgia and the Creeks have seldom taken account of this fundamental distinction. Largely for that reason, previous accounts of Anglo-Creek negotiations and transactions over land have never been adequately analyzed and explained.

There is another historiographic tradition that does focus on the land issues that surfaced in colonial Georgia, though it has little to say directly about Georgia or the Creeks. This separate stream of scholarship consists of legal histories concerned with English colonial dealings over land with North American Indians in general. There are significant older works written by American historians, but for the past three decades most leading scholars have been Canadian. This burst of scholarly activity is largely a welcome consequence of the long struggle between the Canadian government and the Inuits that finally led to the establishment of the Territory of Nunavut (Inuit for "Our Land") in 1999. Insights from this scholarly tradition enable the story of colonial Georgia's interaction with the Creek Indians to be told much more fully.[24]

Once the issue of sovereignty is squarely confronted, the gulf between English and Indian perceptions of land issues becomes plain, and their bitter disputes become more understandable. For the English, ultimate ownership of land belonged exclusively to their "sovereign" king, while for the Indians it resided in their entire people. For the English, a cession of territory normally meant a bargain between two sovereigns that definitively transferred territorial sovereignty from one to the other, as well as the right to rule the inhabitants of the ceded land. As adapted in North America, a land cession was an agreement whereby an Indian chief or chiefs, acting in behalf of an Indian nation (though neither the chiefs nor the nations were recognized as sovereign), permanently relinquished territory (but not the natives' right to self rule) to the king of Great Britain. For the Indians, a grant of territory was simply a gift from one people to another.

Conventions of English property law were also at odds with those of the natives. Under English law, a domestic "conveyance" of landed property required a formal written instrument that specified not only the land conveyed but also the "valuable consideration" (usually monetary) given in return. Most Anglo-Creek land transactions in colonial Georgia did not follow this pattern. In 1825 the first state historian of Georgia, Joseph V. Bevan, noted that the 1773 treaty with the Creeks "is remarkable for having been the first that mentions the fact of any monied consideration being given for their lands." The form that earlier land cessions took was clearly influenced by the Creek predisposition to view them in the context of gift giving—more precisely, reciprocal gift giving. It was not that the Creeks expected nothing in return for their gifts of land; they expected a great deal, but not all at once, and not necessarily in a form that the English would have called valuable consideration. A land cession was an act of friendship, one gift among many between two allied peoples, not an isolated act of commercial exchange.[25]

In most respects, early land transactions involving Georgia followed native rather than English conventions. The main task confronting Oglethorpe was gaining Creek consent for a secure English foothold on land that was, until then, Creek land. He was successful beyond all expectations. In several stages he (as agent for the Georgia Trustees and King George II) obtained a cession of a large tract between the Savannah and Ogeechee rivers "as high as the tide flowed." This was followed by grants of lands within the tidal line as far south as the St. Johns River, along with most of the coastal islands. Although Oglethorpe would negotiate treaties with Creek chiefs in 1733 and 1739, he did not gain the initial cessions by treaty. Instead, each grant began as a gift from Tomochichi, the local Creek leader, acting provisionally for the Lower Creek chiefs. No paper was signed, no "valuable consideration" was agreed upon; it was the kind of thing one good neighbor might do for another. These grants were soon consolidated and confirmed by the Lower Creek leadership. When a large delegation of leading chiefs came to Savannah in May 1733, they orally confirmed Tomochichi's grants of lands between the Savannah and Ogeechee. In July 1736 a similar delegation of chiefs confirmed Tomochichi's later grants. All of these territorial concessions were bundled together and formally ratified in the 1739 treaty, again without a declared quid pro quo.[26]

Oglethorpe's initial success was due in part to his diplomatic skills, but as much or more to Creek determination to make the English welcome. The Creeks' main objective at first was to secure their trade, not their land. Gaining a better source of English goods was initially more important to them than maintaining all of their territory. The Creeks reversed these priorities in 1746, the direct result of two negotiating blunders Oglethorpe made during his final stay in Georgia. Convinced that Oglethorpe had double-crossed them, they resolved that the land grants they had already made would be their last.

Oglethorpe's apparent duplicity poisoned Anglo-Creek relations for more than a decade, and his successors had to cope with his mistakes. The most serious of them proved to be his apparent approval of a Creek grant of territory, not to the Georgia Trustees or King George, but to an individual. The recipient was a half-English, half-Creek woman then known as Mary Matthews. If the Creek land grant to Mary was a grant to an English subject, it was impossible to reconcile with English law. Since Georgia leaders considered it as such, they had to prevent it from taking effect. This included Oglethorpe himself, who soon realized his blunder and did what he could to quash the grant.

Once exposed in 1746, Oglethorpe's apparent double-dealing infuriated the Creek leadership. Since the Lower Creeks were rightful owners of the lands in question, their chiefs assumed that they could grant any such lands to anyone they wished. Most certainly they could grant lands as they saw fit to any of their own people, and Mary (now Mary Bosomworth) was one of them. Thus it appeared to the Creeks that Oglethorpe had not only denied their right to transfer their lands as they chose but had also denied their rights of ownership. To defend those rights, Lower Creek leaders now insisted upon the legitimacy of the original grant to Mary. Georgia leaders were equally insistent that it was void. The result, often called "the Bosomworth controversy," was mutual hostility and diplomatic impasse.

This bitter stalemate was all the more difficult to deal with because much of it took place in the context of three imperial wars. The first began in 1739 between England and Spain, but soon merged into a larger war with France (1744–48). During the "French and Indian War" (1754–63), France again was England's principal enemy, Spain making a late entry as junior partner to France. The English could not afford to alienate the formidable Creeks into the arms of their imperial rivals. For their part, while the Creeks were ready to use the threat of joining forces with the French and/or Spanish, they were extremely reluctant to actually do so. Careful neutrality among the European powers had allowed the Creeks to maintain a regional balance of power and prosper for generations. This proven formula for dealing with the Europeans could not be abandoned lightly.

In the midst of the last, greatest, and most decisive of these wars, the diplomatic impasse between the English and Creeks was finally broken. This was surprising in that it occurred well before British arms had prevailed over the French and Spanish. Georgia's second royal governor, Henry Ellis, managed very patiently to put together a complicated compromise that satisfied all parties—not only the English and the Creeks but the Bosomworths as well. Oglethorpe's costly mistakes were at last repaired. The key event was the 1757 treaty Ellis negotiated with the Creek leadership in Savannah.

Two years later, the first British superintendent for Indian affairs in the southern colonies, Edmond Atkin, undertook a diplomatic mission to Creek country in an effort to build upon Governor Ellis's success. Instead, Atkin's clumsy campaign threatened to nullify it, and he barely escaped assassination by a Creek leader. In 1760 encroachments on Cherokee lands led to war between South Carolinians and Cherokees, encouraged and supported by the French. Cherokee agents, exploiting Creek anger focused on Atkin and encroachments by Georgians, persistently tried to draw the Creeks into the conflict on their side. They very nearly succeeded, but news of the British triumph in Canada persuaded the Creeks to maintain their neutrality.

For all participants, the French and Indian War marked the end of an era. Recent historians have made it clear that many of the most significant changes occurred on the Indian side of the frontier. Steven Hahn argues persuasively that as the Creeks became ever more concerned with defending their lands, they could no longer see themselves in the same way. By the French and Indian War they came "to define themselves more abstractly as a territory rather than as a people united in kinship." The Creek Nation had become "a territorially circumscribed legal entity." Never again would the Creeks give land as gifts.[27]

Defeated, in 1763 France and Spain surrendered their territories in eastern North America to Great Britain. Unlike the Cherokees and other native nations that had supported the losers, the Creeks were not forced to share the immediate costs of their defeat. That was small comfort to them, for now they had to face the British alone. The days when Creek chiefs could parley with British leaders on terms approaching equality were about to end.

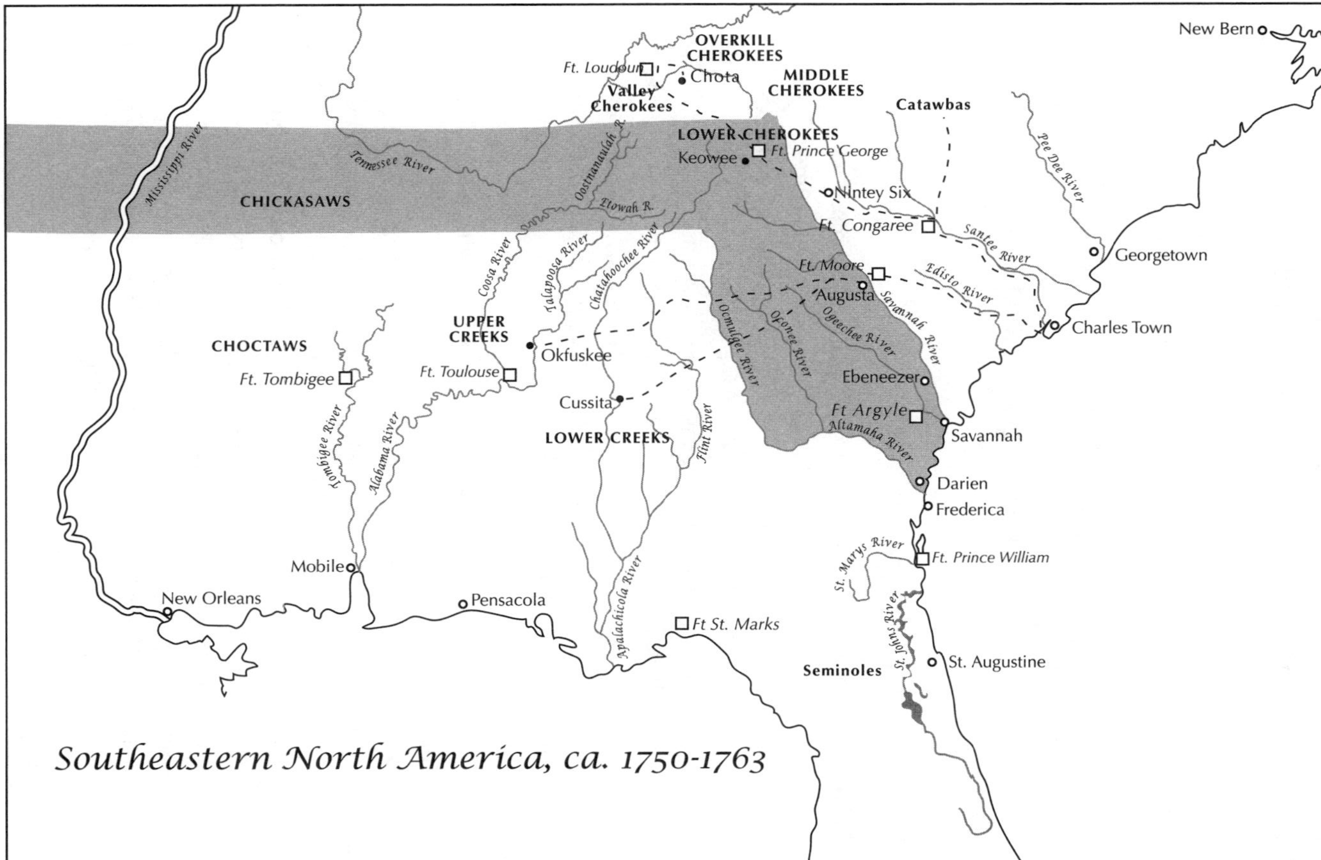

Map 1. Southeastern North America, ca. 1750–1763. Sources: Larry E. Ivers, *British Drums on the Southern Frontier*, 210; Tom Hatley, *The Dividing Paths*, fig. 5; and John H. Goff, "The Path to Oakfuskee," following p. 4. The shaded area depicts Georgia's official boundaries according to the 1732 royal charter. The dashes represent major trading paths. Drawn by Wendy Giminski, Research Media, University of Georgia.

CHAPTER ONE

Carolina Prologue

Unlike settlers in most of the earlier English colonies, those who came to Georgia never had to deal with isolation from other Englishmen. Prosperous South Carolina was just across the Savannah River, which Carolinians had long used as a commercial highway. Upriver at the falls stood Fort Moore, gateway to Indian country and depot for the ever-expanding trade with the Creeks and Chickasaws. Relieved to have the new colony established between themselves and recent foes, Carolinians at first freely gave material assistance and advice to Oglethorpe and the early Georgia colonists. Much of the advice concerned how to deal with the natives of the region. Carolinians had sixty years of experience with that subject.

The English presence in the Southeast began in 1670 with the founding of South Carolina. In less than a decade the Carolinians established a flourishing trade with the surrounding Indians. It was essentially an exchange of European manufactured goods—mainly textiles, metalware, and, not least, munitions—for American peltry, mostly deerskins. The natives were deeply impressed with the utility, availability, and relatively low price of the English goods. The lure of the trade goods spread far and wide, and very quickly, inducing many Indians to move closer to the source. During the 1680s the Yamasees, related by their Hitchiti language to some of the Lower Creeks, deserted what was left of the Spanish province of Guale and moved north to the lower Savannah River. By 1685 they crossed the river to settle the "Indian Land" in the Port Royal area. About that time many of the Lower Creeks were on the move eastward from the Chattahoochee River to the Ocmulgee River, where they reestablished their towns. Some of the Creek migrants, notably the Apalachicolas, continued northeastward to the Ogeechee and Savannah rivers.[1]

Following what the colonists called Queen Anne's War (1702–13), Carolinians became embroiled in trade disputes with the Yamasees and Lower Creeks. The result was the Yamasee War, by far the most dangerous war Englishmen would ever fight with Indians of the region. With crucial help from the Cherokees, the Carolinians evaded possible extirpation at the hands of the Yamasees and Lower Creeks. The main conflict lasted from 1715 to 1717, formally concluding with a treaty between the Carolinians and the Lower Creeks. As Steven Oatis has shown, however, that was only the first phase of a long conflict. Sporadic fighting with the Yamasees continued until 1728. The decimated Yamasees were forced to retreat to northern Florida and Spanish protection. The Lower Creeks likewise withdrew to their old homes on the Chattahoochee, where they would remain for more than a century.[2]

The 1717 treaty was the first and most important of three treaties the South Carolina government signed with the Creeks prior to the founding of Georgia (the others came in 1721 and 1732). Only the text of the 1732 treaty survives. Although the text of the 1717 treaty is not extant, its basic provisions are well established by subsequent commentary: peace, renewed and better-controlled trade at fixed prices, and a boundary between English and Creek territories at the Savannah River. The Earl of Egmont, one of the best-informed Georgia Trustees, summarized the boundary provision of the treaty as follows: "all the lands southward of the Savannah river were agreed to be the Indians' property." This was an extraordinary concession on the part of the Carolinians, reflecting their desperation that year to make peace with the Creeks.[3]

Treaties between the English and Indians that involved land usually saw the latter departing the negotiating session with less land than they came with. The 1717 treaty appears to be a rare example of a treaty that sent Indians home with more land, or at least more extensive land claims, than they had come with. The Creek chiefs agreed to what must have struck them as a novel but advantageous arrangement. While Creeks would continue to see no-man's-lands between their territory and those of native neighbors, henceforth there would be no vacant spaces between Creek lands and those of the English. South of the Savannah River (and, presumably, north of Spanish Florida), the land belonged entirely to the Creeks. The 1717 treaty established the first of a series of negotiated boundary lines between the English and Southeastern Indians, few of which would remain in place for more than a decade.

James Oglethorpe took the South Carolina treaties as the starting point for his dealings with the Creeks and other Indians. Past understandings, however, were of little help for the urgent task at hand. In fact, the Savannah River boundary was a major obstacle. Since Oglethorpe was on a mission to establish a new English colony on Creek land, his first priority had to be gaining Creek consent for this intrusion. He needed a major Creek concession, and very soon. New to the scene, he needed help. He needed people who could help him persuade Creek leaders to accept and cooperate with the Georgia colony. Competent interpreters were one kind of assistant he required, but not the only one. He also needed people whom both English and Creek leaders were comfortable dealing with. He needed diplomatic intermediaries. Very few Carolinians who relocated to Georgia could play such a role. Most of those who could had blood relatives in Creek country as well as South Carolina. A half dozen or so of these mixed-race individuals, three in particular, would provide vital assistance to Oglethorpe.

By the time Georgia was founded, three generations had been born in South Carolina and adjacent Indian lands. At the start of 1733 the regional population included many thousands of native Indians, perhaps thirteen thousand Englishmen and other Europeans in South Carolina, and an even larger number of Africans. It also included at least a thousand persons who did not fit these categories, for they were of mixed parentage. Their numbers were growing rapidly, as were the kinds and complexity of mixtures. By 1733 many individuals had progenitors from all three "races," in ever more complex combinations. Carolinians had a difficult time finding terms that would stick to the slippery reality they saw around them.[4]

Oglethorpe was most interested in one segment of this racial spectrum: people with one English and one Indian parent. Such individuals could claim to be equally sympathetic to both sides and thus ideal mediators. Even this relatively small and simple slice of the mixed population proved difficult to distinguish from others, for observers often had nothing but physical appearance to go on. Since Carolinians dealt with more Euroindians than other English colonists did, they had greater need for terminology to describe these people. Somewhat surprisingly, they never settled upon a term they would assign to the offspring of European and Indian parents, and no one else. Instead, Carolinians called whitered hybrids by a variety of more elastic names, including "mustee," "mestizo," "mulatto," "half Indian," "half blood," and "half-breed." The terms "mestizo" and "mulatto" were borrowed directly from Spanish. In Spanish America the former usually applied to offspring of European and Indian unions, while the latter more often referred to white-black offspring, but both terms could be used for either kind of mixed progeny. The English of early South Carolina generally followed this Spanish usage. "Mulatto" was everywhere the most inclusive term, and the only one was regularly used for any mixture.[5]

In early South Carolina the terms most often used for persons of mixed European and Indian parentage were "mustee" and "half-breed," and both terms were more common there than anywhere else in Anglo-America. The former, which appeared by 1696, was an English contraction of "mestizo." Mustees were often said to be of "yellowish" hue. The term "half-breed," in use by 1719, appears to have been of local coinage. "Half-breed" seems to have predominated in everyday usage, but it rarely or never appears in the formal language of legislation. There we find either "mustee" or "mestizo," the latter (often spelled "mustizo") becoming more common. In the account that follows, Euroindians will be referred to as "mustees," "mixed-bloods," or other terms more acceptable to modern ears than "half-breeds."[6]

By the time the individuals who interest us were born, around 1700, there were probably many scores of other mustees among the native peoples the Carolinians traded with. Their numbers steadily increased. In 1737 John Tanner, an early Georgia agent to the Creeks, reckoned that "there were 400 children So begotten." The colonists generally viewed such people as more Indian than European. Thus, while they often spoke of "half Indians," they rarely or never referred to "half Englishmen" or "half whites." They knew whereof they spoke.[7]

With very few exceptions, these mixed-race individuals were not really "half" Indian, but essentially Indian. Their genetic endowment may have been divided 50–50, but their upbringing was heavily weighted toward the Indian side. Without known exception, each of these mixed-bloods had a European father and an Indian mother. Almost all appear to have been born in or near their mother's home. The European fathers were usually traders, resident only episodically in the mother's town. That being the case, their offspring were "left and bred up by their mothers." Given the matrilineal clan system of Southeastern Indians, these individuals were born into their mother's clan, a permanent status. Furthermore, as members of their mother's clan they were automatically members of their mother's society. Since nearly all of the mixed offspring had been born into an Indian social environment, their native culture was an Indian culture. Thus each of them spoke an Indian language as his or her native tongue, and was much more familiar with native institutions and values than with those of the Europeans.[8]

An Indian child's father—even if he was an Indian born into the same aboriginal community as the mother—was not a member of the child's family and played no formal role in his or her upbringing. The mother's brother or other male relative would have that responsibility. A European father was doubly distant, even during his occasional appearances in the mother's town. Thus the children born to such unions, though they probably spoke a little English, grew up without personal acquaintance with the father's English family or community.[9]

The vast majority of these offspring of white fathers and Indian mothers—nearly all of the females—lived out their lives as ordinary Indians and are invisible in the written record. Yet there were a few—nearly all of them male—who achieved distinction in their native society and left a documentary trail. These exceptional individuals became leaders, sometimes even high-ranking chiefs. We will encounter a fair number of these mixed-blood Indian leaders, including Captain Allick (Yahola Mico) and Half Breed Abraham (Mico Hutke?) among the Lower Creeks; the Half Breed (Heniha Mico) and Mad Dog (Ifa Hadjo) of Tuckabatchee among the Tallapoosa Creeks; Molton (Ifa Mico) of the Alabamas; and Peter Chartier of the Shawnees. They would become ever more numerous.

A smaller cohort of Euroindians, nearly all of them male, was more influenced by their European fathers. Such an individual was more or less comfortable with the father's European culture as well as that of the mother. As befitted their plural ancestry, these people learned to cross the cultural boundary and play plural social roles. They could usually speak their father's language passably well, could interact successfully with the friends and associates of both parents, and often divided their time between Indian and European communities. In other words, they became intermediaries between the two cultures.

Later in life, Captain Allick became a key diplomatic intermediary between the Creeks and the English. Others rendered occasional diplomatic services as translators. Examples include John Musgrove among the Lower Creeks and "Linguister John" among the Upper Creeks. Most, however, became involved in their father's daily pursuits, which usually meant the trade. Such mixed-blood traders included Samuel Brown to the Upper Creeks (son of a Cherokee woman, perhaps by leading trader Patrick Brown), his brother John Brown to the Chickasaws, Thomas Beamer (son of trader James Beamer) to the Cherokees, and George Galphin Jr. to the Lower Creeks. Many of these mixed-bloods lived much of the time near Fort Moore or, after 1736, Fort Augusta on the Georgia side of the Savannah River.[10]

The third and by far the smallest cohort of Southeastern mixed-bloods included individuals who were predominantly English in culture, or at least English enough to spend much or most of their adult lives among the colonists. Living among the English did not guarantee full acceptance into English society. For those born into other societies, Englishness was a status that had to be earned, and the requirements were stiff. Again, nearly all Anglicized mustees that can be identified were male. In South Carolina and other southern colonies, most white-black offspring appear to have been children of white masters or overseers and black slave women. Although Carolinians also held numerous Indian slaves, mostly women, these do not seem to have been the mothers of most white-red offspring. Only two cases have been identified, though there were doubtless more. In 1710 Richard Prize drew up a will freeing his enslaved Indian wife and bequeathing property to their children. In 1725 Robert Johnson did the same thing. Since Prize and Johnson were both traders, their mixed-race children may have been born in Indian country. None of the mixed offspring of Prize or Johnson rose above obscurity in South Carolina, nor apparently did a child of any other enslaved Indian woman.[11]

It appears, therefore, that most of the colony's white-red offspring were born in native communities and only later took up residence within the English settlements. It took something extraordinary to induce such a profound change of life. In most cases, the triggering event was probably the death of the Indian mother, which eliminated the main obstacle to an English father who wished to take his mustee child home with him. Other unusual circumstances that led or might have led to this result were English purchase of a mixed-blood enslaved by Indians, an English father's irresistible quid pro quo to the child's Indian family, abduction by the father, or a child's repudiation by his or her Indian relatives.[12]

The kind of extraordinary conditions that led to a young mustee being raised in an English household were more likely to occur during the early years of the colony. Historians have long observed that during the formative years, Indian traders (colonists engaged in commerce with Indians) included many of South Carolina's leaders—men like Maurice Matthews, James Moore, Thomas Nairne, Thomas Broughton, Theophilus Hastings, Matthew Smallwood, George Chicken, Charlsworth Glover, and Tobias Fitch. Later, however, as the colony's elite switched to rice production, Indian traders were recruited mainly from the opposite end of the social spectrum. Later traders had—and clearly had earned—a reputation for low-life habits and irresponsibility. Elite traders probably behaved better toward Indians than the marginal men who gradually replaced them, if only because they had more to lose and hence more to be careful about. Furthermore, their much broader sources of information gave them a clearer understanding of the colony's precarious situation, and the fact that security could not be had without a more or less cooperative relationship with the Indians. Not least, they had the influence and the means to act on their perceptions.

Although class probably had little or no bearing on how many mustee children an English trader fathered, it appears to have had a significant effect on how many were raised in an English environment. In the late colonial era colonists tended to view a mixed-blood as essentially an Indian of intermediate hue, a person of incorrigibly bad habits and no prospects among the English. The drive to Anglicize Indians, and especially the mixed-bloods, was most conspicuous during the more optimistic early years when colony leaders were involved in the trade. Never numerous, Anglicized Euroindians tended to disappear over time, presumably due either to assimilation within or retreat from English settlements.[13]

The negative stereotype of mixed-bloods had not yet congealed during South Carolina's early years. During the colony's infancy it was no great rarity for a mustee to be reared in an English household and to be predominantly English in culture. Here and there it was even possible to find a full-blood Indian living by choice among the English. The man who brought Pon Pon residents news of the initial Yamasee attack was "an Indian Man (that was born among the Yamasees, but had lived chiefly among the English, having a wife and Children in the Settlement)." Then there was the "Yamasee Prince," who in 1713 accompanied Commissary Gideon Johnson to London and a year and a half later was baptized by the Bishop of London.[14]

There are many parallels between early Carolina and early Virginia three-quarters of a century earlier, including extraordinary individuals who seemed to define certain roles. One recalls Pocahontas, of course, but her son by John Rolfe is a more direct precursor of the Carolina mustees. After Pocahontas's early death and John's return to Virginia, young Thomas Rolfe was raised in England by his father's brother Henry. Brought up as an Englishman, he was assuredly literate and Christian, and did not return to the land of his birth until he was twenty. Back in Virginia by 1635, Thomas claimed most of his father's extensive landholdings as his inheritance. In 1741 he asked the governor's permission to visit his aunt "Cleopatre and his Kinsman Opecancanough," successor to Powhatan. Three years later he fought against Opechancanough's warriors in the second of Virginia's major Indian wars. After 1646, as "Lieutenant Thomas Rolfe," he commanded Fort James on the Chickahominy River.[15]

There probably never was a time when leaders of the southern colonies were more committed to the idea of fostering English-Indian marriages and investing in their mixed offspring than during the early eighteenth century. In fact, two of them published books that boldly brought this argument before a wide public. The first was Robert Beverley's *History and Present State of Virginia* (London, 1705), followed by John Lawson's *A New Voyage to Carolina* (London, 1709). Beverley argued that an intermarriage policy would have prevented violence and war in Virginia. Had such a policy been adopted earlier, Virginia, "instead of all these Losses of Men on both Sides, would have been encreasing in Children to its Advantage." Furthermore, "many, if not most, of the Indians would have been converted to Christianity by this kind Method." Lawson used similar arguments to conclude that "it is highly necessary . . . to give Encouragement to the ordinary People, and those of a lower Rank, that they might marry with these Indians." Thus far most South Carolina readers would have found little or nothing remarkable in the Beverley and Lawson arguments except seeing them in print. It seems clear that some Carolinians had long been practicing what Beverley and Lawson preached.[16]

Lawson went significantly further, however, when he forecast approvingly that mixed Indian-white marriages would eventually lead the Indians to "become as one People with us." He went further yet when he endorsed public subsidies for interracial unions, recommending a program where "so many Acres of Land and some Gratuity of Money, (out of a publick Stock) are given to the new-married Couple."[17]

This would have been a controversial view, and surely a minority view, but not as radical as we might suppose. The French had just appeared on the Gulf

Coast as imperial rivals, and the English were aware that Louis XIV had provided subsidies for Indian-white marriages. To compete successfully, leaders of the southern English colonies would have to at least consider adopting a similar policy. In 1719 the British government went beyond considering. In that year King George II instructed the governor of his new colony of Nova Scotia to "give all possible encouragement to intermarriage between our British subjects and them," the neighboring "Indian nations." Such encouragement was to include a royal "free gift of the sum of £10 sterling and fifty acres of land free of quit-rent for the space of twenty years" to any "white" person of either sex who married an Indian. Contemplated for all of the English colonies, in the end this extreme measure was adopted only for Nova Scotia, a strategically invaluable colony where it was extremely difficult to attract British settlers.[18]

A half dozen or so Anglicized mixed-bloods can be identified on either side of the Savannah River around the time Georgia was founded. All had English surnames and "Christian" given names. Those names, presumably bestowed by English fathers (though probably not at birth), indicate at least an intention to raise these mixed offspring in an English environment. Once again, most were male. At least three of them became important figures in the early history of Georgia, including John Musgrove and Thomas Jones. Far and away the most important of these people was one whose background was doubly improbable, for she was a woman. She first appears in the record as Mary Musgrove, wife of John.

Much of what can be learned about Indian-white unions and their mixed offspring in early Carolina comes from the records of the Society for the Propagation of the Gospel in Foreign Parts (S.P.G.), particularly the field reports various Anglican missionaries sent home. On the eve of the Yamasee War the organized parishes closest to the Lower Creeks (though much closer to the Yamasees) were St. Paul's and St. Bartholomew's. The former was on the east side of the Edisto River, and the latter on the western, much rawer side. These two parishes were among the original ones created by statute in 1706, but both lacked regular ministers until the S.P.G. provided them. Rev. William Tredwell Bull took up his duties in St. Paul's in late 1712, and Rev. Nathaniel Osborne arrived in St. Bartholomew's in January 1713.

On January 20, 1715, Rev. Bull reported that since his last letter he had baptized twenty-two people, including twenty children and one adult. "The other," he continued, was "a Molatto Girl, i.e., one born of an Indian Mother, whose Father was an English Trader amongst them and long deceased. This Girl was sometime agoe taken into a Family of Landgrave Joseph Mortin, who himself and Virtuous Lady became Suretys for her, and accordingly take all imaginable care to give her a Vertuous and Christian Education." This nameless girl's story was strikingly similar to that of her exact contemporary across the river, soon to be known as Mary Musgrove.[19]

Colonel John Barnwell, hero of the Tuscarora War, could not compete with Landgrave Morton for rank, but he was an even more important leader. On July 10, 1717, he paid ten pounds to the colony for a particular servant bound to him for nineteen years. The Indian commissioners who acted for the colony reported that they had agreed with Barnwell "for the Service of a Mustee Boy (purchased at the Charikee Factory and brought down from thence among the Indian Slaves in June last)." As part of the deal, Barnwell was obliged to post a bond "in the penal sum of five hundred Pounds" to ensure that the boy would be released at the end of his term. He also had to promise "to educate the said Boy, Christian-like, and cause him to be instructed in a good Trade." Colonel Barnwell went far out of his way to give this boy a proper English upbringing. Since he apparently ignored Indian slaves and focused solely on this one mustee, it is highly probable that his decision hinged on knowledge that the boy's father was an Englishman.[20]

On March 1, 1715, Rev. Osborne reported that since his arrival in St. Bartholomew's Parish he had baptized more than seventy persons. This total included six adults, "the rest children Five of them Molatto Children being those of our Indian Traders, by Indian women during their abode amongst them." These five Euroindian children very likely included the future Mary Musgrove and probably included Thomas Jones, but almost certainly not John Musgrove. The S.P.G. also sent a schoolmaster, Benjamin Dennis, to South Carolina. Dennis opened his school in the colony's most favored parish outside of Charles Town, St. James Goose Creek. On April 22, 1714, he reported that "My school now consists of about 20 Whites two Mustees or half Indians and one Negroe." On March 21 of the following year he recorded an addition: "I have had lately committed to my care a Mustee or half Indian a Cherokee by Nation." Thus the three mustees we will follow into Georgia had considerable company in South Carolina, and surely knew some of the other mixed-bloods we have stumbled across.[21]

John or "Johnny" Musgrove was the son of John Musgrove of South Carolina by a Creek Indian woman, probably from Apalachicola. The elder Musgrove started out as a trader to the Creeks, as "Captain" Musgrove served as interpreter for a significant 1705 agreement, and rose to prominence in 1712 as a member of the Board of Indian Commissioners. He was one of the Carolina commanders during the Yamasee War, and the colony's chief negotiator of the treaty that officially ended it. A few days after the November 1717 treaty he was promoted to "Colonel" Musgrove. He made his home in St. Andrew's Parish, south of the Ashley River, not far from Charles Town.[22]

Colonel Musgrove's half-Creek son Johnny would play a leading role in early Georgia as a supplier of English goods to the natives and as an interpreter between them and the colonists. Following the death of the elder Musgrove in 1719, young John became an Indian trader and later an interpreter. His career as an interpreter began accidentally in 1725, when another employed by Indian agent Tobias Fitch fell ill. Fitch related that "young Musgrove . . . is as good as any I believe; only he wants some English." When James Oglethorpe took a group of local Indians to London in 1734 he chose John Musgrove to go along as interpreter. His English had not improved much, for the Trustees had trouble understanding him. Nevertheless, had he not died the following year John surely would have continued to be an important intermediary between the English and the natives. Yet even while he lived, in Georgia his influence was overshadowed by that of his wife, who was perfectly fluent in English. She would soon emerge as a figure everyone had to reckon with. We meet her first as Mary Musgrove; subsequent marriages would alter her name to Mary Matthews and, finally, Mary Bosomworth. Her original name, however, was Coosaponakeesa.[23]

Most improbably, Mary wrote an autobiographical sketch that survives. It appears in the opening pages of a memorial or petition she addressed to Colonel Alexander Heron in 1747. Mary stated that she "was born at the Cowetaw Town on the Oakmulgee River which is . . . the Chief Town of the Creek Indian Nation." This must have been around 1700, a decade or so after Coweta and other Creek towns had relocated eastward to the Ocmulgee. She avowed that she was "by Descent on the Mothers Side (who was Sister to the Old Emperor) of the same Blood of the Present Mico's and Chief's now in that Nation." She thus declared herself to be a member of Coweta's most influential matrilineal clan (unfortunately unnamed), a claim to imperial lineage that Savannah leaders would eventually dispute. She also presented herself as a niece of Brim, the greatest of Lower Creek leaders.[24]

Mary went on to relate that she, "about the Age of 7 Years, was brought Down by her Father from the Indian Nation, to Pomponne in south Carolina; There baptized, Educated and bred up in the Principles of Christianity." Most likely it was at her baptism that she acquired her English name. Already her story was extraordinary. Mary, apparently born into an elite Creek family, claimed to be—and in fact was—literate in English and a practicing Christian. Compounding the odds against her actual situation, Mary was married to another half Indian whose upbringing was very much like her own.[25]

It was hardly a secret, but Mary neglected to mention that her father was an Englishman. Savannah leader Thomas Causton reported that she had a brother, "One Edward Griffin." Oglethorpe described him as "Griffin, a half-Indian brother to Musgrove the interpreter's wife." In 1719 Mary's "half-Indian" brother had joined her half-Indian husband, Johnny Musgrove, in a raid on Yamasee Indians near St. Augustine. Colonel John Barnwell, who led this attack, described the pair as "Musgrove and Griffin half breed[s] or Mustees." The likely father of Mary and her brother Edward was another Edward Griffin, an Indian trader.[26]

In 1703 the elder Edward Griffin makes his first appearance in the record. In January "one Edward Griffen" was briefly under arrest for having uttered "Contumelous and Reflecting words" against a member of the Commons House of Assembly. In 1707—about the time he brought his daughter Mary to Pon Pon—Griffin was a trader employed by Thomas Broughton, the then governor's son-in-law and a future lieutenant governor himself. The following year Griffin and a fellow Broughton trader, John Dickson, swore to depositions alleging that Thomas Nairne had made treasonous statements in November 1707. Nairne complained that his accusers were "two very infamous Wretches . . . one [Griffin] a perfect Lunatick and the other a mere villain whom I formerly put in prison for Buggery."[27]

It begins to be clear why Mary never boasted of her paternal lineage. Nevertheless, her father seems later to have become more or less respectable. In March 1711 he and his current partners—the firm of Holford, Peirce and Griffin—posted the bond required of traders. In November 1714 he posted a similar bond on his own account, suggesting some upward mobility. Edward never rose far, however, for there is no indication that he ever became a landowner.[28]

The experiences of the young Mary Griffin differed from those of most mustees in several crucial respects. Most obviously, from about age seven she was not raised in the Creek community of her birth, but in her father's English community. Mary adjusted. The fact that her father resettled her as a young girl in his Carolina community, together with the fact that she clearly acquired a basic English education, implies that he had a strong and probably dominant role in shaping her development.[29]

When Edward Griffin brought his young daughter to Pon Pon, it was a mere hamlet on the west side of Edisto River in St. Bartholomew's Parish, Colleton County. On March 1, 1715, the newly arrived rector, Rev. Nathaniel Osborne, described the parish as "very large and scattered," adding that its more than twelve hundred square miles included only 120 families. Pon Pon was nevertheless a good location for an Indian trader like Mary's father, for it lay upon the great trading path from Charles Town to Lower Creek towns far to the southwest. Here the path crossed the wide Edisto (known locally as Pon Pon River) over a strategic bridge.[30]

Whether or not Mary experienced a major trauma as a young girl, she definitely lived through one a few years later during the Yamasee War. As far as Carolinians were concerned, the war began on April 15, 1715, with a fiendish massacre of innocent negotiators and traders by faithless savages. This would have been the interpretation Mary heard, as her Pon Pon neighborhood was suddenly thrown into terror and confusion. The war-triggering event was the massacre (it is the right word) of Thomas Nairne's party at Pocataligo, a Yamasee town about thirty miles southwest of Pon Pon. Within a very short time, probably hours, a Yamasee loyal to the English brought news of the attack to the Pon Pon area. Rev. Osborne reported that this alarm "came so very seasonably and providentially that the greater part of my Parish Escaped [with] their lives, though with the loss of almost all their Effects." Apparently nearly all residents dropped everything and ran for their lives. Osborne related that, with Indians less than three miles away, he himself had been "forced to run away with nothing but the cloaths upon my back." As a result of the Yamasee assault, he lamented, "My Parish is intirely deserted."[31]

The refugees from Pon Pon doubtless first crossed the bridge into St. Paul's Parish. If Mary was still there on July 15, she surely had to run again. On that day five hundred or more warriors crossed Pon Pon bridge into relatively well developed St. Paul's, and began to undevelop it. Over the next five or six days they "burned about 30 houses, Destroyed all the Horses, Cattle and Plantations they could, and did a Damage of £30,000." Some even pushed their advance northward, "as far as within Twenty Miles of Charles Town." Ironically, this rampage seems to have been led by Chigelli, Mary's purported uncle; she later learned that it was he "who at the Head of 600 Creek Indians at that time Advanced as far as Stono River." Following this bold sortie, the Indians retreated much the way they had come, burning the Pon Pon bridge as they recrossed.[32]

In 1714 Mary's father was an established trader; he is apparently never mentioned again in the surviving records. During the early stages of the war, most—reportedly a large majority—of perhaps a hundred traders then in the backcountry were killed. It seems highly likely that Edward Griffin was among them. However that may be, it is clear that during the Yamasee War Mary suffered at the hands of the Indians, and had good reasons for identifying more strongly with the English.[33]

So far as the Creeks were concerned, the war ended in 1717. In July, Captain John Musgrove undertook a long and dangerous mission to Coweta, and there managed to negotiate a provisional peace agreement with Brim. In early November, Musgrove escorted eleven Creek leaders to Charles Town, where a formal treaty was signed. Now Colonel John Musgrove, early in 1718 he made one more trip to Coweta, which he entered "bearing a white flag." The dramatic final scene occurred on March 4. One of Brim's younger sons, Malatchi, recalled it about thirty years later. Echoing the Europeans, Malatchi boasted that "my Father was Emperor of the Creek Nation." He went on to relate that at the close of the war "the Governour of Carolina sent his Beloved Man [Musgrove] up to make peace with us. He then broke his Sword and buryed it in the Ground as a token of peace, and we likewise broke our Arms and buryed them in the Ground also."[34]

Colonel Musgrove was not the only Musgrove to play a role in the peace process. A few months before he set off for Coweta in 1717, his son John married another mustee, Mary Griffin. In a 1753 petition designed to reclaim her land rights in South Carolina, Mary stated that "about the year 1716 your Petitioner's first Husband John Musgrove" had purchased 650 acres of land from Thomas Jones, upon which the couple made their home. She thereby implied that she and John were already man and wife when John made the purchase. To support her petition, Mary located an old friend, Elizabeth Hunt, who corroborated her main contentions. Elizabeth stated that in 1713 she had married her first husband, Alexander Clark (another Indian trader), "at Pon Pon." She related that "she has known the said Mary Bosomworth from a child," suggesting that in 1713 Mary was still a child. Elizabeth also claimed to be well acquainted with both Mary's husband and Thomas Jones, and the land transaction between them. Significantly, she stated that it was not until "soon after their Marriage" that John purchased the land upon which the Musgrove couple made their home. Finally, Elizabeth declared that she had "delivered the said Mary Bosomworth (then Mary Musgrove) of a Child upon that very tract of Land, [that] Musgrove Purchased from Jones." Largely because of Elizabeth's testimony, Mary's petition was successful.[35]

Mary was young when she wed, not much above sixteen, and now probably an orphan. Perhaps it was the recent death of her father that made her receptive to an early marriage. Or perhaps Captain Musgrove calculated that a marriage of Brim's half-English niece Mary and his half-Creek son John would smooth the way toward a desperately needed peace with the Creeks. At any rate, the match, if not exactly a marriage alliance, doubtless helped Musgrove make his successful approach to Brim.

Young John Musgrove followed his father into the life of an Indian trader. In 1722 he complained that the commander at Fort Moore had unlawfully seized some of his skins. On February 2, 1726, he renewed his trading license. The following summer Carolina authorities suspected that Lower Creeks were behind the recent murder of noted trader Matthew Smallwood and four of his assistants by Yamasees. In early August lower house leaders decided to send two mustee traders, John Musgrove and James Welch, up to the Chattahoochee to find out what these Indians had to say about the incident. Before the month was out the plan was altered so as to place Musgrove and Welch at the head of armed troop of twenty whites and more Indians. If the Lower Creeks did not come clean, a much larger force was provided for. Two years later John volunteered to lead Creek warriors supporting a Carolina attack on St. Augustine. This action ("Palmer's raid") was spectacularly successful, and Musgrove was awarded £140 currency for his part in it.[36]

Contrary to earlier accounts, there is no evidence that John and Mary Musgrove ever made their home among the Creeks. Such speculation probably grew out of Mary's statement in her 1747 memorial that she had been "Settled in Carolina upwards of Seven Years till June 1732." Does this imply that from her marriage until 1725 or so she and John had been settled *outside* of South Carolina—in Creek country, for instance? Probably not, though around 1725 they may have made a brief sojourn there or elsewhere out of Carolina. According to Elizabeth Hunt, the land John purchased soon after he and Mary wed was in Pon Pon, "on the west side of Pon Pon River." She went on to say that the Musgroves "lived many years in undisturbed and Peacible manner in the Possession of the said Lands," which "always went by the name of Musgrove Tract." Mary likewise declared that in 1731 she and John "had been 14 or 15 years in undisturbed Possession of the said Tract and Improvements."[37]

Furthermore, an incident from 1722—a year John and Mary have been assumed to be absent from Carolina—implies that they had been there since 1717 or 1718. On January 5, 1722, the Commons House of Assembly asked Governor Francis Nicholson to issue a proclamation to enforce an act passed the previous September. That act provided that "no Indian . . . shall presume to come within the Settlement" unless the governor "shall order and permit the same." As a example of such impropriety, the house pointed to "a Creek Indian named Whitlemca with his people . . . who now live on the other side of Pon Pon River." The governor issued the desired proclamation that very day.[38]

Soon afterward Nicholson asked the lower house to approve an exception for the individual they had named. On March 8 he explained that "Young [John] Musgrove's Uncle Witlemico an Indian has desired me to give him the liberty to live on his Cousins Land as he had done for these four or five years past." It is highly unlikely that this Witle Mico would have been living on John's land unless John were living there too. Probably this man was the same "Wettly . . . a Palachicola Indian" who helped lead the 1719 raid that Musgrove and Griffin had joined. If so, it indicates that Musgrove's mother was from Apalachicola. Nicholson favored the Indian's request, he said, because he had a good opinion of the man's character, expected him to be "serviceable to us in many cases," and—above all—"he promises to behave himself well and to suffer no Indians to come to him." The house promptly agreed. Thus it seems very likely that John and Mary Musgrove maintained their home at Pon Pon during all or nearly all of their married years, until their move to Yamacraw Bluff in 1732. Moreover, by 1722 they had a reputation for having, over the previous "four or five years," entertained their Creek relatives and friends in uncomfortable proximity to their English neighbors.[39]

The Pon Pon area remained an exposed and periodically frightened neighborhood. To Carolinians during the 1720s, crossing the Pon Pon (Edisto) River meant entering the danger zone where clashes between whites and Indians could erupt at any time. Periodic raids from Yamasees, aided by some Hitchiti-speaking Lower Creeks, continued until at least 1728. The bridge burned by the Indians during the war had not been rebuilt, and the ferries that substituted for it no longer allowed for a reliable quick escape toward Charles Town. On November 16, 1727, acting governor Arthur Middleton reported that "about ten days agoe there came 35 of the Lower Creeks and Yamasses and Cut off a family on the out side of Pon Pon." Indians too recognized that this river, along with the Savannah, continued to bracket a conflict zone. In 1725 Sepeycoffee, "Emperor" Brim's son and presumed successor, reluctantly agreed to visit Charles Town. He would come, he said, guarded by forty warriors, "for he Lookes upon it as [being as] Dangerous between the Savana town and Edisto [as] any other part of the way."[40]

Despite their difficult environment in South Carolina, by the time John and Mary Musgrove moved to Georgia in 1732 they had managed to prosper. They had acquired at least three tracts of land totaling more than seven hundred acres, ran numerous livestock, and evidently even operated "Musgrove's Ferry" across the Edisto. They had also become the parents of three sons.[41]

The third Carolina mustee to play an important role in early Georgia was Thomas or Tommy Jones. He was probably the son of Thomas Jones, an Indian trader. In August 1711 the colony's Indian commissioners took legal action against the elder Jones and eight other traders "who are settled in the Limitts of the Yamosse Settlements." Like the younger Musgrove and other mixed-bloods, the younger Jones followed his father into the Indian trade. In September 1723 the Tuckabatchee Captain, a major Upper Creek leader, complained that "Thomas Jones the halfe Breed" had insulted him and tried to thwart Creek plans for a raid against the Yamasees. Two years later Jones was one of three Carolina traders who made a daring trading expedition to the remote Choctaw country.[42]

It is not clear what native society Thomas was born into. The uncertainty is party due to the fact that he was not merely bilingual but was multilingual. Later in Georgia he would serve as official interpreter for English meetings with the Creeks, Choctaws, Chickasaws, and possibly even Yuchis. As a boy Tommy Jones was probably a childhood friend of Mary Griffin, and he apparently continued to live in Pon Pon. "Thomas Jones, Trader" is on a list of nineteen men from St. Bartholomew's Parish who were late or delinquent on their taxes for 1732–33. Six years later Oglethorpe reminded William Bull, South Carolina's lieutenant governor, that Jones hailed from Pon Pon.[43]

For most English colonists the question of Englishness or Indianness was an either/or question. "Mustee" and other terms for Euroindians never became well established. A memorable illustration of this either/or mind-set comes from New York (the northern colony whose Indian relations most closely resembled those of South Carolina and Georgia). In August 1682 a party of Iroquois Indians held talks with Anglo-Dutch leaders at Albany. One of the two interpreters was the Dutchman Aernout Cornelisse Vielle. He was "assisted" by "Akus Cornelis formerly an Indian." It seems highly probable that the assistant Cornelis was the son of the interpreter Cornelisse, the son by an Indian woman. It also seems that he remained fond of his Indian name, Akus, and perhaps even preferred it to his Christian name, Jacques. At any rate, Akus/Jacques was not seen as a "half" Indian, but as "formerly" an Indian. He had shed his Indianness. One of the most embarrassing truths of the era was that it was far more common for colonists to shed their Englishness and become Indians.[44]

Even before they moved to Georgia, the Musgrove couple and Thomas Jones were accepted by their English families and neighbors as full members of the English community. All three went by their English names and had a basic English education. All three were not only more or less fluent in spoken English, they were literate. Still more significant for their status within South Carolina and Georgia, all three had access to English law and willingly exploited it for their own advantage. In this they acted much as ordinary English colonists did, but as ordinary Indians (or other non-Christians) did not and could not. In South Carolina, Georgia, and other southern colonies, an individual unable to give "sworn" (Christian) testimony could not sue or even testify in an English court of law.[45]

Here as elsewhere, the crucial eligibility test for full acceptance in an English society was Christianity. John Musgrove, Mary Musgrove, and Thomas Jones were all accepted as Christians. Abundant evidence supports this conclusion for both Musgroves; there is less for Jones, but it is decisive. In July 1737, Rev. John Wesley himself baptized a child of Tommy Jones. In August a Savannah grand jury found in this another indictable offense by Wesley, though not for the reason we might think. The indictment states that Wesley had violated the king's peace by going ahead with the ceremony with only one set of grandparents, "notwithstanding that Jacob Matthews and Mary [Griffin Musgrove Matthews] his wife, near relations of the said child, did offer to stand godfather and godmother at the same time." Note too that if Mary was a near relation to the child, she had to be even more closely related to Tommy. Four years later, when he was called upon to testify about Oglethorpe's siege of St. Augustine, Thomas was first "duly sworn on the Holy Evangelists of Almighty God."[46]

Although John and Mary Musgrove, and Thomas Jones too, were solid citizens in South Carolina, few would have mistaken them for gentry. It does not appear that any Carolinian prior to the founding of Georgia ever referred to Thomas as

"Mister" Jones. John Musgrove had a more distinguished English pedigree and more property, but he was almost never called "Mister" Musgrove. That Jones and Musgrove could not command this gentlemanly title in South Carolina is not surprising; very few Englishmen in the colony or in England itself were deemed qualified for it. What is surprising is that in Georgia these half Englishmen were regularly saluted as "Mister Musgrove" and "Mister Jones." James Oglethorpe himself was probably responsible for this honor. For example, in his letter to Bull he referred to the latter as "Mr. Jones of Pon Pon." He was even more explicit regarding Musgrove, referring to him as "John Musgrove Gent." John's spouse was almost invariably called "Mrs. Musgrove."[47]

Oglethorpe showed extraordinary favor to these individuals because he knew he needed people like them. These Carolina mustees transplanted into Georgia had two precious qualities: facility with both English and at least one Indian language, and, still more important, proven commitment to the English. Mixed-bloods indifferently provided with such assets would still be welcome, people like Edward Griffin, Jack Smallwood, or James Welch. There were many other individuals such as these in the backcountry, especially around Fort Moore on the Savannah River. In June 1736 Oglethorpe reported that Carolina traders and Indians had approached him with plan to build a town three hundred miles up the river at their own expense. It was to be settled by forty families, "all to be white People or half-bred Indians." He seized the opportunity, and a few days later Augusta was established.[48]

The founding of Georgia was welcome news to the vast majority of Carolinians, to whom it meant security. A few Anglicized half Indians—notably John Musgrove, Mary Musgrove, and Thomas Jones—were equally enthusiastic for a different reason. For them it meant opportunity.

Map 2. Creek country in 1757. Source: William Bonar, "A Draught of the Creek Nation" (C.O. 700, Carolina no. 21). Names of rivers modernized; spellings of some Creek towns altered to accord with those used in this book. Town locations are necessarily approximate. Drawn by Wendy Giminski, Research Media, University of Georgia.

CHAPTER TWO

Georgia Dawn

From the first, Georgia was peculiar. Unlike the other English colonies in North America, it was originally established as a philanthropic enterprise, a refuge for the disadvantaged of England and Europe. It was also to be a place where enslavement of blacks and exploitation of Indians were prohibited. Like most other English colonies, Georgia officially began with a royal grant of territory and governing authority to a group of colonial promoters.

In June 1732 King George II formally conferred such a charter upon "The Trustees for establishing the Colony of Georgia in America." In general, the original twenty-one grantees were public-spirited gentlemen who saw colonization abroad as a way to rehabilitate some of the "worthy poor" at home. Institutionally, the Trusteeship was a charitable corporation supported by private donation and, in most years, by the British Parliament. The last of its kind, the Georgia charter had more restrictions on both grantees and colonists than earlier North American grants. The king gave the Trustees authority to rule the colony in his name, but only for twenty-one years, all the while serving without pay or prospect of gain from the colony. No colonist could receive more than five hundred acres from a single land grant or a combination of grants.[1]

The king went on to grant the Georgia Trustees territory extending from the Savannah River southward about eighty air miles to the Altamaha River, "and westerly from the heads of the said rivers respectively, in direct lines to the South Seas." As with earlier such charters, there was no admission that the fact that this territory was already inhabited in any way constrained the king's ability to grant it to his subjects. Nevertheless, the aboriginal inhabitants of this vast domain did not entirely escape the royal notice. Early in the document the king recalled the Yamasee War, when Carolinians were ravaged by "the neighboring savages." Toward its close he encouraged those willing to undertake commerce with "the wild people" of the region.[2]

Foremost among the original Georgia Trustees was James Edward Oglethorpe. With the possible exception of William Penn in Pennsylvania, no individual dominated the early history of any English colony as Oglethorpe dominated that of Georgia. Like Penn two generations earlier, Oglethorpe was well born, well educated, relatively young (thirty-seven in 1733), high minded, ambitious, and prodigiously energetic. The two also shared serious personal problems: both were careless with money and politically tainted by earlier associations with the repudiated House of Stuart. Nevertheless, Oglethorpe differed decisively from Penn in that he was a dutiful Anglican and had military experience, the latter a necessary prerequisite for the leader of a frontier colony adjacent to rival Spanish and French provinces. One other Trustee, though he never left home, also played a leading role during the colony's early years: John Perceval, after 1733 the first Earl of Egmont.[3]

Although Oglethorpe lived in Georgia during most of its first decade, and acted as its governor and military commander, he held no formal office under the Trust other than resident Trustee. Nor did anyone else hold such offices for the colony. Under the Trusteeship, Georgia never had a governor. Furthermore, during its first decade it had no colonial government at all, that is, no government for the colony as a whole. Two provisions in the royal charter helped produce this strange situation: a prohibition against Trustees holding provincial offices, and a provision that any governor the Trustees might appoint for Georgia had to be approved by the Crown before undertaking his duties.[4]

The decisive factor, however, was the Trustees' determination to insulate the Georgia experiment from court or provincial politics by keeping as much of the colony's administration as possible in their own hands. Rather than seek royal confirmation for a governor, they simply did without one. Furthermore, wary that any official they appointed with jurisdiction over the entire colony might be considered a governor, for ten years they appointed no such official. As a result, the only standing agencies of government that the Trustees established in early Georgia were municipal: the town (and, after 1741, county) council of Savannah and the town council of Frederica. Unwilling to commission provincial officials with general authority to deal with the colony's overall problems, the Trustees instead delegated a series of limited "powers" to various individuals, notably Oglethorpe, to implement policy decisions they themselves had made in London. It seemed plain to them, as Egmont explained, that "the Trustees . . . are the Legislature of Georgia." Oglethorpe not only agreed with his fellow Trustees that they ought to keep maximum control in their own hands, in their name he aimed to exercise nearly all of it. It was an awkward arrangement, and one certain to produce misunderstanding and conflict between the Georgia settlers and the mostly distant Trustees—and the one who was all too present.[5]

This odd institutional context is one of several major reasons the Georgians' early relations with the native Indians were also unusual. During the first decade, negotiations and other interactions between the two peoples were not conducted by a provincial or even (with few exceptions) municipal government. Instead, they were almost entirely in the hands of the Trustees' sole resident member, Oglethorpe. Trustee Oglethorpe purported to speak and act in behalf of the entire Trust, and it was not easy—on either side of the ocean—to dispute him. In fact, Oglethorpe's views on Indians and how to deal with them did not differ markedly from those of fellow Trustees. Inevitably, the point of view of these benevolent but mostly remote figures differed from that of the struggling Georgia colonists. Yet Oglethorpe's initial diplomacy with the natives was so conspicuously successful that its warm afterglow lingered to blur his subsequent missteps. So long as he remained in Georgia, the colonists' ever growing resentment toward the Trustees never came to focus on Indian affairs.

Oglethorpe set sail from England in November 1732 with the "first embarcation" of 114 settlers. They had a favorable passage, losing only two people, and arrived off the coast of South Carolina on January 13, 1733. Oglethorpe went ashore to meet with Robert Johnson, the province's veteran governor, recently reposted as its first royal governor. As Johnson had advised, Oglethorpe left his colonists aboard ship rather than expose them to the temptations of Charles Town. The Carolina governor, delighted that others were about to place themselves between his people and potential menaces from the south, offered the new arrivals generous assistance. He also offered advice based on his long service and experience in the region. Whatever else Johnson said, we can be confident his advice touched on three main points.[6]

First, Johnson undoubtedly explained that the native people Oglethorpe would encounter south of the Savannah River were Creeks, with whom he had signed an important treaty with just seven months earlier. Johnson had concluded that treaty with eleven Upper and Lower Creek leaders. The governor probably also told Oglethorpe that he could expect to have most dealings with the less remote Lower Creeks. The Lower Creek leaders who had met with Johnson were not a representative group. There were only four of them, all from the Hitchiti-speaking towns of Apalachicola, Ouseechee, and Chehaw. Leaders from the dominant towns, Muskogee-speaking Coweta and Cussita, were conspicuously absent. In fact, most of the natives Oglethorpe first encountered came from the same lower towns whose leaders had met with Johnson. The text of the Carolina treaty has long been known, but only recently has it been correctly dated. It was signed in Charles Town on June 14, 1732.[7]

Governor Johnson most likely told Oglethorpe that satisfactory relations with the fickle and dangerous Creeks depended upon following the leads outlined in his treaty, and not only the specific provisions but the language. Several rhetorical flourishes stand out. In the final article on English obligations, Johnson promises to sign and seal the treaty so that "you and your People may have this Chain of friendship fixed in your Minds and fixed in your Hearts." In the final article on Creek obligations, the chiefs promise to sign in order to "keep this Talk in our Hearts as long as the Sun shall shine or the Waters run in the Rivers." These were novel images in South Carolina and sound as though they were transplanted from Pennsylvania or New York. In fact, they were.[8]

The pacific images in the 1732 Creek treaty were borrowed with little change from the 1730 Cherokee treaty, which was signed in London. Not by chance, the two treaties are consecutive documents in the journal of the South Carolina Commons House. Not by chance, Governor Johnson was with the Cherokee delegates in London, and sailed with them back to Charles Town. In the Cherokee treaty, for the first time in a formal agreement with Southeastern Indians, we read of a "chain of friendship" and look forward to its duration "as long as the Mountains and Rivers shall last or the sun shine." When the Board of Trade, new to such matters, wanted expert opinion on how to compose a treaty with American Indians, it called upon Sir William Keith. Knighted for his service in a difficult job, Keith had recently retired as deputy governor of Pennsylvania and returned to London. It was Keith who provided the board with a working draft of an appropriate treaty text, doubtless including the arresting locutions his Pennsylvania service had familiarized him with. This well-tested imagery from the middle colonies would prove to be almost as fetching to leaders in the Southeast, including some native leaders, and would tint diplomatic discourse for the remainder of the colonial era.[9]

The second matter Governor Johnson must have advised Oglethorpe on was the likely reaction of the Creek Indians to the new colony. Oglethorpe doubtless knew that the Carolina treaty with the Creeks ending the Yamasee War had limited English settlement to the north side of the Savannah River. Did that mean the Creeks would contest English settlement on the south side? Would they become enemies to the Georgia colony? If Oglethorpe and the other planners and promoters of the colony had thought that a likely outcome, the Georgia project would never have come this far. The Trustees and British officials knew that the Carolinians had built Fort King George at the mouth of the Altamaha River in 1721 and maintained it for six years, without significant Creek protest. But that was then. Even if the Creeks were still willing to accept English settlement on the Altamaha, the real question was whether they could agree to English settlement on the Savannah, a river that mattered much more to them. Oglethorpe surely asked such questions. Johnson probably gave reassuring answers: provided the newcomers behaved themselves, negotiated fairly, and attended to the needs of Creeks for trade goods, the natives would not prove to be serious obstacles.

The third bit of helpful advice doubtless offered by Johnson would have come in response to another obvious question from Oglethorpe: Where exactly was the best possible site to plant the new colony? Johnson would have preferred a site far to the south on the Altamaha, but if Oglethorpe was set on the Savannah—as indeed he was—the governor knew just the spot. It had to be Yamacraw Bluff. This was a high bluff about a mile in length along the south bank of the Savannah River. It was well watered, well timbered, and partially cleared; even the soil was tolerably good. The riverfront below had long been used as a staging area by Carolina Indian traders, and the river was deep enough that oceangoing vessels could make a close approach to the shore. Anticipating the current situation, the year before Johnson had taken steps to ensure that Oglethorpe and his colonists would not face resistance from the natives. With any luck the newcomers would instead receive a warm welcome.

Sailing south from Charles Town, Oglethorpe landed the colonists at Beaufort on January 20. He continued on with a small advance party to select the site for Georgia's first settlement. The group included several influential Carolinians, William Bull for one, and apparently Jonathan Bryan. It was on or about January 22 that Yamacraw Bluff became Oglethorpe's definitive choice for the townsite of Savannah. Atop the bluff Oglethorpe found, doubtless as Governor Johnson had told him he would, a trading post and a small Indian settlement led by an aged chief, Tomochichi. The *South Carolina Gazette* soon reported that after he "chose a Situation for a town," Oglethorpe "entered into a Treaty with Tomo chi chi, the Mico, or Chief." The word "Treaty" here does not necessarily mean anything more than formal conversation, but probably more than that occurred. Certainly by February 1, and very likely from the first contact, the Yamacraws signaled welcome to the newcomers. Returning for the colonists on January 24, Oglethorpe conducted them to their new home on the first of February.[10]

Nine days later Oglethorpe wrote his first letter from Savannah to the Trustees. He had the most agreeable news: "A little Indian nation the only one within fifty miles is not only at amity but desire to be subject to the Trustees to have land given them and to breed their Children at our Schools. Their Cheif and his beloved man who is the Second man in the Nation desire to be instructed in the Christian Religion." The Indian settlement Oglethorpe referred to was the Yamacraw town, located less than half a mile upriver from his tent. What he called a "little Indian nation" was certainly little; according to storekeeper Thomas Causton it consisted of "about 100 Indians." Oglethorpe may have been unaware of a few Yuchis farther upriver, but he was correct about the scarcity of native inhabitants. In fact, in almost every direction from Savannah within the charter bounds, there were no permanent settlements of any kind for a hundred miles or more. The territory of Georgia was wondrously vacant, moist clay nearly ready to be shaped into the desired form. It even seemed that Oglethorpe had found his man Friday to assist in the person of Tomochichi, the Yamacraw chief.[11]

The Yamacraw town was not a typical Indian town. By Creek lights it was not a town at all, for it had no square ground and its leaders had no regular place at Lower Creek council meetings. It was not even a "daughter" village, for its population was mixed and acknowledged no dependence on a particular Creek town. Moreover, though Tomochichi's wife (Senauki) and her daughters were present, women and children were probably underrepresented in this population. The Yamacraws were a mixed band of refugees, opportunists, and outcasts, predominantly Lower Creeks, who had only recently settled in the area. Like those who met Johnson in Charles Town the previous year, most of them apparently came from Apalachicola, Ouseechee, Chehaw, or other Hitchiti-speaking towns along the lower Chattahoochee River. One of these towns, Chehaw, had formerly been a Yamasee town. Samuel Eveleigh, a prominent and knowledgeable South Carolina merchant, in 1736 described the Yamacraws as a miscellaneous people "composed partly of Creeks and [partly of] Yamasees." A Creek spokesman in 1733 described them as a mixed people "out of each of the Creek towns." Another related that they had been "banished" from the Lower Creek towns and that these "banished Men" had chosen Tomochichi as their leader. Tomochichi himself acknowledged that "I was a banished Man." Egmont gathered that they had been expelled for "cutting down a Popish Chappel, which the french were endeavouring to erect, with design to convert it into a Fort." Mary Musgrove had played a major role in recruiting them to Yamacraw Bluff. Yamacraws told Thomas Christie that the only trade partner they trusted was Mary, "for whose Sake they Settled here."[12]

While there has been some confusion about Tomochichi's ethnic background, it is now clear that he was a Lower Creek from the town of Apalachicola. Spanish contact with the Lower Creeks had long centered on the "province" of Apalachicola. One of many violent encounters in that abrasive relationship gave Tomochichi a permanent grudge: "His father was taken by the Spaniards and burnt because he would not be a Christian." Tomochichi had attended the treaty conference with Governor Johnson in Charles Town in June 1732. That spring Creek leaders had requested permission to visit Charles Town in order to "pay their Respects to the Governor." Around the first of June "about 65" Indians from both Upper and Lower Creek towns were escorted into the Carolina capital by a military honor guard. They were conducted directly to the council chamber, where they met the governor and council. The text of the treaty finalized on June 14 records the most important of the agreements then made in Charles Town, but not all of them. Samuel Eveleigh described one of the latter. He related that some of the Indians settled (or, more likely, about to settle) at Yamacraw Bluff came to Charles Town "and desired his Excellency Robert Johnson Esq. then Governour, That they might have Leave to settle there and have a trader amongst them, which his excellency granted and that Tomochichey . . . was one of them." The treaty described him as "Tomeechey of the Pallachucolas Town." Likewise, the leading chief of the Lower Creek confederacy, Chigelli, in 1735 referred to "the place the present Pallachucolla people dwell in, and from whom Tomo Chachi is descended."[13]

It also seems probable that the predominant element among the Yamacraws came from Apalachicola. "Palachicola Town" on the Savannah River, a natural crossing point, marked the northernmost settlement of Lower Creeks during their brief stay in central Georgia. It was also the one closest to Savannah, only about twenty-five miles upriver. Tomochichi later remarked that "he was not a stranger to the English, for that his father and grand father had been very well known to them." According to one English observer, Tomochichi was "above fourscore, and says he remembers the first settlement of the English at Carolina." The Indians of Apalachicola on the Savannah—Tomochichi, his father, and grandfather apparently among them—would have been among the Creeks best known to the earliest Carolinians. The Yamacraws not only chose Tomochichi as their leader; they also named a nearby stream "Pally Chukola creek" and sent at least one and probably more Apalachicola men to London in the delegation that returned with Oglethorpe in 1734.[14]

The "trader" whom Governor Johnson in June 1732 licensed for the Yamacraw village was John Musgrove. It was probably no coincidence that Musgrove's Creek mother seems to have been an Apalachicola woman. That very month John and Mary opened their trading post on Yamacraw Bluff. Mary later wrote that in "June 1732 . . . She and her then Husband (at the Request of the Creek Nation, and with the Consent and Approbation of His Excellency Governor Johnston) Moved all their Goods Cattle, and Other Effects to the southward of the River savannah, and settled a Trading House at Yamacraw." The Musgroves had economic as well as political backing in Charles Town; Samuel Eveleigh was among their chief suppliers and creditors. Very likely the Yamacraw village Oglethorpe found a few months later owed its existence to the lure of John and Mary's well-stocked trading post.[15]

The journal of Peter Gordon and a Thomas Causton letter of March 12 provide us with our best glimpses of the first few weeks of the infant settlement of Savannah. On February 1, about an hour after the colonists climbed the bluff, a party of Yamacraws headed by Tomochichi walked over to welcome them. They were accompanied by John Musgrove, about to play his initial role as interpreter. The Indians announced their arrival into the bare English camp (Oglethorpe's tent was the only one standing) with a fanfare of musket fire. They then filed into the camp dancing and chanting. When Oglethorpe emerged from his tent, the lead dancer approached him with "a spread Fan of white Feathers in each hand" and "Stroked him on every Side with them." According to Causton, "this continued more than a Quarter of an Hour." The exotic implements were clearly "white wings of peace" or "eagle wands," Creek friendship tokens. Following these feathery felicities, Tomochichi and his wife Senauki headed separate files of male and female natives who introduced Oglethorpe to another local custom. "Then the King and all the men came in a regular manner and Shook him by the hand; after that the Queen came and all of the Women did the like." Causton, with his storekeeper's eye, noticed that the ranking natives wore English clothing, no doubt largely acquired from the Musgroves: "the King and the Chiefs wear Coats and Drawers and a piece of Cloth tied about their Legs like Boots. The Queen and her Daughters wear Common printed Calicoe, Jacket and Petticoat without any Head Cloaths."[16]

Unfazed by the unfamiliar theatrics, Oglethorpe seemed to know what was expected of him. Reciprocating the Indian gestures of goodwill, he invited his visitors into his tent for a session of verbal stroking. "Seating Tomo Chachi upon his right hand," with Musgrove standing between them, "they continued on conference about a quarter of an hour." After what was probably mainly an exchange of courtesies, the Indians "returned to their town . . . in the same order as they came." That evening Gordon and a few others were made welcome at the Musgroves' house and the adjacent Yamacraw village. "As soon as the Indians were informed that we were come to Musgroves house, they began to entertaine us with dancing round a large fire which they made upon the ground, opposite to the Kings house." Afterward the Englishmen dined and slept at John and Mary's house. The following day Oglethorpe was able to deliver gifts to Tomochichi's people that he knew would be appreciated, "Presents to make them Cloathing."[17]

The first few weeks saw the town of Savannah take shape in a whirlwind of activity. In November, just before sailing, the Trustees authorized Oglethorpe to "set out, Limit, and Divide five thousand Acres of Land in Georgia" for the initial settlement. Oglethorpe quickly imposed a design on Savannah that remains much admired to the present day. The Trustees' official records do not say so, but Egmont relates that Oglethorpe was also authorized to make direct land grants to settlers "not exceeding fifty acres besides their houses and gardens." From other sources we learn that these grants were designed for the colonists whose passage was paid by the Trustees, and that the lands so granted were to be held by "tail male" tenure. Lands held by this tenure could be inherited only by males, and could not be divided, sold, or otherwise alienated without prior approval from the Trustees. Close adherence to these restrictions would produce primogeniture and entail. This antique and restrictive regimen was of course soon highly unpopular among the colonists. Reflecting upon the Trustees' refusal to record essential elements of this "controversial" land policy in their official minutes and journals, Phinizy Spalding is persuasive in concluding that their secretive practice was due to "fear of government interference." It would not be long before Oglethorpe's fellow Trustees discovered that he had extended this practice in an unexpected direction.[18]

Initial contacts with the Indians had gone well, very well, so well that Oglethorpe appears to have been euphoric. His February 10 letter to the Trustees, already quoted, radiates optimism. In due course events would reveal that his hopes were extravagant. His conjectures that the Yamacraws "desire to be subject of the Trustees . . . to breed their children at our schools," and "to be instructed in the Christian religion" would all prove soon enough to be wishful thinking. These were recurrent illusions among all European colonizers, false hopes that no amount of previous experience could exclude from a new colony. Oglethorpe's truly surprising claim was that the Yamacraws "desire . . . to have land given them." Probably he thought he was following another precedent set by the Carolinians, who in 1707 had set aside a large tract for the Yamasees. In Georgia, however, the Yamacraws already lived on land that was theirs by treaty; why should they wish to have the English give them their own land? This was the most extreme of Oglethorpe's February 10 claims, and the one he abandoned first.[19]

Echoing Oglethorpe's early mind-set, Gordon reported that on February 25 "Mr. Oglethorp, Coll. [William] Bull, and Tomo Chachi went up the river in order to give the Indians possession of the lands alloted for their setlement." The land supposedly "alloted" to the natives, which contemporaries usually called "the Indian Land," historians have long designated as "the Yamacraw Tract." This was a tract of about four thousand acres immediately adjacent to the new town of Savannah, a rough rectangle extending about four miles up the Savannah River to Pipemaker's Creek, and a mile or two back from the river to the road that would soon be extended to Augusta. Oglethorpe first reported his land dealings with the Indians on March 12. He then wrote the Trustees that the Yamacraws had "concluded a Peace with us giving up their Right to All this part of the Country, and I have marked out the Lands with they had reserved to themselves." The idea of allotting lands to native Indians had vanished, never to reappear. Oglethorpe had not granted lands to the Yamacraws; they had granted lands to him. Rather than receiving lands, they had "reserved" a choice tract as their own.[20]

Historians have long been puzzled about Oglethorpe's early land cession agreements, and even the best scholarly works are ambiguous or confused about this vital matter. The immediate problem is that, contrary to the established practice of most other English colonies, these agreements were simply oral understandings. Hence the crucial early agreements produced no definitive texts, but rather a number of partial and derivative reports that are not easily reconciled. None provides a comprehensive picture of any one agreement, and some appear to conflate several of them. Oglethorpe seems to have chosen to approach questions of land rights through oral agreements rather than written treaties because he worried that the latter would attract attention and second-guessing in London. Unfortunately for the historian, Oglethorpe's modus operandi included near total control over information on land negotiations. In fact, his grip on the written record was so tight that we sometimes learn more about what was going on from the illiterate Indians.

Oglethorpe negotiated two pairs of land cession agreements, the first in 1733 and the second in 1736. The reason these accords came in pairs is evident from a statement Tomochichi made to Oglethorpe in the latter year. In March 1736 Oglethorpe reported that Tomochichi was willing to make a land cession "provided the lower Creek Nations agree to it." The Yamacraws were not independent from the Lower Creek confederacy, and had no wish to be. Any concessions they made regarding territory claimed by the Lower Creeks would be meaningless unless confirmed by the latter. Accordingly, both the 1733 and the 1736 land cessions took the form of a preliminary agreement with Tomochichi and the Yamacraws, followed by a confirmatory and final agreement with the Lower Creek leadership. Mary Musgrove later took full credit for both 1733 agreements, claiming that both were fashioned in the teeth of strong Indian opposition. She later asserted that she had "used the Utmost of her Interest and Influence . . . to bring about a Treaty betwixt Mr. Oglethorpe in behalf of his Majesty and the Indians that were then there, in behalf of the Creek Nation, which Treaty was Provisionary till the Consent of the Nation could be Obtained which Also, was with the Greatest Difficulty effected by your Memorialist's Interest and Influence."[21]

The land cession of 1733 presents numerous problems of interpretation, starting with the question of when it occurred. A few years later Francis Moore, Oglethorpe's secretary, wrote that "the first thing Mr. Oglethorpe did in his first voyage, was to obtain the grant from the Indians." The authors of *A True and Historical Narrative*, no friends of Oglethorpe, likewise stated that "the first thing he did after he arrived in Georgia, was to make a kind of solemn treaty with a parcel of fugitive Indians." Commenting upon this statement, which he perceived to be a malicious understatement, Egmont added that by this agreement the Indians "yielded to him a great tract of land."[22]

These tantalizing later assertions indicating that "the first thing" Oglethorpe did in Georgia was to negotiate a major land cession appear to be essentially correct. Were they precisely correct, it would follow that Oglethorpe achieved the cession via his "Treaty" with Tomochichi during his brief reconnoiter of Yamacraw Bluff in January. This can be ruled out. A less literal reading of the sources would place the cession on February 1, the day Oglethorpe brought the colonists to the bluff. Yet the Gordon and Causton accounts contain no hint of a significant land cession. Having noticed so much, it seems unlikely either writer would have overlooked something of such obvious importance. Or perhaps the cession envisioned by Egmont occurred a day, or two, or a few, later. Perhaps, but probably not.

Closer attention to the sources suggests that there was no single agreement over land with Tomochichi and the Yamacraws. Rather, it appears that the agreement was an evolving one which took shape over several weeks or even a month. If it is highly likely that Oglethorpe's "Treaty" with Tomochichi in January contained a general statement of welcome, it is at least plausible that it also included a specific relinquishment of the Savannah townsite. Whatever the exact date, the evolving Yamacraw cession appears to have begun with the footprint of the town. What seems to be the first stage of the agreement was recalled twenty years later by Creek leader Malatchi: "we gave them as much [land] as might build them a Town and live upon." Oglethorpe never described this agreement, probably because he hoped shortly to enlarge it, and succeeded in doing so. We may suppose that he next prevailed upon Tomochichi to yield some vaguely defined portion of the surrounding countryside. The Yamacraw leader no doubt understood perfectly well that the residents of Savannah needed to raise crops to feed themselves.[23]

It nevertheless seems probable that no substantial cession had occurred by the time Oglethorpe wrote his February 10 letter to the Trustees. Had he already achieved this priority goal he would have been hard put not to mention it in his triumphal relation of good news, but he said no such thing. Yet on February 25 Oglethorpe marked out the bounds of the tract the Yamacraws had "reserved," thereby implying that the Indians had earlier made a major land grant. It follows that this cession agreement must have occurred between February 10 and February 25. It was probably closer to the latter date, for the restless and decisive Oglethorpe would have been eager to move quickly before the Indians changed their minds.

Another obvious interpretive problem is the size of the land cession. Since the 1733 documents are silent on the question we must have recourse to later sources. The most detailed and interesting is a 1746 "Talk" from Chigelli, at that time the principal Lower Creek chief. Chigelli dictated his account to Mary (Musgrove) Bosomworth, his niece, who committed it to paper. Significantly, he declared that "all the Indians say they never talked about any Land, but when you [Mary] was the interpreter." Chigelli likewise relayed Santachi's account of "what was given to General Oglethorp." Santachi, one of the Yamacraws who had accompanied Oglethorpe to London, evidently had witnessed the 1733 cession. Chigelli related that Santachi described what Oglethorpe had been given as follows: "as far as the

Tide flowed up the River Savannah and all along the Sea Coast, particularly reserving to themselves the three Islands upon the Sea Coast known by the Names of Ossabbah, St. Catherines and Sappolo and likewise the Land upon Ogeachy River."[24]

In 1747 Malatchi gave a similar account but added an important detail. He related that upon Oglethorpe's arrival Mary Musgrove sent a runner to the Creeks urging that "some of the Headmen should come down and talk" with the English leader. They did, and "then agreed" to cede lands "as far as the Tide flowed," reserving the same coastal islands listed by Santachi. Malatchi plainly referred to the initial conference with Lower Creek leaders in May 1733. In 1765, Lower Creek spokesman Tallechea echoed him when he said the tidal line was agreed upon "at their first meeting," which he claimed to have attended. Thus it was in May 1733 that Lower Creek chiefs agreed to cede lands as far as the tide flowed, presumably confirming a preliminary agreement between Tomochichi and Oglethorpe in February. Since these accounts of Creek concessions are consistent and come from elite Creek informants, they are unusually credible: surely the Creeks gave as much as their top leaders publicly acknowledged giving.[25]

The Creek grant of mainland "all along the Sea Coast" evidently had a definite southern limit: the Ogeechee River. Egmont seems to rule out the other obvious candidate, the Altamaha. In early 1736 he and fellow Trustees tried to divert Oglethorpe from settling new colonists at the Altamaha, urging instead that they be landed at the Ogeechee. One of the arguments they used was that "the Ogihee River is within that district of land purchased of those [Indian] nations when we settled Savannah." The clear implication is that the Altamaha lay outside the ceded area. Moreover, the 1739 treaty, written by Oglethorpe, seems to paraphrase the original oral agreement when it states that the Lower Creeks have granted the Trustees "all the Lands upon the Savannah River as far as the River Ogeeche." Santachi appears to have provided Creek corroboration when he declared that, in addition to islands, the chiefs had reserved "the Land upon Ogeachy River." On the other hand, since all three of the reserved islands lay south of the Ogeechee, the grant of coastal islands was probably vague or unlimited toward the south.[26]

It is clear that Oglethorpe kept much about his initial land negotiations off the record. Having unlimited confidence in his own abilities, he was extremely reluctant to share information or decision making with anyone. He had no circle of trusted advisers; he generally acted on his own. Contrary to common sense and much precedent, the text of the 1733 treaty does not mention the two-stage land agreement that later documents have enabled us to outline. The fact that we can learn more about this transaction from Indian leaders years later than from Oglethorpe at the time is telling. The most surprising thing about Oglethorpe's secretiveness is that, to a large degree, it extended to his fellow Trustees. Although he wrote to them more or less regularly, he told them remarkably little about his negotiations with Indians over land. Oglethorpe knew he had earned the right to be proud of his successes to date, which seemed due to prompt and decisive seizure of opportunities. More than likely he supposed that time-consuming transatlantic deliberations on how to proceed could only get in the way of further successes.[27]

The land cession of 1733 had two stages: a preliminary agreement with the Yamacraws followed by a confirmation from the Lower Creek chiefs. Significantly, Mary Musgrove was not the official interpreter at the formal treaty conference, which steered clear of any particular land transfer. Yet Mary claimed, and probably deserved, credit for interpreting and facilitating both phases of the 1733 agreement over land. The preliminary agreement with Tomochichi and the Yamacraws was a revolving one, which may have begun as early as January, but did not take final shape until mid- or late February. The mainland that was provisionally ceded extended along the coast from the Savannah River down to the Ogeechee, and inland as far as the tides flowed up the rivers, usually estimated at around thirty miles. The Yamacraws reserved a small but critically important tract adjacent to Savannah, upon which they continued to live. Most likely at the same time, or very shortly afterward, these Indians ceded an ill-defined string of coastal islands, reserving the three that were most valuable to them.[28]

Oglethorpe, aware that these concessions required Lower Creek approval, through Mary invited their leaders to Savannah for a parley. Lower Creek headmen recognized this overture as important, for in mid-May a delegation of forty-eight of them from all eight of their towns appeared in Savannah. They arrived at an awkward moment, for Oglethorpe—accompanied by Tomochichi and his "nephew" Tooanahowi—was off in Charles Town. As usual, the Lower Creek chiefs were headed by the current leader of the Cowetas, Yahoulakee, who told the English "We are come 25 Days Journey to see you." It happened that the leadership of Coweta, and thus of the confederation, was then in a state of transition. The redoubtable "Emperor" Brim had recently died, and definitive selection of his successor or successors had yet to occur.[29]

If the men of Coweta had a succession problem in 1733, what they apparently did about it has perplexed scholars ever since. The interpretive problem is this: what the written record seems to show about the line of successors who followed Brim appears to contradict Creek rules of succession. It is beyond dispute that the Creeks reckoned family (clan) connections through the female line and that certain offices ordinarily were supposed to be filled by men from particular clans. Foremost among these offices was that of Coweta Mico, the town's peace chief. Thus if Brim was Coweta Mico, his successor in that office should not have been one of his sons, but a son of one of his sisters. Yet the written record compiled by

English observers indicates that his successor—and his successor's successor—were biological sons, seemingly a patrilineal line. Either the English observers misunderstood Coweta family connections or there is something wrong with the established view of how Coweta leaders were chosen. We will return to this puzzling matter, but for the time being we will take the written record as we find it.[30]

Brim was survived by two young men, Malatchi and Essabo, who are invariably described as his sons. At the meeting with Oglethorpe in May, the latter was identified as "Essoboo, their Warrior, the Son of old Breen, lately dead." In a great many later references Malatchi is likewise described as Brim's son. The two men were not only brothers, they were twin brothers. This alone marked them for preferment. In Creek culture twins were supposed to have extraordinary spirit power, a prerequisite for successful leadership in peace or war.[31]

The council of Coweta chiefs evidently decided that one brother or the other should succeed Brim. Since the twins were only in their early twenties, underage by Creek standards, guardians were designated for both. Chigelli, Brim's brother and the chief warrior of Coweta, was appointed guardian for Malatchi, and Yahoulakee for Essabo. Whichever son was finally chosen to succeed Brim, an older man would serve as regent during his minority. By the time Lower Creek leaders had decided to come down to Savannah, Essabo had somehow gained the ascendancy over his brother. Malatchi's speech to Heron indicates that he did not personally attend the conference with Oglethorpe, and Chigelli apparently stayed home too. Essabo and Yahoulakee came, the latter identified as "Mico of Coweeta" and "their King or Mico." Thus it was Yahoulakee who headed the delegation of Lower Creek chiefs for their first meeting with Oglethorpe and the Georgians.[32]

Oglethorpe's intermediaries must have sung the praises of this new brand of Englishmen very sweetly, for the Lower Creeks came prepared to make territorial concessions to the new colony that they had long denied to the Carolinians. As Malatchi indicated, the influence of Mary Musgrove was probably crucial. Also important was Thomas Wiggins, until recently an established Indian trader in South Carolina. In the process of transferring his residence, business, and loyalty to the new colony, he was now a very influential Georgian. In May 1733 Wiggins escorted the Creeks from their homes to Savannah. Then, assisted by John Musgrove, he served as the main interpreter for the treaty conference. Wiggins likewise was chief interpreter for Oglethorpe's other treaty conference with Lower Creek leaders, in 1739, and the interpreter Oglethorpe relied upon to assist the agents he sent up into Creek country.[33]

If any formal minutes were kept of the negotiations that occurred from May 18 to May 21, they have not survived. We do have a fairly detailed contemporary account, though it is obviously an incomplete record of what transpired. Doubtless written by one of the Carolina gentlemen who sailed down to advise and assist, it was printed in the *South Carolina Gazette* on June 2. Describing it as a "pretty faithfull account," Oglethorpe sent a copy to the Trustees in lieu of any description of his own. It was at least pretty faithful to the account of the meeting Oglethorpe wished to propagate.[34]

This newspaper description can be supplemented in a few places by another source largely based upon it. This was the relevant section of a much longer narrative of the colony's early history published in 1748. This work is obviously very well informed; James Boswell, Oglethorpe's friend later in life, supposed that Oglethorpe himself had written it. It now seems clear that it was written by the Trustees' secretary, Benjamin Martyn, and hereafter will be referred to as Martyn's "History."[35]

When Oglethorpe returned from Charles Town on May 18, he found Wiggins and the Lower Creek chiefs waiting for him. Promptly "Mr. Oglethorpe received the Indians in one of the new Houses." The first recorded and most important speech was made by Oueekachumpa of Oconee, "called by the English long King" (apparently a translation of the Creek title Mico Chupko). He was "a very tall old Man." The Oconee chief "first claimed all the Land to the southward of the River Savannah, as belonging to the Creek Indians." He then declared that "they were firmly persuaded, that the GREAT POWER, which dwelt in Heaven . . . had sent the English thither for the Instruction of them, their Wives and Children." For that reason, he said, "they gave them up freely, their Right to all the Land which they did not use themselves." This far-reaching decision, he continued, "was not only his Opinion, but the Opinion of the 8 Towns of the [Lower] Creeks, each of whom having consulted together had sent some of their Chief Men with Skins, which is their Wealth." At this point a chief from each town produced a bundle of buckskins, "and laid 8 Bundles, from the 8 Towns, at Mr. Oglethorpe's Feet." Even the ever optimistic Oglethorpe must have found this opening almost too good to be true.

Oueekachumpa concluded with a reference to the Cherokees, the Creeks' longtime enemies, that helps explain his people's extraordinary welcome to the English. Alleging that "the Cherokees had killed some Englishmen," he proposed that if Oglethorpe "would command them," the Creeks "would enter with their whole Force into the Cherokee Country, destroy their Harvest, kill their People and revenge the English." The chief's solicitude for alleged English suffering at the hands of the Cherokees was pretty clearly a gambit designed to elicit English support for a Creek attack upon their old foes.

Tomochichi then rose to deliver a ringing testimonial to the good behavior of the English: "I feared you would drive us away, for we were weak and wanted Corn, but you confirmed our Land to us, gave us Food, and instructed our Children." Noting that "the chief Men of all our Nation are here," he concluded: "before them, I declare your Goodness; and that here I design to die; for we [Yamacraws] all love your People so well, that with them we will live and die. . . . and be numbred amongst the Children of the Trustees."

Yahoulakee was the final speaker. He began by pointing out that he had "been often desired to go down to Charlestown" but had spurned all such invitations. Echoing Oeekachumpa, he said that "when I heard . . . that you were good Men, I knew you were sent by Him who lives in Heaven, to teach us Indians Wisdom." So he came to Savannah. Since the Lower Creek leadership wished to be "reconciled to our Brethren, who are here amongst you," he authorized these offcasts from many towns to "come together and make one Town." Yahoulakee had two specific requests: the usual one that prices of trade goods be lowered, and a surprising one. "We must pray you to recal the Yamasees, that . . . then our Nation shall be restored again to its ten Towns." Since wounds from the Yamasee War were scarcely healed, proclaiming close Creek connections with the Yamasees could not have gone over well with the English. Martyn's "History" omits the Yahoulakee speech, simply adding that other chiefs "made Speeches to the same Purpose as Oueekachumpas."[36]

Then, abruptly, according to the *Gazette* account, Yahoulakee "agreed upon Articles of a Treaty, which were ordered to be engrossed." If Yahoulakee was the only spokesman at this key moment, presumably he agreed in behalf of all of the chiefs present. According to the Martyn "History," after the Creek leaders had finished speaking "they agreed with Mr. Oglethorpe on a Treaty of Alliance and Commerce." According to the *Gazette* account, all of the treaty talk and the agreement on the terms of the treaty were completed on May 18, while the signing ceremony occurred three days later. No surviving copy of the treaty contains any signatures, but it concludes with the Lower Creek chiefs declaring that "we have each of us set the marks of our Families" to the document. Oglethorpe was almost certainly the only English signer, as he would be for the 1739 treaty, and as Governor Johnson had been for the 1732 Carolina treaty. Martyn's "History" confirms that both Oglethorpe and Creek leaders affixed their signatures: the treaty "was signed by him and them." Afterward valuable presents were distributed and gratefully received. These included laced coats and hats for the chiefs, guns and ammunition, textiles, "and 8 Cags of Rum." The rum, presumably a keg for each of the eight towns represented, was issued with the cautious proviso that it was "to be carried home to their Towns."[37]

So far as the record reveals, there wasn't much negotiation at this conference. The English got about all that they could have wished for, seemingly without asking. Three Indian leaders made speeches offering extraordinary concessions without seeking much in return, and they got little of what they did request. In angling for overt English aid against the Cherokees they were seeking what no English leader would provide. In seeking a return of the Yamasees from the St. Augustine area they requested what no English leader could desire, much less provide. Both requests were brushed aside. Oglethorpe made his only recorded statement during the conference when he promised to inform the Trustees of the Creek "Desire of being instructed," but declared the report of Cherokee murders of Englishmen "groundless." While the *Gazette* report depicts native leaders as loquacious, it portrays the English as nearly mute. Oglethorpe at least must have said quite a lot, most of which somehow went unrecorded.[38]

Most articles of the treaty were closely patterned after the 1732 Carolina treaty. In Article 1 the English promised the Lower Creeks trade "at the Rates and Prices settled and agreed upon . . . and annexed to this Treaty." Article 2 promised them justice for murders, robberies, or other injuries they suffered at the hands of Englishmen. Those accused of such offenses "shall be tryed and punished according to the English Law," not Creek laws or customs. Article 3 warned that in the event of Creek misbehavior, the English "will withdraw the English favour from the Town so offending" (a muted threat to cut off trade, explicit in the Carolina treaty).

In Article 5 the Creeks promised the Georgia colonists justice for murder, assault, or robbery suffered at their hands. They pledged "to deliver up any of our People who shall be guilty of the crimes aforesaid to be tryed by the English Laws or by the laws of our Nation as the Beloved Man of the Trustees shall think fit." At first sight it might appear that the Creek chiefs not only conceded to Georgia officials sole authority to pass judgment upon English violators of Creeks, but likewise granted them sole authority to judge Creek violators of Englishmen. Creek leaders had not been so careless about the fate of their own people. The chiefs had not agreed that the English could arrest and bring a Creek to trial; an English trial of a Creek could only begin when Creek leaders concluded that he was "guilty" of a "crime" against the English. In other words, the Creeks would try and convict him first. Oglethorpe and his successors would have little reason to ponder whether to try a Creek by English or Creek law, for Creek chiefs apparently never surrendered one of their people to the Georgia officials for trial.[39]

In Article 6 the Indians promised "to apprehend and secure any Negro or other slave which shall run away from any the English Settlements to our Nation," while the English pledged rewards for such service. By the final article the Creeks promised that "we will not have any correspondence with the Spaniards or French." The newly naturalized rhetoric from the north is there too: the English wish the Indians to keep "this Chain of Friendship in your minds and linked to your hearts," while the natives promise to do so "as long as the Sun shall shine or the waters run in the Rivers." All of this was lifted with little change, often word for word, from the Carolina treaty. Even the apparently irrelevant article on the return of slaves was borrowed whole. The only significant provision of Carolina treaty that

Oglethorpe ignored was a promise to provide ammunition "to go to War against your Enemies."[40]

One article in the Georgia treaty, the fourth, had no counterpart in the South Carolina treaty. Article 4 was special, for it dealt with territory. Oglethorpe doubtless had at hand a draft of the treaty he aimed for when the conference began. If it contained any projected agreement over land, it would likely have been a provision by which the Lower Creeks confirmed the Yamacraws' recent cession of lands along the coast. Whatever his original intention regarding territory, Oglethorpe instantly changed direction and treaty text when he sensed a glorious opportunity. It came with Oueekachumpa's astonishing announcement that Lower Creeks "gave" the English "their Right to all the Land which they did not use themselves." No quid pro quo was demanded; it was a gift, though surely one given in the expectation of reciprocal favors. Moreover, the verb used in translation, "gave," probably misrepresents the Indians' intent. At any rate, Oglethorpe seized upon this statement and made it the foundation of Article 4. As hastily written or rewritten, this pivotal article has the Lower Creeks stepping aside in favor of the English: "we make over unto them . . . all such Lands and Territories as we shall have no occasion to use." While no one could have described precisely what had here been given, it must have seemed to Oglethorpe that here was a gift that might go on giving and giving. That was an illusion, as Oglethorpe probably realized very quickly.[41]

Neither Oueekachumpa's statement nor the treaty article based upon it seems to have had any significant effect on subsequent negotiations or agreements over land. All cessions of territory from Creeks to the English after 1736, and most of the earlier ones, involved lands that were more or less clearly bounded. If Oglethorpe reached for uninhibited future expansion in the formal treaty, he did not neglect to nail down the quite specific grant of territory that the Yamacraws had already conceded. As noted earlier, the evidence indicates that it was during their initial conference with Oglethorpe that Lower Creek leaders agreed to cede lands as far as the tide flowed between the Savannah and Ogeechee Rivers. This cession must have occurred between May 18 and May 21, 1733.[42]

Oglethorpe arrived in Savannah on May 18, the day of the conference, and three days later, the day the treaty was signed, he promptly departed for Charles Town. There is no indication in the record that the confirmation occurred during the two formal meetings, so it was probably arranged during the convivial interlude between them. After Oglethorpe met with the chiefs on May 18, "Tomochichi invited them to his Town, where they passed the Night in feasting and dancing." We may imagine that a bottle or two were uncorked, perhaps at Mary Musgrove's house a few yards away. As noted earlier, Chigelli asserted that the Creeks "never talked about any Land" except when Mary did the translating. So, although she had not been the official interpreter for the formal treaty, Mary almost certainly acted as interpreter—and facilitator—for the land deal.[43]

As for trade prices, a matter of great concern to the Creeks, they received only minor concessions. Appended to the treaty text is a "Schedule of Prices of Goods agreed on," a list of prices for twenty-four items in terms of buckskins or (twice as many) doeskins. This list is nearly identical to its model, which is appended to the 1732 South Carolina treaty with the Creeks. All prices are exactly the same except those for hoes, hatchets, and brass kettles, which were now lower in Georgia. Only the reduction for a hoe (two buckskins rather than three) was substantial.[44]

The successful treaty conference immediately elevated three residents of the Savannah area in stature: Oglethorpe, Mary Musgrove, and Tomochichi. Especially back home, Oglethorpe's achievement seemed almost miraculous. He appeared to have charmed the most dangerous native nation in the region to sing in eight-part harmony to the British tune. Almost overnight Mary metamorphosed from keeper of a country store to an elite figure in the new provincial capital. With a nearly unique ability to communicate easily with both Creek and English leaders, she immediately became indispensable. Almost as quickly, she became a diplomat as well as a translator. In the eyes of the Lower Creek chiefs, Tomochichi was rather suddenly transformed from an old troublemaker into an elder statesman. He clearly had access to English ears and English goods; what he thought, said, and did on Yamacraw Bluff now mattered in council houses on the Chattahoochee. As Oglethorpe and the English satisfied themselves that such was the case, Tomochichi's influence with them grew apace. Altogether this cast of lead actors was half English and half Creek: Oglethorpe was English, Tomochichi was Creek, and Mary split the difference.

The treaty conference evidently did nothing to enhance the stature of Lower Creek leaders who participated, probably because hindsight suggested that they had been overgenerous to the newcomers. Nothing further is heard from Oueekachumpa. Yahoulakee died shortly after the conference. Essabo died at Silver Bluff in March 1735. Malatchi then emerged as Brim's political heir apparent, a role he was obliged to play for a decade. From 1735 to the close of 1746, his guardian, Chigelli, was recognized as the big man in Coweta and head of the Lower Creek confederacy. Malatchi was finally able to claim his place in 1747, and would preside over Lower Creek polity until his death in 1756.

Since Malatchi and Chigelli would be dominant Lower Creek leaders for decades to come, the issue of their exact leadership roles must finally be confronted. To this writer, it seems all but certain that Malatchi and his twin brother were not Brim's nephews, but his biological sons. As noted earlier, Oglethorpe and numerous other Englishmen uniformly identify them as such. That can be and has been dismissed as the result the English cultural blinders toward matrilineal institutions. It is not so easy to dismiss Creek sources that identify Malatchi as Brim's son. There are at least three.[45]

In April 1735 Thomas Causton produced an invitation list of Creek leaders designated by Tomochichi as suitable recipients of English presents. Causton explained that he had "taken the Enclosed List from Tomochichis own Mouth." Tomochichi identified Malatchi as "Twin Brother to Saphia [Essabo?] Son to the Emperor Brem." In December 1747 Malatchi made an important speech to Colonel Alexander Heron in Frederica. He then stated that "My Father was Emperor of the Creek Nation." In August 1749 Lower Creek leaders then in Savannah signed a document recognizing Mary (Musgrove) Bosomworth as "our Rightfull and natural Princess." The document was clearly written by Mary and her then husband. At any rate, it identifies Malatchi as chief spokesman, and describes him as "Malatchie Opiya Mico; by the paternal line: being the son of the old Emperor Rightfull and natural prince of the upper and Lower Creek Nations." The paternal line![46]

An entrenched assumption has stood in the way of recognizing that Malatchi was the son of Brim, and that Tugulki was the son of Malatchi. That assumption is that Brim's essential leadership role was that of Coweta Mico, and this office is what his son and grandson aspired to succeed to. Brim may have been—probably was—Coweta Mico, but the sparse evidence does not establish that connection. More to the point, there is no clear evidence that Malatchi, or Chigelli, or Tugulki, ever claimed that title. The only title we know for Brim was Hopoihithli. That was not a title of office, but a very prestigious war title, that is, a personal title denoting rank. It shows up (variously spelled as Hoboyetly, Hopoeheathly, Opohethle, Opoithly, etc.) adorning numerous other Creek leaders. According to several recent studies, the approximate meaning of the title is "the one who does the thinking about war."[47]

What is important about Brim's leadership is not so much his influence in Coweta as the fact that it extended to all of the Lower Creek towns. He was proud to claim as least as much. In 1716 Brim told a visiting Spanish officer that he was the one "to whom all render obedience" within the "seven provinces which are subject to his order and authority." About a decade later an English officer, after a visit to "Emperor Bream's Dominions," related that Brim "stiles himself the Emperor of Seaven Nations." Colonial leaders believed him. Both the Spanish government in St. Augustine and the English government in Charles Town gave him commissions that recognized him as Creek "emperor." Brim's leadership role beyond his hometown was probably self-created, perhaps too new to have a formal title of office affixed to it. If he had such a title, it undoubtedly signified a war chief rather than a peace chief. No office in Creek society was strictly hereditary, but civil or town offices were almost certainly more closely tied to clan membership than military offices were. Creek war leaders were typically self-made men who were likely to come from any of the clans, not just a "correct" one. Thus, if patrilineal succession was highly unlikely for civil offices, it was better suited than its opposite for military offices.[48]

It was Brim's expanded leadership role over other Creek towns—the Lower Creek confederacy he largely created—that his successors aspired to. His brother Chigelli probably came closest to achieving it, and seems to have thought that he had. In 1735 he told Savannah leaders: "I am of the Eldest Town and was chosen to rule after the death of the Emperor Bream. I have a strong mouth and will declare this resolution to the rest of the nations, and make them comply therewith." When he returned for a talks the following year he was described as "the Chief of the Lower Creeks," not Coweta. Recall that Chigelli had been a great military leader, the man who led Creek warriors to the outskirts of Charles Town during the Yamasee War. Although he is not known to have claimed the title Coweta Mico, Chigelli did claim a title of office, perhaps one first worn by Brim. In December 1746 Chigelli dictated a talk addressed to Major Horton to Mary, who wrote it down and sent it to Horton. Chigelli began by proclaiming his title: "TUSKEE-STONNECAH MICO War King or King of the Warriors in the Creek Indian Nation." This title clearly signifies a military office whose sway extended beyond Coweta to the other Lower Creek towns.[49]

Within a year Chigelli stepped aside in favor of Malatchi. The following December Malatchi and other Lower Creek leaders met with Colonel Alexander Heron in Frederica. On December 14 sixteen of them set their marks to a document recognizing "Malatchi, Opiya Mico to be our Rightful and Natural Prince." Military leaders in many other Creek towns had the same title, rendered here as Hopoya Mico. (The first term is spelled many different ways: Hoboye, Hopoya, Hopoye, Hupei, Oboi, Opaya, Uppoya, etc.) Swanton gives the title as Hobayi Miko, translating it as "Far away miko." Indian superintendent Edmond Atkin probably gave a better translation for a Tuckabatchee chief with that title: "Opoyamico War hunting King and Leading Warriour of Tuckabatchee." Thus the title Malatchi shared with many others was that of a war chief. In his case the authority of this office—or perhaps another he held—was supposed to extend to all of the Lower Creek towns.[50]

Following the treaty, Oglethorpe continued shuttling back and forth between Charles Town and the new colony. One of the tasks he undertook in June was a direct outgrowth of the land cession in May. Among the most appreciated assists from South Carolina was the loan of a company of rangers commanded by Captain James McPherson. Oglethorpe at first stationed these troopers at Horse Quarter, a little upriver from the Yamacraw Tract. Their presence here reassured the colonists that the friendly disposition of the Yamacraws would continue. Oglethorpe returned from Charles Town on June 12. The same day he ordered McPherson and his men to accompany him on a reconnaissance of the interior, and apparently set off almost immediately following the Savannah River. Oglethorpe's main objective was pretty clearly to block out what he understood to be the tract the Lower Creeks had just ceded, or at least the part between the Savannah and Ogeechee Rivers. The survey party proceeded up the river to a spot a little short of the tributary that soon would be known as Abercorn River. Here, at what Oglethorpe likely supposed was a reasonable approximation of the tidal limit, he veered away from the Savannah River and headed southwesterly toward the Ogeechee.[51]

Before the party reached the Ogeechee, it crossed a major Indian path running southward from the old Apalachicola town (now the South Carolina fortified settlement of Palachacola). This path bent off toward the south, and so crossed the Ogeechee well below the limit of its tidal flow. Because this crossing was of obvious strategic importance, Oglethorpe decided to build the fort he had been contemplating here rather than further upriver at the tidal limit. McPherson's men were set to work building a fort on the north bank of the river. The famous "Map of the County of Savannah," apparently based on a 1734 sketch by Oglethorpe, calls it "Old Fort." Having moved quickly as usual, on June 18 Oglethorpe was back in Savannah.[52]

A construction blunder doomed Old Fort. By August fallen trees and debris that the rangers had dumped into the river had choked it off and blocked access from the coast. Oglethorpe promptly ordered the building effort relocated about five miles downstream, the result being Fort Argyle. Although Old Fort was a shell, it was not an empty one. It continued to mark the limit of English possessions up the Ogeechee River, for ten of the rangers under Lieutenant William Elbert were stationed here. Marking a new road from Fort Argyle to Palachacola, a party headed by Oglethorpe "found a River at about 12 miles from this place to which we gave the name of Abercorn." Since "this place" was Savannah, he supposed that the new river emptied into the Savannah about thirty miles from the sea, that is, about at the tidal line. Shortly afterward he would found the town of Abercorn close by that river junction. Significantly, Oglethorpe declared that Abercorn River "divides this part of the Province from the Western Country."[53]

In Oglethorpe's eyes, Abercorn marked a boundary. Oglethorpe had outlined a more or less rectangular area with corners at the mouth of the Savannah River, the mouth of the Ogeechee River, Old Fort on the Ogeechee, and Abercorn on the Savannah. The interior points approximated the tidal line, and altogether the area was about the size of an English county. Around year's end Oglethorpe urged his fellow Trustees to designate it as such: "this County if You think fit to make it such is on the West secured by the River Abercorn." To promote this objective he sketched a prototype map of "the County of Savannah" that was soon engraved in London, and published in Germany in 1735. His fellow Trustees, perhaps annoyed at being pushed, did not act to create this county until June 1741. (A quarter century later, roughly the same area was transformed once again into Christ Church Parish.)[54]

A few days after his return from the Ogeechee, Oglethorpe met with native leaders he had not seen before. By early March he had learned that "there are in Georgia on this Side the Mountains three considerable Nations of Indians." He named the Lower Creeks first, estimating that they could muster "about 1000 Men able to bear Arms." He went on to say that "the other two Nations are the Uchees and the Upper Creeks the first consisting of 200, the latter of 1100 men." At the commonly used four-to-one ratio, Oglethorpe indicated that there were about four thousand Lower Creeks, eight hundred Yuchis, and forty-four hundred Upper Creeks. The first two figures seem about right, but Oglethorpe most likely underestimated Upper Creek population.[55]

Gordon tells us that at some point, probably during or after the Lower Creek meeting, Oglethorpe decided to invite the Yuchis and Upper Creeks to a similar conference. Accordingly, he had sent "two Indian traders and interpreters . . . up to the nations on purpose to bring them down." In late June or early July, Yuchi and Upper Creek chiefs and their followers, about eighty in all, arrived in Savannah. Gordon thought they came "to enter in to a Treaty of Friendshipp with Mr. Oglethorp, and receive the presents usual on those occasions." The visitors were welcomed with much pomp on this occasion: cannons thundered and "all owr people being under arms lined the way on each side they were to pass through from the Bluff to the house where Mr. Oglethorp was."[56]

This time there would be no formal treaty, nor is there any sign of serious negotiation. "The talk," which Gordon mentioned but did not describe, was probably little more than an exchange of greetings and pleasantries. Oglethorpe never mentioned the meeting at all. Unlike the Lower Creeks, the Yuchis and Upper Creeks did not claim lands that Oglethorpe was then interested in. After presents were distributed, the Yuchis and Upper Creeks stayed for a week in separate encampments outside town. The most significant thing about this meeting is what did not happen: the Upper Creeks evidently were not asked to ratify either the Lower Creek treaty or the Lower Creek land cession. Like Carolina leaders, Oglethorpe saw the Lower and Upper Creeks as distinct political entities with distinct territories. Accordingly, he supposed that British development of the coastal region was to be negotiated exclusively with the Lower Creeks.[57]

In June, Oglethorpe sent a copy of the Lower Creek treaty to the Trustees, who received it on August 8. On October 18 the Trustees' Common Council duly ratified the accord, "the articles whereof were engrossed on a large sheet of parchment full embellished." All known copies of the treaty derive from this edited text. It omits the opening and closing formalities, including the date and the signatures.[58]

Oglethorpe had every reason to be content with his diplomacy to date, but soon he made plans to compound his gains by means of a dramatic pilgrimage to London. The pilgrims he would conduct to the seat of British power would be Tomochichi and a suitable company of Indian attendants. The appearance of a large party of unspoiled natural men would excite the curiosity of influential Londoners, inspire confidence in the Georgia leadership, attract new financial support and settlers to the colony, and solidify the understandings achieved in 1733. Moreover, as had happened with the Cherokee visit four years earlier, opportunities for a further advantageous agreement might be cultivated. Once the pilgrims had returned home, the effects on the Indians would be equally salutary: news of British might and generosity would spread far and wide, the prestige of a loyal ally would be enhanced, and the message that it paid to cooperate with the English of Georgia would be unmistakably clear.[59]

Despite his advanced years, Tomochichi was intrigued with the prospect of such a journey and readily fell in with Oglethorpe's plan. Prompted by Tomochichi, the Lower Creeks lent their support to the mission, and various of the Chattahoochee towns sent eagle wands for delivery to the British monarch as tokens of friendship. The delegation of nine Indians that was finally assembled for the grand tour was one of the largest ever to visit England. It consisted of Tomochichi, his wife Senauki, a boy named Tooanahowi ("his nephew, as he calls him"), his "Cosen" Hinguithi, "his chief warrior" Hillispilli (evidently Tooanahowi's father), the Apalachicola "Beloved Man" Umpichi, and three young "Attendants," Santachi, Apokutchi, and Stimaletchi. John Musgrove agreed to go along as interpreter.[60]

Oglethorpe and the Indians began their journey in early March 1734 by sailing up the coast to Charles Town. Coincidentally, the first embarkation of Lutheran exiles from Salzburg bound for Georgia arrived there about the same time. Oglethorpe immediately put his travel plans on hold while he dealt with the Salzburgers. Returning to Savannah with these German colonists, Oglethorpe decided to settle them up the river just beyond Abercorn. There he would mark out the town the immigrants called Ebenezer. In Georgia, as elsewhere in the English colonies, foreign immigrants would usually be directed to settle in frontier areas. There was a parallel example a few miles upriver on the Carolina side: Purrysburg, a Swiss town founded three years earlier. The site Oglethorpe chose for Ebenezer had the potential to become a major embarrassment or worse, for it was located about seven miles beyond Abercorn, and thus seemingly well beyond the tidal line. Oglethorpe probably excused this indiscretion on the ground that the Yamacraw war leader, "Captain Tuscany," had accompanied him upriver and helped choose the site. As Oglethorpe had hoped, the Yamacraws never made an issue of Ebenezer. From the founding of the original town, Ebenezer Creek replaced Abercorn River as the practical boundary of the land ceded by the Lower Creeks the previous year.[61]

Oglethorpe returned to Charles Town in early April, but John Musgrove had unfinished business to attend to before he followed. Like Musgrove, many of Georgia's earliest setters were prosperous men from South Carolina who sensed opportunity across the river. The major attraction was land. Though the Georgia Trustees were parsimonious with land grants to settlers whose passage they paid, they were more generous with those who paid their own way. The royal charter placed a limit of five hundred acres on all grants; the Trustees transformed this limit into the standard for gentlemen grantees. On December 7, 1732, they approved five grants of five hundred acres each to Roger Lacy and four other gentlemen. Unlike their reticence on common grants, they did not hesitate to specify their terms for such elite grants. Each grantee had to agree to transport himself and "four Male Servants" to Georgia within a year, pay a certain quit-rent after ten years, and hold their lands by tail-male tenure. These early five-hundred-acre grants set the basic pattern the Trustees would follow for gentlemen grantees over many years to come.[62]

The main financial burdens on the recipients of these grants were various costs of transportation. These were threshold expenses, due at the outset and usually in cash. Such outlays would obviously be much lower for those crossing a river than those crossing an ocean. Thus gentlemen immigrating to Georgia from Britain were at both a cost and experience disadvantage compared to counterparts from neighboring South Carolina. The Trustees themselves, through their Common Council, made all such major grants; Oglethorpe could merely recommend men he considered worthy of them.[63]

Mary (Musgrove) Bosomworth later wrote that in June 1732 "her then Husband Mr. John Musgrove brought, Considerable Effects into Georgia, as Horses, Cattle, etc." Musgrove had probably driven his stock down the dirt road to Purrysburg, one of the most favorable crossing points along the lower Savannah River, then eastward along the south bank toward Yamacraw. Most likely he left his cattle about six miles above the bluff at a place soon known as "Musgrove's Cowpen." This ranching area was clearly a going concern long before Tomochichi's party departed for England. In February 1734 Oglethorpe described it as "the Lands of John Musgrove Gent." Just before the Indians returned from London the Trustees conveyed the cowpen area to Musgrove as a five-hundred-acre gentleman's grant.[64]

Other Carolina gentlemen settled on either side of Musgrove: Robert Williams on the adjacent tract upriver, and Joseph Watson downriver, between the Musgrove's place and Pipemaker's Creek. John and Mary would have multiple contacts with both of them. The Williams-Musgrove-Watson section of the riverfront, and especially the Musgrove tract, would become the nursery of endless troubles for decades to come.[65]

John Musgrove had to settle two legal matters before setting off for England. First, he had to negotiate a business contract. Since neither his wife nor any other woman was fully competent legally, during his absence from the colony John needed a partner to take legal responsibility for his trade goods and storehouse. Musgrove settled on his neighbor, Joseph Watson. The exact terms are unknown, but Musgrove and Watson signed a partnership contract. Second, on April 29, probably a few days later, Musgrove signed his last will and testament in Savannah. By this will John reportedly left the five-hundred-acre "Cow pen" to his two surviving sons, James Musgrove and Edward Musgrove (the latter presumably a younger son named after Mary's father). He also designated Mary as his "sole executrix and residuary legatee," a provision that would soon become very significant.[66]

Once John Musgrove joined Oglethorpe and the Indians in Charles Town the party was complete and ready to embark. They sailed on May 7. Arriving off the Isle of Wight on June 16, Oglethorpe hurried ahead to make arrangements and entered London on June 20. The next day he told fellow Trustees that Tomochichi, though "ninety years old," was "a sensible, cunning man" whose influence might make or break the colony. Aroused, the Trustees dispatched an elegant barge manned by liveried boatmen to convey the visitors to the capital city. Arriving at the Trustees' offices at Westminster on June 28, Tomochichi and his companions were lodged in handsome apartments upstairs.[67]

On July 3 the Trustees held a formal reception for the Indian visitors, with the Earl of Egmont presiding. Tomochichi proved to be as impressive as Oglethorpe had promised. At the reception he made a moving speech expressing hope that his declining years would see a permanent peace established between his people and the English. He would not have undertaken this journey, he said, had he not had complete trust in his good friend Oglethorpe. He had come "for the good of his Posterity, that they might be instructed in What is right and necessary for them," and he promised to convey to his people all that he saw in England. Clearly touched, Egmont responded with an eloquent speech of his own, forecasting that "Your Children shall be Ours, and Ours shall be Yours." This affecting scene was recorded in the famous painting by William Verelst. Since the likeness of each participant was an actual portrait, the painting took years and many sittings to complete. Verelst lavished particular effort on his individual portrait of Tomochichi. Commissioned by the Trustees, it hung in a place of honor in the Trustees' office. Tomochichi was well satisfied with his meetings with the Trustees, for three weeks later he had a message sent home to his people "to let them know he is doing a great deal of good for them all and their Children." He would do even more good for the Trustees and the king.[68]

Oglethorpe and the other Trustees soon prevailed upon Sir Robert Walpole, the prime minister, to arrange an audience for Tomochichi's party with King George II. Walpole also agreed to provide several royal coaches to convey the Indians around London and a sentry to stand watch outside the Trustees' offices. As Oglethorpe explained to the prime minister, a guard had become necessary for these fascinating guests "to protect them from the curiousity of the Mob who begin now to grow troublesome."[69]

On July 31 Oglethorpe was able to inform his fellow Trustees that King George had decided to deal with the visiting Creeks "on the same foot as the Iroquois Indians were treated in Queen Anne's reign." The Trustees knew that meant first-class treatment, Oglethorpe adding that it included an audience with the king the very next day. Before this day was out, despite the ministrations of Sir Hans Slone, Tomochichi's "Cosen" Hinguithi died. Egmont reported that the Indians "sat up all night, crying and bewailing his loss." So, when they were driven to Kensington Palace the next morning, they were not at their best. But then, neither was the king.[70]

Tomochichi's company, resplendent in their new court costumes and their old paint, made a good show on August 1. After an impressive display of courtly obeisance, Tomochichi addressed the king in much the same way he had the Trustees. "I am come for the Good of the Children of all the Nations of the Upper and Lower Creeks," he declared. An admiring witness reported that the Indian leader "spoke his speeches mighty gravely, and well, and with much emphasis." Pausing briefly, he advanced to the throne and laid several animal skins at the king's feet. As three of his companions came forward with wands of eagle feathers, Tomochichi explained that in his country these were treasured emblems of peace. Pointing out that these particular eagle feathers had come from the various Creek towns, he laid them atop the skins "as a Sign of everlasting Peace." He concluded by promising that "whatsovever Words you shall say unto me, I will tell them faithfully to all the Kings of the Creek Nations."[71]

The king responded to this cue, but he had no prepared speech to deliver. What he did manage to do was to briefly and simply express his appreciation for the peace tokens and declare his fatherly goodwill toward the Creeks. The Indians were then conducted to Queen Caroline, who received them in the company of the ladies of the court. Tooanahowi caught the fancy of the queen, who "Stroked his face" and invited him to return to receive a present. "He answered her in English, and was forward in his learning." Afterward someone asked one of the visitors "which he thought the finest woman there." Embarrassed, the Indian "begged pardon if he made an improper answer, in owning that all white people were so much alike to him, that he could not easily distinguish one from another, and that it was some time before he could distinguish their friend Mr. Oglethorpe from the rest." Later that day meetings were held with the king's two surviving sons, Frederick, Prince of Wales, and William, Duke of Cumberland, along with his five daughters. The thirteen-year-old duke presented a gun and a "gold repeating watch" to Tooanahowi, who later reciprocated by naming Cumberland Island in honor of his benefactor. Tomochichi left the palace "well Satisfied, only he wished his People had been allowed to dance their War dance, which was the highest compliment they could make."[72]

Tomochichi's formal audience with the king was not very substantive, but there was another meeting between them that was. This was a private conference of elite figures that left almost no record. The participants were probably limited to the king, Tomochichi, Oglethorpe, the Duke of Newcastle, interpreter John Musgrove, and very few others. One result undoubtedly was that predicted by Egmont a few weeks earlier when he said the Indians had come "to confirm the Treaty made with them." Harman Verelst, the Trustees' treasurer, most likely captured his employers' motive for financing the trip more exactly. He wrote that Tomochichi's party was in London "to secure the Lands to the Trustees." Very likely Tomochichi did confirm both the treaty and the land cession negotiated with Oglethorpe the previous year. That was not all he was induced to do regarding territory.[73]

Shortly after his return to Georgia in 1736, Oglethorpe wrote an important letter to the Duke of Newcastle, secretary of state, from the new town of Frederica near the mouth of the Altamaha River. He reported that Tomochichi had just accompanied him southward "to the utmost Limits of the King of Great Britain's Dominions." The Yamacraw leader had done this, Oglethorpe reminded the duke, "pursuant to the assurances he gave to His Majesty and your Grace in England." It seems clear that these "assurances" went beyond those Tomochichi gave the Trustees. When North American Indians visited the British court an effort was usually made to maneuver them into some sort of acknowledgment that they and their lands were under British sovereignty. Egmont had broached this delicate subject on July 3 when he told Tomochichi's party that "You are under a King, Who is good and gracious to all his People." The Indians had made no objection to that pregnant sentence: it remained to get them to positively endorse it. As we shall see, later events indicate that this was the main purpose of Tomochichi's private meeting with the king. It would have major consequences for Georgia. If the other Trustees were aware of this meeting, they apparently knew nothing about what transpired until two years later.[74]

During the three months following their audience with the king, the Indians were taken to see the major sights of London and environs, including the Tower, St. Paul's, the old city, Greenwich, Eton, Windsor Castle, and Hampton Court. Usually they traveled in two royal coaches-and-six, and seldom failed to attract crowds. Along the way they were introduced to many British notables, including Prime Minister Walpole, the Archbishop of Canterbury, and several members of the Royal Society. Tomochichi was duly impressed with what he saw of English life, but was not dazzled, remarking that he "doubted if we were happier, Since we live worse than they, and they more innocently."[75]

By mid-August Tomochichi was tiring of it all and ready to return home, but he was determined to resolve trade issues before he left. From late August until early October the Trustees held a series of talks with the Indians on the state of the trade in Georgia. Probably acting on instructions impressed upon him by the Lower Creek leadership, Tomochichi proposed a number of significant changes. He urged that weights and measures be standardized, that "Nobody may be allowed to trade in Georgia without a License from the Trustees," that each Creek town have a single trader, and that the Trustees "forbid the Selling of Rum." He proposed that a storehouse be established in each Creek town, "which shall be obliged to supply them at the fixed Prices." Egmont reported that the Indian leader also proposed that the English "mend their firearms at our expense," thereby following the French example. The Trustees decided that they could not act on these proposals without more information and referred the whole matter to Oglethorpe. He proceeded to draft an act for managing Indian affairs in Georgia, which would be the first of three laws the Trustees approved the following spring.[76]

The Trustees also put Oglethorpe at the head of a committee to draft a memorial to the king asking him to defray the expenses of the Indian visit. This memorial had the desired effect, and early in October the king granted the Trustees £1,000 for these expenses, with £400 earmarked for royal presents to the visitors. Oglethorpe was then placed at the head of a committee to select and purchase these presents. John Musgrove was not forgotten. As the only individual in England who could communicate easily with the Indians, he must have accompanied them everywhere and had an exhausting time. Egmont complained about Musgrove's drunkenness and unsatisfactory interpreting of complex trade questions, but overall he must have done tolerably well. On October 16 the Trustees rewarded him with £100 from the royal subsidy and a grant of five hundred acres of land in Georgia.[77]

The Indians were disappointed that Oglethorpe would not be returning with them. As Oglethorpe saw them off on October 30, Tomochichi said he was glad to be going home, but parting with his great friend was "like the day of death." As a final gesture of reciprocity, he presented carefully preserved gifts to the Trustees.

Among the benefactions received during 1734 and 1735, the Trustees recorded one from Tomochichi: "Left by him, at the Trustees Office, on his going from England, as a Token of Friendship, to subsist between his People and the People of Georgia, twenty Five Buck Skins, One Tyger [panther] Skin, and Six Buffalo Skins." Entrusted to the care of Peter Gordon, the Indians sailed from England on October 31 and on December 28 arrived in Savannah.[78]

They returned laden with gifts. Among the things that struck their fancy in England were portraits, doubtless including Verelst's sketches of themselves. At their trade conference with the Trustees, Tomochichi requested "the picture of the Great Lyon they Saw at the Tower." He got his wish, along with a portrait of Oglethorpe. Shortly after his return, Tomochichi sent word to Oglethorpe that "your picture is gon to the nation." Following this traveling exhibition, the portrait was hung in its permanent place of display, Tomochichi's new three-room house. In 1737 John Tanner told Egmont that Tomochichi "keeps his parlour locked, wherein is the picture of the lion we gave him, as also Mr. Oglethorpe's picture."[79]

Oglethorpe was to remain in England for another year. He must have enjoyed his stay immensely. His diplomacy had succeeded so brilliantly that he was lionized as a national hero. Of more immediate importance, his fellow Trustees recognized him as the indispensable man when developing further plans for the young colony that seemed to be flourishing beyond all expectations.

CHAPTER THREE

Staking Out the Territory

During Oglethorpe's long absence from Georgia, his strong hand was missed. As the cruel difficulties in the way of making the colony a success steadily became apparent, the colonists' high hopes faded and they fell to squabbling among themselves. By mid-1735 a faction of "malcontents" was prepared to openly challenge existing authority. The only real government in the colony, the municipal council of Savannah, was barely able to preserve order in the town and lacked authorization to do more. In particular, the Savannah magistrates had not been empowered to deal with Indians. Just before his departure for England, Oglethorpe had entrusted that responsibility to Patrick Mackay, a decision he would regret.

Patrick Mackay was the head of a prominent Highland Scottish family that had fallen on hard times. Disastrous commercial speculations had forced him to sell the family estate and, apparently, declare bankruptcy. Moreover, according to Egmont, he had "Fled Scotland for Felony." By September 1733 Mackay arrived in Savannah with his wife, daughter, three younger brothers, and an imposing entourage. Oglethorpe was impressed with Mackay's commanding presence and the size of his retinue, seeing the Scottish adventurer as a major addition to the colony. On September 27 he informed the Trustees of an agreement he had made with Mackay's group to found a town of forty men, and argued that appropriate grants should be expedited. He recommended gentleman's grants of five hundred acres for Mackay and three others. Those grants were made, and the Scots were soon settled at what was called Joseph's Town. It was less a town than a string of plantations along the river ten or twelve miles above Savannah. From this time forward, Scotsmen, especially Highlanders, would be conspicuously represented in the Georgia backcountry.[1]

Oglethorpe had spent most of the last two months of his first American sojourn in Charles Town trying to reach an understanding with the South Carolina leaders. While the Carolinians welcomed Georgia as a buffer against the Spanish and the French, they saw it as a mixed blessing. For more than a half century they had carried on a long-distance overland trade with the Southeastern Indians, a trade that the new colony placed at risk. If Georgia now separated Carolinians from potential European enemies, it also separated them from all of their most important native trading partners except the Cherokees. The potential loss or contraction of their most profitable trade, that with the Creeks, was especially disturbing. A significant conflict of interest was inevitable between the two colonies. Governor Johnson and Oglethorpe made some progress toward an accommodation, but Mackay's claim that the Carolinians "willingly surrendered" control over the Creek trade to Georgia was mere bluff.[2]

The main agreement Oglethorpe and Johnson reached focused on the Upper Creeks. For a decade and a half Carolinians had gnashed their teeth over French influence among the Alabamas and Creeks emanating from Fort Toulouse. To counter that threat, Oglethorpe and Johnson agreed to attempt to establish an English fort among the Upper Creeks. South Carolina would provide the funds to build it and maintain it for two years, about £8,000 in provincial currency, while Georgia would provide the garrison. Accordingly, on March 13, 1734, Oglethorpe commissioned Mackay captain of an "Independent Company" of rangers. The project obviously would require some delicate negotiations with the Indians, and Oglethorpe decided to entrust that too to Mackay.[3]

On April 27 Oglethorpe provided Mackay with one set of instructions as ranger captain, and another as "Agent to the Creeks." Mackay was to proceed to Coweta as soon as possible and hold a conference with Creek leaders. Oglethorpe supplied Mackay with a script he hoped this conference would follow, including a speech from himself. The general objectives were to solidify the peace, win vacillating Creeks away from the French and Spanish, and establish better trading relationships. Above all, Mackay was to do whatever was necessary to secure Creek assent to an English fort ("House") on the Tallapoosa River. To further these aims, Mackay was to visit all of the major Creek towns, both Lower and Upper, and hold whatever talks he saw fit. Oglethorpe apparently also won Johnson's agreement to appoint Mackay as South Carolina's agent to the Creeks. Johnson did so, but Mackay later complained that the governor had evaded furnishing him with a notice to this effect addressed to the Carolina traders.[4]

Mackay began to organize his expedition to the Creek country shortly after Oglethorpe's departure for England. By mid-August he had expended at least £315 for Indian presents, including eighteen British flags made of silk. Illness and difficulty in securing an interpreter helped delay his departure until November, and he did not arrive in Coweta until mid-December. Thomas Wiggins served as his guide and adviser, evidently as Oglethorpe had arranged. Throughout the winter Mackay made Coweta his headquarters. Following his instructions, he visited many of the Lower Creek towns, distributing presents and sounding the natives out on the projected fort. He also established contact with the distant Choctaws, reporting that the French were exerting themselves prodigiously to prevent the Choctaws from slipping into the British orbit.[5]

On March 27, 1735, Mackay reported that the previous week he had held a general conference with the Lower Creek headmen at Coweta. There he delivered a formal talk from Oglethorpe and announced that King George and the Trustees would soon provide a large store of presents. A short while later Mackay held a similar meeting with the Upper Creek headmen at Okfuskee. There he made it clear, too clear, that the principal British objective in dealing with the Upper Creeks was strategic. He called upon their leaders to rid their country of Fort Toulouse; after all, it was defended by only thirty men. If they could not bring themselves to do that, they must consent to a major British fort at a site of his choosing. He concluded with a naked threat: if the Upper Creeks refused to cooperate, he would cut off all trade to their towns. Taken aback by Mackay's effrontery, the Upper Creek chiefs deliberated for a week before finally yielding their grudging consent to a British fort.[6]

Mackay's mission was nonetheless a resounding failure. He clearly had no respect for the Creeks. Their reputation for bravery was, he felt, undeserved, "for if I was to demand all their territories, they have not a Countenance to deny me." He described them as "a Sullen morose people of few words, . . . deceitfull and Covetouse, . . . I can't observe they are governed by any virtuoise principle." Numerous sources indicate that the Indians fully reciprocated his scorn. Mackay's browbeating had antagonized all of the Creeks, and the Upper Creeks would soon revoke their assent to a major fort. Only an insignificant and short-lived post was established at Okfuskee.[7]

Mackay even managed to antagonize the Yamacraws. The same ship that returned Tomochichi's party from England brought King George's presents to the Creeks, along with instructions from the Trustees that Tomochichi should decide how they should be distributed. Tomochichi dispatched "his brother" Hillispilli and young Santachi upcountry to invite various headmen down to Savannah to receive portions of the royal presents. In March Santachi was delivering such invitations along the banks of the Chattahoochee. This welcome development smoothed somewhat Mackay's bumpy ride through Creek country, but he was not happy with Tomochichi's choices. Mackay complained that Tomochichi and Santachi were "inclined to have their own private friends Carried down, and not the Leading men." For that reason, he said, "*I forbid him to Invite any without my knowledge*." While Tomochichi had favored friends, especially Lower Creek friends, Mackay's peremptory reaction was another misstep.[8]

Mackay's swashbuckling tactics also provoked serious conflicts on Georgia's other border areas. Intending to confine the Indian trade to responsible men willing to submit to direction from Georgia, Mackay expelled five Carolinians from the Upper Creek country and three from among the Lower Creeks. This unauthorized and ill-considered action ignited a long and bitter wrangle between the two colonies over the Creek trade. Things degenerated further when Governor Johnson died in May and was succeeded by Lieutenant Governor Thomas Broughton, a former trader. True to his roots, Broughton was in full sympathy with the Carolina traders and determined to defend his colony's long-standing trade with the Creeks. The dispute was carried to the Board of Trade and not fully resolved until 1738, when King George himself ordered Georgia to license all Carolina traders with proper recommendations from Charles Town.[9]

More serious yet, Mackay helped create an international incident. Hearing that the Spaniards had plans for "building a fort at the Appalatche old Fields," he lent a ready ear to plans for a preemptive anti-Spanish raid being developed by a headman named Licko. On March 29 Mackay reported that Licko had told him that "I want to be revenged on the Spaniards for killing my Brother, out of whose Scull they drink at Augustine." Mackay cared nothing for Licko's grudge but supposed that his warriors might distract the Spaniards from establishing their intended fort. Claiming he had told Licko that he "neither would advise or disswade him," Mackay affected surprise that he "is with 25 men gone to war." Two days earlier, however, he had warned Causton that "some of the Spaniards may suffer" and to prepare for reprisals. The ensuing raid resulted in the death of a Spanish master gunner at Fort Pupo, vehement protests from St. Augustine, and a retaliatory raid by the Yamasees in which seven Yamacraws were killed. Although Mackay was later able to shift much of the blame for fomenting this raid to his interpreter, he could not shed all of it.[10]

Reports of Mackay's mismanagement of Indian relations undoubtedly had a great deal to do with Oglethorpe's decision, which he announced in late July, to return to the colony. Assured that Oglethorpe would return to repair the damage, the Trustees now took action against Mackay. On July 18 their treasurer, Harman Verelst, wrote Mackay upbraiding him for his attempt to prevent the distribution of the royal presents to some of those designated by Tomochichi, "and taking upon you to name others." He was ordered henceforth "in all things whatsoever to assist and Support the Interest of Tomo Chachi." Furthermore, Mackay was to confine himself to Savannah until Oglethorpe arrived to take charge. After learning more about Mackay's activities, and being especially upset by his provocation of the Carolinians, the Trustees on October 10 dismissed him from their service "for notorious ill behaviour."[11]

Although Oglethorpe had delegated responsibility for Indian relations to Mackay, the Savannah municipal council inevitably became involved. The council, consisting of three bailiffs (magistrates) and a recorder, was increasingly dominated by Thomas Causton, keeper of the Trustees' storehouse. The Trustees had named Causton one of the original bailiffs in 1733 and promoted him to second bailiff the following year. Causton attempted with some success to dominate events in the colony through his obvious ability, powerful personality, and—not least—control over vital supplies.

The most promising Indian conference during Oglethorpe's absence involved the remote but populous Choctaw Nation, hitherto allies of the French. Shortly before his departure, Oglethorpe had reached an understanding on the Choctaws with mustee Thomas Jones. This transplanted Carolinian surely made Oglethorpe aware of the fact that he was multilingual—able to understand and make himself understood in Choctaw and Chickasaw, as well as several languages spoken by the Creeks. Eight years earlier Jones had undertaken a trading venture to Choctaw country, another unique entry on his résumé. Oglethorpe moved quickly to take advantage of Jones's special skills. They agreed that, if Jones could induce an influential delegation of Choctaws to make the long journey to Savannah and establish amicable relations, Oglethorpe would see that he had exclusive rights to the Choctaw trade "for 3 or 4 years." He also promised Jones a choice lot in Savannah.[12]

On July 1, 1734, Jones triumphantly entered Savannah with a party of Choctaws and a few Upper Creeks led by "the Taloupouse King" who had helped persuade them to come, nineteen Indians in all. Oglethorpe had probably instructed the Savannah authorities that if it became necessary to meet with native leaders they should follow the direction of Mackay or William Bull. Thus, on news of the visitors' approach Causton sent off to Charles Town for advice from Mackay and/or Bull, promising the Indians a conference in about two weeks. Mackay wrote back that he would not attend the talks. He advised Savannah leaders to court the Choctaws with a grand reception, provide them with suitable entertainment and "proper presents," and then send them on to Charles Town. A visit to the Carolina capital would pay off, he thought, for "as the Chactaws have never been in any of our British Settlements before they should see the best appearance we can make."[13]

The same day the Choctaws appeared, Bull unexpectedly arrived and immediately agreed to preside over talks. After the most impressive reception the town could manage, an initial meeting took place that very day. First Bailiff Thomas Causton and Recorder Thomas Christie represented the Savannah government, and Jones acted as interpreter. The "Choctaw King" related that his people was beset by unwelcome French attentions, including "building Forts." In the circumstances "we are very glad that the English have taken notice of us." He continued that "we are come to see who are our friends and whose Protection we may rely on," and, most pointedly, "we desire a trade very much." Causton implausibly assured the Choctaws that "they might depend on our Protection" and promised that Mackay would soon confer with them about trade.[14]

Pledges of mutuality were even warmer at a second meeting, six days later. Emphasizing that at present the Choctaws were "very poor and have not a trade to maintain them," their leader now told the Englishmen that "he and all his People are ready to Serve us." As if to demonstrate his good faith, he then requested "a Commission from the Trustees." Causton promised to procure one for him, and in the meantime "sent for a Breast Plate and hung it about his neck." Other fetching presents bestowed upon him included a suit trimmed with silver braid. Jones told Eveleigh that the Choctaws were "very well pleased" with their presents and were considering relocation much closer to the English.[15]

The engaging speeches and behavior of the "Choctaw King" excited English visions of a great diplomatic coup at the expense of the French. Oglethorpe's long shot seemed to have hit the target. He seemed not only omnicompetent but lucky as well. Enthusiasm for the Georgia-Choctaw connection soared higher yet when the Choctaws spurned the invitation to visit the Carolina capital.[16]

It was beginning to seem too good to be true, and so it was. The "Choctaw King" turned out to be no such thing, but rather an audacious war leader and trader known as Soulouche Oumastabe, or Red Shoes. Moreover, his influence did not extend over the Choctaw Nation or even a large fraction of it, but only over a few of the remote western towns. Though keenly attentive to personal gain, Red Shoes was also a Choctaw patriot already experienced at playing the Europeans off against one another. His request for an English commission was not, or not only, to gratify his vanity, but a calculated bid for the kind of recognition he knew would raise his value in the eyes of the French. Red Shoes returned to Choctaw country in September and for a few months played the role of Englishman's advocate, but by 1736 he was back in French favor as a major war leader against the Chickasaws. Never a tool of either the French or the English, until his death in 1747 Red Shoes continued to intrigue against both, concentrating first on one, then the other. Although this would not become clear for some time, from the English point of view the Choctaw talks in Savannah achieved nothing.[17]

Other dealings with Indians in Savannah centered on the nearby Yamacraws. Much as he had done with Thomas Jones, Oglethorpe used the promise of choice real estate to help persuade John Musgrove to accompany him and Tomochichi's party to London. Shortly before their departure, Oglethorpe apparently not only promised him a Trustees' grant of his original homestead adjacent to Savannah but a gentleman's grant about five miles upriver, the first available riverfront beyond the Yamacraw tract. Already known as the "Musgrove Cowpen," it was the grazing area where John had kept his livestock since driving them across the river. On October 16, as Musgrove was about to return to Georgia, the Trustees made a five-hundred-acre grant of the tract to him "and the Heirs Male of his Body." Before the year was out (and before John's return), Recorder Thomas Christie reported that "we have . . . made a Path a Considerable way between the Town and Musgrove Cowpen."[18]

When Musgrove arrived with Tomochichi's party in December he found that the Yamacraws were most unhappy about the operation of the Indian storehouse during his absence. The Musgroves ran this store in partnership with Joseph Watson under a contract with merchant Samuel Eveleigh of Charles Town. In November, Eveleigh wrote Oglethorpe that he intended to resettle near the Musgrove place, but he soon changed his mind. Oglethorpe had given John and Mary Musgrove a joint license to trade with Indians (the inclusion of Mary as co-licensee being an extraordinary concession), and had issued a similar license to Watson. A former seaman, Watson had spent at least five years in South Carolina before crossing the river into Georgia.[19]

During John's absence, Mary and Watson had quarreled repeatedly over their business, with Indians increasingly preferring to deal with Mary. Watson drank like the ex-sailor he was, and often went on binges with local natives, as Oglethorpe later put it, "running naked about the town, etc." His favorite drinking partner was an influential Yamacraw named Skee. Since the early days of the colony Skee and his brother Istinnocecheby had been known as "Captain Skee" and "Captain Tuscany," for Oglethorpe had appointed them captains of two militia companies of "Indian Allies." In September Watson further alienated himself from the local Indians by boasting that he would drink Skee to death, and then apparently proceeding to do it. Bragging of his success helped convince Yamacraws that Watson had "poisoned his liquour." According to Eveleigh, Watson had kept Skee "drunk in his store for [a] fortnight." Things quickly went downhill from there.[20]

As the partners continued their struggle for control of the storehouse, in November the now isolated Watson resorted to a lockout. This was the last straw for Estichi, Skee's "Lieutenant," already incensed over Skee's death and a beating he had received from Watson. Other Yamacraws shared his feelings, and a party of them led by Estichi broke into the storehouse. While pursuing Watson, Estichi killed Justice, an Indian slave belonging to the Musgroves, reportedly by accident. This was the first test of Article 5 of the 1733 treaty, which obligated the Lower Creeks to "deliver up" any of their people charged with murder or other serious "crimes" against "English traders or their people." The accused were to be tried, at the option of Oglethorpe (or, presumably, those substituting for him), "by the English Laws or by the laws of our Nation."[21]

The Savannah magistrates, fearful over possible native reaction, wanted no part of this. They not only refused to prosecute Estichi for murder under English law, they declined to invoke Creek custom to demand "satisfaction" for the killing of Justice. Instead, Estichi was quietly escorted to the boundary of the Yamacraw tract, where he doubtless was told to go away. It was Watson they decided to prosecute, on misdemeanor charges. On November 20 the jury found Watson "Guilty of unguarded Expression." When Causton stormed off the bench to insist on a sterner verdict, the jury reluctantly added a recommendation that Watson be confined for mental incompetence. The court (Causton) then declared him a "Lunatick" and placed him under house arrest. As Causton later told it, Watson "was, as well for his own preservation from Indian resentment as public safety, committed to a close confinement in his own lodgings within the town."[22]

When word of this incident reached the Trustees, Oglethorpe now among them, they were even more alarmed than the Savannah authorities had been. Following Oglethorpe's lead, they quickly concluded that Watson was to blame. In a March 17 letter to the magistrates, the Trustees approved the course followed thus far but reacted strongly against the further steps they had heard were under consideration. Reports had reached London that some Savannah leaders hoped to end the affair by banishing Watson, while others—notably First Bailiff Peter Gordon—wanted him released, arguing that "it is Cruel to imprison on account of an Indian."[23]

The Trustees indignantly forbade both actions. They found the latter especially distressing, "for if Injustice is done to an Indian, the Person who does it should be more severly punished, for doing it to one who is helpless, from his Ignorance of our Language; and because it is a breach of Treaty." The Trustees therefore revoked Watson's trading license and ordered that he remain confined. When he had "recovered his Senses," they would send over a special commission to try him for some unspecified crime. They also ordered that a major gift be made to Skee's large family "to pacify their resentment" and that the magistrates provide Mary Musgrove with another servant. Finally, in September they removed Gordon as first bailiff and replaced him with Causton. This resolution satisfied the Yamacraws and most of the colony, including the Musgroves.[24]

On May 15 the Trustees jointly awarded John and Mary "sole Licence for Trade with the Indians at Yamacraw, and as far as the Uchee Indians." The couple and their two boys had already moved from their old place adjacent to Savannah to the five-hundred-acre tract recently granted to John. There they reestablished their storehouse for the Indian trade. John never learned of the Trustees' license, for he died of a fever on June 12. Causton reported that "as he was a Coastable [constable] we buried him in a Millitary manner." In the will he drew up before leaving for England, John had devised his estate to his two surviving sons, James and Edward, and named Mary his "sole executrix and residuary legatee." Mary was now not only sole proprietor of the local Indian trade but (during her sons' minority) one of the colony's largest landholders.[25]

The Musgrove land was located less than a mile upriver from Pipemaker's Creek and the Yamacraw tract. (Watson's tract, now untended, and two small Trustee reserves intervened between them.) In order to maintain easy access to Mary's store, the Yamacraws relocated their town from its old site adjacent to Savannah to Pipemaker's Bluff, the high ground adjoining Pipemaker's Creek at the upper end of the Yamacraw tract. In February, Tomochichi (Noble Jones acting as his amanuensis) had written the Trustees that the Yamacraws had been joined by a party of peripatetic Savannahs (Shawnees). The newcomers had agreed, he said, "to Joyn Me in building on Pipe Makers blough and we intend to live to Gether." In July, Jones, the colony's surveyor, posted notices warning colonists not to poach timber or otherwise trespass on the Yamacraw tract. He had seen to it that the boundary between Savannah and the Indian land was unmistakable: it was marked by "a blazed line (Distinguished by a Red Cross)."[26]

In early June fifty-four Lower Creeks headed by Chigelli arrived in Savannah to receive the promised royal presents. As Mackay had feared, most were Lower Creeks. His efforts to alter the balance in favor of the Upper Creeks, though provocative, nevertheless had some effect. Causton was relieved when Tomochichi decided to divide the presents equally between Lower and Upper Creeks. Although Mackay had sent word to delay the meeting until he arrived with the Upper Creeks, Tomochichi and the Lower Creek leaders insisted on going ahead without them. After the distribution of the presents, Chigelli and other headmen provided the Georgia magistrates with a detailed migration legend of the Cussitas and Cowetas. At their request, Causton had this valuable traditional account inscribed (in English) in red and black characters on a buffalo skin, which he forwarded to the Trustees.[27]

Mackay finally arrived on June 18, followed a few days later by a party of Upper Creeks. Accompanying them was the now notorious Licko, whom the embarrassed magistrates ignored publicly but interviewed privately. Irked that only half the presents had been reserved for the more numerous Upper Creeks, Mackay tried to persuade the Savannah authorities to increase their share, but at Causton's insistence they finally supported Tomochichi's fifty-fifty allocation. During the meeting with the Upper Creeks, Recorder Thomas Christie delivered a prepared talk to them, the main point of which was apparently to warn them against any repetition of Licko's raid.[28]

After Tomochichi's party left London, Oglethorpe was active in leading the Trustees to approve the only three laws they ever enacted for Georgia. One prohibited rum and strong liquors; another forbade "the Importation and use of Black

Slaves." The first and much the longest dealt with the matter of most immediate importance: "An Act for maintaining the Peace with the Indians in the Province of Georgia." The Trustees approved the Indian act on January 9, 1735, and the king gave his assent to all three laws in April.[29]

Although the Georgia Indian act was closely patterned after the South Carolina Indian act of 1731, the Carolinians immediately mobilized against it, for it proclaimed the Trustees' exclusive jurisdiction over the "Indian Country" within Georgia's chartered limits. Indian affairs within this vast domain were to be managed under the direction of one or more commissioners. This included the trade, which was to be regulated much as Tomochichi had requested. The Trustees appointed Oglethorpe "first Commissioner" on September 24, and on the same day named him sole commissioner for the subordinate function of issuing trading licenses.[30]

His colleagues also assigned Oglethorpe the task of making their case to Parliament for a major appropriation for Georgia's defense. Mounting signs of Spanish antagonism toward the new colony convinced him that securing its southern boundary was a matter of the highest priority. A well-fortified outpost near the mouth of the Altamaha, the southern limit of the province according to the charter, was an obvious means toward this end. After the Yamasee War the Carolinians had maintained Fort King George there until 1728, and had urged Oglethorpe to reestablish it. Since the Altamaha lacked an adequate harbor, Oglethorpe favored a base on nearby St. Simons Island.

Oglethorpe ran a defense plan and budget by fellow Trustees before taking it to Parliament in March. The request would total £25,800. If granted this sum, "he proposes to erect 2 Forts of 80 men each and 18 Forts of 40 Men each, to be built on the banks of a certain river." His colleagues were proud of their philanthropic aims, but they were not pacifists. They made no objection to Oglethorpe's grandiose plan. The river was the Altamaha. One of the larger forts surely was intended for St. Simons Island, the other no doubt far upriver. Oglethorpe must have been equally persuasive when he spoke in Parliament, for his fellow MPs topped out his request and granted the Trustees £26,000. In September, six months before its founding, Egmont reported that "we named our new town Frederica."[31]

That fall, distance began to develop between Oglethorpe and the other Trustees. None of the others could rival his influence at court or in Parliament (most were regarded as supporters of the opposition), and Oglethorpe was gradually drawn away toward service of the Walpole ministry. He was especially close to the Duke of Newcastle, secretary of state. In the fall of 1735, primed by personal reports from Oglethorpe, British officials made significant policy decisions regarding territory south of the Altamaha River. They were reacting to two recent developments. One was Spanish activities in Cuba and Florida that looked suspiciously like preparations for an attack on Georgia. The other was a response to a South Carolina initiative. The old royal charters to the Carolina proprietors had granted them territory far to the south of the Altamaha. According to the 1665 charter the southern boundary of Carolina extended all the way to 29° north latitude, well south of St. Augustine. Relying on the old charters, Governor Broughton let it be known that he intended to reassert Carolina's right to territory south of the Altamaha by making land grants there.

Learning of this from Carolina informants, Oglethorpe alerted the other Trustees. On November 8 they petitioned the king to forbid Broughton from "making any such Grants to the Southward of the River Alatamaha." Egmont doubtless reflected the views of most Trustees when he observed that "neither the Spaniards nor Indians are like to suffer this of the Carolinians, nor even of us." Any attempt to settle Englishmen south of the Altamaha "would disturb our settlement though we should have no hand in it." Soon afterward the Trustees were gratified when they heard that the king had "forbid the Carolinians to take up grants there." If any of them noticed that this prohibition applied only to South Carolina, it did not seem a significant deviation from what they had requested.[32]

By attempting to simultaneously serve the Georgia Trust and the British government, Oglethorpe obliged himself to perform a balancing act.. Over the next few years it is sometimes difficult to determine whether he was acting as an agent of the Trust or the government. Awkward at best, Oglethorpe's straddle would become nearly impossible should the Trust and the ministry disagree about a fundamental policy. Such a policy difference appeared even before Oglethorpe set sail for his return to Georgia. He had no qualms about choosing to back government policy, partly, no doubt, because he had helped formulate it.

Sometime that fall Oglethorpe received what Egmont later described as "orders and instructions . . . from his Majesty" on what to do during his second stay in Georgia. Also that fall, Oglethorpe finalized plans with the other Trustees for establishing a new settlement near the mouth of the Altamaha. By November they had informed the king that "they have given Directions for erecting a Fort upon the Island of St. Simon," but not the other forts Oglethorpe had proposed. The Trustees also agreed that when Oglethorpe returned he would be well provided to gain additional Indian concessions. In April they had appropriated £1,000 "for presents to purchase lands from the Indians." To ensure that these presents had the desired effect, in July they decided that "600 double Sighted guns be bought for the Indians."[33]

The Trustees' original plan was for the new settlers who went over with Oglethorpe to spend some time in Savannah before moving down to St. Simons Island. On November 10, however, as he prepared to embark, Oglethorpe received additional royal instructions that required swifter action. As he later confided to

Broughton, "just before I sailed I received fresh Orders from his Majesty to go immediately to St. Simonds and fortify it without Delay for fear of Accidents which might happen on a Change of the Situation of Affairs in Europe." What precisely the earlier royal instructions or those of November 1735 said is unknown, but one provision probably was not very different from what was said in another set dated May 8, 1738. There the king directed Oglethorpe to defend all the territory he claimed that was "included in Either of the two Charters . . . in the Years 1663, and 1666 [1665]," that is, the old Carolina charters.[34]

Oglethorpe did not explain his dealings with the British government to the other Trustees, most likely because he had been instructed not to. His colleagues, having induced the king to forbid South Carolina outposts south of the Altamaha, must have supposed they had heard the last of the matter. They had no inkling that Oglethorpe had similar plans, much less that he would be acting with the support of the government.

On February 5, 1736, Oglethorpe arrived at Savannah with "the great embarkation" of nearly three hundred settlers. The group included John Wesley and Benjamin Ingham, who intended to become missionaries to the Indians, and John's younger brother Charles, whom the Trustees had appointed Oglethorpe's secretary for Indian affairs. On February 14, Tomochichi and a party of local Indians boarded the anchored ship to greet the new arrivals. Mary Musgrove came along as interpreter. Both clergymen recorded accounts of this meeting, as did Francis Moore. Ingham reported that Mary Musgrove was "a Sensible well civilized woman" and that she had agreed to teach the prospective missionaries the Muskogee language. Tomochichi shrewdly extended a particular welcome to the missionaries, but his speech focused on more worldly concerns. He warned of imminent conflict with the French and Spaniards, spoke of continuing difficulties with the Carolina traders, and relayed Yuchi complaints about encroachments on their lands by the Salzburgers at Ebenezer.[35]

About the same time, 160-odd Highland Scots recruited at Oglethorpe's direction founded the town of Darien at the former site of Fort King George, a few miles up the Altamaha. Oglethorpe had trouble conveying the colonists he had come with to St. Simons. Reluctance of shipowners and masters to risk their vessels in uncharted waters off the island stranded the newcomers near the mouth of the Savannah River until March 2.

By the time he got these settlers to the site he chose for Frederica, Oglethorpe apparently had made progress toward an additional land cession. He implied this in his March 16 letter to the Trustees, but his account is tantalizingly vague. He wrote that Tomochichi, Tooanahowi, Umpichi, and other Yamacraws were with him at Frederica and that they had "agreed that we shall possess the Island of

St. Simons, but reserve that to St. Catherines to themselves." There would be no problem with settling St. Simons, but would the Yamacraws also stand behind the other concessions they had made? Might they even be willing to go further? Oglethorpe was sure that they would. His letter goes on to say that Tomochichi "is willing that we should Settle upon any place within his lands provided the lower Creek Nations agree to it." As in 1733, a 1736 land cession would have to be a two-stage transaction: a Yamacraw concession followed by a Lower Creek confirmation.[36]

But if Tomochichi was willing to part with any of "his lands," what lands were his? The letter explains how Oglethorpe intended to answer this question: "Tomo-Chachi and I at his Desire go out to morrow to hunt the Buffaloe as far as the utmost Extent of his Dominions towards [St.] Augustine." It was not a likely direction for buffalo hunting. Acknowledging that the hunt was a "pretence," Moore later disclosed the real motive of the trip: it was "in pursuance of this agreement" to cede lands "as far as St. Johns river." A mixed party headed by Oglethorpe and Tomochichi sailed south past Cumberland Island, Amelia Island, to the very mouth of that river. Landing on a small island at what Oglethorpe called St. George's Point, he reported that "on the point of the opposite Side the Spaniards keep a Guard." He promptly concluded—or, much more likely, confirmed his already settled opinion—that this river was the dividing line between Spanish and British/Lower Creek lands.[37]

On April 17 Oglethorpe reported his audacious action to the Duke of Newcastle: "The Indian King Tomo Chachi (pursuant to the assurances he gave to his Majesty and your Grace in England) went down with me to the utmost Limits of the King of Great Britain's Dominions to put us in Possession of all the Lands held by their Nation, from this Island [St. Simons] to the Spanish Frontiers. . . . I am in quiet Possession as far as the Spanish Outguards." Oglethorpe wrote again to Newcastle in July, reminding him of this incident. He added revealing details: "I have apprized Your Grace, that the Creek Indians, pursuant to the Treaty made with his Majesty in England, carried me down to the Frontiers of his Dominions in America which are divided from the Spanish by the River St. John's and of which the English or their Allies the Creeks have been in quiet possession [since] before the Treaty of Utrecht." In the second letter Tomochichi's concessions have been recast as Creek concessions, and the St. Johns has been named as the southern boundary of the land ceded. Furthermore, the date the Creeks acquired possession of the southernmost area has been clarified as pre-Utrect, that is, pre-1713. Elsewhere Oglethorpe indicated that 1705 was the date he had in mind.[38]

Most strikingly, however, Oglethorpe now states that these Creek concessions were made as a result of "the Treaty made with his Majesty in England." Thus, according to Oglethorpe, Tomochichi's private meeting with King George and

Newcastle had been highly substantive. In addition to making some gesture interpreted as an acknowledgment of the king's sovereignty, Tomochichi evidently had promised to yield him Yamacraw lands as far south as the northernmost Spanish outposts. In March 1736 he delivered on that promise. Oglethorpe took immediate advantage by sending a small force to build Fort St. George at the mouth of the St. Johns.[39]

With his April letter Oglethorpe sent Newcastle a defense of "the King's Title to Georgia." He began with an argument that had been conventional for more than a century: the King of England had acquired "dominion" in North America by virtue of first discovery and subsequent possession. ("Dominion" traditionally meant ultimate ownership, but by this time, when attributed to a king, it was essentially equivalent to territorial sovereignty.) Oglethorpe identified Sebastian Cabot as the discoverer but was vague about how English monarchs had managed to gain and maintain possession of the vast territories they claimed. Ambiguity was prudent, for their was no thoroughly convincing answer to that question. As is well known, conflicting claims of dominion led to endless disputes among the imperial powers.[40]

Aside from regular challenges from rival European states, the British monarchy's claims of overseas dominion were almost never questioned. The acquisition of territory was a matter of royal prerogative beyond challenge by the king's subjects, including his law officers and judges. Oglethorpe never questioned King George's order to defend his claim to territory under the 1665 charter, though he knew that reviving a British claim reaching below St. Augustine was merely a bargaining point: an extreme counterclaim to the even more extravagant claims of Spain.

Nor did Oglethorpe question the king's right to claim lands that had been occupied by Indians for centuries. In fact, like the king himself, Oglethorpe carefully avoided that issue. How then describe a royal seizure of dominion over those lands? The English never directed arguments based on discovery, so useful against European rivals, against Indians. Insofar as there was an official answer directed against Indians, it was "conquest." Dominion was imposed upon lands occupied by the Indians without asking their leave and without their knowledge. A British claim to American territory was harder to challenge if supported by some sort of native assent, but such assent clearly was not deemed necessary. It was a fictive conquest that could only become reality over the course of time. It was not supposed to be a military conquest but a bloodless one where the natives, grateful for benefits received, cheerfully accepted subordination to the British Crown.[41]

Oglethorpe's argument then took an unusual turn designed to make the royal claim of possession more plausible. He did have precedents. Since New York had no royal charter to define its boundaries, colonial officials there lacked clear authorization for the territorial extent of their jurisdiction. Largely for that reason, since 1701 they had developed the theory that the Iroquois, as the king's subjects, possessed lands (dominion) far into the interior in behalf of the English Crown. Iroquois territory was English territory. This did not mean that these Indians did not own their land; they did. As the Privy Council later put it, the Iroquois "had yielded to Us the Dominion but not the property of those Lands." They had the same natural right as previously, but now within a framework of English sovereignty. The land rights belonging to native peoples and the English monarch were not mutually exclusive, for they existed on different planes. When the king claimed to possess vast territories in North America he was claiming dominion—territorial sovereignty—over them. This was not to deny Indian ownership: it was simply to impose a higher form of ownership and control. In modern terminology, we see here "the fundamental distinction between territorial sovereignty and title to land."[42]

Oglethorpe attempted to apply similar logic to the southern frontier. Since he supposed that the Creeks had subordinated themselves to the British Crown, Creek territory was British territory. The Creeks continued to own their lands, but now beneath a canopy of British sovereignty. Oglethorpe found, as many Carolinians had before him, that the king's sovereign title extended southward all the way to the St. Johns River. From 1705 until the previous month, the Creeks had acted as the king's proxies to maintain that title. Tomochichi and the Yamacraws (subject to confirmation by the Lower Creeks) had just relinquished ownership of those lands as high as the tide flowed.[43]

The Indian title to lands that the English recognized was a natural rights title based on "immemorial possession." Oglethorpe reflected this understanding when he told Governor Broughton that Tomochichi's people had just shown him "how far their Claim and possession extended." Since their claim of ownership depended entirely upon their possession, when the Creeks ceded possession they ceded all that they had. Oglethorpe's memorial goes on to assert that the Creeks had maintained possession for the king from early in the century "to the very Hour that they delivered the Possession thereof to James Oglethorpe for the use of his Britannick Majesty, pursuant to a Treaty Concluded between his said Majesty and that Nation." Until that hour the king had "dominion" over the territory, while under him the Creeks had immediate possession and ownership. Now the king had everything. The treaty alluded to clearly is another reference to Tomochichi's private meeting with King George. Noteworthy too, in the cession agreement with Tomochichi, Oglethorpe was acting as an agent of the Crown, not the Trustees.[44]

By early April, Frederica was taking shape as a strongly fortified town. As agreed with the other Trustees, Oglethorpe established a Frederica municipal government patterned after that of Savannah. He named his secretary, Francis Moore, as the town's register. In mid-April he returned briefly to Fort St. George. He mentioned this fort to the Trustees on May 18 but did not tell them where it was. They soon found out. On June 23 the London Trustees learned that Oglethorpe "had erected a strong fort 60 miles beyond our province of Georgia." They learned this from John Bromfield, their newly appointed register in Savannah. Brownfield reported that Oglethorpe intended to fortify "a place directly opposite to the Spanish Look out upon the River St. Juan about 60 Miles distant from Frederica." The day they read his letter the Trustees commended Bromfield for "his diligence in informing us of what passes." Planting Fort St. George, which incensed the Spaniards, went beyond audacity. The thin rationale Oglethorpe offered for this short-lived outpost was that it was designed "to prevent the Indians from invading the Spanish Province." That was a genuine concern, but not the main one. He soon constructed other sub-Altamaha forts: Fort St. Andrews and Fort William on Cumberland Island, and Fort Amelia on Amelia Island.[45]

While Oglethorpe was making preparations to plant the British flag south of the Altamaha, the Trustees back home decided that even the projected settlement at the mouth of that river was too risky. This reversal was precipitated when Parliament on March 26 declined to appropriate the £20,000 they had requested for Georgia, granting only £10,000. Three days later, five of the Trustees held an emergency meeting. They promptly agreed that it was now "impossible to proceed on the new Settlement on the Allatamaha River." Accordingly, they drafted a letter to Oglethorpe directing him "to abandon the design of that new Settlement, and to Settle the new people either on the Ogeeky [Ogeechee] river, or at Savannah." This letter was unanimously approved two days later and sent on April 1. Similar communications followed on May 10 and June 10.[46]

Upon receipt of these letters, Oglethorpe probably cursed the other Trustees for timidity—the Ogeechee was only about twenty miles below the Savannah—and wished he could be on both sides of the ocean at once. Evidently his only reply was the terse comment that opens his letter of July 26: "The Town on the Alatamaha is already settled." He did not bother to counter their arguments for a change of plans, and, still more striking, he did not inform them that he had been acting under instructions from the king. The Trustees only learned of the existence of these royal orders on June 16, when they read several packets of documents from Oglethorpe dealing with his negotiations with the Spaniards.[47]

Oglethorpe had intended that most fellow Trustees not see these documents. He had sent the packets to two of them he trusted, James Vernon and Thomas Tower, with instructions to pass them on to Newcastle. The enclosed papers included Oglethorpe's April 17 report to Newcastle, his memorial on the king's title to Georgia, and other documents on the Florida-Georgia issue. Oglethorpe sent these papers unsealed, so Vernon and Tower read them. Vernon decided that he could not keep these documents from the other Trustees, and showed them around. Suddenly the tale of the buffalo hunt evaporated and the London Trustees realized that Oglethorpe had been misleading them. They found some of the diplomatic documents, especially an April 1 letter to Oglethorpe, to be especially provocative.[48]

What upset them most were apparent references to instructions from the king to Oglethorpe, "to which the Trustees were strangers." Shocked that he had been dealing over their heads, the Trustees were thrown into turmoil, protesting that "Mr. Oglethorp concealed those orders from us when he went." They promptly complained to the government about these secret "Orders, and Instructions from the King." The particular "Orders" implicit in the Florida documents were probably mainly directions from Newcastle.[49]

Oglethorpe's colleagues were not only provoked by his past duplicity but were alarmed that his high-risk maneuvers could drag them into open-ended conflicts in which they had much to lose and over which they had no control. Perhaps most disturbing, they gradually became aware that British sovereignty was not the only thing Oglethorpe aimed to stretch to the St. Johns. A week after returning to Georgia, Oglethorpe wrote to Governor Broughton. He reminded Broughton that the king in council had recently forbade South Carolina land grants beyond its Savannah River boundary, and went on to caution against any pretense that "Lands lay[ing] to the Southward of the River Alatamaha were out of Georgia." In March Oglethorpe estimated the distance between the Savannah and Altamaha rivers as "ninety miles." Writing to Newcastle a month later, Oglethorpe said he was working on "keeping a Province two hundred miles in length." If Georgia extended two hundred miles south of the Savannah River, it reached to at least the St. Johns. About the same time he argued that the king's title "to Georgia" extended to the St. Johns.[50]

Had Oglethorpe's aggressive activities south of the Altamaha been unauthorized, he quickly would have been disowned as a filibusterer and punished for endangering Britain's peaceful relations with Spain. In fact, his actions helped bring on a war with Spain three years later. Oglethorpe was not disowned or punished; he was made a general and given command of British forces in the region. The inescapable conclusion is that Oglethorpe's basic objectives and tactics had covert government approval.

Having decided to defend antique royal claims to the territory between the Altamaha and St. Johns, and then deciding to deny South Carolina pretensions to the area, the government had to decide what to do with it. The obvious alternatives were either to create an entirely new administration for this territory or to place it under the adjoining provincial government—that of Georgia. The first alternative was not considered. The southern boundary of Georgia would be moved southward, but not until 1763 and then only to the St. Marys River. Until then, insofar as the region had a government, it was Georgia's. Though it seems that no formal decision was made, Oglethorpe must have had some authoritative assurance, probably from Newcastle, that Georgia was likely to be enlarged.

As much as the other Trustees disliked Oglethorpe's daring drive toward the St. Johns, there was not much they could do about it. They were equally unhappy that he had been spending their money on this clandestine operation. There was something they could do about that. Washing their hands of operations south of the Altamaha, they declared that "We confine our Selves within the Limits of our charter." Accordingly, in July they wrote Oglethorpe "expressing the impossibility of our disbursing the Publick money upon any undertakings of his beyond the Limmits of our Province." The Trustees took to same message to the government. To appease them, Newcastle gave the Trustees a nicely ambiguous letter to be forwarded to Oglethorpe. It directed him "not to fall out with the Spaniards, but to follow the things recommended to him when he left England." Egmont reconciled himself to the government's intervention with Oglethorpe, "because thereby it lay on the Crown to justify and Support him in his conduct." In other words, if there were to be sub-Altamaha adventures, it was up to the government to take the heat and pay the bills. And, not least, "we shall remain wholly free from blame."[51]

During his March foray with Tomochichi toward the St. Johns, Oglethorpe found a way to claim that nearly anything he might do in that direction would take place within the bounds of the Georgia charter. By that charter King George granted the Trustees the territory between "the most northern part" of the Savannah River and "the most southern stream" of the Altamaha River. The mouth of the Altamaha near St. Simons Island is at 31°19' north latitude. On his second day's sail south from Frederica, Oglethorpe leaped to the welcome conclusion that there were more southerly branches of the Altamaha. That day, March 18, as Oglethorpe's party sailed the inland channel along Cumberland Island, "they past the Clothogotheo, another Branch of the Allatamaha." That might have been the Satilla River (30°58'), or its southern branch, the Cumberland River (30°53'), but most likely was the St. Marys River (30°44'). Following the trip, Brownfield informed the Trustees that Oglethorpe "has been with a Party of Indians to trace the Southernmost Branch of Alatamaha and found that it included a much larger Tract of Land than he had ever till then supposed."[52]

It appears that as Oglethorpe sailed south, what he took to be the most southern stream of the Altamaha moved south with him. Three years later he wrote that "the Southernmost mouth" of the Altamaha "is in 30.30 D.M.," that is, 30 degrees, 30 minutes. If this latitude reading was perfectly accurate (not to be assumed), Oglethorpe would have identified the Nassau River as the southernmost mouth of the Altamaha. The mouth of the Nassau is at 30°31', only about seven miles above the mouth of the St. Johns (30°24'). It would have been difficult to conclude that this minor stream was a branch of the Altamaha, but Oglethorpe seems to have managed it. A year and a half after abandoning Fort St. George, he described its location to Newcastle: it was "upon that Part of the Alatamaha nearest to the River which the Spaniards call St. Johns. . . . it is on the Alatamaha and not the River Saint Johns, though it is not far from it." There was no branch of the Altamaha south of St. Simons Island, but Oglethorpe's convenient geographical error would not be corrected while the war with Spain continued.[53]

Though Oglethorpe in 1736 did not bother to justify his activities south of the Altamaha to fellow Trustees, he was careful to do so with the British government. What survives of this confidential communication are mainly his April and July letters to Newcastle and his April memorial on the king's title, also sent to Newcastle. These documents are by far the most revealing of Oglethorpe's accounts of his sub-Altamaha operations. Moreover, all three allude to Tomochichi's "treaty" with King George, something Oglethorpe thus far had failed to mention to fellow Trustees. As for his title defense, he did not write it to persuade Spaniards, much less Indians, or even fellow Trustees. He wrote it to convince Newcastle and other superiors in the British government, and probably himself.

The new Spanish governor in St. Augustine, Francisco de Moral Sánchez, of course protested Oglethorpe's recent efforts as a violation of Spanish territory. He demanded that the English withdraw back to South Carolina. A special emissary dispatched from Havana, Don Antonio de Arredondo, personally confronted Oglethorpe with the same message. Oglethorpe snapped back that "the Spaniards should evacuate as far as the 29th degree of North Latitude conformable to King Charles the Second's Charter." This impasse was perfectly predictable. What the two leaders did about it was less so. In October, Oglethorpe and Moral signed a provisional disengagement agreement: Oglethorpe agreed to dismantle Fort St. George, and both leaders agreed to refer the boundary issue to their home governments.[54]

The role Oglethorpe saw for the Yamacraws in this territorial drama was twofold, both based on the assumption that they were Lower Creeks. First, since the purported "humble submission" of Creek chiefs to the English Crown in 1705, they had been subjects and/or allies of the English or (after 1707) British Crown. Second, the Yamacraws were local custodians of Creek rights to land, subordinate to the ultimate proprietors of those lands, the Lower Creeks. Oglethorpe described those rights as being held "by the Creek Nation as Tenants in Common." The Lower Creeks claimed lands from the Savannah River in the north to the limits of the Spanish possessions in the south, and from the coast as far as their settlements on the Chattahoochee. Oglethorpe was happy to endorse those claims, for they could be interpreted to validate British claims.[55]

Though there was a clear distinction between subjects and allies in Europe, that distinction faded when Englishmen attempted to apply either term to American natives they dealt with. They did attempt to apply both, awkwardly, equivocally, sometimes interchangeably. The first term was especially troublesome. Indians who were dubbed subjects were fundamentally unlike any of the king's European subjects, all of whom were obliged to obey his laws. They were also unlike any of the subjects—Indian or European—claimed by the kings of Spain and Portugal. Claims of sovereignty in the New World by the Iberian monarchs were absolute and complete, that is, they applied to both territories and peoples. Accordingly, Indians in Spanish America and Brazil were defined as subjects, who, like their new king's old subjects, must obey his laws. A great deal of coercion was required to force American natives into this role, but the Iberians were more than willing to supply it.[56]

The English (along with the French and Dutch) were not willing to follow that model, largely because of the expense. British claims of sovereignty were not absolute, for they did not immediately apply to the aborigines. Until Indians were willing to subject themselves to English rule, the English were content to let them govern themselves as they saw fit. In effect, British claims of dominion or sovereignty were limited to territorial sovereignty—sovereignty over lands claimed by, and acknowledged to belong to, native peoples. In general, during the colonial era British authorities did not attempt to impose English government or English law upon Indians, even those they called "subjects." (There were exceptions for some "settlement" Indians, especially the "praying towns" of Massachusetts.) Gaining Indian acceptance of English law was supposed to be a gradual, peaceful process. At the end of the colonial era it had hardly begun. As was generally true across the English colonies, Indians in and around Georgia had no legal personality. They could not be sued, forced to pay taxes, or convicted of crimes. On the other hand, they had no legal rights.[57]

The term "ally" was also problematic, for Englishmen did not consider the native peoples they called allies to be sovereign or independent nations. Moreover, neither the Indians nor the English behaved toward the other as allies were supposed to. The natives seldom delivered the military assistance the English expected of allies, while it was even rarer to find the English assisting an Indian nation against its enemies. Neither of the traditional status terms fit Indians. An intermediate expression (something like "domestic dependent nations," perhaps) would have been more accurate, but Englishmen seemed stumped to come up with one.

Oglethorpe usually referred to the Creeks as allies, but his usage was inconsistent. Thus in April 1736 he wrote that the Creeks "are only Allies and not Subjects to our King," yet a few months later he told a Spanish officer that the Yamacraws were "subjects to the King of Great Britain." Similarly, in 1739 he wrote that, prior to the Yamasee War, "the Creek Indians acknowledged the King of England for their Sovereign." Evidently frustrated with the usual terms, Oglethorpe once tried one that was even less suitable: he called the Creeks "Vassals to his Majesty." Another time he dubbed them "the English Confederate Indians." Turning that around, Moore referred to "the Creek English Indians." It seems plain that all of these locutions were tentative and more or less unsatisfying. In contexts where Indians could be cast as supporters of British claims of dominion, they might be called subjects. Otherwise, however, they were likely to be seen as allies, extremely unreliable allies.[58]

Following his trip with Tomochichi to the St. Johns, Oglethorpe supposed that the king of Great Britain's title to the territory and islands between that river and the Altamaha was nearly complete. The Yamacraws having ceded the area, it remained for Lower Creeks to confirm that concession. On July 26 Oglethorpe hinted that this final step had been accomplished. That day he wrote the Trustees that he had been forced to "give the Indians large Presents to procure their Confirmation of the Cession of the Islands." This seems to be the only notice he gave fellow Trustees that he had received a cession of coastal islands other than St. Simons. Notably absent from Oglethorpe's sparse report is a clear description of what had been ceded, and any indication that it included mainland territory. At any rate, the "Confirmation" he alluded to had occurred during a major conference with Creek leaders about three weeks earlier.[59]

Oglethorpe met with Creek chiefs in Savannah between June 27 and July 3. Minutes of the June 27 and July 3 meetings survive. In the initial meeting, called the "1st Audience," Oglethorpe and the Savannah magistrates met with some sixty Lower Creeks. The visitors were led by "the Chiefs of Seven Towns," including Coweta leaders Chigelli and Malatchi. Mary Musgrove acted as sole interpreter. By July 3 the Lower Creeks had been joined by a delegation of Upper Creeks. There were two meetings that day, labeled "2d Audience. 1st Part" and "2nd Audience. 2nd Part." In these sessions Mary was assisted by two other interpreters, Alexander Wood and Thomas Wiggins. The meeting on June 27, a Sunday, was essentially an exchange of greetings. The first session on July 3 focused entirely on the Watson affair, while the second dealt with trade problems and Creek hostilities with the Cherokees. Oglethorpe gave Chigelli "the Coat off my own Back," adding that Malatchi, "who is to succeed Chigillee," should later wear it. As the conference was about to break up, Oglethorpe gave the Indians a dazzling array of presents. Chigelli said he was headed home, "but how to get up there with so many Presents he did not know." His parting words were: "I was never so well pleased in my Life as with this Talk."[60]

At first sight these records do not indicate that anything very important occurred, and Oglethorpe's extraordinary generosity with presents seems surprising. Toward the end of the final session, however, Oglethorpe made a telltale comment. As he turned over supplies of ammunition, he said he expected "your young People will all take notice that you had a Talk at this time about my settling upon the Islands of the Sea. We give You these Presents in token of this Agreement." So Creek leaders did make a concession about the coastal islands, which Oglethorpe reciprocated with "large Presents." Since the surviving minutes say nothing about the negotiation of this agreement, it must have occurred earlier than July 3, but not on June 26. Yet the minutes deny that as a possibility. They declare that it could not have happened before June 26, for the meeting that day was the "1st Audience," and could not have happened between June 26 and July 3, because the "2nd Audience" took place on the latter day. In fact, there was an intervening session.[61]

Charles Wesley's job as Oglethorpe's secretary for Indian affairs required that he play a role in these proceedings. His journal for June 27 is blank, but the entry for July 1 reads as follows: "I was at court while the Creek Indians had an audience with Mr. Oglethorpe; which I took down (as several afterwards) in shorthand." The minutes he recorded for several later meetings are clearly those for the two sessions on July 3. The minutes he took for the meeting on July 1 are nowhere to be found. John Wesley, who had just returned from Frederica with Oglethorpe, was also present. With some annoyance, he reported that on June 27 public worship at the courthouse was canceled. The cause was the imminent arrival of the Creeks at the courthouse, "in which they were to have their audience." His journal entry for July 1 confirms that of his brother: "The Indians had an audience; and another on Saturday [July 3], when Chicali, their head man, dined with Mr. Oglethorpe." After dinner, John discussed religion with Chigelli, describing him as a "grey-headed old man."[62]

If the disappearance of Charles Wesley's July 1 minutes is suspicious, his mislabeling of the July 3 meetings as the "2nd Audience" is clear evidence of tampering with the record. It is not credible that Wesley would have dared to do it unless Oglethorpe ordered him to. It therefore seems clear that Oglethorpe deliberately suppressed evidence of the July 1 meeting, thereby continuing to mislead fellow Trustees about his land dealings. Just as in 1733, in 1736 Oglethorpe conducted the serious business about territory off the record during an intermediate meeting between the two recorded ones.

It is certain that the July 1 meeting involved Creek concessions of territory, at least insular territory. On July 26 Oglethorpe wrote fellow Trustees that he had recently prevailed upon the Creeks to confirm the Yamacraw cession "of the Islands." Likewise, Wesley's minutes of the July 3 Creek conference and a later report by Trustees' secretary Benjamin Martyn declare that the new land cession agreements dealt entirely with the islands. These reports, all traceable to Oglethorpe, were deliberately inaccurate, omitting what he wished to conceal. Thus he gave no account of his provocative activities at the St. Johns River.[63]

What Oglethorpe was most careful to conceal from fellow Trustees was that his efforts south of the Altamaha were aimed at mainland territory, not just islands. In particular, he was unwilling to reveal that his ultimate objective was to stretch Georgia southward until it reached Spanish Florida. Evidently aware that the London Trustees already knew something about his plans for coastal islands, on July 26 he gave them a vague acknowledgment that his negotiation for islands had succeeded. When writing to British officials, however, Oglethorpe could reveal that the 1736 agreement was not confined to islands. On July 26 he wrote another letter to an unnamed lord. Here he referred to the "Lands" which had been ceded. Similarly, on April 17 he informed Newcastle that Tomochichi had accompanied him to the St. Johns "to put us in Possession of all the Lands held by their Nation." Again, in his memorial on "the King's Title to Georgia" that he sent to Newcastle, Oglethorpe related how the king had acquired "the Lands as far as St. John's River." Lands, not just islands.[64]

In 1733 Tomochichi and the Yamacraws had ceded islands and territory on the mainland to Oglethorpe, concessions confirmed by the Creeks. In 1736 Tomochichi surrendered his "lands" or "dominions" down to the St. Johns—more islands, more mainland—to Oglethorpe. When Oglethorpe held a meeting with Creek leaders on July 1, 1736, to secure a "Confirmation" of Yamacraw concessions, it cannot be supposed that he neglected to seek a confirmation of the mainland cession he had invested so much to gain. In all probability he succeeded. In the 1739 treaty the Creeks acknowledge that they had previously granted to the Trustees "all the Lands along the Sea Coast as far as the River St. Johns and as high as the Tide flows," along with most of the islands down to the same river. What was clearly new about the 1736 Creek agreement was the cession of a swath of mainland thirty miles deep from the Altamaha to the St. Johns. The only plausible time for this concession is July 1, 1736, for the conference that July is the only time between 1733 and 1739 that Oglethorpe met with a large delegation of Creek chiefs.[65]

On July 26 Oglethorpe told the Trustees that "Opposition from Carolina" had obliged him to seek confirmation of the Creek grants of islands. What he referred to occurred in Charles Town on July 3. That day, Hopoya Hadjo, "King" of the Abeikas, and two other chiefs met with Governor Broughton and his council. Hopoya Hadjo told the Carolina leaders that land on "the other side [of Savannah

River] was for the red People and their Land." Oglethorpe concluded that this eminent Upper Creek leader had repudiated all land concessions south of the river, and that Carolinians had put him up to it. Writing to an unnamed lord, Oglethorpe marveled that this Creek could "deny the concession of those Lands which he himself had before consented with the rest of the Nation to grant." Charles Wesley later told Egmont that "at length Mr. Oglethorp had got him to confirm it again."[66]

In his July 26 letter Oglethorpe informed the Trustees that Charles Wesley would soon bring them "a more particular Account" of Indian affairs. Wesley, fully disillusioned, was about to return home. He sailed from Savannah that very day, but travel problems and poor health delayed his appearance at the Trustees' office. On December 7 he finally delivered "my secretary's book" to Thomas Tower, and seemed to think he was done with Georgia. The following day, however, "I obeyed a summons from my Lord Egmont," and that evening he met with him for two hours. Wesley told Egmont that Hopoya Hadjo's recantation had finally settled the land issue. "We have possession by consent of all the nations of the sea coast and islands and six [*sic*] miles within the coast of our Province," along with most of the adjacent islands. Thus Wesley described Indian cessions of mainland as limited to territory "within" Georgia, omitting those south of the Altamaha. Probably aware that the Trustees had known about the fort on St. George's Island for nearly six months, Wesley justified it as an isolated measure required to protect settlements on the Altamaha, Frederica and Darien. He admitted that this outpost was "60 miles beyond our province of Georgia." Nevertheless, he added, it was "still on the lands claimed by the Crown as part of Carolina, and belonging to the Indians in alliance with us." He did not mention the forts on Cumberland and Amelia islands. Before parting, Egmont asked Wesley to meet with the other Trustees. He did a week later, and then delivered "papers containing Mr. Oglethorp's conferences with the Indian nations," evidently minus minutes for the Creek meeting on July 1. It seems plain that Wesley was acting on Oglethorpe's instructions to divulge as little as possible about activities south of the Altamaha.[67]

Oglethorpe discussed two other matters involving mainland territory with the Creek chiefs, again evidently on July 1. He asked them for permission to build a fort far up both of Georgia's two boundary rivers, the Savannah and the Altamaha. Since the sites of both projected forts were "within" Georgia, Oglethorpe was open with fellow Trustees about his efforts to establish them. We will consider the Creek replies shortly.

In 1736 Oglethorpe also had to deal with a conflict between the Salzburgers at Ebenezer and the neighboring Yuchi Indians. The Yuchis apparently inhabited the Savannah watershed long before the Creeks, and spoke a completely unrelated language. Since the Yamasee War, and possibly earlier, the Yuchis were gradually being incorporated among the Lower Creeks. Perhaps it would be better to say that they were incorporating themselves into that confederation, for Yuchis who moved to the Chattahoochee insisted on remaining together in one very large town and retaining their separate culture. The lands they moved from—the Yuchi tract—extended from Ebenezer Creek nearly two hundred miles up the twisting river to Briar Creek.[68]

Only two significant Yuchi settlements remained in 1736. The nearest to the colonists was "Euchee Town," located about thirty miles upriver from Ebenezer Creek opposite Palachacola Fort. After the founding of Ebenezer, the Yuchis—"chusing to settle farther up," said Stephens—seem to have gradually withdrawn from this site to another about 140 miles upriver. This new town, at Silver Bluff on the Carolina side, was occupied only a little more than a decade. With the renewal of the Creek-Cherokee War in 1749, the remaining Yuchis there sought Lower Creek protection and retreated to the reconstituted Euchee Town on the Chattahoochee. Yuchis chose their townsites well: Thomas Wiggins would establish a major trading store at the old town, calling it "Mount Pleasant." George Galphin, a recent immigrant from northern Ireland, would soon build a much bigger and more significant trading establishment at Silver Bluff.[69]

The Salzburgers had quickly discovered that the lands Oglethorpe had assigned to them were not nearly as good as first appeared, and began to pine for more attractive lands beyond Ebenezer Creek. Shortly after Oglethorpe's arrival in 1736 they moved to New Ebenezer, across the creek and closer to the river. The Salzburgers yearned to make further use of Yuchi lands, at least to graze their cattle. The Yuchis were seldom seen but were often heard as they protested encroachments both from New Ebenezer and the South Carolina side of the river. Oglethorpe accepted the Salzburgers relocation but drew the line there, warning that any further advance "will certainly draw on an Indian War."[70]

According to Oglethorpe, stray Salzburger cattle had been able to "eat the Uchees Corn 20 miles above Ebenezer." Worse, Carolinians "swam a great Herd of Cattle over Savannah, and sent up Negroes and began a Plantation on the Georgia side not far from the Uchees Town." Shortly after his arrival, Oglethorpe wrote Causton that "they must be dislodged, for we will never break Faith with the Indians." Later he proudly reported that he had "ordered back the Cattle and sent away the negroes which I did as soon as ever I arrived." In early May the Yuchi "King" and twenty warriors came down to Frederica to express thanks. Most satisfying to Oglethorpe, "they told me that my having done them justice before they asked it made them love me."[71]

This Yuchi visit produced some of the best graphic evidence on Georgia's Indians (Baron von Reck's now famous drawings) but little written evidence, and no official record of proceedings. Von Reck says that "the Indian king gave a long speech, an alliance was concluded, and gifts were exchanged." Oglethorpe adds that the Yuchis promised to provide a hundred warriors for a year "to help me against the Spaniards." This meeting, which seems to have been the first and nearly the last between Yuchi and English leaders, apparently allowed Oglethorpe to claim another achievement. Five years later he described the Yuchis as "affectionate Subjects to his Majesty." However they were supposed to have acquired this status, most likely it occurred during their meeting with Oglethorpe in Frederica.[72]

The Salzburgers did not give up, but appealed to the London Trustees for permission to settle on the seemingly abandoned Yuchi lands. Replying for the Trustees on June 10, Benjamin Martyn denied their request, explaining that since these lands "belong to the Indians, the Trustees have no power to grant them." That same day he wrote Oglethorpe asking him to resolve the problem by securing an appropriate (Yuchi) land cession. Oglethorpe may already have tried this, but he was never able to accomplish it. Three years later he wrote that the Yuchis "will not part with the same."[73]

In June, Oglethorpe appointed Roger Lacy agent to the Cherokees and about the same time named John Tanner agent to the Creeks. As they sought to establish their authority in the Indian country, both were soon involved in conflicts with the Carolina traders and their Indian friends. Tanner reported that he spent "4 months in driving away the Carolina Traders" who lacked Georgia licenses. Of the Creeks he encountered, he said that "there are now few Indians that do not Speak English enough to be understood." He added, however, that "they do not care to do it but when drunk."[74]

Lacy's appointment was closely connected with the establishment of what was unquestionably colonial Georgia's most important outpost: Fort Augusta. The following year a palisaded fort would be erected on a site about 230 river miles above Savannah which had been recognized as strategic for half a century. The Carolinians had maintained Fort Moore nearby on their side of the river since 1717. The site was at the headwaters of navigation on the river, very near where the path to the Creeks crossed it, and the Cherokees would soon mark out a new path along the river that connected both forts to their country. Oglethorpe was not exaggerating when he called Augusta "the Key of all the Indian Country."[75]

Establishing a commercial center near this strategic location must have been on the Trustees' to-do list for more than a year, ever since they legislated to control the Indian trade on their side of the Savannah River. According to Oglethorpe, Augusta "was laid out by the Trustees' orders in the Year 1735/6." Anticipating having to deal with a new set of regulators, many of the traders operating out of Fort Moore decided it would be prudent to move across the river. This relocation had begun by February, for in March the Spanish governor indicated that he had received Yuchi complaints that Englishmen were making ready to build a fort on their land. In June Oglethorpe wrote the Trustees that "Indians and traders and Cherikees" were with him in Savannah "and offer to build a Town at their own Expense 300 miles up the River, to consist of 40 families the first year." These settlers, he added, "are all to be white People or half bred Indians."[76]

Oglethorpe was ready for this opportunity. On June 11 he appointed Lacy captain of a ranger company organized to build and garrison a new fort at Augusta. To assist Lacy in his capacity as Cherokee agent, Oglethorpe also appointed ten Carolinians as constables to discipline fellow traders in the Cherokee country. On June 14, Noble Jones was directed to plan a survey of the projected fort area. Before construction could begin, however, it would be necessary to seek and gain Creek consent for the fort. Luckily, Creek leaders were expected in Savannah at the end of the month.[77]

During his conference with the Creeks, Oglethorpe made the necessary request. Wesley's minutes for June 27 and July 3 say nothing about the proposed fort, presumably because this matter too was discussed in the July 1 meeting devoted to land issues. Once again Oglethorpe got his way, and again the evidence appears in later sources. In 1747 Malatchi summarized Creek land cessions down to 1736 in a speech to Colonel Heron. He then declared that "These were all the Talks we had with the General [Oglethorpe] about Lands, only he asked leave to build a House [fort] at Augusta." The Creek leader here implied that this request had been granted, but in 1755 he openly acknowledged that "the Creeks consented that he should build a Fort on this Side by Savannah River." The English must have supposed that this consent included a cession of the land around the fort, for the Savannah authorities soon began making land grants outside the palisade. The Creeks never objected.[78]

Following Creek agreement for a fort on the Savannah, Oglethorpe went on to solicit their consent for a similar base on the Altamaha. This time he had to report that "they have refused as yet to give leave to settle the Inland Parts up the Alatamaha." The Creek chiefs doubtless replied differently to the two requests because they recognized that the two projected outposts would affect them differently. An English fort at the falls of the Savannah would expand existing trade connections; a fort at a similar site on the Altamaha would merely plant troublesome Englishmen in Creek hunting territory. Unwilling to take the Creeks' no for their final answer, in September Oglethorpe went "several days Journey" up the river, no doubt scouting for a suitable site. Denied Creek permission to build, that was all he could do.[79]

Though fortified bases far in the interior would encourage commerce with Indians and discourage attacks from them, at first their main purpose was to support British claims of territorial sovereignty against the Spaniards and French. After English outposts far up both the Savannah and the Altamaha had become a reality, Savannah leader William Stephens wrote in 1740 that "Forts were erected upon the Extremities to keep up Marks of Possession." The following year Benjamin Martyn published a major defense of the Trustees' management, which by then needed a major defense. Martyn enumerated British forts in the region, including those on Cumberland and Amelia islands, and used them to demonstrate British possession from Savannah to the Gulf of Mexico. Even the tiny outpost at Okfuskee was assigned a leading role: Martyn described it as "a Mark of Possession within 40 Miles of the French Fort."[80]

The dimensions of the 1736 Lower Creek cession can now be delineated with some confidence. During the talks with Oglethorpe between June 27 and July 3, evidently on July 1, the Lower Creek chiefs confirmed the cession agreement made three or four months earlier with Tomochichi and the Yamacraws. They agreed to cede a tract extending inland to the tidal limit and southward to the St. Johns, along with most of the coastal islands. Specifically exempted were the Yamacraw tract and three of the islands: Ossabaw, Sapelo, and St. Catherines. In addition, in the only aspect of the cession not mentioned in the 1739 treaty, the Creek leaders either ceded the site for Augusta or at least granted permission to settle it. Lacy and his fourteen rangers would finally reach the site on May 29, 1737, Jones finished his survey in July, and construction was essentially complete the following April.

An Indian land cession appears to be a simple exchange of property: agents of the English king buy a certain tract of land from Indians with guns, textiles, and other manufactured goods. We again and again read that Oglethorpe or other British officials have "purchased" land from Indians willing to "sell" it. The everyday terminology is misleading. In the Anglo-American legal tradition, a transaction concerned with landed (real) property differs fundamentally from one involving movable (personal) property, and is always more highly regulated. For centuries many things have been required by law for landed property that are not required for movable property. Likewise, many things are forbidden in connection with landed property that are perfectly legal for movable property. In the English colonies one such prohibition applied to any attempt to acquire legal title to land by buying it from Indians. In the eyes of English law, a cession of lands by Indians was not a legal "conveyance" of property but rather a renunciation of property. Had Indians been able to make legal sales of land to colonists, it would have meant (barring a rare claim that their right to the land originated with a grant from the king) that they, not the king, had ultimate "sovereign" title to such land. Accordingly, purchases of land from Indians were repeatedly prohibited.[81]

In November 1734 Samuel Eveleigh asked Oglethorpe if "I might have Liberty to purchase of the Yamacraw Indians Twenty Acres of Land Somewhere by Musgroves." Replying for the Trustees the following May, Benjamin Martyn wrote Eveleigh that his request "must on second thoughts appear to You impossible to be granted, because it is contrary to Law for any Private Persons to purchase any Lands of the Indians; and indeed the Indians cannot alienate their Lands." Eveleigh knew that, or he would not have made his request. Others did not know that, or preferred not to, and attempted to make such purchases. Invariably this got them into legal trouble. We will shortly encounter a major example in Georgia.[82]

No one but the king could acquire land from the Indians, but even he did not "buy" it from them in any ordinary sense. The natural rights title of the natives was not something the king wanted or had any use for. What he and British officials wanted was that this inconvenient title disappear, so that formerly Indian lands could be treated as vacant. The king, as sovereign over this vacant territory, could then make land grants to his subjects under English law. A few decades later, colonial officials began to say that the result of an Indian land cession was that the native title was "extinguished." The Indian right was not transferred to the king; it was erased. Following the American Revolution, "extinguishment" became a dominant concept in United States Indian law.[83]

According to English law, Indians did not sell lands to the king; they gave lands to him. The king did not regrant or otherwise preserve the Indian title; it quietly disappears, never to be cited in legal records that trace "chain of title." In the colonies, as in England, all lawful titles to land (all those that an English court would uphold) began with a grant from the king. Since an Indian cession was not a legal conveyance of property, it followed that whatever the king or his agents gave the Indians in return did not constitute a payment ("valuable consideration") for lands. Instead, what the Indians received were "presents," that is, reciprocal gifts. Accordingly, the records of land negotiations do not mention any bargaining over price. Moreover, Indian concessions of land always preceded English grants of goods, and often several days separated the two events. The Indians thus rarely, perhaps never, knew precisely what they would receive in return for their land. Formally, the guns and other valuable goods Oglethorpe gave the Creeks in July 1736 were not the final requirement for closing a deal; they were simply gifts. The Creeks agreed, for mutual gift giving was the heart of their traditional diplomacy.[84]

The English had good reason to be confident that they got more on July 1 than they gave on July 3, but there is no evidence that the Creeks felt cheated. On the contrary, Chigelli and his followers behaved as though they had been beneficiaries of a windfall. They were not being naive. Unlike the English, the Creeks did not consider what happened on July 1 or the day of any land agreement as a discrete occurrence, separate from all others and complete in itself. They did not compute the value of their lands and the value of the English goods, then compare them to determine if the land they had surrendered had fetched a "fair price." Rather, what they had given the English and what the English had given them that day were small parts of an ongoing pattern of mutual gift giving, necessary nourishment for an ongoing relationship between friends.

Even if the Creeks believed that the value of the lands they had yielded on July 1 far exceeded the value of the goods they had received—as they surely did—that was of no particular concern. What mattered most to them was not short-term value but long-term reciprocity. Insofar as value mattered, it was value over the long term. The Creeks believed that they had given the English so much valuable land that they could expect the English to reciprocate with valuable gifts for a long time to come. They could expect this even on occasions when they gave the English little or nothing. English observers could easily misconstrue this as the behavior of spoiled children—"Indian giving." Thus later that year Samuel Eveleigh complained that "the Indians have been so used of late Year's to receive presents That They now expect it as a Right belonging to them, And the English French and Spaniards are in Some measure become Tributary to them."[85]

While Oglethorpe was engaged with the Creek chiefs, he learned that a party of Chickasaws had appeared near Augusta. They were on the other side of the river visiting a band of separatist Chickasaws that had settled near Fort Moore. Oglethorpe shared the Carolinians' perception that the Chickasaws were the most valiant and reliable Indian allies the colonists had. Moreover, not only were they supposed to be British subjects in some vague sense, but they actually claimed to be British subjects. Eager to learn how they were faring in their war with the French and the Choctaws, Oglethorpe sent a scout boat up the river to invite them down to Savannah. It returned on July 6 with twenty Chickasaws aboard, including a few wives and children.[86]

In talks a week later, Thomas Jones acted as one of the interpreters. One of the Chickasaw leaders, Mingo Bemingo, apparently expected to find that Oglethorpe too was a mixed-blood: "We heard you was a Red Woman's Child." Oglethorpe deftly replied, "I am a Red Man, an Indian in my heart." In much the same spirit, Mingo Bemingo declared that "We are come into our own Town, and our own People." Other Chickasaw spokesmen went on to inform Oglethorpe that the French and their numerous Indian allies had mounted a strong new offensive. The Chickasaws were hard pressed and had no allies other than the distant Cherokees; they required immediate military assistance, and as British subjects they were entitled to it. Oglethorpe agreed that as subjects these Indians were "intitled to the

Help and Protection they sought for." He responded with advice about weaponry and tactics as well as a major outlay of presents, mainly in the form the Indians had requested: powder and shot. Afterward Oglethorpe wrote that the Chickasaws "have been here to demand protection as the Kings Subjects" and that they had provided valuable intelligence about French machinations.[87]

Oglethorpe had good reason to be satisfied with his brief second stay in Georgia. In the space of a few months he had succeeded in overcoming much of the suspicion and hostility that had developed among the Indians during his absence, and he had won important new concessions from the Yamacraws and Lower Creeks. In keeping with his instructions from the government, the de facto southern frontier of the colony had been advanced far beyond the Altamaha without, so far, provoking a Spanish attack. With the colony now seemingly more secure than ever, and internal conflicts muted, he could turn his attention back home. There he had plenty to worry about. He had the ear of high officials, but in 1736 Parliament had slashed the appropriation for Georgia. Furthermore, the Trustees were already furious over what they knew of his recent activities, and lately they had been sending urgent warnings that serious trouble was brewing with Spain. He had a lot of explaining to do, but he also had results. Having "left me in the charge of the whole colony," wrote Causton, on November 23 Oglethorpe sailed for England to help prepare the next moves in the imperial contest.[88]

CHAPTER FOUR

Faltering Diplomacy with the Creeks and War with Spain

By the time Oglethorpe returned to London the Spanish government was protesting forcefully against Georgia, and evidence continued to accumulate that it was organizing for an attack on the colony. When Oglethorpe rejoined his fellow Trustees he finally gave them a straightforward account of what he had been up to south of the Altamaha. On January 9, 1737, three days after Oglethorpe reached London, Egmont met with him for more than four hours. Egmont related that "his account of affairs in Georgia and of his own behaviour and conduct there was very satisfactory to me and has cleared up divers matters whereof the Trustees were in doubt." Oglethorpe gave the other Trustees a similar briefing on January 12 and January 19. He explained that establishing Fort St. George was one of several measures he took in response to intelligence that the Spaniards were planning an assault on Frederica. It was a necessary defense measure "to keep the Spaniards from interrupting his building a Fort at Frederica." Evidently he also told them about instructions from the king and the ministry, for they never again protested what he had done or would do south of the Altamaha.[1]

Parliament was then in session, and Oglethorpe was still a member of the House of Commons. That month, in behalf of the Trustees, he introduced an appropriation bill for Georgia. He told Egmont that he had argued for £30,000, but hoped for £20,000. In March Parliament appropriated £20,000. Oglethorpe, urgently concerned to provide for the defense of Georgia, now had to turn to the ministry. He was repeatedly at odds with Prime Minister Walpole, whose priority was to avoid war with Spain. In February Oglethorpe bluntly told Walpole that unless the government embraced Georgia as "a National Affair," the colony would fail and he would be remembered as "a Don Quixot." Walpole offered to have him appointed governor of South Carolina, as he had the year before. Oglethorpe again declined, his excuse being his desire to keep his seat in Parliament. The prime minister then offered him the command of the military forces of both South Carolina and Georgia, but Oglethorpe was willing to accept only if he were given a regiment of regulars. This stiff condition was finally agreed to, and in June Oglethorpe was appointed "General and Commander in Chief of the Forces in South Carolina and Georgia." Shortly thereafter Parliament appropriated about £13,000 for Georgia's defense, most of it earmarked for the new regiment. This new unit was the Forty-second Regiment of Foot, with an authorized strength of 684 under Oglethorpe as colonel.[2]

While military arrangements were being worked out with the government, the Trustees considered several other matters that would affect Georgia's relations with the Indians. One, already noted, involved Mary Musgrove Matthews's appeal regarding the Musgrove five-hundred-acre grant. Another involved Joseph Watson, still detained in Savannah. A sympathizer complained that Watson had been "kept in Confinement under a strong Guard for upwards of two years." Early in 1737 Watson's wife arrived in London and petitioned the king in council for his release. Mrs. Watson pursued her legal case with determination, and the Trustees were forced to reconsider the matter in March. Oglethorpe told his fellow Trustees that he believed Watson "not only drank the Indian dead by design . . . but that he poisoned his liquor, as the other Indians alleged." He went on to declare that "Watson would certainly have been found guilty, of murder, if Indian evidence had been allowed to be taken."[3]

Oglethorpe thereby raised a much larger issue: the Savannah magistrates' policy of barring Indian testimony from their courts. Here the Savannah leaders were following the lead of South Carolina and other colonies. Oglethorpe explained to the other Trustees that Indian statements were excluded from colonial courts because "by the laws of America they are not allowed to be evidence." The rationale for this exclusion was the idea that nearly all Indians (exceptions were made for Christian converts) were incapable of giving sworn testimony. Persuaded that the natives had been denied justice, the Trustees ordered that an act "for allowing of Indian evidence in our Courts" be drafted. Presumably it would have extended to Indians the Quakers' right to testify by affirmation. That was as far as the matter went, evidently because the Trustees feared that such a law would intensify their ongoing conflict with South Carolina. The issue of Indian testimony would resurface in a much more serious case nine years later. As for Watson, in May the Trustees directed the Savannah magistrates to free him, provided he had "returned to his right Senses." He was released in November.[4]

Still suspicious that they could not rely on Oglethorpe to keep them fully informed about what was going on in Georgia, his fellow Trustees had already begun casting about for an alternative source. In April, with Oglethorpe's approval, they appointed William Stephens to be their resident secretary in Savannah. Stephens was a Cambridge M.A. who had been a member of Parliament for twenty years before business losses led him to flee his creditors, first to Scotland and then to America. In early 1736 he had agreed to supervise a survey of four large tracts on the Carolina side of the Savannah River claimed by Colonel Samuel Horsey. (Horsey would soon be named Governor of South Carolina, but died before he could take up his post.) Stephens arrived in Charles Town that April and, in Savannah a month later, met and impressed Oglethorpe.

Stephens took up residence in Savannah in October 1737. With his education and political experience, he was no ordinary colonist. Even his physical constitution was extraordinary: he was already sixty-six years old when he gratefully took up his new post. Over the next thirteen years he proved to be an able and loyal servant to his employers, and soon emerged as the most influential resident of the colony. The detailed journal he kept for the Trustees, which survives for the years down to 1745, remains the premier historical source for the period.[5]

Not the least of Oglethorpe's achievements during his 1736 stay in Georgia was the close working relationship he forged with the widowed Mary Musgrove, who was not easy to deal with. Her willingness to intercede for the colony with her influential relatives and friends among the Lower Creeks was an important factor in the colony's survival during the seven difficult years that followed.

When John Musgrove drew up his will in early 1734 he had two surviving sons, James and Edward, who were to inherit the bulk of his estate. Both sons were alive when their father died in June 1735, and still alive in April 1736, when Benjamin Ingham agreed with Mary to teach them to read. Ingham reported that "I am to spend three or four days a week with them." John Wesley, who stayed in Savannah, soon informed the Trustees that he and Ingham had established "*Irene*, a house built for an Indian School on a Small round hill." This was a major blunder. They had built their large Indian schoolhouse atop Irene mound, a prehistoric earthen platform at the upper end of the Yamacraw tract. The Indians avoided these haunted relics, and so of course they avoided the school. Completing the disaster, Ingram soon lost his high-profile pupils. James Musgrove died sometime after April, and in late November his younger brother also died. For Mary the loss of Edward or "Ned," her father's namesake and her last and perhaps youngest child, must have been particularly painful. In February 1737, when Ingham left Savannah for England, the school was a quaint memory.[6]

Mary was no longer the widow Musgrove, however, for she had recently married Jacob Matthews. Stephens described him as "a hail, lusty, young Fellow," evidently considerably younger than Mary. In June Causton twice hosted a midday meal for the colony's most important mustees and their spouses. On June 25, "Mr. Mathews and his wife, and Thomas Jones and his wife dined with me. I gave each of them a Dozen bottles of English beer." Among Mary's very numerous troubles, she must have been acutely aware that the lack of a male Musgrove heir in tail-male Georgia meant that if she died her five-hundred-acre tract would revert to the Trustees, and in the meantime she could not sell it or any part of it to relieve her growing financial distress. Before Ingham sailed, Mary persuaded him to argue her case for exceptional treatment before the Trustees.[7]

In June the Trustees were startled to learn that Ingham, "who Shewed So much zeal for converting the Indians," had deserted the colony. When he showed up at their office in July, he explained to the suspicious Trustees that he had returned "to take Priests orders." Perhaps the best that could be said of this fiasco was that the Trustees were now better prepared for the news a few months later that their second Indian missionary, John Wesley, had left the colony in high disrepute. Wesley in particular was totally disillusioned with Indians. On the Creeks, he opined that "they know not what friendship or gratitude means," and "show no inclination to learn anything" except "European vices." This was true even for Chigelli, for whom "neither age, wisdom, nor reputation can restrain him from drunkeness." The Yuchis were worse, notorious "as well for their cowardice, as their superlative diligence in thieving, and for out-lying all the Indians upon the continent." Since Charles Wesley had returned to England the previous December, the retreat of Georgia's Indian missionaries was now complete.[8]

In fact, by late 1736 the colony itself seemed on the verge of collapse. After three years of disappointments, dreams of prosperity were evaporating. Rather suddenly, Trustee policies, especially the ban on slavery, seemed calculated to drive the colonists into poverty and keep them there. A faction of "Malcontents" surged into prominence. Among the bad news Charles Wesley brought the Trustees, he reported that "the Carolinians have distressed our Colony by seducing away from the first settlement of our people 700 persons." A sea captain who visited Savannah a little over a year later claimed that "there are more houses in the town than inhabitants" and that the people who remained were embroiled in factional quarrels. Even William Stephens was privately discouraged. Three months after undertaking his duties in Savannah, he wrote that until Georgia produced a valuable export, it "must be a place of Want."[9]

On July 20 Ingham presented Mary Matthews's petition to the Trustees. He asked that "she might have leave to appoint a successor to her lot (her children by Musgrove being all dead), and to assign the same for payment of her debts." Ingham added that "if she obtained this favour, it was her intention to leave the Colony and settle with her new husband in Carolina." Oglethorpe told the others he did not believe she would return to South Carolina, "for she owed there a thousand pound." The Trustees took no immediate action on Mary's petition, but apparently did approve it later.[10]

As Oglethorpe understood, it was already clear that Mary's trading business was failing. There simply were not enough hunting Indians settled at or near the new Yamacraw town to support it. Moreover, Mary complained that during 1736 and 1737, whenever Creeks appeared at Frederica, she was called down to serve as interpreter. The result, she charged, was that her business and property near Savannah "went to Ruin, being in her Absence on publick service entirely Left to the Care and Management of Servants."[11]

One of William Stephens's earliest journal entries concerns the original Yamacraw townsite, vacated two years earlier, and Mary and Jacob Matthews. The old Yamacraw town stood in a wooded area extending from the Savannah town line a short distance upriver to a creek, evidently the one the Indians called Palachacola Creek. In December 1737 Stephens reported that Tomochichi had just given the site "to Mrs. Matthews and her Husband." Although he did not say so at the time, Stephens later recalled thinking that "it foreboded no Good." It was much worse than he imagined. Tomochichi's gift to the Matthews was just a "Spot of Land . . . about two or three hundred Acres." Or maybe a little bigger: five years later the Matthews estimated its size at "450 acres." Despite its insignificant size, Tomochichi's grant of the site to Mary and Jacob marked the inconspicuous beginning of a problem that would eventually metastasize into a mortal threat to the colony.[12]

By early 1738 most of the Trustees had concluded that war with Spain was imminent and that they could no longer take any responsibility for the defense of Georgia. On March 23 a Trustees committee voted unanimously to reject "all branches of expenses of a military nature," including even "the building of a fort at Augusta." Forewarned of what was afoot, Oglethorpe made himself scarce. Egmont commented that "since he is not thoroughly pleased with our proceedings, he choses to be absent as often as he can with decency." The Trustees promptly sought to place military responsibility where they thought it belonged: "In the beginning of the Year 1738 . . . they applied to his Majesty to take upon him the Protection of the Colony."[13]

The Trustees' meeting on May 10, the last Oglethorpe attended before returning to Georgia, was long and contentious. Over his strenuous objection, the rest of the board reiterated their determination not to pay for any expenses "relating to the defence of the Colony." Further restricting Oglethorpe's room for maneuver, the Trustees resolved that presents for the Indians henceforth were not to be purchased in America, but were "to be sent from England only," and only by them. They went on to divide Georgia into two parts: the "Northern Division" around Savannah and the "Southern Division" around Frederica. Against Oglethorpe's wishes, they dismissed Thomas Causton, "that wastfull Man," as their Savannah storekeeper, replacing him with Thomas Jones (an immigrant, not the mustee). A few weeks later they also removed Causton as first bailiff in Savannah, appointing Henry Parker in his place.[14]

The fleet transporting Oglethorpe and his regiment finally got under way in July and on September 18 arrived at St. Simons Island. During the next five years Oglethorpe kept his headquarters at Frederica, which temporarily became the colony's most important settlement. Throughout his third sojourn in America he was preoccupied with preparing for, and then fighting, a war with the Spaniards. Relations with the natives received less attention than before, except insofar as they might affect the looming conflict. Indian assistance would be valuable, but Oglethorpe never supposed that it could be decisive. With his regiment at Frederica, he had the largest offensive force on the continent and good reason to rely mainly on British arms. There was no way to break the Spanish hold on Florida without taking the fortress at St. Augustine. That would require a protracted siege, a task ill-suited to Indian allies.

Although this would not become apparent for years, the most important meeting Oglethorpe held with Indians during his final stay in Georgia occurred less than a month after his arrival. This meeting has scarcely been noticed before, because until recently the only source was an anonymous letter from Georgia dated October 22, 1738, published soon afterward in the *Gentleman's Magazine*. Two much more revealing documents—Recorder Thomas Christie's minutes and Robert Williams's deposition—have lately come to light. Significantly, it was visiting Indians who took the initiative for this meeting, doubtless under prompting from Mary Matthews and Tomochichi. Oglethorpe was caught off guard.[15]

On October 6 Oglethorpe heard from the leaders of four Lower Creek towns that they were on their way to Savannah to see him. The four towns represented were Apalachicola, Chehaw, Ouseechee, and Ocmulgee (the three last were clustered at a bend of the river and were often collectively called "the point towns"). All four were Hitchiti-speaking towns, and Apalachicola was Tomochichi's native town. The visiting chiefs were clearly his friends: "Tomo Chachi said these Indians were his own Towns People." Aware that it might be insulting and dangerous to beg off, Oglethorpe dropped his military preparations at Frederica and sailed north to meet the visitors. He arrived in Savannah on October 10, shortly after the Indians camped at Tomochichi's new town near the Matthews' place. The chiefs did not come alone, but were accompanied by more than eighty of their townsmen.

The following day Tomochichi came down to see Oglethorpe. "He had been very ill, but the good old Man was so rejoiced at the General's Arrival, that he said it recovered him." He reported that the visiting chiefs "were at his house" and ready to meet with Oglethorpe "to assure him of their Fidelity to the King of Great

Britain." Two days later the Indians came down the river to Savannah. "As they walked up the Hill they were saluted by a Battery of Cannon, and conducted to the Town Hall by a Party of Militia, where the General received them." The meeting took place over October 13 and 14.[16]

There were three significant developments at this meeting. One was old business. Although Oglethorpe's imposing force near the mouth of the Altamaha diminished the case for a fort far up the river, he had not given up on the project. Mackay and Oglethorpe had both failed to gain the Creeks' permission, but they might speak differently to Mary. Having determined that Mary and Jacob Matthews were willing to relocate their failing trading establishment to the Altamaha, Oglethorpe recognized this as a way to finesse Creek objections to a fort. Even if fortified, such a trading post would have little military value, at least in the short run. It would, however, help support British territorial claims and foster closer relations with the Lower Creeks. The Indians were sure to see readier access to Mary's trade goods in a positive light.

Assured that the visiting chiefs would welcome such a post, Oglethorpe apparently proposed that the Matthews establish it far up the river at "the forks," where the Ocmulgee and the Oconee rivers converged to form the Altamaha. The Indians demurred: "they wanted Mrs. Matthews to settle on the Alatamaha River about a Mile and a half from Darien." One of them explained that the lands around the forks "are continually overflowed" and, worse, were "in the Path to the Spaniards," and thus highly vulnerable to attack. Furthermore, a site near Darien and the coast provided "a better Path to go down to his Excellency at the southward." In the end a compromise site midway between the forks and the coast was chosen. Mary later related that "at the Request of his Excellency general Oglethorpe" she had established Mount Venture about sixty miles up the river. This small but fortified post was established sometime in 1739. It was planted on the south bank of the river—outside the charter bounds—probably at Oglethorpe's insistence. In February 1740 Oglethorpe mentioned "Mr. Matthews new Settlement," and Stephens noted that Jacob and Mary were now living there.[17]

The second major development looked to the future. Having enticed Oglethorpe to travel a long way to Savannah, the Indians now wished him to draw him much farther: all the way to their settlements on the Chattahoochee. In both Indian and European cultures, who came to see whom was an indicator of who was subordinate and who was dominant. According to the October 22 letter, "They invited the General to come up in the Summer to see their Towns, which he promised to do." Christie's minutes merely have Oglethorpe saying "he would Endeavour to see them" and inquiring about the best time to visit. They answered: "the Latter end of June or beginning of July at the Busk." Oglethorpe's later statements likewise indicate that his answer was equivocal, for he plainly was not eager to go. At any rate, he must have given at least a qualified acceptance to the Indians' invitation.[18]

The third development was by far the most important. As intended, it caught Oglethorpe completely by surprise. On October 13, after Oglethorpe made a formulaic speech reviewing good relations in the past and promising better ones in the future, the Indians suddenly changed the subject and took control of the proceedings. According to Christie's minutes: "Indians then spoke and said that they gave all the Tracts of Lands belonging to them lying between this Place and Tomo Chachis to Mrs. Matthews and that no Indians after this can demand the same again. Being asked by the General if they would not desire it again when the White People had got possession of it and when the Trees are cut down and especially when they should find the white Peoples hearts not straight towards them. They answered no, no Body will trouble them." Evidently the Indians' reply satisfied Oglethorpe, or perhaps it merely flummoxed him. At any rate, Christie's minutes indicate that nothing further was said on the subject, and the meeting moved on to other business. It ended in routine fashion when Oglethorpe distributed £93 in presents to the visiting chiefs.[19]

Two aspects of this remarkable episode stand out as especially remarkable. First, it seems all but certain that the land in question was not merely the old Yamacraw town, as had been the case a year earlier, but nearly the entire Yamacraw tract. When the visiting chiefs granted lands "between this Place and Tomo Chachis," they pretty clearly meant the lands between Savannah and Tomochichi's place five miles up the river, where they had spent the previous three days. Oglethorpe may have misunderstood. He may have remained passive on October 13 because he was slow to realize that what was at stake was not the old townsite but essentially the entire Yamacraw tract (all but the new Yamacraw town).

New Yamacraw not only was not a Creek town; it was not even a stable community. People were constantly coming and going, lately mainly going. From the start, Indians who came to Tomochichi's town were attracted by Mary's nearby trading store. Now that she had made it known that she and her husband planned to relocate their trading operation to the Altamaha, life by Pipemaker's Creek lost much of its appeal. With the natives drifting away, granting the Yamacraw tract to Mary would repay old favors at minimal cost and help ensure that her trading business survived.

Note too that this grant was intended to supersede the original reservation of the tract by Tomochichi and the Yamacraws: "no Indians after this can demand the same again." Tomochichi had played host to the visiting chiefs at his place, acted as advance man for their visit to Savannah, accompanied them to town, and to some degree participated in making the grant. According to Robert Williams, his participation was active. Williams swore he recalled that he and various Savannah gentlemen "were desired by the King Tomochichi and several other head men and Warriors of the Creek nation to be Witnesses of their Surrender of all their Right to a Certain tract of Land called the Indian Land adjacent to the town of Savannah."[20]

The second outstanding feature of the 1738 grant was that it was not simply a transaction among Indians governed by Indian rules. Mary Matthews had an English education, was a practicing Christian, was married to an Englishman, had an English land grant for the maximum acreage allowed in the colony, and was already accustomed to sue and be sued at English law. In short, although she was half Creek by birth, Mary's lifestyle was predominantly English and she was accepted as an influential member of the colony.[21]

Mary clearly intended to receive this grant as an Englishwoman and hold it under English law. All other lands within the colony, including her five hundred acres, were held by tail-male tenure. The Yamacraw tract, however, was granted to Mary without tenurial restrictions. (Lawyers would say that her tenure was allodial.) Should the Indians' grant take effect, none of the Trustees' landholding rules would apply to it. Most conspicuously, since the Yamacraw tract contained "about 4000 Acres" (probably more), it was about eight times the five-hundred-acre maximum the Trustees allowed to elite landholders. More important to Mary, since the Trustees' restrictions on alienation applied only to lands they had granted, she could freely sell all or parts of the tract. There would be no shortage of buyers, for Mary could offer disgruntled colonists larger tracts unburdened by the despised restrictions on alienation.[22]

Thus the intended grant could solve Mary's financial problems with plenty to spare. It would immediately make her one of the largest landowners in all of North America, and allow her to profit from land sales for many years to come. Oglethorpe seems to have had a momentary inkling that something like this was in the works. He therefore asked the Indians if they were sure they would not want the land back "when the White People had got Possession of it," presumably by purchasing sections from Mary. When the chiefs immediately assured him that their minds were made up, Oglethorpe apparently put aside whatever doubts he had about what he had just witnessed.

The visiting chiefs, having publicly granted Mary their right to the Yamacraw tract, made a separate public move to grant her possession of that land. This surprising dual action demonstrates beyond doubt that the native grantors, doubtless well coached, were attempting to act in accordance with English common law. That law distinguished sharply, though not absolutely, between title to landed property and possession of that property. Title was conceived to be an abstract right, while possession was considered a matter of fact. Accordingly, there were separate rules and procedures for dealing with them. In English law, possession is demonstrated by "a sufficiently close physical relationship between a person and a parcel of land, due to his presence on or control over it." In medieval England, land transactions among the largely illiterate populace were validated not merely by a written deed transferring title but by "livery of seisin," a public display signifying transfer of possession. This was accomplished by the grantor presenting a clod of earth with vegetation still growing upon it to the grantee in the presence of neighbors. The point of this, the venerable "turf and twig" ceremony, was to enable even illiterate witnesses to testify in court about the transfer.[23]

One of many contemporary discussions in Savannah about land tenure occurred in June 1737. The participants were Thomas Causton, Thomas Christie, Lieutenant William Horton, and Robert Williams. According to Causton, Horton expressed doubts about land titles in the colony: "the Reason he gave was, that the true way of giving possession was, by a Twigg and a Tuef [Turf], and that no other way was legall." That had once been true, but by this time English law recognized other ways to accomplish livery of seisin, as well as ways to get around it. Nevertheless, Christie and Williams evidently believed Horton's assertion. Causton states that "this seemed to stick with the other two." Clear evidence that it did stick appeared at the Savannah meeting between Oglethorpe and the visiting Creek chiefs in October 1738. Whoever planned the Lower Creek grant of the Yamacraw tract to Mary Matthews decided that, to demonstrate strict adherence to English law, possession should be transferred by the turf-and-twig ceremony. Though others were doubtless involved, the key planner was surely Williams.[24]

The sworn deposition Williams gave years later asserts that such a ceremony was performed in Savannah that October, apparently a day or two after the exchange with Oglethorpe. Williams says that he, Stevens, Horton, and "some of the Magistrates and Several other Gentlemen of the Town" were present as "Witnesses" invited by the Indians. Christie was there as town recorder. Oglethorpe himself may have been present, though Williams does not say so. Williams then relates that "in a very Solemn manner Livery Possession and Seizen of the above mentioned Lands According to the Ancient manner and form of Twig and Turff was given and Delivered by King Tomochichi and the Rest of the head men and Accepted by . . . Mary Mathews."[25]

Williams goes on to say that on "that day or very soon afterward" the Indians requested that "a Court might be Called at Savannah which was Accordingly done." When it convened "King Tomochichi and the said head men did then Insist that the said Surrender and Investments [investiture] should be then and there Recorded." In other words, they demanded that their grant to Mary be entered in the official land records of the colony as a lawful conveyance, and thus ever afterward enforceable in Georgia courts. At this point, if not before, Christie and the magistrates realized that something was amiss. They refused. Williams coyly supposed that they did so because they feared that complying "might not be agreeable" to the Trustees.[26]

Compliance with the Indians' insistent demand would indeed have been disagreeable to the Trustees, very disagreeable. The official record of the meeting, Christie's minutes, identified Oglethorpe as the principal British witness to the Indians' attempted land grant. Oglethorpe and Savannah officials had been set up to witness proceedings that, though formally more or less in accord with English common law, were such that no English official or judge could dare to pronounce them lawful. It seems clear that the Indians were acting at the behest of Mary and Jacob Matthews, but it is highly unlikely that the couple could have hit upon the turf-and-twig ceremony on their own. Most probably they were following what they took to be good legal advice from Williams and other Malcontents, their friends and political allies. It was not good legal advice, but it was mischievously effective as political advice.

The critical issue here is whether a subject of the king of England could acquire legal title—a title enforceable at English law in English courts—by virtue of a direct grant from the native Indians. This issue goes back almost to the beginning of colonization and was "resolved" over and over again, always in more or less the same way. The answer was always no. A lawful grant of land from Indians always had to be directed to the king or his agent. Nevertheless, this issue refused to stay resolved and would persist to the very end of the colonial era. The most famous cases involved Roger Williams, the Maryland Jesuits, the Kennebec proprietors—and Mary Musgrove Matthews (after her third marriage, Mary Bosomworth). English and later British officials over and over again dismissed Indian land grants to individual colonists or groups of colonists as contrary to English law, and forbade the king's subjects to accept them. They might as well have forbade the rivers to flow downhill. Allowing such grants would have opened a nearly foolproof path to profit for alert British colonists, for it would guarantee them an opportunity to buy cheap (from Indians) and sell dear (to other colonists). As often as that golden path was fenced off, potential beneficiaries would find ingenious ways to get around the obstruction.

If the Lower Creek leaders had attempted to grant Mary their annual accumulation of deerskins, or their corn harvest, or their horses, or any other movable property, there would have been no legal issue and no political problem. Land, however, is fundamentally different from movable property, and land law differs profoundly from other property law. Oglethorpe could not stand by as a prime witness apparently giving official sanction to a proceeding that would be anathema to the British government. He had to object, but he did not. It was the worst mistake he or any leader of the Georgia colony ever made about Indian relations.

Oglethorpe had no choice but to deny the legitimacy of the intended land transfer from native Indians to a British colonist. There were compelling reasons why British leaders had to uphold the established precedents at almost any cost. First, to accept such native land grants as lawful conveyances was necessarily to violate the "theory of tenures," the foundation of English land law since the time of William the Conqueror. According to that theory, all subjects of the king of England in England or any English dominion held all of their lands in those places directly or indirectly from the king of England. The Indians, however, did not claim their territories because kings of England had granted such lands to them, but because they and their ancestors had lived upon them for ages. The English recognized that title. In their view, passage of time had converted the natives' possession into title. Europeans would call it a title by "occupation" or "natural right."[27]

Since the 1707 union of England and Scotland into the Kingdom of Great Britain, all lands in both kingdoms and their dependencies had to be held of the king of Great Britain. That's the way it was in England, Scotland, Ireland, the Isle of Man, Jersey, Orkney, etc. etc.; that's the way it had to be in the American colonies. To acknowledge an Indian grant to a colonist as a legal conveyance necessarily implied that the grantor Indians, not the king of England, had ultimate title to the lands in question. It would force the king into the subordinate role of enforcement officer, who by means of his court system enforced decisions about lands made by sovereign Indian leaders far away. Moreover, if Indians were sovereign over their lands, it followed that they had ultimate authority over the laws that prevailed within those lands—including lands they might grant to individual Englishmen.

The notion that the native Indians, not the English king, had sovereign authority over North American lands had other obnoxious corollaries. If the king did not in fact have that authority, then the territorial claims he made in North America had no legal basis. That in turn would imply that the grandiose concessions of territory he made to English colonizers via royal charters were legally invalid. And that would imply that no British colonist had a secure title to landed property, for nearly all of them traced their title to colonizers who were recipients of such charters. (The rest, a handful of royal favorites, traced their title to direct grants from the king himself.) The charters could no longer be viewed as "constitutions," but would have to be regarded, as John Marshall put it a century later, as "blank paper." No British official could tolerate a practice that led to such results.

When, however, native leaders granted land to the king of England or his duly constituted agents—such as the Trustees of Georgia—all such difficulties vanished. An Indian grant to a colonist or group of colonists created an apparent title which contradicted that of the king; an Indian grant to the king himself erased a title that might otherwise contradict his. Thus, from early Virginia to the end of the colonial era, British officials repeatedly attempted to forbid private land purchases from Indians. All of the colonial governments took similar steps, and most would enact penal statutes prohibiting the practice.[28]

Though Georgia did not enact such a law until 1758, the Trustees followed the well-understood official line from the start. As noted earlier, when Samuel Eveleigh in 1734 sought special permission to purchase land from the Yamacraws, he promptly received a sharp rebuff from the Trustees' secretary, Benjamin Martyn. Soon afterward their accountant, Harman Verelst, reminded Eveleigh that "none can purchase Land of the Indians in Georgia without the King's Authority, and that Royal Authority is Granted only to the Trustees for all the Land in the Province of Georgia." The iron rules that applied to purchases from Indians likewise applied to gifts or any other form of land acquisition.[29]

As a witness to one or both of the Indians' public efforts to transfer the tract to Mary, Oglethorpe seemed to endorse the legitimacy—the legality—of those actions. He could not possibly do that, as he surely understood on some level, but the purported grant to Mary had been sprung on him in a context that made it very difficult for him to avoid doing so. Somehow Oglethorpe had to publicly disassociate himself from the intended grant to Mary—possibly by walking out, or repudiating what was taking place before him, or demanding a reconsideration, or at least by recording his objection. He knew, however, that it was impossible to do so without offending Tomochichi, major Lower Creek leaders, and Mary Musgrove. He needed all of them, hesitated, and failed to object. It was a trap, but he didn't see it in time. So far as the record shows, the other Savannah leaders didn't either.

Since the snare worked as intended, those who set it never forgot about it. The document that proved the authenticity of the grant was lovingly preserved by Mary Matthews and her last two husbands, Jacob Matthews and Thomas Bosomworth. The key point supporting Mary's claim to the Yamacraw tract under English law was made most clearly years later by Bosomworth: "The Lands there called Indian Lands had been Solemnly reserved by the Indians in Treaty with Mr. Oglethorpe on the first Settlement of the Province; and the Property thereof, so long agoe as the Year 1738, Conveyed by them, in Open Court, to Mrs. Bosomworth in the presence and by the Approval of Mr Oglethorpe who then represented the Body of the Trustees." In Georgia, Oglethorpe acted in behalf of the Trustees; unless they specifically contradicted him, his "Approval" was their approval. Thus, even if there were some sort of a technical flaw in Mary's title, Oglethorpe—speaking for the Trustees—had risen above pettifoggery to pronounce that title good.[30]

Before he left Savannah, Oglethorpe almost certainly realized that he had blundered into an ambush set by people he was obliged to consider his friends. That may have occurred by the day of the turf-and-twig ceremony, for then someone, likely Oglethorpe himself, sounded the alarm that led the magistrates to refuse to record the event in the town records. Later he did what he could to repair the damage, but his options were few. He could warn Mary not to attempt to make use of her tainted grant, and he could attempt to conceal what had occurred. Probably he did both. There is no further reference to Christie's minutes in Savannah's surviving official records. Evidently neither Oglethorpe nor the town magistrates sent a copy of this embarrassing—possibly even incriminating—document to the Trustees in London. The Trustees apparently first learned of the purported Creek grant to Mary more than three years later.

It seems evident that Christie's minutes were suppressed, and highly probable that Oglethorpe ordered them suppressed. He was the individual most threatened by the document and, in the Georgia of 1738, it was all but impossible to dispute his authority. Pretty clearly his effort to erase the memory of what he must have regarded as a greedy charade did not stop there. Not only the official Savannah records, but the unofficial ones as well are henceforth silent about Christie's minutes or the October events it described. Christie probably gave Mary a copy, or perhaps even the original document, after it was decided not to record it. If Oglethorpe had been aware of any effort to pass the document on to Mary, he surely would have objected. Suspicion of Christie's ties to Mary and Jacob Matthews had much to do with the Trustees' gradual loss of confidence in him. On December 9 Christie and Matthews publicly became political allies when both signed a "Malcontent" petition. The following June, shortly after the petition reached London, the Trustees replaced Christie as recorder.[31]

Most revealing, astonishing really, is the complete absence in Stephens's journal of any reference to the Creek grant to Mary on October 13, though he witnessed it. Stephens faithfully filled his journal with detailed, day-by-day reports on what transpired in Savannah and vicinity. Yet he draws a shroud over the events of October 11 through 14 with a single remarkable sentence: "These Days were variously taken up in attending the General, to receive his Orders, and execute such Commands as he saw proper, wherein nothing passed that was uncommon or extraordinary." He even failed to mention that Indians came to town. Stephens could not have written that sentence unless someone heavy was leaning on him. Oglethorpe, of course. Nearly three years went by before Stephens, very cautiously, alluded to the problem. In August 1741 he questioned "how far it is consistent with the Honour and Sovereignty of the King of Great Britain, for a Subject of his in the Province of Georgia, to hold lands by Virtue of any Grant from the Indians within the said Province."[32]

Oglethorpe would also have been glad to forget his vague promise to visit the major Lower Creek settlements the following summer. Although the Indians renewed their invitation several times, he was reluctant to mount up for a two-hundred-mile ride into the deep interior. He finally yielded in June. On June 15 Oglethorpe wrote that the present and future top leaders of Coweta, Chigelli and Malatchi, "insist upon my coming up to put all things in order, and have acquainted me that all the Chiefs of the Nation will come down to the Coueta Town to meet me." He also heard that the chiefs of "All the Towns of the Creek Nation" (that is, the Lower Creek chiefs) would be joined by Upper Creek counterparts from the Abeika and Tallapoosa divisions ("the Cousees and Talapousees") and that the Choctaws and Chickasaws would also send "Deputies." What was planned, Oglethorpe wrote, was a "General Assembly of the Indian Nations." He added that "Tomo Chachi and all the Indians advise me to go up." Creek leaders evidently wished to suggest that anticipation of Oglethorpe's journey had galvanized native nations as far as the Mississippi to send delegates to Coweta, there to consider commitment to him and his king.[33]

The Lower Creeks also sent Oglethorpe negative messages designed to launch him into the saddle. The letters he wrote shortly before his departure indicate that the Coweta leaders had captured his attention with dark warnings that their nation was on the brink of three decisions with ominous implications for the English. Most alarming was the possibility that the Lower Creeks might respond favorably to recent Spanish blandishments and take the wrong side when the expected hostilities broke out. Oglethorpe wrote Egmont that a "general meeting" of the Lower Creek chiefs was to convene in July, when "they either will renew their Assurances of Fidelity to the King or go into the Spanish Interest." Wishfully, he assured Egmont that "my presence will entirely settle them in an unanimous Resolution to Adhere to his Majesty." The Creek leaders apparently also suggested that they might decide to join the Chickasaws and some Choctaws in their ongoing war with the French, perhaps forcing the English to take part. More worrisome, recent price increases and abuses by the traders led the Creeks to threaten that "if I do not come up to them they will take Arms and do themselves Justice." Finding the Creek warnings more persuasive than their promises, Oglethorpe began making preparations for the long journey to Coweta.[34]

Oglethorpe set out from Frederica on July 8. His escort consisted mainly of Highland Scots, partly officers from his regiment and partly leaders of Darien. Ascending the Savannah River to the old Yuchi town, he was there joined by a party of rangers from Augusta. The company, now grown to about twenty-five

Englishmen and Scots and a few Indian guides, set out on horseback on July 24. As the travelers neared the Lower Creek towns, the Indians' welcome was palpable. Oglethorpe related that "they met me forty Miles in the Woods, and layed Provisions on the roads in the Woods." Oglethorpe's party reached a tributary of the Chattahoochee on August 6. Here they were joined by Thomas Wiggins, a key figure in the enterprise. Wiggins was easily the most important Georgia trader among the Creeks. He maintained trading houses not only at Yuchi Town and Apalachicola but also at one of the dominant Lower Creek centers, Cussita. Both the Creeks and Oglethorpe had great confidence in him, and few colonists could match his command of the Muskogee language. As in 1733 and 1736, Wiggins was the chief interpreter for the 1739 conference. This time he was also its chief organizer.[35]

Two or three days later, Oglethorpe's party was ceremoniously escorted across the river to the Coweta town square. There he was greeted by "the Indian King," probably Chigelli, beguilingly holding one of the British flags Mackay had distributed. The welcome became even more animated after the black drink was passed around. The festivities continued for several days while the Creek leaders assembled. No minutes survive for the conference that followed, so any account must be pieced together from fragmentary reports and the text of the new treaty that resulted.[36]

It is highly significant that Oglethorpe undertook this mission as a representative of King George II, not the Trustees. The opening sentence of the treaty proclaims that Oglethorpe "was present in behalf of His Majesty." In October he wrote the Trustees to explain that he had been forced to incur major expenses, but not to worry. He expected, he said, that these "will be laid before the Parliament not as the Trustees, but as a Governmentall Expence." The London Trustees must have read this with mixed feelings: relief about the financial responsibility, but concern that their role in shaping the colony had been further diminished.[37]

Oglethorpe opened the formal conference on August 11 with a speech, whose main purpose was doubtless to persuade the Indians that the Spaniards were a common threat requiring a common response. The following day the conference adjourned across the river to Cussita, whose *mico* also received the visitors with a Union Jack in his hand. The sharing of the meeting between Coweta and Cussita was probably due in part to the Indians' concern to honor their two leading towns equally. The fact that Wiggins's storehouse was in Cussita may have been an even more important reason for the move; he would supply about half of the presents Oglethorpe distributed at the close of the conference. There is no indication in the sources of any significant presence of Upper Creeks, Choctaws, or Chickasaws at any stage of the proceedings. The treaty text begins by listing fourteen chiefs as present; all were Lower Creeks. It was essentially a meeting between Oglethorpe and Lower Creek leaders, primarily those of Coweta and Cussita.[38]

Most of the serious discussion seems to have taken place at Cussita on the thirteenth. Deferring to Indian custom, the parties first agreed to reaffirm their previous agreements, including the 1733 treaty, the 1733 understandings on land, and the 1736 land cession. For this purpose, as Lieutenant Thomas Eyres related, Oglethorpe distributed copies of the former treaty to various Creek chiefs. The new treaty text formalized eight days later states that the Creek deputies duly produced their copies of the original treaty.

The new treaty dealt almost entirely with land. In its most far-reaching statement, the assembled Lower Creek chiefs are said to acknowledge that their nation "hath for ages had the Protection of the Kings and Queens of England." This was not as clear a statement as Oglethorpe would have liked, but to British readers it would have been tantamount to an admission by these Indians that they held their lands under British sovereignty. The text purports to confirm the land cessions of 1733 and 1736 and also the 1736 reservations. The separate previous agreements are not described, but instead all are run together. The composite picture of former cessions and reservations is given more exactly than in any previous account, in the case of the cessions probably more exactly than the original agreements themselves.

The Lower Creeks acknowledge that they have previously granted to the Trustees "all the Lands upon the Savannah River as far as the River Ogeeche and all the Lands along the Sea Coast as far as the River St. Johns and as high as the Tide flows and all the Islands as far as the said River," with certain reservations. There was one curious omission: once again there was no mention of Augusta. The Creeks thus far had welcomed Augusta, but evidently they were unwilling as yet to make a definitive cession of a tract so deep into their territory. As for the exceptions, "they did and do reserve to the Creek Nation the Lands from Pipe makers Bluff to Savannah and the Islands of St. Catherine's Ossebaw and Sapphelo and they farther declare that the said Lands are held by the Creek Nation as Tenants in Common."[39]

These declarations had to be extremely gratifying to Oglethorpe. Regarding the lands between the Altamaha and the St. Johns, he could bask in vindication. Hitherto the grant of this strategic strip of coastline depended on an oral and probably ambiguous concession, and had been challenged back home. Now it had definite boundaries and, as he was pleased to inform Verelst, it had been confirmed by "a regular Act," a formal treaty.[40]

The Creek declaration regarding the reservations may have been even more welcome to Oglethorpe. Important here is the fact that there was an addition to the expected list of reservations: "the Lands from Pipe makers Bluff to Savannah," that is, the Yamacraw tract. The previous October four Hitchiti-speaking chiefs had granted that tract to Mary Matthews. The leading Lower Creek chiefs, those of Muskogee-speaking Coweta and Cussita, had had no part in and perhaps no knowledge of that affair. Doubtless at Oglethorpe's urging, they now in effect repudiated that purported grant, for they declared that the Yamacraw tract was among the lands that the Lower Creeks had reserved. The treaty then concludes with Oglethorpe vowing that "he will punish any Persons that shall intrude upon the Lands which the Creek Nation hath reserved as above." To show that he meant business, he added a codicil warning "all His Majestys Subjects," including Mary, that violators "shall the same at your Peril answer."[41]

Thus the treaty text quite literally cut the ground out from under Mary Matthews. If she tried to make good on her 1738 grant, Oglethorpe would see that she regretted it. Inducing the Lower Creek leaders to reserve the Yamacraw tract was a neat and ingenious solution to a dangerous problem—provided that Mary was permanently intimidated, that the chiefs would not change their minds, and that nothing else went wrong. All of these hopeful assumptions would prove to be mistaken. Oglethorpe's negotiating skill, perhaps enhanced with some verbal manipulation in the treaty text, had seemed to solve the problem. In fact, he had succeeded only in concealing and prolonging it.

Oglethorpe had not only failed to solve the problem of Mary's grant for the Yamacraw tract, he made it worse. In addition to copies of the 1733 treaty, he gave Lower Creek leaders copies of another document of crucial importance. Malatchi later referred to it as "a Paper General Oglethorpe gave us when in the Nation." The chiefs evidently had no inkling of the import of this document. They kept it with their other papers from the English, but of course could not read it. Oglethorpe had unwittingly planted a ticking bomb. When Chigelli and Malatchi had it translated seven years later, it exploded. We shall be better able to understand this document when we reach the events of 1746. Most likely we will never understand it completely, for no copy is known to exist. Suffice here to say that it had something to do with Oglethorpe's effort to get the Lower Creeks to acknowledge (in his view, re-acknowledge) British sovereignty over them and their lands.[42]

Oglethorpe probably soon satisfied himself that the alleged dangers of major Creek defections to the Spaniards or Creek attacks on the French had been ploys calculated to bring him to Coweta, for nothing further is heard of them. He solicited Lower Creek support for the English in the approaching imperial conflict—successfully, he supposed. Upon returning to Savannah in September, he told town officials that he now regarded the Creeks as "a Wall of Defence." On October 5 he reported that he expected the assistance of four hundred Creek warriors, and on October 20 he submitted a plan for employing them that was probably a creative enlargement upon an understanding reached at the conference.

These warriors were to be organized into "A Regiment of Creeks" commanded by Wiggins as captain. In addition to provisions, each warrior was to be recompensed for a year's service with a gun, a hatchet, and a blanket, while war leaders and interpreters would receive more.[43]

The treaty text is silent on all this, and Creek promises very likely were vaguer and more qualified than Oglethorpe later made them appear. While the Creeks were willing to contribute a few mercenaries to the British forces, they were characteristically unwilling to commit themselves to the British cause. The notion that Indians could be induced to provide a full year of military service was pure fantasy.

After this engagement with high policy, Eyres reported that "the General then redressed Several Grievances which the Indians complained of." As far as the Creek were concerned, that was undoubtedly the main purpose of the meeting. Despite the price schedule fixed by the 1733 treaty, with the risk of war growing daily the traders had raised their prices. The Creek headmen demanded a rollback. Oglethorpe now "recommended" that the traders comply. What the master of their trading licenses had traveled more than three hundred miles to recommend to them, they could not refuse. The Indians were satisfied. As he later wrote Verelst, Oglethorpe was convinced that his decisive action had averted Lower Creek violence against the traders. This "would probably have occasioned their beginning a War."[44]

On August 21 the treaty was formally approved and signed. Surprisingly, it appears that Oglethorpe was the only signer. His apparent decision not to procure Indian signatures to the treaty is hard to explain, for the omission would make it harder for the British to hold the Lower Creeks to its terms. Eleven of the thirteen British witnesses listed Highland Scots, most of whom had accompanied Oglethorpe from Frederica. Finally, Oglethorpe distributed a large supply of presents, nearly all of which he bought from Wiggins and other traders.

It was an expensive meeting in terms of time and effort, as well as money, but Oglethorpe had reason to consider it worth the costs. He had gained important confirmations of previous Creek cessions, cleverly stymied the Matthews land scheme, probably prevented attacks on the traders, and made some progress toward securing Creek aid against the Spaniards. He did not yet know that he had made another major blunder regarding Mary Matthews, this time an act of commission. The Indians were probably at least equally pleased with the outcome. They had new guarantees regarding their lands, while their other major concerns had been addressed and at least partly satisfied. And, so far as they knew, they got these things for nothing, for they had made no new concessions in return. They had obliged the British not only to come to their turf but to dance to their tune.[45]

At the conclusion of the conference, Oglethorpe was stricken with a fever that delayed his departure until August 27. Arriving at Augusta on September 5, he met with the local band of Chickasaws the following day. The next ten days were spent in anticipation of a meeting with the Cherokees, and on September 17 major trader Samuel Brown escorted thirty-four of them into the fort. The Cherokees were in great distress. A smallpox epidemic that had ravaged Charles Town the previous year had been carried up to Cherokee country by traders. Oglethorpe reported that "above 1000 of the Indians died and the sickness raged so that they could not attend their Corn fields." Before they could ask, he offered fifteen hundred bushels of corn for their relief. About the same time he appointed Lieutenant Eyres as agent to the Cherokees, "as they live in Georgia" (a gross exaggeration). As with the Lower Creeks, he sought Cherokee promises of assistance against the Spaniards. The grateful Cherokees were more forthcoming than the Creeks had been, agreeing to contribute six hundred warriors. On October 20 Oglethorpe submitted a plan for organizing them into "A Regiment of Cherokees" under Brown as captain, to serve on the same terms as the Creeks.[46]

When a messenger brought premature word that war had been declared between Great Britain and Spain, Oglethorpe hurried down to Savannah, arriving on September 21. Two weeks later he issued a declaration of war, though the British government did not do so until October 19. Feverish military preparations were briefly suspended when Tomochichi died on October 5. In his final illness the aged Yamacraw leader had requested that he be buried among the English, and Oglethorpe responded with an elaborate military funeral. Oglethorpe himself, Stephens, and officers of the regiment served as pallbearers, and Tomochichi was buried in Percival Square in Savannah. Meanwhile, Oglethorpe completed his "Introductory Discourse" on the state of the colony, which he sent home to the Trustees on October 11. By this time he must have at least suspected that his 1736 contention that the southernmost branch of the Altamaha was very near the St. Johns was wishful thinking. Nevertheless, the tract opens by declaring that "the Southernmost mouth" of the Altamaha was at 30°30', only six or seven miles north of the St. Johns.[47]

During the next four years the English got somewhat the better of the tactical struggle with the Spaniards and achieved a strategic victory. They did it essentially by holding what they had. There was no decisive battle. There were two major campaigns during the war: Oglethorpe's first siege of St. Augustine in 1740 and the Spanish invasion of St. Simons Island in 1742. Both were dismal failures. The eventual British success likewise owed little to assistance from the Lower Creeks and Cherokees. The Creek and Cherokee regiments never materialized, and aid from these Indians consisted mainly of small war parties that scouted around St. Augustine for a few days or weeks, then returned home.

Only the small groups on the Savannah River provided significant support. These included local Yamacraws under Santachi and Tooanahowi, Chickasaws from the Augusta area under the Squirrel King (Fanne Mingo), and a few Yuchis. Tom Jones, the mustee ranger captain, also rendered important service at both St. Augustine and St. Simons. Jones was Oglethorpe's main intermediary with his revolving company of Indian allies, and apparently led most of their sorties. He proudly claimed that Oglethorpe had directed him "to head them in all Actions." In late 1741 some of his Indians—at the moment a mixed party of Lower Creeks, Yamacraws, and Yuchis—captured a Spanish officer and soldier. Jones led the victorious party and their captives to Frederica in November.[48]

Recruitment of Indian auxiliaries was doubtless hampered by the Trustees' unwillingness to share the expense. In December Verelst reiterated their 1738 decision to pay Indian expenses relating "only to those which immediately border on the Settlements, not to Indians that come down from the Nations in their Way to General Oglethorpe for the King's Service." Native involvement would also have been greater but for Oglethorpe's humanitarian scruples, which struck the Indians as absurd. At least in part to prevent atrocities, he always tried to keep native auxiliaries under close supervision, if possible under officers of his choosing. When the Squirrel King proudly presented him with the severed head of a Spanish Indian, Oglethorpe "refused to receive it, calling it Barbarity." He also insisted that enemy Indians captured in battle be treated as prisoners of war, not enslaved or tortured to death. To prevent the latter, he ransomed some captives taken by his Indian allies with the only thing they would accept in return, horses.[49]

The Cherokees were in no position to provide much assistance to Oglethorpe's forces. After Eyres was appointed agent to the Cherokees he undertook missions to their country in late 1739 and early 1740. He found that the Cherokees were far from recovered from the recent epidemic. Moreover, Carolina traders discouraged them from sending any of their warriors to Oglethorpe's aid, doubtless to preserve what was left of their trade. The Cherokees were also anxious over recent raids from northern Iroquois (Senecas), their ancient enemies. One such raid in 1741 led to the death of the "Emperor" Moytoy. Skiagunsta, head warrior of the upper towns, succeeded Moytoy as "the white Men's King."[50]

Still worse, in the fall of 1740 Upper Creeks fell upon a Cherokee war party en route to the Choctaw country. This seemingly minor incident reignited the old Creek-Cherokee hostility into a major war that flamed on and off for the next fourteen years. From time to time both sides sought English mediation in both South Carolina and Georgia. Oglethorpe sometimes thought he had arranged peace, but never achieved more than a temporary truce. Given this conflict, the

Creeks and Cherokees could not simultaneously provide substantial assistance to the English. In the end, neither did.

A final impediment to Cherokee assistance is more difficult to assess. Since 1736 a German visionary named Christian Priber had lived among the Cherokees, patiently working to establish what he called the "Kingdom of Paradise." Priber sought nothing less than a grand union of all the Southeastern nations under a benevolent government based on "the natural rights of mankind." He had progressed so far with his design as to crown a Cherokee follower emperor, who in turn named Priber "principal secretary of state." The new utopian state was to be fully independent, so Priber urged the Indians "to throw off the yoke of their European allies, of all nations." The plan also called for the establishment of a free town in Cherokee country that would serve as "an Asylum for all Fugitives." Priber's influence among the Cherokees was clearly growing and might have developed much further had he not been captured and turned over to Oglethorpe early in 1743. In his report on this astonishing prisoner Oglethorpe neglected to mention that the Indians who turned him in were Creeks. Their probable motive was to make trouble for the Cherokees.[51]

Lower Creek inactivity during the Spanish war was more a matter of deliberate policy. Full commitment to any of the imperial powers remained impossible because the Creeks were divided over their preferences for Europeans and united in their determination not to become tools of any of them. Having just contracted a major treaty with Oglethorpe in 1739, Chigelli listened attentively to French emissaries who came to Coweta that winter. The following April he led two hundred of his people to Fort Toulouse to hear French proposals for ending the long-standing Creek-Choctaw conflict. Interested in what the French might have to offer, Chigelli turned a deaf ear to Oglethorpe's call for Creek support in his first siege of St. Augustine. Unhappy with his guardian's leadership, Malatchi refused to attend the French parlay, but instead came down to Frederica to talk with Oglethorpe. Assuring the general that "the main Body" of his people would be glad to cooperate against the Spaniards, Malatchi threatened to unseat Chigelli if he continued his supposedly unpopular course. A few days later in Savannah, Malatchi told Stephens he intended, "if Chigellie opposed him, to cut off his Head."[52]

At Fort Toulouse, Chigelli found the French unwilling to make substantial concessions unless the Lower Creeks broke off all relations with the English. A total severance of contact with any of the imperial powers was one demand the Creeks would never agree to. The Coweta leader returned home in a huff, telling his people "they had no Business to interpose among the white Mens Quarrels." That was not his last word on the subject. Chigelli's experience at Fort Toulouse, combined with the rift that had developed between him and Malatchi, persuaded the Coweta leader to reconsider Oglethorpe's appeal for military assistance. Chigelli had probably also learned that the siege was going badly, which lessened the danger that Creek aid might lead to a decisive British victory. At any rate, on June 30 Oglethorpe reported the best news he had: "Mallachi and Chigilli with all the Lower Creeks have declared for us, and some of them have been down." Actually, as he admitted a few weeks later, at that time his Indian auxilliaries were melting away and he was "obliged to give very large Sums to get them to stay a few Days." On July 4 he lifted the siege.[53]

The war required administrative changes in Georgia. Following up on their earlier division of the colony into two parts, on April 15, 1741, the Trustees elevated the two sectors into "the County of Savannah" and "the County of Frederica." Each was now to be governed by a president and assistants. William Stephens was immediately appointed president in Savannah, and Oglethorpe was told to nominate a counterpart for Frederica County. Such appointments were made, but the government of the lower county scarcely functioned. Two years later, on April 18, 1743, the Trustees decided that the president and assistants in Savannah would henceforth be the government "for the Whole Province." At last, ten years after its founding, Georgia had a provincial government.[54]

Oglethorpe was not part of it. Exasperated over his free spending and frequent inattention to their directives, the Trustees moved to ease him out of civil administration. The most important step came on January 23, 1740, when they "totally excluded General Oglethorpe from handling our money" and transferred fiscal control to the Savannah authorities under Stephens. On September 10, 1741, they also appointed Stephens to be Oglethorpe's co-commissioner for issuing trading licenses. Since Oglethorpe remained the sole commissioner for executing the 1735 Indian act, he retained exclusive control over negotiations with the natives. It seems clear that Oglethorpe resented his loss of authority to the Savannah magistrates, for henceforth he seldom bothered to keep them informed of his activities.[55]

As the commander of a British army funded by Parliament, Oglethorpe could and did continue to be open-handed toward the Indians, at least those who fought in his cause. Early in 1741 he reported that every native warrior he put into the field against the Spaniards cost a minimum of £10 a year. Even if the Trustees had been willing to share this cost, they no longer had the means to contribute significantly. The days when they could deliver lavish presents to Indians were over. Verelst's accounts show that for the six fiscal years beginning in 1734–35 the Trustees spent an annual average of £735 on Indian presents, with a peak expenditure of £1,167 in 1739–40. During the four years that followed, such presents averaged only £197 per year.[56]

One transaction that the Trustees would have been glad to provide amply for could not be arranged. The most promising avenue for the future expansion of the colony was the Savannah River, but the small band of Yuchis who lived on the tract above Ebenezer blocked the way. Attempts as early as 1736 to persuade these Indians to agree to a land cession had been fruitless. Around 1738 they abandoned this site and moved upriver to resettle at Silver Bluff. Still, they refused to relinquish any of their lands. In October 1739 Oglethorpe wrote that the Yuchis "will not part with the same. Therefore it cannot be Planted." Thomas Wiggins had long maintained a trading store in the old Yuchi town. Early in 1740 Oglethorpe "ordered him to build a Fort there." The Yuchis allowed Wiggins to build a small fort called Mount Pleasant adjacent to their abandoned town. Garrisoned by a ranger company captained by Wiggins, Mount Pleasant became the most important way station between Savannah and Augusta. Leaders from the northern part of the colony continued to agitate for a Yuchi cession, but Oglethorpe in September 1741 refused to consider it. He remembered with gratitude the assistance "the Uchee Indians, affectionate Subjects to his Majesty," had rendered during his siege of St. Augustine. Accordingly, he wrote Stephens that "it would not only be unjust but very Impolitick at this Time to attempt buying Lands from the Indians especially the Uchees." There the matter rested.[57]

During the war Mary Matthews became indispensable to Oglethorpe as an intermediary with the Lower Creeks. Her place outside Savannah (the Musgrove Cowpen) became the main assembly point and supply depot for Indians on their way to attack Spanish targets. She reported that she had a "standing Order" from Oglethorpe to furnish "provisions, Ammunition, etc. To different parties of warriors" serving the British cause. Moreover, she was often called down to Frederica to act as interpreter. On at least one occasion a minor Indian talk was held at Mary's home. When "the Wolf" (better known as "the Wolf King") from the Upper Creek town of Mucklassee appeared there in 1741, Oglethorpe was otherwise engaged. Concerned that this important visitor not take offense, Mary then arranged for Stephens and the Savannah assistants to talk with him at her place. It took special circumstances to bring the Savannah president and Mary Matthews together, for they clearly did not get along. Stephens acknowledged that when it came to dealing with Indians, she alone "knows how to prevail with them," but he found her "haughty temper" almost insufferable. For her part Mary found Stephens parsimonious in authorizing issues from the Trustees' remaining stores, and they had several raucous squabbles on this score. The Indians also found Stephens tight-fisted and tended to avoid him.[58]

Mary's second husband was even more difficult to deal with than she was. According to Stephens, once Jacob Matthews had acquired freedom and a wife, he "grew vain . . . and began to behave insolently." In late 1739, shortly after Jacob and Mary established Mount Venture on the south bank of the Altamaha, the Spaniards responded by planting a small fort on the north bank of the river. Oglethorpe answered back the following October by appointing Jacob captain of a company of rangers to be stationed at Mount Venture. Matthews was slow in organizing this company, and continued to spend most of his time in Savannah or at home.[59]

It is abundantly clear that Mary and Jacob became more and more discontented as the war dragged on. It appears that as their fortunes deteriorated they tried to stay afloat on illicit rum. Speaking of Jacob in August 1741, Stephens reported that rum was the source of "that Influence he thinks he has over those neighboring Indians." He elaborated that the Indians, "by half Dozens, or more at a Time, have daily of late been flocking about his House in Town, where they continually get drunk with Rum, and go roaring and yelling about the Streets, as well at Nights as Days." In February 1742 several casks of rum Mary had dispatched to Mount Venture for the Indians were seized and staved at Frederica. Mary "was so provoked, that she could not forbear uttering many hard words and threats," notably "what Revenge we might expect from the Indians." Stephens's comment was prophetic: "In such manner are we to be terrified, if any Obstruction is given to the Domineering Will of that Family."[60]

The following month Mary and her husband became so angry at a letter Thomas Wiggins had given several Creeks on their way to see Oglethorpe that they burned it and advised them not to go. Bad blood between the Matthews and Wiggins is evident earlier. Jacob and Mary likely blamed him for helping Oglethorpe cheat them out of the Yamacraw tract in the text of the 1739 Coweta treaty. Soon afterward they came to blows. In October 1740 Jacob was indicted for "beating and Imprisoning" Wiggins and two others in Coweta. The three victims had been acting "in the Execution of their Office as Constables" to police the traders.[61]

With their ever-lengthening list of grievances, Mary and Jacob Matthews had naturally gravitated toward the organized opposition to the Trustees' regime that had been developing since 1735. Branded "the Malcontents" by the Trustees, these disaffected colonists were united by economic complaints. Their most important objective by far was to overturn the prohibition of Negro slavery, and they also strongly opposed the ban on rum and tail-male land tenure. The Matthews fully agreed with this program, and by late 1738 they had joined the Malcontent opposition. In December disgruntled Georgians, including the prominent Malcontent leaders, petitioned the Trustees to reverse themselves on land and slavery. They asked for fee simple land tenure and, "with Proper Limitations," Negro slavery. Discontent was so general that two of the Savannah magistrates, Henry Parker and Robert Gilbert, along with Recorder Thomas Christie, headed the list of 121 signers. One of the others was Jacob Matthews.[62]

The ringleader of this alienated faction was a transplanted Carolinian, Robert Williams, whose riverfront plantation was adjacent to the Matthews.' Most of the other important figures were disillusioned Scottish gentlemen, notably Dr. Patrick Tailfer (Williams's brother-in-law) and Patrick Mackay. By late 1740 many of them had already bolted to South Carolina, and many lesser figures followed them. There they were free to import and employ slave labor and continue their noisy agitation for basic change in Georgia. Mackay had moved to the older colony shortly after the Trustees dismissed him from their service. According to Stephens, although Mackay spent most of his time on "his Negro Plantation" just across the Savannah River, he remained "an Arch Incendiary" in Georgia. Williams complained that the four years he spent in Georgia cost him more than £2,000. According to Egmont, Williams stayed that long only because of "the prospect he had of having the monopoly of Negroes brought into the Colony." Williams was already a slave trader, and would become a major one. His offer of easy credit to purchasers of slaves, should the Trustees relent on their prohibition, made him a formidable recruiter for the Malcontent cause. Jacob Matthews was not as important a leader of this faction as he imagined, but he often hosted its meetings. Thus many streams of discontent converged at the Matthews place, described by Egmont as "the great rendevouse of the malecontents." In July 1741 one of their formal complaints, a "Petition to his Majesty" with sixty-one signatures, was "Signed . . . at Mr. Mathews's."[63]

Early in 1741 Williams proudly introduced Sir Richard Everard into this company. Everard was the last proprietary governor of North Carolina, whose final year in office had been marred by a major land scandal. Sir Richard evidently was in the midst of some sort of midlife crisis. Early that spring he went upriver to Augusta. There he borrowed £300, which "enabled the Baronet to take a Journey to the Cowetas." In April he arrived at Coweta, where he was granted a audience with Chigelli. When the old chief asked his guest whether he had come to deliver "a Talk from the Great King," Everard answered that he had not. Well, why then had he come? Aware that Indians valued straight answers, Everard gave them one: "He came there to lye with their Women." Insulted, the Cowetas sent him on his way.[64]

The civil strife in Savannah provoked by the Malcontents came to a head in the summer of 1741. During July and August, Everard used his rank and legal learning to help lead the disaffected in a series of battles to gain practical control of the town government. To broaden their appeal, Williams and Everard added other complaints to the old reliables concerning slaves, rum, and land tenure. These included the tyrannical excesses of Thomas Causton, the unjust conviction of Joseph Watson, and the arbitrary denial of the just claims of Mary and Jacob Matthews. Stephens observed that while Mary "has a very great Influence upon many" of the Indians, who showed "some Regard" to her, "they shew none to him." Fellow colonists were obliged to pay some respect to Jacob, despite his arrogance and "drunken Frolicks," for he was now the legal owner of Mary's five hundred acres. Stephens reported that it was their neighbor Robert Williams who had recruited the couple into the organized opposition. Regarding Jacob: "our Malecontents so blowed up their new Favorite among them, that he was taught to believe he ought to be . . . gratified in whatever he asked; . . . having such a powerful Body of Men to stand by him." Stephens observed that when Jacob came to town, he, Williams, and Tailfer "were never long asunder."[65]

In September Everard left for England, followed shortly by Williams. Stephens believed that their ultimate objective was to overthrow the Trust so that the king would take Georgia "under his own care." In that event, he said, Everard hoped "to return hither as Governor of it, or Chief Justice at least." Both men carried documents designed to advance the Malcontent cause that they would deliver to the Trustees.[66]

The Trustees first learned of the Indians' purported grant to Mary more than three years after it occurred. Their source was not Oglethorpe or the Savannah authorities, but Mary and Jacob Matthews. On February 2, 1742, the Trustees read and considered two documents delivered to them by Robert Williams. One was a letter of attorney authorizing Williams and Everard, acting in the Matthews' name, "to apply to the Trustees for a Grant of Land alledged to be given them by the Creek Indians." The other was Christie's minutes of the meeting on October 13 and 14, in which Oglethorpe "is mentioned to have been then present." Surprised, the Trustees resolved to send copies of both documents to Oglethorpe in Georgia, "and that he be desired to make a Report to the Trustees how the Claim stands." Verelst sent the documents to Oglethorpe with a cover letter noting the impropriety of the Matthews' receiving such a grant. Verelst observed that if it was "necessary" to acquire the tract, "The Trustees themselves, or your Self as one of them, should have obtained the Indians Consent, and not Captain Mathews or his Wife."[67]

Verelst went on to suggest that, "if you are of Opinion the Tract should be granted," there was a straightforward way to get it done. Two simple steps were required: "some Care must be taken to express in the Grant; That the Indians Cession thereof being first made to You on behalf of the Trustees, and You recommending the said Captain Mathews and his Wife for a Grant thereof, the same was so granted." What seemed simple in London was not so simple in Georgia. There seems to be no evidence that Oglethorpe replied to Verelst's letter. There was little he could say to excuse his blunder. Most likely he had already tried, without success, what the Trustees now recommended. Oglethorpe could not reconvene the meeting with the visiting chiefs, and he apparently could not persuade Mary and Jacob to give up the grant they had for one they might have.[68]

The main thing the Trustees didn't yet understand was the size of the supposed grant described in the Christie minutes. When they read there that the Indians granted Mary all their lands "between this Place and Tomo Chachis," they assumed that the document referred to Tomochichi's old place adjacent to Savannah, not to the place five miles upriver where he had lived for more than three years. Accordingly, the Trustees went on to assume that the Creek chiefs had granted "Part of what the Yamacraw Indians had at first reserved," not the entire Yamacraw tract. They were meant to assume that. The Matthews and everyone else in the colony knew that the Trustees were certain to reject any request for a land grant of more than five hundred acres.[69]

Having failed to have Christie's minutes recorded in the colony's official records, Mary and Jacob aimed to get the Trustees themselves to give legal effect to at least one of their grants from the Indians. Their letter of attorney authorizing Williams and Everard to represent them requested that the Trustees make a grant to Jacob of land the Indians had previously given to Mary and him. Doing so would give Jacob an ironclad legal title to the land. The letter of attorney does not survive, but there are revealing references to it in the Trustee minutes, Egmont's journal, and Verelst's letters to Oglethorpe and Stephens. Most significant, Egmont says that by this letter Jacob Matthews requested "a grant of 450 acres made out to him, being land made over to him by the Indians near Savannah." The land they now requested was what Tomochichi had granted them in December 1737, the old Yamacraw townsite. Having no written record of that gift, they sent the record they did have, the Christie minutes of the October 1738 grant.[70]

If the Trustees were wrong about the land Creek chiefs granted in 1738, they were right that what the Matthews now sought was only part of the Yamacraw tract. A small part too, for 450 acres was only about a tenth of the entire tract. It is impossible to believe that the Trustees would have defied the royal charter and their own land policies to grant Jacob Matthews perhaps ten square miles of the most valuable land in Georgia. Robert Williams, Richard Everard, and the Matthews knew that. So, even though Jacob and Mary sent a copy of Christie's minutes to the Trustees, they did not request a grant of the entire Yamacraw tract. They merely requested what they knew they were most likely to get: the site of the original Yamacraw town adjacent to Savannah. They did not get that either. The Trustees simply turned the matter over to Oglethorpe for his recommendation on how to solve the problem. He didn't have one, and evidently did not even reply. Had their request for the old Yamacraw townsite been successful, Jacob and Mary most likely would have been satisfied. If so, they probably would have shelved their 1738 grant from the four Creek chiefs. Denied the relatively small grant they had sought in London, they hung on to their claim to the entire Yamacraw tract. Another day it might look quite different.

Since the Christie minutes of the 1738 meeting implicated Oglethorpe as a witness to an unlawful land grant, his fellow Trustees must have soon realized that the document was at least a serious embarrassment. They evidently became almost as eager as Oglethorpe himself to forget about it. No copy is to be found among the voluminous Trustee records or in the comparable collection preserved by Egmont. Today we would be just as ignorant of Christie's minutes as the Trustees were prior to 1742, were it not for the fact that Mary and her last two husbands carefully preserved the document. Fifteen years after the events it detailed, her third husband, Thomas Bosomworth, had it recorded in the "Miscellaneous Records" of South Carolina. It is the only copy known to survive.[71]

Three months after the Trustees considered the Matthews petition for Yamacraw land, Jacob died. In London the problem of the Creek grant to the Matthews must have seemed half solved. Without Jacob the Mount Venture settlement dwindled as most of the Indians he and Mary had attracted drifted away. On November 7, while most of the rangers were absent in Frederica, a band of Yamasees attacked and destroyed the post. They carried the five surviving Indian defenders to St. Augustine. Once again Mary was widowed and impoverished. According to Thomas Bosomworth, Oglethorpe promised her that the British government would cover her losses, for he knew that Mount Venture had been established "for the sole Benefit of his Majestys Service." She would wait in vain. The new provincial government in Savannah was equally unhelpful. The following year it refused to reimburse Mary for "the Expence of entertaining the Indians going to Warr." It must have seemed to her that things could not possibly get worse.[72]

Oglethorpe's relations with Mary Matthews had turned cool during his final stay in Georgia, and his mistakes ensured that worse was to come. To a lesser degree, the same was true for his relations with pivotal Lower Creek leaders on the Chattahoochee. The close relationship he had hoped to establish with the Cherokees had not developed, and would not. Despite numerous reverses, he had been more successful with his first priority: defense of the colony against the Spaniards.

The crisis of the war came in June and July 1742 with the long-expected Spanish invasion of St. Simons Island. The defenders included Tooanahowi's Yamacraws, Jones's rangers, and a few Creeks from Mount Venture. According to one witness, however, it was the Savannah River Chickasaws that did most to break the Spanish assault. Daniel Pepper later recalled that these Chickasaws "behaved bravely at the Discent the Spaniards made upon Frederica and were in great measure the saving of the Place." After this seemingly minor military action, the Battle of Bloody Marsh, the defenders watched in amazement as the invaders sailed away. Evidently concerned that the British were now on the verge of complete victory, the Creeks now shifted some of their weight into the other scale. Renewed Lower

Creek contact with the Spaniards began with Estichi, who, banished from Savannah nine years earlier, now turns up as the *mico* of Apalachicola. After murdering a Carolina trader, Estichi fled to St. Augustine, where he was received as a visiting potentate. That summer the Hispano-Creek relationship warmed and Chigelli seriously considered Spanish appeals for an alliance against the English.[73]

The November destruction of Mount Venture at the hands of Spanish Indians led Chigelli to backtrack again, for most of the victims had been Creeks. The following spring he dispatched a large war party to help Oglethorpe in his second unsuccessful assault on St. Augustine. During that shorter and even more ineffectual effort, Tooanahowi was killed. After the 1743 campaign stalled, the exhausted parties sank into a long stalemate.[74]

Worn down in both body and spirit, in the summer of 1743 Oglethorpe made plans to return home. Having expended more than £60,000 of his own funds in Georgia's defense, he was financially ruined if he could not persuade Parliament to reimburse him, and soon. Before his departure he pacified Mary Matthews as best he could. He gave her £180 for her services as interpreter and a diamond ring off his hand. According to Mary, he also promised her an annual salary of £100 for her continued services, and to do what he could to have her recompensed for her losses. On July 22, 1743, he sailed from Georgia for the last time.

CHAPTER FIVE

A Wider War and Deeper Discord

The situation in the Southeast became more complex and more dangerous on March 25, 1744, when George II finally took the long-anticipated step of declaring war on France. The conflict between the British and the allied Bourbon powers during the next four years was for the most part fought elsewhere. In the English colonies, where it was known as King George's War, the major campaigns were in the north. In the Southeast the moment France became the principal adversary the focus of the conflict shifted from the south to the west. Now facing a much stronger enemy, Georgia's role was overshadowed by that of the far stronger colony of South Carolina.

None of the imperial powers was able to mount a major offensive in the region because none was able to assemble a sufficiently formidable force of Indian allies. The quest for such a force occupied them all, and eluded them all, for the duration of the struggle. The coalition the British built included the Chickasaws (as always), elements among the Upper Creeks and Cherokees, and a few Choctaws. It was an unstable coalition, for the Creeks and Cherokees could not be brought to cooperate with each other. Still, British leaders hoped that their force of native auxiliaries would reach critical mass when enough of the Choctaws were won away from the French. For their part, the French at Mobile and Fort Toulouse strove to recruit supporters for their cause among the Upper Creeks, and succeeded well enough to offset British gains among the Choctaws. It was a standoff, exactly the result intended by the central players in the game, the Lower Creeks. Under the Coweta leaders Chigelli and Malatchi these Indians welcomed the attentions of all three imperial suitors, kept them all waiting, and went their own way. The Lower Creeks were not only the recipients of favors from all three powers, they were "the only Indians" in the region who regularly received presents from both South Carolina and Georgia.[1]

Although Georgia now had a rudimentary government—the president and assistants in Savannah—it had little to do with Indian relations. When in 1738 the British government relieved the Georgia Trustees of responsibility for military affairs, it thereby relieved them of nearly all responsibility for negotiating with the natives. Since then the Trustees' subordinates in Savannah had confined their dealings with Indians to the few who lived nearby and occasional visitors. As British commander in chief, Oglethorpe had shouldered the main responsibility for Indian relations during his final tour in Georgia. Upon his departure he transferred this task to the acting commander of the regiment in Frederica, not the provincial government in Savannah. Thus it came about that Oglethorpe's successor as chief negotiator with the Indians in Georgia was a relatively obscure junior officer, Captain (after July 1745, Major) William Horton.[2]

Even without the broadening of the war, Horton's negotiating position was bound to be even more precarious than Oglethorpe's had been. Short on rank and political experience, Horton had little chance of establishing a firm command or securing adequate funding for Indian diplomacy. The responsibility that had nearly bankrupted Oglethorpe quickly threatened to do the same for him. Still, Horton was a man of ability and somehow struggled through more successfully than anyone had a right to expect for nearly four years. During his command, especially after March 1746, Lower Creek resentment toward the Georgia colony steadily grew. This occurred for reasons that were beyond Horton's control, and his success in forestalling a bloody confrontation was a major achievement. One influential Carolinian even credited Horton's "good Management of the Creek Indians" with bringing Red Shoes's Choctaws back into the British alliance.[3]

Around the first of June 1747 Horton was relieved by his old superior in the regiment, Alexander Heron, recently promoted to lieutenant colonel. Problems with the Lower Creeks had grown more acute, and Heron strove to avert disaster with a more active and therefore more expensive diplomacy. By January 1748 he was loudly complaining that the only resources he had to support this essential effort had to be diverted from his fund for regimental provisions, which was now exhausted. Worse, although Heron was far more popular with the Lower Creeks than Horton had been, his diplomacy had created new difficulties. By January 1748 the pivotal Lower Creeks were on the brink of a major confrontation with Georgia.[4]

Surprisingly, this had little to do with the war or the machinations of the French or Spaniards. The conflict was provoked by long-standing British policies toward Indian lands and, especially, by the way those policies had been implemented in Georgia. It is usually known as the Bosomworth Controversy. This label understates the importance of this conflict, for it dominates the story of Georgia's Indian relations for more than a decade. This bitter struggle began with

Tomochichi's 1737 grant to Mary Matthews of several hundred acres adjacent to Savannah, the abandoned Yamacraw townsite. It became much more serious in October 1738 when Tomochichi and other Lower Creek headmen, in the presence of Oglethorpe and the Savannah magistrates, enlarged the grant to include the entire Yamacraw tract. In 1741 Mary and Jacob Matthews petitioned the Trustees to grant the old townsite to them. This would have given them, for the first time, a title to this small but valuable piece of land that was valid in English law. The Trustees would not and could not do it, so Mary and Jacob (during the brief time he yet lived) were left to nurse their frustration. Still, Mary's disappointment did not become dangerous to the colony until she wed her third husband, Thomas Bosomworth.

Little is known about the background of Thomas Bosomworth. He related that he came from a large family of small means and until 1741 "spent my time in the usual studies for Holy Orders." Financial distress, he said, led him to lay aside his plans for the ministry to seek his fortune in Georgia with his friend Christopher Orton. The Trustees had appointed Orton minister in Savannah. The best they could offer Bosomworth was a clerkship to President Stephens. This was not what Thomas had in mind, but he accepted, he avowed, "in hopes of preferment in some other capacity."[5]

Just twenty-two when he arrived in Savannah on December 3, 1741, Bosomworth quickly impressed Stephens as "a studious young man" with talent and ambition. Observing that "his sprightly Temper, added to a little Share of Classical Learning, makes him soar above the low Employment that was here prepared for him," Stephens nominated his young assistant for more responsible positions. These efforts were unsuccessful, except that Bosomworth was appointed secretary for Indian affairs. This position, another clerkship, was no more satisfactory to Bosomworth than it had been to Charles Wesley. It did bring him, however, into regular contact with Oglethorpe and Mary Matthews. After Oglethorpe told him that the regiment needed a chaplain and Orton died in August 1742, Bosomworth concluded that his future lay with his original calling. Borrowing the money for his passage, in late 1742 he sailed for England. Stephens hinted that he left more than one scandal behind.[6]

Bosomworth was soon ordained by the Bishop of London, then applied to the Trustees for a pastoral appointment in Georgia. On July 4, 1743, they chose Thomas to succeed to Orton's pulpit in Savannah, with the expectation that a salary would be provided by the Society for the Propagation of the Gospel. The society did grant Bosomworth an annual salary of £50 "for 3 years from Midsummer 1743." On December 21, 1743, the Reverend Thomas Bosomworth arrived in Frederica, where he soon made it clear he wished to stay. Although he made the southern town "his chief place of Residence," Bosomworth took up his duties in Savannah two months later. He was seldom seen in the northern town except on Sundays, but he performed his duties creditably. He was especially popular with Savannah's small German community, "being in great Esteem for his Volubility of Speech and manner of Preaching among them."[7]

On one of his trips back to Frederica, in June 1744, Thomas sailed in the company of the widow Matthews and about thirty Creeks on their way to see Captain Horton. It proved to be a voyage of destiny, for on July 8 Thomas and Mary were wed in Frederica. Given their vastly different backgrounds and the fact that Thomas must have been about twenty years younger than Mary, it was an astonishing match. When the news reached Savannah it at first "appeared so incredible . . . that 'twas looked on as a piece of Merriment." On August 5 the Reverend Bosomworth and his bride returned to Savannah to begin their new life together.[8]

Although Bosomworth continued to officiate as minister in Savannah, it quickly became apparent that he took a more than ordinary interest in his wife's business affairs. On September 5 he complained to Stephens that Joseph Watson continued to encroach on Mary's legal monopoly of the local Indian trade. A week later Thomas returned to Stephens with a new complaint. How was it, he wanted to know, that his spouse had never been paid the bounty money she was due on grain raised at the Matthews place in 1739? Stephens promised to look into the matter. By November the Bosomworths had moved from Savannah to Mary's riverfront tract (now sometimes called "the Grange"), and again Thomas was seldom seen in town except on the Sabbath. By that time too they had apparently decided to appeal Mary's claims for compensation as interpreter and grain bounties to England. Oglethorpe was expecting to see the couple in London in February 1745, but their travel plans were postponed.[9]

Thomas Bosomworth did return to England that summer. In early June he and magistrate Charles Watson left Savannah in "a clandestine Manner" for Charles Town, where they arrived on June 12. There they met with Patrick Mackay to complete plans for a voyage to London. All three planned personal appeals for redress of grievances: Watson sought vindication against charges that he had disgraced his office by public gambling (for which the Trustees suspended him in August); Mackay wanted settlement of his old claims against the Trustees while agent to the Creeks; while Bosomworth was prepared to present all of his wife's old claims and more. The departure of "the Triumvirates who lately made such haste for England" created resentment and anxiety in Savannah. It appeared that a new leadership had suddenly coalesced to head what was left of the old Malcontent movement. Bosomworth in particular was vulnerable to criticism, for he had abandoned his pulpit without notice and without providing for a substitute minister.[10]

In England Watson achieved his goals, Mackay made some progress toward his, but Bosomworth came up far short of his expectations. In London on September 3, Thomas tried to explain his absence without leave from his Georgia pulpit to his superiors at the Society for the Propagation of the Gospel. He related that he had wed Mary "the better to enable me to carry on the great Work of promoting Christian Knowledge amongst the Natives of America." He declared that his return to England was a matter of "absolute necessity" in order to preserve the "Friendship and Alliance" of the Creek Indians. He claimed that negative reaction to his unusual marriage had placed that critical alliance in jeopardy: "Such vile and base means have been made use off [*sic*] in order to murther both our Reputations and distress us in every shape; that the Indians have threatned to take their own Satisfaction in Case Justice was not done." He would elaborate on this argument for many years to come.[11]

After some mutually unsatisfying contacts with the Trustees, Thomas went north to Yorkshire, where Oglethorpe was busy with preparations for the military campaign against the Pretender. On October 12 he wrote Verelst that he intended to join the patriotic effort and did not expect to return to Georgia for some time. Since Thomas also extended best wishes to "my Successor," the Trustees concluded that he had resigned his ministerial office in Savannah and immediately nominated Bartholomew Zouberbuhler as his replacement.[12]

Bosomworth's unexpected personal appeal evidently had some effect on Oglethorpe. According to Thomas, Oglethorpe assured him that after the Scottish disturbances were quelled, "Mrs. Bosomworth might depend upon his Honour for full satisfaction for all her services, and that in the Interim Mr. Bosomworth might draw upon him for any sum not Exceeding £1000." On November 13 Oglethorpe also gave him a brief letter of recommendation to Captain Horton in Frederica. Oglethorpe could apparently not be moved to endorse any of Mary's land claims, for Thomas was silent on that issue. At any rate, Bosomworth was disappointed, and later groused that "this is all the satisfaction" he had been able to obtain by his troublesome journey.[13]

On December 5 the Trustees received a memorial from Mary Bosomworth in the post from Portsmouth. Thomas evidently had carried this memorial with him, and posted it just before setting out on his return voyage. The text of this document is lost, but it clearly made new demands upon the Trustees. The strongest of the Bosomworth claims was Mary's demand for compensation as interpreter. She seems to have been genuinely and perhaps rightly convinced that Oglethorpe had promised her an annual salary of £100; over a decade that came to a balance of £1,000 due. Thomas probably showed Mary's memorial to Oglethorpe in Yorkshire, which may have jogged his memory, or otherwise helped persuade him to commit his own £1,000 to the Bosomworth cause. Mary's memorial to the Trustees began with the matter of her services as interpreter, but it went on to claim a £50 bounty for the first crop of wheat in the colony, £150 under the 1739 grain bounty, and £4.9.8 under the 1742 grain bounty. The Trustees immediately declared that they had never promised Mary an annual salary for her services or offered a reward for the first wheat crop, and summarily dismissed both claims. As for the 1739 and 1742 grain bounties, those were matters for the Savannah magistrates to settle.[14]

The most extraordinary claim Mary presented in her memorial dealt with land. She called upon the Trustees to issue a grant to her husband for "a Tract of Land called Yamacraw from the West Line of the Town of Savannah to Pipemaker's Creek." Thus for the first time the Bosomworths demanded that their claim to the entire Yamacraw tract be validated in English law by a grant of this land from the Trustees. Presumably their claim was based on the 1738 grant from Lower Creek headmen to Mary, though there is no indication that a copy of the Christie minutes documenting that grant accompanied Mary's memorial.[15]

There could be little doubt that the Trustees would react much as they had in 1742 to Jacob Matthews's bid for a grant of a small part of the tract. They were bound to reply that no such grant could be considered until such time as the Trustees had a grant of the land in question from the Indians made out to themselves. For the time being they referred Mary's demand to their Common Council, which apparently took no action. Thus in her 1747 memorial Mary complained that her petition for an English grant of the Yamacraw tract had been "in Vain."[16]

If reading Mary's petition informed Oglethorpe of Mary's exact salary claim, it must also have made him aware of her astounding claim to the entire Yamacraw tract. For Oglethorpe, this was a ghost from the past. It seems likely that Thomas not only raised the issue but reminded Oglethorpe of the awkward matter of his presence at the 1738 Creek grant to Mary, as proven by Christie's minutes. For the next ten years Bosomworth agitated tirelessly for Mary's right to the Yamacraw tract, yet until 1756 he carefully refrained from mentioning Oglethorpe's involvement in the 1738 grant. While he attached scores of supporting documents to memorials he wrote in this cause, his key document—the Christie minutes—was never among them. It seems likely that this uncharacteristic restraint was suggested to him, directly or indirectly, by Oglethorpe in 1746. The £1,000 that Oglethorpe then in effect contributed to the Bosomworth cause evidently gave Thomas hope that Oglethorpe might eventually be persuaded to support Mary's land claim. That hope probably explains his silence over the next ten years on Oglethorpe's role in 1738.

Thomas Bosomworth returned to Georgia in January 1746 and was often seen thereafter around Frederica. According to Stephens in March, "he has thrown aside his Sacredotals, and appears to be wholly employed in carrying on the Indian Trade, under the Influence of his Spouse." He was also acting with help from

Oglethorpe. Thomas related that he used his line of credit with Oglethorpe to purchase "a Large Cargoe of Indian Goods." The Bosomworths were preparing to establish a trading station at the forks of the Altamaha. Horton's letter of November 18, 1745, to Mary indicates that this was part of the Bosomworth plans by that date. Like their decision to press the Trustees for a grant of the entire Yamacraw tract, this project had been settled upon before Thomas's departure for England the previous June.[17]

The Bosomworths' trading post at the forks was established sometime early in 1746, probably in April or May. There Thomas built "a very good Dwelling House, outhouses, a large store and Fortifyed the whole round." Malatchi related that "I carryed her [Mary] myself up to the Forks of the Altamaha and settled her upon our own Lands." It is evident from Horton's letters to the Bosomworths in 1746 that he considered their influence with the Creeks invaluable and that he often called upon them for assistance. Mary avowed that during Horton's command, as during Oglethorpe's before and Heron's afterward, she had a "standing Order" to issue supplies to Indian war parties "as were thought necessary for his Majesty's Service."[18]

During the war the most effective native auxiliaries Oglethorpe and his successors had were probably the Lower Chickasaws. Even their aged chief, the Squirrel King, took part in the fighting. The Lower Chickasaws were an offshoot of the Chickasaw Nation on the Mississippi. As a defensive measure following the Yamasee War, the South Carolina government invited any or all Chickasaws to relocate to the outskirts of the colony. Around 1723 one Chickasaw band did resettle near Fort Moore. The Carolinians respected and trusted Chickasaws more than other Indians, and treated them differently. As Thomas Nairne put it early in the century, "The Chickasaws are to the Talapoosies as men of Quality among us are to the peasants." By treating them more like Englishmen the hope was that they would become more like Englishmen, or even Englishmen. Probably to attract more of them, in 1739 the Carolina authorities granted these Chickasaws a huge reservation. The tract was surveyed, a plat was drawn up, and the governor in council approved the grant of "Twenty one Thousand seven hundred and Seventy four acres in New Windsor Township." A few years later, trader Enos Dexter related that these Indians were settled in two villages: about fifty families under the Squirrel King opposite Augusta, and about twenty families under Mingo Stoby ten miles away near Fort Moore.[19]

"Squirrel King" was the traders' translation of "Fanne Mingo." Nairne's recently published 1708 journal establishes that this was a special title among Chickasaws and neighboring peoples, bestowed by members of one clan or nation upon an outsider from another willing to act as "a protector or Freind" to the grantors. "The Chicasaws call these protectors Fane Mingo or Squirrell king," Nairne wrote, and their job was "to make up all Breaches" between the two groups. Presumably the particular responsibility of the Fanne Mingo who assisted Oglethorpe and Horton was to serve as protector to Chickasaws from their Mississippi homeland who visited the Augusta area.[20]

Lower Chickasaws who went down to Florida to aid the British war effort were at least nominally commanded by Tommy Jones, one of very few Georgians conversant with their language. In June 1744, for example, one such contingent was recruited around Augusta by the "half Indian Capt. Thomas Jones of the Rangers." By the following year, however, some young Lower Chickasaw warriors were committing numerous depredations around Augusta, "which occasioned most of the Inhabitants to partake themselves to the Fort for Security." In August, Horton made the long journey from Frederica and calmed things down. According to Stephens, Horton's success was partly due to an imaginative exercise in role playing: "he got a Convention with them in a Solemn manner, wherein he personated the Beloved Man (i.e. the General) in behalf of the English; and the Chief of the Chickassaw Indians (called the Squirrel King) appeared at the head of them."[21]

Early in 1746, active hostility toward the English suddenly erupted among a wider circle of natives, particularly the Lower Creeks. In February Horton turned away a party of Creek warriors who had trekked to Frederica expecting employment against the Spanish Indians. According to Malatchi, this was bitterly resented and the spurned war party vented its frustration with a raid against the Yuchis near Augusta. That was far from the end of it. By late March Horton had received reports that the Lower Creeks were seething. That month a party of Cussitas, probably the one Horton had turned away, had demanded powder and shot from Captain Richard Kent, commander at Augusta. He had replied aggressively. According to Malatchi, "Capt. Kent's answer was, that if we wanted any, we should have it out of the mouth of his Great Guns."[22]

This and other provocations, Horton was told, had brought the Lower Creeks near to joining forces with the Cherokees, Chickasaws, and even the Catawbas "to declare War against the English." Similar accounts reached Charles Town. One trader reported on March 17 that a war party of thirty-six Cussitas was expected to join some of the Lower Chickasaws in an attack on Augusta "to cut all the White people off." Most ominously, he added that Indians had told him that "old [Chi] Geally is very much for it." According to George Galphin, "old Chiggilli" expected to "see the Town of Savannah in flames."[23]

It was not long before some Georgians were blaming the Bosomworths for inciting the Lower Creeks to hostilities. George Galphin was one of them. Since his arrival in the colony a decade earlier as an indentured servant, he had transformed himself from a nobody into a somebody. In 1746 Galphin, whose main business was in Coweta, was one of the most successful traders in the colony. In

May 1748 a letter from Galphin and other traders was considered in council by Governor James Glen of South Carolina. It stated that "till the time Mr. Thomas Bosomworth settled the Forks the Indians of the Nation were quiet and Peaceable." Since then growing Creek misbehavior was directly traceable to the Bosomworth family: "these disturbances are occasioned by bad Talks the Indians receive from the Reverend Mr. Thomas Bosomworth or Abraham Bosomworth," his brother.[24]

Whatever its origin, the emergency was serious and was immediately recognized as such in both colonies. In late March Horton made plans to journey to Augusta to meet Chigelli in an effort to relieve the tension. Governor Glen was so alarmed that he prepared to lead a peace mission to confer with the Catawbas at Congarees, the Cherokees at Ninety-Six, and the Lower Creeks and Lower Chickasaws at New Windsor (the new name for old Fort Moore).

Meanwhile, an incident in Savannah in late March 1746 involving the Yamacraw tract threatened to provoke the Lower Creeks beyond any possibility of reconciliation. For several years some Savannah residents, despite Indian protests, had been cutting timber on this reserved Yamacraw land. The tract contained the best stand of hardwood trees near Savannah. The trees poachers chose to harvest included the most valuable ones, walnut trees. As this illicit timbering continued, the remaining Yamacraws, especially Tomochichi's widow, Senauki, became "Very clamorous." Confronting Stephens and the magistrates, the aggrieved natives told them "they might see with their own Eyes such a Number of Walnut Trees and other Timber at such a white Man's Door."[25]

Finally, when the Indians threatened to take matters into their own hands, Mary Bosomworth drafted a formal protest. Though she had claimed the tract as her own a few months earlier, she now supported the Yamacraw claim of proprietorship. Thomas likewise backtracked, pointing out that the tract was "Reserved by Treaty," the 1739 treaty. President Stephens received the Yamacraw protest on Saturday, March 29, and replied immediately. He invited the Indians to send "any Christian Person" to a meeting of the president and assistants the following Monday to give sworn testimony regarding their complaint. The Yamacraws understood Stephens's reply as an official notification that "their Evidence signified nothing unless some Christian People was to swear to the Fact." They had interpreted Stephens's letter correctly, for the Trustees had never followed through on their 1737 decision to enact "A law for taking Indian Evidence." The Savannah magistrates were following established legal precedent, but their rote denial of mutuality infuriated the Yamacraws.[26]

At this point, Santachi, who as a young man had accompanied Oglethorpe to England in 1734, arrived on the scene. He joined Senauki at the head of a Yamacraw delegation that returned to Savannah to renew the protest, apparently on March 31. After hearing the Indians out, Stephens and the assistants made a totally unexpected response. According to Santachi, the Savannah authorities now denied the Indians redress on the ground that "the Indians that were over the great Water had given away their Lands to the King." According to Bosomworth's narrative, they declared that "the Land was not the Indians for they had given it all to the Great King when in England."[27]

This sensational pronouncement provoked consternation among the Indians. Santachi and Senauki, both of whom had been in England and witnessed no such thing, could hardly believe their ears. In reply, Santachi "talked very Strong" to the magistrates, upbraiding them as "Lyars." Although Stephens and the assistants evidently took no significant action to meet the Yamacraw protest, they appreciated the gravity of the situation and looked for a way to calm the aroused Indians. They therefore agreed to a demand by Santachi and Senauki for twelve kegs of wine. According to Santachi, the Yamacraws interpreted this as compensation "for the Injury done them and as an Acknowledgement of their Rights."[28]

Further light on the Savannah magistrates' provocative declaration emerges from Malatchi's 1747 speech to Heron. Malatchi related that after the bitter confrontation in Savannah, Santachi went up the river to Augusta. He arrived in time to meet with Chigelli, who had led a Lower Creek delegation to confer with both Governor Glen and Major Horton. Glen held his conference with the Lower Creeks at New Windsor on May 8 and 9, and a few days later Horton met with them at Augusta. At these talks the British leaders succeeded, temporarily, in defusing the conflict with the Lower Creeks. The minutes of Horton's conference do not survive, but Chigelli reported that he and Horton had established a good relationship and that he had promised to meet Horton again at the forks around September.[29]

After his talk with Chigelli, Horton met with the neighboring Lower Chickasaws. While the British at all levels continued to be highly respectful of the Chickasaws on the Mississippi, they no longer felt the same way about those settled near Augusta. Governor Glen would describe them as "a few who dare not go Home to their own Country." During the spring of 1746 troubles with the Lower Chickasaws were even more serious than those that had driven Augusta settlers into the fort a year earlier. A few days before Horton arrived, Glen met with the Squirrel King and Mingo Stoby. He later had this to say about the meetings he and Horton had with these Chickasaws: "I found it very Necessary to speak pretty Roughly to them and Major Horton who then Commanded the Troops in Georgia spoke to them in the same manner. This had a very good Effect for they have been very humble and tractable ever since."[30]

It happens that this portion of Horton's journal does survive. It appears to be the only firsthand record of Horton's Indian diplomacy now extant, and it provides a very different picture of his meeting with the Lower Chickasaws. According to Horton, Lower Chickasaws led by a fierce young warrior named Tuscasuccy had lured Cussitas (the frustrated war party mentioned earlier) to join them in a marauding band that terrorized the area. The old chiefs, the Squirrel King and Mingo Stoby, had lost their influence with their young men, and Glen's bluster had apparently failed to solve the problem. Though Tuscasuccy had refused to attend Glen's talk, and had never attended any previous meeting with the British, he came to meet with Horton. That alone indicates that Horton was a surprisingly skillful diplomat, and this impression grows.

In response to Horton's tactful criticism, and a suggestion from the visiting Chickasaw "Doctor" that the young troublemakers accompany him back to the Chickasaw homeland, Tuscasuccy said he was "very willing" to go if that was what "the Squire" wanted. ("The Squire" was a term Indians commonly applied to Oglethorpe; evidently Tuscasuccy was recalling Horton's role-playing exercise the year before.) Horton replied that he did not want that, for "I did not want them to disperse their People for that it would weaken them very much and give their Enemys advantage over them." Horton thus managed to convert his complaint into an expression of sympathetic concern. Tuscasuccy pledged to restore order, and the old chiefs deferred to him. He promised Horton that "the white People should have no more reason to Complain of them." The Squirrel King told Horton he thought that Tuscasuccy's change of heart would do the job, for "all the Young Fellows were afraid of him." Evidently it did. Moreover, Santachi showed up at this meeting and, like Chigelli, apparently was conciliated. He went away promising Horton that if his party came upon any "Frenchmen in the Nation They will send them down to me."[31]

Santachi needed to be conciliated. Just before his encounter with Horton he had met with Chigelli, giving him an account of the recent storm in Savannah. Chigelli related that Santachi asked him "if I or any of my people had given all the Lands away." The Lower Creek leader of course denied it, promising he would shortly "call all the Head Men together" to get to the bottom of the problem. After his return to Coweta, Chigelli waited for Malatchi, his soon-to-be successor, who was then involved in settling Mary Bosomworth at the forks. When Malatchi came home, probably in July, Chigelli recounted all he had heard from Santachi. He then produced "a Paper General Oglethorpe gave us when in the Nation" in 1739. Suspicious that this document might have something to do with the outrageous pronouncement of the Savannah magistrates, Chigelli took it to George Galphin to be read and translated. Barely literate himself, Galphin obliged. Sure enough. According to Malatchi, Galphin told the Coweta leaders that "the Contents of that Paper was that we had given away all our Lands to the King."[32]

Chigelli related that this sensational revelation "Vexed us very much," for the Lower Creek leaders quickly concluded that they had been betrayed. As astounding as the deed itself, the perpetrator was none other than James Oglethorpe. Malatchi reported that Oglethorpe's deception "made us very uneasy, to think that he should impose upon us so, and give us a Paper to take away our Lands and not let us know any thing of it." This shocking news doubtless lay behind the bitter message Mary Bosomworth gave Malatchi to carry to the Creeks a few months later. According to the mangled prose of Galphin's summary, Mary now denounced her old friend as "a Roge" who had attempted to swindle the Creeks out of their lands in order to save his own skin. He would have "had his heed Cut of . . . if it had not been for the Land that he tooke from the Indians and Give it to the King to Save him." This treachery had no equal. "And this is the thanks they know git for saving federico from been tacken by the Spanards." The injustice of it all cried out for relief, and Mary saw just how it might be obtained. Accordingly, she "beged that all the head men in the nation might be a Quented of it that they might Come Down and Demand there Lands before it was too late." Early in 1748 Galphin and other traders reported that this was only one of the "bad talks" the Creeks received from the Bosomworths during the next year and a half. These talks, they added, put the lives of all traders in danger.[33]

That summer Malatchi delivered a speech in the Coweta square enlarging upon Mary's accusations. The traders who heard it regarded it as menacing, and their reports caused alarms in Frederica, Savannah, and Charles Town. Malatchi's talk must have been hot, for even Mary Bosomworth was "uneasy" about it. Horton shared the general concern, and on November 11 he sent Mary a copy of the reports he had on the speech. Trying to put the best face on things, Horton wrote her that "it is possible Malatche might misapprehend something you said to him but more probable that the Persons who say they heard his Talk Misunderstood him." Chigelli related that Malatchi's speech was "about our Lands concerning which so many Lies have been told" and was directly inspired by Santachi's account of the confrontation with the Savannah magistrates. Whatever Malatchi said, it clearly went beyond what Mary had.[34]

The document that had provoked this hostile reaction, the "paper" Oglethorpe gave to the Lower Creeks at the Coweta treaty conference in 1739, does not appear to survive. Nevertheless, its general content can be inferred from allusions to it in the accounts of Chigelli, Malatchi, and Thomas Bosomworth. To begin with, it was almost certainly the same document that lay behind the obnoxious pronouncement of the Savannah magistrates in March 1746. Second, it obviously did not say exactly what the Indians thought it said. Had Oglethorpe foisted a document claiming all of their lands on the Creeks in 1739 he would have flagrantly contradicted the treaty he had just negotiated with them. That is not credible.

Still, the document had to sufficiently resemble a claim that the Lower Creeks had surrendered all of their lands to the king to sound that way when clumsily interpreted for them by Galphin. A decade after the confrontation in Savannah, Thomas Bosomworth reported what the Yamacraws thought they had heard from the Savannah magistrates. Significantly, he also admitted that "the Magistrates have since Denied that they told the Indians the Lands belonged to the Great King."[35]

It seems clear that the misunderstanding was due to confusion over the crucial distinction between territorial sovereignty and land ownership. The offending document planted by Oglethorpe did not contain a claim that the Lower Creeks had surrendered ownership of their lands, but rather an assertion that they had yielded sovereignty over those lands to King George. Moreover, since the magistrates alleged that the Indians made their concession "when in England," they must have been referring to the visit of Tomochichi's party in 1734. The main purpose of all government-sponsored visits by Indian delegations was to reinforce British claims of sovereignty. As noted earlier, there is good evidence that in London the Yamacraw leader delivered as Oglethorpe had hoped. During a private audience with King George, Tomochichi made some sort of a gesture that his hosts could—and did—interpret as an acknowledgment of British sovereignty over Creek lands.

When Santachi and Senauki vehemently denied having witnessed a surrender of their lands when in England, they were surely correct. Even had they been present at the private audience with the king, it is not likely they would have divined the significance British leaders attached to the meeting. Tomochichi himself probably did not fully understand. At any rate, Santachi and Senauki were almost certainly not present. Like other American Indians, the Creeks did not normally allow boys or women to participate in important diplomatic meetings. As British leaders then understood Tomochichi's kingly status, only his participation was essential. Were any other members of his party present when he met King George, they would have been the only other adult males, Umpichi and Hillispilli.

Whatever Tomochichi said or did to gratify British territorial ambitions would have been of little use to the British unless the Lower Creeks ratified it. The document that had so incensed Chigelli and Malatchi apparently was intended by Oglethorpe to facilitate such a ratification. Significantly, Chigelli's concern to learn whether Mary had been the interpreter when the alleged surrender was made indicates that the offending document was not drafted during Tomochichi's visit to England, but afterward in Georgia. It also implies that the document was not composed during Oglethorpe's 1739 Coweta conference (Chigelli being well aware that Mary had not been present), but earlier. The 1733 meeting obviously can be ruled out. Most probably the document was not written during the 1736 meeting either: then the leading Creek participants were Chigelli and Malatchi, who after 1746 surely would have denounced an effort to bamboozle them personally. Oglethorpe probably drafted the document in the wake of the October 1738 meeting in Savannah, most likely in the spring of 1739 while preparing to meet the Creek chiefs in Coweta.[36]

Whatever its exact content, it seems clear that the document never satisfied Oglethorpe, for he never publicly invoked it. Probably it fell short of his hopes because few Creek leaders, possibly even Tomochichi alone, had subscribed to it. Why then did he leave a copy with the Creeks during the Coweta conference, and apparently give them another copy the following year? Probably because at Coweta he had failed to get what he most wanted: an explicit acknowledgment of British sovereignty in the treaty text. He likely supposed that he would have another go at the desired result at a future Creek conference. At that time, retrieval of the document from the Indians' own archive might help persuade them to yield the desired acknowledgment. But Oglethorpe never had another major conference with Creek leaders, and his maneuver backfired disastrously in 1746.

If the troubles that erupted in 1746 resulted from confusion between land ownership and territorial sovereignty, why did Oglethorpe, other British leaders, or interested colonists not attempt to explain the distinction to the Indians? Perhaps some did, but there were powerful reasons to maintain the ambiguity. For one thing, a straightforward explanation was likely to provoke Indian indignation and resistance. A question of sovereignty, then as now, was essentially a political or military question, not a legal or ethical question. For British and colonial leaders, British sovereignty was a given, whatever native leaders thought or did about it. The task of converting pretention into reality necessarily was a long-term project. One essential part of that task was to pressure or persuade Indian leaders to give at least some appearance of recognizing British sovereignty. Over time, as the disparity between British and native power grew, it was reasonable to suppose that the Indians would be forced to move further in the desired direction.

On the other hand, to prevent violent and expensive conflicts, it was essential that British officials be able to assure Indian chiefs that colonization did not threaten them. Again and again they assured native leaders that they had no wish to deprive them of their right to govern themselves or their ownership rights to their ancestral lands. And, for the most part, they meant it. To the extent that natives were confident that the British respected their rights of self-rule and land ownership, they might be unguarded about requests that they honor the British king. They might then be induced to assent to declarations that went far beyond their intentions, declarations that the British could interpret as acknowledgments of British sovereignty. From the point of view of British officialdom, the less the

Indians knew about sovereignty the better. The British were duplicitous toward the Indians, but mainly about sovereignty, not land ownership.

Ambiguity about the distinction between sovereignty and land ownership also served the interests of the Bosomworths. Thomas Bosomworth certainly understood the distinction. He did not try to explain to the Indians that the British claimed sovereignty over their lands, not property in their lands, because he saw advantage in continued confusion. Thomas and Mary understood full well that the success of their effort to make good on Creek land grants depended crucially on the Indians' support for those grants. When colonial officials denied the legitimacy of Creek grants to the Bosomworths, Thomas and Mary could and did tell the Indian grantors that the perfidious British had attempted to deny them their rights to their own lands. Confusion of a sovereignty issue with an issue of land ownership served the Bosomworths' cause by provoking Creeks to rally to their support—and to the land grants Creek chiefs had given them.

The Bosomworths were emboldened by Malatchi's speech denouncing British duplicity, which Thomas may have witnessed, to further defy the Georgia authorities. In August Stephens informed the Trustees that Thomas had sent to South Carolina for six Negro slaves to be employed at the forks. About the same time, Thomas also purchased some Carolina cattle on credit and turned them loose to multiply on St. Catherines Island. Presumably, Lower Creek leaders had given permission to do so on this island they had reserved. Stephens at first interpreted the Bosomworth cattle herd as an effort "to make good that claim" by demonstrating possession on behalf of the Creeks. That may have been the immediate purpose of bringing cattle to the island, but the growing herd could also be used to demonstrate Bosomworth possession.[37]

Thomas and Mary apparently soon heard rumors, probably passed on to them by Malatchi, that caused them to doubt Major Horton's goodwill. It came to their ears that Horton was planning to establish a post at the old site of Mount Venture, a potential competitor to their trading operation at the forks, and that he challenged the Creek claim to St. Catherines. On November 13 Horton wrote Thomas to assure him that both rumors were false. He had no plans to challenge Mary by settling Mount Venture, for "I always apprehended that Land belonged to her." Presumably, since the old post lay in Lower Creek territory, he supposed it was hers by Indian right. Moreover, "I never had any objections to the Indians doing what they thought proper with the Island of St. Catherines, because I always knew it belonged to them." Thus he had no objection, if the Creeks did not, to Thomas's using St. Catherines to become a cattle baron.[38]

Early in December, Chigelli came down to the forks intending to meet with Horton, as they had arranged at Augusta. After Horton sent word that he could not come, probably because he lacked presents, the Creek leader sat down with his niece. Mary told him she knew nothing of Oglethorpe's offensive paper or any other pretext for a British claim to all of the Lower Creek lands, but said she would have to read "all our Papers." Chigelli promised to bring them down to Frederica the following spring so Mary could interpret them to the Creek leaders in Horton's presence. For the present, on December 4 he dictated a long talk to Horton outlining his understanding of the background of the current troubles. Often cited already, it is one of the most important documents of the period.[39]

Chigelli never again met with Horton. Malatchi related that during the remaining months of Horton's command the Creeks heard reports that he intended to seize and hang Thomas and Mary "for settling at the Forks upon the King's Land." Directly or indirectly the Bosomworths doubtless inspired these rumors. Horton's plans during early 1747 were quite different, as his letters of May 31 to Mary and July 6 to Thomas demonstrate. Horton had decided to provide Mary with an annual allotment of £200 worth of Indian presents to distribute in the king's name. This was intended, he explained, "to prevent Expenses here by Stopping Indians at the Forks," an idea that both Chigelli and Malatchi had endorsed.[40]

In Savannah the Bosomworths reiterated their demands deriving from the 1739 grain bounty, but without success. By February they were planning to sail to England to press their various claims more forcefully at a higher level. On February 23 Horton encouraged Thomas to "Draw up a State of Mrs. Bosomworth's Case, with her Demands for Services before the General Left the Colony," promising to send it to Oglethorpe before their departure. While supporting Mary's claims for "Services," Horton was loudly silent about her land claims. By March 10 Thomas had delivered the invited memorial to Horton, who forwarded it to Oglethorpe along with his supporting recommendation. The document does not survive, but it had no apparent effect and the Bosomworths again postponed their trip.[41]

By the end of 1746 the effects of Horton's successful meeting with Chigelli that spring had worn off and the British were again faced with potential disaster in Lower Creek country. Horton's successor, Lieutenant Colonel Alexander Heron, later blamed the renewed troubles on bungling in South Carolina, and he was at least partly right. In late October, Governor Glen convened a Creek conference in Charles Town that, due to the dangerous and deteriorating situation, had attracted native participants of the highest rank. They included the most influential leaders of both Upper Creek divisions: the Abeika chief Enochtanechi of Oakchoy, better known to the English as the Gun Merchant; and the leading Tallapoosa chief, the Wolf King of Mucklassee. Malatchi led the Lower Creek delegation. Both Upper Creek leaders agreed to assist the Carolinians in an assault on Fort Toulouse and to permit them to build a fort near Mucklassee. Malatchi and the Ouseechee "King," withstanding a great deal of pressure, showed "the greatest unwillingness" to participate in the proposed attack. Glen informed the Georgia magistrates that Malatchi declared that "as long as he lived he would neither permit us to take that Fort or to build one of our own there." Disappointed in the Carolinians, Heron complained that "this Scheme was So ill Concerted, and so Publickly talkt of that it had like to have Brought an Indian War upon themselves, and us."[42]

After his return to Coweta, Malatchi promptly dispatched runners to French and Spanish leaders to inform them of what had passed in Charles Town. Alarmed, the French hastened to take advantage of Malatchi's estrangement from the British and schemed to use him to strike first. Guns and ammunition were sent "to every Town in the Upper and Lower Creeks." After several meetings with French emissaries, at least one of them in Fort Toulouse, Malatchi emerged at the head of a Creek party determined to teach the British a lesson. Upper Creek headmen were persuaded not only to revoke their permission for a British fort but also to join in a concerted assault on British traders. According to one report to Horton, "Evry Head man Had Consented to it." But at this point an unexpected attack by the Cherokees temporarily threw the Creeks on the defensive. Had it not been for this, "evry White Man in the Nation had been Murdered this Spring." About the same time, Malatchi sent word to Governor Glen that any attempt by the Carolinians to cross Lower Creek territory to attack Fort Toulouse would be resisted, by force if necessary.[43]

Amid these fears of imminent Creek attack, in early June 1747 Heron relieved Horton of his command. Heron quickly decided that in order to prevent such a disaster he had to call upon Mary Bosomworth to intercede for the colony by arranging a meeting with the Lower Creek leaders. On July 8 he sent Mary a copy of the latest ominous intelligence from Creek country and implored her to use her influence with the Indians "to prevent them from falling upon his Majesty's Subjects." He added that he lacked the means to implement Horton's plan for an annual allotment of Indian presents to be entrusted to her, but assured her that his appeals to England would soon lead to the establishment of a permanent fund. According to the comment appended to this letter by Thomas Bosomworth, Mary had already "sent a Messenger to the Creek Nation and Satisfyed the Indians," but she now recommended that Heron dispatch an agent of his own. Heron promptly agreed, and also accepted the Bosomworths' nominee for this delicate task: Abraham Bosomworth, Thomas's brother. This was the beginning of a close relationship between Heron and the Bosomworths, much to the disgust of the Savannah authorities.[44]

On July 20 Heron commissioned Abraham Bosomworth to undertake an immediate journey to Coweta. The Frederica commander expected Abraham to arrange a meeting between himself and the Lower Creek leaders. Thomas Bosomworth carried Heron's commission to his brother waiting at the Bosomworth place at the forks, and probably accompanied Abraham to Coweta. Thomas also delivered Heron's letter of July 20 to Mary, in which Heron asked her to furnish supplies necessary for the mission, promising to reimburse her. Mary accordingly provided her brother-in-law with suitable presents for the Creeks, along with men and horses to transport them. Thomas later claimed that this cost Mary "upwards of £300 Sterling which she never was yet Repaid by the Government."[45]

Abraham arrived in Coweta on July 31 during the annual busk. As the Bosomworths had doubtless anticipated, his host was Malatchi, who had just succeeded the aged Chigelli as leading chief among the Lower Creeks. Abraham was well received with a white wing of peace and many professions of friendship. He later related that he then "pacified" the Lower Creek leaders with promises that generous presents would soon be forthcoming, "as they usually had been during Mr. Oglethorpe's Administration." Abraham also won Malatchi's agreement to come down to Frederica for talks with Heron. On August 18 he apparently also prevailed upon George Galphin and four other traders to sign a memorial "from all the English Traders in the Creek Nation" to Heron. According to this document, its subscribers credited "the providential Interposition of Mr. Abraham Bosomworth" with averting a Creek defection to the French and a disastrous war. The Bosomworths attached great importance to this document, but its obvious special pleading invited disparagement. The Savannah magistrates promptly ridiculed it, contending that most traders, "except two or three of no Note," had refused to sign it. Galphin soon repudiated it as "entirely false and forged."[46]

While Abraham Bosomworth was busy in Coweta, probably with Thomas at his side, Mary Bosomworth presented Heron with a lengthy memorial that she wished forwarded to the Duke of Newcastle, secretary of state. Heron had probably already agreed to do so during his talks with Thomas in July. Mary's memorial of August 10, 1747, already often cited, is another of the most important documents of the period. It is the longest and most informative of her extant writings, and the earliest of numerous Bosomworth statements of their case to survive.[47]

Mary presented her grievances against the colony in the context of a fascinating narrative of her life, beginning with her birth in Coweta and removal as a young girl to Pon Pon by her father. Since she had been born into the ruling family of Coweta, she now declared herself to be the "Rightfull and Natural Princess" of the Lower Creek Nation. Despite her "Maternal Affection" toward the infant colony of Georgia, and many extraordinary services for its benefit, she was now "Destitute of even the Common Necessaries of Life." Adding insult to injury, she was forced to endure abuse from "those ungrateful People who are indebted to her for the Blessings they Injoy." Oglethorpe appears as the chief ingrate, for his promises to secure her a decent reward for her services and restitution for "her Losses Sustained in his Majesty's service" had proven empty. Those losses, "upon the Most Moderate Computation," now stood at £5,714.17.11, which she trusted would be made good by "the Justice and Compassion of a British Parliament."[48]

Mary opened the issue of her land claims, very carefully, toward the end of the document. Laying the groundwork, she mentioned the Georgia charter, but clearly implied it had no relevance to the ancient inhabitants of the region. In particular, the Creeks "never owed Allegiance, to or Acknowledged the sovereignty of any Crownd Head whatever." The Creeks were a free and independent nation merely allied to, not subordinate to, the British Crown. Their lands were their own to do with as they chose. They had chosen to make certain land cessions to the Georgia Trustees, which concessions had been readily enough honored in London, but they had also made a cession to her, which had been treated with contempt. She complained that she had been "Branded and Stigmatized with the Odious Name of Traytor, for Making any Pretensions to those Rights she is Justly entitled to by the Laws of God and Nature." She was no traitor, for "she has in Vain made Application for a Grant from the Crown." Despite the injustices she had suffered, she was still hoping to secure one.[49]

Mary concluded that she was "Willing to hold What Possessions she is there entitled to by the Laws of Nature and Nations, as a Subject of great Britain." Willing indeed, for holding the lands she claimed by Creek grant as a British subject was the fundamental objective of her struggle. While Mary had raised the issue of her land claims, she was careful not to say what lands she claimed. Most probably she and her husband were preparing to reassert her 1745 claim to the Yamacraw tract. What Abraham accomplished in Coweta would enable them to do that, but it seems unlikely that he or Thomas could have returned by August 10. Mary went on to imply that she was so determined to have her lands that, if she could not have them via a British grant, she would hold then under her Indian grant as a hostile Creek princess. "With the greatest Reluctancy," she suggested that Georgia would suffer disaster if her appeal for justice was ignored, for she would then be "Drove to the Necessity of Flying to her Indian Friends for Bread." The influence of Mary's husband on this section is clear. A memorandum Thomas later wrote for his lawyers outlining the Bosomworth position likewise relies on "the Law of Nature and Nations."[50]

On September 8 Heron forwarded Mary's memorial and various supporting documents to Deputy Secretary of State Andrew Stone for delivery to Newcastle. Heron made it clear that he believed her influence with the Creeks to be fully as important to the colony as she claimed, and that he was sympathetic to her case. In a postscript he added that he had just received word of the success of Abraham Bosomworth's mission and expected to meet with Creek leaders soon. The strong support that Heron gave the Bosomworths over the next months probably owned something to his discomfort at being unable to reimburse them for the expense of outfitting Abraham's expedition. According to Thomas, Heron's appeal for help had led Mary "to strip her store of her Indian Goods," and the expedition eventually wound up costing her over £650. When Heron proved unable to repay her, the Bosomworths abandoned their settlement at the forks as a total loss. Twelve years later they still had not been repaid.[51]

Around the first of December, Heron welcomed to Frederica a large Lower Creek delegation headed by Malatchi. It was soon apparent that the Creek leader had come to talk about what had been on his mind for over a year: the land question. On December 7 Malatchi delivered a major speech to Heron, his officers, and other notables of the town. Mary apparently served as interpreter. When the Savannah authorities learned of it they were convinced that it showed signs of Bosomworth authorship, and found it significant that Major Horton had chosen to absent himself from "this idle Farce."[52]

Malatchi's speech focused on Anglo-Creek dealings over land since the founding of the colony. These had been satisfactory to the Creeks until the previous year, when they had learned of Oglethorpe's attempt "to give us a Paper to take away our Lands and not let us know any thing of it." This duplicity and recent unfriendly talks, he related, by the past summer had led him to conclude that the French were speaking truth when they charged that "the English only wanted to take away our Land and enslave us." Fortunately, Heron's arrival had forced him to reconsider, for "We find your Heart is straight towards us Indians." Malatchi wanted this misunderstanding over lands settled once and for all, "and presents for our Wives and Children as usual." To advance these ends, he asked that Abraham Bosomworth be appointed to convey his talk directly to King George. The king should take note that "I am now Emperor of the Creek nation" and hear his complaints accordingly. His people looked forward to a favorable reply and in the meantime would continue to rely on the counsel of Mary Bosomworth, "our Sister, in whom the whole Nation confides."[53]

Heron's reply the same day must have been deeply gratifying to both the Indians and the Bosomworths. He could not resolve the land question himself, he said, because he did not know "what portions of your Lands you have resigned, nor what Considerations You have received for them." Coming from the chief British negotiator with the Indians of Georgia, this was an extraordinary statement. It appears that some of the most important documents dealing with Anglo-Creek land agreements, including the treaty of 1739, were nowhere to be found in Frederica. Even if all of them had been ready at hand, Heron might well have hesitated to grasp this thorn, for Oglethorpe's oral understandings with Indians over land inevitably created uncertainties for his successors. Heron now did what the Creeks had asked him to do: he agreed to send Abraham Bosomworth to

England with Malatchi's speech. Or, rather, he made his intention public. Months earlier he apparently had agreed with Abraham to undertake such a mission to England. It was becoming difficult to distinguish Heron from the Bosomworth cause. Heron declared himself convinced that the king, after he heard from Abraham, "will do you Justice." Not only that, he would provide a suitable reward for Mary Bosomworth.[54]

Losing no time, the next day Heron wrote two letters to Deputy Secretary Andrew Stone, which Abraham was to deliver along with Malatchi's speech. These letters were strongly supportive to both the Creeks and the Bosomworths. In the first, Heron asked the ministry to grant him the means to satisfy Malatchi "in relation to the Acts of Injustice he complains of." Furthermore, he was now convinced that Mary Bosomworth "is looked upon by the whole Creek Nation, as their Natural Princess." That made it advisable, he thought, for the government not only to redress her grievances but to provide "an Annual Support for her for the future." In the second letter he recommended Abraham Bosomworth for an officer's appointment in his regiment.[55]

During the next two weeks, various supporting documents were provided for Abraham Bosomworth to convey to England. The most striking was a declaration signed on December 14 by fifteen Lower Creek headmen. The document was "Signed and Sealed in the Presence of Alexander Heron" and five other Georgians, who added their own signatures as witnesses. The fifteen leaders now declared that Malatchi "has full Power and Authority as our Natural Prince to Transact all Affairs relating to our Nation." Three days later, twenty leading inhabitants of Frederica, headed by Heron and some of his officers, subscribed to a statement attesting to the importance and good character of the Bosomworths.[56]

On about December 23, Heron and Abraham Bosomworth set off together for Charles Town. Thomas Bosomworth, returning to Savannah, accompanied them most of the way. Heron and Abraham avoided Savannah, turning up the Ogeechee, then overland to Ebenezer, and finally to the Carolina capital, where they arrived by January 2, 1748. In Charles Town they took care to have three documents generated by Abraham's past and present missions recorded in the South Carolina secretary's office. These were the traders' declaration of August 18, the December 17 testimonial of Frederica residents in favor of the Bosomworths, and, most important, the Lower Creek chiefs' December 14 declaration that Malatchi was their "Natural Prince." All three were among the documents Abraham would deliver in England a few months later. Heron personally recorded the December 14 document, for his sworn statement testifying to its authenticity appears on the reverse.[57]

The Savannah magistrates had already begun to learn that the Bosomworths and Lower Creek leaders had concerted plans that had a much more immediate impact on the colony. On January 1 an unidentified Frederica informant, most probably Major Horton, wrote Stephens that "the Family of the Bosomworths have brought Malatchee here and made a formal Speech for him denying that any Lands in Georgia belong to the Trustees" except those specifically ceded by treaty. This source went on to say that "the honest Parson," Thomas, "publickly tells the Indians they have a Right of killing or taking away all the Cattle they find on their Lands." Most significant, the writer professed to be "well informed that several Indian Grants of Lands will be soon made." He was well informed.[58]

On January 4, 1748, Malatchi signed a deed conveying to Thomas and Mary Bosomworth the three islands the Lower Creeks had reserved in 1736, and again in the 1739 treaty: St. Catherines, Ossabaw, and Sapelo. Thus, with crucial assistance from their kinsman Malatchi, who other Creek chiefs had declared had "full Power . . . to Transact all Affairs relating to our Nation," the Bosomworths had won an astonishing new concession. The Creek leader may also have signed a similar deed for the Yamacraw tract. In 1756 Thomas referred to a Creek "Ratification" of Mary's right to the Yamacraw tract that occurred in "the year 1747." The text of the January 4 deed gives the date as that day in "1747," that is, 1747 old style, or 1748.[59]

The Bosomworths now had Creek grants for all lands the Creeks had specifically reserved, including the Yamacraw tract. In fact, they had them four or five months earlier. While on official business for Heron, Abraham had also attended to some family business. One result was a Creek ratification of the Bosomworth claim to the Yamacraw tract. Another was that, for the first time, the Bosomworths acquired a claim to the three coastal islands. Two sources point toward this surprising development. First, on October 2, 1747, President Stephens and the assistants charged that Thomas now claimed St. Catherines Island "by a Grant from the Indians." The second is Noble Jones's very revealing deposition of January 7, 1748. As Thomas Bosomworth acknowledged, this sworn statement was "the principal" and "most Material" piece of evidence behind the charges of treason that the Savannah authorities were soon preparing against him. Well aware of the danger that his document posed to him, and normally tireless in rebutting accusations, Thomas nevertheless never disputed the assertions set forth in the Jones deposition. They may therefore be presumed accurate.[60]

Jones related that on January 1 he had an eye-opening encounter with Thomas in Savannah. Bosomworth had shown him a deed issued by Lower Creek leaders to himself, his wife, and his brother Abraham for the Yamacraw tract and St. Catherines Island. Jones testified that this document "was Signed with several Marks said to be the Marks of Chicalee [Chigelli], Malatchie, and about six or eight other Indians with Seals affixed against each respective Mark." Thomas also told him that he had a similar deed for Ossabaw and Sapelo islands and that he was about "to settle the Island Ussabaw in like manner that he has already done Saint Catherines." The fact that Abraham Bosomworth was one of the original grantees strongly suggests that these deeds originated during Abraham's mission to Coweta the previous summer. Chigelli's participation makes that all but certain, for he had not accompanied Malatchi's delegation to Frederica in December. Jones's deposition thus establishes that by August 1747 the Lower Creek leadership had already been persuaded to grant the Bosomworths all of the lands they had reserved in the 1739 treaty.[61]

The Coweta deeds, one of which Jones was allowed to inspect, were never seen again. Thomas most likely destroyed them after January 4, the day Malatchi signed a more defensible deed or deeds. The motive for seeking new deeds to supersede those signed in Coweta arose from the fact that Abraham Bosomworth was one of the original grantees. Once Colonel Heron had committed himself on December 7 to dispatch Abraham on a mission to England, Mary's brother-in-law was potentially most useful to the Bosomworth cause if he could secure appointment as a British official. This promising avenue of influence would vanish if Abraham appeared to have a direct interest in the Bosomworth land claims. Accordingly, a new rendition of the deeds purged of any reference to Abraham was required.

The January 4 deed for the three coastal islands not only survives, it exists in two different versions. In addition to the elimination of Abraham Bosomworth as one of the grantees, these documents differ from the Coweta deeds described by Jones in two significant ways. First, they were not signed by a number of Lower Creek leaders, but by Malatchi alone. Second, the distribution of the lands in the original deeds was altered. In the Coweta documents St. Catherines Island was linked with the Yamacraw tract in one deed, apparently because these were the areas of greatest consequence to the Bosomworths, while Ossabaw and Sapelo islands were granted together in the second, perhaps as an afterthought. On the other hand, geographical logic prevailed in the document or documents of January 4. St. Catherines was now linked with the other two islands in one deed, while the second deed, if there was one, presumably dealt with the Yamacraw tract alone.[62]

The existence of two distinct versions of the January 4 deed is at first puzzling. The earlier and briefer version clearly was drafted well before January 4, and probably before December 14. The revised version was written afterward, for it echoes the Creek recognition that day that Malatchi had "full Power and Authority to Transact all Affairs" in their behalf. It seems clear that the revised version was intended to supersede the original, for the date remained unaltered and our copies of both have annexed (among others) the same affidavit sworn by the same subscribing witnesses. These five witnesses were probably all Carolinians, and their statement was sworn in Frederica on March 1 before John Mullryne, a South

Carolina justice of the peace. If the Bosomworths had a growing list of enemies in Georgia, they still had friends in Carolina.[63]

In this affidavit the witnesses "declare that Possession Livery and Seizin of the within mentioned Lands Islands and Heriditaments was in their presence given and Delivered by the said Malatchi Opiya Mico unto the within named Thomas Bosomworth and Mary his Wife." Evidently Horton's lesson on the importance of livery of seisin a decade earlier remained persuasive to the Bosomworths. It seems likely that the original version of the deed was used on January 4 because the revised version was not yet complete, with the substitution coming shortly afterward. An additional affidavit dated January 22 and attached to the revised version indicates that this had been done by that date.[64]

In a second notable alteration, the opening sentences of the revised deed, unlike those in the original, describe Lower Creek territory in a close paraphrase of the 1739 treaty. On December 7 Heron had indicated that no copy of this treaty was available in Frederica. Thomas Bosomworth apparently decided to improve his intended deed by including a direct reference to the 1739 treaty and perhaps other documents, then went off to Savannah to procure copies. His old friend Charles Watson could supply them, for Watson had been appointed recorder the previous August. Thus when Noble Jones met Thomas on January 1, he found him to be carrying many documents, including copies of the 1733 and 1739 treaties.[65]

With these in hand, Thomas immediately returned to Frederica. Stephens reported that he had been in Savannah only a "few hours." One of the changes Thomas made in the deed was probably in response to an afterthought by Malatchi. Unlike the original, the revised deed has Malatchi reserving to the Creeks "forever" the use of the granted islands for fishing, hunting, and planting. Sometime after the Frederica meeting dispersed, Thomas gave Watson a copy of the original deed to record in the colony records. Watson complied, but it is doubtful that the document remained there for long. It would have given the magistrates a powerful weapon to use against the Bosomworths, but they never mentioned it.[66]

Thomas Bosomworth almost certainly intended to secure a second deed for the Yamacraw tract. The Coweta deeds of summer 1747 could not be fully replaced unless there was a second deed, and Stephens's anonymous informant reported that "several" Indian grants were being prepared in January 1748. Furthermore, Thomas later asserted that "the main Land [Yamacraw tract] had been conveyed to Mrs. Bosomworth by the Indians ever since the Year 1737 and the Islands (together with a Ratification of the main Land) ever since the year 1747." Thus there was some form of ratification for the grant of the Yamacraw tract in January 1748, but most likely this did not take the form of a written document. If such a document was produced, the Bosomworths soon thereafter suppressed it. No text seems to exist, and there are no references to it where we might expect to find them. The Yamacraw tract evidently was treated more cautiously than the coastal islands, doubtless because it was a much more sensitive piece of real estate.[67]

The Lower Creek grant or grants of January 1748 to the Bosomworths inevitably brought Thomas and Mary into confrontation with the Savannah magistrates, the Georgia Trustees, and eventually the British government. Upon learning of the events in Frederica in December and January, the Savannah authorities quickly concluded that Thomas Bosomworth was the mastermind and driving force behind the recent Creek grants. The evidence abundantly supports that conclusion. Thomas's unguarded conversation with Noble Jones on January 1 exposed his ultimate objective. Upon perusing several documents Thomas showed him, Jones warned him that "no British Subject could accept any Grant from the Indians." Thomas brushed this aside. He acknowledged himself a British subject, "but was well advised that having . . . obtained a Grant from the Indians He could by Law oblige the King to allow of the same." Bosomworth surely knew that there was no precedent for the king authorizing any of his subjects in America to lawfully hold lands under an Indian grant, and little chance that he would be the first to gain such an authorization.[68]

If Thomas meant exactly what Jones said he said, he would have to rely on "the Law of Nature and Nations" to influence the king in his favor. An opening gambit perhaps, but not one likely to prevail over English property law in an English court. Thomas never sued to gain the land rights he claimed because he knew that would be futile. He realized that the only way to gain the protection of English law for his Indian land grants was in the political arena. He saw that intolerable pressure from the Creeks was the only thing likely to "oblige" the king to validate their land grants to the Bosomworths. The obvious way for the king "to allow" Thomas and Mary full benefit of those grants, nearly the only conceivable way, was by making a royal grant of the same territory to them. That is the course he would steadfastly pursue from now on.

The Bosomworth strategy was not entirely new. In 1741 and 1742 Mary and her previous husband, Jacob Matthews, had petitioned the Trustees (as agents of the British Crown) to grant him the old Yamacraw townsite, which Tomochichi had already granted to her in 1737. Likewise, in late 1745 Mary petitioned the Trustees to grant Thomas the entire Yamacraw tract, which the Creeks had granted to her in 1738. These early efforts had been summarily dismissed, but after the summer of 1747 Thomas and Mary were in a position to hope for a much different outcome. What was new about the Bosomworth strategy was the insistent political support they had persuaded Creek leaders to give to their land claims. Noble Jones might lecture Thomas on what British law required, but Thomas had been busy creating American facts.

From the moment the Coweta deeds were signed, the old Bosomworth demand for a British grant of the Yamacraw tract, now augmented by a demand for a grant of the three islands, no longer rested on legal aphorisms or theoretical arguments. Those might prove useful, but from that time forward the Bosomworth claims depended almost entirely upon the support the Lower Creeks were prepared to give them. With that nation now led by the Bosomworths' "cousin" Malatchi, that support appeared to be absolute. With Malatchi periodically threatening to bolt to the French, it was not easy for British officials to contradict him. A tight knot had been tied in the British relationship to the Lower Creeks, and it was hard to see how it could be loosed without gratifying at least part of the Bosomworth demands.

The legal advice Thomas Bosomworth mentioned to Noble Jones probably came mainly from his South Carolina friends. As noticed earlier, in 1737 lawyers retained by South Carolina had argued before the Board of Trade that "the Indians within the limits of Georgia were not reckoned subjects, but allies to his Majesty." That was the basic premise of the Bosomworth legal position. Some of the Bosomworths' Carolina friends, notably Port Royal justice of the peace John Mullryne, were with them in Frederica in December 1747 and January 1748. Their assistance goes far to explain the sophisticated legal language found in the revised deed for the islands.[69]

These Carolinians were not disinterested observers, but participants in land development schemes in the vicinity of St. Catherines and Ossabaw islands. Thomas Bosomworth's fateful conversation with Noble Jones began with his disclosure that he intended soon to settle Ossabaw, as "he had already done St. Catherines." On December 12, 1747, Mullryne presented the Savannah authorities with a petition seeking grants of five hundred acres for himself and eleven others near Ossabaw Island. The magistrates approved such grants to Mullryne and three others. In January they received similar requests from four other Carolinians for grants near St. Catherines. This time the board balked, declaring that "they will receive no more Petitions from any of the Inhabitants of South Carolina" until the Trustees' pleasure was known. They explained that these petitions seemed to be part of a campaign undertaken with Colonel Heron's support to introduce Negro slavery into Georgia. Later they charged that Heron "was promised a Good Portion" of the lands the Creeks had granted to the Bosomworths in January.[70]

On January 12 Stephens reported to Secretary Martyn on Thomas Bosomworth's furtive visit to Savannah, noting that "he avoided any conference with me the few hours he was in Town." As yet unaware of the January 4 deed, Stephens denounced the earlier Creek deeds to Mary, Thomas, and Abraham Bosomworth. He enclosed three affidavits taken on January 7 from those whom Thomas had talked to on January 1. Notably included was that of Noble Jones; notably absent was any statement from Recorder Charles Watson. As Stephens saw it, the Creek concessions to the Bosomworths were part of a nefarious land speculation scheme. He charged that Thomas had already "made offers of granting divers Tracts to others" out of those the Creeks had deeded to his family. The January 7 affidavits of Jones and others could be, and were, used to support a much more serious charge than illegal land-jobbing. Later that year the Savannah magistrates relied on them (not the January 4 deed, which they apparently could not lay their hands on) in preparing an indictment of Thomas Bosomworth for treason. As Thomas reported, his alleged offense was "holding Lands in the Colony independent of the Crown of Great Brittain, or Authority from thence Legaly derived."[71]

Around the first of March, Abraham Bosomworth arrived in England to make Heron's case for an annual fund for Indian presents. On March 4 he delivered Heron's letter to Verelst, probably after conveying the main packet of documents he carried to Secretary at War Henry Fox. These included the representation of the Creek traders in August 1747, Malatchi's speech to Heron in December, Heron's reply, and the Lower Creek recognition of Malatchi as their prince. The January 4 deed from Malatchi was not included. On April 1 the now discouraged and nearly moribund Trustees received copies of these papers from Fox, along with a request for their opinion on what ought to be done to ensure the safety of the southern frontier. Three days later they stirred themselves to endorse the idea of a permanent annual fund for Indian presents.[72]

Abraham's stay in London was also good for family business. Fortunately for the Bosomworths, the Savannah magistrates' accusations against them and the dangerous supporting affidavits they enclosed did not arrive in England until sometime that summer. Had these documents reached London a few months earlier, Abraham would have been forced onto the defensive and the outcome of his mission surely would have been very different. A second stroke of luck involved a change in the ministry. In February the Duke of Newcastle, who had ignored Mary Bosomworth's 1747 memorial, was succeeded by the Duke of Bedford as secretary of state for the Southern Department. Abraham apparently made a very favorable impression on the inexperienced secretary, who seems to have agreed to every proposal that Bosomworth laid before him.[73]

As Heron had instructed him, Abraham appealed for an annual royal fund of £3,000 for presents to the Indians of Georgia and South Carolina. On April 26 Bedford wrote similar letters to Heron and Governor Glen informing them that the king had agreed to this proposal. Distribution of these presents was to be entrusted to two agents, one appointed by the Georgia Trustees and the other by the government of South Carolina. The secretary concluded these letters with statements revealing that Bosomworth had succeeded in winning a sympathetic hearing for his sister-in-law's 1747 memorial. Bedford wrote to Glen: "Colonel Heron having transmitted a Petition of Mrs. Bosomworth, of Indian Extraction, and related to some of the Indian Chiefs, His Majesty left it to the Consideration of the Persons who are to distribute the Presents to the Indians, whether it may not be for the Service of His Majesty that some Part of those Presents should be given to her." Finally, in his most stunning coup, Abraham persuaded Bedford to back him for a position that would allow him to play a key role in making that decision. On June 9 Bedford wrote Glen to recommend that Abraham be appointed South Carolina's agent for distributing the presents.[74]

As Abraham prepared to return to America, his reports to his brother on his extraordinary success must have brought joy to the Bosomworth circle, including the couple's Carolina creditors. The struggle, however, had really just begun. The central issue, not yet clearly appreciated in England, was sovereignty over the lands reserved by the Lower Creeks in the 1739 treaty. While the British government was usually willing to negotiate questions of land ownership, British sovereignty over Indian lands was non-negotiable, a sensitive matter to be avoided if at all possible.

After Malatchi's deed of January 4, 1748, this issue was no longer avoidable. The stakes had been raised. It was one thing to have the Bosomworths in 1745 petitioning for a British grant; it was another to have the "Emperor" of the Lower Creek Nation in 1748 proclaiming that, acting in behalf of his people, he had granted various lands to the Bosomworths. The former could be dismissed by British officials and forgotten; the latter were neither dismissible nor forgettable. With the January 4 deed the Bosomworths forced the issue of sovereignty—or, rather, that part of the issue they were comfortable with—into the open. The Bosomworths were now willing to have it known that they now claimed various lands freely given to them by the "Emperor" and other leaders of the Lower Creek Nation. Such news improved their credit rating and helped them line up potential purchasers for prime rice land along the coast. They were not willing, however, to expose their main title deeds—Christie's 1738 minutes and Malatchi's 1748 deed—to inspection by anyone outside their clique.

Thomas Bosomworth was astute enough to recognize that the 1738 and 1748 grants were two-edged weapons, as dangerous as they were promising. The moment they became known in England they became hanging dangerous. Thomas's one slip-up so far, his unguarded encounter with Noble Jones, was about to get him indicted for treason in Savannah. There must be no further slip-ups. Hence copies of the key Indian deeds are conspicuously absent from the bundles of documents the Bosomworths sent to British officials, and no clear reference to them is to be found in any of their numerous memorials. Nevertheless, after January 1748 enough was known about the Creek-Bosomworth deeds to guarantee a major confrontation between the British and Georgia governments on the one hand and the Lower Creeks and the Bosomworth family on the other. The Indians, loudly seconded by the Bosomworths, would insist that as an independent nation they could grant their lands to whomsoever they chose. British and Georgia authorities would insist that no Indian nation within the chartered limits of Georgia could grant territory to any British subjects except the king's authorized agents.

Once the fundamental issue of sovereignty was joined, there was no easy way for either side to back down. The Lower Creeks would find it very difficult to annul their grants to the Bosomworths under British pressure without undercutting what most mattered to them: their claim to be a free and independent nation. The British government was at least as unlikely to acknowledge the legitimacy of the Creek grants, for there was no way to do so without undermining its claims of territorial sovereignty in Georgia and vast other stretches of North America. Thus, by January 1748 it had to be clear to disinterested observers, if any such there were, that the contest would be long and bitter, and that it could only be resolved by a diplomatic accord between the British government and the Lower Creeks. It was also clear that, barring some unimaginable collapse on one side or the other, any arrangement calculated to settle the Bosomworth land claims would have to be an elliptical one that somehow allowed both sides to save face.

CHAPTER SIX

The Bosomworth Ordeal

In October 1748 the treaty of Aix-la-Chapelle ended the war between the European powers. As peace returned to the southern frontier, in November the British government decided upon a drastic reduction of the military establishment in Georgia and South Carolina. Oglethorpe's regiment was to be disbanded, along with the three independent companies. Three new companies, recruited mainly from veterans of the regiment, were to be entrusted with the defense of both colonies. Like the units they replaced, they would be stationed in South Carolina. On May 29, 1749, Colonel Heron reviewed the regiment for the last time in Frederica. Of the 500-odd soldiers, 151 elected to become colonists in Georgia, a few enlisted in the new independent companies, and the rest prepared to return home. On July 7 Heron embarked most of the veterans from Savannah, then departed for Charles Town to command one of the new companies.

The only troops now remaining in Georgia were seven men Heron left on Cumberland Island. The disbanding of the regiment triggered a general exodus from the southern part of the colony, as hundreds of settlers relocated to safer and more promising lands on the Ogeechee and Savannah rivers. Even Major Horton, whose plantation on Jekyll Island had been the most impressive agricultural effort near Frederica, was discouraged. Concluding that "Jekyl Island being at length totally unfit for Cultivation," he sought a gentleman's tract on the Ogeechee. He died shortly afterward, a great loss to the colony. In September, President Stephens and the assistants reported that "there are not above one third of the Freeholders left" in Frederica. The following July the Trustees admitted that there were "few or no Persons now left at St. Simons."[1]

This rapid transformation had at least three major implications for Georgia's Indian relations. Most obviously, the removal of the regiment left the colony more vulnerable to Indian attack than it had been since its earliest days. As Stephens and the assistants noted on September 8, while the troops had been stationed in

Georgia "they were not less a Check on the Indians than on the Spaniards." Second, the focus of Anglo-Indian contacts shifted permanently from the Altamaha to the Savannah River. Third, after sixteen years, authority to deal with the Indians had finally devolved upon the provincial government in Savannah.[2]

The first such task it faced was distribution of the £3,000 in royal presents authorized the previous year for the Indians of Georgia and South Carolina. This project had not been well thought out in London, and implementing it produced dissension every step of the way. Over the strong objections of Oglethorpe, on May 24, 1748, the Trustees urged the Duke of Bedford to see to it that all presents were purchased in England, which he agreed to do. A week later they appointed Stephens to be their agent for distribution of the Georgia presents. Allowing for Stephens's advanced years (he was now seventy-seven), they also named Dr. Patrick Graham "Coadjutor to Mr. Stephens in the said Agency."[3]

On July 1 the Trustees approved instructions to Stephens stating that the presents would all be sent from England apportioned into "equal Quantities" for the two colonies. Stephens was to inform the Indians that such presents were "intended to be renewed annually to them," a major innovation designed to make them more reliable allies. He was to caution them, however, that they must not come down to the colony to take delivery until "due Notices shall be sent them, when Presents for them are ready to be distributed."[4]

South Carolina authorities took no action until Abraham Bosomworth arrived from England in April 1749. He was accompanied by the youngest of the Bosomworth brothers, Adam, who soon set out to join Thomas and Mary in Georgia. With them came the royal presents, packed in separate consignments for the two colonies. It may have been the largest and most diversified array of Indian goods ever sent to either colony; the Georgia portion included 300 guns, 12 "fine guns," 90 half-barrels of gunpowder, and a broad assortment of textiles and metal implements.[5]

Despite the unaccustomed plenty of Indian goods, a committee appointed by the South Carolina assembly to recommend procedure was soon spouting complaints. It judged the value of the presents consigned to South Carolina to be only £1,260 and those allotted to Georgia only £1,120, figures that had to be reduced because some of the goods were "bad in Kind and unfit for Indians." The committee's main complaint was that it would be absurd to allow Georgia officials a predominant role in the distribution of half of the presents. If that were done, it forecast that since Georgia had "little or no Connexion at present with any other Indians but the Creek Nation, almost the full Moiety of all these Presents will probably fall to the Share of that Nation only." In that event other native nations would surely become resentful, a problem that South Carolina would have to face alone. Seizing on the fact that Bedford's letters had not specified that half of the goods were to be delivered to the Georgia agent, the South Carolina government sought to retain control over part of the goods earmarked for Georgia as well as its own share.[6]

On May 9 Patrick Graham arrived in Charles Town to collect the presents consigned to Georgia. When he immediately encountered resistance, Graham resorted to prevarication. In order to make Georgia's need for the Indian goods appear urgent, on May 23 he told Governor Glen and his council that the Creeks "were on their way down to Savannah, upon an Invitation from the magistrates of Georgia, to come and receive Presents sent them by his Majesty." No such invitation had been sent, but Graham's rash words would soon become a major embarrassment for Georgia officials. Unmoved, the Carolinians offered only to allow Graham to "take so much along with him, as would gratify the said Indians." Graham retorted that he would take Georgia's full share or none, and threatened to protest South Carolina's action to London. The threat was more effective than the lie. Realizing that his subordinates were overreaching, on June 1 Glen ordered the entire Georgia consignment released to Graham.[7]

Carolina leaders refused to go along with Bedford's recommendation that Abraham Bosomworth be appointed their sole agent for distribution of the royal gifts in both provinces. On May 31 the assembly committee proposed that John Dart should be the colony's agent for distributing the presents in South Carolina, but that Abraham Bosomworth should be its agent for distributing the Indian goods in Georgia. Whatever difficulties Abraham's participation might cause would thus be confined south of the Savannah River. This recommendation was accepted, and on July 12 Glen finally issued Abraham his commission and instructions.[8]

In late June, transport ships arrived from England to carry the mustered-out troops home, the return voyage expected to begin in three weeks. The Bosomworths had been quietly watching events unfold from their place on St. Catherines Island. A great deal depends on how Thomas Bosomworth's next move is interpreted. On July 1 he set off for his abandoned store at the forks, then proceeded on to Lower Creek country. He was accompanied by his servant Joseph Piercey, who knew enough of the Muskogee language to act as interpreter. Thomas spent a few days at Coweta, then headed for Savannah. With him came Malatchi, two Cussita headmen, and a few other Indians. On July 21 the party arrived at the old Musgrove place and promptly requested a meeting with the Savannah magistrates. Three days later Mary Bosomworth informed President Stephens that "all the Chiefs of the Creek Nation would be here in a few Days." The stage was set for the most famous confrontation in the history of colonial Georgia's Indian relations.[9]

The sudden and totally unexpected appearance of demanding Creeks, with many others on the way, threw Stephens and the assistants into an uproar. By July

24 they were convinced that Thomas Bosomworth had summoned a menacing horde to the gates of Savannah to intimidate them and promote his own foul designs. Thomas had acted "without previous Orders or Authority to bring down such a body of Indians, at a Time when no Provision was made for them." This aggressive move was a patent violation of the 1735 Indian act, Trustee instructions, and the magistrates' own orders. The following day they wrote the Trustees that "near Two hundred of the Creek Indians including their Chiefs are expected here in a few days." Clearly frightened, they charged that the Bosomworths had contrived with Lower Creek leaders a scheme "intended to sap the very Foundation of this colony."[10]

Stephens and the assistants were most alarmed by details Mary gave them. The Indians were looking forward to meeting Abraham Bosomworth, expected at any moment from Charles Town. If he did not bring them a satisfactory answer to their complaints, "they intend in a very absolute and open manner to forbid any of His Majesty's British Subjects to settle in this Colony above the flowing of the Tide." Such an ultimatum would be catastrophic, for "Augusta Ebenezer and some others of our best Settlements must fall a sacrifice." Furthermore, Creek leaders were ready to "insist" that Thomas and Mary's right to the Yamacraw tract and the three islands be recognized, and intended "publickly to possess the Bosomworths" with these lands. In short, now that the colony was "destitute of all Protection," Thomas had mustered his savage friends to force a crisis over land issues and "frighten us into compliance with his unreasonable demands."[11]

Thomas Bosomworth later gave a much different account of his actions. He maintained that the only purpose of his journey to the Chattahoochee was to preserve the peace. He related that when news reached him in late June that the troop transports would sail for England in three weeks, he came to a sudden resolution to book passage with Mary. In England they would further appeal their just claims, and Thomas would defend himself against the magistrates' misguided accusation that "I had Committed an Act of Treason by Purchasing Land from the Indians." He explained that he was entitled to free passage, "having officiated as Chaplain to the Regiment," and had informed Mary of his new plan on June 30. Aware, however, that rumors had been circulating among the Creeks that Mary was to be "sent Home in Irons," he decided that to prevent trouble the Indians had to be assured that Mary was sailing voluntarily. Accordingly, he set off to Creek country "with no other view than to quiet the Minds of the Indians." To accomplish this, he invited Malatchi and the two Cussita headmen, but no others, "to see Mrs. Bosomworth before she went for England." The other Indians who came down to Savannah came because the magistrates had earlier invited them down to receive the royal presents. To prove that such an invitation had been issued, Thomas cited Graham's statement to this effect before the South Carolina governor and council.[12]

Neither interpretation of Thomas's journey is persuasive. In their initial alarm Savannah leaders had leaped to the conclusion that his purpose was to provoke what they most feared: a crisis with the Lower Creeks over land claims. In all probability, as they seem to have realized a few days later, Thomas's original aim was much more limited. His account of his journey is even less credible. Written seven years later, it was obviously fashioned to exculpate himself from serious charges. It was a clever argument, but at odds with the 1749 sources at several key points. Most conspicuously, his contention that it was not he, but the Savannah magistrates, who had invited the Indians to town was an artful lie.

On July 25 Stephens and the assistants reported that Thomas himself "acquaints us that he has engaged the Chiefs of the Creek Nation to follow him who he expects here in Ten or Fourteen days." This account of what Thomas said is secondhand, but there is convincing firsthand testimony to the same effect. Mary Bosomworth was unwittingly the main witness against her husband's later account. In her July 27 letter to the magistrates, she conceded that the Creeks "did not come here at the Invitation of the Publick." Rather, before setting out from Coweta, Malatchi had "ordered all the Heads of the Nation to be down in six Days after him." Three days earlier she told them that Thomas had intended that Malatchi issue such an order: "Mr. Bosomworth hurried up into the Nation to bring Malatchee and other Chiefs, that he could then most conveniently get, to come down with him."[13]

In her July 27 letter Mary said the Indians had come for two reasons: to satisfy themselves that she was not being shipped off against her will, and to meet with Abraham Bosomworth to hear the king's response to their complaints. The first of these alleged motives was the core of the Bosomworths' cover story, but it was also probably genuine, at least for Malatchi and the two chiefs who accompanied him. Thomas and Mary likely did consider a July departure for England, but not very seriously. They surely knew that even the quickest round trip to Coweta would take three weeks and jeopardize a departure with the troopships. In fact, when Thomas and the three chiefs reached Savannah on July 22 the transports had already sailed. But the main reason for doubting the Bosomworths' commitment to that voyage was that from their point of view July 1749 was the wrong time to make it. After years of unsuccessful maneuvering for a substantial British payment to satisfy Mary's ever mounting claims, a golden opportunity to realize this priority goal now beckoned in Savannah.[14]

The Bosomworths knew that the royal presents had arrived in Savannah the first week in June, that the Duke of Bedford had left it up to two agents to decide whether some portion of them ought to be given to Mary, and that at Bedford's recommendation Abraham Bosomworth would probably be named agent for South Carolina. Thus primed, as soon as Thomas returned to Savannah he sent Adam to fetch Abraham from Charles Town. Meanwhile, the Bosomworths' South Carolina creditors were closing in on them and they were in danger of losing everything they still had. This could hardly have failed to focus their attention on gaining a major share of the Indian presents. On September 8 Stephens and the assistants wrote that Thomas had "reported to some of us that he expected near one half of the presents sent for the Indians." They added that "he wrote to the same purpose to some of his Creditors at whose Suits he was then under arrest," but that even half of the presents would not have covered his debts. Thomas later denied writing such letters, but conceded the rest by vowing to "Prove by the most Authentic Testimony that it was his Majesty's gracious Intention Mrs. Bosomworth should receive a Moiety of these Presents."[15]

The only thing that appeared to stand between the Bosomworths and a £600 windfall in July 1749 was the consent of the Georgia agent for the presents. Only if and when the goods were distributed to the satisfaction of Thomas and Mary would they have been likely to consider pressing their land claims. It was just possible that this might be done at the very end of the meeting between the magistrates and the chiefs, but this would have been very difficult to arrange. Colonial authorities normally distributed presents to Indians only after they were sure that substantive discussions had concluded. The fact that President Stephens was the Georgia agent was a serious obstacle to the Bosomworths' scheme, for he had long been their chief adversary. Yet the old man was now frail and weak, and perhaps more vulnerable to pressure than he had been in the past.

The main motive of Thomas's swift ride to Coweta was almost certainly to marshal that pressure. Piercey later swore that Thomas had nothing to say to the Indians except to inform them that he and his wife would soon depart for England, and that Mary would welcome a visit from Malatchi "or some of her Relations" before they sailed. Nevertheless, it seems certain that Thomas conveyed at least two other pieces of information to the Lower Creeks. First, he informed them that his brother Abraham, their agent to the king, was expected shortly in Savannah with His Majesty's reply. The Lower Creeks who came to town in July came anticipating a meeting with Abraham. Second, Thomas surely mentioned that the presents they had so long hoped for had at last arrived in Savannah. Piercey referred to the main body of Creek visitors as "the Indians that came for presents."[16]

Whatever their reasons, Malatchi and the other headmen who came to Savannah obviously believed that an important meeting was in the offing. Having recently received an invitation from Governor Glen to attend a formal conference in Charles Town in late August, they had declined specifically in order to go to Savannah instead. Even more remarkably, the three chiefs who accompanied

Thomas to Savannah and other early arrivals had chosen to absent themselves from the main occasion on the Creek calendar, the annual busk ceremonies.[17]

The presence of a large assembly of expectant Lower Creeks in and around Savannah was bound to affect the still incomplete plans for distribution of the presents, if only to force quicker action. With the Indians' impatience and expenses for entertaining them mounting, when Abraham Bosomworth appeared to make his predictable recommendation that Mary receive a large share of the presents, Stephens would find it very difficult to refuse. Moreover, the Bosomworths had good reason to suppose that the Indians would actively support them.

The company of natives who arrived at the old Musgrove place in late July came almost entirely from two Lower Creek towns, Coweta and Cussita. It was thus weighted in favor of Mary's relatives and friends. Furthermore, the urgency of the situation and the lack of traders nearby would likely compel the magistrates to employ as interpreter the only well-qualified local resident; her name was Mary Bosomworth. Finally, Abraham's reunion with the Creeks in Savannah promised to be a triumphal one. The Bosomworths could plausibly claim to the Indians that it was brother Abraham's dedicated efforts in their behalf that had opened the royal purse to them. In gratitude to their benefactors, Creek leaders could be expected to strongly support the Bosomworths' claims for a suitable reward. It was a well-laid plan.[18]

For the first few days after Thomas arrived with Malatchi, Stephens and the assistants were obliged to communicate with the headmen through Mary. On July 25, however, they unanimously decided that "the first and most expedient Step was, to get a good Interpreter; former experience having convinced them, that no trust can be given to Mrs. Bosomworth in an Affair concerning the Interest of herself and Family." They believed none was to be found "nearer than Augusta or Charles Town." The following day, "just as we were sending Messengers to Charles-Town and Augusta for an Interpreter, Providence provided us with one." John Kenard, the Augusta trader they had hoped to recruit, and "the second best Interpreter in the Nation," unexpectedly appeared in Savannah and agreed to take the job.[19]

On July 27 Stephens received a letter from Mary announcing the imminent arrival of "all the Heads of the Nation" and setting forth the Bosomworth version of their reasons for coming. She went on to convey Malatchi's complaint that he and his companions had yet to be welcomed, a discourtesy Indians never inflicted upon unexpected guests. On the advice of the assistants, Stephens responded with an invitation to Malatchi and the two Cussita chiefs to dine at his house the next day. The dinner was congenial, but no serious business was conducted then or for the next ten days.[20]

The Georgia leaders were determined to proceed with extreme caution and evidently resigned to await the appearance of Abraham Bosomworth. On August 4 Adam Bosomworth arrived from Charles Town and told them his brother would follow the next day. More to their liking, the Creek company was swelled by the arrival of twenty-odd Indians led by a mixed-blood chief known to the English as Captain Allick. The newcomers were apparently a disaffected element from Cussita, where Captain Allick had recently been ousted as leading chief. It would now be more difficult for Creek leaders to present a united front to the Georgians.[21]

On August 7 Abraham Bosomworth still had not appeared. Out at the old Musgrove place, Creek leaders began "to behave very clamorous, demanding large quantities of Provisions, and other things not less expensive." Since the magistrates found themselves reacting to the visitors "hourly," they decided to "postpone all other business" and concluded that a conference could no longer be postponed. Kenard was dispatched to invite the chiefs down to Savannah on Friday, August 11. He was expected to detain them where they were until Friday morning, when boats would be provided to carry them down the river. As soon as Thomas Bosomworth learned of this, on August 9, he sent his own boats for the Indians, doubtless counting on them to reckon this as one more of his favors. The last party "came down the River in the middle of the Night, Fireing their Guns all the way." Although the magistrates surely knew that Indians often fired such volleys as salutes, in their anxious state they interpreted the Creeks' behavior as "menacing and insulting."[22]

While most of the headmen who came down the river camped on the Yamacraw tract, Malatchi and Estepoyichi (the Cussita *mico*) stayed with the Bosomworths in their Savannah house. On Thursday Stephens and the assistants revised their plans for the meeting. Kenard was now to inform the Indians that the Savannah militia would receive them Friday morning "on their own Lands at the place where Musgrove formerly lived," then escort them into town. It was also ordered that the path from the Yamacraw tract into town should be cleared of brush "for their better accomodation." Before the work could begin, the Bosomworths sent one of their Indian slaves to forbid it. He warned the workers that "they must not cut over his Master Mr. Bosomworth's Line." When the magistrates ordered the work detail to ignore this warning and proceed, all three Bosomworths and a party of Indians headed by Malatchi confronted the workers on the path. "Mrs. Bosomworth then repeatedly threatned them at their Peril to go any farther, and immediately the Indians seized their Tools, and carried them without their Line, and threw them down."[23]

A great and now familiar issue lurked beneath this game of bluff: ownership of the Yamacraw tract and by implication all of the coastal lands reserved under the 1739 treaty. Stephens and the assistants maintained that the Yamacraw tract still belonged to the Lower Creeks, but the Bosomworths insisted that it belonged to them. The Georgia authorities had provoked the incident, surely deliberately. By doing so they had ensured that the talks about to begin would deal to some extent with the land question, an unwelcome development to the Bosomworths. Two days later one of the chiefs, as quoted by Thomas, declared that "he could not understand what the Gentlemen [magistrates] Meant by troubling themselves so much about the Indian Lands." Though they did not dare to press the issue, the magistrates obviously hoped to maneuver the Creeks into disavowing their grants to the Bosomworths. That evening they invited the chiefs (but not the Bosomworths) to a supper. They used the occasion to attempt to persuade the Indian leaders that they had been "misled" by the Bosomworths on the land question, and claimed some success.[24]

On August 11 the formal meeting finally got under way. That morning Noble Jones as commander of the militia headed a troop of horse to the Yamacraw tract to escort the Indians into town. At the head of the Indian procession (or, as he later maintained, at the rear of the English) marched Thomas Bosomworth "in his Canonical Habit," along with his wife, brother Adam, and Malatchi. When the procession reached town, a fifteen-cannon salute was fired and the Indians were conducted to President Stephens's house. Stephens presided over the welcoming ceremonies, but his infirmities forced him to relinquish direction of the British negotiating effort to Assistant Henry Parker. After the magistrates made it clear to the Bosomworth brothers that this welcome did not include them, they were obliged to withdraw. Pipes and glasses were then handed around, and the talks began—very slowly.[25]

If this had been an ordinary meeting between British and Indian negotiators, the hosts would have delivered an opening speech that outlined an agenda. The Georgia leaders declined to behave in the ordinary way. Instead, they invited Malatchi to deliver the opening speech. The magistrates' passive stance was probably adopted partly as a reminder that they had not agreed in advance to this conference and were participating against their will. More importantly, it appears to have been part of a deliberately defensive negotiating strategy. Unsure of what the Indians were up to, the magistrates evidently planned to draw the chiefs out with leading questions, watching for opportunities to discredit the Bosomworths. But if the colonial leaders for once chose to play the reactive role usually left to Indians, the Creeks did not readily yield it. When called upon to make an opening statement, Malatchi responded that "they had no Talk to deliver, untill they saw Abraham Bosomworth, and knew what he brought from the great King in answer to a Talk, they had Sent by him." With both sides reluctant to say the first words in hopes of having the last, the talks seemed about to sputter out.

Then one of the Savannah leaders asked Malatchi "what induced him to come down unsent for," and words were soon flying. The Creek leader replied that it was to assure himself that Mary was not being sent to England as a prisoner, but if she was, to free her. The magistrates countered that "no such design was known here, but if She had done any thing to deserve it, as we looked upon her as a Subject of the King of Great Britain, we should tie her, and send her home without asking their Liberty." Ignoring this challenge, Malatchi then raised an issue of more immediate concern to the Bosomworths: the exclusion of Mary as interpreter. He now demanded that she alone "was to give and receive all Talks from them and us." When the magistrates brushed this aside, Mary could endure it no longer and seized the floor. Denied the role of interpreter, she now demanded recognition as the principal Indian negotiator. She was, she declared, "Empress and Queen of the Upper and Lower Creeks," and as such "could command every Man to follow her." The tension thickened when Malatchi appeared to endorse her claim.

It seems clear that Mary would never have made this extraordinary declaration had she been accepted as interpreter. Her outburst appears to have been an impulsive effort to claim a central role for herself in the conference. Although Malatchi was obviously on their side, the Bosomworths evidently had little confidence in him and regarded Mary's active participation in the talks as crucial to a favorable outcome. Not entirely surprised at Mary's new pretensions, the magistrates sought to draw her in deeper by asking her if she were not a subject of King George. Mary obliged them by replying that "She owed him no Allegiance otherwise, than in Alliance, being herself a Sovereign."

With these ill-considered words Mary put the entire Bosomworth cause in jeopardy. Mary's pretensions to sovereign and even imperial rank could only hurt her standing with British officials and might well do the same with jealous Creek chiefs. Unless the Creek leadership solidly supported her claims, Mary would be branded an imposter and left looking foolish. The magistrates must have quickly realized that she had handed them a likely tool to separate the Bosomworths from both the English and the Indians. After trading a few more barbs, supper was served, but Mary stalked out with Malatchi and five other chiefs.

Troubles resumed late that afternoon when the nervous townspeople were alarmed by a procession of Creeks marching through town to the beat of a drum. Rushing to the scene, the magistrates immediately arrested Adam Bosomworth and Joseph Piercey, who had accompanied the marchers. They then persuaded the Indians to retire to Stephens's house "to drink a Glass of Wine, and talk the Affair over." Barely arrived there, Mary stormed in "like a Mad and Frantick Woman." In her frustration she again let her tongue get away from her: "You talk of your White Town, your General and his Treaties, a fig for your General, you have not a Foot of Land in the Colony, and Stamping with her Foot on the Ground impudently said, That very Ground was hers." The Savannah leaders charged that she went so far as "to threaten the Lives of some of the Magistrates, and the destruction of the Colony."

Mary was briefly confined, then returned to Stephens's house where she and the Indians received some "very Sharp Talk" about their "unsufferable Behaviour." Malatchi then pleaded for Adam's release, explaining that "He had drawn him into this Scrape." This was agreed to on condition that Thomas be responsible for Mary and Adam's attendance at the next meeting with the Creeks at 8:00 the following morning. When Thomas appeared that evening he must have been shocked to discover how badly things had gone the first day. According to the magistrates, he "with Tears condemned his Wife's and Brother's conduct," begged for favor, and promised to have them appear the next morning. Thomas later acknowledged the promise, but denied the rest. If he did shed tears, they were probably tears of frustration over the way his wife and brother had disfigured a beautiful plan. Before they dispersed for the night, Parker could not resist asking, first the Indians, then Mary, "whether Mrs. Bosomworth was an Indian or a White Person?" When both the headmen and Mary replied that she was an Indian, Parker shot back: "Madam if I had told you so, you would have spit in my face."[26]

Thomas Bosomworth probably slept little that night trying to figure out how to salvage something from the talks that had seemed so promising until they had begun. At 8:00 the next morning—Saturday, August 12—he sent a message to the magistrates that "the Indian Chiefs were all Drunk, and could not attend." After the board again summoned all three Bosomworths, Mary and Adam appeared and seemed apologetic over their behavior the day before. They also made excuses for the absent Thomas, who the magistrates believed was also nursing a hangover. Actually, Thomas was busy that morning preparing a document purporting to validate another major Creek concession to his spouse. Two objectives seem to have guided this effort. First, Mary had rashly claimed to be Empress and Queen of the Creeks, words that would have to be eaten unless supported by the Creek leadership. The document went some way toward supplying such an endorsement. Second, Abraham's continued absence and Mary's exclusion as interpreter meant that no Bosomworth was in a position to participate directly in the talks. The document aimed to rectify that too.

The freshly drafted instrument was dated August 12 and purported to represent the will of Malatchi and nine other Lower Creek chiefs. According to this document, these leaders insisted on Mary's identity as a Creek Indian, referring to her has "our beloved Woman Cowsaponckesa alias Mary Bosomworth." (This is the first invocation of Mary's native name in the record.) The headmen proceeded to support Mary's claim of Creek royalty by recognizing her as "the Rightfull and Natural Princess of the said upper and lower Creek nations." Finally, and most important, the document granted her exclusive authority to negotiate with the British on all matters related to "Lands Territories dignities or Royalties." Although this authorization explicitly anticipated that Mary would go to England to confer with the king or his principal officers, it implicitly applied to any such negotiations in Georgia. The document clearly was not intended solely for use on the other side of "the Great Water," for it served notice to officials "on this side" of Mary's new role, and five days later it was formally presented to the Savannah magistrates. Thus the immediate message was unmistakable: if Stephens and the assistants wished to talk to the Creeks about lands, they would have to speak with Princess Cowsaponckesa.[27]

This hastily composed document was below Thomas Bosomworth's usual standard, for at key points it was difficult to reconcile with obvious facts. It was most vulnerable in its claim to represent the judgment of both the Upper and Lower Creeks: no Upper Creeks were present, and Lower Creek leaders had rarely presumed to speak for them. Even a more modest claim that the document reflected the will of the Lower Creeks would have been suspect. So far as the magistrates were aware, the visiting headmen came entirely from Coweta and Cussita. Furthermore, any document dated August 12 could not readily be accepted in Savannah as a product of the sober judgment of the Creek leaders, for Thomas himself had reported that they were too drunk that morning to meet. Finally, the new grant of authority to "Princess" Mary was in direct conflict with the similar grant to "Prince" Malatchi a year and a half earlier.[28]

That afternoon Stephens and the assistants held informal talks with "some of the soberest and leading Men of the Chiefs." The Bosomworths did not keep their promise to attend. Malatchi too, complaining that "his Head Ached," at first refused to participate, but a threat to arrest the Bosomworths if he did not soon brought him. The magistrates received him by avowing their suspicion that "He had two Tongues" and was "closely attached to the French Interest, notwithstanding his pretended Friendship to the English." Malatchi's professions to the contrary were allowed to pass without further comment, but were not believed.[29]

The Savannah leaders were now ready to discuss the presents. They began with another leading question designed to plant a wedge between the Creeks and the Bosomworths. The Indians were asked "if they were willing to receive only two Blankets and let Bosomworth have the third, and so in proportion of all that the Great King had sent them?" Evidently it was at this moment that the Creek chiefs learned from the magistrates, as they had not from the Bosomworths, that any reward Thomas and Mary received would be subtracted from the presents that otherwise would go entirely to them. They answered as the Savannah leaders had anticipated: "they declared No." Pressing their advantage, the magistrates assured the chiefs that they were the real guardians of Creek rights: "it was their Duty to protect the Indians in their rights to these Presents." Artfully, they added "and likewise to their Lands, which Bosomworth pretended to claim."[30]

With their loaded question on possible sharing of the presents, the Savannah leaders had scored their most telling point. The Creek chiefs now realized that Thomas and Mary had not been completely open with them, and that they stood to lose if the Bosomworth claims for compensation were met. According to the magistrates, the headmen now acknowledged "how much they had been imposed on," and even Malatchi admitted that "the Bosomworths deceived him." The Savannah leaders were so pleased with this session that Stephens closed it with a promise that the Lower Creek presents would be delivered early the following week.[31]

On Tuesday, August 15, Stephens and the assistants resolved to go ahead with the allocation of the presents before the chiefs had second thoughts about cutting the Bosomworths in. Abraham Bosomworth had still not appeared. The magistrates now decided to make "a proportionable division of all the Presents, and deliver a proper share of them to these Indians." The shares allocated to Coweta and Cussita would be distributed forthwith, while similar shares would be reserved for the other Lower Creek towns, the Upper Creek towns, and some of the Chickasaws and Choctaws. The Cherokees were left entirely for South Carolina. Patrick Graham spent the next day and a half on this task of apportionment, and on Wednesday the Lower Creek leaders in town were informed that their presents would be delivered that afternoon.[32]

Wednesday, August 16, loomed as a day of disaster for the Bosomworths. Unless Abraham Bosomworth suddenly arrived on the scene, it was clear that a major portion of the presents would be distributed, the rest committed, and Thomas and Mary would receive little or nothing. When Abraham still failed to appear, through Malatchi the Bosomworths attempted a last-ditch diversion designed to force further consideration of Mary's claims and postpone the distribution a little longer.

That afternoon the visiting Creek men, over seventy in all, were escorted to the courthouse for delivery of the presents. Malatchi immediately arose and delivered a long harangue. According to the magistrates, he proclaimed that Mary was "the Queen and Head of their Nation," that it was she who had given the English "liberty to Settle" in Georgia, that "the Lands they now lived on were held under her," and that the same would be true for any additional lands they acquired. Malatchi then produced the August 12 document, still unsigned, and gave it to Henry Parker, who was presiding. When Recorder Charles Watson read it aloud, the English reacted "with Abhorrence and Astonishment, and especially that any

Brittish Subject could be capable of being the Author." According to Adam Bosomworth, Kenard asked various Indians whether they owned this document as accurate and their own, and all affirmed that it was both. The chiefs then asked to "sign and deliver the said Instrument of writeing in Public court," but Parker "absolutely denyed" this request.[33]

The magistrates believed that of the nine chiefs named in the document, only Malatchi and one other were present, but they chose not to make that an issue. What they found most abhorrent about the document was the purported grant to Mary of authority to negotiate in behalf of the Lower Creeks "on this side" of the ocean. Casting about for the quickest way to dispatch it, they at first considered confiscation. They decided, however, that "if it had been kept, it would have been a sufficient reason for them [the Indians] to imagine, it was Approved of." So instead they returned it to Malatchi, who said he would "return it to the Person he Had it from." Thomas later acknowledged that "Malatchi returned the Paper to Mrs. Bosomworth."[34]

The Savannah leaders answered Malatchi's provocative speech with one of their own. They charged that, far from being a Creek princess, Mary was "a Daughter of a Woman of the Tuckabachee Town (of no Note or Family) by a White Man." Mary did have relatives in Tuckabatchee, but they were wrong about her mother. Thomas later happily observed that "Every Indian in the Nation, knew of what Family she was, much better than the Gentlemen did," so that their wild charge had the effect of "disgusting the Indians." The magistrates then argued that it was only Oglethorpe's patronage that "made her the Woman she now appears to be." As for Thomas, he was simply a cunning fortune hunter, now a desperate one, and they went on to explain his troubles with his Carolina creditors. Thomas was present with a law officer, apparently from South Carolina, at his side. Relishing his predicament, the town leaders called the Indians' attention to it: "He was now tied, (meaning a Prisoner) and they might themselves see, He had a White Man to take care of him." It was to evade imprisonment for his debts that Thomas had hatched a scheme to defraud the Indians of a large part of the presents the king had sent them.[35]

The magistrates then demanded a formal answer to the pivotal question: Were they willing for Thomas Bosomworth to receive a share of the presents? "They all answered No, that he should have none of theirs." Malatchi did not join this chorus, but became "so angry as to foam at his Mouth." When he ordered his people to leave the courthouse, but "only the Young Men obeyed," he was finally humiliated into compliance and professions of friendship. At this point the Savannah leaders demanded that he prove his friendship by surrendering the instrument of August 12 to be publicly burned. Malatchi declined on the ground that this would be discourteous to its author. "He was then told, that the White People looked upon that Paper, to be of no more consequence, than that He now saw burnt before them (a piece of Paper being then burnt)." According to the magistrates, Malatchi responded that "he looked upon it as the same."

Savannah leaders believed that Malatchi was now almost alone in willingness to divert a share of the presents to the Bosomworths. Lest he recover from the rout he had just suffered, they decided to proceed immediately with the distribution of the presents. The goods allocated to the men of Coweta and Cussita were then brought in and delivered to the chiefs "in the most Publick and Shewey Manner." Malatchi, his good humor restored, then suggested that presents for the women and young people be delivered the next day, and that the leaders of the two sides spend the evening together "in Mirth." This was readily agreed to.[36]

There was no mirth in the Bosomworth household that day, for their scheme to secure part of the presents now lay in ruins. That evening the magistrates and the Creek headmen met at a tavern in a mood of celebration. At Malatchi's request, they had just joined hands in a circle symbolic of peace and friendship when Mary burst into the room. She arrived "in the most violent outrageous and unseemly manner, that a Woman Spirited up with Liquor, Drunk with passion, and disappointed in her Views could be guilty of." In her fury she proclaimed that "She was Empress and Queen of the Upper and Lower Creeks, Yea, went so far in her imaginary Sovereignty, as to call herself King, and that She could command every Man in those Nations to follow her, and We should soon know it to our Cost." Provoked, the Savannah leaders ordered her to go home or face detention. At this Malatchi sprang to Mary's defense, declaring that if the magistrates tied her, "He would untie her." Accepting the challenge, the town leaders had Mary seized and confined. Malatchi again lost face with the other headmen, who "one after another" privately told Savannah officials that "they were ashamed of his Behaviour." The magistrates were now pretty confident that the Bosomworth-brewed "Poison has only been swallowed by their Tool Malatchee and another Chief," probably the Cussita *mico*.[37]

As Mary was being led away, Thomas appeared and took his turn at venting bitter frustration. After assailing the magistrates with a stream of oaths and curses, he calmed down enough to acknowledge that his wife had been guilty of "ill conduct." Nevertheless, he "endeavoured to justifye and support her pretended Rights" and vowed to "spend the last drop of his Blood" defending them. Most revealingly, his despair overcame his usual reluctance to identify the villain he believed responsible for the injustices Mary had suffered, "Swearing by G_d that General Oglethorpe had ruined her."[38]

The following afternoon Thomas appeared before the Savannah authorities at his own request. He came to plead for leniency. Apologizing for Mary's and his own recent excesses, he "burst into a flood of Tears" and promised that they would behave differently in the future if their errors were overlooked. Mary was then brought in and gave similar assurances. Hopeful that they had an opportunity to end the Bosomworth problem once and for all, the magistrates demanded that Thomas publicly express the same sentiments before the Creek leaders. He agreed to do so.

An hour later Stephens and the assistants met the Indians in the courthouse. There Thomas kept his word. He censured Mary's recent behavior and said she deserved her confinement. Then, in what must have been the most galling part of the price the magistrates exacted from him, he went on to renounce any claim that Mary might have to participate in future negotiations. From now on, the Creeks "must deliver their Talk to the Beloved Man (pointing to the President) and his Beloved Men, and receive all Talks from them, and to have no regard to what Mrs. Bosomworth said for the future, except She spoke from them." After Thomas's speech was translated, the Indians "declared they were well satisfied . . . desiring this Talk might be for Ever dropped." Thomas later admitted the tears, but charged that the magistrates had misrepresented his concessions, which were invalid anyway because "extorted." Moreover, he had only submitted to this oppression "to quiet the Minds of the Indians who were now discovered to be so enraged that they had determined to send forward their Women and Children and fall on the Town."[39]

During the Savannah confrontation, both sides had at least some inside information on the other's tactics. The magistrates related that throughout the meetings Captain Allick behaved as "a Friend of the English, and has, during this whole Affair, distinguished himself as such by discoverying the intrigues of the Bosomworths with Malatchee." Probably aware of Allick's role as stool pigeon, Malatchi refused to cut him and his followers in on the presents. When Allick complained to the magistrates, after Malatchi's party was safely gone they made a separate allocation "to Ellick and Landlord Two Headmen of the Cussitaws." Thomas Bosomworth later denounced Allick repeatedly.[40]

Charles Watson passed intelligence in the opposite direction. A year and a half later, President Parker and the assistants charged that Watson was in the "Interest" of the Bosomworths, "having formerly publickly supported this Cause." Soon afterward Thomas deposed that "some days before" the Savannah altercation Watson wrote him that the town leaders "were Predetermined to find some pretext to lay this Deponent and his wife in Custody." He advised Thomas "to Comply with the request of the said Magistrates whatever, . . . as the only means to preserve his Liberty." Thomas implied that it was this warning that later led him to submit to public humiliation. Watson asked Thomas to "burn the letter as soon as perused," which he did. On August 12, during Mary's eruption at Stephens's house, Watson came to warn Thomas that things were not going well and that he should come at once—timely advice that prevented a worse outcome. According to Thomas, Watson came "as a Friend (Not by orders of the Board)."[41]

After the rest of the presents were distributed, tension gave way to outwardly amicable socializing. The meeting finally broke up on August 18. The Indians requested boats to carry them and their now considerable baggage up the river, and "as their absence was very agreeable," the magistrates readily complied. By 11:00 the next morning most had departed. Three hours later, Abraham Bosomworth at last arrived from Charles Town.

The Savannah authorities were certain that their first conference with Indians had been a huge success. Careful management had turned a sudden menace into a decisive triumph over the Bosomworths and the limited group of Creek leaders they could influence. In their September 8 report on the meeting, the magistrates were confident that the "monstrous conduct" of an "Ambitious dissolute and avaricious Family" had been exposed for what it was. The mastermind of this evil scheme, Thomas, had designed it to support "his extravagant and voluptuous way of Life." Their countereffort began with the premise that, unless the Bosomworths were "discountenanced from having the least concern with the Indians, We can expect no settled peace with them." Accordingly, they had spared no pains to isolate the Bosomworths by opening a rift between them and the Creek chiefs, and had succeeded. The Georgia leaders acknowledged that their tactics had "offended" Malatchi, but they did not believe he had sufficient influence to threaten the colony. In general, relations with the Lower Creeks, though still strained, seemed to be on a better footing than at any time since Oglethorpe's departure.[42]

For the Creeks the results of the conference were mixed. They had received the windfall of presents that had brought most of them down in the first place. They had also received a promise that this largesse would be renewed annually (a promise that would not be kept). In addition, they had been given solemn assurances that the lands they had reserved under the 1739 treaty would continue to be respected as their own.[43]

If renewed promises to respect their lands pleased some of the headmen, Malatchi and several others must have regarded it as doubletalk. The disgruntled chiefs assumed that since the lands in question belonged to them, they could do with them as they pleased and, if they wished, convey them to whomsoever they chose. As one of them is supposed to have said about the disputed lands: "surely they could do what they would with them, without being Directed by the White People, who knew that the Indians had given those Lands to Mrs. Bosomworth and her Husband."[44]

Many of the Creeks probably left Savannah unhappy over their failure to aid their kinswoman in her quest for a just reward. Most of them were probably distressed over the demonstrated inadequacy of their own leadership. Malatchi had not proven to be a leader with political skill, firm resolve, or great influence over other chiefs. One of the headmen, probably Captain Allick, had even ridiculed him to the magistrates: "His Heart is like the Wind, or rather that He had no Heart at all." Many others probably resented the lack of respect the Georgia leaders had shown them. A year later a Bosomworth-inspired document has the Lower Creek chiefs complaining that the magistrates, "who refused to hear our Talk, called us a parcell of old Women." Finally, the division that had developed among the Creek leaders during the meetings had enabled the magistrates to manipulate them.[45]

For the Bosomworths the conference had been an unmitigated disaster. The reasons were many: cousin Malatchi and brother Abraham had let them down, Mary had not been able to control her temper, and Captain Allick's party had compromised support from the Indians. Perhaps most important, they had underestimated the magistrates. Various efforts to place Mary at the center of the talks had backfired, and she wound up entirely excluded from the negotiating process. Her extraordinary claims of authority and influence had been followed by impotence and isolation, memorably climaxed by Thomas's public humiliation before both Georgia and Creek leaders. The Bosomworth land claims also depreciated badly. The Creek chiefs had not provided the insistent support that alone might have forced Savannah leaders to seek some sort of accommodation. The magistrates later said that Thomas even "promised to take the Cattle off" the islands. Finally, the Bosomworths' scheme to restore their financial position with a major share of the Indian presents sank like a stone. Thomas left town even before his brother arrived and went to Charles Town, where he was promptly arrested for his debts.[46]

When Abraham Bosomworth arrived on August 19 he sought out President Stephens and presented his credentials as South Carolina's agent to distribute the royal presents in Georgia. He was in a hurry, telling Stephens he had to be back in Charles Town on August 25. When the magistrates next met on August 22, Stephens informed the others that Abraham "had been very Urging and pressing with him" to deal immediately with the article in his instructions that concerned his sister-in-law," but ignored the rest, "whereby it too evidently appeared, that his Views in coming here, were only to serve his own Family." After considering this and a piteous letter from the imprisoned Thomas, the magistrates decided upon an ambiguous response to Mary's claim to a share of the presents. Stephens was advised to withhold all remaining presents from the Bosomworths, but "not to give them a determinate Answer, least it might drive them to some desperate Act, and to inform them, that when their future Behaviour should recommend them, due Notice would be taken of it."[47]

The following day, Abraham proposed that Mary should at least be given a share of the presents sufficient to "enable her to carry on a Trade at the Forks for her future Support." In reply, the magistrates first recounted the recent behavior of Mary and Thomas, denouncing it as "inconsistent with their duty to his Majesty." Significantly, the Savannah authorities thus refused to accept Mary's impulsive renunciation of her British allegiance. They concluded by conveying the ambiguous answer they had settled on the day before. Abraham made no effort to justify the late conduct of his kin, saw that his appeal was hopeless, and promptly returned to Charles Town.[48]

Malatchi and his followers had come to Savannah rather than attend a conference in Charles Town scheduled for late August. Governor Glen had planned to meet with both Creeks and Cherokees in hopes of brokering a permanent peace between them. Although Malatchi and other Lower Creek leaders had told Glen that their business in Georgia made it impossible for them to attend, they had also "promised to agree to every thing done in Charles Town." After leaving Savannah nearly all of the Lower Creek leaders headed home. Captain Allick, however, went to Charles Town to participate in the conference. Glen was disappointed that only a handful of Lower Creeks showed up, but he went ahead with the meeting in early September. The result was a tenuous peace agreement between the Cherokee delegation and a mainly Upper Creek delegation headed by the Wolf King. In the event that the peace was violated, both parties agreed that the Carolina governor should punish the aggressor with a trade embargo.[49]

On August 31 Savannah leaders made plans to distribute presents to the Lower Creek towns that had been entirely or almost entirely unrepresented at the just-concluded talks: the Hitchiti-speaking towns. Stephens opened the meeting by announcing that his deteriorating condition obliged him to relinquish his agency to his coadjutor, Patrick Graham. When Graham requested advice, his colleagues recommended that he employ interpreter Kenard for a special mission to the hitherto unrewarded towns. Kenard should personally invite their headmen down to receive their presents, and then escort them to Savannah. And so it was decided.[50]

Earlier reports that many Creeks had left Savannah discontented were confirmed on September 6, when a party of Ouseechees arrived. There were twenty of them, led by "Stinlapoegee King of Oseechees." They apparently had come down in response to Malatchi's original call, but had participated in the annual busk ceremonies before setting out for Savannah. The following day they met with the magistrates at Stephens's house. The Ouseechees reported that on the path they had met Malatchi's company making its way home. Malatchi "gave them a bad Talk, and would have turned them back." Other chiefs in his party, however, said "the whole Uneasiness proceeded from Mary and Melatchee, and advised them to proceed here."

Although it had been chiefs from the Hitchiti-speaking towns who had made the original grant to Mary, they were now unwilling to follow Malatchi in giving unqualified support to that and related grants. On the recent altercation, Ouseechee leaders gratified the magistrates by declaring that "all the Indians were obliged to Us for preserving their Properties to their Lands" and that Malatchi "had no superior Right to them or any other Chiefs in the Nation to give away their Lands." As proof of their feeling on this score, they even offered to destroy the cattle the Bosomworths had stocked on the islands. The meeting concluded cordially two days later when the Ouseechees received their share of the presents and their chiefs dined with the magistrates at Stephens's house.[51]

On November 12 Kenard returned from Lower Creek country with ninety Indians from most of the towns yet to receive their presents. He reported that Malatchi had created "great Difficulty" for him. The Coweta leader had issued dark warnings that "the white People wanted to make War with them," and the Indians were sufficiently agitated to alarm the traders. Kenard went on to relate that his mission had been saved by Wioffki, the Long Warrior of Oconee. "It was entirely through his influence," said Kenard, that he had been able to persuade these Indians to disregard Malatchi and set off for Savannah.[52]

Wioffki also acted as "the Mouth of the whole" when this party met with the magistrates on November 18. He expressed "great Satisfaction" at the reception accorded his people, and denounced Malatchi's recent pronouncements as "Lies." The Savannah authorities were much taken with him, so much so that they evidently schemed to set him up in Malatchi's place. According to Thomas Bosomworth, they offered him a commission "to command the whole Nation, and told him that all Talks concerning the English should be sent to him for he (Malatchi) was a French Man and did not love the English." Wioffki was a formidable leader, and would later become "Chief King of the Siminoles." If Thomas's charge was true, Wioffki refused to go along. The Indians, eager to return for their autumn hunts, received their presents that very day and soon departed. Only one of the Lower Creek towns had yet to receive its presents.[53]

After his ignominious exit from Savannah, Thomas Bosomworth spent the next four months in Charles Town licking his wounds and extricating himself from his legal difficulties. No doubt his brother helped him, for in November Abraham married a wealthy woman. In December the Georgia leaders learned that they had not heard the last of the Bosomworth land claims. Savannah residents again had been cutting timber on the Yamacraw tract, and some had justified their activity "by virtue of Leases from Mr. Thomas Bosomworth." Unlike their passivity in 1746, the magistrates immediately put a stop to this poaching. The difference was that the current activity implied a Bosomworth title to the tract. Confronted with this harbinger of vexations to come, the magistrates must have cursed their failure to compel Thomas to renounce his land claims when they had the chance.[54]

Three weeks later, Abraham returned to Savannah. Since Stephens and the assistants had not foreclosed the possibility that Mary might yet be rewarded out of the remaining presents, he had come to make one last appeal. On January 5, 1750, he presented the Georgia leaders with a memorial which assured them that Mary was now "extremely sorry" for her recent "imprudent Conduct" and was ready to do whatever she could for the welfare of the province. She had changed her ways, as the magistrates had demanded, and was in urgent need. He concluded by proposing that she be allowed a share of the presents. If this were done promptly, he said, "She will proceed directly for the Forks to be in Time for the Indians Winter Hunt."[55]

The answer the magistrates gave Abraham on January 13 showed that Thomas's renewed pretension to the Yamacraw tract was much on their minds. After reviewing the Bosomworth activities over the past six months in detail, they declared that they were not satisfied that Thomas and Mary "were yet sensible of their Errors." Therefore no presents would be given to Mary. The town leaders then spelled out what the Bosomworths might have done, and still could do, to effect a different outcome. If Thomas and Mary provided the board with "an indisputable Satisfaction; That they had relinquished all their idle Claims of Lands and Sovereignty and that they would behave for the future as loyal Subjects to his Majesty of Great Britain; They might expect (notwithstanding they had forfeited all pretences of Favours) a proper Countenance." Abraham "seemed truly affected" by this reply, the indictment of Thomas and Mary "so just, that He could say nothing in their Favour, nor would own them as Relations, until they had made satisfactory Concessions."[56]

Although Stephens and the assistants had warned the Trustees about the Bosomworth land claims in January 1748, the demoralized board had not paid much attention. Oglethorpe apparently avoided the issue, and attended his last Trustees' meeting on March 16, 1749. On July 7 Secretary Benjamin Martyn took note of the controversy over the Yamacraw tract in a letter to the Savannah leaders. He observed that the tract "cannot be given up to any private Person, and any pretended Agreements or Contracts, made with the Indians, for that Purpose, are ipso facto void." Martyn continued in a vein which indicated that whatever interest the Trustees still had in the Yamacraw tract concerned its potential as a new area of settlement in the growing northern part of the colony. In particular, they hoped to use some of it as a glebe for the Savannah minister, as Rev. Zouberbuhler had requested. Accordingly, Martyn relayed the Trustees' order that the magistrates "enquire if any of the Yamacraws are in being, and whether, if there are, They have abandoned that Tract of Land, or if they may be induced to Surrender it to the Trust."[57]

Martyn had, probably unintentionally, altered the Trustees' meaning. It was not a mistake born of haste, for the decision he referred to had been made more than two months earlier. On May 29 the Trustees approved directions to the magistrates "to inquire whether the Yamacraw Indians have abandoned that Tract of Land, . . . and Whether those Indians may be inclined to surrender the said Land to the Trust." When the two ideas are connected by "or" rather than "and," the meaning is significantly different. By the time they received Martyn's letter the Savannah magistrates had scant interest in the Trustees' views on Indian affairs, but they did take notice of Martyn's "or."[58]

Since the disbanding of the regiment, Stephens and the assistants had ignored many of the Trustees' instructions, seeming to regard them as ill-informed homilies from an irrelevant body whose days were numbered. Its days were numbered: the royal charter would expire on June 9, 1753. The exasperated Trustees—the few who still attended meetings—demanded on January 7, 1750, that the magistrates henceforth provide "Paragraph by Paragraph" responses to their directives. This must have been good for a laugh in Savannah.[59]

Stevens and the assistants finally answered Martyn's letter of July 7, 1749, on July 19 of the following year. They interpreted Martyn's rendering of the Trustees' order as directing them to either treat the Yamacraw tract as abandoned or seek to purchase it from the Yamacraws. They dismissed the second option as impractical until such time as they had an ample supply of Indian presents. As for the first, they piously replied that a unilateral appropriation of the tract, which the Trustees had seemed to suggest, would be unwise because it would antagonize the Lower Creeks. The Indians would probably infer that Savannah officials had refused to recognize Creek grants of the Yamacraw tract to the Bosomworths so that they might seize it themselves. The Bosomworths could be counted on to help the Creeks reach that conclusion. The magistrates concluded that all action on the Yamacraw tract should be deferred.[60]

In November the Trustees learned of the confrontation in Savannah, but they were slow to appreciate its seriousness. On January 7, 1750, Secretary Martyn wrote the magistrates that the Trustees were "pleased with the whole of your Conduct" in the affair. He also informed them that the Trustees intended to report the matter to the secretary of state, and expected that Bedford would soon issue orders that "shall put it out of the Power" of the Bosomworths to create such disturbances. Three days later Martyn prepared this report and sent it on, but the only corrective step the Trustees proposed was that Abraham Bosomworth be removed as agent for the presents.[61]

On July 14 Martyn wrote to Henry Parker, now vice-president, about the Yamacraw tract. This letter makes it plain that the Trustees failed to grasp how seriously Bosomworth maneuvers had damaged their hope for a Lower Creek cession of the tract. In fact, they thought the Creek grants to the couple had helped, for they showed that these Indians were "ready to surrender this Land." Accordingly, the Trustees now directed the Savannah leaders to approach the Creeks about a cession of the Yamacraw tract and the three islands "the first time any Presents are delivered to them." They envisioned no difficulty with this, and even supposed that the Indians might agree to the cession without any additional presents. Should the magistrates feel that more were required, the Trustees would provide them. Finally, Martyn related that the Trustees thought it "absolutely necessary" that the colony's surveyor perform an immediate survey of all the lands claimed by the Bosomworths.[62]

To the Savannah leaders, the most welcome news in these letters was the prospect of intervention by the secretary of state. As they wrote on July 29, they looked forward to that "with some Impatience." As for the survey of the contested lands, the magistrates declined to employ either of their surveyors on the project. It could not be done by a public surveyor without Thomas Bosomworth's learning of it, and he "doubtless would improve such a Circumstance with the Indians." Noble Jones, however, had volunteered to undertake the task covertly.[63]

If the Trustees were now interested in the Yamacraw tract as a potential area of new settlement, they had long nursed similar hopes for the vastly larger Yuchi tract upriver. By 1749 the Yuchis' gradual evacuation of the tract was essentially complete. For nearly a decade the Trustees had been urging the colony's leaders to negotiate with the Yuchis for a cession of this territory. They continued to issue such directions in letters of January 2, 1749, and January 7 and July 14, 1750, but had yet to receive a reply.[64]

Stephens and the assistants finally took notice of these "repeated Orders" in their July 19 letter to Martyn. Dismissing the Trustees' directives as impractical, the magistrates explained that they had decided upon a different course the previous summer. They had concluded that "to treat with the few Indians called Euchees about these Lands, would induce the Creeks to make Pretensions to them likewise, as they look upon the Euchees as their Vassals, which might create endless Disputes and Expenses." To avoid such difficulties, the magistrates had settled upon a bolder policy: to appropriate the nearest portion of the Yuchi lands "without taking any Notice of it to the Indians, who have deserted them." They had begun by authorizing Rev. Bolzius to settle a few families beyond Ebenezer Creek, but he had opted to wait until an expected new contingent of German settlers arrived. The magistrates very likely got the desertion idea from the Trustees' supposed plan for the Yamacraw tract (which they rejected in the very same letter). The distracted Trustees apparently did not object.[65]

Early in 1750 Thomas and Mary Bosomworth returned from Charles Town. From this time forward the couple seldom appeared in Savannah, spending most of their time on St. Catherines Island. On March 1 they sold both the old Musgrove place and their town house in Savannah, thereby divesting themselves of all property they held under Trustee grants. The only lands they now maintained a title to were those they claimed under their Creek grants, and they were more determined than ever to make those claims good. On July 29 the magistrates reported that Thomas had repeatedly declared that "He will leave no Means untryed to carry his Point." They did not doubt him.[66]

Stephens and the assistants also heard that Mary had told some of her relatives in Tuckabatchee that, because of the land dispute, she planned to move there. She reportedly would bring her cattle and other effects and was expected in time for the busk. More ominously, Malatchi and various Upper Creek leaders had lately returned from visits to Mobile and Fort Toulouse laden with French presents and "very well pleased." The Savannah leaders were now convinced that most Creeks were dangerously disaffected. If it were not for the continuing "hot War" between them and the Cherokees, the magistrates thought it "more than probable" that the Creeks would be "meditating some Mischeif against us."[67]

Thomas and Mary did attend busk ceremonies that summer, but in Coweta, not Tuckabatchee. Their plan was not the rumored one, but to lay further groundwork for an appeal of their land claims to the highest levels of the British government. They would sail for England armed with fresh confirmations of all their claims contributed by major Creek leaders at their most prestigious council square. On August 2 they were able to secure three confirmatory deeds signed by Malatchi and six other headmen in the name of both Upper and Lower Creeks. Only one of these chiefs was an Upper Creek, "In Clechumbey" of Tuckabatchee, perhaps a relative of Mary's. All three documents were witnessed by Adam Bosomworth, Joseph Piercey, George Galphin, and Galphin's Coweta storekeeper, William Lindin.[68]

One of the new documents was a confirmation of that of August 12, 1749, recognizing Mary as princess and sole representative on land questions. Adam Bosomworth later deposed that when he arrived in Coweta on July 29 he found the French colors flying. When he asked Galphin about this, the trader explained that a recent visit by "three or four French Officers" and a few French traders had exploited a "general Dissatisfaction" among the Lower Creeks. That ill feeling was due to "the treatment which the Indians had Received at Savannah last Summer." Adam continued that on August 2, with Mary present, the "whole Assembly" of the Lower Creeks composed a talk "to send home to England by her for his Majesty's Consideration." This, he said, occasioned "a General Joy in the Face of the whole Assembly and the French Colours were taken down." He neglected to mention the three confirmatory deeds Malatchi and other chiefs signed that day.[69]

The other two Creek-Bosomworth documents dealt with the lands the Lower Creeks had reserved under the 1739 treaty: the Yamacraw tract and the three coastal islands. All were now regranted to Thomas and Mary Bosomworth. The new deed for the islands simply confirmed the similar deeds signed by Malatchi on January 4, 1748. The only noteworthy addition was a statement that the Creeks now recognized Thomas as "our beloved Man."[70]

The companion deed for the Yamacraw tract was more elaborate and far more important. This now valuable land was the physical focus of the conflict with the Georgia authorities. The new deed for the Yamacraw tract was the only one of the three documents for which the Bosomworths seem to have lacked a usable substitute. Malatchi and the other subscribing headmen are represented as confirming the Yamacraw tract to the Bosomworths in recognition of Mary's "many signal Services," along with "Sundry Valuable Merchandize" just received from Thomas. The fact that it was thought necessary to mention "valuable consideration" in this deed (but not the one for the islands) is another indication that the Bosomworths lacked a Yamacraw tract counterpart to the 1748 deed for the islands.[71]

In September Thomas returned to St. Catherines, where he made arrangements with a shipmaster to carry him and his spouse to England. To support their appeal there, the Bosomworths intended to present the three Coweta documents as evidence. To enhance the credibility of these documents, on September 29 Adam Bosomworth and Joseph Piercey swore to three identical affidavits before magistrate Samuel Marcer. One was affixed to the outside of each of the three Coweta documents, which were folded and sealed. In each affidavit Bosomworth and Piercey swore that in Coweta on August 2 they had witnessed "the within written Paper" signed, sealed, and delivered from chiefs "of the said Creek Nations" to Mary and Thomas. They also deposed that they saw George Galphin and William Lindin "sign their names as Subscribing Witnesses."[72]

As an assistant, Marcer had participated in the provincial government's campaign against the Bosomworths, but he had been suspended from that office in April and had become a Bosomworth ally. On October 22 he mentioned these affidavits to two assistants, who pressed him for details. After seeming to admit that he had taken copies of the three Coweta documents, Marcer denied it and avowed that he had copied only the affidavits, the "three Instruments of writing." He continued that "a fourth was offered Him; but He knew it to be so barefacedly untrue, that He refused to Swear them to that." Marcer then rendered an opinion on the controversy that might have come from Thomas Bosomworth himself: "these Affairs had better be decided at Home, for they never could be concluded here."[73]

With even Marcer refusing to notarize the fourth document, the Bosomworths were unable to get it done. Another of their allies, Recorder Charles Watson, was more helpful. Watson recorded not only all three affidavits in the colony's archive but the fourth document as well. All were recorded without date or comment. When Thomas later recorded the August 2 deed for the Yamacraw tract in Charles Town, he included the fourth document as an attachment. This peculiar document is an endorsement of "the within Written Paper" but does not identify who is speaking, or when, or where. Nevertheless, the clear implication is that the purported speakers were Creek leaders. Like the August 2 deeds, it appears to be written in Thomas's acidic prose.

The document is especially remarkable in that, for the first time, the Bosomworths unsheathed their sharpest weapon in the land contest: the fact that Oglethorpe had witnessed the Creek 1738 grant of the Yamacraw tract to Mary—the grant that lay behind the recent Coweta deed of the tract to both Thomas and Mary. The document asserts that the original grant occurred on October 13, 1738, at a "Public Meeting . . . between his Excellency James Oglethorpe Esq. and several Chief Men of our Nation."[74]

Obliged to proceed without copies of the August 2 documents, the Savannah authorities gathered what information they could about them. On September 15, Galphin, "desirous of becoming a Freeholder of Georgia," appeared before the magistrates to request a five-hundred-acre grant across the river from his Silver Bluff estate. Duly impressed by his remarkable success in the Indian trade, the board approved his request. Grateful, Galphin apparently then volunteered an account of the recent events in Coweta.

Galphin related that the Bosomworths had arrived with "Papers ready wrote for the Chiefs to sign" but had been disappointed that so few headmen were willing to meet with them. Aware that the three Coweta documents might cause personal trouble for him, Galphin neglected to mention that he had subscribed his name to all three as a witness. Instead, he allowed that his knowledge of these documents was secondhand and general, though he gathered that "they related to Lands down here." He added that he could have learned "the Contents" of these documents from his Indian friends, "but did not chuse it, not caring to enter into Disputes in the Nation." This was the last magistrates' meeting William Stephens presided over, or attended. On September 26 his colleagues, citing his "Infirmities, and confused Mind," asked the octogenarian to step down. He did so gladly. Henry Parker immediately succeeded him as acting president.[75]

When Marcer brought one of the three affidavits to his former colleagues on November 8, the magistrates saw that it named Galphin as a witness to one of the August 2 grants. This was startling news, for Galphin's recent report was now seen to have been dishonest. They immediately put a hold on his land grant. Yet while the other witnesses might easily be discredited, as a self-made man and the chief trader in Coweta, Galphin was a formidable character whose signature had to be taken seriously. Accordingly, the magistrates wrote him complaining of his assistance to the Bosomworths in August, and suggesting that he had better repudiate it. Galphin did so in his return letter. He conceded that in Coweta he had signed one Bosomworth document, and also admitted that Adam had told him that it was a Creek concession "to give away there lands and Ilands abought Georgia to Mary."[76]

Galphin excused himself by insisting that he had only signed out of fear. He offered to carry a new document repudiating what had been done on August 2 to Creek country, promising that he could induce more chiefs to sign it than Mary had recruited for hers. Galphin went on to say that when Mary proffered her prepared text to the Creeks, "what was therein sitt forth was never interpreted to them wille She was in the nation and to my Knowledge th[e]y were Egnorant to what they Signed." Moreover, when he had told the Coweta war leader that the document just signed had conveyed the reserved lands to Mary, the chief had shown displeasure and declared that these lands "Co[u]ld not be given away without all the nattion was wiling."[77]

By October 22, before Mary was able to come down from the forks, the ship Thomas had booked passage on sailed without them. A year and a half would pass before they made another attempt to reach London. Forced to postpone their travel plans, the Bosomworths put the Coweta deeds of August 2 in storage.[78]

Encouraged by Galphin's letter, on November 14 Parker and the assistants enlarged the scope of a mission to Creek country that Patrick Graham was already organizing. "Notwithstanding Mr. Galphin's late double Dealings," the magistrates decided to employ him to assist Graham. The original purpose of the mission, set forth on October 4, was for Graham to personally deliver the Upper Creeks' allotment of the royal presents. The new and more important objective was "to frustrate the mercenary Intentions and wicked designs of the Bosomworths" by negotiating a Creek cession of the Yamacraw tract and the three islands.[79]

Parker and the assistants were not simply following what the Trustees had directed nearly two years earlier. It had never before been considered necessary or desirable to deal with the distant Upper Creeks on land questions. The instructions the magistrates issued to Graham reflect revised thinking. The Upper Creeks were not only to be included in the projected negotiations, they were to be the focus: Graham was to address his first and most important talks to them. Parker doubtless spoke for his colleagues when he wrote in April that, while the Lower Creeks were "insolent," the upper townsmen were "by far the most deserving" Creeks.[80]

There were strong reasons for anticipating that the Upper Creeks would prove more cooperative on the land question than the Lower Creeks: they had no known grudges toward Georgia, few ties to the Bosomworths, and much less interest in the disputed lands. Moreover, a conference with them would almost certainly open with an effusion of goodwill. Arriving with a trove of royal presents, Graham was bound to be very welcome. Plans were accordingly made to ship the goods to Augusta in time for delivery to the Upper Creeks in February, but complications intervened and the Graham mission was postponed to the spring.

One complication grew out of renewed Creek attacks on the Cherokees, which provoked both the victims and the South Carolina government. The Carolina leaders were convinced that the peace agreement of September 1749 had broken down because of Lower Creek aggression, that Malatchi was personally responsible, and that the Coweta leader was acting as a pawn of the French. On September 5, 1750, Lachlan McGillivray and several other traders told Governor Glen and his council that "Malatchi never rested three days at Home upon his Return either from Carolina or Georgia before he either went or sent to the Alabama Fort [Fort Toulouse] Acquainting them with every thing he had heard or Observed in either Place." When Glen asked the traders the likely effect of a trade embargo against the Lower Creeks, they gave him the answer he wanted, being "Unanimously of Opinion that it would . . . Mortify and Humble them very much." Glen and his council then decided to cut off all trade with Coweta and Cussita until the Creek-Cherokee peace was restored. They asked the Georgia government to do the same.[81]

Georgia leaders had long been aware of Glen's effort to broker a lasting peace between the Creeks and Cherokees, but had never agreed with it. On October 4 they reported that their policy had always been to avoid involvement in conflicts among natives. They added that the traders uniformly maintained that "the Indians never behaved better to them, than when they have War among themselves." A few days later the magistrates received Glen's letter recounting the recent troubles and requesting that they join the embargo. This request posed a dilemma for Parker and the assistants. If they complied, they would not only reverse their established policy but spoil plans for Graham's mission to the Creeks. On the other hand, knowing that Glen's complaints were well founded, they were reluctant to reject his appeal. They did so silently, for they did not reply for six months.[82]

The Georgia leaders also had to deal with the meeting of the colony's first elected assembly. The Trustees had authorized this assembly the previous June, not to make laws, but only to make recommendations on law or policy for the Trustees to consider. The assembly met in Savannah from January 15 to February 8. Its main accomplishment was the drafting of ten "representations" to the Trustees. The first of them, presumably the one of highest priority, dealt with the

Bosomworth land claims. Neither the text of this document nor the minutes of the assembly survive, but on March 8 Parker and the assistants reported that the assembly had found Thomas Bosomworth's machinations "illegal and treasonable, and we concur with them." Thomas later complained that "In January 1751 the people of Georgia sent home a most flaming Representation against me setting forth the dangerous Consequences of Monopolizing of Lands in the Colony by Indian Purchasers etc. etc."[83]

Another of the representations dealt with Indian affairs. The assembly charged that "the Indian Trade in the Province is almost entirely monopolized by a Company of seven Persons at Augusta." The accused company was known as Brown, Rae and Company; Lachlan McGillivray and George Galphin were prominent members. The assembly recommended that partners in this alleged monopoly be denied future trading licenses, and the Trustees later concurred. The company was soon howling in protest, but no significant action seems to have been taken against it.[84]

After the Bosomworths learned that the assembly had denounced them, on March 1 Thomas, Mary, and Adam each drafted a petition to Parker and the assistants. Thomas demanded a copy of the charges against him; Mary pressed for an official explanation of why she had been denied a share of the royal presents; and Adam requested that Mary's trading license be transferred to him. Adam delivered these petitions on March 5 and three days later received the magistrates' answer. All were denied.[85]

The Trustees considered the assembly's representation on the Bosomworth land claims on May 18. They declared themselves "much concerned to find Mr. Bosomworth persists in so unnatural, undutifull, and illegal an Attempt as to enter into Treaties with any Indians for the purchase of Lands within the Bounds of his Majesty's Charter." Invoking their treaties with the Lower Creeks in 1733 and 1739, they roundly asserted that "No Title can be made to the Reserved Lands but by an Agreement to be made between the Trustees and the Lower Creek Nation in general." The Trustees then agreed on a set of directives to Parker and the assistants. First, they were to inform the Lower Creeks that the Trustees were now "ready to treat with them for the purchase of the aforesaid Lands." The presents necessary to effect this purchase would be provided. The magistrates were also directed to inform the Bosomworths that "if They persist in this unjustifiable Attempt of theirs, They will be prosecuted with the utmost severity of the Law." Finally, the Savannah leaders were to issue a public notice in the Trustees' name warning all Georgians not to enter into any bargains with Thomas for these lands, "to which the Bosomworths have, and can make no Title."[86]

On May 24 the Trustees adopted instructions to Parker and the assistants for managing a Lower Creek conference they were to call. The Indians were to be reminded of their obligation under the 1733 treaty not to dispose of any land except to the Trustees, and warned that their grants to the Bosomworths were invalid. The lands Thomas Bosomworth claimed under Creek grants "by the Laws of England he cannot hold, or dispose of." The magistrates were then to persuade the Indians to make the desired cession. Finally, the Trustees directed that British sovereignty over Lower Creek country was to be asserted: the Indians were to be informed that "they, as well as the English, are all under the Protection of his Majesty King George."[87]

These instructions were irrelevant even before they were written, for about the first of May Patrick Graham set off on his mission to the Creeks. The Trustees learned of preparations for this diplomatic adventure by early July, though the magistrates had neglected to inform them about the plan to concentrate on the Upper Creeks. Supposing it was to be a mission to the Lower Creeks, similar to the one they had envisioned, the Trustees were "glad" to approve the effort.[88]

Parker and the assistants issued instructions to Graham on April 25. He was to proceed to the Upper Creeks' country, distribute the royal presents, and then attempt to win their consent to a cession of the Yamacraw tract and the three islands. Borrowing a leaf from the Bosomworths, he was given two already prepared "Deeds of Conveyances" ready for Indian signatures. If he succeeded with the Upper Creeks, he was to stop among the Lower Creeks on his return trip and attempt to gain their concurrence to the cession. He was authorized to spend up to £150 to help them think correctly. If the Lower Creeks went along, he was to have their headmen sign the same or similar deeds.[89]

On the eve of Graham's departure, Parker finally answered Governor Glen's October letter requesting Georgia's cooperation with his colony's trade embargo against Coweta and Cussita. He replied that he and the assistants "thought it prudent not to shew any publick Resentment, untill we had confered with them." Therefore, nothing would be done until the results of Graham's mission were known. The Savannah magistrates were clearly bent on following their own counsel, and not much concerned with what the Trustees or Carolina leaders thought about it.[90]

On May 4 Graham arrived in Augusta, which he found to be in turmoil over reports that the Cherokees were threatening to murder the English traders among them. After passing this news on to Savannah leaders, he continued on toward Upper Creek country. Parker and the assistants supposed that the traders had brought the trouble on themselves. As bad as Indian traders were in general, those who dealt with the Cherokees—nearly all of them Carolinians—were "reputed to be the worst set of People of any." The magistrates concluded on June 6 that "this Colony had at present very little Connection with these Indians or their Traders, and that it almost wholly laid on the Government of South-Carolina to conduct this troublesome affair." A few days earlier the Georgia leaders had received a request from Governor Glen that they cut off the colony's minor trade to the Cherokees. This time they complied, and on June 6 Parker so informed Glen.[91]

Graham was warmly greeted by the Upper Creeks and promptly delivered their presents on May 20. Eight days later a conference convened at Oakchoy, the Gun Merchant's town. Graham began his speech warning of the evil designs of the French and the Bosomworths, ending with an offer to purchase the reserved lands. In reply, the Gun Merchant assured Graham that the Upper Creeks paid no regard to "false and malicious reports" about the English, whose friendship they valued highly. He concluded that the English "should possess" the Yamacraw tract and the three islands, and his chiefs were ready to sign "a paper" to that effect. That same day twenty-four of them, headed by the Gun Merchant, signed the deed Graham produced. The witnesses included McGillivray, who had served as interpreter for the conference, and Galphin.[92]

Hoping to repeat their success at Oakchoy, Graham's party headed for Coweta. There on June 3 Graham repeated the speech he had delivered at Oakchoy. Replying for the Lower Creeks, Malatchi made a perfunctory profession of friendship, "But declined selling or disposing of the Lands." Still, he and his people were willing "to lend the whole, or any part thereof During Pleasure." The Coweta chief then denied that the Lower Creeks had ever granted the reserved lands. Furthermore, he declared that the Lower Creeks "utterly reject and Disown any Claim that Mr. and Mrs. Bosomworth pretends to have, to said Lands, and positively affirms they never Executed any Deed concerning the same that they knew of." Malatchi did recall that Lower Creek headmen had recently signed a paper for Mary (again, one paper, not three), but they had understood it to be a protest to Savannah leaders over a rogue trading store on the Oconee River. Prompted by "some of those that were witnesses therto"—Galphin and Lindin—Graham concluded that Mary Bosomworth had misrepresented the document(s) she got them to sign in 1750.[93]

There was a lot of lying in the Coweta square that day. On the English side, Galphin and Lindin probably planted the story of Mary's deceit. These Coweta traders apparently aimed to suggest that they had been duped into witnessing a Bosomworth deed, just as the Indians had been gulled into signing it, and therefore were blameless. Galphin had told a more believable story in his letter of November 4, 1750. There he admitted he had known the day the paper was signed that it was a Creek "talk to give away there lands and Islands abought Georgia to Mary," and had so informed the Coweta war chief. He added that when he heard that chief ask Mary if the signed document was a protest talk against the Oconee store, she had answered "it was not."[94]

Malatchi and his clique won the day's prevarication prize. Probably many, perhaps even most, of the Lower Creek headmen had been misinformed about the Bosomworth deeds they signed on August 2, 1750. Artfully, Malatchi declared they had all been in the dark, for they had never signed such a deed "that they knew of." It passes belief that he and all headmen who had signed three separate sets of Bosomworth deeds could have been completely ignorant of the content of every one of those documents when they met Graham. Malatchi certainly was not, as we shall see. It is hard to see why he and others who had signed the Bosomworth deeds now denied knowledge of them and their substance to Graham—unless they had agreed with Thomas and Mary that these things should be kept secret until a more propitious time arrived.[95]

On June 21 Graham reported the results of his mission to President Parker and the assistants. He regretted that the talks at Coweta had not gone as well as those at Oakchoy, but he was neither surprised nor discouraged. An Upper Creek deed was in hand and a parallel Lower Creek deed seemed possible in the not distant future. Graham apparently bought Malatchi's tale that the Lower Creeks had never knowingly executed any deeds for land to the Bosomworths. It was not easy to dismiss Malatchi's claim, for no Georgia official except Noble Jones had ever seen one of those deeds, and he could not know that the Indians understood what they had signed. After hearing Graham's report, the magistrates supposed that "notwithstanding Malatche and two or three Head men in the Cowetaws remain disaffected on this Head," most Lower Creek leaders would "readily comply" with a renewed request for the cession if the price were right. When the overdue shipment of royal presents arrived, even Malatchi might be won over.[96]

Meanwhile, the magistrates had gone ahead with their plan to unilaterally appropriate the nearest portion of the Yuchi tract. When that met no resistance, the plan was soon extended to encompass the entire tract. A new company of German settlers, ably led by William De Brahm, arrived in the fall of 1750. Before the year was out, twenty-four Germans received fifty-acre grants between Ebenezer and Mount Pleasant. In 1751 De Brahm established the town of Bethany in the area and surveyed the site for another at Briar Creek. The latter settlement, located at the far end of the Yuchi tract, was founded the following year. This was just the beginning of a major land rush. As news spread that the Trustees had abandoned their effort to prohibit slavery, and seemed about to surrender their authority altogether, a tide of settlement from South Carolina and other colonies began to flow into Georgia, mostly into this area. Even then, neither the Yuchis nor their Lower Creek overlords seem to have lodged any serious complaint about the new settlements.[97]

Emboldened by this success, in 1752 the Savannah authorities decided to follow a similar course toward the Yamacraw tract. The only show of Indian consent they had for an appropriation of this land was Graham's deed from the Upper Creeks. The Trustees had reasonably declared that they had "not thought this a sufficient Foundation for their Entering on, and taking Possession of the said Lands," and continued to call for a Lower Creek cession. Down to the summer of 1752 the magistrates had not dared to disagree, but several things combined to change their minds. In May Thomas and Mary Bosomworth left the colony for Charles Town, the first leg of their long-contemplated trip to England. In June the rump Trustees announced that they would surrender their royal charter that very month, a year before it was due to expire.[98]

In July the magistrates hosted unusual visitors. The Savannahs were some of the first natives the English had encountered in the region. Settled at a site near Augusta until the Yamasee War, since then they had lived mainly in western New York and Pennsylvania. Some had returned episodically, like those who in 1736 had joined the Yamacraws in Tomochichi's town. A decade later they sent a message to Charles Town that "they wanted to return to their own Lands," and they began showing up in larger numbers. Most were settled among the Upper Creeks, but there were others among the Lower Creeks and Cherokees as well. Graham had met some of them during his talks at Oakchoy, heard from traders that they were "capable of doing a great deal of Service, or Mischief," and invited them down to the Georgia capital.[99]

Upon their arrival, the thirty or so Savannahs had friendly talks with the assistants (President Parker having just died). Since the Upper Creeks had not chosen to share their presents with the Savannahs, Graham recommended that some now be found for them. The magistrates scrambled to do so, then took advantage of the resulting good mood. Had the Georgia leaders been consistent with their abandonment theory, they would not have considered acknowledging that the Savannahs retained any rights to their old homeland. The visitors seemed so cooperative, however, that the assistants were ready to overlook a thirty-five-year absence. As they reported on July 28, since the Savannahs "formerly lived on the Bank of this River near Augusta, and lay some Claim to the Lands, We got their Head King to sign the Deed" that Graham had won from the Upper Creeks.[100]

This signing added only the weight of the ink to the Graham deed. What the incident reveals is that the magistrates were worried enough about the legitimacy of the Graham deed that they seized the opportunity to add to it almost any additional Indian signature. Though the Trustees had warned that this deed did not justify appropriation of the Yamacraw tract, leaders in the colony—Graham now acting as president—chose to disagree. Sometime in 1752 they apportioned the Yamacraw tract among several settlers, and these grantees had occupied their allotments. This is what Malatchi was referring to when he complained the following year to Governor Glen that "of late" the Georgians had taken Mary Bosomworth's lands from her "by Force."[101]

There were no significant dealings between the provincial government and the Indians during the next two years, which were mainly occupied with the liquidation of the trusteeship and the transition to royal government. Though a merciful calm followed the Bosomworths' departure, the land controversy was not the closed book the magistrates had struggled to make it. Thomas and Mary were soon at work on the next chapter in Charles Town.

In April 1752, just before the Bosomworths arrived, an incident occurred just outside Charles Town that was to alter their travel plans once again. Late in March an uninvited party of three dozen Creeks entered the Carolina capital. Most were Lower Creeks, but their spokesman was Acorn Whistler, a minor headman from Okfuskee. The following day a party of twelve Cherokees arrived claiming that menacing Creeks had forced them to seek sanctuary. Charles Town's residents were immediately apprehensive that violence might erupt between the two groups, but Glen saw their accidental presence together as an opportunity to promote the precarious peace between their nations. The governor held separate talks with both groups, reminded both of their obligations under the 1749 accord, and finally presided over an outwardly amicable meeting between them. After the talks ended on April 4 both visiting parties took their leave, but "within the Sight of Charles Town" the Creeks fell upon the outnumbered Cherokees and killed four of them. When Cherokee leaders learned of this Creek treachery they were enraged, accused the Carolinians of complicity, and demanded that they prove the contrary by punishing the Creeks. By April 28 Glen and his council concluded that the only way to avert serious trouble with the Cherokees was to send an agent to the Creeks to demand satisfaction.[102]

Like the Georgia magistrates, most members of the South Carolina lower house believed that Glen's interventionist policy was misguided. On May 8 the house served notice on the governor that it opposed the intended agency. Unmoved, on May 25 the council unanimously reaffirmed its plan for a special Creek agent. Two days later Glen reported that his first choice for this doubly dangerous mission, William Pinckney, had declined the assignment. Having learned that the Bosomworths were in town, Glen then suggested that Mary might be "a very proper Person" to serve as agent. The council demurred at this, but was willing to have her assist a more suitable agent as interpreter.[103]

After several other Carolinians declined the appointment, on June 16 the job was offered to Thomas, with Mary to assist him. Sensing opportunity, the Bosomworths agreed to undertake the mission, on certain conditions. The most important were that Glen would protect Thomas from his creditors during his service and that, if the mission were successful, the governor would recommend Mary to officials in England. Glen had already promised as much in earlier negotiations, the deal was struck, and the governor signed Thomas's commission and instructions on July 2. Thomas would later interpret Glen's promise to write a letter of recommendation for Mary as a commitment "to recommend Mrs. Bosomworth['s] Case Home to Great Britain."[104]

Glen instructed Thomas to persuade the Lower Creeks to execute "some of the most considerable" of the murderers in order to appease the Cherokees. If they refused, he was to attempt to persuade the Upper Creeks to force them to comply. Should he succeed in gaining this satisfaction for the Cherokees, but only then, he was to attempt to mediate a formal peace between the Creeks and Cherokees. Upon learning of the Bosomworth mission, Georgia leaders were stricken with forebodings. On July 28 the assistants predicted that "this Embassy . . . will in the End prove very injurious to the Welfare of this Colony."[105]

On July 3 Thomas and Mary set out on the path to Creek country. During the next six months they were involved in complex negotiations with both the Lower and Upper Creeks. Much to their credit, they were generally successful in achieving the goals Glen had set for them: Acorn Whistler was executed, and both Lower and Upper Creeks declared themselves ready for a permanent peace with the Cherokees. Thomas and Mary also succeeded with private aims. While preparing their trip, they had made friends with and done favors for many of the traders, notably Lachlan Mackintosh and even their old enemy John Kenard. They could look forward to return favors.[106]

From September 21 to 23 the Bosomworths held a major conference with the Upper Creeks at Tuckabatchee. The official result of these talks was an Upper Creek agreement to certain gestures of satisfaction and provisional consent to a peace with the Cherokees. Fifteen chiefs affixed their marks to the conference proceedings. No sooner was the public business out of the way when Thomas and Mary broached some private business, the matter of their land claims. That very day they prevailed upon Upper Creek chiefs to sign a second document, doubtless prepared in advance, that breathed new life into their cause.[107]

That document was, first of all, a repudiation of the deed Upper Creek leaders had signed for Patrick Graham the previous year. The fifteen headmen who set their marks to this document were essentially the same individuals who had signed the earlier agreement that day. More important, at least nine of them had signed Graham's deed. One signature notably absent was that of the most influential Upper Creek chief, the Gun Merchant. Thomas said he was out on a hunt. The document states that the chiefs were compelled to repudiate Graham's deed because the Georgia agent had misrepresented it when he laid it before them.

They now alleged that Graham had told them "at the time of signing thereof that the intent and meaning was only to know the names of the Head Men of every Town in the Nation that the People of Georgia might know to whom to send their presents." They went on to "absolutely deny" that a land cession "was ever so much as mentioned to us at the signing of our names to the said Paper." Then the pièce de résistance: "in justice to our beloved Woman and Sister," the signers ratified and confirmed Malatchi's grant of the Yamacraw tract and the three islands to Mary Bosomworth.[108]

Since the official objectives of the mission had been achieved, on November 15 Governor Glen ordered Thomas back to Charles Town, clearly intending that Mary accompany him. Thomas came, but left Mary behind. He arrived on January 6, 1753, and two days later made an impressive report to the governor. Glen sent him back to the Creeks with an invitation to attend a major conference, evidently at Fort Moore, in order to ratify the new understandings and seal a formal peace with the Cherokees. That accomplished, Thomas again returned to the Carolina capital. When the assembly served notice that it would not pay for the conference, Glen canceled it and simply sent presents for the Creeks up to Fort Moore. In April Mary conducted a large Creek delegation expecting talks with Glen and the Cherokees to Augusta, where Thomas met them. According to Thomas, the failure of Glen and the Cherokees to appear "concurred to disgust" the Creeks. Perplexed at "how to act in that critical situation," he consulted with the Augusta traders. They "Unanimously" advised him to conduct the murmuring Creek chiefs down to Charles Town for a meeting with the governor. Needing no persuasion, for the second time Thomas made a surprise entrance into a colonial capital with an uninvited company of Creeks.[109]

The Indians met with Governor Glen and his council from May 28 to June 4. About a hundred Upper and Lower Creeks were present, including nearly all leading chiefs except the Gun Merchant. In his absence Malatchi served as chief spokesman for both nations. Malatchi now confronted Glen with a claim he had never before made to a colonial official: he invoked and defended the Lower Creek grants of territory to Mary Bosomworth, though he did not specifically endorse the written deeds. He began by declaring that "My Sister, Mrs. Bosomworth, I do not look upon as a white Person." He insisted that she was an Indian, and as "an Indian . . . was entitled to the Lands she possessed." That land, which the Georgians were attempting to deprive her of, was rightfully hers because it "was given her by the Indians, and it belonged to us, when it was given her." He then called upon the Upper Creeks present to orally repudiate Graham's deed, which they did. He concluded with a peroration: "A Grant of Land cannot be made by one or two, it must be done by all the Head Men as the Act of the whole Body of the Nation." Graham's deed certainly fell short of that standard, but it is not clear that the most formidable combination of Bosomworth deeds (the 1750 Lower Creek deeds and the 1752 Upper Creek deed) came any closer.[110]

According to Glen, Mary's land claims were "not only urged in Publick, but pressed much more in private, and not only was I pressed by King Malatchi who is her near relation but by every other Headman." Moreover, it seemed to him that Malatchi "is now looked upon by all his own People as the greatest Leader they ever had." He went on to confirm that the Upper Creek leaders explicitly repudiated the deed they had signed for Graham: "they absolutely disavow their knowing of any such Conveyance, but with one voice affirm that when Doctor Graeme desired them to put their marks to a paper he acquainted them that he only wanted to know the number of Headmen and what Town they belonged to that he might apportion the Presents he had brought up accordingly."[111]

Glen's report echoes the Upper Creek repudiation drawn up by Thomas Bosomworth, but since it was based on what the Creek leaders said to him, it is much more credible. Graham may have been deceitful with some Upper Creek chiefs when soliciting signatures for his deed, but not all of them. In 1755 the Gun Merchant acknowledged that when Graham requested a cession of the lands claimed by the Bosomworths, "he did consent to give them." Furthermore, before he gave this consent to the Graham deed, he had "called all the head men and Warrriours together, and made the strictest enquiry if any of them knew anything about the said Islands therein mentioned." None did. Thus before the deed was signed the Gun Merchant had informed other headmen that it related to the coastal islands. Few could have come away believing it was a mere census of chiefs. The "one voice" Upper Creek leaders gave in support of the census story was insincere. The Gun Merchant did not go along. He did not sign the repudiation document or accompany the others to Charles Town. In 1755 he regretted his consent to the Graham deed, but on a different ground: the Upper Creeks were then unaware of Malatchi's grants to Mary.[112]

Malatchi ended his talk to Glen with an appeal that the governor use his influence to resolve the controversy. Glen replied that he lacked authority to settle disputes in another province, but promised "to represent what you complain of" to higher officials. He did that right away. In his July 30 report to the Board of Trade, Glen hinted transparently that he was sympathetic to the Bosomworth land claims. He thought the Graham deed fraudulent, but even if not, invalid. Glen declared that "among Indians, Lands are generally deemed to belong to that part of the Nation next to which they lye." When South Carolina negotiated with the Cherokees, it was guided by this Native American principle. Accordingly, his government dealt "only with the lower Towns." It followed that only the Lower Creeks could cede lands in coastal Georgia and that any instrument executed by the Upper Creeks purporting to do so was worthless. Glen omitted such reflections from the terse and tardy report on Malatchi's talk he sent the Savannah magistrates in October.[113]

Georgia leaders had long since concluded that Glen had become Thomas Bosomworth's "Patron." Few in Charles Town would have disagreed. Despite the assembly's opposition to any such mission, Glen had commissioned Thomas special agent to the Creeks. Upon Thomas's return the governor had praised his work and supported his claims for compensation from the hostile assembly. He went on to represent the Bosomworth land claims in Georgia in a favorable light to the Board of Trade. Not least, for more than two years Glen had shielded Thomas from his creditors by taking him into his special protection. Finally, as we shall see in the next chapter, Glen appears to have rendered important assistance to Thomas in preparing the legal defense of his Georgia land claims that he was about to carry to London.[114]

After an long wrangle with the South Carolina assembly over compensation, early in July 1754 Thomas and Mary finally set sail for England. Their activities over the previous seven years had completely dominated Georgia's relations with Indians. With the absolute territorial sovereignty of the Indians as their first principle, the Bosomworths had secured numerous Creek deeds purporting to convey to them the Yamacraw tract and three coastal islands. Three separate sets of these grants were signed by Malatchi and other Lower Creek leaders in 1747, 1748, and 1750. Partly to bolster their claims, the Bosomworths had forced two unplanned Creek conferences upon colonial authorities, first in Savannah in 1749 and then in Charles Town in 1753. When Georgia officials in 1749 had insisted that no unauthorized British subject could receive land grants from Indians, Mary seemingly had renounced allegiance to King George and secured what purported to be a Lower Creek recognition of herself as princess.

Although apparently soundly defeated in 1749, the Bosomworths persevered and made a spectacular recovery after their arrival in Charles Town in 1752. In September they secured an instrument from the Upper Creeks that repudiated the Graham deed and confirmed their own. That and the subsequent conference in Charles Town undermined official Georgia diplomacy with the Creeks since 1749. Finally, their difficult mission for Glen brought them important new allies for the next phase of the struggle. As for the Savannah magistrates, with the Trust defunct, they were now lame-duck placeholders. With the Bosomworths ascendant in Creek relations, it was the magistrates who now seemed isolated and discredited.

What the Bosomworths did not do is almost as revealing about their strategy as what they did. When Thomas and Mary had their deeds confirmed in Coweta on August 2, 1750, they did not back down a bit from their previous pretensions, though there were powerful reasons to do so. Far more than Mary, Thomas had incurred the hostility of the Georgia magistrates and assembly, and was in real jeopardy of dire punishment. Mary was at least partly an Indian, and therefore likely to receive some forbearance. Her husband was every inch an Englishman, allegedly a traitorous Englishman. The fact that Thomas had risked having himself named as a grantee in the deeds he and Mary procured from the Creeks made those documents mortally dangerous to him.

Given Thomas's extreme legal vulnerability, the Bosomworths could not afford to allow any of their deeds from the Creeks, or even copies of them, to fall into the hands of the Savannah magistrates, at least not so long as the couple remained in Georgia. Accordingly, they maintained a tight grip over their deeds until they left the colony in May 1752. These written documents provided the best evidence, as understood by Englishmen, of the Creek grants to Thomas and Mary. The deeds would be essential exhibits when they presented their case in England. Yet before their departure from Georgia they did not dare to transmit a copy of a single one to British authorities, presumably to avoid word of it coming back to afflict them in Savannah.

Once safely out of Georgia, Thomas and Mary relaxed their grip on their title deeds and their heretofore resolute refusal to link Oglethorpe to their land claims. On May 4, 1753, Thomas recorded two of the three 1750 confirmation instruments in Charles Town, and the third one a few months later. This would have been pointless if these documents had already been recorded in Georgia, more evidence it had not been done. The second statement attached to the confirmation grant for the Yamacraw tract (the one Marcer refused to notarize) was essentially a summary of the 1738 Christie minutes from an allegedly Creek point of view. In August Thomas recorded the full text of the Christie minutes in Charles Town. For the first time Oglethorpe's role in the 1738 grant of the Yamacraw tract to Mary was a matter of public record. Anyone could procure a copy, provided he knew where to look. A few weeks later the Bosomworths prevailed upon Mary's old friend Robert Williams to record a fresh deposition corroborating the Christie minutes.[115]

The Christie minutes, the work of Georgia's early recorder Thomas Christie, had been written as the official record of the events of October 13, 1738. That was the day four Lower Creek chiefs made the original grant of the Yamacraw tract to Mary. This document was the Bosomworths' ace, for it seemed to prove that Oglethorpe—and by implication the Trustees he represented—had given at least tacit approval to the grant. It was a card that had to be held close to the chest and played carefully. Thomas and Mary could not exploit this document without exposing one of Oglethorpe's worst official mistakes, which would have negative consequences for them in London. They did not wish to do this except as a last resort. Their motive for this restraint was almost certainly to avoid humiliating Oglethorpe, who, although he had often spurned their requests for help, might yet be induced to play a key supporting role in their long-planned appeal to British authorities. They wanted his help, not his scalp. For years the Bosomworths had been remarkably disciplined in containing their resentment toward Oglethorpe. Only when reduced to despair in Savannah in 1749 had they allowed any of it to show.

Had Mary been the sole grantee in the Bosomworth deeds, and had she continued to insist with the support of the Lower Creeks that she was one of them, the threat of a treason trial for Thomas would have evaporated. A treason trial for Mary was theoretically possible, but it would have been political lunacy. The Georgia leaders' whole case against Mary depended on the debatable assumption that she was an Englishwoman; if she was an Indian they had none. It was an either/or question, and the answer had large consequences. Suppose for a moment that Mary was what she and Malatchi said she was, a Creek Indian. If she was an Indian and sole beneficiary of the Lower Creek grants, what she would have had was a clear Lower Creek title to enjoy exclusive use of the Yamacraw tract and the three islands so long as she lived. That appears to have been Malatchi's understanding of her situation. As an Indian, he told Glen, Mary was "intitled to all the Rights and Privaledges of an Indian, and was entitled to the Lands she possessed, . . . which was given her by the Indians." If only that were at issue, the Bosomworth grants would have been an internal affair among Lower Creeks, and British authorities would have had no reason to object or interfere.[116]

The Bosomworths did not share Malatchi's view of Mary's land grants. Thomas's repeated insistence on having himself named co-beneficiary in the Lower Creek land grants, at great risk to himself, indicates that an Indian grant to Mary alone would not have been acceptable to the Bosomworths. The reason is perfectly clear: lands held by Indians under Indian custom enjoyed no protection from English law. If Mary held lands in this manner, she might have conveyed portions of them to other Indians or even Englishmen, but there would not likely be much profit from such transactions. The parcels she conveyed to her grantees would still be held by Indian right for a lifetime only, still beyond the pale of English law, still worth about what she had paid for them.

But if a Bosomworth conveyance somehow led to a secure title under English law—so that the grantee could rest assured that English courts would enforce his rights and those of his heirs or assignees—the Bosomworth lands would be worth a fortune in potential sales to Englishmen or other colonists. In effect, the Bosomworths were claiming that since Mary was both Indian and English, she had both Indian rights and English rights. When it came to acquiring lands from natives, she was an Indian named Cousaponakeesa. She therefore was not subject to inconvenient English laws or regulations, such as the five-hundred-acre limit on Georgia land grants that King George had imposed in the colony's charter. On the other hand, when it came to selling or encumbering her land rights to Englishmen, she was an Englishwoman named Mary. She was therefore entitled to the time-honored protections of English property law. Furthermore, when she married Thomas, by English law her property became his.[117]

Thomas Bosomworth had to know that land purchases from Indians in Georgia or South Carolina had never led to secure English titles, and must have been at least vaguely aware that no such result had ever been reached in any other English colony. Yet in his case, he was determined to have it so. The only place such a radical alteration of English law could be effected was in London, so there he must go. Thomas Bosomworth was not only amazingly tenacious, his grand design was incredibly bold.

CHAPTER SEVEN

Royal Government and Imperial Crisis

For more than a year after the Georgia Trustees surrendered their royal charter the colony drifted along on momentum, for it had no formally constituted government. In April 1753 the Board of Trade was ordered to prepare a plan for governing the orphaned colony. Three months later it adopted a plan that closely followed the pattern set for other royal colonies in America. Authority was to be placed in the hands of a governor appointed (theoretically) by the king, a council likewise appointed, and an elective lower house of assembly. With the Trust out of the way, Georgia officials would now have to take orders directly from the British government, especially the Board of Trade. The Privy Council approved the reorganization in March 1754. John Reynolds, a former naval officer and future admiral, was named the colony's first royal governor. The plan went into effect when Reynolds reached Savannah in late October. The acting president and assistants surviving from the last days of the trusteeship were converted into members of Governor Reynolds's council.[1]

In one respect the new plan reverted to an earlier model. James Oglethorpe's persistent efforts to extend Georgia's territory southward from the Altamaha River, the southern boundary according to the royal charter, were ignored. The Altamaha was reaffirmed—for the time being—as the southern boundary of the colony. From that river south to the northernmost Spanish possessions, unspecified, the territory was British but was supposed to be administered by South Carolina according to its seventeenth-century charters.[2]

Six months before Reynolds arrived in Savannah, French forces clashed with Virginians at the forks of the Ohio River. The long-anticipated war for control of North America had begun. It was clear to both sides that support from Indians would be crucial to the outcome. Hopelessly outnumbered by the British, this was especially clear to the French. Three years earlier Governor Vaudreuil of Louisiana had been confident that nearly all Choctaws were loyal to the French, and optimistic about support from many of the Creeks, especially Lower Creeks. He said he was sure that "the Emperor of the Kawitas," Malatchi, "was on our side." His successor was even more confident. In December 1754 Governor Kerlérec called the Coweta leader "this faithful ally."[3]

In early October the Louisiana governor hosted a conference with Creek chiefs, mainly Upper Creeks, in Mobile. Kerlérec later reported that Malatchi had "been ill for six months" and could not attend. According to a secondhand report from Daniel Clark, Lachlan McGillivray's partner, the climax of this "grand Conference" came when Kerlérec showed the chiefs "a fictitious Letter wrote with red Ink." This bogus paper purported to be an invitation from English governors to the French "to join together in Order to destroy the Indians." Kerlérec manfully assured his visitors that the French were above such things, while the perfidious English "wanted nothing but the Indian Lands." He concluded that "it was high time for the Indians to begin upon the English; and they (the French) were ready to support and assist them." McGillivray, who had forwarded Clark's report, thought Kerlérec's performance "silly, and shallow" but feared it could have "a great Effect" on the Indians. He later warned that "the french have the Indians hearts; but the English have only the present trade of their deer-skins."[4]

Another report on the Mobile meeting from McGillivray reached Savannah on November 1, the day after Reynolds took his oaths of office. According to McGillivray, Kerlérec had "prevailed upon Head Men out of every Town to go to Mobile." The following day members of the council urged the inexperienced governor to send to both Upper and Lower Creeks "a Letter, or what is usually called a Talk," countering the French blandishments. On November 5 Reynolds signed identical letters to the Upper and Lower Creek leaders. McGillivray was to deliver the former to the Gun Merchant, and George Galphin the latter to Malatchi. These talks were not outstanding examples of the genre. In a brief paragraph Reynolds simply assured the chiefs that he would do his utmost to "preserve the good Understanding" between Creeks and Englishmen, and looked forward to meeting them. He would inform them when the time was ripe.[5]

Three weeks later the council minutes stated that this "was all that could be done, unless they had Presents to give them." Nothing further was done until royal presents finally arrived on September 30, 1755, nearly a year later. Only then did Governor Reynolds invite Creek leaders to meet with him.[6]

Since Reynolds was an experienced military man facing an all-out war, it is difficult to explain his prolonged inaction toward Indians except as one aspect of the political paralysis that soon crippled nearly all aspects of his administration. It is not much of an exaggeration to say that Reynolds was at war with his council long before he was seriously engaged with the French and Indians. Much of what Reynolds was blamed for was actually the work of his crony William Little, a former naval surgeon and now the governor's secretary and factotum. The governor's autocratic style, and especially the wide range of extraordinary powers he conferred upon the detested Little, had quickly alienated most of the colony's notables. It appeared that Reynolds was out of his element on dry land and was likely to face a mutiny.[7]

The main actions concerning Georgia's Indian relations during Reynolds's first year in office occurred on the other side of the ocean. In 1755 Edmond Atkin presented a major report on relations between the southern colonies and the native Indians to the Board of Trade, along with a comprehensive plan designed to remedy the problems he had identified. Atkin was a leading merchant and longtime member of the South Carolina council who in 1750 had returned to England for his health. With the outbreak of war, the board approached him for advice on the situation in the Southeast. Atkin's report and plan were painstakingly compiled and studded with shrewd insights.

Atkin argued that "the Indian Trade and Commerce . . . is so closely connected and interwoven with the Affairs of Government, that it cannot be separated from them." This was so because the Indians seemed bound to lean toward the imperial power that gave them the most rewarding trade. The British had enormous advantages here, for they were able to provide regular supplies of coveted manufactured goods, tailored to native tastes, delivered to their homes, at prices the French and Spanish could not match. Nevertheless, Atkin warned, the British were losing, a startling message that surely captured the board's attention. He wrote that "the British Interest among the Indian Nations . . . must, on the present footing, . . . continue to decline while we have any to lose."

Atkin pointed out that the French had advantages too and that they had learned to make the most of them. Their direct river connection to the Upper Creeks and Choctaws made it possible for them to deliver large quantities of ammunition to native towns, something the British could never do on horseback. The French effort was heavily subsidized by their government and controlled by gentlemen, not avaricious traders. Gentlemen made it their business to learn how to deal with negotiating partners, no matter how lowly, with respect and attention to their needs and wants. The French were accordingly much more effective with native leaders than the British were. The French honored old chiefs with presents, not the fearsome war leaders favored by most British traders. Unlike the penny-pinching British, they also repaired Indian firearms gratis. In short, unless the British adopted paternalistic policies more like those of the French, the tide of native affections would continue to run against them.[8]

In order to ensure that such policies were consistently implemented, Atkin recommended that the British government create a new official responsible for the entire southern region. This new imperial officer would be a southern counterpart to Sir William Johnson, superintendent of Indian affairs in the northern colonies. The Board of Trade and other British officials were impressed with Atkin's recommendations, though not so much with him. After some hesitation, in the summer of 1756 Atkin was appointed to the new office he plainly sought: "Superintendent of Indian Affairs in the Southern District of North America."[9]

Sometime in the late summer or early fall of 1754, Thomas and Mary Bosomworth arrived in London. They came more determined than ever to make good on Mary's various claims for services and their Georgia land claims, for they had nearly exhausted their resources to make the trip. Accordingly, their first step was to gain financial backing for their struggle. Very likely it was brother Abraham who located a financial angel for them, merchant Isaac Levy. On October 14 both Thomas and Mary signed articles of agreement with Levy. The basic bargain was as follows: Levy would provide the couple with up to £300 to meet their needs "during their stay in England" and would finance efforts to gain legal confirmation of their land claims; in return, Thomas and Mary agreed to give Levy a half interest in the three coastal islands. Abraham was one of the three witnesses.[10]

A related document Thomas wrote about the same time also deals with the land claims. Titled "Usefull hints," it evidently was intended as a guide to Levy and his lawyers, outlining the kind of legal defense of his land claims he wished to make before British authorities. His argument was based on precepts of Roman law, ideas that Thomas clearly derived in large part from Governor Glen. Thomas's central point was that the fundamental issue was property, not sovereignty. Prior to the establishment of the colony, the entire territory described as "Georgia" in the royal charter belonged to the Creek Indians. These natives were entitled to those vast lands by "that Natural Right and Property which by the Law of Nature and Nations is allowed to be vested in them." To demonstrate the relevance of the "Law of Nations," a basic concept of Roman law, he cited several maxims from the famous *Digest* of the Emperor Justinian. King George's charter to the Georgia Trustees had no effect on the Creeks' property rights, for "no Charter from any Crowned Head whatever could give the Grantees a Right or Power over a free and Independent people or their Properties; but by treaty or Conquest." Only the treaties of 1733 and 1739 diminished Creek rights to land, but those concessions involved only a small fraction of Creek territory. If the Creeks had ceded some lands to the Georgia Trustees, they could cede other of their lands to other grantees (Thomas and Mary, for instance). To hold that "the Creek Indians cannot give or dispose of their Reserved Lands to whom they please" was necessarily to deny their rights "by the Law of Nature and Nations."[11]

Thomas and Mary stood to gain more from their land claims than Mary's claims for services, but pursuing the former was far riskier. It would not be easy to convince the reigning king that he could not do what kings of England had been doing since the Virginia charter of 1609: publicly proclaiming their own sovereignty over vast stretches of North America. It would be easy, however, to provoke prosecution for treason. To publish challenges to the king's long-maintained sovereignty over a particular territory was to attempt to "unking" him there. It was to provide British officials with evidence, written and signed, of treasonous behavior. Thomas was daring, but he was not reckless. He had generally been careful to keep his Creek deeds out of sight; he was even more cautious with the extreme legal argument he based upon them.[12]

Over the next nine months Thomas and Mary presented six major memorials or petitions to high officials of the British government. The first two went to the Board of Trade in November: one from Mary ("Coosaponakeesa"), the other from Thomas "in behalf of Himself and Wife." Three others were delivered early in 1755. Thomas sent one to the Lords of the Treasury in February, and another to the Board of Trade in April. Finally, in June Mary presented a fifth to the lords justices of the Privy Council. The daring argument on the land issue found in the two private documents drafted in connection with Isaac Levy is absent from these five petitions. In these documents neither Bosomworth makes any direct reference to their land claims; all five focus on Mary's claims for services.[13]

But there was a sixth petition. Two years later Thomas described it to Governor Henry Ellis. He said that he and Mary had presented a memorial to the Board of Trade "setting forth their right and title to certain Islands . . . and a certain Tract of Main Land upon Savannah River." The Bosomworths had clearly decided to separate their two kinds of claims, perhaps on the advice of Levy's lawyers. The memorial on their land claims was the most important of the petitions the Bosomworths delivered in England, and the most closely held. No copy is known to survive, but it evidently was a companion piece to the one on services that Thomas presented in his and Mary's name.[14]

Yet even the five petitions that focus on claims for services contain hints on the Bosomworth strategy regarding the lands. All five present Mary as a Creek Indian, not a British subject. All say or imply that she was merely "allied" to the king of England, and none mentions her English father. Her memorial to the Board of Trade explains her relationship to the king as "being by Marriage allied to his Subjects." Accordingly, the two memorials submitted under her name were submitted under her Indian name, Coosaponakeesa, with no mention of her English name. Mary's claim to Indianness was irrelevant to her demands for services, but fundamental to the Bosomworth case regarding lands. If it were determined that Mary was English, the board could easily resort to precedents and declare that neither she nor her English husband nor any of the king's subjects could lawfully receive land grants directly from Indians.[15]

If Mary were an Indian, however, that easy exit from the controversy was blocked. Furthermore, the Coosaponakeesa introduced to the British government was no ordinary Creek Indian. As Thomas described his spouse to the Board of Trade, she was "of Indian Extraction, and Related to many of the leading Chiefs of the Creek Indian Nations and by their Laws and the Voice of the said Nation Esteemed their Rightfull and Natural Head." In her memorial to the Board of Trade she presented herself as the "Rightful and Natural born Princess of the upper and lower Creek Nations of Indians." Thus Mary did not petition as subject to sovereign, but as one sovereign to another.[16]

Although the surviving memorials did not refer to the Creek grants to the Bosomworths, two of them clearly aimed to turn the government's attention to the land claims. To her memorial to the Board of Trade, Mary appended the 1750 Creek recognition of herself as princess with "full power and Authority" to act for both Lower and Upper Creeks on all land questions. She explained that this authorization provided a way to settle "all past Differences and Animosities" between the Creeks and the British, no doubt including Creek ire that Savannah officials had dismissed their land grants to the Bosomworths. She concluded by requesting an "Audience" before the Board of Trade. This was a thinly veiled invitation to a deal: in return for the board's favorable consideration of Mary's land claims, Coosaponakeesa might consider an additional cession of Creek lands to the king.[17]

The veil came off in the memorial Thomas submitted to the board in behalf of himself and his wife about the same time. The document purports to be expressed in Mary's words. She there declares: "Your Memorialist (as Natural head or Chief of those Nations is fully Authorized and Empowered to make such further Concessions of Lands for the Use of his Majesty on their [the Creeks'] behalf, as she shall think proper." It was a transparent bid to gratify both the Bosomworths and the British government at the expense of the Creeks. Much to its credit, the British government ignored this disgraceful overture.[18]

On November 26 the Board of Trade read the two memorials and granted Mary's request for a hearing. When the Bosomworths appeared before the board on December 3 they reiterated their now familiar arguments for compensation for Mary's services. More important, they finally laid out their case for their Creek land grants, and finally revealed the evidential bases of their claims. Most likely it was at this hearing that the Bosomworths presented their lost memorial on the land claims. Thomas later said that on this occasion he produced "the Title Deeds . . . to the . . . Islands." In fact, he laid most of the key documents in his private archive. Discussion of these documents in the board's report a week later shows that what Thomas produced that day included at least the following: the 1748 deed for the islands; all three documents of August 2, 1750; the Graham deed of 1750; and the 1752 Creek repudiation of the Graham deed. The Bosomworth cards were now on the table. At the close of the session Thomas and Mary were told that because of the complexity of the issues, the board would need some time to consider them.[19]

Members of the board promptly set to work on the Bosomworth case and acted with unusual dispatch. They deliberated upon the case on December 4 and December 6, and on the latter day apparently decided what to do. That day they "ordered a state of the case to be prepared," that is, a report explaining the Bosomworth claims and what they thought the evidence revealed about them. That lengthy report was complete on December 10, and the Bosomworths were ordered to appear two days later.[20]

The "State of the Case relative to . . . the Bosomworths" was a confidential document for the use of members of the Board of Trade, and almost certainly was never shown to Thomas and Mary. Had they read it, they would have been furious. The report generally takes the form of a point-by-point refutation of the memorial that Thomas had put before the board. Early on it invokes the "known and established Principle in Law that no Subject can acquire a Title in Lands in any of His Majesty's Colonies, by purchase from the Indians." At the end it denounces the Bosomworths for "the many Signal Proofs which they have given of a Seditious and turbulent Temper." The report's last few pages drip with sarcasm: "If marrying a man who had ignominiously deserted his Ministry and Profession, and concerting with him a Scheme fraudulently and illegally to divest the Indians of Lands which the Crown has consented should be reserved to them . . . be a Meritorious Service, that merit is justly due to her. . . . If threatening destruction to the Colony, and calling in question his Majesty's Title to it, and the Rights of His Subjects to the Lands they possess, be a meritorious Service, this too will evidently appear from the foregoing Narrative."[21]

Members of the board were all too aware, however, that the couple had managed to create a very difficult problem for them. The problem was not legal but political. The nub of the difficulty was that, if the government took steps to give the Bosomworths the punishment it felt they deserved, it risked converting the Creeks from unreliable allies to implacable enemies in the midst of a momentous war with the French. The board was not willing to run that risk.

On December 12 the Earl of Halifax and other board members gave Thomas and Mary a carefully restrained statement of its findings. It was much like what the Savannah magistrates had told Abraham Bosomworth five years earlier: nothing Thomas and Mary had petitioned for would be granted, but everything they had requested might be granted at some future date. In the meantime no action would be taken against them. The board announced three "resolutions," the first two relative to the land claims and the third to the claims for services. The first two were written in gentle and measured tones but represented severe setbacks for the Bosomworths. The third, on the less serious issues, was expressed more forthrightly and handed them another defeat.[22]

First, Mary was not a Creek princess but "a natural born subject, being the daughter of an Englishman." In London, even more than in the colonies, ethnic identity remained an either/or question. Mary had claimed to be an Indian; the board now ruled that she was an Englishwoman. Evidently the sole basis for this finding was the patrilineal bent of English law, which made children more the offspring of their fathers than of their mothers. The board was unwilling to consider that Mary's Creek mother made any difference to her status or, in general, that mustees might have a status different from those of either Indians or Englishmen. (Much less would they consider the logical corollary to their ruling on Mary that English paternity must make Englishmen out of the thousands of mixed-bloods in North America who lived as Indians.) The board took note of "the pretence of Mrs. Bosomworth . . . that she came over here fully authorized by them [the Creeks] to treat with his Majesty . . . and to make concessions of lands." It did not characterize this shameful offer to betray the Creeks, but simply dismissed it on the ground that "a subject not authorized by any Commission from his Majesty" could not be an intermediary between the king and Indians.

Second, the board ruled that the Bosomworths had raised "a question of property, which must be heard and determined by a legal process in the Courts of Common Law or Equity in the colony." The second clause was the important one. The board told the Bosomworths that they had come to the wrong place: since they claimed a legal title to landed property in Georgia, they would have to sue in the colony's courts to validate that title. The board declined to characterize for the Bosomworths the land claims it had privately called fraudulent, illegal, and apparently even seditious. Instead, it challenged Thomas and Mary to initiate a lawsuit, confident that a Georgia court would rule against them if the matter ever went to trial.

The board's third resolution was that Mary must present her claims for services to Governor Reynolds, who would be ordered to investigate and report back to the board. On this matter, the board hinted at its current opinion. It declared that the records of the president and assistants in Savannah alleged that "instead of service Mrs. Bosomworth and her husband had done very ill offices to the prejudice of the colony, and been the authors of great disorders there." The board now challenged Thomas and Mary to dispute these allegations. Accordingly, it would direct Reynolds to give them "liberty to take copies of all such records" compiled by the former president and assistants.

These resolutions were skillfully drawn. The board had taken pains not to provide Thomas and Mary with anything they might show to the Creeks as evidence of British perfidy or even disrespect. The lords commissioners did not use the harsh words of the confidential "Case"; they did not say that the Creeks could not grant their lands to whoever they pleased; they did not even say that Mary's claims were tainted. Yet, despite its nonjudgmental pose, the Board of Trade had made two judgments that struck crippling blows to the Bosomworth land claims. If Mary was the king's subject, the land issue was resolved on its face. The second ruling was almost as bad for the Bosomworths. According to common law, title to lands was established by showing that they had been derived directly or indirectly from the king. No royal grant, no title. What Thomas and Mary were striving to establish was that certain lands, though granted to them by Indians and not by the king, nevertheless gave them a title good in English law. They could not expect to arrive at that result before judges or juries, for both were obliged to follow established precedents. To get to the novel place they wished to go the Bosomworths needed an innovative ruling, something they could reasonably hope to obtain only from top government officials. Understanding this, they had always directed their land appeals to executive rather than judicial bodies.

Thomas and Mary remained in London for six or seven more months. Realizing that their land claims had run into a wall, henceforth they devoted nearly all of their efforts to the pursuit of compensation for Mary's services. In this quest they sent additional memorials to the treasury officials, the Board of Trade, and even the Privy Council. As part of this effort they recorded in London some of the numerous documents they had brought from Georgia. Always able to persuade a few in high places to become his allies, Thomas engaged the lord mayor of London, Stephen Jenssen, to serve as his recorder. On April 19, 1755, Thomas appeared before Jenssen to swear to the authenticity of five documents relating to his wife's claims for services in Georgia. Five days later he returned to do the same for a copy of the 1733 treaty he had procured in Savannah and a copy of the 1739 treaty he had recorded in Charles Town.[23]

In a remarkable illustration of his tenacity, Thomas had somehow located Thomas Marriott, Oglethorpe's secretary during the 1739 treaty conference, and brought him to Jenssen. Marriott then swore an affidavit before the lord mayor attesting to the authenticity of the treaty text. Thomas also tried to involve Oglethorpe in his behalf, and claimed some success. A year later in Georgia, he referred to "General Oglethorpe's having Countenanced and supported every Claim on the Government when Mrs. Bosomworth and self were in England."[24]

Near the end of their stay the Bosomworths made one last effort to keep their land claims alive. On June 30, Mary, again as Coosaponakeesa, sent a memorial to the lords justices of the Privy Council. Defiantly, she again maintained that her relationship with King George was one of "Friendship and Alliance." She even managed to exceed her previous claims of authority: she was "Princess of the upper and lower Creek Nations . . . (over which God and Nature had ordained me head)." Divine right redux. She went on to complain of the Board of Trade's finding six months earlier that she "is a subject because her supposed Father was." She begged their lordships to consider "whether your Memorialist forfeits the Right of her [Creek] Inheritance by Reason One of his Majesty's Subjects violated the Laws of God and Man?"[25]

Despite an all-out effort, the Bosomworths received precious little satisfaction in London. The Board of Trade had repudiated one of their key contentions and had sloughed off the rest to the Georgia courts. Mary complained that "no Answer ever yet could be obtained" to their petition to treasury officials. The same was true for Mary's final appeal, for the lords justices of the Privy Council simply referred the matter to the Board of Trade. Toward the end, the money they had from Isaac Levy ran out. It was time to return home to St. Catherines, if it was still home. Thomas later complained that in order to pay for their return passage he was obliged to sell "the reversion of a paternal Estate in England." Frustrated and broke, the Bosomworths apparently had no choice but to forget their spurned claims and move on.[26]

During the Bosomworths' absence the administration of Georgia's first royal governor had, in most respects, quickly approached paralysis. In one way, however, it was very active. Since the lifting of the ban on Negro slavery, a tide of settlement had begun to flow into Georgia. Coming mainly from South Carolina and other southern colonies, the large numbers of immigrant whites were rivaled by large numbers of the blacks they brought with them. Most of this new settlement sought out potential rice lands along the damp coastline or the lower courses of the Ogeechee and Savannah rivers. Georgia officials prior to Reynolds had usually devoted one meeting a month to requests for land grants, almost always based on "headrights" of fifty acres for every person settled. A monthly meeting was completely inadequate for the crush of land business that had developed by 1754. Most meetings of Governor Reynolds and his council were devoted entirely to consideration of petitions for land grants.

The meeting of April 4, 1755, is particularly instructive. On that day Reynolds and the council considered sixty-seven petitions for land grants. Forty-seven of these dealt with lands on the Ogeechee, all but four seeking town lots in Hardwicke. The first petition considered was that of Jonathan Bryan, preeminent among transplants from South Carolina, and now a member of the council. Bryan sought, and received, five hundred acres on the south side of the Ogeechee. The petitioners for Hardwicke lots included three men Reynolds would soon nominate to the council: James Edward Powell, Samuel Marcer, and James Mackay. This hitherto insignificant settlement had been established by Oglethorpe at the practical limit of navigation for oceangoing ships, about fourteen miles inland.[27]

The governor himself was responsible for most of this sudden interest in the Ogeechee. As Reynolds explained to the Board of Trade on May 1, the Ogeechee was "a fine fresh water River" that originated far in the interior, as far (he thought, wrongly) as "the Nation of the Upper Creek Indians." Hardwicke possessed a "charming situation," along with a gentler bluff and deeper water than Savannah. All in all, he concluded, the colony's principal town had been planted in the wrong location: Hardwicke "is the only fit place for the Capital." He admitted, however, that "only one House is yet built there." By September 2 Reynolds had a warrant for his own five hundred acres on the Ogeechee.[28]

Governor Reynolds's fixation upon developing the Ogeechee goes far to explain why he cast a blind eye on a serious problem that had been developing there. Three months before the council meeting noted above, another such meeting had dealt with another petition for lands on the Ogeechee. On January 13 Reynolds and the council considered a petition from thirty-eight men headed by Edward Brown. The petitioners explained that "they had been at great Expense in removing themselves and Families many Hundreds of Miles from several of the neighbouriing Provinces in order to settle in this." Beginning in the early spring of 1754, they had come at their own cost and risk (mainly from Virginia and North Carolina) and had settled upon "uncultivated and vacant Lands" on the north bank of the Ogeechee. The petitioners went on to request that "the Lands they now dwelt upon might be granted to them." These lands, they explained, were "about one hundred Miles from the Mouth" of the Ogeechee, that is, about seventy miles beyond the tidal line agreed upon with the Creeks. This fact explains the petitioners' second request: that Governor Reynolds would take appropriate "Measures with the Indians . . . to secure them from their insults they having used many Threatnings and thereby put them in fear of their Lives." Unless the governor was able "to satisfy the Indians," the petitioners declared, "they would be under a Necessity of leaving the Province."[29]

Reynolds and his council did not wish to lose this large contingent of hardy backwoodsmen as Georgia settlers. On the other hand, they knew that this unauthorized settlement deep in Creek territory was bound to be provocative, and might well lead to bloodshed. So, what to do? So far as the record reveals, they did nothing. The minutes for the January 13 meeting conclude with the colony's leaders postponing any decision on the petition "untill they could get better Information respecting the Matters therein set forth." Over the next eighteen months Reynolds and council members undoubtedly received a great deal of information on the Ogeechee settlement, and the Indians' angry reactions to it, but none of it appears in their journal. The only further reference to the offending settlement in their proceedings during that period is oblique: on July 6, 1756, Andrew Lambert, another of its leaders, applied for a grant of three hundred acres on the Ogeechee. This petition too was postponed, this time without comment.[30]

The absence of further references to the Ogeechee settlement in the council journal is suggestive in another way: evidently the Creeks had yet to make a formal protest to Reynolds over the intrusion. That implies that there was a significant number of Creeks who found the rogue English settlement welcome. For them, most likely illicit trade anesthetized the pain of flagrant encroachment. Reynolds's successor later explained that the Ogeechee squatters, "having furnished themselves with dry Goods, and Rum, carry on a Trade with the Creeks, and have drawn such numbers about them, as greatly annoy the other Settlers." That September the colony would pay for Reynolds's inaction.[31]

In mid-July 1755 Thomas and Mary sailed from the Thames, arriving in Savannah on the last day of September. The ship that carried them also brought instructions from the Board of Trade on how to deal with the troublesome couple and a fresh supply of Indian presents. Those instructions, which doubtless directed that the Bosomworth land claims should be decided in a Georgia court, were read on October 3. Thomas, defiant again, had anticipated this. The same day "a Memorial of the Reverend Thomas Bosomworth in Behalf of himself and Mary his Wife was likewise read." He was ordered to attend the following week. On October 10 he came with a more detailed brief, "the Case of Mr. Thomas Bosomworth," along with supporting documents. This material was referred to the colony's attorney general, William Clifton, for an opinion on how to proceed.[32]

Neither of these petitions survives, but Clifton's opinion a week later reveals Thomas's immediate objective. Clifton ruled that the Bosomworth land claims were "only cognizable by a Court of Law, and cannot properly be determined by your Excellency and the Councill." When Reynolds gave this news to Thomas the governor also returned his petitions and supporting documents. It seems clear that Thomas, aware that his land claims had little or no chance in a Georgia court, tried to steer his case before the governor and council instead.[33]

When that stratagem failed, Thomas did not give up on executive action. The Board of Trade's third 1754 resolution on the Bosomworth case had directed Reynolds to make relevant evidence available to Thomas and Mary for their prospective lawsuit. The governor was to see to it that, provided they paid the usual fees, the Bosomworths were to have copies of all pertinent records in the colony, including "the journals of the President and Court of Assistants." Reynolds provided these records, which Thomas used to structure the longest and best of his numerous memorials. Entitled "A Narrative In Answer to the Charges and Alegations of the late President and Court of Assistants . . . ," it was not designed to support a lawsuit. Addressed to Reynolds, the document's first and only use was again as a petition to executive officials. The "Narrative" is impressive for its vigor and detail, the more so because bolstered by near a hundred appendices of more or less relevant documents. Strikingly, however, these attachments did not include copies of any of those most relevant: the Christie minutes or any of the Creek "deeds" to the Bosomworths. Reynolds forwarded Thomas's magnum opus with his letter of September 25, 1756, to the Board of Trade.[34]

Shortly before the Bosomworths' return, Governor Reynolds clashed with members of his council over his ubiquitous secretary, William Little. On September 12 six of them presented the governor with a memorial demanding that he remove Little from his numerous official positions "and your Excellency's Counsels." The same councillors repeated this demand eleven days later. Reynolds refused. Instead he fired one of them and appointed two new members, James Mackay and James Edward Powell. By this time the governor was almost completely isolated politically. Conspicuous among his few remaining supporters were old Malcontents like James Mackay, Samuel Marcer, and Charles Watson. These men were longtime friends and allies of the Bosomworths. When Thomas and Mary returned to Georgia they had to be surprised that they now found this the friendlier side of the Atlantic. Entirely apart from their own efforts, circumstances had conspired to breathe new life into their cause.[35]

The instructions the Board of Trade sent Reynolds on the Bosomworths do not survive, but the board referred to them several times in a report to the king on the governor's mismanagement. Board members recalled warning that Thomas and Mary "had affected a peculiar sort of title of Managers in all Indian Treaties in their own right, against which pretension the Governor had been sufficiently cautioned." They had directed Reynolds (1) to secure "the Friendship of the Creeks" and (2) to settle disputes with these Indians, including those involving the Bosomworths, "by an explicit Treaty or Conference at the time of the distribution of the presents." The board added that Reynolds "had been fully instructed with respect to the Second of these points by the Letters which Arrived at the same time with the presents."[36]

On October 8 Reynolds informed the board that the royal presents had arrived and that he had sent letters to all the Creek chiefs "inviting them to an interview at Augusta, as soon as the presents can be carried there." Distributing the king's bounty at Augusta rather than Savannah was an innovation, most likely mandated by the board's instructions. The board in turn may well have got the idea from Edmond Atkin, who pointed out that the French distributed presents from their king at forts near the Indian towns. When the Indians received British presents, however, "they earn them much too dearly" by long journeys and lost time.[37]

Reynolds apparently did not inform members of his council of his plan to meet the Creeks at Augusta until November 7. That day he told them he would be off to Augusta "shortly" and asked that three council members be chosen to accompany him. The governor had scheduled the meeting for the first week in December. According to the Board of Trade, he set off for Augusta on about November 17, which should have brought him there about four days later. According to Reynolds, he stayed in Augusta for ten days, but the Indians did not appear. He then returned to Savannah, "leaving Mr. William Little Commissioner and Agent for Indian Affairs, to deliver my Speeches, and the Presents to them."[38]

Reynolds went on to relate that the Creeks, three hundred of them, arrived "a week after I came away; and Peace and Friendship were renewed between us." That was the sum and substance of his only report on the meeting, which he sent to the Board of Trade on January 5. Only one other document, "Abstract . . . [of] a Conference held at Augusta," gives an account of the meeting. The talks extended over four days, from December 15 to December 18. What transpired was a question-and-answer exchange between Little and the Gun Merchant, "Speaker on behalf of the Indians." Henry Ellis, Reynolds's successor, later observed that "Insnaring questions were asked that led to the desired answers." The "Abstract" notes that Mary Bosomworth was present and that on the last day she contributed the final and decisive question for the Indians.[39]

Little showed the 1751 Graham deed to the Indians, then asked "if they allowed the Validity of that Deed." When this did not produce a straight answer, he tried another question: Which of two grants, the Upper Creek grant to Graham or the Lower Creek grant to Mary, yielded the "most valid" title? This query caused the Indians "much uneasiness" and a sleepless night, clearly because of the apparent conflict between the authority of Lower Creeks and Upper Creeks. The next day the Gun Merchant delivered the Indians' answer in favor of the grant to Mary. This answer, however, remained unsatisfactory: "having made use of the Words, viz. 'That Mrs. Bosomworth was an old woman and by the course of nature could not live long;' without explaining his meaning upon these words; the interpreters concluded that his meaning was that Mrs. Bosomworth should enjoy these Lands only for her Life." The document adds only "But this being a Misconstruction," then has the meeting adjourn for the day. The supposed misconstruction would be explained on the final day of the encounter.[40]

If Mary had merely a grant for her lifespan, she had the sort of land rights that Indians generally recognized. That was not the answer Little or Mary wanted. On December 18 Little asked the Indians how their grant to Mary "was consistent with the Promise they had made that none should possess those lands without the Authority of the King"? That was an easy one: "they gave the Lands to Mrs. Bosomworth as an Indian and one of themselves." Then, "at the Request of Mrs. Bosomworth," the final question was put to the Lower Creeks: "Whether they intended that Mrs. Bosomworth should have full power to alienate or dispose of the said Lands and Islands"? The Indians answered that she "might give them, sell or dispose of them as she pleased." Having arrived at last at the intended destination, the meeting ended. The extraordinary finale has Creeks granting Mary lands as an Indian, but not by Indian land tenure. The Board of Trade's instructions to Reynolds on how to deal with the Bosomworths and the Creeks had been entirely subverted.[41]

From Augusta the Gun Merchant and about ninety followers proceeded to Charles Town for a conference with Governor Glen. There Creek grievances were discussed at length. The main ones involved the trade, especially the premium over Cherokee prices Creeks paid for the same goods, and the illicit settlement on the Ogeechee. On September 12 Reynolds and his council had supported Glen's plan to lower Creek prices. Glen used price concessions to gain tentative Upper Creek approval for a fort in their country. Like Atkin, he hoped to build an English fort in every major Indian nation, a project inspired by the French example and designed to counter it. He had earlier prevailed upon the Lower Cherokees to approve a fort near Keowee, built as Fort Prince George in late 1753. Negotiations were under way with the Overhill Cherokees to build what soon became Fort Loudoun. The lowered prices and the Creek fort were bundled into a deal that became a formal treaty signed on January 23, 1756. This treaty, "the Gun Merchant's Treaty," became a dead letter when the Upper Creeks refused to ratify it because of the fort.[42]

Governor Reynolds's obvious mismanagement of the Creek conference quickly led to a storm of protest, including letters to the Board of Trade from two of the councillors who had followed him to Augusta. On July 29 the board petitioned the king to order Reynolds home to face an inquiry and asked that an interim successor be appointed. The board complained that despite the clear instructions it had given Reynolds regarding a Creek meeting and the Bosomworth problem, the governor had not listened. Reynolds had never consulted with his council on the matter, had never negotiated for the desired treaty or agreement, had abdicated his responsibility to his secretary, and had never sent the board a genuine report on what had occurred at the Augusta meeting. Perhaps worst of all, Little had "admitted Mr. and Mrs. Bosomworth to be present at it, although they are persons interested in points prejudicial to your Majesty's interests and those of the Colony."[43]

On September 25 Reynolds reported his findings on the Bosomworth affair to the Board of Trade. He appended Thomas Bosomworth's "Narrative," brief letters from the four surviving assistants, and various other documents. The board had directed him to form a general opinion on the state of the controversy. He did. "It is . . . my opinion that Mr. Bosomworth and his Wife have been very Ill used by that Court of President and Assistants, who I think acted in a very Injudicious Unwarrantable, and Arbitrary manner."[44]

The most serious charge against Reynolds involved court packing. In December 1756 he reconstituted the colony's three-man general court. He dismissed two judges and pressured the third to resign. One of those removed was the chief justice, Noble Jones, long a Bosomworth foe, who was also suspended from the council. In January Reynolds appointed Little to replace Jones, and two others to fill the other vacancies. Savannah residents smelled Bosomworth influence, "and Mr. Little chosen to preside there with a view to facilitate the establishment of these peoples pretensions at the approaching Tryal." At the last minute Little resigned. Ellis later explained that this left Patrick Mackay on the bench "as senior Justice, and one of the most partial ones imaginable. He it was that Mr. Reynolds fixed upon to manage Bosomworths affair." He supposed that this would allow Mackay "to share the spoil."[45]

In the spring of 1756, Alexander Kellett, member of council and provost marshal, sailed for England at the request of "most of the Councillors, Representatives, Public Officers, Planters of Substance and Character" in Georgia. He carried a fourteen-count indictment of the colony's governor. Reynolds was forced to defend himself from these charges before the Board of Trade in 1758. He described Mary to the board as "being Indian," but otherwise gave a very different version of the Augusta meeting. Struggling to exculpate himself, Reynolds now turned on the Bosomworths. In his telling, he had advised Thomas and Mary not to stay away, but when they decided to come along he had no power to prevent them from attending a public meeting. If anything untoward occurred at Augusta, the blame did not belong to himself or Little but to the Bosomworths: "Mrs. Bosomworth in private conversation with the Indians prevailed upon them to bring the matter of her Grant from Malatchi in question during the conference." Attentive to his duty, Little had done what he could to thwart them. He had seen to it that consideration of any and all Creek grants was put off "to a future General Meeting of the Upper and Lower Towns."[46]

Since this version of events directly contradicted the "Abstract," Reynolds strove to discredit that document. What seemed to be a transcript of the talks was actually a Bosomworth fabrication. According to Reynolds, "this pretended Abstract" was "false in every essential point" and, though the Bosomworths had often tried to foist it on Little, "it was as often rejected by him as fictitious." To expose the falsity of the document, Reynolds explained that the issue of Mary's grant had been avoided at Augusta in order to avoid "a Contest with the Indians." Such a contest was pointless "because Mrs. Bosomworth herself could not in the course of nature Live long and whenever she dyes all disputes upon that head will be at an end." Thus Reynolds echoed the Gun Merchant's very words, thereby endorsing the idea that the grant was temporary and reversing the message of the "Abstract." If the Creek grant to Mary was an ordinary Indian allotment, the entire controversy was a tempest in a teapot that would soon dissipate. Surely it was no cause to unseat a conscientious governor.[47]

The British government was not inclined to agree. The Board of Trade's July 29 report quickly won royal approval, and Henry Ellis was appointed lieutenant governor on August 3. This most welcome news did not reach Georgia until October, and Ellis did not arrive until the following February. Reynolds was summoned home, and sailed in March. A year later he made his formal defense to the Board of Trade, which the following month recommended his dismissal from office.[48]

Unprecedented trouble with the Creeks darkened Governor Reynolds's final months in Georgia still further. For two and a half years Lower Creeks had protested the Ogeechee settlement deep in their territory. Reynolds apparently took no notice. On August 30, 1756, a petition signed by all the major traders and inhabitants of Augusta warned Reynolds that things could not go on this way. The petitioners declared that "we seriously wish there had been no Settlement made on Ogechee as yet for . . . the Creek Indians . . . are continually Exclaiming against it and more so this Summer than ever." They urged that the settlement be abandoned "by degrees." The inevitable clash occurred four days later when a party of Tuckabatchee hunters stole some horses from the offending settlement, and two of them were killed by pursuing settlers. One Englishman was reported to have died from his wounds afterward. It was the worst episode of violence between colonists and Creeks since the founding of Georgia, and perhaps the first instance of intentional bloodshed.[49]

More worrisome, with Britain and France now officially at war, the French could be counted upon to exploit Creek resentment. They would surely use the incident in their effort to persuade the Creeks to fight in their behalf. If they succeeded, the British cause in the Southeast would be placed in mortal peril. Believing that the instigators were Lower Creeks, on September 14 Reynolds protested the armed horse thievery to Tugulki, son and presumed successor of the recently deceased Malatchi. To William Lyttelton, the new South Carolina governor, he confided that "I have avoided mentioning therein that the White people returned the fire of the Indians, and that two of them were seen to drop, because I think it will be best to conceal that part of the story." Both Lower and Upper Creeks had already noticed, for the two victims were Upper Creek "runagates." Reynolds organized a company of rangers, but he seems to have taken no further action. When news of the incident reached London, it was recognized as a potential disaster and extraordinary measures were taken. To defend against a feared French and Indian attack, early in 1757 a force of a thousand army regulars was shipped to Charles Town, where they were joined by other troops from the northern colonies.[50]

The Creek leadership, which had shown remarkable restraint about the Ogeechee settlement, was equally distressed by the violence. On September 17, before they heard from Reynolds, Lower Creek chiefs sent him an account of the incident. They wanted a quick resolution. They reported that two of the young Upper Creek raiders had been killed and one wounded, but supposed that two white men had also been killed. With blood for blood already shed, the incident should be forgotten: "we hope our loving Brother will let the Thing die." They then made the first recorded formal protest of the settlement to Georgia officials: "we beg of you for to draw your People from Ogeechee," for their "living so high up spoils our hunting Ground." They also asked the governor to order home two men "who trades away back in the Woods." Far from the Creek towns, these trouble-makers intercepted young hunters before they could bring their skins home.[51]

In a follow-up talk on October 13, Lower Creek headmen again asked that "you will not let any of your People settle at Ogeechee." Elaborating on the illicit trade, they explained that their hunters could not resist the lower prices offered by rogue traders, or their rum. This created serious problems in the Creek towns: "they buying Goods cheaper below makes them often quarrel with the White People in the Nation, besides they often get drunk." This was apparently the first serious complaint about trading "in the woods," the first of many. There was another first in the October message: "we are resolved not to sell any of our Lands, nor let the White People settle any nigher us, for our Hunting Ground is already too small." There is no record that Reynolds replied.[52]

The Upper Creeks, though they at first talked of demanding satisfaction for their casualties, soon also came around to seeking a speedy resolution. The Gun Merchant dispatched a renowned war chief, Hopoya Thluko of Okfuskee, generally known to the English as Handsome Fellow, to settle the matter with Reynolds. On November 16 he met with the governor and council in Savannah. The Upper Creek leader promptly conceded that "the Indians were the first Agressors." They were "a Parcel of Stragling runagates" acting without encouragement from his nation, "and it was natural for the White People to protect themselves." He also accepted Reynolds's claim that at least one of the Ogeechee pursuers had been killed. With the burning issue now flickering out, the governor finally took notice of what had caused it: "If the Settlement of Ogechee is offensive I will order the People to remove from thence." Handsome Fellow replied that "I have no Authority to talk about the removal of the Ogechee Settlement" and indicated that this was a Lower Creek problem. Reynolds later claimed to have settled the killings issue with Handsome Fellow, but continued to take no action on the offensive settlement.[53]

Handsome Fellow also volunteered that "We have no Objection to the Settlement of Augusta which is usefull for the Trade of our Nation." Then he went further: "We have no Objections against Peoples settling on the Waters of Savannah River." It was one more indication of a nonchalant Upper Creek attitude toward Lower Creek lands. Even so, it relieved remaining English concerns for the safety of settlements from Mount Pleasant up to Augusta. These unsolicited concessions were strong evidence of Upper Creek determination to maintain peaceful contacts with the British.[54]

A dangerous problem, the first serious bloodshed, had been laid to rest. Significantly, the Creeks had taken the initiative to solve it. Rather than gravitate to the French in anger, they had reached out to the English. Georgians and South Carolinians allowed themselves a great sigh of relief. Though it is not clear that any Englishman had died during the skirmish, both Lower and Upper Creeks seemed glad to suppose that several did. Their diplomatic credulity on this point was a strong signal that they wanted no part of the French war effort. Rather than make common cause with the French, they would maintain their neutrality. So far as the British were concerned, this was the best possible outcome. The Southeast would not be a major battleground of the war. In the spring of 1758 nearly all of the British troops would be withdrawn to the northern colonies.

Lieutenant Governor Henry Ellis reached Charles Town in late January 1757 and Savannah about two weeks later. On February 16 he formally relieved Reynolds. To Georgians then, and historians since, it was a case of day following night. Ellis proved to be a sure-handed diplomat. Though in private he often referred to the natives as "savages," he was unfailingly respectful in public. Ellis found that a party of twenty-nine Lower Creeks, headed by Occouthla of Chehaw, "had been many days in Town without being taken any notice of by Mr. Reynolds." The new governor immediately treated the visitors as honored guests. Noting that the party was "in great want of provisions," Ellis ordered supplies for them. Occouthla was given an audience with Ellis and the council on February 19 and again six days later. The Creek leader was given the commission he requested, along with gifts for himself and his followers. Having found the entire experience "highly pleasing," the Indians departed in good humor.[55]

It is clear that Ellis not only had a talent for diplomacy but had done some homework on how best to speak to and behave toward Indians. When native visitors showed up unannounced, as happened with increasing frequency, he made them feel welcome, often at his house. For example, when one such group of twenty-four Cussitas appeared on April 21, Ellis used the occasion to wish that "the Chain of Friendship might be continued bright and the Path strait between them and us." He then invited them to his house to receive some presents, ordering the commissary to provide "some Provisions and Liquor."[56]

Ellis could turn a phrase but, perhaps more important, he could recognize conventional phrases that played well on both sides of the ethnic divide. He seldom let slip an opportunity to invoke the "Chain of Friendship," and sometimes his call elicited an Indian response with sympathetic vibrations. Thus when Ellis opened a formal conference in November 1757 with a call for "brightning the Chain and making the Path Strait for ever between Us," the Lower Creek spokesman responded with the hope that "no Rust may sully the Chain of Friendship between Us any more." Similarly, after receiving a (lost) talk from Ellis nine months later, Lower Creeks replied: "We hope . . . that our Chain of friendship still bright and unsullied will continue so long as the Sun Shines and the Water runs."[57]

The governor could pick up on Indian statements too. In July he observed to an Okfuskee chief, another uninvited visitor, that the English were famous for bravery, "as might be seen by the Bones of their Enemies scattered over the Appalachian Fields." This was a deliberate echo of the Lower Creek boast quoted in the 1739 treaty. Ellis added that "the French were become so Perfidious that even their Friends the Spaniards . . . were ashamed of their Behaviour and refused to join with them agains Us." Ellis was unusually receptive to Indian visitors, who for many months were all unofficial visitors. A little over a year after his arrival, he reflected that he had "already seen no less than thirteen hundred Red People." Above all, he was patient.[58]

Two items were at the top of Ellis's agenda. First, of course, was the war. Under pressure from London, Ellis had to try to recruit native allies who would fight for the British cause, or at least dissuade them from joining the French. In August he wrote William Pitt, the new prime minister, that a good relationship with the Creeks was so vital that "the very being of this Government depends upon it." Second was the Bosomworth problem. It was less pressing for the time being, but for more than a decade it had tied the relationship between the Georgia government and the Creeks in knots. Ellis had to try to untie them.[59]

The French had been actively attempting to recruit Creek auxiliaries for more than a year. Ellis's first attempt to do so occurred during his first contact with Creeks. Meeting with Occouthla's party on February 19, he "urged every thing I was capable of to fix them in our interest and excite them to annoy our enemies." Ellis told the visitors that "we would give 20 shillings for every scalp of our Enemies and 40 shillings for every prisoner." He explained that "I did this with the advice of Council whom I convinced of the expediency of it." He was aware of, and clearly approved of, the example set by South Carolina, Virginia, and other colonies. Although Ellis regularly sought to recruit auxiliaries from among friendly Indian visitors, there is no sign that he made a direct approach on this subject to the leadership of either the Lower or Upper Creeks.[60]

On May 18 Captain Allick came to town with his brother Will and several other Creeks. As Ellis noted to the council, the mustee Allick "had lived amongst us some Years." Captain Allick had staked out a plantation on Penholloway Creek, a tributary of the Altamaha, and came mainly to request an English grant of this land. His brother, however, came seeking the governor's reaction to a recent Cherokee talk to the Creeks. Will related that the Cherokees said they were about to join the French "and wanted the Creeks to do likewise." The Cherokees had argued that the recently established Fort Loudoun was a sign that the British were plotting to "take away their Lands." After countering that the fort had been built "at the particular Request of the Cherokees themselves," Ellis argued that it was the French who schemed to expropriate Creek lands. The crafty French kept their evil design well hidden, but "they were creeping upon them like old Age, which they could not see." The governor again concluded with a bid for military aid from individual Creeks and a promise of bounties. He explained that the bounty offered for prisoners was twice that for scalps because, unlike the French, the English "never took Pleasure in Spilling human Blood." Captain Allick, who was not returning to Lower Creek country, said that what Ellis had propounded "was very true and just." His brother, who was returning, said nothing.[61]

It seems clear that most Creek reaction Ellis heard to his war wooing was negative. He tried once more. On September 13 he hosted a visit from fifty Lower Creeks, mostly Oconees, who had relocated far to the south and would soon become known as Seminoles. The party was headed by the war chief the English knew as the Cowkeeper. He and the Oconee peace chief, Wioffki, would be paired for decades to come as principal Seminole leaders. Ellis reminded the Cowkeeper of Oglethorpe's first treaty, the foundation of Lower Creek–English friendship. Now the Cowkeeper, as a special friend, had "a Special opportunity of manifesting his Friendship to the English by making War on the French." The Indian leader avoided a direct reply, and Ellis soon concluded that his bids for Creek military assistance were not working. After his most important conference with Creek leaders in November, Ellis reported that "during the whole negotiation I never instigated the Indians to make war upon our Enemies." In December he wrote Pitt that Creek neutrality was the best that could be hoped for. He explained that "the french have acquired so strong a party in their Nation, that to propose to the Indians to act offensively against them, would have given great umbrage, and been employed to our disadvantage by the Enemy."[62]

Though characteristically deliberate, Ellis was surprisingly slow to move against the major irritant of his predecessor's last days, the illicit settlement on the Ogeechee. Creek condemnations of the settlement continued, notably from an abrasive voice heard more and more often, the Mortar of Oakchoy. Attacks on the settlers' livestock followed. Intimidated, many of the settlers abandoned the area. On April 12, 1757, Ellis and his council considered a petition for aid from the Ogeechee setters. Now "reduced to 25 or 30 Families," they lamented that they were "obliged to let the Indians do as they thought fit." Ellis linked the Ogeechee settlement with another a few miles away on Briar Creek, a tributary of the Savannah. He thought that Creek depredations at both places could be curbed by cracking down on illicit traders. Two days later Ellis took action against trader John Fitch, who admitted selling rum to Indians "in the Woods." He told the Ogeechee settlers that his efforts to end trade abuses would make them "more Secure."[63]

The conference Ellis held with the Lower Creeks in November appeared to vindicate his reluctance to move against the Ogeechee settlement. The Indians' spokesman, Stumpe, declared that "I will say nothing as to the Lands above the flowing of the Tides." On the way down his people had "observed a few Settlers there," but fewer than they had expected. Except for one cattle drover, "We are content that every one should continue unmolested where they are Settled." Their contentment did not last. What apparently changed their mind was a report that none of the Ogeechee settlers who had killed the two Upper Creeks were themselves slain. Relatives of the deceased concluded that "no satisfaction was given" because the English killers "are yet alive [except] only one that died in Savannah Goal." In other words, Reynolds had lied to them.[64]

Governor Ellis's wartime diplomacy with the Creeks was not designed to support British offensive operations against the French. No such attack was seriously considered until 1758 and, unlike Lyttelton, Ellis was not brought in on the planning. Ellis saw his essential task as negative: to prevent the French from gathering enough Indian allies to mount an assault on the British. Since his aim was to prevent something bad from happening, his negotiating strategy was reactive and defensive. No such strategy was likely to be effective with the governor's other major diplomatic problem: Creek support for the Bosomworth land claims. Here Ellis's task was the more challenging one of undoing something bad that had already happened. Earlier attempts to do this had been ill prepared and ineffective. Except for the Graham mission, Georgia and British officials had simply reacted to Bosomworth initiatives. This had produced some temporary successes, but no settlement. If the Bosomworths were ever to give up their fight, the Georgia government had to carry the struggle to them and their Creek protectors.

Ellis quickly realized that his essential diplomatic task was to maneuver the Creeks from being participants in the struggle to bystanders. In May 1758 he outlined his strategy to Governor Lyttelton of South Carolina: "It is of importance that the Indians should be disengaged, and that the dispute should rest between the King, and his natural born Subjects," Thomas and Mary Bosomworth. Heretofore, when the Savannah authorities had gone after the Bosomworths, Creek headmen had come to their rescue. It was vital to Thomas and Mary that the Creeks continue to serve as a shield between themselves and the colonial government. If the chiefs could be persuaded to discontinue that role, the Bosomworths would have to abandon their struggle or fight on almost alone. If they chose to fight, the odds would have changed and the government could safely confront them. Either way, the conflict would probably soon be over. Ellis was soon convinced, however, that it would be unwise to inflict a total humiliation on the couple. Thomas was "a most mischievous, crafty and obstinate fellow," and he and Mary had proven again and again that they were capable of striking back with surprising effect. After less than three months in the colony, Ellis was already suggesting to the Board of Trade that the only lasting solution to the problem had to be some sort of a compromise.[65]

It would help persuade the Indians to retire quietly from the controversy if new clashes with the Bosomworths—especially with Mary—were carefully avoided, so for the time being Ellis did what he could to prevent confrontations with the couple. Instead of ostracizing them, he contacted Thomas and Mary through intermediates, dropping hints of a possible compromise. Thomas evidently did file the lawsuit he had contemplated the previous year. A court battle managed by the wily Thomas could be highly disruptive or worse. As Ellis explained to the Board of Trade on October 22, he had acted to deny the Bosomworths that opportunity: "I confess I have used some art to put off the tryal as the peoples notion of their power with the Indians is such that it is doubtful with me whether that alone on a hearing would not influence them to decide in their favor."[66]

Governor Ellis could easily have been more positive about the diplomatic progress he had already achieved. On May 18 a £1,500 consignment of royal presents for Indians was delivered in Savannah. In the past this had promptly initiated plans for meetings with the Creeks and other natives to air grievances, settle differences, and deliver the goods. This time, plans for a Creek meeting moved ahead much more deliberately. Ellis was unwilling to schedule a conference until he understood the situation thoroughly and had created enough goodwill among the Creeks to provide some chance of gaining the concessions he sought.[67]

On August 7 he sent Joseph Wright up to the main towns of both Lower and Upper Creeks. He instructed Wright to invite "the chief men of both Nations" to meet him in Savannah. Ellis also wrote to "each" of the Creek traders, urging them, as their patriotic duty, to help persuade leading chiefs to attend. "They all . . . exerted themselves to oblige me." In an extraordinary gesture of respect, Ellis did not set a time for the meeting. Instead, he left that up to the Creek leaders, "and You are to send me early notice of the time fixed on to meet me." Ellis also instructed Wright to conduct the visitors himself, taking care "to avoid Augusta and the inhabited parts of the province." And one more thing: "You are not to insinuate any knowledge of the Subjects upon which I intend to treat." The chiefs who came were not likely to arrive nursing a fresh grievance suffered on the trail or well primed to resist what he asked of them.[68]

Creek leaders had spurned several recent invitations from Governor Lyttelton to meet with him in Charles Town, but they readily agreed to see Ellis. On October 25 the governor informed the council that agent Wright and the lead party of Creeks had reached the forks, and were hourly expected at Fort Argyle. Ellis was ready with what was probably the most elaborate welcome Englishmen had ever extended to Indians. When Oglethorpe had trekked to Coweta in 1739, he reported that Creeks had met him forty miles away, "and layd Provisions on the roads." Having arranged an analogous courtesy, Ellis told the council he had sent Captain John Milledge and his ranger company to Fort Argyle. There the rangers were to "accomodate" the Creek visitors, provision them, and then escort them to Savannah.[69]

On October 29 about 150 Indians, Upper Creeks and Lower, approached Savannah behind their ranger escort. They had come from twenty-one towns, all of the major towns of both nations. They were met about a mile outside of town by Captain Jonathan Bryan "with the Principal Inhabitants of the Town on Horseback." These Savannah worthies then welcomed the Indians in the governor's name, "and regaled them in a Tent pitched for that Purpose." Mounting up again, "the Cavalcade" resumed its march. "Captain Bryan at the Head of the Gentlemen led the Way, the Indians followed according to their Rank, and the Rangers brought up the Rear." As the procession came in sight of the town, a circular salute of cannon fire went round from one bastion to the next. At the gate Bryan's horsemen divided to the right and left, forming "two Lines through which the Indians marched." At this point there was another handoff of escort duty. Noble Jones, colonel of the local militia company, then conducted the visitors toward the council house. "As they passed the Governors House they were Saluted with Seven Cannon from his Battery, which was Succeeded by the Cannon at the Water Side and from Vessels in the River." And a good deal more of this sort of thing. "For us?," Indians must have thought.[70]

Ellis met the Creeks at the council house, where he gave them a short welcoming speech. He told them he had ordered his people "to supply you with every thing the Plantations afforded" and would make that his personal business. "And that you may enjoy each others Company under one Roof and receive no Injury from the Weather, I have built a large House to Shelter You," doubtless similar to the Indian house the French had built in Mobile. After their long journey, Ellis was concerned not to "detain you longer from Repose" but promised a meeting soon at which he would deliver them a talk from King George. (In fact, he had no royal talk, but Wright had led the Indians to expect one.) "And in the mean Time I Recommend to you to get your Guns and Saddles repaired which I have

Ordered our Workmen to do if you desire it," another good idea borrowed from the French.[71]

Surprisingly, the visitors had chosen the Wolf King of Mucklassee to deliver their reply as "Speaker for the whole." There was no precedent for Lower Creeks choosing an Upper Creek to speak for them. Moreover, the Wolf King was the most outspoken Anglophile among the Upper Creeks. Before he said a word it was clear that the Creeks had not come to talk tough. The Wolf King said he and fellow Creeks had made many previous trips to meet English governors, "but never had more Satisfaction than we feel on this Occasion." After Tugulki added a few comments, Ellis "invited the Head Men to dine with him at his own House where they were entertained in the kindest and most Friendly manner to their entire Satisfaction."[72]

Thomas Bosomworth had been watching all this with growing anxiety. For more than a year the viability of his and his wife's land claims had suffered. Governor Reynolds and his few political allies had been swept from office. Malatchi was dead, and his presumed successor, his son Tugulki, was still a boy. The Ogeechee incident had made it plain that Creeks were in no mood for confrontation with the English. If they were not willing to threaten the English for shedding Creek blood, was it likely they would do it in support of the Bosomworth land claims? Indications were accumulating that Governor Ellis was on the verge of a diplomatic triumph, one that could flush the Bosomworth land claims down the river. Seeing the trend, Thomas rushed to salvage something while it was still possible.

On October 31 Thomas Bosomworth did what he had never done before: he sent Ellis a compromise proposal to settle the old dispute, all of it. With the exception of St. Catherines Island, Thomas now said he and Mary were ready to surrender all of their land claims. They were also ready to declare their claims for services satisfied. In return for these startling concessions, they had two essential demands: £3,000 sterling within a year, and a royal grant of St. Catherines Island "to the said Thomas Bosomworth and his heirs upon the terms that other Lands are held in the province." Orally, Thomas also promised Ellis that, if his terms were accepted, he and Mary would assist "to obtain an absolute [Creek] Cession of those Lands."[73]

Governor Ellis would not convene a formal meeting with the Indians until November 3. During the previous four days—and nights—he entertained the most influential Creek leaders at his house. The private talks that ensued are undocumented but clearly went about as well as Ellis could have wished. It appears that the Creek leaders not only shared his concern to end the debilitating wrangle over the Bosomworth land claims but were receptive to his suggestions on how to go about it. An understanding was reached that would decisively shape not only the coming conference but the entire Bosomworth controversy. The idea was that at the public conference Creek leaders would appear to take the initiative to end the conflict. There they would formally propose an ostensibly temporary measure that was actually tantamount to a permanent solution.

The council chamber was crowded with Indians and most of the colony's notables when the conference finally began. After a few formalities, the governor opened by solemnly reading "a Paper he had wrote for the Purpose," which he introduced as the promised speech from King George. The distant monarch was in better form than usual. As Ellis intoned the purported royal words, His Majesty explained to "you my most beloved Children" that the French king had initiated the current war with a surprise attack. As part of his treacherous scheme, he had seduced "some of my Children among the Red People inhabiting the Borders of the great Lakes," and was trying to do the same with the Creeks. The speech went on to urge that the Creeks remain firm in their "Obedience and Affection to me" and always consider "my Friends as your Friends, and my Foes as yours." The speech stopped short, however, of soliciting Creek participation in the war.[74]

The governor then elaborated in his own voice. He informed his Creek audience that the king "has commanded me to take Care of his Children the red People but especially of you the best beloved." Accordingly, he asked: "Is there any thing I can do for you? Let me know and it shall be done." This opportunity to strengthen the bonds uniting the English and Creek peoples must be seized, "that our Children may have Reason to remember this Day with thankfulness when our Bones are cold." Again there was no appeal for military aid. When Ellis paused for the chiefs' reaction, the meeting got down to the real business of the day.[75]

The Creek response was delivered by Stumpe of Coweta, uncle and guardian of the seventeen-year-old Tugulki. He expressed "great Satisfaction" with the king's speech and that of the governor. "There is nothing we desire more than . . . renewing our ancient Friendship with our Brothers the English." Accordingly, "We will now open our Hearts and entirely unburden our Minds." What had been weighing on their minds was a certain quarrel over land. Stumpe then recalled that his people had granted lands along the coast to Oglethorpe, but had reserved three islands: "these we left in the Hands of an Old Woman (meaning Mrs. Bosomworth) to keep for Us." Unfortunately, she had taken advantage of them, "She Pretending to have bought [them] and that they belonged to her." This pretence had led to "great Animosities and Disturbances between Us and the White People." This must stop. "We now declare that we did not Sell them to her and we desire that your Honour will take them under your Care in Trust to put an End to future disputes concerning them." Stumpe added that there were many other things that had "caused Uneasiness among Us," but he would forbear mentioning them now "for Fear of raising new Difficulties." The one thing the Creeks wanted settled immediately was the dispute over the islands.[76]

As all who heard it understood, Stumpe's denial that the Creeks had granted Ossabaw, Sapelo, and St. Catherines to Mary was not exactly unsullied truth. It was, however, what the occasion required. The important thing to arrive at was not the truth but the diplomatic answer that would liberate both English and Creeks from a crippling conflict. The fact that the speaker represented Coweta only magnified the impact of his words. If the Indians were relieved, the Englishmen present must have been beaming. No one doubted that Ellis spoke truth when he replied that "The Confidence you repose in me in regard to the disputed Lands gives me great Pleasure." A few minutes later the governor called for the treaty text he had prepared. After "each Article was fully and distinctly interpreted and explained," the chiefs "heartily and unanimously approved" the treaty. Finally, they "put their Hands and Seals to it before a numerous Audience."[77]

Most articles of the 1757 treaty were routine provisions renewing peaceful relations, but the fourth was new and riveting. It begins by stating that there had been reports that "the head Men and States of the Creek Nations had alienated and sold to Coosaponakesee alias Mary Bosomworth" certain lands. These were the three coastal islands and "the Lands from the town of Savannah to Pipe Maker's Creek." (Stumpe had apparently forgotten to mention the Yamacraw tract, but no Creek questioned the addition.) These reports were mistaken: "We the head Men and States never did sell or alienate the same to the said Coosaponakesee alias Mary Bosomworth, or to any private person whomsoever." Furthermore, "we now deliver the said Lands and Islands in Trust to his Honour the present Governor Representative of the Great King." Nothing specific was asked or given in return.[78]

Article 5 was also novel. The parties supposedly agreed that "the Friends of the One, shall eternally be considered the friends of the Other, and the Enemies of Either as the Enemies of Both." There were similar provisions in treaties between Europeans that established military alliances, but no such alliance was conceivable between the English and the Creeks. The Creeks had no intention of helping the English fight their French enemies, and the English were even more unlikely to help the Creeks fight their Cherokee enemies. Everyone on both sides knew that. Article 5, perhaps inserted to please Ellis's London superiors, was potentially embarrassing to both sides. From the start it was a dead letter. The imperial war would continue for six more years, but neither Ellis nor his successor ever tried to convince the Creeks that they were treaty-bound to send their warriors against the French.[79]

After the treaty was signed, the Wolf King stood up and warned his peers not to do what he said they had done in the past, "deny in your own Towns the Contracts you have made in those of the White People." The conference thereupon adjourned, and the chiefs accompanied Ellis to his house for dinner. Afterward Ellis distributed the presents "with my own hands knowing that would make them go much further and be better received."[80]

The land agreement was largely, but not simply, the governor's work. Ellis's private diplomacy with the chiefs had probably persuaded them to go beyond what they had intended. He certainly thought so: "The Indians of their own accord made this proposal in Council to which however they were induced by the impressions that I had been making on them for several days before the Talk during which time I constantly entertained select parties of the leading men at my own house." In particular, Ellis must have sold them on the trust arrangement, an idea alien to the Indians but familiar enough to the English. In fact, there were already trust arrangements with Indians in Virginia and other colonies.[81]

Creek leaders were also partly responsible for the new agreement. In the wake of the Ogeechee incident, they had in effect assured the British that they would watch the imperial war from the sidelines. They did not intend, however, to be marooned there for the duration without powder, shot, cloth, and other goods from their normal suppliers. The trade already mattered far more to the Creeks than it did to the English. This was especially true during wartime, when the English had good reasons to focus their attentions and resources in other directions. Determined not to be forgotten and to make a good start with the new regime, the Creeks had come in unusually large numbers and prepared to make concessions. When Ellis sent the treaty text to Pitt he reported that "the article respecting Lands and Islands was inserted at the desire of the Indians themselves."[82]

The 1757 treaty was a diplomatic triumph for Governor Ellis. He and the council were so pleased with Joseph Wright's work that they doubled the £30 they had promised him for his services. They were so delighted with Article 4 of the treaty that they uncharacteristically extended their hospitality several more weeks. The Creeks also seemed glad to wash their hands of the Bosomworth problem. One notable exception was Tugulki. The Bosomworths prevailed upon him to visit them after leaving Savannah, and persuaded him that they had been victimized. Ellis related that Tugulki then returned to Savannah with Mary "in order to disavow the cession of those Lands which the Indians by treaty made over to me in Trust." Mary demanded a hearing before the council "at which she should be present." Ellis refused and strove to persuade the young Creek leader that he would undermine his own reputation if he continued trying "to cancel what had been done by the unanimous consent of the Head Men." The governor claimed success and said that Tugulki departed "to all appearances entirely satisfied." Mary, of course, was not. Ellis was concerned over a report that she planned to accompany

Tugulki home "to solicit a New Grant of the Lands," but that did not happen. The treaty had fundamentally changed the situation. When the Creeks left Savannah they abandoned the Bosomworth cause for good.[83]

Reporting his success to the Board of Trade on November 25, Ellis wrote that the Creek grant of the disputed lands to him in trust "paves the way for obtaining an entire grant of these Lands, greatly invalidates the Bosomworth's Pretensions, and leaves them in a manner at the mercy of the Crown." Though he now had Thomas and Mary cornered, Ellis knew that might make them more dangerous. On December 7 he wrote the board that if the Bosomworths were "drove to despair" he thought they would resort to "very violent steps," presumably with help from Mary's Creek relatives and friends. He did not intend to let that happen, and continued to bide his time. Summing up for the board, he wrote: "Nothing that I have hitherto done in this matter is conclusive my intention being only to amuse and procrastinate till a more favorable season."[84]

The new year brought a more favorable season. Having already planted a wedge between the Bosomworths and the Creeks, Ellis first sought to drive it deeper. To ensure that there would be no more Bosomworth deeds, on February 15, 1758, he prevailed on the Georgia assembly to enact a law forbidding private land purchases from Indians. Each infraction carried a £1,000 penalty, "one half thereof to his majesty." A week later leaders of Apalachicola, the one Lower Creek town that had not been represented at the treaty conference, came to town to meet with Ellis. They came in part to add their weight to the treaty agreement, but actually went further. Their spokesman declared that "he and his People desired to resign all Right and Claim to those Islands and all Disputed Lands." He said nothing about a trust arrangement, asking rather that these lands "might be Settled . . . as his Honour the Governour should think fit to grant."[85]

Governor Ellis intended the trust agreement to pave the way for a complete cession of the disputed lands. The unsolicited declaration of the Apalachicola leader indicated that some Lower Creek chiefs were ready for that. Hoping the others could be brought around, Ellis sent Wright back to Creek country to try to secure an absolute cession. This would be one of the most important meetings ever held with the Creeks, but no documentation survives on what was said. Somehow Wright succeeded completely. Like Graham seven years earlier, he traveled first to Upper Creek country. In Mucklassee on April 22 the Wolf King and twenty other Upper Creek leaders signed a document that cleared the way toward a final resolution of the conflict. The Upper Creeks thereby "granted, and for ever quitted and resigned" to the king all rights to the Yamacraw tract and the three islands. It was an absolute cession. The Indians ceded these lands in "consideration," not of some new favor, but "of the great Love, and Esteem we bear the English Nation, and the many presents and other favours we have from time to time received from them."

For full closure, they went on to "revoke and disclaim all former gifts grants, or Sales" of the troublesome lands.[86]

Nine days later, in Apalachicola, fifteen Lower Creek leaders added their marks to the same document. Tugulki was not among them. In fact, only two of the signers were from Coweta or Cussita: Stumpe ("Stump Finger") of Coweta and the "Cusseta King." This meeting at Apalachicola was one of the first signs that Lower Creek leadership was passing from Coweta and Cussita to the Hitchiti-speaking towns. A Creek delegation then carried the document to Savannah. On May 29 Ellis wrote Lyttelton that more than forty Creeks, "amongst whom are some principal Men," were with him in Savannah. He explained that "they are come down with a full Ratification of our late Treaty, with them; and in a formal manner to resign to the Crown, for ever, some Indian Lands, and Islands." Ellis was still entertaining the same group, grown somewhat larger, on June 28.[87]

It was another triumph for Governor Ellis's diplomacy, but the Creek declaration at Mucklassee and Apalachicola could not have been signed without the willing cooperation of Creek leaders. It was approved in their own leading towns at meetings they presided over; it had been accomplished very quickly; they demanded nothing in return; they even sent envoys to Savannah to ratify the cession. Most telling, hereafter neither Upper nor Lower Creeks ever questioned its legitimacy. So far as the Creeks were concerned, a major distraction was over and done with.

But the Indians were not the only ones concerned. With the definitive Creek cession in hand, the governor could have proclaimed victory, evicted the Bosomworths from their home on St. Catherines, and proceeded to make grants to other settlers covering all of the long-contested lands. He did none of those things. Or, had he chosen a milder course, he could have negotiated some sort of a compromise settlement with the Bosomworths anytime after the treaty. Thomas had proposed one the previous October, and the Creek cession now left him nearly bereft of defenders. Yet for more than a year after the cession Ellis refrained from that too.

One factor leading Creek leaders to abandon the Bosomworths was the continuing challenge of the Ogeechee settlement. Most apparently saw reestablishing good relations with the Georgia government as much more important than gratifying the Bosomworths. So long as the British were obsessed with the old land dispute they seemed unable to see the Ogeechee issue. If this obstruction were removed, surely their vision would clear. Although the Creeks had refrained from bringing the matter up at the treaty conference, they returned to it more loudly than ever in the months following. On May 26 Ellis and the council met with Whoyanni of Chehaw, spokesman for a visiting delegation of forty Lower

Creeks. They "had brought down to his Honour a Talk from the Nation in Writing." The document does not survive, but Ellis informed the board that in it the Indians "complain heavily of the Settlements on their hunting Grounds at the Ogeechee . . . and desired such Settlers may be ordered to remove from thence." The council urged the governor to send the Creeks "an Answer by Letter" and have Joseph Wright explain it to them. Though presumably sent, that letter also does not survive.[88]

Another inducement to abandon Thomas and Mary applied particularly to Coweta. On July 29 Ellis wrote Lyttelton that the Creeks were "well affected to us, if we except the Cowetas, where the Interest of our Mischievous people the Bosomworths principally centers." Tugulki, despite the assurances he had given in Savannah, "is at length become very troublesome." Probably at prompting from Ellis, trader George Galphin decided that he could no longer tolerate the situation in Coweta. Accordingly, he moved "to withdraw his Goods from that Town, and is resolved not to return thither, until there is an evident alteration in the temper and Manners of these Indians." Ellis was confident that "to withhold their Trader will bring this speedily about." To maintain the pressure, Ellis asked Lyttelton not to grant a trading license for Coweta to anyone except Galphin.[89]

As Ellis reported on June 28, the Bosomworths were not prepared to go quietly. He described Thomas as "cunning industrious and desperate." Ellis thought the Bosomworths saw his present inaction toward them as "a forbearance which is to last no longer than convenient," which was true enough. Accordingly, Thomas and Mary continued "to employ every means to keep the Indians on their side." They still had friends and supporters among the Creeks, and "the disagreement of a small number of leading men greatly impedes and in some degree invalidates their public Resolutions." He charged that the Bosomworths were creating new "Jealousies" among their Creek friends "by disclosing the secrets of our policy." This was "instigating them to plunder the out settlers which having been repeatedly done with impunity discovers our weakness," good news for the French. Having provoked this and other "flagitious practices," Thomas and Mary deserved severe punishment. "Yet how can we punish the authors of them upon Indian Evidence?" Unsworn evidence remained inadmissible in Georgia courts, "and no other can be obtained."[90]

In short, the embittered Bosomworths remained capable of causing unacceptable damage, had demonstrated that they intended to do so, and could not be stopped by fair means. Despite the diplomatic coup with the Creek leadership, a huge problem remained. Ellis wrote the Board of Trade that he saw only one way to solve this problem: "I am clearly of opinion that a compromise with these troublesome people will be the most prudent speedy and effectual method of terminating it with advantage both to the Crown and the Colony." Given an acceptable settlement, the grateful Bosomworths might even help the colony in the continuing struggle against the French.[91]

Ellis concluded, however, that it was still too soon to talk to them. He realized that Thomas and Mary could not be pacified unless they received at least a substantial portion of what Thomas had outlined in October. He also knew that if he entered into negotiations with them he would be obliged to overlook their past behavior. For both reasons, any conceivable accord he was able to negotiate with the couple would be highly vulnerable to repudiation by the British government. To eliminate that risk, Ellis had to convince his superiors in London to approve his unprecedented course in advance. It would take more time and trouble, but the governor bent himself to the task.

At length, his efforts succeeded. Three years earlier the Privy Council had commissioned the Board of Trade to do a report on Mary Bosomworth's 1754 memorial. The board finally completed this task on December 6. The report began with Mary's claims for services, which the board supposed had some merit. The document quickly moved, however, to the more important issue omitted from her memorial, the land claims. On this matter, the board found that "her Conduct since the Year 1747 has been highly criminal with respect to His Majesty's Government and much more deserving of punishment than Reward." Nevertheless, having the "greatest Confidence" in Ellis's judgment, it reluctantly approved his compromise plan as a necessary expedient. It then recommended the plan to the Privy Council. At some point, probably while the Privy Council was considering Ellis's plan, the king in council also focused upon the merits of the Bosomworth land claims. The Privy Council approved the compromise plan the following January 11. Appropriate royal instructions to Ellis were put to paper on January 31. Finally, on February 2, 1759, the king in council adopted an order in council giving final approval to royal instructions for Ellis. About the same time in Savannah, Ellis learned that he had been promoted to governor.[92]

It was probably July when Ellis received the Board of Trade report, the pursuant royal instructions, and another document from the king himself. The governor soon called several meetings with the Bosomworths: a long private one with Thomas and Mary that produced the general outline of a settlement, and another in the council chamber on July 20. Describing the former, Ellis said that "after a great deal of discussion," certain "preliminaries" were agreed upon, "each party reserving a liberty of receding from them" at a later stage of the negotiation. The three points agreed upon were similar to those proposed by Thomas in October 1757, and essentially the same as the three points of the final agreement. In order to nudge the Bosomworths toward settlement, Ellis doubtless shared with them at least the general tendency of the three key documents he had received from London. He also told them to come to a subsequent council meeting with a detailed statement of their claims for services.[93]

Along with other elements of Ellis's compromise plan, the Board of Trade report approved and the royal instructions authorized the grant of St. Catherines Island to Thomas and Mary. It is important to note the official rationale for this grant. It was not any or all of the Creek grants; those were irrelevant. What was relevant, as both documents emphasized, was that the Creeks had the previous year granted St. Catherines, along with the other disputed lands, to the king. For British officialdom, that was what made the compromise possible. The royal instructions observed that because of the Creek cession, "the said Lands and Islands are become subject to our royal Grant or Disposal." Two further justifications for the grant were provided. The instructions explained that it was approved because "the Island of St. Catherine is settled and now actually possessed and improved by Thomas Bosomworth Clerk and Mary his Wife." Also, this grant would "make them ample Recompense for the Services alleged by them to have been performed."[94]

On Friday, July 20, Governor Ellis and the council considered the case of *Bosomworth* v. *Evans*. From 1752 onward the president and assistants, and later the governor and council, had authorized a few land grants on the Yamacraw tract, Ossabaw Island, and Sapelo Island—probably to see what happened. What happened was that Thomas filed caveats protesting these grants in the colony's general court. The particular case in question began on August 6, 1755, when Middleton Evans petitioned for, and was granted, five hundred acres on Ossabaw. Now armed with authoritative directives from the British government, Ellis summoned Thomas and Mary to the council chamber "to show cause why those Caveats should not be rejected." The council minutes report that on July 20 the governor and council ordered that "the litigation of this Cause be this Day heard." Thomas was accordingly called in to present his case. This he did in the familiar way, relying upon "certain Deeds of Conveyance made to him and Mrs. Bosomworth by the Creek Indian Nation." After Thomas was "fully heard," Ellis announced that he had no case.[95]

The governor explained that Thomas's "Claim and Title aforementioned had been laid and examined before his Majesty in Council, where it had been disallowed." Moreover, the king "had been pleased to signify such his disallowance under his royal Sign Manual," his personal signature. Ellis then produced this document, which was read aloud. This royal directive, the third of the key documents Ellis had recently received from London, does not appear to survive. Its disclosure had the intended effects: the council "Ordered the Caveats to be dismissed" and, more important, Thomas abruptly turned submissive. He "thereupon waived his pretentions, declaring that he never meant or intended to hold the said Lands against his lawfull Sovereign." His disclaimer was technically accurate: what he had intended was to "oblige" his sovereign to recognize his claim to these lands. Now that he had it from the king's own hand that this would not happen, he "said it was his Duty to submit, and he did so."[96]

After his earlier discussion with Ellis, Thomas could not have been much surprised at this turn of events. Something else he said that day suggests not only that he had a clear idea of the probable final outcome but that he thought his previous efforts to involve the Creeks had helped bring it about. Thomas said he "had entertained hopes, as Mrs. Bosomworth had been a faithfull Servant to the Crown, and himself a Dutifull Subject, that his Majesty would have been graciously pleased to have admitted his Claim." Thomas thus declined to abandon his contention that Mary was an Indian, apparently still hoping that Creek grants to her—along with her faithful services—would help the government decide to grant St. Catherines to him. He would get the grant he sought, but only on the basis of the services. The same day, Thomas delivered to the governor and council an accounting of his wife's claims for past services, along with his own commentary. Mary's claims totaled £5,420.[97]

Sometime late Friday or over the weekend, the council decided what to do about these claims. Ellis and his advisers already knew what to do about any compensation they decided was due to Mary. It was not to be an up-front payment. Rather, as suggested by the Board of Trade, the royal instructions directed that it be paid only after the appropriate sum had been raised by sale of portions of certain lands at public auction. St. Catherines excepted, such lands were those claimed by the Bosomworths.[98]

When the governor and council reassembled on Monday, July 23, Thomas and Mary were present. They had already publicly agreed to do what the compromise agreement required of them, renounce their old land claims. It remained for Ellis and the council to do the two things the compromise required of the government. That is what brought everyone to the council chamber that morning. The governor and council went through the motions of considering Mary's accounts, but Ellis quickly announced a decision that must already have been made. Most of Mary's claims were scaled down or dismissed, but a substantial balance remained. The governor and council had decided that she was entitled to a salary of £100 a year for sixteen and a half years, plus £450 for goods advanced on Colonel Heron's orders in 1747 and 1748, a total of £2,100. Ellis accordingly announced that in consideration of "the many Years Services of Mrs. Bosomworth as Interpretess," along with her losses and sums advanced, she would finally receive an appropriate compensation. That sum would amount to £2,100, "provided so much should be produced from the Sale of the Islands Ossabaw and Sapala." Second, "in further Recompence" and because they had for years settled upon and improved it, Thomas and Mary would receive a grant of St. Catherines Island. The Bosomworths had come equally primed to effect the compromise, and "gratefully accepted" the terms Ellis offered.[99]

The following day, "Articles of Agreement" incorporating the three points of the compromise were signed by Thomas and Mary for the one part, and by Governor Ellis and members of the council for the other. After advertising five-hundred-acre lots on Ossabaw and Sapelo for four months, these were put up for auction in December. When the bids fell short of the required minimum, this auction was canceled. Ellis then advertised another auction to sell each of the islands as an undivided unit. The winning bidder for both islands was Gray Elliott. On April 14, 1760, he paid £1,350 for Ossabaw and £700 for Sapelo. Five days later, Ellis passed this £2,050 on to the Bosomworths and provided for a royal grant to them for St. Catherines Island.[100]

It was over. Relief was palpable on all sides, and there was no doubt who deserved most of the credit. In retrospect, Governor Henry Ellis had undertaken a complicated and time-consuming triple negotiation: first with the Creek Indians, then with the British government, and finally with Thomas and Mary Bosomworth. He had succeeded with all three. The sequence of these negotiations was crucial to the success of the entire effort. Without the Creek cession to the Crown, Ellis could not have convinced the British government to accept an inglorious compromise with a "criminal" element, or convinced the Bosomworths that it was time to deal. Without advance approval from his superiors, he could not have negotiated any agreement with Thomas and Mary certain to stick. He aimed for a permanent solution, saw what was necessary to gain it, and followed through unflinchingly. Finally, a problem more than two decades in the making had been solved. At last, after more the a dozen years, the debilitating struggle with the Bosomworths and their Creek friends had been resolved. And, perhaps the most remarkable aspect of Ellis's achievement, he had resolved the conflict to the satisfaction of all concerned.

Only after the Bosomworth problem was safely out of the way did Ellis move decisively on the Ogeechee problem. On October 11, 1759, he directed preparation of a proclamation ordering the removal of settlers on the upper Ogeechee. They needed no further prompting, and abandoned the site on their own. Most of them moved north to the Broad River. With both major irritants removed, relations between the Georgia government and the Creeks were now more harmonious than at any time since Oglethorpe's early days.[101]

CHAPTER EIGHT

The Atkin Mission

The resolution of the seemingly endless Creek-Bosomworth problem by Governor Henry Ellis proved to be permanent. For the next year or two, English relations with the Creeks were—or, from Ellis's vantage point, appeared to be—satisfactory to both parties. Furthermore, as the governor had hoped, Mary Bosomworth once again became an important asset for the colony's diplomacy with her native people. Ellis himself was much less active than he had been, for the hot zones of diplomatic activity were shifting far upcountry into Indian territories. When at war with each other, Europeans came to Indians.

Ellis had taken up his duties in Savannah knowing that sooner or later he and other southern governors would have to share authority over Indian diplomacy with Edmond Atkin, the newly appointed superintendent of Indian affairs for the southern colonies. For Ellis, it turned out to be twenty months later. While British officials had eagerly supported William Johnson for the northern superintendency, they had serious doubts about Atkin. In 1755 Johnson had been appointed the king's "Sole Agent for and Superintendent" for Indian affairs, but Atkin's commission omitted the word "Sole." His defined role was limited to diplomacy and treaty making. Atkin pleaded for Board of Trade instructions directing the southern governors to yield him substantial control over the trade. The instructions the board finally issued merely urged the governors to cooperate with him. Atkin not only lacked specific authority over trade and traders, he had no funding commitment from the London government. Disappointed, he was at first inclined to spurn the appointment. When the South Carolina agent and other influential Carolinians then in London assured him that, if necessary, their colony would pay his expenses, he changed his mind. Atkin was directed to secure instructions and funds from Lord Loudoun, the British commander in chief in North America. Privately, Secretary of State Henry Fox instructed Loudoun to replace Atkin if he felt the Carolinian was not up to the task.[1]

Obliged to work out the particulars of his charge with his immediate superior, Lord Loudoun, Atkin followed the British commander to New York in October 1756. Over the next six months he trailed Loudoun from place to place, seeking to have his office fashioned into a decent approximation of the one he had imagined in his "Plan." Loudoun eventually provided a salary for him, along with a supply of Indian presents, but that was as far as his material support went. The British commander apparently never did get around to giving Atkin written instructions. Most disappointing to Atkin, Loudoun denied his requests for £2,000 to cover expenses, and authority to draw upon him for emergency outlays. The British commander referred Atkin to the governors of the southern colonies for all additional financial support. This arrangement, rather than lifting Atkin's authority above that of the governors, in effect made him their subordinate. Atkin's hope for a superintendency independent from the provincial governments was thwarted almost before his service began.[2]

Atkin told Loudoun that his main diplomatic objective was "to retrieve our declining interest" among the Choctaws, a people he despised. In his "Report" he made this very clear: "Of all the Indians the Chactaws bear the worst Character." They were devious and they were mercenary, "in a manner selling the French just as much Friendship as they pay for." Nevertheless, the populous Choctaws were potentially so formidable that the English must reach out to them, even while holding their noses. Atkin went on to offer a simple plan on how to reopen active contacts with these Indians. He argued that the South Carolina Indian commissioners had been ineffective because they never traveled into Indian country. That left them almost totally beholden to traders for information about the natives. Atkin proposed to remedy this problem by establishing and maintaining direct contacts. He told Loudoun that he intended to visit Choctaw country every year, and along the way to visit both Lower and Upper Creeks. Loudoun may well have doubted the practicality of this plan. Atkin was nearly fifty, portly, and suffered from gout and rheumatism, while a one-way trip to Choctaw country from Augusta involved about five hundred miles on horseback.[3]

Whatever the merits of Atkin's original plan, by January 1758 British leaders had decided that there was a better way to defeat the French in the south. Because little came of it, the British "southern strategy" long went little noticed by historians. The general idea was that it would be much easier to attack the French in Mobile and Fort Toulouse than New Orleans, and easier to recruit auxiliaries from among the Creeks than the Choctaws. Predicated upon the arrival of a British naval force, the plan called for coordinated land and sea attacks on Mobile and Fort Toulouse. A successful assault on the latter would depend almost entirely upon the cooperation of the nearby Creeks, who might also assist in a siege of

Mobile. Atkin's assignment was to cajole the Creeks into abandoning their traditional neutrality and protection of Fort Toulouse.[4]

There was much to be said for Atkin's continued interest in the Choctaws. These Indians were by far the most numerous native nation in the Southeast, and Atkin was right to conclude that the Creeks "stand in fear of the Chactaws." If the superintendent's main task was to get the Creeks to help the British war effort, closer ties between the Choctaws and British would bring pressure upon the Creeks to behave as desired. The most formidable military threats the Creeks could possibly face in 1758 would come from the Choctaws to their west and the English to their east. Being centrally located was not an unmixed blessing. If the British and Choctaws ever decided to make common cause, the Creeks would be forced to defend themselves on two fronts.[5]

The Choctaws had long been by far the strongest and most reliable allies of the French in Louisiana. The Franco-Choctaw alliance depended largely on the always erratic flow of French goods to these Indians. The irregular delivery of goods during peacetime dwindled to a trickle during the war, as British naval power choked off most French shipping to the Gulf. From the onset of war until August 1758, not a single ship carrying Indian goods that set out from France reached New Orleans. According to McGillivray, without Spanish help the French would have lost all credit with the Indians. Earlier that year Spaniards at Pensacola "purchased a large quantity of English goods at Charlestown," then delivered this cargo at Mobile. The waning ability of the French to supply their Choctaw allies inevitably weakened the ties between them. Choctaw leaders began to look for an alternative source of supply, and they knew where to look.[6]

In December 1756 an alarmed Governor Kerlérec had reported that both public and private stores of Indian goods were exhausted and that Choctaws were welcoming contacts with English traders. A month earlier two Choctaws had crossed into Creek territory to meet with South Carolina agent Daniel Pepper. In January 1757 Governor Reynolds heard reports that "the Chactaws have proposed making an alliance with us." In May the Louisiana governor wrote that Choctaw leaders "have just told me that the nation could no longer do without receiving the English among them" if he could not promptly supply them with goods and ammunition. Of these items, he added, "we are entirely destitute." Some Choctaws had already moved beyond words. That month a Choctaw party appeared in Oakchoy, telling the Gun Merchant they wanted an English trade. In the fall, fifty Choctaws seeking English goods brought deerskins into Upper Creek towns. Since the enemy's main allies had taken the initiative to establish ties with the English, the Choctaws had given Atkin a diplomatic opportunity impossible to overlook.[7]

In March 1757 Atkin traveled south to Virginia, and there began his public duties as superintendent. His Virginia activities included settling a minor dispute with the Catawbas at Jamestown and several negotiations with Cherokees at Winchester and Fort Loudoun. He badly mishandled one of his encounters with the Cherokees when he impulsively locked up ten of them as French spies. Colonel George Washington managed to extricate Atkin from the dangerous situation he had created. Governor Robert Dinwiddie thought Atkin's service had been worthwhile but expensive. In an observation that would be echoed by Ellis and others, Dinwiddie added that Atkin was "very slow in all his Affairs."[8]

After half a year of indifferent accomplishment in Virginia, in the late fall Atkin set off for South Carolina. On his ride through North Carolina he suffered a serious attack of gout, which incapacitated him for months. He did not reach Charles Town until March 23, 1758. Shortly afterward serious trouble with the Cherokees began in Bedford County, Virginia. There in May a Cherokee war party, returning from frustrating service with General John Forbes, stole some horses. A pitched battle with pursuing settlers ensued, with casualties on both sides. From this point on Anglo-Cherokee relations steadily worsened, and violent incidents became commonplace.[9]

Atkin did not return to Virginia, but spent the next six months in Charles Town. There he was deeply involved in negotiations, not with Indians but with the Carolina government. His objective was to gain financial support from the provincial government most likely to provide it. Since Atkin had never resigned his seat on the council, by reason of seniority he now presided as its president. There was also something of a personal tie between Atkin and Governor Lyttelton. While in England, Atkin had become friendly with the governor's brother, Sir George Lyttelton, chancellor of the exchequer, who had supported him for superintendent. In May, Governor Lyttelton urged the provincial assembly to provide financial assistance to the superintendent. As promised in London, it did commit to pay his necessary expenses. It balked, however, at paying salaries for all the military escorts and assistants Atkin wanted, agreeing to pay only his interpreter and secretary. Atkin would later single out Lyttelton as the only southern governor who had really supported him.[10]

Despite the rapidly deteriorating relationship with the Cherokees, the superintendent's gaze was fixed in a different direction. Historian John R. Alden pointed out long ago that "Even before he reached Charleston, he determined, for reasons unknown, to negotiate with the Creeks first, and the Cherokees later." It now seems clear that Atkin focused on the Creeks because Lord Loudoun had ordered him to. Having received similar written orders from Secretary Pitt, Governor Lyttelton doubtless strengthened Atkin's resolution to be off to Creek country—that is, once he was ready. In the meantime there were so many options to be considered, tasks to be done, and things to be acquired. In addition to appropriate Indian presents, especially gorgets and other prestige items for chiefs, the superintendent's shopping list included items intended to impress observers with the dignity and noble purpose of his office. He purchased green uniforms for the troop of rangers he intended to escort him into Indian country, a staff with his personal standard attached, a supply of English (not British) flags, and a special flag he intended to carry during his progress through Creek territory. The special flag bore the image of "an Indian arm (the Creeks) and an English arm (King George) clenched in a bond of friendship." This image was Atkin's elaboration upon a conventional gesture among the Southeastern Indians: their special way of shaking hands, "or rather arms."[11]

Around the first of October, Atkin set off for Savannah. With his secretary bearing his standard marching before him, the superintendent paraded into town a few days later. On October 10 Ellis met with his council to decide how they might assist him. The governor explained that Atkin was on his way "to visit the Creek Indian Nations." He added that in private the superintendent had "complained much of having been neglected in Carolina and by the Commander in chief at the Northward." Ellis said he had already given Atkin what assistance he could on his own, having ordered twelve rangers to accompany him as "an Escort" up to Fort Moore and Augusta. He then proposed that the Indian presents remaining at Augusta be turned over to Atkin and that he be sworn as a justice of the peace. The latter was no formality, but the source of the only legal authority Atkin could claim over the traders. Both proposals were promptly approved.[12]

During the next several weeks Ellis and Atkin had more private talks, which did not go well. On October 25, Ellis wrote the Board of Trade that he had rendered Atkin all the assistance in his power, along with "giving him my sentiments on Indian Matters with the utmost plainness and candour." Atkin and his host came down on opposite sides of the never-ending debate among British officials on grand strategy toward Indian nations: whether the security of the colonies was better served by promoting unification of all friendly Indians or by relying instead on divide-and-rule tactics. The superintendent was in the former camp. They likewise disagreed about English participation in the native practice of scalping. Ellis saw providing rewards for the scalps of Indian enemies in time of war as a necessary expedient, while Atkin saw it as not only shameful ("unworthy of any Christian people") but self-defeating ("so many Temptations to some Indians to kill others that are our Friends").[13]

The two men disagreed most strongly over Atkin's intention to proceed next to Creek country. Since Atkin was under orders to do so, he probably dismissed Ellis's objections as pointless. In no position to alter British military strategy, Ellis probably argued that Atkin should at least postpone his mission to the Creeks until a more pressing problem had been addressed. He wrote the Board of Trade that he was "not entirely convinced of the expediency of his visiting that Nation where every thing at *present* is perfectly quiet and whilst affairs of an alarming nature are left unsettled behind him." He explained that recent reports had convinced him that "the Cherokees and Virginians were upon the verge of a quarrel." Undeterred, Atkin replied that he had "taken some measures in consequence thereof," by which he meant he had sent advice to his Virginia deputy and "applications" to the Cherokees. Resigned that Atkin would go to the Creeks, Ellis worried about his intention to press them to join the war against the French. The governor supposed that this would not only be fruitless but might provoke the French to set Choctaws upon Georgia's frontier settlements.[14]

There was a case to be made that diplomacy with the Creeks could help relieve the mounting tensions with the Cherokees. Atkin may or may not have made such a case in his talks with Ellis, but he certainly did so later. Since the end of the Creek-Cherokee war four years earlier, contacts between disaffected Creeks and Cherokees had steadily developed. The principal Creek supporters of this rapprochement were the Mortar of Oakchoy and Escotchaby of Coweta. Both were war chiefs reputed to have extraordinary influence over Cherokees. According to a Cherokee spokesman, the Mortar was "our King of Chote" (Chota, the main town of the Overhill Cherokees). According to Ellis, Escotchaby "is a Cherokee King, and much attached to the French."[15]

What drew Creek and Cherokee malcontents together were common grievances: the numberless abuses and indignities inflicted upon their people by the traders, alarm over accelerating English expansion, and lately the issue of English forts. It was one thing for Creeks to tolerate Fort Toulouse, which had helped maintain a power balance between French and English; it was another to permit the stronger English to build a fort that might destroy that balance. The English had already built two major forts among the Cherokees, and had long schemed to plant one among the Creeks.

About the time Atkin was in Savannah, the Mortar was establishing an encampment far to the north on Coosawaittee Creek. This outpost, Etoahatchee, was not far from the Overhill Cherokee towns. With him was his brother, who was married to a Cherokee woman. The Mortar's settlement became the meeting ground for nativists of both nations hatching schemes to drive the English from Indian lands. Both saw British expansion as a menace and sought to use the relatively inoffensive French as a counterweight. The French were already supplying both Creeks and Cherokees with a great deal of ammunition. Most was shipped up the Alabama-Coosa River system, but some came from the Ohio country via the "Cherokee" (Tennessee) River. Since the French were able to transport this heavy cargo by water, while the English had to haul it on horseback, French ammunition was usually more readily available. In 1757 Governor Kerlérec said the

French supplied the Cherokees with about ten thousand pounds of gunpowder a year. Moreover, the French were often able to undersell the English for this coveted commodity. In 1759 the Tuckabatchee Mico complained to Atkin that forty bullets for a deerskin was too few. Atkin's interpreter tacitly agreed, pointing out that a French trader in Oakchoy "sells 60 Bullets for a Pound of Leather."[16]

French agents had given both Creeks and Cherokees reason to believe that they would soon build a fort and trading house adjacent to the Mortar's outpost. Such an establishment, easily accessible from the Tennessee River, would radically increase French influence in the region. According to Captain Allick, "the Talk was, that when a Fort should be built there, Then the Cherokees should be supplied with Goods there by the French." Atkin reported that when he set out to meet Lower and Upper Creek leaders, "by the Opinion of our Traders the Majority were in the Interest of the French." Like many other British officials, Atkin was convinced that the Mortar was the nativist mastermind behind a nefarious plot to throw the English back on themselves. "The Scheme he had formed was an Union among the Red People in favour of the French, and against the English. . . . He had gained over to him most of the greatest Warriours, and those of the most Sense and strongest Mouths." Thus it was reasonable for Atkin to argue that his personal diplomacy with the Creeks could counteract the growing intimacy and dangerous chemistry among Creeks, Cherokees, and Frenchmen.[17]

On October 25 Ellis reported that Atkin "is just now setting out for the Creek Nation." The superintendent was not happy with his experience in Savannah. He later complained that Ellis was the least cooperative of the southern governors, and had wounded him with "cruel Treatment." Atkin and his entourage took the road to Augusta, where they arrived before the end of the month. The superintendent was not satisfied with preparations for his arrival at Augusta. No gunpowder was available for cannon salutes until he sent some forward. At length he choreographed a welcoming ceremony to his liking. Disgusted at Atkin's minute attention to the inessential, Ellis called it "a very pompous entry."[18]

On November 2 Atkin issued a proclamation that must have provoked most of the traders: he forbade anyone to carry rum to the Creeks. Soon afterward he forbade the Augusta traders from carrying any goods to the Creeks until he had held a conference with those Indians. He also wrote traders then among the Creeks to halt business until he arrived. As Corkran observes, these actions amounted to "an unprovoked embargo." Outraged traders were soon venting to a sympathetic Governor Ellis. On February 24 Ellis wrote Lyttelton that Atkin's plan to control the traders was not promising: "I am afraid he is rather too hasty, and sanguine a temper, to deal properly with the people he intends to reform." In general, Ellis confided, "Mr. Atkin's projects alarm me, not less for their object, than the manner in which he will attempt to carry them into execution."[19]

To the frustration of all but the French, Atkin remained in Augusta for the next six months. The superintendent's "dilatoriness" infuriated Ellis, who later complained that it "forewarned the French so it gave them time to provide presents to counteract him." Atkin doubtless justified his refusal to move by pointing out that a December arrival in Creek country would occur after most of the men had just departed for their long winter hunts. While he waited for a better season to visit the Creeks, Atkin might have gone north to see if the situation in Cherokee country was as bad as reported. He didn't. Instead, along with attempts to overawe the traders, he busied himself with recruiting a military escort from hangers-on around Augusta, and drilling them in parade and formal battle maneuvers.[20]

James Adair witnessed some of this, and was appalled. Atkin's military exercises with "swivels, blunderbusses, and many other sorts of blundering stuff" would have been laughable had they not distracted him from his real problems. Ellis was right: Atkin's dithering enabled the French to take countermeasures. Some of these, notably larger deliveries of ammunition, were effective enough to worry Anglophile Creeks that their people were falling prey to Gallic seduction. According to Adair, "Indian runners were frequently sent down by our old friendly head-men, urging the absolute necessity of coming up soon, otherwise it would be too late." Augusta traders told Atkin that, with Frenchmen again active in Creek country, it was imperative to respond positively to these appeals from friendly chiefs. As Adair saw it, the danger was such that Atkin should "have immediately proceeded to their country." He didn't. After he made it clear he was staying put, the traders tried again. Adair said Atkin should have "listened to the entreaties of the Indian traders of that place, to request one . . . to go in his stead." He didn't. Adair was amazed by "his pride, his obstinacy, and unskillfulness."[21]

In February, Atkin wrote to Ellis about something that had been gnawing at him for a long time. He lamented that "my Success depends in a Manner intirely on the Behaviour of our Traders." The problem was that, so long as he lacked authority to revoke their licenses, "it cannot be imagined that they will pay the least Regard to any Orders of mine that do not square exactly with their own private Interest." Back in London, Atkin had tried to gain exclusive authority over trade licenses but had been rebuffed. That authority remained with the southern governors. Since then the superintendent had tried to persuade each of them to relinquish licensing authority to him, but only Governor Arthur Dobbs of North Carolina had done so. Dobbs's gesture was of no help to Atkin in Creek country. This issue likely had provoked much of the ill feeling between Atkin and Ellis in Savannah.[22]

Scaling back a bit, the superintendent tried again from Augusta. He now requested a "Declaration under Hand from each Governour that any Act of mine as to the suspending or vacating any Licence shall have their Confirmation."

When Governor Ellis presented this proposal to his council on March 8 he did not pretend to have an open mind. He supposed that Atkin's authority "was as the Government intended it," and did not think himself at liberty "to strengthen his Hands by any new Authority." Significantly, Ellis added: "nor had he any Encouragement from the Agent's Conduct hitherto." The council "intirely" agreed.[23]

Atkin knew that achieving his goals would require an extended stay among both Lower and Upper Creeks. It was clear to him, if not to Ellis, that the former would be much more difficult to deal with. For more than a decade, Georgia officials and Lower Creek chiefs, especially those of Coweta, had periodically confronted each other over land and trade issues. Georgia leaders had found it much easier to deal with the distant Upper Creeks. Proud of the recent success of his Creek diplomacy, Ellis consistently overestimated Creek goodwill toward the English. In July 1758 he wrote that, except for Coweta, "all the Towns of the Upper and Lower Creeks are well affected to us." In October he opined that "the influence we have acquired with them adds greatly to our Security." In April of the following year he wrote that "all the accounts from their Country are uncommonly favorable." Atkin had more detailed, and more disturbing, information. Numerous reports of Lower Creek fraternization with Frenchmen and Cherokee militants reached him in Augusta. Doubtless included were some dealing with Tugulki's 1758 summer visit to Mobile, where the young Coweta leader reportedly agreed to join a French effort to take Fort Loudoun. Apparently recognizing that his nephew had crossed a red line, in August of that year Sempoyaffi told Joseph Wright that Tugulki "has Behaved ill and is not worthy a Commission."[24]

As frustrating as Atkin's delay in Augusta was for the English, it was much worse for the Lower Creeks. Our best account of this comes from Sempoyaffi, now apparently *mico* of Coweta. Outraged by the superintendent's performance, in October 1759 the Coweta leader led a delegation to Savannah to protest to Ellis. According to Sempoyaffi, Atkin had been disrespectful and provocative from the start. Shortly after he arrived in Augusta, the superintendent sent a message to the Lower Creek chiefs that "he was coming up with a Talk from the great King himself." Bitterly, Sempoyaffi recalled that "we waited many Months at Home in Expectation of his Arrival, whereby we suffered Hardships." Feeling that they must remain close to their towns, food gathering lagged and "Famine" appeared; "the Loss of our Winter Hunt" perfected their destitution. Furthermore, Atkin was not just a passive tormenter: "he stopped all the Goods from coming into our Nation as usual, which very much alarmed Us."[25]

Cleverly, Sempoyaffi charged that Atkin, by making the Lower Creeks very angry at him months before they ever saw him, was responsible for making them vulnerable to French deceit. At Fort Toulouse, the French had assured Creek visitors that Atkin was coming at the head of an army "to cut us off, which our young

Men were almost inclined to believe." Sempoyaffi knew whereof he spoke, for he had been among the Lower Creek visitors to the French fort. The superintendent apparently sent no further messages to the Creeks from Augusta. Just before departing, however, he sent one to Choctaws who had been floating trade overtures. Atkin later reported that "an Interview therefore in the Creek Nation between me and some of the Chactaws was concerted before my setting out." He also issued a proclamation forbidding Choctaws to visit Savannah or Charles Town.[26]

In early April, Atkin rode out from Augusta at the head of his honor guard, impatient traders, and a long pack train carrying Indian goods and supplies. The convoy took the well-beaten Lower Creek path southwest toward Coweta and Cussita on the Chattahoochee. About two weeks later the superintendent called a halt twenty-two miles from the river. Atkin later boasted that there "I was met by a great many Beloved men, Mico's, and head Warriours." The superintendent added that he had heard "a great many bad things before I came into the Lower Towns; but when I came there, I was received by them in the best manner they could." Sempoyaffi recalled the occasion somewhat differently. He complained that Atkin had failed to give the Chattahoochee townsmen respectful notice of his approach. Instead, when he "arrived within a Days March of our Nation, he dispatched a Talk expressing his Desire that our Head Men should come and meet him." Although taken by surprise, they complied, "and conducted him with the Greatest Respect and Ceremony to the Cusseta Town, whither he chose to go."[27]

One reason the superintendent chose Cussita over Coweta as his local headquarters was the fortuitous presence there of Captain Allick, the friendliest face among Lower Creek leaders. Allick had returned to his hometown the previous August, and almost immediately had been pressed into service. A few days before his arrival, Lower Creeks had been thrown into turmoil by a rare incident of violence against Englishmen in their country: the murder of a man and two women by Yuchis. Atkin reacted by cutting off trade to Yuchi Town and demanding satisfaction for the killings. Wright reported that Captain Allick had been "impowered by the Heads of the Lower Creeks with the assent of the Upper Creeks" to satisfy the English. As the husband of three Yuchi wives, Allick had close ties to the Yuchis. The Lower Creeks had promptly captured and killed one of the murderers, and Allick promised that the same fate would soon befall the other one. The mixed-blood leader acted as Atkin's host at Cussita and continued to act as spokesman for the Lower Creeks throughout the superintendent's mission. Atkin was pleased to report that "from the time I came to Cussihta till the day I left it, the English Colours stood set up in that Square."[28]

Atkin turned away from Coweta because he already had abundant information that it was the center of Lower Creek intrigues with the French and Cherokees.

More was soon forthcoming. Although Tugulki was supposedly being groomed to succeed Malatchi as principal leader of the Lower Creeks, Coweta politics was dominated by four or five of his kinsmen. Atkin branded four of them "the 4 vile Brothers owners of the Town Ground." Sempoyaffi, the *mico*, was first in prestige but not in influence. His brother Escotchaby, eldest of the four, was war chief. According to Atkin, he "overrules all when on the Spot." A third brother, Ufylegey, was a Beloved Man of the town. The superintendent reported that when Escotchaby was away, Ufylegey was "the ruling man in his Absence." The more Atkin learned about the Coweta chiefs, the more he despised them. As he later wrote to Ellis, "I can scarce speak bad enough of those who bear sway there." All were two-faced: "The French have not better Friends any where among those who pretend to have any connection with us."[29]

Soon after his arrival, Atkin learned about the most recent Coweta contacts with the French. In November more than 130 Lower Creeks led by Tugulki and Escotchaby had gone to Mobile, drawn by news that French goods had slipped through the British blockade. Governor Kerlérec reported that they received "very Handsome presents" and departed "saying openly that the English were scoundrels and liars." About the time Atkin had set out from Augusta, a Lower Creek party had gone to Fort Toulouse for more French goods. The group was led by Sempoyaffi, Escotchaby, and Tugulki. A few days before Atkin's arrival, Sempoyaffi and Tugulki returned to Coweta. Back home they spread news of French largesse and French-inspired suspicions of the superintendent's motives. Coweta leaders were also deeply involved with Cherokee malcontents. Sempoyaffi was not home when Atkin arrived, because he was off to Cherokee country to share what had passed at Fort Toulouse. The superintendent never saw Escotchaby, he "not coming once home while I was in the Nation."[30]

Coweta headmen were indignant over Atkin's conduct toward their town. Sempoyaffi charged that the superintendent never set foot in Coweta and other disfavored towns, but to avoid them "purposely turned aside and travelled through the Woods." When Coweta leaders crossed the river to see Atkin, he gave them a "contemptuous Reception," saying he would send for them when he wished to see them. Unwilling to accept this as the final word, Tugulki "forced past the Sentry at his Door" and thrust his hand out to Atkin. The superintendent "scornfully rejected" the gesture. Taken aback by this "galling Affront," Tugulki said he had shaken hands with governors of South Carolina and Georgia, "and desired to know if he was greater than they?" Atkin welcomed the question. "Yes," he replied, "inasmuch as he was the King's own Mouth," which the governors were not. As a parting shot, the superintendent "added that he knew my [Sempoyaffi's] Nephew was a French Man, and all his Town."[31]

The last straw for Atkin came when he learned that Cherokees had brought to

Coweta some of the English scalps they had taken in North Carolina. He declared that these terrible trophies had been "received in that Square" and that Escotchaby was "the greatest offender" in receiving them. The superintendent promptly prohibited all trade with Coweta. Shortly afterward, Issulgy, Second Man of Apalachicola, returned home with Cherokee war beads and a talk inviting Lower Creeks to join Cherokees against the English. Atkin reported that when the Apalachicola headmen did not send the beads back, "it was adjudged by the Upper Town Headmen an Acceptance of the Proposal." To punish this hostile act, Atkin ordered a halt of the trade to Apalachicola.[32]

Superintendent Atkin remained in and around Cussita for two months, long overstaying his welcome. He spent much of that time talking to headmen about their commissions. This lengthy exercise was triggered when Atkin got Ufylegey to produce his French commission. The Tuckabatchee Mico later told Atkin that Ufylegey had acquired it in Mobile in 1756 at the onset of the war. It pledged the Coweta headman and his subordinates "to be Friends with the French, and Enemies to their Enemies." On its face, this required them to join the French war effort against the British. Atkin soon demanded to see all French and Spanish commissions. Some of the French commissions contained the same pregnant phrases as Ufylegey's. The superintendent ignored the fact that Governor Ellis's 1757 treaty included similar language. No matter, Atkin went on to demand that all French commissions be surrendered to him. Reluctantly, Lower Creek leaders complied.[33]

The ammunition and other goods Atkin had carried up remained under guard during his protracted stay in Cussita. Meanwhile, the thirty or so Choctaws who had traveled far seeking to reopen a trade with the English were camped in Mucklassee, where the Wolf King was trying to make them wait for Atkin. A few, however, were sent ahead and found the superintendent in Cussita on May 14. Atkin sent them back with instructions to gather their chiefs, promising to meet with them soon in Upper Creek country. If, as seems likely, he gave these Choctaw emissaries a few presents, another of Sempoyaffi's complaints began in Cussita. Rather than "bestowing the smallest Mark of his Bounty out of those Goods which were originally designed for Us," he charged, Atkin "before our Faces gave Presents and friendly Talks to the Choctaws." Though Atkin had in fact given some prestige goods to Lower Creek chiefs, when he finally packed up and rode out past sour faces his inventory of ammunition was almost entirely intact. He also took at least eight of the lower town traders with him. Before he left he doubtless alerted the Lower Creek chiefs that soon he would hold a grand meeting with both Upper and Lower Creeks at which the king's presents would be distributed.[34]

The superintendent could not have been long among the Lower Creeks before he realized that the main errand the British government had sent him on—

inducing the Creeks to support the war effort against the French—was hopeless. Reporting on his experiences among the Creeks to Secretary Pitt, he wrote that when he had set out to their country, "the Leading men were divided into two Parties." One tended to favor the English, the other the French, but the Francophile party was larger. This was an excuse for non-performance, but a well-founded one. Before he left Cussita Atkin had plenty of evidence of Lower Creek support for the French, if only to put obstacles in the way of the more threatening English. He learned that the French had been effective in fanning Creek suspicions that the English were scheming to erect forts in their country. According to Daniel Pepper, the Wolf King related that the Creeks "looke upon the Words Fort and Slavery to be synonomous Terms."[35]

The French had gone on to warn that forts were merely the first step of an English scheme to seize Creek lands. The superintendent acknowledged that his own people had given "too just Grounds" for these fears. As a result, he said, "the natural Jealousy of the Nation is raised within a few late Years with regard to Land to a Pitch almost beyond imagination." Atkin also heard reports that Lower Creeks had been consorting with Lower Cherokees with fresh English blood on their hands, and hatching joint schemes to spill more. He supposed that "the Plot concerted between the Lower Creeks and Lower Cherokees was but one Branch" of the Mortar's anti-British project.[36]

Atkin had no choice but to conclude that he would be doing well simply to maintain Creek neutrality. He told Pitt he had done what had to be done: "upon my first Arrival in the Nation, I dissipated their Fears and Apprehensions, by declaring in the Publick Square of Cussihta, as well as in other Town Squares afterwards, that his Majesty wanted nothing of them, neither Land nor Leave to build a Fort." The king had sent his agent to the Creeks merely to see "if they were his Friends," settle problems with traders, and consult "for our mutual Good."[37]

As he prepared to move on to the Upper Creek country, Atkin showed that he had learned his lesson about arriving on short notice. After a delay forced cancellation of his first notice, during the last week of June he sent word to Upper Creek leaders that he would appear in about five days. He related that Captain Allick and Half Breed Abraham "proposed voluntarily to attend me up there." This did not happen, "for such bold things were said in the Upper Towns about me, as well as of Aleck on my Account," that the two mixed-bloods backed out. The superintendent arrived at a camp ten miles outside of Tuckabatchee on July 2. The Indians who came out in the rain to meet him the following day assured Atkin that the notice he had given was "long enough." The fact that only fourteen men headed by a single chief took the trouble to greet him, without ceremony, indicated otherwise. The superintendent did not attempt to conceal his irritation over the spare welcome.[38]

Though off to a bad start, things went better for the superintendent among the Upper Creeks. Atkin had chosen his intended headquarters there for much the same reason as he had chosen Cussita among the Lower Creeks. The Tallapoosa division of the Upper Creeks had long been a more hospitable place for Englishmen than the Abeika division further north. Among the Abeikas the one town Atkin would have avoided above all others was Oakchoy, headed by the Gun Merchant and energized by the Mortar. The superintendent described the pair as "the heads of the French Party." In fact, Atkin did not visit any of the Abeika towns until the very end of his mission. Among the Tallapoosa towns, the two that attracted his interest were those with the most Anglo-friendly leaders. One was Mucklassee, headed by the Wolf King, while Tuckabatchee was home to Old Bracket, honored by the English as their oldest friend among the Upper Creeks. Atkin chose to operate from Tuckabatchee, largely because Mucklassee was uncomfortably close to Fort Toulouse, only seven miles away.[39]

Concerned to mollify the superintendent, four days later the Upper Creeks orchestrated a more impressive welcome. About eighty of them led by a dozen chiefs, along with some of the visiting Choctaws, went out to his camp. They came painted, singing, dancing, and firing salutes. Waiting at his tent, Atkin got into the spirit "with a Discharge of his Brass Blunderbusses." After the usual ceremonies of hand shaking, stroking with eagle wands, and presentation of a white wing, Atkin indicated he was satisfied. "I [had] begun to think of turning back," he said, but now agreed to proceed to Tuckabatchee square. His hosts assured him that there "the Headmen from every Town in the Upper Creek Country are met, and ready to receive you." That evening the superintendent was conducted into the square with great ceremony. The promised great assembly of chiefs was there; even the Gun Merchant was there. According to Atkin, the Oakchoy *mico* had tried to prevent the meeting but had been pressured to go along. Atkin gave him an ostentatious snub by shaking the hand of a chief who sat next to him but not that of the Gun Merchant.[40]

Business got under way on July 9. Preceded by bearers carrying his personal standard and french horn, Atkin was again conducted into the square. After drinking black drink, he gave a long speech making the same points he had made to the Lower Creeks. The king did not want to build forts and did not want Creek lands; he wanted to find out which Indian nations were his friends. Thus "if I find there are more Friends to the French among you than to the English," he would know he had come to the wrong place. "The Great King . . . has given me his own Mouth, and what I say is the same as if he said it." He said he would also work to resolve trade problems. "And after I have done this, then I intend to talk with all your Headmen both of Upper and Lower Towns together, to set things right." Asking for the best place to hold this joint meeting, the Wolf King assured him that

Tuckabatchee was best, "as it is the most Central." Significantly, the Musklassee leader added that he and his fellow chiefs would "defer saying any thing" until the general meeting.

The superintendent wrapped up by taking notice of the numerous Choctaw visitors in the area. They had come in response to the vague invitation to meet he had sent them from Cussita. As the French had discovered earlier, when the Choctaws came, they came in strength. Atkin reported that there were now 460 Choctaw men and 20 Choctaw women camped nearby. Since provisions were extremely scarce, Atkin was "very Sorry that so many are come." He assured his Creek audience he had tried to send some of the Choctaws home. When he asked for the best place to hold his Choctaw meeting, the Wolf King named the village of Waulyhatchee about two miles away. Atkin indicated he would now turn to dealing with the Choctaws because "I want to dismiss them as Soon as possible." The Creeks did not complain, for they were even more anxious to be rid of them than he was. Gun Merchant then made it clear that he wanted the Anglo-Choctaw talks to fail. Those talks would focus on trade and, like most of his people, Gun Merchant opposed the opening of a trade between the English and the Choctaws. "I have often forewarned the White People going into the Chactaw Nation; but they would not mind me, and they were knocked in the Head." He sneered that the Choctaws had come seeking trade, but "not one of them have Skins enough to buy a Blanket." His real motive surely was to prevent these recent enemies from acquiring arms and ammunition from English traders.[41]

Atkin now turned his attention to the Choctaws. These Indians, who for months had been doggedly soliciting the English to open a trade, were in no position to dicker over terms. The first written treaty the Choctaws ever contracted with the English or anyone else was signed at Waulyhatchee on July 18, 1759. Headmen from sixty-two Choctaw towns were present. Spectators included "a Great number" of Creek and Chickasaw leaders and, Atkin claimed, "almost all the British Traders in the Crick Nation." No minutes of proceedings survive, but probably the only thing that required any negotiation was the Choctaw agreement to be at peace with the Chickasaws. The treaty Atkin wrote for the occasion was more lopsided than usual.

The treaty began with a preamble recounting the Choctaw request for peace and trade with the king's subjects. On behalf of the king, the superintendent granted this request, provided the goods would be carried to only two named towns, and "on the following conditions." The Choctaws promised to pay the same prices for goods as the Chickasaws did, provide guards for packtrains and houses for traders, give "Full Satisfaction" for any harm they did to traders or their goods, exclude French and Spanish traders, and set up English flags in their towns. The final condition was the most extreme. It required from the Choctaws what Atkin dare not, despite Ellis's 1757 treaty, ask from the Creeks. The Choctaws were to "be Friends to all the Friends of the British Subjects; and shall be Enemies to all their Enemies both white and Red People; . . . and distress the same to the utmost of their power."[42]

The treaty was "read, interpreted, and fully explained" to the Choctaws, who promptly agreed "to the whole with one Tongue and one heart." Two leading chiefs signed in behalf of "the whole Chactaw Nation," and Atkin signed for the king. Afterward he distributed presents, including flags for towns. Atkin did not suppose that the treaty would induce the Choctaws to take up arms against the French; he had a more attainable goal in mind. As he explained to Pitt, "by this Treaty the hands of the Creeks, who stand in fear of the Chactaws, were tied up from taking any part against us." Well-armed Choctaws in their rear would clarify Creek thinking.[43]

Most of the Choctaws remained in the neighborhood until August 9. Some wished to continue on to Savannah, probably with the hope of additional presents. Atkin forbade them to go, and they obeyed. One chief, however, apparently sent a written message to Governor Ellis via John Spencer. Atkin had been about to expel this notorious trader for "his Behaviour in regard to the Wolf." Against the Mucklassee chief's wishes, Spencer had erected a trading house "in the woods" outside of town. There he had profited from an illicit trade that served, Atkin charged, "to ruin it for other Traders." The superintendent was about to expel Spencer when he suddenly left on his own.[44]

Spencer, who had been denouncing Atkin to Ellis and Lyttelton, evidently saw an opportunity to get even. The disgruntled trader claimed to have acted as amanuensis for "Ebitapogola-Mingo," apparently the greatest of the Choctaw chiefs, Betapoucoulou Mingo. Spencer wrote out a talk supposedly dictated by this chief to Governor Ellis. The appearance of a written talk from any Choctaw leader to a British official inspires skepticism. Unlike the Creeks and Cherokees, the Choctaws did not send written "talks" to the English. Dispatching one—and this seems to be the only one mentioned during the colonial era—would have required much prompting. At any rate, in November Spencer brought Ellis the message, along with a white wing, claiming that he received both from Ebitapogola Mingo at Mucklassee. In the written text the Choctaw leader expressed disappointment that "we were stopped by Order of . . . Mr. Atkin." Nevertheless, sooner or later his people would be able to come: "we are still resolved to see the Governour and compleat the good Work we have begun." Atkin denounced the purported Choctaw letter as "a most impudent falsehood" by Spencer.[45]

Atkin intended to dispatch traders with the first consignment of trade goods to the Choctaws as soon as possible. It apparently took several weeks for those able and willing to go—James Hewitt and George Johnston—to assemble the necessary goods, horses, and packhorsemen. On August 9 "the far greater part" of the Choctaws "set out homeward . . . as a Guard to the first Cargo." Lyttelton heard from Atkin that 380 Choctaws convoyed "Sixty horse Loads of Goods." On August 18 the superintendent wrote Governor Lyttelton with a report on his success to date ("almost beyond the Flattery of my own Imagination") in Upper Creek country. That day, a month after its signing, he also sent the Carolina governor a copy of the Choctaw treaty. Atkin did not keep Governor Ellis as well informed. Evidently learning that Lyttelton had received or was about to receive the treaty text, Ellis on August 27 wrote Lyttelton that he had not.[46]

The superintendent also informed Lyttelton that he had put a stop to the English trade with the Alabamas. These Indians were closely related to the Creeks and less closely to the Choctaws. Soon their towns would be considered Upper Creek towns, but in 1759 Atkin reckoned the Upper Creeks and Alabamas to be "2 Nations." The Alabamas were in a unique and anomalous position, for they lived on Tallapoosa land. Their seven towns were clustered around Fort Toulouse, also on Tallapoosa land. Furthermore, although the Alabamas were regular customers of English traders, they were decidedly pro-French in their sympathies. Atkin said there were two French agents "living in the two principal Towns." He crowed that by cutting off the Alabama trade, he had forced the hard-pressed French to try to fill the void, thereby putting them to a "monstrous Expence."[47]

Since it seemed clear to Atkin that the Alabamas were French allies, he immediately concluded that the English trade with them was illegitimate. Furthermore, the Alabamas were largely supplied from Little Tallassee by Atkin's rival and personal enemy Lachlan McGillivray. Atkin denounced "the Infamous Trade of Little Talsey by which his Family has been getting Estates in Succession already above 30 years." Other goods dealt to the Alabamas came from John Spencer's even "more infamous" store in the woods outside of Mucklassee. The Alabama trade did not exhaust the list of Lachlan's "illegal Dealings at his Store at Little Talsey" (Little Tallassee). According to Atkin, McGillivray and Spencer were guilty of "engrossing the whole Trade of 450 Albahma Indians, and dealing with them and other his Majesty's Enemies." He accused both of crossing him again and again during his Upper Creek sojourn. Among other things, McGillivray was guilty of "the first Disregard paid to my Injunctions" to halt the Alabama trade.[48]

During his travels through Creek country, Superintendent Atkin had many private conversations with native leaders. One of the Upper Creek chiefs, the Mad Dog (Ifa Hadjo) of Tuckabatchee, later told Governor Ellis that his people "had chalked down near forty Talks delivered by the Agent . . . in the Nation." These talks, he fumed, "contained provoking Words and much Abuse." Many of these mostly unrecorded talks related to a major addition to British methods for dealing with Indians that Atkin had been laboring to put into effect. It was not exactly an innovation, for it was closely based on French practice, which in turn was based on an institution widespread among the native nations of the Southeast. Atkin often said that French methods for dealing with Indians were more successful than those employed by the English, and recommended following various French practices.[49]

The native institution underlying the French practice that Atkin aimed to emulate in 1759 has only recently attracted scholarly attention. The spur was Alexander Moore's discovery of three 1708 letters by South Carolina expansionist Captain Thomas Nairne, and their publication in 1988. In one of these letters Nairne describes what he calls a "prety rationable" custom found among "the Chicasaws Yassaws and other people of these parts." It operated at two levels: the "fameily" (clan) and the "nation." At the lower level, "any fameily of a nation who pleases usually chuse a protector or Freind out of another fameily. . . . for the head or Chief of their Fameily, . . . Then he is to protect that Fameily and take care of its concerns equally with those of his own." The clan making the appointment does so in a four-day ceremony featuring an "Eagle pipe." At the higher level, "Two nations at peace, each chuse these protectors in the other," presumably via a similar "calumet" ceremony. In other words, each nation appointed a "protector" chief in the other nation. "His business is to make up all Breaches between the 2 nations," and otherwise to look after the interests of the nation that appointed him. Nairne adds that the Chickasaws "call thes protectors Fane Mingo or Squirrell king."[50]

Atkin's successor as Indian superintendent, John Stuart, also described this aboriginal institution. In a 1764 report to the Board of Trade, Stuart highlighted "another custom common to all the Indians, of which, the French availed themselves to great advantage, in Governing the Nations in their Interest." He illustrated by describing how this institution operated among the Cherokees, the nation he was then most familiar with: "In every Town in the Cherokee Nation, are Beloved men appointed by the Creeks, Chickasaws, Catawbas, and other Nations with whom they are at Peace. A Deputation sent from any of these Tribes for this purpose installs some Cherokee of Influence with much Ceremony, and the Appointment is approved of by the Inhabitants. The Person so appointed ever after and on all occasions interests himself in the affairs of his constituents; and is looked upon by them as conservator of their rights and Protector of their persons." This officer was known as a "Kemitah," the Cherokee equivalent of "Fanne Mingo." The Cherokees likewise appointed protector chiefs for themselves in towns of other nations. As noted earlier, both the Mortar and Escotchaby were Cherokee "kings," presumably because Cherokees had appointed them to act as their protectors in Oakchoy and Coweta.[51]

Superintendent Stuart described the creative use the French had made of this native custom a few pages later:

> The French by their Dextrous Culture of the Indians, under the great disadvantage of inability to supply their wants, were possessed of their affections in a much greater degree Than the English. The System they adopted for governing them was Suggested by observation of their Disposition and Customs. No people are more free than Indians: No Individuals fonder of Power and Influence. . . . The French made this love of Influence coincide with their own Views: And found out a Method of conferring it. I took notice that it is customary for Indians to appoint certain persons protectors of their Rights, in countries with which they are at Peace. This the French fell into and appointed such in every Town in the Chactaw Nation. They found out and pitched upon the most aspiring for this purpose; and after appointing him with great Solemnity hung a Silver Medal around his neck as a badge of office.

Lesser chiefs received smaller medals, and certain "Captains" were given gorgets.[52]

What Stuart described was a French institution he admired, a ranked system of medal chiefs. This institution originated by 1732 as an effort to gain for Frenchmen the benefits that all Southeastern Indians had in "protector" chiefs from other nations. The French effort to acquire reliable Choctaw guardians did not stop with metallic adornments. Those distinguished by the French in this fashion received other special gifts and were given sole responsibility to apportion the annual allotment of presents as they chose. Naturally, the medal chiefs favored "such persons as they judged most capable of supporting their Authority," which necessarily meant supporting French authority. Medal chiefs received special marks of respect in all their dealings with the French, "and all Commissions as leaders of parties were given according to their recommendation." Not least, "The Chiefs bearing Medals determined all Disputes between the Traders and Indians, and the Traders were obliged to Obey their decision."[53]

In talks at Tuckabatchee on July 25, Superintendent Atkin indicated that he had recently concluded that the French practice of appointing "protectors" for Frenchmen in Indian country was shrewd policy. (He had not mentioned this French practice or the Indian custom it was based upon in either his "Report" or "Plan" of 1755.) That morning Atkin met with the four main leaders of the town, singling out one of them for a special honor and responsibility. It was not the peace chief, the Tuckabatchee Mico, but the war chief Hopoya Mico or "Opoyamico" (the same title that had graced the late Malatchi). Atkin told them what he had in mind: "If at any time any Difference arises between any of your People, and the Trader in the Town, I rely upon the Cheif Leading Warriour to put a Stop to it, and make it up. I order the Trader on any such Occasion, to apply to him." Later that morning Atkin repeated this for all the townsmen at a general meeting in Tuckabatchee square, adding that he expected "the Cheif Warriour . . . to take Care of Trader."[54]

At the earlier meeting with the four leaders of the town, Atkin evidently tried to head off any jealousy that three of them might have felt over his announcement. He explained that he had chosen the war chief for the protector role because it was "his Proper Business." His new responsibility might require "Strength or Force," and "old Beloved men should not be troubled with such things." Atkin's auditors promptly agreed that his plan was "very good and we will observe to do it." The superintendent then bestowed presents on the four headmen, including a special present for the newly designated protector of Englishmen. Atkin repeated his Tuckabatchee action at the other Creek towns he visited. He emphasized this in his "great talk" in September: "In every Town where I have been I gave the Charge of the Trader to the Chief Warriour, and I gave him something for the Trouble he might be at." That something included a gorget. In a circular letter he sent to traders the following February, he called attention to the "Head Warriours . . . to whom I gave Gorgets." About the same time, Captain Allick advised Atkin that if he wanted help against the Cherokees, he should send for "the Head Warriours of the several Towns to whom he gave Gorgets."[55]

Atkin met again with the four Tuckabatchee leaders after his July 25 speech in the square. This time the *mico* said he had a message to convey from the young men of the town. They suffered from scarcity of ammunition and felt that they paid their trader too much for it. They requested that a deerskin bring them fifty bullets "instead of 40," and a similar price reduction for gunpowder. Aware that Atkin was transporting a packtrain of presents, the Tuckabatchee leader then suggested that he distribute his town's share before moving on to another. Atkin was not ready to discuss prices. Nor was he willing to deliver any of the ammunition he brought in the usual way, that is, serially to the most compliant leaders of each town. Instead, he would take another cue from the French. He would deliver all the presents he carried at the "General Meeting" he planned to hold with the leaders of all the Creek towns. Furthermore, as he explained to the men of Tuckabatchee: "I have no Presents for Towns. I have some Ammunition which I design to give to the chief Leading Warriour in a Town, and leave it to him to dispose of it as he thinks fit. I think this will be the best way, because it will cause the young

Warriours to pay the more Regard to him." The Tuckabatchee Mico replied that "this is the best thing ever we heard."[56]

On September 28, the day he finally set to deliver his "Great Talk" to the general meeting, about 150 leading men of the Upper and Lower Creeks gathered in Tuckabatchee square. The superintendent had intended to speak earlier, but the Abeika leaders were slow to arrive. The meticulously prepared minutes of the meeting lists eighty-three chiefs by name and/or title, town affiliation, and sometimes office. According to the minutes, the assembly included "almost all the Principal men of the Nation." While many were present, this claim was a gross exaggeration. In fact, most of the *micos* were not present, perhaps in silent protest at Atkin's favoritism toward the war leaders. The most conspicuous absentee was the host, Tuckabatchee Mico. On July 24 he had told Atkin that the numerous Creeks who had French and/or Spanish commissions "mean no harm by it," and he intended to keep both of his. Furthermore, he had accepted a Spanish invitation to visit Pensacola, and intended to go "the next Moon." He neglected to mention that he had already established a Tuckabatchee colony in Spanish Florida, with his son as chief. He did as he said he would: the minutes report that he was "absent at Pansicola."[57]

The Gun Merchant and Mortar of Oakchoy were not present either. When the superintendent saw the former in November, the Oakchoy leader slyly criticized Atkin's September "Great Talk." He went on to suggest that Atkin speak to the Mortar: "He is the Man, that hath the most Wisdom among us; and he has also the greatest Influence or Command over our Head Warriours." Atkin replied that he had heard much about this exceptional leader but had never seen him. He related that the Mortar had briefly been in Tuckabatchee shortly before his September speech, but had spoken only with Creeks. Elsewhere Atkin reported that the Mortar soon left for Fort Toulouse in the company of some Cherokees, telling Creeks "to Send for him there, if he should be wanted."[58]

The other Upper Creek absentees were the Tallassee Mico and all headmen from Hoithlewaulee. The biggest gaps, however, were in the ranks of the Lower Creeks. While the minutes record that the *micos* of Hitchiti and Lower Eufaula were present, corresponding leaders were "Absent from 7 Towns." Four of the Lower Creek towns, nearly half of them, sent no representatives at all. The missing towns were Apalachicola and the three "point towns" of Chehaw, Ouseechee, and Ocmulgee. Coweta was represented, but not by its principal leaders. Rather than attend, Sempoyaffi, Escotchaby, and Tugulki were off to Savannah to give Governor Ellis an earful about Atkin's performance to date.[59]

On the afternoon of September 28, nearly three months after his arrival in Creek country, the superintendent stood in the chiefs' cabin at Tuckabatchee square to deliver his "Great Talk." Joseph Wright, who had done most of the interpreting all along, continued as principal interpreter. Atkin began by asking that he be heard without interruption; afterward, following due consideration of his talk, "I shall be glad to hear your answer." Inquiring who would deliver the Creek reply, he was told it would be the Wolf King, who promised an answer the following day.

Atkin at first planned his "great" talk to achieve a grand objective. As he explained to Governor Lyttelton, however, as the day approached he felt obliged to lower his sights. "It was my intention, to have brought my Speech at that General Meeting to this short decisive point; to insist that the Creeks should positively tell one of us to leave their Country, the English or the French." He dropped the idea because "things wore so gloomy an Aspect" and because it alarmed the traders. Atkin may have first supposed that such a demand would lead to the desired result because word of recent British victories in Canada would convince the Creeks that the French cause was lost. Instead, he found that the Creeks reacted to the news "with profound Silence, and an apparent Want of Satisfaction, or Joy at it, for which Reason I have been very backward in telling them that kind of News. The Meaning of it is this. They have an Opinion, that sooner or later they shall lose their Freedom, and become Subject to one of the European Powers. And they would keep that day as far off as possible. Wherefore the greater our Success is, the more they are inclined in their Hearts to assist and prop up the tottering French; not so much out of Compassion or real Love to them, as out of a true Regard to themselves, and their own Independency." This was a shrewd insight, borne out by recorded admissions from Creek leaders that it was "too late" to take various actions that once might have stopped the oncoming English.[60]

At any rate, Atkin's numerous conversations with Creek chiefs convinced him that the Creeks could not be induced to order the French to abandon Fort Toulouse. He decided therefore to deliver a more attenuated message, a decision already apparent in his July 9 speech. The key change was his adoption of a new and much reduced standard for identifying a friendly Indian nation: nothing more than a plurality of sympathizers.[61]

The superintendent began his September 28 speech by indicating that he had no surprises to spring: in both lower and upper towns "at my first Arrival . . . I told you the Nature of my Errand." He had, he recalled, professed his main purpose in many meetings, both public and private. "I told you it was to see whether you were really Friends to my King and his Subjects? Or whether you were better Friends to the French than to them." Atkin said he had not demanded and did not demand an exclusive friendship for his king, merely a preponderant one. He had also come to settle differences between the Creeks and their traders. The British king "will let no Red People have Goods, but those who are Friends to him and his subjects." Most emphatically, he had not come seeking land or forts: French lies. For King

George, "those who are his Friends are Fort enough." The important point was that "My King wants nothing of you . . . but not to hurt his own People."[62]

Atkin went on to review his proceedings to date. Unnecessarily, he said "I have done nothing in a hurry." He described his activities this way: "I have seen and talked with most of the Headmen of the Nation, and also with the Traders; and I am now pretty well acquainted with the Situation of Affairs between you." He added that his inquiries had enabled him to do "the Red People . . . justice in several Cases." The superintendent said that in his travels through the Lower and Tallapoosa towns, "I don't know that I gave Offence to any." He acknowledged that there had been objections to his frequent requests for information about the men, women, and children of each town, but he maintained that he had simply been asking innocent questions designed to help bring about a more equitable distribution of presents. Bad men at Oakchoy had "threatned to throw (Stones) at me" if he showed up there, so it was the Abeikas' own fault that he had not visited their towns. Atkin then tried to explain why the Alabama towns deserved to have their trade cut off.[63]

Seated behind the superintendent was Tathlahbegey, nicknamed the Tobacco Eater. Tathlahbegey was a high-ranking warrior of Cussita and one of the headmen Atkin had chosen to have charge of his talks. As Atkin began to speak of the Alabamas, Tathlahbegey was heard to say (while staring at the three Sowwicolas present) that "those men are talking of killing me." This was loud and disturbing enough to interrupt the speech, and "it was proposed to remove him." Atkin even "felt his Pulse, and said they were in a flutter." The superintendent nevertheless resumed. A few minutes later Tathlahbegey stood up. When Atkin paused to look back at him, the Cussita leader said "nothing was the matter, he was only tired [of] sitting."

As the superintendent was defending his action toward the Alabamas, Tathlahbegey "started up behind him, and fell on him with a Pipe Hatchet; and made 6 Strokes at him." Atkin reported that four of them landed: two "on my Skull," others on his hand and shoulder. This sensational attack triggered a general uproar. The assembly immediately broke up, and the bleeding Atkin was led to the house where he was staying for attention to his wounds. He was not seriously hurt, but was seriously humiliated. Tathlahbegey's first stroke had been partially deflected by a roof timber, and others were parried by those who subdued him. Ironically, Atkin's main rescuer was an Alabama, the mixed-blood war chief (Ifa Mico) of Tuskegee known as Molton.[64]

What motivated this attack is obscure. Atkin initially supposed that it was a crazed eruption by a single "Madman." As he reported to Secretary Pitt the following March, however, "after some time I found that this thing was concerted at the French Fort, and that the killing me was intended as the Signal for killing all the rest of the white People in the Nation, which must have followed immediately." Two sentences later Atkin described what he took to be a contemporaneous but separate conspiracy: Cherokees had invited "some" Lower Creeks to join them in revenge attacks on North Carolina settlers, "which invitation was accepted." (This apparently was the same invitation conveyed by Issulgy of Apalachicola.) The plot fizzled when Upper Creek leaders learned of it, ordered their people to have no part of it, and warned the Cherokees "not to spoil the white people's path" to Creek country. Years later James Adair supposed that both Tathlahbegey's attack and those contemplated by the Cherokees were part of a broad conspiracy jointly planned and coordinated by the French and by the Mortar.[65]

Atkin's report that some Lower Creeks had accepted the Cherokee call to arms is credible, for a few weeks later Coweta leaders would privately admit this to Governor Ellis in Savannah. Evidence that this pact was part of a larger conspiracy put together by the French and the Mortar is weak, while evidence that Tathlahbegey's attack on Atkin was part of it is still weaker. There may be some truth in the former or even both of these theories, but a simpler explanation better fits the existing evidence.[66]

The apparently shocked and apologetic behavior of Creek leaders toward what had occurred argues against a broad-based conspiracy. Moreover, there is abundant evidence that Atkin had antagonized many Creeks to the point of considering murder. When Tugulki learned of the attack on Atkin from Governor Ellis, he responded that "I would have served him so my self long ago had I not been prevented by the other Indians." Weightier testimony to the same effect came from the Mad Dog of Tuckabatchee, one of Atkin's hosts and one of those he had selected to entrust with his future talks. The following June, Mad Dog told Ellis that Atkin's behavior "became so intollerable to the Indians, they would certainly have killed him had it not been for the Intervention of two or three." It seems likely that Atkin's assailant was moved by a fit of rage that differed from the widely shared anger mainly in intensity.[67]

The following day Atkin continued his speech to a smaller gathering in the yard adjoining the house of the Heniha Mico (also known as Tuckabatchee Half-Breed, father of Mad Dog). Putting up a brave front, he began by minimizing yesterday's "Accident," which was received with relief and approval. He then resumed where he had left off, detailing the Alabamas' actions in support of the French that had led him to stop their trade. Atkin next sought to justify another of his unpopular actions. He said he had ordered the English trader out of Oakchoy "because they had a French Trader there, and the Headmen of that town wanted him there." Since his "Cheif Business here was to prevent Disturbances," he had acted to preserve harmony. He had removed the English trader, he explained, because he was sure "an English Trader, and a French Trader in one Town could never agree."[68]

The superintendent then turned to some of the things he hoped to do for the Creeks in the future: help arrange better trade prices, provide a smith to repair their guns, and offer advice on better ways to provide for their families than hunting the dwindling herds of deer. "All signified their Approbation, at each sentence." The following ones were less well received. Atkin declared that there were two things about the Creeks that "surprize me very much." First, all Creeks agreed that "they can't do without the English." Nevertheless, he said, "there have been *designs to kill the Traders*." Why was that, he wanted to know. Second, Creeks were "all afraid of having Forts among you." Nevertheless, "you have suffered the French to have one a great many years." Was it not time for the Creeks to be consistent and expel this alien and troublesome presence?[69]

Turning positive again, Atkin observed that "the wisest" of their ancestors had given the Creeks excellent advice. "They said, hold fast all three, English, French and Spanish. Take Care, and never Quarrel with any of them." For his Creek auditors this was the high moment of the speech. "Here one and all signified their Approbation with a visible Change in their Countenances." All understood that the superintendent was referring to the neutrality policy initiated by Brim more than forty years earlier. Atkin then alluded to an amendment the Creeks could not recollect as clearly as he seemed to. He asserted that the same wise Creek forebears who had recommended neutrality also advised that "If you let go any, don't let go the English, for you can't do without them." It was an attempt to put his notion of predominant friendship into native idiom, but it drew no sign of approval.[70]

The superintendent then issued several warnings. If the Creeks were to join the Cherokees in attacks on the king's people, "you will let go his hand." In other words, the Creeks would forfeit the king's friendship and all the benefits that went with it. He added that the same result would follow if the Creeks aided the French against the English. Finally, "my King will never hurt you, unless you take part with his Enemies." The implied threat in the second clause was unnecessary and unwise. There was some audible approval for the first of these cautions, but the last two passed in silence.[71]

Reminding the Creeks that he had come "to hear any Complaints you had to make and set things right," Atkin announced that "I am now ready to hear them." The silence was deafening. This lack of response most assuredly was not due to a lack of Creek complaints. It was, rather, an implicit statement that there was no point in talking to Atkin about their complaints because he figured so prominently in them. This refusal to respond to a direct question from the superintendent—in effect to ignore him—was a deadly insult. If Atkin noticed, he pretended not to. The speech was about at an end, but the cold shoulder was not.

Before Atkin spoke, the Wolf King had been designated to reply for the Creeks. The minutes relate that after Atkin withdrew from the square, the Wolf King followed him and began to speak of trade issues. The superintendent told him to hold his comments for his formal reply. At this the Mucklassee leader revealed that "they had *no Answer to make*; he having told him this Morning in his Speech, all that they had to say." Atkin later complained that what the Wolf King said that morning "related only to some Alterations in the Trade in their favour." It apparently suddenly dawned on the superintendent that he was being scorned. His carefully prepared "Great Talk" had been dismissed before it had been fully heard. "What, said the Superintendent, [you replied] before you heard half my Speech!" The Wolf King "persisted that they had no Answer to make." And with that "the Assembly appeared disposed to break up;" the minutes end abruptly with that semicolon. Insult, this time a comprehensive one, had been added to insult. Compounding it further, it had been delivered by the best friend the English had among the Upper Creeks. In November the Gun Merchant rubbed it in by reminding Atkin that "there were no Answers given to your Talks."[72]

It took only a month for the Alabama trade embargo to have its intended effect. The superintendent was able to report that on October 10 he signed a treaty with the Alabamas "on my own Terms" in Tuckabatchee. The treaty text relates that the day before the signing "the cheifs or Head ruling men" of the six Alabama towns had come submissively to him. Since the French had proven "utterly unable to supply their wants," these leaders "did humbly request to be looked upon and treated as well as the Creeks by having the same Trade allowed to them."[73]

Like the Choctaws three months earlier, the Alabamas came hungry for English trade goods, and Atkin's treaties with the two peoples are similar in many respects. Although the treaty text distinguishes the Alabamas from the Creeks, on behalf of the king the superintendent grants them the right to trade "at the same rates as the Creeks now do." This commerce is limited to licensed traders operating out of Little Tallassee (Lachlan McGillivray and William Struthers) or Mucklassee (James Germany and William Trewin), and only upon seven conditions. Of most immediate importance, the Alabamas now pledged not to interfere with the Choctaw trade, as they had earlier. They also promised to give satisfaction for any injury to the persons or effects of English traders, to raise the "English Colours" in all six Alabama towns, and to shun the French. One condition of the Choctaw treaty is conspicuously absent: the obligation to make the friends and enemies of the English their own. Traders likely advised Atkin that the Alabamas were Creeks enough to refuse any such concession. Furthermore, such a provision would have required the Alabamas to attack Fort Toulouse, which they had long defended. Atkin probably did not raise the issue. According to the treaty text, the Alabama headmen promptly and "unanimously" agreed to the treaty.[74]

Later that month, Atkin finally visited some of the Abeika towns. He reported little about his private meetings with Abeika leaders, except to claim that his prohibition of trade to Oakchoy had "helped greatly to bring the Mortar and Gun of that Town, who were the heads of the French Party, to terms." In late October, through the Gun Merchant's mediation, the Mortar agreed to carry a written message from Atkin to the Cherokees. The superintendent later learned that the Mortar had tossed it into a creek.[75]

It was at Okfuskee that Atkin held the last of his major public meetings. It was a conference not with the Creeks but with the Choctaws, evidently at their initiative. According to Atkin, when the packtrain returned from delivering "the first Cargo" to Choctaw country, a party of Choctaws "claimed a right of joining in it." The augmented packtrain made its way to Okfuskee, and there found the superintendent. He related that the Choctaw party, eighty men, was "chiefly the principal Head Warriours of the Nation." Still more significant, it was weighted in favor of the eastern division, the most Francophile part of the Choctaw Nation. The Betapoucoulou Mingo, "the first man in the Nation," did not come himself, but his younger brother and several other lieutenants did. The leader of the party was his principal war leader, the Red Captain, who acted as the group's main spokesman. He would continue to be a dominant Choctaw leader, in both war and peace, over the next eight years.[76]

The impromptu talks extended from October 25 through November 1. Since no Choctaw-English interpreter was available, an awkward double translation was necessary. Choctaw speeches were first translated into Muskogee by Wauthlucko Mico of Muklassee, who had served as guide and interpreter for the packtrain. His Muskogee version was then translated into English by Joseph Wright. Since Atkin had merely acquiesced to the meeting and did not wish to play host, the Red Captain made the opening speech. He explained that he and his companions were "the Chief Warriours of our Nation" and that they had come "to confirm the Friendship that was made with you." More particularly, "Our chief Business was to guard the white People back whom you sent, and to see you." The Red Captain praised Atkin for having brought about peace between themselves and the Chickasaws. "Now the time is come that through your means all Red People are at Peace and Friendship. . . . All the Paths are white." As for the newly bleached path to the English, "I was one of the People who never before would agree to a Peace with the English. . . . but now I have turned." From now on the Choctaws would "hold fast by the English."[77]

The next day other speakers reiterated the Red Captain's main points. One was Shulush Mastabe (Red Shoes) of West Yazoo, regularly associated with the Red Captain in coming years. Shulush Mastabe reminded Atkin that in July he had urged the Choctaws to make peace with the Chickasaws, "and we have paid Regard to what you said." The brother of Betapoucoulou Mingo emphasized a point of more concern to the English: the current Choctaw attitude toward the French and themselves. He related that the Choctaws had hitherto allowed Frenchmen to live in their towns, "but now we think no more about them, nor of any but the English." Toward the end of the meeting, another speaker reported that as soon as the first English trader entered Cousha, the resident Frenchman disappeared. "It will be the same when we go back. The Frenchmen will all run away." It seems clear that it was not merely the trade that had brought the Choctaws to the English. By this time, and probably well before the July treaty, they appear to have concluded that the French were destined to lose the war. They clearly preferred to share the British victory rather than the French defeat. Atkin later reported that the Choctaws were so ripe for action that he cautioned them to wait until a British fleet appeared off the coast. He added that the French were counting on Choctaw support in case of a British invasion, but the wily Choctaws had decided "to turn the Tables upon them."[78]

Superintendent Atkin replied on October 27. He began by stating that the Choctaw visitors had told him that they had been "sent by your Nation, to confirm the Treaty of Friendship that I made with your Headmen" in July. This was not exactly what they had said, but their acquiescence enabled Atkin to reinforce the treaty. Three days later it "was duly ratified and confirmed by the beforementioned Chactaw Head Wariours." The superintendent then declared that King George "did not send me to set one Nation of Red People against another, as the French do, but that all those who are Friends to the English may live together in Peace and Quietness." Near the close of the meeting, Atkin went further when he related that "I have forbid the Traders buying Scalps, or having any hand in Blood." This humanitarian concern, so appealing to us, was not so attractive to the Choctaws or other Indians Atkin met during his mission. It was no pose, but a genuine concern consistently expressed.

Bridging his assertions on political and trade issues, Atkin declared that so long as the Choctaws and Creeks lived in friendship with the English, "you will never want Goods." Never, that is, unless the Choctaws failed to reform a particularly objectionable habit. He criticized Choctaw leaders to their faces for behavior that many Frenchmen and English traders had denounced in private. "Your People have a way of begging Goods different from other Nations, which is like taking them away." If this continued, the traders would not return. The Red Captain's reply was as Atkin hoped it would be: "We have heard your Talk and we will observe it." If the Choctaws could swallow Atkin's scolding on this score, they had a harder time agreeing to pay Chickasaw prices for English goods, as the treaty required. Hence the Red Captain appealed for trade at the lower prices paid by "our elder Brothers," the Creeks. The superintendent explained that this was not yet possible: Chickasaw prices were higher than those paid by the Creeks because a greater distance separated them from the English, which entailed greater expense, trouble, and risk for the traders. Once the English were able to "bring Goods to you by Water, as the French do," the Choctaw rates would be the same as those for the Creeks.

The superintendent remained in Creek country until mid-December, arriving back at Fort Moore on December 23. The Indians' concern over British reaction to Tathlahbegey's assault on him probably explains how he was able to prolong his stay so far beyond his welcome. His last days there were busy. His long report to Lyttelton on his activities among the Upper Creeks, often quoted above, was dated November 30. In the opening sentence Atkin claimed to be "Happy in the final Accomplishment of every thing I have undertaken." Well, almost everything: "except the humbling of the execrable Coweta men, who have been rescued out of my hands into the able hands of Governor Ellis." In fact, Atkin's report repeatedly undermined his opening boast. Most conspicuously, he recommended that South Carolina and Georgia act to interrupt the trade to the Creeks "until a Satisfactory Answer is given to the several Points in my Speech at the General Meeting at Tookybatchey."[79]

Anyone who read the report could not help doubting Atkin's claim that in the end he had cemented relations with the Upper Creeks. "I have closed my Negotiations, by bringing to a private Interview, and reconciling in my presence, the Wolf and the Gun, the Heads of the two Parties in this Nation; who have consented and agreed, to share the Direction of Affairs; the Wolf to have that of the Tallapoosas and Alabamas, and the Gun that of the Abekas." The Wolf King was a reliable Anglophile, but Atkin conceded that he had been losing influence, even among the Tallapoosas. This led the superintendent to try "to restore the Wolf to his lost Credit." As for the Gun Merchant, Atkin observed that the Oakchoy Mico had been "as good a Friend as ever we had for many Years." Lately, however, the aged chief had deferred to the Mortar, who "had acquired the Chief Command over the *Head Warriours*." Furthermore, "even in the Gun merchant's Opinion, he is the man possessed of the most Wisdom; No man equal to him in this Nation, And in high Repute among the Neighboring ones, especially among the Cherokees. . . . No Man durst openly oppose him." The superintendent admitted that his mission had faced resistance from the start. He pointed to the Mortar and Gun Merchant, ringleaders of the pro-French faction, as "my two greatest Opponents."[80]

Atkin made numerous public pronouncements to the Creeks that he had not come to ask them to take up arms. Just before his departure, however, he privately approached two of the most Anglophile chiefs on future collaboration. As Atkin later reported to Pitt: "Before I left the Creek Nation I accomplished one thing hitherto thought to be impracticable considering the neutral Principles of those Indians with regard to white People, that is I engaged two principal Leading men, the most to be trusted, to take small English Colours from me and Head War Parties against the French at Mobile, whenever any of the Kings Ships appear. Others will in that case follow their Example. At present it is kept a Secret." The two Creek leaders who yielded to his persuasions were probably the Wolf King and Captain Allick. The superintendent was convinced that Allick was so useful to the British cause that he must be persuaded to remain in Cussita rather than return to his place on the coast. The problem was that Allick's wives wanted to return. Atkin got him to agree to stay if he were given forty head of cattle, and then got Governors Lyttelton and Ellis to promise at least thirty head. Allick apparently never received them, and returned to the coast.[81]

Facing rising Cherokee belligerence, that fall Governor Lyttelton and the South Carolina council urged Atkin to incite the Creeks and Chickasaws against the Cherokees. The superintendent had refused, for that "would be contradictory to the whole Tenour of all my Talks." The news Atkin heard at Fort Moore dealt mainly with the rapidly escalating conflict between the Carolinians and the Cherokees. By the time he wrote several messages on February 5, that conflict had become open warfare, which led him to change his tune.[82]

Writing to the Creeks that day, Atkin recalled his pleas in their towns to ignore Cherokee attempts to lure them into the conflict. He was pleased to acknowledge that they had done so: "This was a proof of your friendship, and . . . I thank you in the great king's name." Reminding the Creeks of their warning to the Cherokees "not to spoil the white people's path to your nation," he declared that they were "very near to spoiling it now." In other words, Cherokee violence threatened to cut off Creek access to English trade goods. He continued that the Cherokees had accused him of scheming to set the Creeks upon them, "but you know I did not." That, however, was then. In the new situation, Atkin hinted broadly that it was time for such of "your young men who want to go to war" to join the English against the Cherokees, and that this would be rewarded with trade concessions. He was blunt in a letter he wrote to the Creek traders the same day, stating that his "present purpose . . . is to induce them to take part with us against the Cherokees."[83]

Shortly afterward the war leaders from the seven Abeika towns replied to Atkin's message. Their spokesmen were the captains of Okfuskee, Pucknatallahassee, and Oakchoy. Their answer was reassuring. The Pucknatallahassee leader declared that "the Abeckas, Tallapooses, Cowetas, and Coosadices [Alabamas] are resolved to have no hand in the war." They were determined that "our path shall not be spoiled" and that "the goods may continue amongst us." The others made similar statements. The Oakchoy leader added a remarkable explanation of why their words could be trusted: "It was not the white people forced themselves upon us; it was we that sought after them, every one of my own forefathers." It was one of the superintendent's most effective exchanges with the Creeks, perhaps because he was no longer among them.[84]

Apprehensive about Atkin's mission from the start, Governor Ellis soon concluded that so far as relations with the Creeks were concerned, the mission was a disaster. The reports Atkin sent him, like those the superintendent sent Lyttelton and Pitt, no doubt provided ample grounds for criticism. Probably the governor was more influenced by negative reports from traders and by several personal meetings with both Lower and Upper Creek leaders. The anti-Atkin invective poured out to Ellis by Coweta leaders in October 1759 and the Mad Dog of Tuckabatchee in June 1760 has already been noted. On the former occasion Ellis came close to apologizing for the superintendent's behavior; on the latter he did apologize that "the Imprudence of one Man" should have provoked so much Creek resentment.[85]

Any doubts Ellis had about Atkin's Creek diplomacy vanished after his meeting with the Coweta leaders. On October 11 he wrote Lyttelton that "I heartily wish the agent would quit the Nation for the Creeks that are with me complain bitterly of him." He was restrained in his reports to London until there was no chance the superintendent could achieve some last-minute diplomatic coup. He let fly as soon as he learned of Atkin's return to Fort Moore. On January 6, 1760, he unburdened himself to the Board of Trade. He began with a cruel gibe at Atkin, comparing him to "that Philosopher who first concealed truth in a Well, [then] boasted of having brought it out." He went on to ridicule the superintendent's boast of success with the Creeks: Atkin had the nerve to claim credit for "having left Matters there in a settled state, after he had greatly disturbed and embarrassed them." Ellis was so disgusted with the outcome that he suggested that London officials abolish the office of Indian superintendent for the southern colonies.[86]

Governor Ellis's angry assessment of Superintendent Atkin's eight-month mission to Creek country, and especially of Atkin himself, was too harsh. Edmond Atkin was a man of intelligence and integrity. As his "Report" and "Plan" of 1755 demonstrate, he was observant and had a keen analytical mind. Moreover, he was not only able to put his finger on festering problems but had vision enough to propose workable solutions. Some would be followed by his successor John Stuart and even by Governor Ellis. For example, Atkin's plan to make a war leader of each town responsible for the safety of traders and their goods prompted Ellis to design a similar scheme that conceded even more control to the Indians. On June 30, 1760, the Georgia governor told "Ambassadors" from the Upper and Lower Creeks that he intended soon to reopen the trade disrupted by the Cherokee war.

"But first," he said, "I expect that the Head Men of every Town will meet and choose out some powerfull Person to take Charge of the Traders and be answerable to me for their Persons and Effects." Other examples of Atkin practices that inspired imitation include provision for direct consultations between English and Creek leaders on the Indians' home ground, distribution of gorgets and armbands to favored chiefs, making a point to honor elderly leaders, and providing for the repair of Indian firearms.[87]

Atkin was a careful observer of Creek society. Probably no Englishman of his day understood Creek social structure better than he did. In other circumstances he might have been a scholar. He not only was deeply interested in the Indians but sincerely concerned for their welfare and convinced he was promoting it. For a colonial leader of his day he was unusually humane. While many others thought it was wise policy to encourage Indians to make war on their native rivals, Atkin thought it was dishonorable. He was proud that "I have constantly inveighed against the French Practice, of setting one Nation of Indians upon another." Until actual warfare erupted, Atkin refused South Carolina pleas that he incite the Creeks and Chickasaws to attack the Cherokees. While many others thought turning native scalping to European purposes was praiseworthy, or at least expedient, Atkin thought it was shameful. In 1757 he had denounced the bounties and other rewards English and other Europeans offered for the scalps of their Indian enemies. Two years later he blamed former governor James Glen for making it an English practice. When he had a chance to do something about it during his mission, he did: he forbade traders to pay for "enemy" scalps.[88]

Unlike so many of his contemporaries, Atkin admired aspects of Creek culture that we are likely to find admirable, such as its commitment to neutrality in conflicts among Europeans and its disdain for public lying. Unlike so many others, he was normally scrupulous about speaking what he saw as truth to Indians. The only evidence to the contrary is his last-minute recruitment of two Creek leaders to head war parties against the French in the event of a British invasion of the Gulf Coast. He erred much worse in the opposite direction. Atkin knew that the Indians valued frankness; what he failed to grasp was that they also valued withholding harsh words—no matter how true—in order not to give offense. His relentless hectoring offended countless Indians. The fact that he thought he was telling necessary truths was beside the point.

Initiating diplomatic practices that later became more or less standard were not the only achievements of Atkin's mission. Atkin signed—he wrote—the first written treaties with the Choctaws and the Alabamas. The Choctaw treaty was notable for establishing regular commerce between the English and Choctaws. Also significant was the Choctaw commitment to fight against the enemies of the British. This did not lead to any actual military assistance, but it did undermine

French morale by demonstrating to them that their only credible defensive force for the Gulf Coast was unreliable. Choctaw initiative was mainly responsible, but Atkin also deserves credit. Until his superiors redirected him toward the Creeks, establishing closer ties to the Choctaws had been his first priority. Then, when the Choctaw overtures came, he recognized them as significant opportunities, made the necessary adjustments in his schedule, and took full advantage. The most important result of his Alabama treaty was to secure the Choctaw trade by obliging the Alabamas to cease blocking it. Perhaps his greatest achievement was the peace between the Choctaws and Chickasaws.

Not only did Atkin have successes, but some of the failures he has been blamed for were not his fault. He was sent to do a very difficult job, which became a nearly impossible job once he was ordered to focus on overcoming Creek neutrality. He was dispatched with a vague mandate, inadequate authority, and no means. He had nothing with which to pay for any of his activities except what he was able to beg from other British officials. Three months after his return from Creek country he wrote Secretary Pitt that he had "carried on the Service hitherto without one Shilling of the King's Money." The fault most often laid at his door—that he failed to see that the main Indian problem in his district was Cherokee disaffection, and so went off on a Creek adventure—was not his doing.[89]

After all due allowances are made, however, Atkin's mission must be judged a resounding failure. The original goals were not met and, more important, whatever benefits Atkin did achieve were far outweighed by the costs. Two negative results stand out. First, Atkin poisoned Creek feelings toward the English and especially their government, and thereby was largely responsible for making Anglo-Creek relations very difficult during the remainder of the colonial era. Relations between the English and the Lower Creeks in 1759 were not nearly as good as Governor Ellis supposed, but Atkin made them much worse. Although anti-English sentiments had made little headway among the Upper Creeks prior to his arrival, Atkin proved to be the ideal carrier of the infection. Neglect of the Cherokees in favor of the Creeks was not his idea, but he failed to recognize that a major mistake had been made and propose corrective action until it was too late.

Whatever the superintendent's merits, Ellis was surely right when he said that Atkin was "very ill calculated for the employment he is in." Unlike the Georgia governor, Atkin was totally miscast as a diplomat. Ellis was convivial, even when caught by surprise, and could spend half the night palavering and drinking with Indians, seeming to enjoy it. Atkin was almost the reverse: formal, austere, even forbidding, and likely to meet with Indians only by appointment. He was prone to make threats, deliver snubs, and hold grudges. He was also ponderous, vain, insecure, and stubborn. He had a good understanding of the big picture, but often not of the man standing in front of him or, most importantly, the man he saw in his shaving mirror.

Atkin understood much, but he did not understand himself. Recognition of the negative effects he had upon others usually eluded him. It was not just Indians he antagonized: he was almost as unpopular among the traders. He was probably totally unaware of the personal characteristic that most disqualified him from diplomacy: his in-your-face bluntness. Priding himself on his straight talking with Indians, he seems to have been oblivious to the fact that this could be overdone and perceived as verbal aggression. The Creeks found Atkin intolerably censorious. To them his aim mattered less than the fact that so many of his words came like bullets. The wounded would return the fire.

CHAPTER NINE

The Cherokee War and Imperial Triumph

Although Virginia was centrally involved in the onset of the Franco-British war for control of North America, most fighting occurred in the north. After numerous reverses, the capture of Louisbourg in July 1758 turned the tide in favor of the British. The fall of Quebec in September 1759 seemed to resolve the imperial conflict once and for all. But it did not, not yet. Two subsequent events acted to prolong the contest and bring it back to the south. First, in late 1759 the English blundered into a costly war with the Cherokees, who were egged on by the French. Second, a secret agreement between the Bourbon kings of France and Spain brought Spain into the North American war in early 1762. The zone of imperial combat was now enlarged to include Spanish Florida.

While both South Carolina and Georgia had active contacts with the Creeks, only the older colony maintained such links with the Cherokees. Since Oglethorpe's departure, Georgia leaders had been content to leave the unprofitable trade and frustrating diplomacy with the Cherokees entirely to South Carolina. Governor Henry Ellis saw no reason to alter the traditional arrangement. From the start, however, South Carolina governor William Lyttelton was suspicious that the new Georgia governor intended to compete with him for influence with Indians, especially the Cherokees. Recalling his disembarkation in Charles Town in January 1757, Ellis later reminded Lyttelton of their first meeting. The South Carolina governor had asked his junior colleague what he intended to do about the Cherokees. Ellis recalled that his reply had been that he had "no intention of concerning myself with their Affairs."[1]

When the two governors met again that August, Ellis again tried to put the Carolina governor's turf worries to rest. Thus he agreed to have a major Creek embassy, expected in the fall, visit Charles Town first. A few days later he wrote Lyttelton that "I can assure You Dear Sir that I have no sort of ambition of being principal Negotiator with the Indians," well aware that Lyttelton rather fancied that role. On September 25 he denied that he had ever contacted the Cherokees without Lyttelton's knowledge. Furthermore, "though I have often been importuned for Licences to Trade in that Nation, I have constantly refused them." Aware of Lyttelton's suspicions, Superintendent Atkin later assured him that Ellis had no wish to deal with the Cherokees. Atkin related that Ellis had told him that he intended "to concern himself with no Indians but the Cricks." No amount of reassurance on this point seemed to defuse Lyttelton's jealous distrust of his Georgia counterpart.[2]

On another Indian matter, Atkin deepened Lyttelton's suspicion of Georgians. The Lower Chickasaws near Augusta, like their countrymen in the Chickasaw homeland, had a well-earned reputation for ferocity in battle and—more importantly—loyalty to the English. Like the Catawbas in the north, the Lower Chickasaws in the south were extremely valuable to South Carolina as early warning monitors and committed defenders. After that colony in 1739 set aside a huge reservation for them (about fifteen thousand acres), the Lower Chickasaws lived upon it in two small settlements near Fort Moore. In March 1757 Carolina Indian agent Daniel Pepper reported that they had grown in population and now boasted about seventy "gun men." He opined that in case of a French attack these few "would be of more Service to us than four Hundred other Indians."[3]

Around 1748 some of them began crossing the river and resettling near Augusta, encouraged by traders who had made the same move a decade earlier. The Lower Chickasaws soon leased various tracts on the Carolina side to Augusta traders. Toward the end of 1757 the Indians agreed with the leading transplanted trader, Lachlan McGillivray, for an "exchange" of lands. In return for relinquishing their fifteen thousand Carolina acres to him, McGillivray gave them five hundred acres at "New Savannah" below Augusta and a similar tract on the opposite side of the river. In the eyes of McGillivray and fellow Augustans, he had performed a great public service. Carolinians disagreed.

When Superintendent Atkin met with the Lower Chickasaw leaders in November 1758 he scolded them, not only for giving so much for so little, but mainly for giving what they had no right to give: the reserved land "the Governour of Carolina gave you leave *to make use of Some*." The shamefaced headmen admitted that "all of us" signed the deed McGillivray had put before them. Although superficially resembling deeds the Bosomworths had obtained from the Creeks, this one had even less legal merit. (While the Creek deeds dealt with natural rights titles the Indians held before Europeans arrived, the Lower Chickasaw deed dealt with lands reserved to them by agents of the British king.) Under Governor James Glen, McGillivray had been a key intermediary between the Carolina government and Indians, especially the Creeks. After Atkin denounced him to Lyttelton, his services were no longer welcome in Charles Town. His land "Exchange" was repudiated. McGillivray remained a key presence in Creek country, but now in behalf of Georgia.[4]

Trouble with the Cherokees had been brewing since at least 1755. On March 27 of that year, trader Ludovic Grant, whom Governor Glen had sent to gather information on the Cherokee mood, reported that it was bad and getting worse. Grant reported that the smoldering discontent was due, "solely or at least in the greatest Measure," to their ever-increasing trade debts, "they never being capable of paying them." He added that there was no talk of killing traders "as yet," but a month later he was obliged to report that very thing.[5]

The following year Cherokee malaise gained focus as Carolina settlers established themselves beyond Long Canes Creek. This stream, which flowed into the Savannah River from the north, was part of the South Carolina–Cherokee boundary fixed by a 1747 cession. The new settlements were well beyond it. After decades of fruitless efforts to coax Creeks into an alliance against the English, the French now had reason to hope that Cherokee anger over these encroachments would lead to a Franco-Cherokee alliance. In October 1756 the Mankiller of Tellico, a leading Overhill chief, led a delegation of twenty-four to Fort Toulouse. The French had also succeeded in drawing a Creek delegation, which included some of the temporarily resident Shawnees, to the fort. There French officers, the Mankiller, and the Shawnees tried to persuade the Creeks to agree to a joint attack on the English. They failed, but five of the Cherokees went on to Mobile and New Orleans, where on November 25 they signed a provisional treaty with Governor Kerlérec. This agreement provided for Cherokee assistance against the English in return for large quantities of trade goods and presents. Since the handful of Cherokees who signed this agreement had no authorization to do so, there was little likelihood that the document would influence events. But that was before the copy Kerlérec sent home was captured by a British warship. Henceforth most British officials were suspicious that the Cherokees had become secret enemies, devious and dangerous.[6]

Violence between Englishmen and Cherokees began in November 1757 when two Cherokee men and two women were robbed of their deerskins, murdered, and scalped near the Long Canes settlement. In March 1758 Cherokee warriors en route to join General John Forbes's forces near Fort Duquesne killed five settlers in Bedford County, Virginia, apparently in clashes over theft of English horses. On their return journey two months later, Bedford men were waiting for them, killing three and capturing two. Cherokee rage over this incident finally focused the attention of the English in their direction. William Byrd, Superintendent Atkin's nominal deputy, appealed to trader Lachlan McIntosh to placate the Cherokees with presents. Likewise, Governor Lyttelton sent them a talk offering compensation "sufficient to hide the bones of the dead men and wipe away the tears of their friends."[7]

Further raids and counterraids followed in Virginia and the Carolinas. Since the Creeks too were threatened by illicit settlements, many sympathized with the struggle of their old Cherokee enemies against English intruders. Some went further. In March 1759 the Mortar of Oakchoy rode from his northern outpost at Etoahatchee to several of the Overhill Cherokee towns, including Settico, with encouragement and promises of Creek and French support. In April, following a meeting with the Mortar's party, Moytoi of Settico led an attack that left about fifteen North Carolinians dead.

During the spring and summer of 1759 the situation deteriorated quickly. English passions were inflamed by the murders and scalpings committed by Cherokees along the Carolina frontier. The Cherokees, especially those of the lower towns, were equally inflamed by the killings they had suffered. Their rage rose higher still after an incident at Fort Prince George. There in July several British officers—including Lieutenant Richard Cotymore, commander of the fort—raped several Cherokee women. Cherokee hostility now began to focus on the two English forts in their midst.[8]

At the end of June, Tugulki and Stumpe of Coweta unexpectedly arrived, from different directions, at Augusta. The commander of the fort, Lieutenant White Outerbridge, reported that Stumpe acknowledged that he had come from Cherokee country, having "been there some time." Tugulki may have been there too, but he said he merely stopped by while out on a hunting trip. Stumpe told McGillivray that the Cherokees seemed convinced that the English were plotting with the Creeks to mount a joint attack "to Cut them off Root and Branch." The immediate source of this rumor was an account by a Cherokee mustee, Thomas Beamer, of what Atkin had supposedly said at Augusta before setting out for Creek country. Stumpe went on to relate that the Cherokees had appealed to his Creek party for help and had pressed them "to continue in their nation by way of safeguard."[9]

A much more important Cherokee-Creek meeting took place at Keowee on July 28 and 30. Accounts gathered from Cherokee and Creek witnesses differed sharply, but both versions were extremely alarming. The Cherokee account came almost immediately, the Creek account six weeks later. The Cherokee source was a young warrior whom Lieutenant Cotymore induced to spy for him. This Cherokee account was the basis of the ominous report on the meeting Cotymore sent to Lyttelton on August 3. Cotymore related that on July 28 the messenger whom Cherokees had sent to the Creeks "to renew their Friendship and Alliance" returned with four Creeks. Two of the visitors were headmen, "one coming from near the Alabama Fort." These Creeks had come to Keowee with black beads and malicious intent. After their hosts assured them that anyone who revealed what was said "should die," the Creeks proposed that the Cherokees join them and the French "to break out a War with the English." Having just come from Fort Toulouse, where trade goods had just arrived, they promised that henceforth the French would amply supply Cherokee needs. The Cherokees replied that they would have to consult with the Overhill towns before giving a definitive answer, which would require two days. Having anticipated this, the visitors said that another Creek messenger had already carried "the same proposals" to Chota.

On July 30, Wawatchee, war leader of Sugar Town, gave a formal reply in behalf of "all these lower towns." He quickly went to the main point: "we will therefore join you against the English, conditionally, that you will first kill all the white People belonging to the English in your Nation." The Creek messengers accepted this condition, promising that soon after they returned home the Creeks "would kill all their Traders etc." and immediately inform the Cherokees of the deed. Cotymore's informant continued that upon news of this massacre the Cherokees would "begin with their Villany," Fort Prince George being their first target. Cotymore added, from another source, that in the autumn the Upper Creeks, along with some "northern" Indians and a few Frenchmen, would "assist the over Hill Towns in cutting off Fort Loudoun." The prospect of a general war against united native foes was a recurring English nightmare. It would have been a reprise of the Yamasee War, but—because the allied aborigines now would have material support from the French—even more menacing.[10]

Ellis evidently received a copy of Cotymore's August 3 letter a few days later. On August 10 he wrote Lyttelton that reports of a Creek-Cherokee plot seemed exaggerated: "the Creek Nation at least, will not precipitately attack us." On September 6 he reported news of an anti-British "Conspiracy (whether real or imaginary)" between Cherokees and "a few discontented frenchified Creeks." These malcontents allegedly "had projected a design of cutting off the Traders in both Nations and falling upon our back Settlers." Duly concerned, Ellis related that he had sent an express to the Creeks "to put the Traders on their guard and to acquaint the head men there that the Cherokees had disclosed the plot and laid the blame upon them." This must have been in mid-August, for by September 6 he already had a reply: "The Creeks were extremely provoked at this supposed treachery and absolutely denied having been concerned with the Cherokees." Ellis seemed inclined to believe them, but added that he felt it necessary "to send for some of the leading men in order to make them perfectly easy as to our doubts of their fidelity."[11]

Wawatchee soon learned that the secret Creek-Cherokee meeting had been penetrated, and evidently even learned of the Cotymore letter. On August 13 he went to trader John Vann and dictated a rebuttal he wished sent, not to Governor Lyttelton, but to Governor Ellis. The Georgia governor received Wawatchee's talk by August 27. The Cherokee leader declared that the Cotymore letter "Contained nothing but falsehood." He went on to insist that the root cause of Cherokee unrest was that "the People of South Carolina have made encroachments upon their Lands." Wawatchee then asked Ellis to intercede with Lyttelton. He asked the Georgia governor to persuade Lyttelton to order settlers back behind Long Canes Creek, and to invite Cherokee leaders down to Charles Town to confer "upon these Matters."[12]

Ellis promptly forwarded the Cherokee letter to Charles Town, followed by one of his own urging Lyttelton to seize the opportunity. He argued that the Cherokees were behaving defensively and that they genuinely feared coordinated attacks from South Carolina, Georgia, and the Creeks. Moreover, the Creeks had been so provoked by Atkin that there was real danger that they would welcome a pact with the Cherokees. In that event South Carolina might be afflicted, but Georgia "would run a great hazard of being totaly destroyed." The fort at Augusta was in a ruinous condition, "and the large quantity of Indian goods in that Town are great temptations to such people." In order to make sure that the English would not have to face a combined Creek-Cherokee enemy, the prudent course was immediately to make a deal with the Cherokees "upon the best terms we can, the overture they have made opens the way for it." Doubtless concerned that Lyttelton would be reluctant to deal with Wawatchee, a key participant in the secret Creek-Cherokee meeting, Ellis offered to serve as a mediator. He suggested that he and a personal emissary from Lyttelton arrange to meet the Cherokee leader at Augusta.[13]

By the time Ellis's proposal reached Charles Town, relations between the Carolinians and the Cherokees were in crisis. On August 14 Lyttelton and his council ordered the Charles Town merchant who supplied goods to the traders dealing with the Cherokees to cease. It was, in effect, an embargo of the Cherokee trade. Acting on a long-standing authorization from Lyttelton, a week later Cotymore impounded all the guns and ammunition in the hands of traders to the Overhill Cherokees. The following day, Overhill leaders protested to the officers commanding both British forts that without fresh supplies their winter hunt and very survival were at risk. At Fort Loudoun, Oconostota confronted its commander, Captain Paul Demere, with a demand to release the ammunition. The Cherokee leader insisted that this was essential to preserve the peace, an implicit threat to Fort Loudoun itself. Although Demere had no authority to release the ammunition at Fort Prince George, he was so alarmed that he promised to order Cotymore to do so.[14]

Lyttelton received a copy of Wawatchee's talk by August 28, for that day the Carolina governor and council agreed upon a reply. It was a stinging rebuke to the Cherokees for having taken their South Carolina grievances to the governor of Georgia. Lyttelton made it plain that he was insulted that these complaints had not been addressed to him. Stiffly, he declared that "this Government is able to transact the Business belonging to it, without the Intervention of any other Government." If the Cherokees thought they had just complaints, they should send authorized spokesmen to Charles Town to make their case. He promised them safe conduct. The scolding letter thus ended with a backhanded invitation. Concerned that the Cherokees might spurn it, Ellis sent them another talk "exhorting them to accept of that invitation."[15]

The immediate goal of English diplomacy with the Creeks was to dissuade them from joining the Cherokees and French against the English. That aim fit well with the Creeks' long-standing conviction that their interests were best served by avoiding any involvement in warfare against Europeans. Should that defensive goal be achieved, the English hoped to cajole at least some of the Creeks to join them in offensive warfare against the Cherokees and French. That would be far more difficult, for it would require the Creeks to violate their traditional neutrality. With the advantage of frequent contact with Creek leaders, Superintendent Atkin too had been pursuing these objectives, but so clumsily as to put his own life in danger. Governor Ellis handled his limited diplomatic opportunities much more skillfully. His efforts would play a significant role in containing the Cherokee conflict, and he would even manage to instigate a few attacks on Cherokees by Creeks and other Indians. Unwilling to deal through Atkin, his first step was to authorize Mary Bosomworth to inform her Lower Creek friends that they would be welcome in Savannah to meet with him and explain where they stood.

Early in September, Ellis received two reports from Lower Creek country, apparently from the same writer. Both contained intelligence from the Creek side on the secret Creek-Cherokee meeting. On September 14 he forwarded excerpts to Lyttelton without comment, without even identifying the author. That unnamed writer identified his Creek source as Tugulki's "Guardian," that is, Stumpe. In June, Stumpe had made similar comments to McGillivray in Augusta (particularly the reference to Thomas Beamer). That and the unusual quality of the writing point to McGillivray as the author of these reports. The longer and more important of the two is dated "Lower Creeks 10th August 1759." The author was aware that Ellis, through Mary, had invited Creek leaders down to Savannah. The first sentence of this report announced replies: the Mortar and Gun Merchant intended to visit Ellis "this Winter," while Escotchaby, Tugulki, and Stumpe planned to do so "sooner."[16]

The writer went on to relate that Stumpe told him that the secret meeting at Keowee began innocently when a Lower Creek delegation arrived to renew peace. Cherokee spokesmen, however, used the occasion to detail their grievances with the English, then "pressed the Creeks to declare freely what part they would take in the present quarrel." Stumpe reported that the Cherokees implied that they were ready for war "if the Creeks would only stand Neuter." When the Creek spokesman (Issulgy, Second Man of Apalachicola) declined to give a direct reply, the Cherokees "insisted" that he take their question back to "a general Meeting" of the Lower Creeks for a formal answer. From this Stumpe inferred that "as the Cherokees seemed determined to take no resolution of breaking out with the English without the Concurrence and approbation of the Creeks (which he is sure they will not obtain) he thinks there is no danger of a rupture." The second report adds that "a Creek head Man," evidently Stumpe, believes that Cherokee militance was fueled by a wild rumor traceable to Thomas Beamer. This Coweta headman related that "young Beamer" had charged that, while at Augusta, Atkin had let slip his supposed plan to "prevail on the Creeks Catawbas and Chickasaws to Join and cut off the Cherokees."[17]

This intelligence, which doubtless also reached Atkin, was credible because it derived (via Stumpe) from a participant in the meeting. McGillivray's August 10 report to Ellis provided insightful context. He related that "a constant Jealousy subsists between the head Men of the Upper and Lower Towns, the latter of which are more than ordinarily Connected with the Cherokees." He thereby implied that Creek hostility toward the English was concentrated in the lower towns. Moreover, the information not only came from a Coweta leader, but one the English were most worried about, Stumpe.[18]

There are other good reasons for concluding that it was the Cherokees, not the Creeks, who in July 1759 took the initiative in proposing joint action against the English. More than four years earlier, Ludovic Grant heard from Creeks that Lower Cherokees had proposed a similar plot to Lower Creeks. Furthermore, in the later 1750s Cherokee resentment toward the English was far more intense than that of the Creeks. For more than a year prior to the secret Creek-Cherokee meeting there had been bloodshed between the Cherokees and English. In July 1759 the Cherokees had a pressing motive to seek military aid against the English that the Creeks entirely lacked.[19]

Through the early months of 1760, Superintendent Atkin remained convinced that the English had much more to fear from the Lower Creeks than from the Upper Creeks. In January he wrote that Issulgy of Apalachicola had acted as a conduit for bad talks between Lower Creeks and Lower Cherokees, and on August 21 had returned home with the Cherokee proposal for joint hostilities against the English. When the Lower Creeks did not send the beads accompanying this message back, "it was adjudged by the Upper Town Headmen an Acceptance of the Proposal." Most Upper Creek leaders regarded this as a serious mistake, but not all of them did. The Mortar's brother, who had a Cherokee wife, was one of those most out of step. The following spring he sent a message to Coweta stating that "he expected they had not forgot the engagements they entered into, when they received a bloody hatchet and a string of red and black beads from the Cherokees last summer." Atkin reported that this compromising incident caused worried Upper Creek leaders to "order" the beads returned by a different messenger, and himself to cut off trade to Apalachicola. The pattern was repeated at Atkin's "great talk," when most Upper Creek leaders attended but most Lower Creek leaders did not.[20]

If Stumpe was not sowing misinformation, his account indicated that even the most disaffected Lower Creeks, though they were tempted enough to listen to bellicose Cherokees, would in the end refuse to join them against the English. McGillivray endorsed this view when he related that Coweta headmen Escotchaby, Stumpe, and Tugulki had decided to come down soon for talks with Ellis. He believed that these leaders were sincere about easing tension with the English, and saw their forthcoming trip to Savannah as a diplomatic opportunity. "As these are the principal Malcontents their Resolution of having an interview may be productive of good effects."[21]

The reports Ellis sent to Lyttelton on September 14 strengthened the Georgia governor's skepticism about a Creek-Cherokee plot. His decision to send them without comment probably stemmed from concern that he had already sent the Carolina governor as much unwanted advice as he dared on this subject. In fact, the forwarded material had little or no effect on the Carolina governor. Lyttelton chose to believe the more menacing account of the secret meeting provided by Cotymore's Cherokee spy, and his militant response was already well under way by the time he received the reports Ellis had forwarded.[22]

Two of the Coweta leaders named in McGillivray's August 10 report followed through on their stated intention to visit Ellis. Escotchaby and Tugulki spurned Atkin's "great talk" and instead rode down to Savannah. Accompanying them were Sempoyaffi and "several other principal Creek Indians" from Coweta and Cussita. They had "a long Conference" with the governor and his council on October 10, and again the following day. The most surprising of these visitors was Escotchaby, the Coweta strong man Atkin said "overrules all when on the Spot." The meeting of Ellis and Escotchaby was probably awkward for both. Ellis later described the Coweta leader as "the worst person we could have amongst us," for he was "a Cherokee King, and much attached to the French." He sat silent through most of the talks, while his brother Sempoyaffi acted as spokesman.[23]

The conference opened in an unusual way: with a brief speech addressed to Ellis by Mary Bosomworth, once again acting as the governor's chief interpreter. She spoke "in the Creek Language that the Indians themselves might the better understand what she said." Mary recalled that she had been stirred to action by reports that the Lower Creeks "have entred into an actual Confederacy with the Cherokees in a War against the English." She then reminded Ellis that "by your Permission, Sir, I sent for them hither that they might Exculpate themselves and declare to your Excellency the Causes of their Dissatisfaction." Confirming her account, Sempoyaffi said that "understanding from Mrs. Bosomworth that there were bad Talks given out about Us, we came down to Savannah to clear our Selves before You."[24]

Sempoyaffi declared that "Our Wise old Men" had always cautioned against breaking with the English. The Creeks continued to value friendship with the English highly because of the benefits they enjoyed from the trade. Their situation was far better than that of natives who dealt with the French, "whom we frequently see almost without a Flap to cover their Nakedness." Sempoyaffi then admitted that English worries about a Creek-Cherokee plot had some basis. "It is indeed true the Cherokees have strongly sollicited Us to join and break out war with the English under Pretence that the English wanted to take away their Lands and make them Slaves." He maintained, however, that "our People did not heed the Talk, nor ever would consent." In private, the visitors apparently went further. Ellis informed Lyttelton that "they have acknowledged they were privy to and disposed to act a part, in the designs of the Cherokees; They rejoice that they did not, but were induced to come here."[25]

Sempoyaffi continued that, if the governor could satisfy some of their complaints, "we shall return to our Nation with glad Hearts and a lasting Friendship will be established." Ellis replied that his ears were open. Sempoyaffi promptly launched into a vehement denunciation of Atkin, and was still going strong when Escotchaby cut him off with a warning that enough was enough. Ellis could not mistake the fury behind Sempoyaffi's indictment or his own powerlessness to remove the cause. He could only reply that Atkin's indiscretions must have been due to "his being a Stranger to the Manners of their Country" and that the king would eventually call him to account. The governor professed great pleasure to learn that rumors that the Creeks had conspired with Cherokees were "absolutely false" and that they recognized the value of their ties to the English. He noted that only the English could supply them properly, "softly reminding them that they could not live as their Forefathers did."[26]

After Ellis invited them to unburden themselves of anything else on their minds, Sempoyaffi replied that "there was one Grievance more that made their Hearts very heavy." If the Cherokees were provoked by encroachments on their lands, so were the Lower Creeks: "there are a great many Virginia people settled high up in the Countrey, in our hunting Grounds." These "Virginians" (a term for backcountry migrants from the north that Creeks borrowed from Georgians) had rifles, "Guns that will kill Deer as far Distant as they can see them." The intruders were "destroying our Game" and making it impossible for Creek hunters to pay for their trade goods. The offending settlers included those near the headwaters of the Ogeechee River, whom the Creeks had been complaining about for several years. More than once they had threatened to take action on their own, but they now asked Ellis to do so. "We therefore request your Excellency to give Orders that these People do remove off from our Hunting Grounds, and that we may have a Paper given Us to show those people it must be done." The governor replied that he would consider this complaint and attempt to resolve it the following day.[27]

The meeting on October 11 began in alarm and confusion when Ellis, "after much Preparation and Circumlocution," shared with the Indians news of the assault on Atkin. At the first sign of calm, the governor was quick to assure them that he did not blame the Creeks for "so unlucky an Accident." On the contrary, "the Creeks I have always deemed the Eldest Brothers and the best Friends of the English." This would have been an extraordinary encomium even without the unprecedented reference to Creeks as the "Eldest Brothers" of the English. (Still savoring these words six months later, Tupahutke told Ellis he was glad to please the English, "whose elder Brethren we are.") Ellis observed that the attack on the superintendent was especially "unlucky" because it came at a time when it appeared that open warfare between the Carolinians and Cherokees was about to break out.[28]

Deftly turning all this bad news to advantage, the governor grew solicitous for Creek safety. Since Englishmen could not easily distinguish Creeks from Cherokees at a distance, Creeks in Cherokee country might be killed by mistake. Such mishaps would multiply if the war spilled over into Georgia. Ellis therefore advised the chiefs present to "immediately" send runners to both their own nation and the Cherokees. They should tell their countrymen to stay home and should warn the Cherokees that the Creeks would "resent any Injuries done the People of Georgia." The official record apparently omits something the governor said about the intruders on Creek lands. Handsome Fellow later reported that both Escotchaby and Sempoyaffi told him that Ellis "had promised them . . . that as soon as the Cherokee War was over these should be sent off."[29]

Swayed, the Lower Creek leaders promptly agreed to dispatch runners to both their own towns and those of the Cherokees. They added that the governor could rest assured that "no Mischief should be done on this Side Savannah River; nor would any of the Creeks go on the other Side." Ellis could not have hoped for a better outcome. "This point being settled the Governour made them considerable Presents and dismissed them with the strongest Appearance of Satisfaction." The same day he directed preparation of a proclamation ordering the offending settlers to withdraw by the first of January. As in 1757, Ellis's rapport with

Creek leaders owed much to his willingness to spend long hours with them in private talks, often at his own house. On October 16 he wrote Lyttelton: "When our Publick conferences were over, I entertained the Chiefs at my House, where I had then, and afterwards many conversations, in all which they discovered much good sense, and no bad disposition towards us."[30]

Ellis knew whereof he spoke when he warned Sempoyaffi that the Carolinians and Cherokees were on the brink of war, for on October 1 Lyttelton had written to tell him so. Since Oconostota's August 15 threat to isolate Fort Loudoun, many of his warriors had acted to give effect to his words. Violent incidents swirled around the beleaguered outpost, then spread to Fort Prince George. The alarmed commanders sent urgent appeals for aid to Lyttelton. When the governor's dismissive reply to Wawatchee reached Cherokee leaders in early September, they took it as an insult. On September 27 they met Captain John Stuart, en route to Fort Loudoun with a relief party, at Fort Prince George. At Stuart's urging, the next day Oconostota and other Cherokees agreed to act upon Lyttelton's grudging invitation to come to him for talks. A party of thirty-eight leading Cherokees headed by Oconostota was soon on the path to Charles Town, where it arrived on October 16.[31]

The Cherokee mission was doomed. On September 30 Lyttelton had ordered the mobilization of the colony's militia and independent companies for an invasion of Cherokee country, and six days later he announced that he would lead it in person. Learning of the approach of Oconostota's party, the governor and his council agreed that it "should not be received with the usual Marks of Friendship." When the Cherokee leaders met Lyttelton on October 18, Oconostota told him they had come in response to his invitation. The governor icily replied that "I did not invite you to come, I only permitted you to do so." From there the talks went downhill. The Indians wanted injuries on both sides forgotten in the interest of peace; Lyttelton was intent on extorting "satisfaction" for the injuries done to the English. As the impasse became clear, four of the eight councillors present proposed taking some of the Cherokee leaders hostage in order to force surrender of the murderers. Lyttelton, recalling his pledge of safe passage, seemed to reject the idea. Nevertheless, on October 22 he told the Indians that in order to guarantee their safe return they would have to accompany him and his army to Keowee.[32]

Lyttelton's invasion force of about thirteen hundred men set out in early November. Doubtless the Cherokee ambassadors objected, but they were obliged to go along. After a few days on the trail, at Monck's Corner, news arrived that General Wolfe had taken Quebec. Further on, at the Congarees, Oconostota and his companions were under armed guard: they were hostages. If the Cherokees did not surrender those who had taken English lives and scalps, many of their most important leaders were in jeopardy. Four of the prisoners managed to escape and bring word of Lyttelton's treachery to Keowee on November 9. This news so enraged the Cherokees that a peaceful resolution of the crisis became all but impossible. John Oliphant, author of the most recent and best study of the Cherokee War, aptly calls the events that precipitated it "Lyttelton's Folly."[33]

Frustrated that Lyttelton seemed deaf to his cautionary advice, Ellis soon had another reason to fault the Carolina governor. Since 1748 Fort Augusta had been garrisoned by one of South Carolina's independent companies of regular troops. Lately, Lieutenant White Outerbridge had commanded the twenty-odd men in the fort. In order to provide himself with some reserves, early in his march Lyttelton ordered the garrison to evacuate Augusta and relocate to Fort Moore. He neglected to inform Ellis of this step. Ellis learned that his key fort was now empty when an urgent letter arrived from a leading Augusta merchant. Sharing the news with his council on November 28, Ellis declared that Georgia now faced an "Emergency." Augusta, "full of Property, and of great Consequence," was defenseless. The governor and council promptly agreed to send twenty militia men under Lieutenant Edward Bernard to Augusta to serve as a stopgap garrison. Ellis ordered Bernard to suppress illicit trading between Augusta traders and Cherokees. This commerce was unlicensed, unlawful, and unpatriotic, "a villanous trade in the woods." About the same time he began efforts to recruit Creeks to attack Cherokees. On December 7 he informed Lyttelton that he was "employing Mrs. Bosomworth to engage another party from the South [Seminole Creeks] to go upon the same Errand."[34]

Lyttelton did not wish to do battle with the Cherokees, and could scarcely have done so. Smallpox had appeared among his recruits, and desertions were heavy. Rather, he intended to use his Carolina army to intimidate the Cherokees into making acceptable "satisfaction" for the English lives they had taken. When he began his return march in late December he supposed that he had been almost completely successful. There had been no battle, the Cherokees were intimidated, they turned over three of the alleged murderers to him, and on December 26 they signed a formal treaty.[35]

Lyttelton's success was almost completely illusionary. The Cherokees were only temporarily intimidated, but profoundly antagonized. The governor had three of his wanted men, but to get them he had released Oconostota and two other important leaders, all of whom burned with indignation. He confined the twenty-two remaining hostages in Fort Prince George, announcing that they would be freed one-for-one with the surrender of the remaining alleged murderers. That fort immediately became a prime target for Cherokee vengeance. As for the treaty, Lyttelton had dictated it. All concessions were made by the Indians. Article 3 focuses on Cherokee murders of Englishmen, with no notice of reciprocal slayings. The text has the Cherokees agreeing to surrender twenty-two additional men "guilty of the said Murders" to Lyttelton. The following article names the twenty-two Indians who "shall remain as Hostages for the due Performance of the foregoing Article." The final article obliges the Cherokees to treat any Frenchman found in their territory as "one of his Majesty's Enemies" and either kill or capture him for disposal by the governor. These terms were humiliating. Oconostota, Attakullakulla, and the four other signers had put their marks to the treaty only to hasten the departure of Lyttelton's army. He might have guessed earlier, but when Ellis finally read the text the following February he knew the treaty was "too mortifying to be observed by the Cherokees."[36]

Cherokee attacks began in mid-January 1760, first against traders but soon against settlers along the entire Carolina frontier. One settler, John Pearson, reported that "All up Saludy, Little River, Rabourns Creek, Long Cane, and Stevens Creek, are all destroyed." Patrick Calhoun, a refugee from Long Canes, reported the death toll there was "about 50 Persons, chiefly Women and Children." By the end of the month more than a hundred had been killed and many hundreds had fled in panic. Meanwhile, warriors intent upon freeing the hostages had drawn a cordon around Fort Prince George. When Oconostota in mid-February confronted Cotymore to demand their release, the fort's commander refused. Two days later the Cherokee leader lured Cotymore and his second-in-command into an ambush. Both officers were killed. In retaliation, soldiers in the fort killed the surviving hostages. Lyttelton appealed to General Jeffrey Amherst in New York for two regiments of regulars.[37]

Amherst received this request on February 23 and immediately decided to provide the troops for a brief campaign of "punishment." More than three months went by, however, before this formidable force reached Cherokee country. Meanwhile, young warriors ran riot amid abandoned settlements, and a few carried their attacks across the Savannah River. On February 5 Atkin reported from Augusta that the fort, church, and every defensible building in town was "crammed with people flying for shelter." That day, news arrived that Cherokees had killed Thomas Williams's wife and child and now besieged John Vann's house. McGillivray immediately organized a party of fifty men to pursue the raiders, having first sent word to Lower Creek friends imploring them to join him. Cherokees likewise tightened the noose around both British forts. Few supplies reached Fort Prince George, and Fort Loudoun was completely isolated. In March, Ellis related that the confident Cherokees had bragged they would "drive us into the sea."[38]

On February 3 Ellis reported news of the Cherokee attacks to his council, which immediately agreed to send all available ranger units to Augusta. Captain John Milledge was to command. Six days later the governor related that, among the instructions he had prepared for Milledge, one stood out. As entered into the council journal, it reads: "A Publication to be made to our Friend Indians, that for every Enemy's Scalp they brought in they should receive for the same a Trading Gun, three Pound of Powder, six Pound of Shot, a Blanket, a Flap, a pair Indian Boots, and a Cag countaining four Gallons of trading Rum." The board approved of Ellis's generous if inhumane offer "as a proper Reward, and a Matter of Expediency." Announcement of the scalp bounty would have gained more currency had Ellis made it himself. Presumably he ordered Captain Milledge to make it because he wished to avoid difficulties, both with British officials, especially Superintendent Atkin, and French-leaning Indians after the war.[39]

During these fearful months the Lower Creeks were tempted to join Cherokees for a share of the war honors and the spoil. For the most part they resisted. In fact, they generally kept their October pledge to Ellis that they would act to prevent violence on the Georgia side of the Savannah River. In December a settler on Broad River reported that neighboring Creeks had told him that if any Cherokees entered the area to hunt or "do any Mischief to the white people, or steal any of their horses, they will kill them." Beyond the words, there was some action. McGillivray's appeal for aid was answered by a Lower Creek war party led by Escotchaby and Talhichico, head warrior of Cussita. The merchant elite of Augusta met them and some Lower Chickasaws at the fort on February 11. McGillivray tried to persuade the Creeks to take an active role against the Cherokees, but Escotchaby replied that the Lower Creeks remained neutral and would fight only to keep the path from Augusta to their country open.[40]

The mere presence of Creeks helped persuade the Cherokees to withdraw; a few Creek warriors even joined McGillivray to pursue the retreating raiders on the Carolina side of the river. Their greatest service was to rescue several of the attackers' English captives. McGillivray's recruitment of Indian auxiliaries during this crisis later helped the Georgia assembly decide to honor him for heroism. In March Ellis observed that so far Georgians had suffered very little during the Indian war. He thought this was due "chiefly . . . to our engagements with the Creeks, and their menacing to revenge any hostilities that may be committed on the Inhabitants of Georgia."[41]

On February 15 Ellis sent an elaborate appeal for military assistance to all leaders of both Upper and Lower Creeks. He began by recalling that "when you Met me last" an important agreement had been reached, the 1757 treaty. Ellis reminded them that in the final article of the treaty "you engaged that our Friends should be your Friends, and our Enemies, you would treat as your Enemies." When the Creek leaders heard this read to them, they must have wondered anew how the wily Ellis had managed to slip such an entangling article past them. It obviously contradicted their long-standing commitment to the "Coweta Resolution" and neutrality in wars involving Europeans. Toward the end of the message Ellis offered the Creeks a new inducement to help "punish the Madness and Treachery of the Cherokees." If you assist us now, he said, you will "make your Name dear to Us." In gratitude, the British king and his officers would "stand by, assist, and regard, You, and your Children, in War, and in Peace; as long as the Sun shines, and the Rivers run into the Sea." If Creek auditors heard that as a promise of British aid against their native enemies, Ellis no doubt intended that they should. This promise was just as empty as the Creek promise to aid the British against their enemies, an example of Anglo-Creek reciprocity more impressive than most.[42]

There was an important meeting of Lower Creek chiefs at Cussita on March 6. Predictably, they reaffirmed their neutrality between the English and the Cherokees. In addition, however, they agreed to provide guards for traders' packtrains and, should the Cherokees threaten this vital commerce, to take the warpath against them. Although this policy was adopted out of self-interest, it was exactly what Ellis had urged them to do and of great help to the English cause. Soon the Tallapoosas and Abeikas were also supplying guards for the packtrains.[43]

Creeks leaders did not accept the inference Ellis drew from the 1757 treaty. Nor did they reject it; for the most part they ignored it. It appears, however, that some were astute enough to find a less demanding interpretation for the critical article. On March 29 the Gun Merchant issued a reply to Ellis's message that survives only as a summary published in the *South Carolina Gazette*. Coming right to the point, he declared that the Creeks "neither had nor would have, any concern in the present war between the English and Cherokees." To assure the English that this was not empty verbiage, he recalled his April meeting with Cherokees at Fort Toulouse. There, he declared, "he had given the Cherokees a final answer, which was, that the Creeks would persist in a neutrality." Only if Cherokee warriors "attacked any pack horses or traders in the Creek nation, which should always have guards, or spilt any white people's blood on that side of Savannah river" would the Creeks take up arms to support the English. Shrewdly, the Gun Merchant implied that, insofar as the 1757 treaty obliged the Creeks to provide military aid to the English, it applied only south of the Savannah River. He added that some young Creek warriors would have gone against the Cherokees but for "the irresolution, diffidence, and contrary opinions of many of the traders and some interpreters in the nation." If Ellis wanted someone to blame for Creek inaction, it was his own people. They were responsible for "not publishing there the rewards offered for Cherokee scalps, the suppressing parts of public talks, etc."[44]

However attenuated in transit, Ellis's war appeal and news of the scalp bounty did get through to the Creeks. There it had some effect, but probably not as much as persuasions offered directly to Indian visitors in Savannah. Ellis reported that "whilst I am negotiating publickly I am working in private with the stragling parties of Creeks that occasionally visit me in hopes by their means to embroil their

Nation insensibly, and as it were against their inclination." On March 15 he wrote that Thomas and Mary Bosomworth were "very active in promoting my design of setting the Creeks upon the Enemy." Already the gratified couple had "prevailed upon a party to go out against them and bloody the path, on certain conditions of reward, which I have agreed to." Here he referred to a war party from Hitchiti-speaking Lower Creek towns led by Tupahutke ("White Cabin") of Chehaw and Wioffki of Oconee-Alachua. They had been recruited, he said, "by means of Mrs. Bosomworth." This party "was fitted out for War against the Cherokees at the Expence of this Government." On April 7 a party of Yuchis met with Ellis to plan a similar mission. The governor was later pleased to avow that this was a war party "I fitted out from hence." Surprisingly, even Sempoyaffi showed interest. In May, accompanied by twenty warriors, he came to Savannah promising to lead them against the Cherokees.[45]

There were other recruits, especially Lower Chickasaws. Ellis reported in May that "the Chickasaws and some gangs of Creeks which I prevailed on to go against the Enemy" had not only taken Cherokee scalps but had "United in burning Estatoe and Keowee." A newspaper account of the incident applauded "the firing of the Town-House and some other houses at Keowee by the Chickasaws." The Cherokees had not retaliated, Ellis supposed, "for fear of drawing that Nation [the Creeks] upon them." Callously, he added: "I am in hopes however, that in some of these Excursions the Enemy will kill some of the Creeks, whose death their friends must revenge, and so the Nation may be at length compelled to make the Cause its own."[46]

On April 14 Tupahutke and Wioffki returned in triumph to Savannah with three Cherokee scalps. The council minutes report that "they Entred the Town, the Enemies Scalps being born before them, singing their War Songs; and were saluted by a Discharge of the Cannon." After they were conducted to the council chamber, Governor Ellis congratulated them profusely upon their success. At the Indians' request, further talks were postponed until Mary Bosomworth arrived to interpret. Upon her appearance three days later, the meeting resumed. Ellis again congratulated these Creeks for the honor they had earned, not only for themselves, but for "their Nation in general." He thanked them for "having made good the Engagements so lately entred into between them and Us, by being the first of their People who had shed the Blood of the Cherokees." Ellis assured them that English gratitude would go beyond mere words, and promised to see them again "when he had got their Presents ready."[47]

Two weeks passed before the very special presents Ellis had ordered were ready. On April 28 the expectant Creek party, accompanied by Thomas and Mary Bosomworth, was again conducted to the council chamber. Ellis began where he had left off, by attempting to persuade these victorious warriors to repeat their valorous deeds. He reminded them that when they had first brought their hairy trophies to Augusta they had boasted that they had given the Cherokees "one Stroke and . . . would follow it with many." He recounted the similar deeds of the Yuchis and Lower Chickasaws, the latter having just brought in two scalps "taken in sight of Estatoe." These were glorious successes, "but there is a great Deal yet for you to do."[48]

The governor then turned to the business that had kept his visitors in town so long: their reward. Their achievement, he said, was not only to have struck the first blow against the Cherokees but also to have "influenced our Friends among the red People by your Example." To commemorate it, Ellis announced that he was presenting leaders of the Creek party with "silver Gorgets and Arm Plates, on which your Names, your Family Arms, and your Exploit shall be engraven." He concluded by expressing the hope that "you will immediately set out for War again." Tupahutke thanked the governor, but went on to explain that they were unable to return to the warpath immediately. Their wives and children required attention, their horses were scattered, and it would take time to recruit additional warriors. Instead, he promised that his partisans "would make War upon the Cherokees as soon as it was in their Power." Reluctantly accepting this noncommittal reply, Ellis presented the expensive silver presents to Tupahutke and Wioffki.[49]

On May 20 Ellis met with a party of Creeks that had brought him talks given at Tallassee on April. Gliding quietly over his orchestration of recent Creek forays against the Cherokees, he not only thanked the Creeks for their efforts but tried to award them responsibility for taking the initiative. In his telling, "no sooner did the Cherokees do Mischief and spill the Blood of the white People on this Side the River, than Whehoffkee and some other Creeks went out to War and brought in some Cherokee Scalps in Revenge." Noting that Yuchi and Chickasaw warriors had made similar raids, Ellis implied that they too had acted on their own. He added that he and other English leaders never incited Creeks against the French. The wicked French behaved differently. Though they deny it, French leaders "are daily studying to make Mischief between Us and our Friends the Creeks; but we never send any bad Talks concerning them to your Nation."[50]

Beginning with the Savannah meeting of October 1759, Governor Ellis's deft if devious diplomacy with the Lower Creeks helped shift threats to British interests westward into Upper Creek country. Although their towns were near Fort Toulouse, it was not the Tallapoosas who became dangerous. For the past decade or so they had been the Creeks who most valued good relations with the English, and this pattern would continue. Their leaders included conspicuous Anglophiles like the Wolf King and Old Bracket, but no prominent Anglophobes. None of the hostile or even unfriendly acts that the English blamed on Creeks during the war were committed by Tallapoosas. Superintendent Atkin had chosen one of their main towns to deliver his "great talk," and it was not a Tallapoosa but a Lower Creek who had attacked him there.

It was the Abeika Upper Creeks who supplanted the lower townsmen as the main focus of British concern. In the spring of 1759, Cherokee warriors had brought English scalps to Coweta, where they were welcomed and displayed before being carried to Fort Toulouse for French rewards. A year later, twenty Cherokees bearing "a good many English scalps" and two captives to the French fort avoided Lower Creek country and went around by way of the Abeika towns. The Mortar's brother accompanied them. Parting company with them, he gave them a message from the Mortar to the Fort Toulouse commander, which they delivered. This time Lower Creek leaders, including "Stump-finger (Coweta Head Man)," were upset over Abeika assistance to Cherokees bearing scalps.[51]

Stumpe related that on April 17 "we set out to the Alabama Fort with a full Intent to bring back the Prisoners and Scalps, . . . and deliver them up to the English Traders." When Stumpe's party arrived, however, they found that trader John Spencer had already "purchased" the captives from the Cherokees. Stumpe considered both Abeika connivance with the Cherokees and the ransom shameful. Regarding the redeemed prisoners, he charged that "it was intirely the Gun-Merchant's Fault that they were paid for." A later trader's report found no fault, concluding that the Gun Merchant had acted to reward two of the captors "who saved them from being burnt."[52]

Returning home through Tallassee, the frustrated Lower Creeks stopped to meet with its leaders. On April 25 the "Warrior's King" of Tallassee delivered the sense of the meeting, which was sent on to Ellis. He related that the Lower Creek visitors "have engaged to abide by what we determine." The Tallassee leaders had determined that, although the Abeikas had "always pretended great Friendship to the English," they had disgraced themselves by allowing "the English Prisoners to be brought through their Towns and not take them away." Lamely, "the only Excuse they make is that they had no Linguist." He continued that "we are blamed for taking Part with the English, but we don't mind that as all the lower Towns are of our Side." He then boldly proclaimed that "the Cherokees are our Enemies and the English are our Friends; and we are determined to go out against the Cherokees." The Tallassee war captain, Tustunake Hopoya, followed by asserting that "we young Warriors" were eager to do so, and "we hope it is not too late." He added that "the Tallassee King is present at this Talk and will stand to it." But there was a catch. The Warriors' King concluded by stating that his men must "first be provided with Ammunition." The war captain ended with "our Request that the Price of Goods may be lowered," specifying the desired price for each item on a long list of trade goods. The English interpreted this as a bid for a quid pro quo: "they offer to take up the hatchet, if the proposed reduction is granted."[53]

In the end the traders did not reduce their prices, and the Tallassees did not go to war. Nor did any other Creek town. Prompted by Atkin, Captain Allick had been attempting to incite the lower towns to attack the Cherokees. In May the *Gazette* reported that "capt. Alleck, not having prevailed in persuading his countrymen to go to war, is determined not to return to his town, 'till he can introduce a Cherokee scalp into its public square." The editor of the paper was convinced that all of the Creeks had quickly fallen in behind the bargain the Tallassees had proposed: should they receive a substantial reduction in trade prices, "in return to go against the Cherokees." One straw in the wind was Sempoyaffi's cancellation of his advertised plan to lead an attack upon the Cherokees, "he having had a Lesson from his Countrymen upon that Subject." It now seemed clear that unless prices came down, nearly all Creeks would stay home. The editor unhappily concluded that "the whole Nation seems resolved to take advantage of the present Situation of Affairs, and insist upon this Point vigorously."[54]

On April 1 the troops dispatched by General Amherst arrived at Charles Town. They consisted of the better part of two regiments, 1,373 men in all, commanded by Colonel Archibald Montgomery. James Grant, just named lieutenant colonel, served as second-in-command. The arriving army was greeted by Governor Lyttelton, who four days later departed to take up his plum posting as governor of Jamaica. William Bull, among the less bellicose Carolinians, took his place as lieutenant governor. Having other uses for Montgomery's veterans, Amherst had ordered a quick campaign. Barring unforeseen circumstances, as soon as the Cherokees were sufficiently chastised the troops were to return to Charles Town. There the waiting transports would promptly carry them back to New York. On April 23 the British invasion force marched. Grant was convinced that the Cherokees were amenable to peace but that most Carolinians wanted blood. After a month on the march the army reached the last colonial outpost, the trading town of Ninety-Six.[55]

With Montgomery's force poised for the assault, on May 16 the English received a shocking blow from a different quarter. That day Abeika Upper Creeks, mainly from Okfuskee, murdered trader John Ross, his black slave, and one of his white packhorsemen. James Adair related that Ross, "who was surly and ill-natured, they chopped to pieces, in a most horrid manner, but the other two they did not treat with any kind of barbarity." The mayhem began at Sugatspoga, an Okfuskee village, then quickly spread to Okfuskee, Kialegee, and Oakchoy. At day's end five traders and six of their servants were dead. Early reports alleged that the ringleader of these attacks was Hopoya Thluko of Okfuskee, long known to the English as Handsome Fellow. The alarm spread as far as Charles Town. There, Bull ordered troops at Fort Moore to relocate to Fort Augusta and vowed, if the Georgia fort were attacked, to personally lead seven hundred militiamen to its relief.[56]

Historians have struggled to explain the motivation behind these attacks. Several things are perfectly clear. First, the Upper Creeks had little or nothing to gain by the violence. No force of British regulars had ever been this close to their homeland. Had the attacks mushroomed into a general assault on traders, the Indians would not only have lost their trade but would have courted devastation from Montgomery's army. Second, Upper Creek leaders were clearly unaware of any plans for an assault and immediately acted to counteract it. The Okfuskee Captain, the Wolf King, and the Gun Merchant were especially active. Many potential victims received warnings and/or assistance in making an escape.[57]

One was packhorseman Robert French, who witnessed part of the melee outside Ross's trading house. He later related that the list of Creeks to whom he owed his life began with "three or four Indian fellows who told him that they were sent to take Goods away and to kill him but that they would not do the latter." Instead, they "immediately hurried him forceably away to a Place of Safety." There he hid for several hours until "an Indian Wench, a friend of his" ("his wife," said Adair) found him. She directed him to a meeting place she had arranged with her uncle, the Okfuskee Captain. This leading chief told French that Ross had been "cut to Pieces" and that he believed traders at Sugatspoga, Oakchoy, and Kialegee had put up a fight but also had been killed. French gratefully recalled that the Okfuskee Captain then assisted him "with an Horse, sweet flour, a pair of moccossons, and an old Blanket to get him safe off." Staying clear of the path, it took French a week to reach Augusta, where he delivered the initial report of the attack.[58]

Animus toward Ross obviously helped trigger the killings, and even the ordinary course of trade regularly produced bitter disputes. Atkin's mission the previous year had also provoked passions. It seems likely, however, that there were other motives more difficult to fathom. Shortly before the attack, Old Bracket of Tuckabatchee, the venerable Anglophile, became alarmed that Upper Creek antagonism toward the English was much worse than usual and that violence was possible. Unable to travel, he gave Mad Dog a warning message to deliver to Governor Ellis. Old Bracket asked Ellis if he could explain "whence it had arose that the Indians spoke so hard of their best Friends the English." Even Tuckabatchee was simmering. Although "his Town had always shown a particular Regard to the white People, . . . he now feared for them." The talk did not reach Ellis until June 5, nine days after French's initial report of the murders. When the governor asked

Mad Dog how he would answer Old Bracket's question, the Indian said Atkin's excesses were responsible. Ellis knew that was partly true, but he made the safe reply that Creek disquiet was due to "the lying Talks of the Cherokees and French."[59]

Ellis returned to this theme again and again, both to Creeks and his superiors, and thus seems to have genuinely believed that Cherokee and especially French instigation was at least partly responsible. This was and is a reasonable conclusion. On May 16 a few Upper Creeks had done, on a much reduced scale, what for years French officers and Cherokee warriors had been urging all Creeks to do. The French had not only pressed such advice, they had promised large rewards. And for years many Creeks had been listening. In 1755 Ross himself had warned that the Okfuskees had "concluded to cut of[f] the English in that Town." In August 1759 Lachlan McIntosh wrote that three-quarters of Okfuskee townsmen "are become Frenchmen" and that he had been told that "it would not be long before a Blow would be given to the white People." Having received reports for months on the murders, in October 1760 Ellis stated that the main cause was "now pretty well known." It was French instigation: alarmed that the English were succeeding in their efforts "to engage the Creeks in a War with the Cherokees," the French had exerted themselves "in an extraordinary manner to prevent it." Adair too saw the main cause as "the French diabolical scheme."[60]

Cherokee influence was probably less, but more immediate. Aware that the Cherokees were about to suffer a major British assault, their Upper Creek friends might have found the idea of a sympathetic counterstroke attractive. Had the attack resulted from a Creek-Cherokee plot, the Mortar surely would have been a central actor and the first man the English would suspect. Yet at the time of the attack he was apparently far away, either at his Etoahatchee retreat or in Cherokee country. Though historians have made the Mortar a prime suspect, contemporaries generally did not. The only Upper Creek leader ever accused of involvement in the attack was Handsome Fellow. Ellis duly reported that "a Principal Indian" had been "charged with having abetted the late Murders," but he was skeptical. He immediately added that this notable, presumably Handsome Fellow, "in Order to vindicate himself, went out against the Cherokees lately and returned to Augusta with one of their Scalps" on August 20.[61]

The motivation behind the May 16 assault on the traders appears to have been linked to the French and Cherokees in a less direct but more powerful way. By September 1759 the Creeks had learned from Superintendent Atkin and others of the British triumph over the French in Canada. Atkin wrote Governor Lyttelton that he had also told them of "the prospect of the King's stopping up the Rivers of Mississippi and Mobile." The superintendent had hoped that the news would embolden the Creeks to join the British in finishing off French Louisiana, but found instead that they reacted coldly. Atkin quickly realized that, given their considerable success in playing off the French against the English, the Creeks found the rapidly accumulating evidence of a complete French defeat threatening.[62]

The news from Cherokee country was unwelcome for the same reason. By early May the Creeks knew that Montgomery's army was about to inflict a devastating blow upon the Cherokees. If the Carolinians and Georgians no longer had to worry about either the French or the Cherokees, the Creeks would have to confront the English alone. The only conceivable way they could avoid that ugly prospect was to fashion an alliance with the Choctaws, whom they despised. That prospect was evidently even uglier to the Creeks, for they never seriously considered it. This combination of long-smoldering resentments against the English, regularly refueled by French officers and Cherokee malcontents, along with new fears for the future, probably explains Creek motivation for the attack as well as it is likely to be explained. Rather than being the result of an transnational conspiracy or plotting by Upper Creek leaders, the attack appears to have been a spontaneous spasm of violence carried out by a few young and low-ranking warriors.[63]

That certainly was what Upper Creek chiefs wanted the English to believe. Their first message to the English regarding it came on May 26 at the Wolf King's town of Mucklassee, where a few days earlier most of the fleeing traders had found refuge. Speaking for the assembled chiefs, the Gun Merchant hoped that Governor Ellis "will not think what fell out was a concerted thing of the Nation in general." Had that been the case, "none of the white People now alive would ever have got to their own Country." He maintained that "the Mischief was done by a few young Fellows without consulting the Head Men of the Nation." Those headmen wanted Ellis to know that they "think it not prudent that any Satisfaction should be demanded at present least these desperate Fellows should be pushed to greater Lengths." On the contrary, the Gun Merchant "intreats the Governour to let the Traders return speedily with Goods to quiet the Minds of the young People who would be alarmed at the Trade being stopped."[64]

These requests indicate that, while only a few Upper Creeks had drawn English blood, many were unwilling to see the culprits penalized. On or about the same day, the Wolf King sent a message to Ellis relating that he and the Gun Merchant, as a precaution, had "hurried the remaining traders out of the nation." The less involved Lower Creek chiefs echoed their Upper Creek counterparts. Their June 7 talk to Ellis declared that the murderers were "a few young People," that the Creeks would never turn on the English, that they would remain neutral in the Anglo- Cherokee war, and that it was essential to restore the trade.[65]

On May 26 Ellis received Robert French's affidavit on the attack, given at Augusta three days earlier. The same day the governor prepared a written talk for the chiefs and warriors "of the Creek Nations," Upper and Lower. It was remarkably restrained, for he had not yet decided exactly what to do. French's report had given him a pretty good idea of what the chiefs would say about the killings, and suggested an initial response. Rather than blame all Creeks, Ellis supposed that "some of your mad People" were responsible. Rather than threatening retaliation, he called for better communication. Rather than taking revenge or hostages, "the many of your People now amongst Us" would continue to be treated as friends. Most notably, rather than obsessing upon the murders, Ellis focused on preventing new killings: "And though some of your People may have done a mad Thing yet Friends may overlook it and make all straight again." He did not mention "satisfaction."[66]

Ellis sent separate copies of this talk to Upper and Lower Creeks. Both were carried by Creek couriers, a highly unusual move doubtless intended as a further signal that his trust in Creek goodwill remained unshaken. One copy he entrusted to "Fulwygee-opia-Mico," an otherwise unidentified leader, probably an Upper Creek. He gave the other to Mary Bosomworth to forward by a messenger of her choosing, "accompanied with a Talk of her own." She entrusted both to Salechi, head warrior of Ouseechee.[67]

Ellis revealed how he had decided to proceed regarding the murders in his June 5 interview with Mad Dog of Tuckabatchee. As accommodating as he was, he was not ready to forget about the culprits. They must be punished, but "agreeable to treaty I am ready to leave the Satisfaction due to us for the late Murders to themselves." The treaty provision he referred to (and freely interpreted) was Article 3 of the 1757 treaty. Ellis later reported that he had also summoned some of the many Creeks then within the colony ("not less than two hundred," he said). He first assured them that he would not retaliate in kind but that he would demand satisfaction. Had Englishmen murdered Creeks, the culprits would have been put to death, "and we expected that they would punish their People in like Manner." He did not say how many should suffer.[68]

On June 1 Montgomery launched his assault on Cherokee towns. It began with a rare nighttime attack on the lower town of Estatoe, which the British burned to the ground. Over the next few weeks the redcoats burned four more towns and killed scores of Cherokees. Although Montgomery and Grant had carried out their mission of vengeance, they had shown some restraint, especially by sparing the Indians' ripening corn. Satisfied that they had punished the Cherokees enough to comply with Amherst's orders and that they were powerless to do anything for the beleaguered garrison at Fort Loudoun, they began the return march to Charles Town. There they were greeted by angry Carolinians convinced that the invasion had ended too soon with too little pain inflicted upon the Cherokees. Oliphant argues persuasively that the main reason Montgomery and Grant cut their punitive campaign short was that they (especially Grant) were no longer sure they had been fighting in a just cause.[69]

Meanwhile, Governor Ellis and Creek leaders were trying to end the turmoil unleashed by the murder of the traders. On June 30 the governor met with ten Creeks "sent down Ambassadors from the upper and lower Creek Nations with two Written Talks," the Upper Creek talk of May 26 and the Lower Creek talk of June 7. Joseph Wright interpreted. The lengthy reply Ellis gave these envoys glowed with good feeling and hope. He declared himself "extremely pleased" with the Creek talks, which had "removed all Anger from my Heart." Accepting Creek assurances that the murders were the work of "a few of your young mad People," he shrewdly observed that "if so, Satisfaction may the easier be given." The English expected satisfaction but would "leave the Punishment of your People, and the Satisfaction due to Us, to yourselves." He promised that trade would be restored "as soon as it can be done with any Safety." To hasten that end, he proposed that each Creek town choose a "Guardian" for its traders, an unacknowledged variant of Atkin's plan. Ellis's most surprising gesture concerned the Cherokee war. He called upon the Creeks to "make Peace between Us and the Cherokees, as we did between the Cherokees and them." The Creeks had to be pleased that the English had sought a Creek solution to a problem they could not solve themselves.[70]

Aware that his mild response to the murders would raise eyebrows in London, Ellis took pains to justify it in his July 10 report to the Board of Trade. Implicitly, but unmistakably, he contrasted his lenient approach to the Upper Creeks with Lyttelton's disastrous hard line toward the Cherokees. He took special care to defend his decision not to demand some specific satisfaction: "had we specifiyed the Nature and Extent of the satisfaction we expected, and they refused to give it, we must either have retracted, and exposed our inability, or insisted on those terms, which must inevitably have plunged us into a Cruel War." Furthermore, though "stopping or permitting" the trade were both dangerous, the former was more so. He feared that if the Creeks were deprived of their trade with the English, "they would not hesitate, to Join our Enemies." The governor did not neglect to prepare for the worst. Old forts were reconditioned and new ones built. In particular, Ellis had at his own expense (more than £400, he said) erected a new fort at Savannah.[71]

Wright immediately rode off to repeat Ellis's talk to Upper Creek leaders, which he did at Tallassee on July 17. The headmen were greatly relieved at the mildness of the message and eager to seize the chance to mend relations. On August 8 most of "the great Kings and Head Warriors of the Upper Creek Nation" assembled at Tallassee to concert their reply. Tomathli Hadjo ("Tomathla-Hago"), *mico* of Okfuskee, acted as their principal spokesman. Ellis's message was again read, prompting

Tomathli Hadjo to rejoice that "this Day he has heard a great Talk." He and fellow leaders "are now convinced you are a Friend to our Nation." Since the murders "there has been a great black Cloud spread over our Land," but the friendly talk from Ellis put him "in Hopes it will clear away." It was imperative that the traders return, and he immediately agreed to Ellis's request for guardians. In fact, he carried the proposal a step further: traders "must live in such Headmen's Houses as shall be thought proper and able to protect them." Should any such incident occur in the future, he promised that upon the governor's complaint, "Satisfaction shall be given immediately." Notably absent, however, was any mention of satisfaction for the May murders.[72]

The final speaker, the Gun Merchant, confirmed that if one of his people killed an Englishman he "shall dye immediately." As for the May murders, however, "all past Grievances must be forgotten and never more thought about." He quickly had second thoughts about this peremptory pronouncement. After the meeting ended he insisted on an "Addition" to his speech. Softening his message, the Gun Merchant argued that pressing for satisfaction would backfire on the English. If they were to demand it, "he is sure that more Mischief will be done." After passions cooled, "something may be done but not at present for the People are all mad."[73]

On October 20, as the ailing Ellis was preparing to depart for England, the Upper Creek talk of August 8 finally reached him. It was not delivered by Upper Creek emissaries but, strangely, by three Lower Creek chiefs. The long delay in delivering the August 8 talk, the fact that it was not accompanied by a single Upper Creek leader, and the fact that it was finally delivered by Lower Creek intermediaries all suggest that influential Upper Creek chiefs were reluctant to associate themselves forthrightly with this conciliatory message. Their influence over their angry people evidently was tenuous. Ellis professed satisfaction with this "National Talk" and, in general, with the apparent Creek determination "to live in Peace and friendship with us."[74]

Earlier that day, Ellis had his last public conference with Indians. A few days before, a party of ten Choctaws, headed by a "principal" chief, had made a surprise appearance in Savannah. They came with thanks for the several consignments of trade goods steered their way by Superintendent Atkin, and in quest of more. To strengthen their appeal, they presented Ellis with a French scalp and a white wing. They explained that they had taken this scalp in revenge for the murder and scalping of an English packhorseman "in their Nation." Though a Choctaw had killed the Englishman, they argued that the fault was really French, specifically "the very great Temptation the French threw in their Way, being a Reward no less than four Pieces of Strouds, ten white Blankets, ten white Shirts, and a Gorget, to any

Indian who should kill and scalp an Indian Trader." The Choctaw spokesman also related that his people had recently made peace with the Chickasaws, "although by French instigation they had been so long at War with one another."[75]

Ellis was happy to inform the Choctaw visitors of the British triumph over the French in Canada. He said he gave them "very satisfactory answers" to their concerns. He not only accepted the French scalp but swallowed the Choctaw explanation of why it made sense to kill a Frenchman to atone for a Choctaw's killing of an Englishman. Now, he said, "all is again made strait." Likewise laudable was the Choctaws' escape from French deception by making peace with the Chickasaws. As for the trade, Ellis pointed out that it had to go through Creek country. It was the Creeks who had interrupted further trade to the Choctaws by their murdering of traders. He advised them to warn the Creeks that if there were any further molestation of traders, the Choctaws would react "in a hostile way." As soon as the Creeks had given proper satisfaction for the murders, "the Choctaws may expect large Supplies of Goods." According to Ellis, his guests "greatly approved" of his advice, as well as his entertainment and "handsome Presents."[76]

Ellis sailed from Savannah on November 2. His replacement, James Wright, was a forty-four-year-old Carolinian. A London- trained lawyer, he had served as South Carolina's attorney general for more than twenty years and was that colony's agent in London when he was appointed lieutenant governor of Georgia. After several weeks transitioning to his new job in Savannah, he took his oath of office on October 31. Wright doubtless had heard much talk about revenge against the Cherokees and their Creek supporters from friends in Charles Town, but for a time he distanced himself from the Carolinian hard line. He had a darker view of Indians, especially Creeks, than Ellis did, and was much less inclined to trust them. Nevertheless, he came prepared to defer to Ellis's advice on Indian diplomacy, and at first did so. Ellis briefed Wright in detail, as he had earlier done with Atkin. He came away with a much better opinion of Wright. On October 20 he declared himself "much pleased with him," and confident Wright "will conduct the Affairs of this Government in the best manner."[77]

That summer the Cherokee war exploded. Enraged that the English continued to hold hostages, Upper Cherokees laid siege to Fort Loudoun. On August 7 the starving garrison surrendered. The capitulation agreement was negotiated by Captain John Stuart, who had led an inadequate relief column to the fort. From the start Stuart enjoyed unique respect from the Cherokees. Under the surrender terms, the 150 soldiers and other inhabitants of the fort were to proceed under Cherokee guard to either Fort Prince George or Virginia. They were allowed to keep their arms and ammunition. The homeward march of the distraught English began on August 8. The Cherokee guard soon melted away, and two days later the column was ambushed by hundreds of warriors. Captain Demere, three of his officers, and twenty-three others were killed.

The survivors were taken prisoner and marched back to Cherokee towns. There they endured numerous mistreatments; one man was tortured to death. All were obliged to dance for the amusement of their triumphant captors. One day the entire company was marched to Chota for a command performance; the audience included some of the Mortar's gang of Creeks. Stuart, however, along with his servant and an "old doctor," was allowed to escape. This was the work of Attakullakulla, the "Little Carpenter," who was desperately trying to prevent things from getting worse. He ransomed Stuart from his captor and escorted him and the others to safety in Virginia.[78]

Once Stuart brought the terrible news to the English, all talk of reconciliation ceased. On December 15 General Amherst ordered Grant back to Cherokee country to teach "these perfidious Savages" a lesson they would never forget. This time they must be forced "to the absolute necessity of Suing for Pardon." Grant was to spurn any peace overtures from the Cherokees until they had been severely punished. This time their crops would not be spared. Amherst wanted the invasion to begin as soon as possible, perhaps before the end of winter. Grant and his regulars sailed from New York on December 23, just missing ex-governor Ellis, who arrived there a few days later.

Ellis soon met with Amherst. He warned the general, with "a certain bluntness of conversation," that his plan was flawed. Ellis argued that it would be self-defeating to invade without a force sufficient to compel the Cherokees to sue for peace, and Grant had not been given such a force. If the plan went forward, an attack launched before April was bound to fail. Until then there would not be enough forage for the army's animals and no crops to destroy. Ellis's blunt counsel probably helped induce the flexibility Amherst later showed, but effected no immediate change in his plan. Amherst doubtless considered Ellis's military advice amateurish: after all, Grant would command nearly twice as many troops as he had the year before.[79]

Governor Wright's first public act concerning Indians came on November 7, when he replied to the Upper Creek message of August 8. He dryly observed that there were "some good Things" in their talk. Absence of a promise to give satisfaction for the May murders was not a good thing, but he let that pass without comment. He warned against seduction by the Cherokees; they were about to suffer the great king's wrath. Wright had the pleasure of relating that the French had been routed in Canada. "The King's Warriors have now nothing to do at the Northward," and would soon march against the Cherokees. He renewed Ellis's September invitation for two headmen from every Creek town to come down to meet him, promising them presents. Significantly, Wright also promised that the trade would continue. The following day he read this talk to the Lower Creek emissaries, "then invited them to stay and eat Dinner" with him and his council on the king's birthday three days hence.[80]

About ten days later a party of Creek headmen arrived in Savannah in response to Ellis's invitation. On November 19 Wright informed the council that he had met briefly with a dozen of them, mainly to complain that so few leading figures had come. The visitors excused the sparse turnout on the ground that "a great Sickness among them had prevented many from coming who intended it." They were hopeful that more were still on the way, including "two of their Kings."[81]

No *micos* did arrive; all of the headmen present were war leaders. Wright met with them in the council chamber two days later. He opened the meeting by asking "whether they were come down in a national Character?" The Indians replied that "they were charged with nothing from their Nation, that they were come Down on the Invitation given them." Wright regretted that no one empowered to speak for the nation was present, for "we might have renewed our antient Treaties and settled other Matters." The inexperienced governor should have let it go at that and proceeded to distribute the presents the Indians had come for. Instead he went on to deliver the speech he had prepared.

Wright got off on the wrong foot when he went straight to the issue Creeks refused to discuss: Why was it that "some of our People had been killed in your Towns," and what did the Creeks intend to do about it? "Satisfaction should be made; and this is agreeable to your own Customs." He avowed that, like Ellis, he was "not willing to believe that your Nation intended to kill the white People." He therefore approved of his predecessor's muted response to the attack, including "leaving it to your selves to give Us Satisfaction." On the dwindling trade, he said the Creeks could not expect to be "fully supplied" until they fully protected the traders. The leading war chiefs present, the Okfuskee Captain and Duvall's Landlord, both made lengthy replies. Neither said a word about satisfaction. Disappointed, Wright closed the session by distributing the presents. He also gave the visitors a written copy of his unwelcome talk to carry home.[82]

Wright had his first opportunity to confer with a Creek "king" on January 29, 1761. That day he met with the Wolf King and seven followers in the council chamber, but the Mucklassee *mico* had not come to negotiate. Wright gave the Tallapoosa chief an account of his previous meeting with Creek war leaders. He went on to relate that an irresistible British force, including fearsome Mohawks, was now assembling in South Carolina. It would soon march to crush the Cherokees. The Wolf King replied with conventional expressions of friendship and an account of how he had sheltered terrified traders the previous May. Since then his people had complied with Ellis's request that they provide guards for traders and their goods. He complained, however, that none of the promised compensation had been paid. Wright made no reply other than to pass on an invitation from Governor Bull to visit Charles Town. The Wolf King promised to go and did. When he returned, Wright said "he Seemed greatly Struck at Meeting with some Mohawks and their Conversation."[83]

Wright was already unhappy with his dealings with the Creeks. He counted every additional Creek visitor as an additional burden, and he counted them all. On December 23 he reckoned that he had already played host to "upwards of 140 Creek Indians"; on February 20 he noted more than a hundred more; on April 15 his running total reached 371; and on May 16 it was 475. He found them to be "most Troublesome disagreeable and Expensive Guests." Wright was clear about his view of the Creeks in his February 20 report to the board. Overall, "we have Some Friends amongst them, but many more Enemies." To illustrate, he reported that two soldiers had recently been killed near Fort Prince George "by Fellows who spoke the Creek Language." Wright could not help pitying himself, condemned to have "such Perfidious wretches to deal with." He would put up with this onerous task for the present, but he anticipated better days ahead: "I hope I shall be able to keep things quiet till his Majesties arms shall have leisure to Operate at the Southward."[84]

Colonel Grant and his troops reached Charles Town on January 10. His views on the coming campaign were very similar to Ellis's, but even more sympathetic toward the Cherokees. He found various good reasons to delay his march, and three months later was still encamped at Monck's Corner. All the while he sought to moderate Amherst's punitive plan toward an early accommodation. Well aware that the Carolinians were even hotter for Cherokee blood than Amherst was, Grant schemed to gain practical control over negotiations to end the conflict. That was all he could aspire to, for the general had ordered him to defer to Governor Bull on diplomacy. By the end of May, Grant's persistent maneuvering brought him Amherst's permission to secure peace terms from Bull, and on that basis to conduct the preliminary talks.[85]

The Creeks watched the British preparations with growing anxiety. That spring, Creek leaders sought to assure Governor Wright that their people would stay clear of the coming struggle. On April 30 Upper Creek headmen met at Mucklassee, purportedly to answer a talk the Wolf King had received from Mohawks during his visit to Charles Town. Apparently the Mohawks had advised the Creeks to prepare for a final French defeat by reestablishing close ties with the English. The Wolf King reported that both Upper and Lower Creeks had recently held meetings on this subject. The result was that "it's agreed to hold fast the English both here and in the lower Towns."[86]

The Gun Merchant confirmed this message, then forecast that the Cherokees were about to suffer a catastrophe. The Creeks would leave the mountain people to their fate, "and if any Cherokees should run here for shelter we hope it will not be taken amiss if we take and make them our People." He named nine headmen from eight Abeika towns who had sacrificed their winter hunt by staying home "to protect the Traders." The promised rewards, he noted, had yet to appear. His central point was that the Creeks, whether of high station or low, now "want nothing but Peace and Goods, and white People among them." The expensive presents Ellis had given two Lower Creek leaders a year earlier had not gone unnoticed by Upper Creeks: the Gun Merchant's want list now included "Silver Arm Plates and Gorgets."[87]

The talk at Mucklassee was recorded by William Struthers, employed by Lachlan McGillivray to look after his major trading establishment on the Coosa River. On May 17 the Upper Creek leaders finally met to answer Wright's talk of November 21 and another from Bull. Their reply was again recorded by Struthers, but this time at Little Tallassee, a village that had sprung up near the McGillivray place. While the English often called this settlement an Upper Creek "town," the Creeks did not consider it one of their *talwa* (there is no record that it had a square ground, *mico*, or council). What can be said about it was that it was new, small, centrally located between the Abeika and Tallapoosa towns, the home of several Anglophile headmen soon to become extremely influential, and a common meeting site for Upper Creek leaders for the remainder of the colonial era. Little Tallassee thereby became a key linkage between Tallapoosas and Abeikas as they gradually moved toward confederation.[88]

The unidentified spokesman on this occasion, probably the Okfuskee Captain, said he had been fully occupied maintaining order but that he hoped to come down to see both governors soon. He had recently visited Fort Toulouse, where the downhearted French had advised the Creeks "to hold fast by the English, as they say they are the only People that can properly support Us in our Wants." He charged that the devious Cherokees "want to bring Us in their Snare by killing your People and talking our Language." Despite some loose talk among young warriors, there was no danger that the Creeks would take part in the war. If Cherokees ignored last year's warning not to cross the Savannah River, "they may expect more Hatchets on them than they have at Present."[89]

The Hitchiti-speaking towns among the Lower Creeks, notably Chehaw and Ouseechee, were equally concerned to heal relations with the English. The old leadership in the Muskogee-speaking towns of Coweta and Cussita, having clashed so often with colonial authorities, was less resigned to reconciliation. Even there, however, headmen could read the signs. On March 4 Wright reported receipt of "a written Talk" from Sempoyaffi and Escotchaby of Coweta, which does not survive. It contained, he said, "great Professions of Friendship for the English." Later, Wright said this talk included a claim that, unlike the Upper Creeks, the lower townsmen "never spilt the white People's Blood nor never would." *Never* was too strong a word. On June 22 worried headmen from Coweta and Cussita informed Wright that several Cowetas had argued with a packhorseman near Augusta, then killed him. These chiefs were "very much concerned about this bad Accident," though not sufficiently concerned to consider punishment. Instead, they wrung their hands in the now customary way: "some of our young People are mad and we cannot rule them." Sadly, they were probably right about their loss of control.[90]

On August 4 Wright replied to all recent Creek talks with a message addressed to both Upper and Lower Creeks. He began with a bitter observation on the murder of the packhorseman. "That in Consequence of the repeated Requests and Sollicitations by you that your Nation might be supplied with Goods, this Man was actually going up with Goods to trade in your Countrey when some of your People fell on him and Murdered him and carried off his Goods." Furthermore, three children had been murdered in the southern part of the colony, presumably by Lower Creeks. He demanded that the Lower Creeks "convince me of your Sincerity by punishing the Offenders," adding that "I know very well it is in your Power to punish them." Still, he did not threaten to cut off the trade. As for the rewards promised for protection of traders, it was up to the traders to supply them.[91]

Wright was generally careful not to let his rancid personal feelings toward the Creeks control the policies he followed toward them. Like Ellis, he was certain that the safety of the colony, now beset by two wars, depended crucially upon avoiding trouble with the Creeks. The best evidence of this is Wright's consistent determination to maintain the trade connection, his only reliable lever to influence Creek behavior. In late January, Governor Bull had requested that, in order to prevent Cherokees from acquiring supplies from friendly Creeks, Georgia halt the Creek trade for "a short Time." Backed by his council, Wright refused. He was also cautious about Creek land. Shortly after taking office, Wright had observed to the Board of Trade that the colony was "hemmed in" due to "the Indian Claim to Hold all the Land above the Flowing of the Tides." The board responded unhelpfully, suggesting that the governor seek "a Release from our Engagement not to Settle above the Flowing of the Tides." On September 15 Wright politely replied that the time was not right.[92]

Meanwhile, the third phase of the Cherokee war moved slowly toward its conclusion. As General Amherst had ordered, Governor Bull was to have the last word on the peace terms. Grant was certain that the Cherokees did not deserve the harsh terms Bull had proposed in May 1760 and would never accept them. While in Charles Town the following January he had pressed the Carolina governor to moderate them, and won some concessions. The discussion continued by letter as the army made its slow progress toward Cherokee country that spring. Grant wanted Bull's new terms in writing. The governor finally obliged on April 14. Bull agreed to accept fewer executions ("one or two . . . from each of their Four Settlements," rather than fifteen) and to drop his earlier demand for five additional Cherokee hostages. On the other hand, he added two stiff new demands: first, the Cherokees were to cede a swath of territory seventy miles wide; second, they were to accept Attakullakulla as their new "emperor."[93]

Whatever terms might be offered, first the Cherokees had to be persuaded to negotiate. Grant hoped that intimidation would be sufficient to accomplish this. Including Carolina provincials, he now commanded an army of more than twenty-eight hundred fighting men. On May 23, as his troops approached Fort Prince George, Grant received a message from Attakullakulla suggesting that Oconostota and the Cherokees were ready to treat for peace. In direct violation of Amherst's orders to punish first and negotiate later, Grant offered to begin talks. When this produced only Cherokee delaying tactics, on June 7 Grant gave the order to march on the middle settlements.

Once again Cherokee warriors attacked the invading British in the narrow pass outside Etchoe, but they were obliged to retreat when their powder ran out. Etchoe was put to the torch, and this time the crops were also destroyed. During the remainder of June the army made a wide circuit through the abandoned middle towns. All were methodically devastated. Lieutenant Colonel Henry Laurens, second-in-command of the Carolina regiment, reported that Grant's army "burned upward of 800 [houses] in 15 Towns in a circuit of 150 Miles, and plucked up at lea[st] 1,500 Acres of Corn, Beans, Mellons, etc." Little remained that was above knee high or green. On July 4 Grant ordered a return march to Fort Prince George to await peace overtures from the stricken Cherokees. He waited for seven weeks. It was not until about August 21 that the Indians chose an eight-man delegation headed by Attakullakulla to sue for peace. A week later it reached the fort.[94]

Grant had shown great restraint in sitting immobile for nearly two months, all the while sparing the defenseless lower towns nearby. His behavior before, during, and after that period consistently indicates that, despite Amherst's orders and Bull's demands, he was determined to decisively shape the peace. He aimed to give the Cherokees as generous a peace as possible. When Grant read Bull's peace terms to Attakullakulla's party, it was an edited version. Gone were the articles on a land cession and Cherokee emperorship. The demand that was most precious to Bull and most obnoxious to the Indians, the executions, Grant scaled down to four.

Convinced that Cherokees would not agree to any executions, Grant maneuvered to pass the problem on to Bull. On August 31 he demanded that Attakullakulla "Answer to every Article particularly except the first, which they will talk of afterwards." With the offensive article set aside, the rest were read one by one. Attakullakulla, "In the Name of the Whole Nation, agreed to them separately." Grant then pointed out that peace would require a treaty agreed upon and signed in Charles Town. In the end Attakullakulla and other leaders would have to go down to negotiate with Bull, who alone had the power to strike the first article. Why not go now? Grant declared that if Bull agreed to forgo the executions, he would "have no Objection." Recognizing the diplomatic opportunity that Grant had created for him, Attakullakulla immediately agreed to go down to Charles Town.[95]

On September 3, Attakullakulla and five other headmen, escorted by Henry Laurens, set off for Charles Town. Laurens had come to admire Grant, and was the colonel's strongest supporter among the Carolina elite. Most of the others thought Grant had betrayed them. Governor Bull and three members of his council met Attakullakulla's party just outside of town on September 15. The Carolina leadership soon realized that there was little they could do to alter the terms Grant had, in effect, imposed upon them. The articles on executions and a Cherokee emperor were dropped. To assuage their disappointment the Carolinians insisted upon a land cession, though one considerably smaller than Bull had envisioned in April. The Cherokees, judging this an acceptable price for the key Carolina concession, agreed. The treaty was signed by Bull and Attakullakulla on September 23. The Cherokee envoys, again escorted by Laurens, then set off for home to secure national consent to the agreement. This was accomplished by early November, and formal ratification by both parties occurred on December 18 in Charles Town.[96]

The Cherokee war brought major changes to the political landscape of the Southeast. The home government had been put to great expense to rescue Carolinians from the conflict their leaders had provoked and then mismanaged. Henceforth the South Carolina leadership would be viewed with suspicion from London, one reason Carolinians became increasingly recalcitrant in their dealings with imperial authorities. On the other hand, by averting war with the more dangerous Creeks, the Georgia leadership gained stature in London.

Activities during the Cherokee war helped elevate some British leaders in reputation and political influence. All appear to have been those who had worked to avert or moderate the war and to secure a generous peace. Henry Ellis rose highest. Upon his return to London he was greeted as a sage and became a close adviser to the Earl of Egremont, secretary of state for the Southern Department. George Johnstone described him as "a Kind of Underline Minister for Plantation Affairs." Memoranda Ellis wrote for Egremont led directly to the two major initiatives the British government took toward Indians in the next two years: the Proclamation of 1763 and the Congress of Augusta. Lieutenant Colonel James Grant was soon promoted to full colonel, and in 1763 he was appointed governor of East Florida. Captain John Stuart in 1762 replaced Edmond Atkin as superintendent for Indian affairs in the Southern Department. Henry Laurens would soon be recognized as South Carolina's most influential political figure.[97]

The war likewise produced major changes in Indian country. The big losers were the Cherokees, especially the middle towns. The terms of the peace treaty were harsh, but less so than they had feared. Except for a brief relapse during the Revolutionary War, the Cherokees henceforth forswore war with the whites. Diplomacy had served them well in the endstage of their ill-advised war with the English. Afterward they would rely almost entirely on negotiation to secure their interests, and become even more open to Anglo-American influence. The destitution they had been reduced to had one positive effect: it helped them to secure better terms of trade than they had prior to the war.

The Creek towns most friendly to the Cherokees also lost. Most were northern towns closest to the Cherokees: the Abeika towns among the Upper Creeks, and Coweta and Cussita among the Lower Creeks. Henceforth the English naturally preferred to deal with the Creeks that had proven themselves most supportive during the war: the Tallapoosa towns among the Upper Creeks, and the Hitchiti-speaking towns among the Lower Creeks. The Indians reacted accordingly. In the coming years, gatherings of Abeika and Tallapoosa chiefs usually occurred in Little Tallassee. Similarly, major assemblies of Lower Creek leaders now tended to occur at Chehaw rather than Coweta.

While all those who lived in and around Georgia were obliged to pay close attention to the Cherokee war, most colonists and many Indians knew that events far away were likely to have a greater impact on the region. Crucially important was the British conquest of French Canada in 1759. French Louisiana, strangling behind the British blockade of the Gulf ports, was now also cut off from aid from the north. The remaining French foothold in North America was now nearly defenseless. The British could take their time to polish off Louisiana, but did not bother, for more tempting targets had appeared.

In 1761 the Bourbon monarchs of France and Spain renewed their "family compact." The beleaguered French needed all the help they could get, while the Spanish foresaw dire consequences for their empire if the British succeeded in driving the French from North America. While outwardly a defensive alliance, the Franco-Spanish compact had a secret clause obliging Spain to enter the war as an ally of France as soon as the annual treasure fleet arrived safely. Learning of this, in January 1762 the British preemptively declared war on Spain. A large expeditionary force, already being prepared to attack the French sugar islands, was given an enlarged mandate. The ultimate objective was now Havana, the nerve center of the Spanish American empire. The British effort was spectacularly successful. After capturing Martinique and other French islands, the British force invaded Cuba. Following a two-month siege, Havana capitulated in August.

Almost miraculously, the British now had both of their rivals for American empire at their mercy. The French and Spanish had no prospect of reversing their staggering losses by force, so they braced themselves for a humiliating settlement. Doing what they still could to limit British gains, in November the French signed a secret treaty with the Spanish. To prevent even more of North America from falling into British hands, while compensating their hapless allies, the French ceded trans-Mississippi Louisiana and New Orleans to the Spanish. The terms ending the imperial war were negotiated in January 1763, and the three parties signed the Treaty of Paris in February. Desperate to recover Havana, the Spanish agreed to the British price: the cession of Florida. Finally, to regain their profitable islands, the French reluctantly ceded all of their North American possessions to the British. As far as Europeans were concerned, Great Britain was now sovereign over all of North America east of the Mississippi except New Orleans. Europeans were not the only ones concerned.

The triumphant British would have to work out new understandings with the Indians before they could fully enjoy their victory. Yet for two full years Governor Wright made no effort to negotiate with the Creeks. He would see them if they came to Savannah, but he did not invite any to do so. He doubtless would have invited Creek leaders down had any of them signaled readiness to provide satisfaction for the 1760 murders, but by this time it was plain that that would not happen. When in late 1762 Wright finally invited Creek chiefs to Savannah, his aim was not to discuss the future but the past, the old murders. To the lawyerly Wright a heinous crime had gone unpunished. Having now vanquished their imperial rivals, the British were finally in a position to insist that the Creeks honor their treaty commitment to render justice. The governor intended to see that they did.

It was clear that Wright suddenly wanted to talk with Creek leaders, for he chose a time he knew would make it difficult for them to attend: the first week in January, the height of the Indians' hunting season. Few if any Lower Creeks heeded his invitation, but on the last day of the year a delegation of Upper Creeks arrived. Most and perhaps all were Abeikas. They too wanted to talk, for they were headed by their leading chiefs: the Gun Merchant, the Okfuskee Captain, and Handsome Fellow.[98]

Wright opened the conference on January 4, 1763, with a long speech. He first informed the Indians of the death of the old king and the accession of young George III. He promptly proceeded to remind them of the long simmering issue: the murders in the Abeika towns three years earlier. Wright did not renew his demand for satisfaction in so many words, but it was clear that that was what he was driving at. He did so by speaking hypothetically about any repetition of the attack. The Creeks must understand that Englishmen, "though of long forbearance, cannot put up with bad Usage forever." Reminding them of what English arms had done to the Cherokees, he made a veiled threat that another attack by Creeks would bring the same misery to them. Should the Creeks abuse the English, "the great King George will be angry, and his Warriors will be angry also and take Satisfaction." Most undiplomatically, he declared that "You know you cannot do well without us, but we can do without you."[99]

Satisfaction was not what the chiefs had come to talk about. Their spokesman, the Gun Merchant, managed to be diplomatic while making their chagrin perfectly clear. This veteran leader said he supposed he had been invited "to talk of those antient Treaties, and for that Purpose he now came down." To his surprise, however, the governor seemed most interested in the misbehavior of "their rash young Men." The Gun Merchant replied politely but defiantly: "he did not expect to have heard it mentioned at this Time, nor was it possible for him to answer to it." Not now, evidently not ever. The meeting promptly broke up, having achieved nothing but intensification of Creek resentment toward the English.[100]

Ever since Governor Ellis's departure, the Creeks had been obliged to face ever stronger gusts of bad news. At Fort Toulouse and Mobile there were unmistakable signs that the French were discontinuing operations and preparing to leave. Recently, the Spanish at St. Augustine and Pensacola seemed to be making similar preparations. The ascendant British seemed poised to seize control of the territories long dominated by the French and Spanish. Day by day it was becoming clearer that the Creeks would soon have to face the English alone. With the French and Spanish focused on their own straightened circumstances, already it was no longer possible to play one imperial power off against the others. With deep foreboding, Creek leaders foresaw an approaching British encirclement. Most alarming, growing British dominance of the region had led to a flood of new settlers coming overland from the Carolinas, Virginia, and even farther north. Many of these newcomers were staking out illicit settlements on Creek lands.

When Governor Wright next heard from the Upper Creeks, it was clear they were in an ugly mood. In April and May they sent him two written talks from Oakchoy, the Gun Merchant's town. Ominously, their principal spokesman for both talks was not the Gun Merchant but rather the Mortar, their renowned warrior and Anglophobe. The April 5 talk conveyed the sense of a meeting of the chiefs that day. Omitting the usual pleasantries, the Mortar went straight to the point. By treaty the land south of the Savannah River above Augusta belonged to the Upper Creeks, yet they now "find it settled all over the Woods with People Cattle and Horses." This intrusion must end. The Mortar called upon Wright "to clear the Virginia People from their Lands." If they remained they alone would be responsible for the consequences. Handsome Fellow followed with a briefer speech to the same effect. Tellingly, however, these growls were not followed by Creek attempts to expel the intruders by force.[101]

The May 8 talk was labeled as coming from both the Mortar and the Gun Merchant, but only the Mortar spoke. He began by renewing the previous protest in stronger language. The English not only seemed to think that his people "have no Lands," but they apparently "intend to stop all their Breaths by their settling all round them." More provocatively, he raised a larger issue. He had heard reports that the English "are going to take all the Lands which they lent to the French and Spaniards." All along, the departing Europeans had been mere tenants on Creek lands. The Creeks were "surprized how People can give away Land that does not belong to them." The Mortar, presumably backed by the Gun Merchant, thus served notice that the Upper Creeks were prepared to dispute the transfer of Louisiana and Florida to the British.[102]

Georgians and Creeks alike could feel that an era was ending, but they felt it differently. The French and Spanish were on their way out of the region, a great relief to the English but a disaster for the Creeks. The English could look forward to establishing new colonies in Louisiana and Florida; the Creeks could look forward to the English coming at them from three directions. The Creeks were also newly insecure on their western flank. The Choctaws were far more populous than the Creeks and bitter enemies, but they had never been able to acquire a comparable stock of arms and ammunition from the French. The English would prove able and willing to narrow the arms gap substantially. In their view, well-armed Choctaws made for better-behaved Creeks.

Most basically, because the English no longer had much reason to fear the Creeks, these Indians were no longer in a position to deal with the English on anything like equal terms. The Creeks had long been accustomed to charging their English muskets with French powder and shot, but that source had dried up. Now they had no choice but to get their ammunition from the English, and were soon complaining loudly that the supplies they received were inadequate. English traders had always found it troublesome and unprofitable to carry these heavy items on their packhorses, but now Governor Wright deliberately discouraged them from carrying more. It was evident that he could also forbid them from carrying anything. Down to 1763 the Georgia government had never employed a trade embargo against the Creeks, largely because the Indians had alternative sources of supply. Now they did not, and because they did not, an embargo or even a threat of one had become a potent instrument of coercion. As the Creeks feared, the English would soon put it to use.

The Creeks felt their rapidly growing vulnerability most keenly regarding their lands. Recall that nearly all of the territory the Creeks had ceded had been turned over to Oglethorpe in 1733 and 1736. The only other cession since then was the 1758 grant of the Yamacraw tract and three coastal islands. Here the acreage ceded was relatively small and was relinquished to end a political dispute both the English and the Indians wished to be rid of. This agreement owed much to cajoling by Governor Ellis, but it was not coerced. Most likely in 1758 the English still could not compel the Creeks to do anything.

It was a different story three years later. The Creeks could not be coerced about their lands so long as they were able to defend them, or at least convince Englishmen that they could and would defend them. A forbidding snarl would deter most would-be intruders, but a few would take their chances. To prevent a slaughter of English people, no matter how provocative or lawless they were, any Georgia government would be spurred to remove the offending settlement. Without that spur it might act flaccidly or not at all. The first serious intrusions onto Creek lands came in the 1750s on the Ogeechee and Satilla rivers. Creek threats to take action if Governor Ellis did not persuaded him to do so. Both rogue settlements were abandoned. A tipping point was reached in 1760 or 1761. The Creeks witnessed the catastrophe that befell the Cherokees when they tried to repel white encroachments by force. That straightforward method no longer seemed viable. Furthermore, the force Creeks could actually muster now was limited by their precarious supplies of ammunition.

The Creeks continued to warn squatters off their lands above Augusta, but rather suddenly their threats had little effect. Many of the intruders now calculated that the Indians would not dare, and the provincial government would not care, to use force to remove them. In general, they were right. Governor Wright scolded the trespassers, but most often other problems seemed to have greater claims on his attention. Creek leaders could anticipate that, unless they became much better at persuading British officials to support their just claims, one way or another they would lose vast tracts to the newly aggressive colonists.

As Steven Hahn brilliantly elucidates, during the era of the French and Indian War the Creeks took major steps to transform themselves to meet the challenge. Like other Indian nations, hitherto they had understood themselves to be a people or peoples connected by bonds of kinship. The ever-intensifying threat to their lands from the British was ever more obvious to all divisions of Creek society. To repel this common menace, all had a powerful reason to coordinate defensive measures with the others. The various Creek entities had to find a way to unite so they could speak with one voice and act accordingly. As Hahn explains, "the defense of their land from the territorially inspired British stimulated among the Creeks a need to define themselves as a territory and thus led to the invention of the Creek Nation." It would take several decades to develop institutions that fit the new model, notably a national council and dominant single chief, but the die was cast.[103]

Notes

Abbreviations

APC: Col. *Acts of the Privy Council of England: Colonial Series.* Ed. W. L. Grant and James Munro. 6 vols. Hereford: His Majesty's Stationery Office, 1908–12.

Atkin, *Report* *The Appalachian Indian Frontier: The Edmond Atkin Report and Plan of 1755.* Ed. Wilbur R. Jacobs. Columbia: University of South Carolina Press, 1954.

B.C.T. "The Bosomworth Controversy Transcripts." Library of Congress.

Bevan Papers Joseph V. Bevan Papers, Georgia Historical Society, Savannah.

CGHS *Collections of the Georgia Historical Society.* 21 vols. to date. Savannah: Georgia Historical Society, 1840–.

C.O. Great Britain, Public Record Office, Colonial Office Papers, London and Kew.

CRG *The Colonial Records of the State of Georgia.* Vols. 1–19, 21–26, ed. Allen D. Candler et al. Atlanta: Franklin Printing and Publishing Company, 1904–16. Vols. 20, 27–32, ed. Kenneth Coleman and Milton Ready. Athens: University of Georgia Press, 1976–89.

C.R.G. "The Colonial Records of the State of Georgia." Vols. 33–39 (typescripts), GDAH

DAR *Documents of the American Revolution, 1770–1783.* Ed. K. G. Davies. 21 vols. Dublin: Irish University Press, 1972–81.

DRIA, I *Documents Relating to Indian Affairs, May 21, 1750–August 7, 1754.* Ed. William L. McDowell. Columbia: South Carolina Archives Department, 1958.

DRIA, II *Documents Relating to Indian Affairs, 1754–1765.* Ed. William L. McDowell. Columbia: South Carolina Department of Archives and History, 1970.

EAID *Early American Indian Documents: Treaties and Laws, 1607–1789.* General ed. Alden T. Vaughan. 20 vols. Bethesda, Md.: University Publications of America, 1979–2004.

Egmont, *Diary* *Diary of Viscount Percival, Afterwards First Earl of Egmont*. Ed. R. A. Roberts. 3 vols. London: Historical Manuscripts Commission, 1920–23.

Egmont, *Journal* *The Journal of the Earl of Egmont: Abstract of the Trustees Proceedings for Establishing the Colony of Georgia, 1732–1738*. Ed. Robert C. McPherson. Athens: University of Georgia Press, 1962.

Egmont Papers The Phillipps Collection of Egmont Manuscripts, University of Georgia Libraries, Athens.

GCCB Georgia (Colony), Register of Records Office. *Abstracts of Georgia Colonial Conveyance Book C-1, 1750–1761*. Comp. Frances Howell Beckemeyer. Atlanta: R. J. Taylor, Jr., Foundation, 1975.

G.C.J. Georgia (Colony), Council Journal (unpublished, in various locations).

GDAH Georgia Department of Archives and History, Morrow.

GFT *Georgia and Florida Treaties, 1763–1776*. Ed. John T. Juricek. Vol. 12 of *EAID*.

GHQ *Georgia Historical Quarterly*

GT *Georgia Treaties, 1733–1763*. Ed. John T. Juricek. Vol. 11 of *EAID*.

JBT *Journal of the Commissioners for Trade and Plantations* (the Board of Trade). 14 vols; London: His Majesty's Stationery Office, 1920–38.

JCIT *Journals of the Commissioners of the Indian Trade, September 20, 1710–August 29, 1718*. Ed. William L. McDowell. Columbia: South Carolina Archives Department, 1955.

Lyttelton Papers Sir William Lyttelton Papers, William L. Clements Library, University of Michigan, Ann Arbor.

Moore, "Voyage" Francis Moore, "A Voyage to Georgia Begun in the Year 1735" [London, 1744], in *CGHS*, 1:79–152.

MPAED *Mississippi Provincial Archives: English Dominion*. Vol. 1 (all published). Ed. Dunbar Rowland. Nashville: Brandon Printing Co., 1911.

MPAFD *Mississippi Provincial Archives: French Dominion*. Vols. 4 and 5. Ed. Patricia Galloway. Baton Rouge: Mississippi Department of Archives and History, 1984.

RSUS "Records of the States of the United States of America." Ed. William Sumner Jenkins. Library of Congress microfilm, 1949.

SCCHJ South Carolina (Colony), *Journal of the Commons House of Assembly*. Ed. J. H. Easterby et al. 14 vols. to date. Columbia: South Carolina Archives Department, 1951–.

S.C.C.H.J. South Carolina (Colony), Journal of the Commons House of Assembly (unpublished, in various locations).

S.C.C.J. South Carolina (Colony), Council Journal (unpublished, in various locations).

SCDAH South Carolina Department of Archives and History, Columbia, South Carolina.

SCHM *South Carolina Historical Magazine*

S.C./P.R.O. South Carolina Department of Archives and History, Columbia: "Records in the British Public Record Office Relating to South Carolina, 1663–1782" (the Sainsbury Transcripts). 36 vols.

S.C.S.M.R. South Carolina (Colony), Secretary—Miscellaneous Records
S.C.U.H.J. South Carolina (Colony), Upper House Journal
Shelburne Papers Earl of Shelburne Papers, William L. Clements Library, University of Michigan, Ann Arbor.
SPG Society for the Propagation of the Gospel in Foreign Parts, London.
Stephens, *Journal* *The Journal of William Stephens, 1741–1743*. Ed. E. Merton Coulter. 2 vols. Athens: University of Georgia Press, 1958–59.

Introduction

1. Serious scholarship on diplomatic interaction in colonial Georgia between the English and the Creeks begins with Corkran, *The Creek Frontier*. Subsequent works that do not focus directly on Anglo-Creek diplomacy nevertheless make significant contributions to that subject. The major titles are Braund, *Deerskins and Duffels*; Hahn, *The Invention of the Creek Nation*; and Piker, *Okfuskee*. Sweet synthesizes much of the previous scholarship on the Trustee era in *Negotiating for Georgia*. Sweet revives Corkran's diplomatic focus and corrects some of his errors.

2. *CRG*, 28, pt. 1:252 (Ellis); Adair, *History*, 276.

3. The classic work on this era, often reprinted, is Crane, *The Southern Frontier*.

4. Noteworthy recent works dealing with this depopulation include Worth, *Struggle for the Georgia Coast*; Hann, *Apalachee*; Gallay, *The Indian Slave Trade*; Oatis, *A Colonial Complex*; Ramsey, *The Yamasee War*.

5. Estimates of the number of Creek towns vary. In 1734 two Carolina merchants wrote Oglethorpe that there were "at least Eighteen" of what they called "Chief Towns" among the Creeks. In 1756, South Carolina Indian agent Daniel Pepper reported that he had delivered a speech to representatives of twenty Creek towns. When major towns that had not sent representatives are added, the total rises to at least twenty-five. The most careful list, compiled by Superintendent Edmond Atkin in 1759, identifies thirty-five Creek towns (including two Alabama towns and one Shawnee). Some of Atkin's towns (including "Suckaspoga," "Loustyhatchy," and "Chowwaogley") were pretty clearly satellite villages of major towns. On the other hand, there are obvious omissions from his list (Chehaw, Ouseechee, and Ocmulgee). An estimate of thirty-five Creek towns at midcentury seems about right. *CRG*, 20:79 (1734 merchants); *DRIA*, II, 256–57 (Pepper); *EAID*, 14:78–81 (Atkin).

6. Edmond Atkin, superintendent for Indian affairs for the southern colonies, later described the Hitchiti-speaking towns as "the Ancient Possessors" of the Chattahoochee valley. Atkin, *Report*, 57. The Cussitas and Cowetas first relocated to the upper Chattahoochee (probably from the Tallapoosa River) about a half century earlier. Hahn, *Invention*, 27–28. In 1675 Bishop Calderón placed both Cussita ("Cazithto") and Coweta ("Cabita") among thirteen Lower Creek towns in "the Province of Apalachocoli." See "A Seventeenth Century Letter of Gabriel Diaz Vara Calderon, Bishop of Cuba, Describing

the Indians and Indian Missions of Florida," *Smithsonian Miscellaneous Collections*, 95, no. 16 (Washington, D.C.: Smithsonian Institution, 1936), 9 [hereafter cited as Calderón letter]. On classification of languages, see Swanton, "Social Organization," 248.

7. By far the best account of the evolution of Creek society is Hahn, *The Invention of the Creek Nation*. On the precedence accorded Coweta and Cussita by Upper Creeks, see the exchange between Richard Sattler and me in *Ethnohistory* 40, no. 2 (1993): 307–9. There I cite two English sources that make the point (*GT*, 54, 239). See also *GFT*, 61, 97. There are French sources too. In November 1763 the new governor of Louisiana, Jean Jacques Blaise D'Abbadie, informed Major Robert Farmer that the Abeikas ("Abuas"), Chehaws ("Chuashas"), and Cussitas ("Kashetas") were all "Dependants on the *Kowitas* [Cowetas]." *MPAED*, 1:83. The results of ball games between Creek towns could change moiety affiliations. See Mary Haas, "Creek Inter-Town Relations," *American Anthropologist* 42 (1940): 479–89.

8. Atkin, *Report*, 43. See the classic study by Morton H. Fried, *The Notion of Tribe* (Menlo Park, Calif.: Cummings, 1975).

9. Creeks evidently referred to Brim more often by his "war title" of Hopoihithli. In his dissertation research, Steven Hahn found two sources that referred to Brim by this title. Hahn, "Invention," 435–36. First, the 1705 "Submission" of Creeks lists "Hoboyetly" first as "King of the Cowetas" (*EAID*, 13:91). This is confirmed in a 1734 manuscript letter from a Spanish spy shadowing Tomochichi's party in England. Reporting various conversations with the Indians, he repeatedly refers to Brim as "Opujisli," pretty clearly a Spanish version of the same title (Joseph Ramos Escudero to the Conde de Montijo, October 10 and/or October 15, 1734, AGI-SD 2591, Worth transcripts, quoted in Hahn, "Invention," 436). Hahn reported these findings more briefly in his book (*Invention*, 66 and n. 55). Though Brim was a rare individual, his war title was not rare. Other eighteenth-century leaders known by this title included those from Tallassee, Tuckabatchee, Coolamee, and Packana. According to Hahn (elaborating on a finding by Janis Campbell), "Hopoihithli" might be translated as "the one who does the thinking about war" ("Invention," 435). To me the title appears to be a compound of *hopoya* ("seeker") and *hithli* ("fog"), whose literal meaning is something like "one who sees through the fog." Although some scholars render this leader's name as Brims, the best-informed English sources (including Oglethorpe, William Stevens, and Edmond Atkin) give the name as Brim.

10. Hahn, *Invention*, 110–20.

11. After the Revolution, Spain did negotiate written treaties with Indians. By the Peace of Paris in 1783, Great Britain turned over East Florida and West Florida to Spain. The Spanish promptly followed British practice in negotiating written treaties with the Indians. One motive for this dramatic change was probably that the Spanish supposed that the natives had become so reliant upon treaties that it would be dangerous to discontinue them. Another, probably more important, was that they now recognized that the British had proven such treaties to be a formidable instrument of manipulation. The Spanish then carried their new practice to the trans-Mississippi west. Jack D. L.

Holmes, "Spanish Treaties with the West Florida Indians, 1784–1802," *Florida Historical Quarterly* 48 (1969): 140–54; Lawrence Kinnaird, "Spanish Treaties with the Indian Tribes," *Western Historical Quarterly* 10 (1979): 39–48. The French signed a few written treaties in Canada (notably in 1701), but not in Louisiana.

12. James M. Anderson, *History of Portugal* (Westport, Conn.: Greenwood Press, 2000), 40.

13. *GT*, 265 (Ellis). The classic account of Southeastern Indians' dual leadership is Fred Gearing, *Priests and Warriors: Social Structures for Cherokee Politics in the Eighteenth Century*, American Anthropological Society Memoir 93 (Menasha, Wisc.: American Anthropological Society, 1962).

14. Corkran, *Creek Frontier*, 172–76. The text of the aborted treaty is in *EAID*, 13:309–12.

15. Braund, *Deerskins and Duffels*, 90–92; Meriwether, *Expansion of South Carolina*, 117–18. A major branching of the Creek path into upper and lower paths occurred just west of the Flint River. See John H. Goff, "The Path to Oakfuskee," *GHQ* 39 (1955): 1–36, 152–71.

16. *GFT*, 97.

17. Waselkov, "Indian Maps," 302–3, 324–29, and figs. 4 and 12.

18. Superintendent Atkin's talks with Upper Creek leaders at Tuckabatchee, July 9, 1759, *EAID*, 14:66–71, quotes at 70–71. Likewise, Robert Beverley commented that the English had long noticed that Indians "were without Boundaries to their Land." Beverley, *History*, 17. Relevant studies include Harold Hickerson, "The Virginia Deer and Intertribal Buffer Zones in the Upper Mississippi Valley," in *Man, Culture and Animals*, ed. Anthony Leeds and Andrew P. Vayda (Washington, D.C.: American Association for the Advancement of Science, 1965), 43–65; E. Randolph Turner, "An Intertribal Deer Exploitation Buffer Zone for the Virginia Coastal Plain–Piedmont Regions," *Archeological Society of Virginia Quarterly Bulletin* 32 (1978): 42–48; and Paul S. Martin and Christine R. Szuter, "War Zones and Game Sinks in Lewis and Clark's West," *Conservation Biology* 13 (1999): 36–45. Buffer zones appear to have been the norm for North American Indians. According to Rik Hoekstra, in Mexico "the *altepetl* [native "principalities"] only occupied rather small areas in prehistoric times." Lowlands "were often the no-man's-lands between the *altepetl*." This pattern "occurred throughout the whole of prehispanic Mexico, with the exception of the valley of Mexico." Even there, prior to Aztec rule "all *altepetl* had been separated by some two kilometres of uninhabited area." Hoekstra, *Two Worlds Merging: The Transformation of Society in the Valley of Puebla, 1570–1640* (Amsterdam: CEDLA, 1993), 22–23, 93.

19. *GT*, 354 (Oconostota).

20. *GFT*, 262. For Emistisiguo's later references to his "vine" speech, see ibid., 35 (1767), 51 (1768), 519 n. 65 (1771), 383 (1771), 392 (1771), *DAR*, 5:74 (1772), and *GFT*, 136 (1774).

21. *GFT*, 262–63 (Mortar), 373 (belt).

22. Ibid., 392 ("thorns and Weeds"); *GT*, 267 (Creek spokesman), 271 (1757 treaty).

23. The reference here is to Richard White's pathbreaking study, *The Middle Ground: Indians, Empires, and Republics in the Great Lakes Region, 1650–1815* (New York: Cambridge University Press, 1991). See especially his second chapter.

24. Four Canadian scholars stand out: Kent McNeil, Ken MacMillan, Geoffrey Lester, and Brian Slattery. MacMillan is a historian; the others are legal scholars. Important early works in this tradition include Lester, "Primitivism versus Civilization"; and Brian Slattery, "The Land Rights of Indigenous Canadian Peoples, as Affected by the Crown's Acquisition of their Territories" (Ph.D. diss., University of Oxford, 1979; printed in Saskatoon the same year by the University of Saskatchewan Native Law Centre). The outstanding recent works are MacMillan, *Sovereignty and Possession*, especially on territorial sovereignty; and McNeil, *Common Law Aboriginal Title*, especially on land ownership. Significant earlier works by American authors include Julius Goebel, "Discovery and Occupation in International Law," chapter 2 of his *The Struggle for the Falkland Islands* (New Haven: Yale University Press, 1927); and Harris, *Origin of the Land Tenure System*. I rely most upon my own work: John T. Juricek, "English Claims in North America to 1660: A Study in Legal and Constitutional History" (Ph.D. diss., University of Chicago, 1970) and "English Territorial Claims."

25. *Governor's Message to the General Assembly of the State of Georgia, at the Opening of the Annual Session, November 7, 1825, With the Documents Accompanying the Same* (Milledgeville: Camack and Ragland, 1825), 36. Bevan edited the documents section.

26. Though his two treaties with the Creeks did not mention payment for lands, in 1736 Oglethorpe acknowledged making reciprocal gifts. He then told the visiting chiefs: "We give You these Presents in token of this Agreement" regarding "the Islands of the Sea." Presumably he had bestowed similar gifts upon receiving the 1733 cessions. *GT*, 74.

27. Hahn, *Invention*, 258–70, quotes at 263 and 270.

Chapter 1. Carolina Prologue

1. These migrations are discussed in Oatis, *A Colonial Complex*, 24–29; and Worth, "The Lower Creeks," 278–86 and fig. 10.2 (tracing of 1715 map). A 1707 law drew boundaries around the Port Royal lands of the Yamasees. It was not a land grant, but a reservation "for their use only." *EAID*, 16:144–45.

2. Oatis, *A Colonial Complex*, chap. 8.

3. Crane, *Southern Frontier*, 259. The 1717 treaty was evidently renewed with little or no change in the 1721 treaty. The Creeks repeatedly recalled that the Savannah River was the southern limit of English settlement that they had agreed to, and the English sometimes confirmed this. *CRG*, 1:238, 4:663; Egmont, *Journal*, 117; Egmont, *Diary*, 2:204 (quote); *GT*, 141, 149; Martyn, "Impartial Enquiry," 57; *GFT*, 67–69 (1768 treaty), 457. On the 1721 treaty, see Moore, "Voyage," 121. Corkran (*Creek Frontier*, 64–65) misidentified the 1732 treaty as that of 1717. This error has misled many later scholars, including me (see *GT*, 4).

4. For credible population estimates on whites and blacks, see Peter Wood, *Black Majority: Negroes in Colonial South Carolina from 1670 through the Stono Rebellion* (New York: Knopf, 1974), table IV, p. 152.

5. My account is based mainly on Forbes, *Africans and Native Americans*, 214–34, esp. 219, 222.

6. Ibid., 208–9, 225–27. South Carolina laws mentioning Indians and mustees are collected in *EAID*, vol. 16, chap. 2. "Mustees" first appeared in a 1696 act. Ibid., 121. In 1719 John Barnwell wrote of a pair of "half-breed or Mustees." S.C./P.R.O., 8:1–5. It is possible that the former term also had a Spanish origin. In 1559 Luis de Velasco, viceroy of Mexico, warned Tristán de Luna to beware of "half-breeds, mulattoes, and Indians." Quoted in David J. Weber, *The Spanish Frontier in North America* (New Haven: Yale University Press, 1992), 327.

7. Egmont, *Journal*, 273 (Tanner).

8. Ibid. ("left and bred up"). The clans of the Creeks and other Southeastern nations were rigorously matrilineal, that is, based entirely on genetic kinship through the female line, and not at all on affinal kinship (that deriving from marriage or adoption). In these societies a person's clan membership was permanent, for it was derived entirely from his or her mother (one of the reasons that James Adair and others supposed Indians were descended from Jews). Driver, *Indians of North America*, 274; Hudson, *The Southeastern Indians*, chap. 4, esp. 186. Nearly everything written since on Creek society is heavily indebted to the great work of Swanton, "Social Organization and Social Usages of the Indians of the Creek Confederacy."

9. Perdue, *Mixed Blood Indians*, chap. 2; Richard Godbeer, *Sexual Revolution in Early America* (Baltimore: Johns Hopkins University Press, 2002), chap. 5; Barker, "'Much Blood and Treasure,'" chap. 4.

10. C.O.5/428, p. 137 (Musgrove); *GFT*, 352 (Linguister John); *DRIA*, II, 246 (S. Brown), 301 (J. Brown); *GT*, 299 ("young Beamer"). Half a century later, Robert Goudey made a will leaving small sums of money to "his three Indian daughters." Meriwether, *Expansion of South Carolina*, 132 (T. Beamer and Goudey).

11. On the Prize and Johnson wills, see J. Leitch Wright Jr., *The Only Land They Knew* (New York: Free Press, 1981), 236–37. For their status as traders, see Barker, "'Much Blood and Treasure,'" 161, 178.

12. William L. Ramsay joins Eirlys Barker in paying due attention to Carolina mixed-bloods, but goes too far. Ramsay supposes that some traders reacted to conflict with native wives "by simply removing their children from the mother's influence and sending them to be raised in Charles Town." Ramsey, "'Something Cloudy in Their Looks': The Origins of the Yamasee War Reconsidered," *Journal of American History* 90 (June 2003): 50. There would have been nothing simple about removing children from an angry Indian wife; very likely such an abduction would have been life-threatening to the Englishman who tried it. At any rate, while this may have happened, no clear evidence that it did has been encountered.

13. David D. Smits, "'Abominable Mixture': Toward the Repudiation of Anglo-Indian

Intermarriage in Seventeenth-Century Virginia," *Virginia Magazine of History and Biography* 95 (1987): 157–92.

14. Nathaniel Osborne to the SPG secretary, May 28, 1715, SPG, A10 (series A, volume 10), p. 100. (Since all SPG letters cited herein are addressed to the secretary, hereafter they will be identified only by author and date.) Frank J. Klingberg, "The Mystery of the Lost Yamasee Prince," *SCHM* 63 (1962): 18–32, esp. 22.

15. Philip L. Barbour, *Pocahontas and Her World* (Boston: Houghton Mifflin Co., 1970), 183–84, 214; "Thomas Rolfe," *Virginia Magazine of History and Biography* 21 (1913): 209–11; Richard L. Morton, *Colonial Virginia*, 2 vols. (Chapel Hill: University of North Carolina Press, 1960), 1:178n.

16. Beverley, *History*, 38–39; John Lawson, *A New Voyage to Carolina*, ed. Hugh T. Lefler (Chapel Hill: University of North Carolina Press, 1967), 244.

17. Lawson, *New Voyage*, 244–45.

18. Leonard W. Labaree, ed., *Royal Instructions to British Colonial Governors, 1670–1776*, 2 vols. (New York: D. Appleton-Century Co., 1935), 2:470.

19. SPG, A10, p. 90.

20. *JCIT*, 198–99.

21. SPG, A10, pp. 92–93 (Osborne); ibid., A9, pp. 266–67, A10, pp. 83–84 (Dennis).

22. Basic facts on Musgrove can be found in Crane, *Southern Frontier*. More on Musgrove and his relatives, including Mary, are in a valuable 1967 research report by William L. McDowell, "John Musgrove," on file at SCDAH. In 1716 Musgrove signed a petition as a member of the St. Andrews congregation. SPG, B4, no. 47. He was in trouble with the Carolina government in 1706. Among other charges, he was accused of having "threatned the lives of the Tuckesaw Indian King and another unless they would give him Four Slaves upon pretence that they had taken away his the said Musgroves and one William Steads Indian Wives." Musgrove and Stead eventually accepted "three Slaves in Satisffacion For their wives." No children were mentioned. This Indian wife was probably not Musgrove's first, and not the mother of Johnny Musgrove. *SCCHJ*, 1706–7, p. 21. "Tuckesaw" was the Creek town mentioned by Bishop Calderón in 1675 as "Tacûsa." It soon disappeared. Calderón letter, 9.

23. Tobias Fitch to S.C. Council, August 4, 1725, C.O.5/428, p. 137.

24. Mary Bosomworth's Memorial to Heron, August 10, 1747, *GT*, 140–44, quotes at 140. The Coweta town was located on the Ocmulgee only between about 1690 and 1715. Since she was married in 1716 or early 1717, and died in 1765, Mary must have been born around the turn of the century. Fisher, "Mary Musgrove," 73, 75 n. 3, 518. See also Crane, *Southern Frontier*, 36; Hahn, *Invention*, chap. 2.

25. *GT*, 141.

26. Causton to Trustees, January 20, 1736, *CRG*, 21:71; Oglethorpe to Egmont, January 25, 1741, in Lane, *Oglethorpe's Georgia*, 2:536. Similarly, Moore reported that Mrs. Musgrove's brother was "an half Indian called Griffin." Moore, "Voyage," 145. On the 1719 raid see Crane, *Southern Frontier*, 264 n. 27 (Barnwell); and Milling, *Red Carolinians*, 154–55.

27. At least three other Griffins had come to South Carolina by 1700. The first to appear came very early. In February 1671 John Dowden arrived from Barbados with a servant, "his boy named John Griffin." John apparently returned to Barbados with Dowden the following year. This or another John in 1695 received a warrant for fifty acres as "his arrival rights" (headright). John P. Thomas Jr., "The Barbadians in Early South Carolina," *SCHM* 31 (1930): 92; *The Shaftesbury Papers*, ed. Langdon Cheves (1897; reprint, Charleston: Tempus Publications, 2000), 271–72, 359; Alexander S. Salley and R. Nicholas Olsberg, eds., *Warrants for Land in South Carolina, 1672–1711* (Columbia: University of South Carolina Press, 1973), 526. If the 1695 John was poor and obscure, Richard Griffin and Joseph Griffin were not. Both were in the colony by 1700, and both promptly became major landholders in elite Berkeley County. Agnes Leland Baldwin, *First Settlers of South Carolina, 1670–1700* (Easley, S.C.: Southern Historical Press, 1985), 107; Salley and Olsberg, *Warrants for Land*, 580, 607; S. Emmett Lucas, ed., *An Index to Deeds of the Province and State of South Carolina, 1719–1785, and Charleston District, 1785–1800* (Easley: Southern Historical Press, 1977), 138; C.O.5/398, ff. 10, 12. It seems highly probable that Richard and Joseph were brothers. John may have been another brother, but more likely was a cousin. Trader Edward Griffin was surely related to at least one of these other Griffins, and probably all of them. All four Griffins appear to be of the same generation. My guess is that Edward was a brother of the 1695 John and a cousin of Richard and Joseph. For the 1703 quote see *Journals of the Commons House of Assembly of South Carolina for 1703*, ed. A. S. Salley (Columbia: Historical Commission of South Carolina, 1934), 19–20. For the Nairne quote see Gallay, *The Indian Slave Trade*, 220–21, quoting Nairne to Earl of Sunderland, October 16, 1708, HM22268, Maggs 498, Henry E. Huntington Library. My thanks to John Rhodehamel, Norris Foundation Curator at the Huntington Library, for checking this document and sending me copies of the enclosures. Two of them make it clear that Dickson was the man accused of buggery.

28. *JCIT*, 6–7, 63; Crane, *Southern Frontier*, 127. Griffin's partners were even more obscure than he was. One was Charles Peirce (*JCIT*, 5, 51), but there is no further mention of Holford.

29. What little we know about Mary's brother Edward suggests that he was not literate or Christian and that he lived as a more typical "half breed"—as a Creek warrior. Early in 1736 Chigelli employed him to carry a message from Coweta to Tomochichi in Savannah. *CRG*, 21:71. It seems likely that Edward was older than Mary and that he shared little of her experiences in their father's Carolina home. In 1740 he was apparently among Oglethorpe's Indian auxiliaries at the siege of St. Augustine. Mary reported that "her own brother" was among those who died there. *GT*, 142.

30. Osborne, March 1715, SPG, A10, pp. 92–93. On the name Pon Pon River, still in use very recently, see Salley and Olsberg, *Warrants for Lands*, 328 n.

31. Osborne, May 28, 1715, SPG, A10, pp. 99–100. Osborne's fellow missionaries William Tredwell Bull and William Guy confirmed that St. Bartholomew's Parish was now totally deserted. Ibid., 59, 68. Bull's important letter of August 15 is printed (from SPG, B4) in Klingberg, "Mystery of the Lost Yamasee Prince," 23–26.

32. Le Jau, August 23, 1715, in Frank J. Klingberg, ed., "The Carolina Chronicle of Dr. Francis Le Jau, 1706–1717," *University of California Publications in History* 53 (1956): 164 ("burned"); Rev. Thomas Hasell, December 1, 1715, SPG, A11, pp. 97–98 ("as far"); *GT*, 141 ("at the Head"); Crane, *Southern Frontier*, 171–73. For locations of Pon Pon and other major features 1717–32, see maps in Ivers, *British Drums*, 8; and Larry E. Ivers, "Scouting the Inland Passage, 1685–1737," *SCHM* 73 (1972): 118.

33. On May 28, 1715, schoolmaster Benjamin Dennis reported that the Indians "have killed most of our Indian traders." SPG, A10, p. 102. In June, Charles Town authorities guessed that ninety of about a hundred traders in the field had been slain. Much later, an informant of William Bartram guessed that "almost all" were killed. In November 1717, twenty-four members of the Commons House of Assembly, including the Speaker, along with "the rest of the Inhabitants of the Province"—568 of them—signed an anti-proprietary petition to the Crown. The signers included Richard Griffin, "Joseph Griffith [Griffin?]," and Benjamin Griffin (probably a son of Richard or Joseph), but not Edward Griffin. S.C./P.R.O., 7:90, 94; Sirmans, *Colonial South Carolina*, 117.

34. *GT*, 149 (Malatchi); Crane, *Southern Frontier*, 259–60. Spanish witnesses summarized by Barcia provide additional or slightly different details, one of which is very important. According to Barcia, when Musgrove's party entered Coweta on March 4, Brim was no longer "emperor" or "grand cacique." Five days earlier, this office, "with the consent of the ancient emperor," had passed to Brim's son Sepeycoffee ("Chipacafi"). Other details: the exact date; Musgrove's entry "bearing a white flag"; Musgrove "broke a knife," while Indians broke a bow and some arrows. Andrés González de Barcia Carballido y Zúñiga, *Chronological History of the Continent of Florida*, trans. Anthony Kerrigan (Gainesville: University of Florida Press, 1951), 361–62, 364, 375.

35. Petition of Mary Bosomworth, June 30, 1753, S.C.C.J., July 3, 1753, SCDAH, No. 21, Part 2 (RSUS, South Carolina, E.1p, reel 6), p. 501 [hereafter Mary's petition of June 30, 1753]; "Declaration" of Elizabeth Hunt, July 1[8], 1753, in ibid., August 7, 1753, p. 561 [hereafter E. Hunt Declaration]; petition of Mary Bosomworth, August 7, 1753, in ibid., August 7, 1753, p. 558 [hereafter Mary's petition of August 7, 1753]. On August 7 Governor Glen and Council approved Mary's June petition. Ibid., p. 562. Mary was using an "Old Style" date of 1716 (through March 24, 1717). Steven Hahn informs me that he has found the deed from Jones to Musgrove, dated February 5, 1717. Misfiled, it is found in South Carolina (Colony), Register, Conveyance Book F, 1707–1711, SCDAH, unnumbered pages. The seller was not Thomas Jones the trader but another of that name, a cordwainer.

36. S.C.C.J., February 11, 1723, C.O.5/425, f. 391v (seizure by Captain Gerard Monger); McDowell, "John Musgrove," 2, citing S.C. Treasury Ledger A, 1725–30, p. 62, SCDAH (license). On Smallwood incident see Barker, "'Much Blood and Treasure,'" 264–66, 272; Fisher, "Mary Musgrove," 52. On Colonel John Palmer's raid see Crane, *Southern Frontier*, 249–51. When William Stephens explored up the Savannah River in 1736, he hired a guide "earnestly recommended" by Jonathan Bryan: "an Indian . . . who went by the name of Jack Smallwood." This man, whom Stephens found to be "a shrewd

observing Fellow," was most likely a half-Indian son of Matthew Smallwood. Stephens, *Journal*, 1: appendix A, pp. 239, 248. Early in 1728 the South Carolina council resolved that James Welch, "who is related to the Chickesaws," be encouraged to live among the Lower Chickasaws near Fort Moore. S.C.C.J., February 29, 1728, C.O.5/430, f. 12.

37. E. Hunt Declaration, p. 560; Mary's petition of June 30, 1753, p. 501.

38. S.C.U.H.J., January 5, 1722, RSUS, A.1a, reel 1, unit 1 (transcript, ca. 1890, S.C. Hist. Comm.), p. 144. The relevant section of the act of September 19 is in *EAID*, 16:234. The proclamation is in S.C.C.J., January 5, 1722, C.O.5/425, ff. 223v–224.

39. S.C.U.H.J., March 8, 1722, RSUS, A.1a, reel 1, unit 1, pp. 209–10; Crane, *Southern Frontier*, 264n.

40. *Journal of Colonel John Herbert, Commissioner of Indian Affairs for the Province of South Carolina, October 17, 1727, to March 19, 1727/8*, ed. A. S. Salley (Columbia: Historical Commission of South Carolina, 1936), 21 (Middleton); "Tobias Fitch's Journal to the Creeks, 1725," in Mereness, *Travels in the American Colonies*, 212 (Sepeycoffee).

41. Fisher, "Mary Musgrove," 52–53. On March 11, 1738, Lieutenant Governor William Bull gave final approval to "An Act for making and keeping in Repair the Road which leads from the Head of Westow Savanna Road on the East Side of Pon Pon River to Musgroves Ferry and from thence to Parker's Ferry Road in St. Paul's Parish." *SCCHJ*, 1736–39, p. 543. Elizabeth Hunt stated that after he sold his land to John Musgrove, Thomas Jones "Lived upon another Tract of Land belonging to John Godfrey where the Ferry was Kept upon Pon Pon River and at that time, commonly called Godfrey's Ferry." E. Hunt Declaration, p. 561.

42. *JCIT*, 16–17. Barker supposes that Thomas was the son of a much more prominent trader, Colonel John Jones. Barker, "'Much Blood and Treasure,'" 288n. She cites no evidence, but might be reacting to the fact that by 1717 John Jones was "Commander at Edistoe Garrison." *JCIT*, 149, 151. Thomas Jones is a better candidate. The Edisto garrison was not near Pon Pon, but twenty miles to the north. On the Tuckabatchee Captain's complaint, see Gerard Monger to Nicholson, September 24, 1723, C.O.5/359, ff. 63–64. The other traders who accompanied Jones to the Choctaws were Thomas Wiggins (later a major figure in Georgia) and John Gillespie. This venture turned out badly. As Jones told the story, shortly after he left with his packtrain for home, Choctaws plundered the other traders and "killed a White man," presumably a packhorseman. "Fitch's Journal," in Mereness, *Travels in the American Colonies*, 206.

43. Ivers (*British Drums*, 75) says that the mother was "probably Creek." Barker ("'Much Blood and Treasure,'" 165) declares that she was "Choctaw." Neither cites evidence. Because of the ties between the elder Thomas Jones and the Yamasees, and the ties between the younger Jones and Pon Pon, Ivers's hunch seems more likely. Jones translated for the Choctaws in 1734 (*GT*, 38) and the Chickasaws in 1736 (ibid., 75). In 1740, Jones, "being of Indian Extract, was employed by him [Oglethorpe] as a Linguist to the Creeks and Euchees." *SCCHJ*, 1741–42, pp. 99, 192. On Jones's tax problem see ibid., 1736–39, p. 408; for Oglethorpe's comment see ibid., 1741–42, p. 166.

44. *Documents Relative to the Colonial History of the State of New York*, ed. E. B.

O'Callaghan and Berthold Fernow, 15 vols. (Albany: Weed, Parsons & Co., 1856–87), 3:323. On Akus's Christian name, see *EAID*, 7:336, 385–86. Important scholarship on ex-Englishmen begins with James Axtell, "The White Indians of Colonial America," *William and Mary Quarterly* 32 (1975): 55–88.

45. Virginia apparently set the pattern for other southern colonies when in 1705 it enacted a law declaring that "negroes, mulattoes, and Indian servants, and others, not being christians . . . to be persons incapable in law, to be witnesses in all cases whatsoever." Quoted in Kathleen M. Brown, *Good Wives, Nasty Wenches, and Anxious Patriarchs* (Chapel Hill: University of North Carolina Press, 1996), 182. On the Musgroves' literacy, see Mary to Oglethorpe, July 17, 1734, John to Oglethorpe, January 24, 1735, and Mary to William Stephens, July 27, 1749, *GT*, 38–39, 43–44, 173–74. As for Jones, on March 23, 1741, the clerk of the South Carolina lower house was ordered "to write" to him, requiring that he testify on the failed St. Augustine expedition. He appeared in person on April 9 and gave a sworn deposition, which he presumably read before he signed. *SCCHJ*, 1739–41, p. 550; ibid., 1741–42, pp. 192–94, quote at 192. On recourse to English law, in 1734 Mary twice sued Joseph Watson, and won both cases. *GT*, 40. In South Carolina, John was the recipient of several warrants for land and paid taxes. Mary later stated that just before leaving for Georgia, John "made his will and Left her Sole Executrix with all his Estate Real and Personal." Likewise he gave "a Power of Attorney" to Captain Daniel Green to perfect his land titles. Mary's petition of June 30, 1753, pp. 501–2; Mary's petition of August 7, 1753, p. 559. In Georgia, John in 1734 signed "Articles between Musgrove and Watson" that established a "partnership." *CRG*, 20:174. That year when Jones returned to Savannah with Choctaws he found Robert Parker in possession of the town lot that Oglethorpe had promised him. Jones brought "an Action of Trespass and Ejectment" against Parker, and won his case. Ibid., 122–23, 284, 438.

46. True Bill, August 31, 1737, *The Works of John Wesley* (Bicentennial Edition; Nashville: Abingdon Press), vol. 18 (1988), *Journals and Diaries I (1735–38)*, p. 561; *SCCHJ*, 1741–42, p. 192 ("duly sworn").

47. *SCCHJ*, 1741–42, p. 166 (Jones); *CRG*, 20:51 (Musgrove). For other Georgia examples of "Mr. Musgrove," see *GT*, 8, 13, 45; *CRG*, 20:163, 200, 389. For other examples of "Mr. Jones," see *GT*, 36, 38, 39; *CRG*, 21:344. Among many references to John Musgrove in the South Carolina records, one is to "Mr." Musgrove, perhaps a slip. S.C.C.J., February 15, 1724, C.O.5/427, p. 79.

48. Lane, *Oglethorpe's Georgia*, 1:276.

Chapter 2. Georgia Dawn

1. Georgia charter, June 9, 1732, *CRG*, 1:11–26, esp. 12 (21 years), 16 (pay), 22 (500-acre limit).

2. Ibid., 11 ("neighboring savages"), 18 (boundaries), 21 ("wild people").

3. Egmont was the most active and best-informed of the Trustees in London. His *Journal* and especially his *Diary* are among the best sources we have on early Georgia

history. See Betty Wood, "The Earl of Egmont and the Georgia Colony," in *Forty Years of Diversity: Essays on Colonial Georgia*, ed. Harvey H. Jackson and Phinizy Spalding (Athens: University of Georgia Press, 1984), 80–96.

4. Georgia charter, *CRG*, 1:11–26, esp. 16 and 24.

5. A 1740 incident illustrates the Trustees' consistent policy. In that year Trustee James Vernon proposed appointing a Georgia official capable of checking Oglethorpe, only to conclude that it would be better to rely upon "a President and Council for the North Division of the Province, and a President and Council for the Southern Division." That way, he said, "we should avoid the constituting one person to govern the whole province, and so preserve the colony to ourselves." All members present "readily" agreed to the scheme, but Frederica and the southern area were all but abandoned before it could be implemented. Egmont, *Diary*, 3:171. Vernon was simply proposing an expanded geographical jurisdiction for the two existing town governments (and, for Savannah, county government), both consisting of a president and several bailiffs. Savannah's team (whose presiding officer was initially called "first bailiff") was named just before the original colonists set sail in late 1732. Corresponding officers for Frederica were appointed in September 1735, just before its settlers embarked for St. Simons Island. Egmont, *Journal*, 7–8, 101, 110. Egmont, *Diary*, 2:371 ("Legislature of Georgia").

6. Temple and Coleman, *Georgia Journeys*, chap. 1.

7. The treaty text is in *EAID*, 13:150–52. The correct date was first reported in Fisher, "Mary Musgrove," 49 n. 84.

8. Both images are usually linked with William Penn's legendary first treaty with the Delawares (1682?), of which no text survives. According to early historian Robert Proud, this treaty "was solemnly ratified by the usual token of a *chain of friendship* and covenant indelible, never to be broken, so long as the sun and moon endure." *EAID*, 1:58. Conceptualization of the "chain of friendship" or "covenant chain" was largely the work of New York governor Sir Edmund Andros five years earlier. See Francis Jennings, "The Constitutional Evolution of the Covenant Chain," *Proceedings of the American Philosophical Society* 115 (1971): 88–96.

9. On the 1730 Cherokee visit, see Vaughan, *Transatlantic Encounters*, 137–50. On Keith's role, see Crane, *Southern Frontier*, 298–99. The text of the 1730 Cherokee treaty is in *EAID*, 13:137–38. A draft of the 1722 treaty Keith negotiated with the Iroquois recalls how "We brightened the chain together that it might be clear, strong and lasting as the Sun and Stars, . . . and last as long as the Mountains and Rivers and the Sun and Moon shall endure." Ibid., 1:251–52. This rhetoric goes back to the Old Testament. In the King James version, Psalm 72:7 reads: "In his days shall the righteous flourish; and abundance of peace so long as the moon endureth." The following verse, which includes the phrase "from sea to sea," was inspirational from the first days of English colonization. Juricek, "English Territorial Claims," 13–18.

10. *South Carolina Gazette*, March 31, 1733; excerpt in *GT*, 7. On Bryan, see Gallay, *Formation of a Planter Elite*, 20.

11. Oglethorpe to Trustees, February 10, 1733, *CRG*, 20:10; Causton to his wife,

March 12,1733, *GT*, 10. Egmont's estimate of "not above fifty fighting men" seems in line with Causton's, while Gordon estimated only "forty souls." Egmont, *Diary*, 2:36, 113. Oglethorpe's "Curious Account of the Indians," enclosed in his June 9 letter to the Trustees, also refers to these early days. The date is uncertain, but February 1 and March 7 are most likely. There Oglethorpe recalls that "Tomo Chichi, in his first set speech to me, . . . said, here is a little present; and then gave me a buffalo skin, painted on the inside with the head and feathers of an eagle." The chief went on to explain that "the feathers of the eagle were soft, and signified love; the buffalo's skin warm, and signified protection; therefore he hoped that we would love and protect their little families." *GT*, 10.

12. *SCCHJ*, 1736–39, pp. 153–54 (Eveleigh); *GT*, 13 ("banished"), 14 ("out of each"); *A True and Historical Narrative*, 45 (Egmont); Thomas Christie to Oglethorpe, December 14, 1734, *CRG*, 20:122. In 1713 "King Lewis" of the Yamasee town of Pocotaligo told the South Carolina Indian commissioners that the "Cheehawes" were living among the Creeks. As a people "formerly belonging to the Yamassees," King Lewis asked for help that they "might return." *JCIT*, 42 (quotes), 50.

13. Egmont, *Diary*, 2:122 ("His father"); *EAID*, 13:149 ("about 65"), 150 ("Tomeechey"); *SCCHJ*, 1736–39, p. 154 (Eveleigh); *GT*, 54 (Chigelli). Of course, the Indians sought Johnson's approval for a resident trader, not "Leave to settle there."

14. Atkin, *Report*, 57; *GCCB*, 352; *GT*, 9 ("not a stranger"), 23 ("above fourscore").

15. Mary Bosomworth's memorial to Col. Alexander Heron, August 10, 1747, *GT*, 140–46, quote at 141. Statements Mary wrote or instigated in 1753, while generally compatible with her 1747 account, differ in at least three ways. First, as already discussed, the 1753 documents and others seem to contradict the suggestion in the 1747 memorial that prior to 1725 or 1724 Mary and John had lived outside South Carolina. Second, in 1753 Mary claimed that she and John moved to Georgia "at the Request of his Excellency the Governor" rather than at the Indians' request. Perhaps both the governor and the Indians asked that they go. Third, in 1753 Mary alleged loss of "Cattle, Horses, Hogs etc. left by Musgrove at the aforesaid place, when he went for Georgia." Perhaps it was a loss not worth mentioning in 1747 Georgia, for no redress was to be found there. Mary's petition of June 18, 1753, p. 501; E. Hunt Declaration, p. 561; Mary's petition of August 7, 1753, p. 560. In 1749 Savannah officials noted that in 1733 the first settlers found the Musgroves "setled in a small Trading-House by License from the Government of South Carolina." *GT*, 182.

16. *GT*, 7–9 (Gordon), 10–11 (Causton). The Yamacraws' handshaking was a native custom, not borrowed from the English. William Bartram later reported that the Cowkeeper, a Seminole leader, "shook our hands (or rather arms) a form of salutation peculiar to American Indians." Bartram, *Bartram on the Southeastern Indians*, 50. Many Europeans noted that the Indian custom was different, but none seems to have described it in detail. According to Swanton, "Instead of shaking hands individuals meeting in a friendly way rubbed each other's arms and bodies." According to Wright, "Indians shook each other's elbows and stroked parts of the arms and torso." John R. Swanton, "Aboriginal Culture of the Southeast," in *Forty-second Annual Report of the*

Bureau of American Ethnology (Washington, D.C.: Government Printing Office, 1928), 702; Wright, *Creeks and Seminoles*, 36. See also Merrell, *The Indians' New World*, 147. My guess is that each Indian reached out with right arm to grasp the right elbow of the other, while with left hand stroking the other's right shoulder and side.

17. Peter Gordon's account of early contacts, February 1–March 7, 1733, *GT*, 7–11.

18. *CRG*, 2:9 ("set out"); Egmont, *Journal*, 7. For a concise overview of the Trustees' land policies, see Reese, *Colonial Georgia*, 41–44. See also Spalding, *Oglethorpe in America*, 61.

19. *CRG*, 20:10 ("desire to be subject . . . to have land"); *EAID*, 16:144–45 (Yamasee land). Oglethorpe was probably also influenced by the 1730 Cherokee treaty, which states that the king "gives to the Cherokee Indians the privilege of living where they please." Ibid., 13:137.

20. Gordon said that the tract extended "six miles above us." *GT*, 8. This was an overestimate, probably because he meant river miles. Future governor Henry Ellis said the tract contained "about 4000 Acres," probably a slight underestimate. *CRG*, 28, pt. 1:254. The 1735 map, which has a believable scale, tends to support Ellis's estimate. There the tract appears as an irregular area extending about four miles up the river and a mile or two back from it. *GT*, illustration 2.

21. *GT*, 61 ("provided"), 142 ("the Utmost"); Temple and Coleman, *Georgia Journeys*, 18–19.

22. Moore, "Voyage," 121; *A True and Historical Narrative*, 44–45.

23. Malatchi's speech to Gov. James Glen, June 2, 1753, *GT*, 227.

24. Chigelli's talk to Major William Horton, December 4, 1746, ibid., 132–34.

25. Ibid., 149 (Malatchi). Francis Moore told essentially the same story. Moore, "Voyage," 121. In 1765 Tallechea related that "the first time he had met the English was at Tuffuskie, ... That at their first meeting it was agreed that the white people should not settle beyond the flowing of the tide." *GFT*, 457. "Tuffuskie" apparently is a variant of Daufuskie, a name still current. Daufuskie Sound and Daufuskie Island are at the mouth of the Savannah River. See Ivers, *British Drums*, map on 24.

26. Egmont, *Diary*, 2:252 ("Ogihee"); *GT*, 96 (1739 treaty), 133 (Santachi).

27. In 1756, Georgia's first royal governor, John Reynolds, reported that Creeks had told him about the original land deal. They claimed, he wrote, that "they never gave up their Land to this Province any farther than the tide flows, and so far they allow they have given up to Mr. Oglethorpe, but that treaty is not to be found here." It was not found because never written. Reynolds to Lyttelton, September 8, 1756, Lyttelton Papers.

28. In 1736 Stephens said that the tides flowed sixteen miles above Savannah, and so about thirty-three miles from the coastline. Stephens, *Journal*, 1: appendix A, p. 238. A few years later Moore said the Indians had granted land as far as the tidal limit "and two hours walk above it." Moore, "Voyage," 121. Perhaps the additional walking distance was supposed to represent the distance from Abercorn or Ebenezer up to New Ebenezer. It was in the interest of the Salzburgers to detect the tide still further up, and so they did.

In 1736 Baron von Reck declared that "the ebb and flood . . . can be detected as far as Purrysburgh." Jones, "Von Reck's Second Report," 322. In 1757 Governor Ellis said "tides do not flow above 30 miles up." *CRG*, 28, pt. 1:22. The only surviving cartographic representations of the tidal line, the De Brahm and Yonge maps of 1763, render it as a straight line about thirty miles inland. De Vorsey, *The Indian Boundary*, 172–73 and fig. 17.

29. The first conference with the Lower Creeks, May 18–21, 1733, *GT*, 12–14, quote at 13; ibid., 149 (Mary sends invitation).

30. Swanton, "Social Organization," 191–97, 276–90. All scholars of Creek history during the colonial era have struggled with this issue. The earliest, David Corkran, concluded that Brim's successors did constitute a patrilineal line. Corkran, *Creek Frontier*, 15, 79. Two of the most recent, Kathryn Braund and Steven Hahn, favor the view that the English misidentified nephews as sons. Braund does so without reservation, Hahn very cautiously. Braund, *Deerskins and Duffels*, 20; Hahn, *Invention*, 192–93.

31. First conference, *GT*, 12. On Creek twins, see John R. Swanton, "Religious Beliefs and Medical Practices of the Creek Indians," in *Forty-second Annual Report of the Bureau of American Ethnology* (Washington, D.C.: Government Printing Office, 1928), 615–16. The belief that twins had special powers extended beyond Creek culture to other Southeastern cultures, and to American Indian cultures in general. Hudson, *The Southeastern Indians*, 322, 337; Driver, *Indians of North America*, 438–39.

32. First conference, *GT*, 12–13; Corkran, *Creek Frontier*, 78–79; Hahn, *Invention*, 196–98. In 1740 Malatchi told Stephens that he was "near Thirty." *GT*, 102.

33. Stephens, *Journal*, 1:105. In addition to acting as lead interpreter for Oglethorpe's two treaty conferences with the Lower Creeks, Wiggins was one of the interpreters for the 1736 conference. *GT*, 12, 70, 97. Oglethorpe retained Wiggins to assist Patrick Mackay in 1734 and John Tanner in 1736. Wiggins's main trading house was in Cussita, where he became close to Captain Allick, a major character in the story that follows. He died in 1742. Ibid., 35; *SCCHJ*, 1736–39, pp. 92, 118, 138–39.

34. This newspaper account, reprinted in *GT*, 12–14, is the main source for the following paragraphs. Oglethorpe's comment is in his June 9 letter to the Trustees; ibid., 17.

35. Martyn, "History." On Oglethorpe's supposed authorship, see Spalding, *Oglethorpe in America*, 180 n. 90. The opening section of the "History" (324–26) is a point-by-point recapitulation of the first eleven pages of Martyn's *An Account Shewing the Progress of the Colony of Georgia in America from its First Establishment* (London, 1741). In particular, the last four paragraphs of this section in the 1741 *Account* (pp. 10–11, beginning "When the Trustees . . .") are repeated nearly word-for-word in the 1748 "History" (326). Martyn's description of Oglethorpe's conference with the Lower Creeks is based on the *Gazette* account, but is somewhat shorter and differs in some details. One indication that it was the work of a knowledgeable author is that it corrects the "old Breen" of the newspaper account to "Old Brim."

36. Martyn, "History," 327.

37. *GT*, 14, 16; Martyn, "History," 327.

38. *GT*, 13 (quote).

39. Oglethorpe's first treaty with the Lower Creeks, May 21, 1733, ibid., 15–17; South Carolina treaty with the Lower Creeks, June 14, 1732, *EAID*, 13:150–52. Beverly Sylvester has called my attention to what appears to be a unique example of a Creek tried for crime under English law. On October 31, 1764, South Carolina hanged a Creek named Wholanawidtma, convicted of murdering a Long Canes setter named Bedingfield. *South Carolina Gazette*, November 5, 1764. This trial and execution took place because "the Gun Merchant and others" gave prior permission. As the *Georgia Gazette* reported on August 16, "if the fact was proved according to our laws, they had no objection to his being put to death."

40. Oglethorpe's first treaty, *GT*, 16 (article 6); S.C. treaty of 1732, *EAID*, 13:151 ("go to War").

41. Oglethorpe's first treaty, *GT*, 15 (article 4); ibid., 13 (Oueechachumpa).

42. Ibid., 149 (Malatchi); *GFT*, 457 (Tallechea). Superintendent John Stuart supposed that this cession extended southward to the St. Johns River. Hence he saw to it that the text of the Picolata treaty refers to the earlier Lower Creek cession this way: "all the Sea Coast as far as the tide flows, in the manner settled with the English by the great Tomachiché, with all the Country to the Eastward [northeast] of St. Johns River." Ibid., 465.

43. *GT*, 14 ("feasting"), 134 (Chigelli).

44. Compare the South Carolina price schedule in *EAID*, 13:152, with its Georgia counterpart in *GT*, 16–17. The 1739 treaty states that in that year some Creek towns "produced" their copies of the 1733 treaty. Ibid., 96.

45. Hahn notes that "not once is the term 'nephew' used" to describe Malatchi. Hahn, *Invention*, 300 n. 13. If the English confused a man's nephews for his sons, we might expect that the Muscogee terms for these relatives sounded a lot alike. Not so. The term for a man's son was "kputci" and that for his sister's son was "hopwiwa." Likewise the Muscogee term for a man's father ("iki") sounded nothing like the term for his maternal uncle ("pawa"). Swanton, "Social Organization," 85. Savannah president William Stephens was one Georgian who could distinguish between Creek sons and nephews. In 1740, speaking of Chigelli, Stephens observed that "his Nephew Malatchie . . . was the Son of old Bream." *GT*, 102.

46. *GT*, 52 (Tomochichi), 149 ("My Father"; repeated on 151 and 152), and 179 (1749 document). Mary knew the facts. Since she translated for Malatchi's 1747 speech (and probably had a hand in composing it), and almost certainly helped write the 1749 document, presumably she agreed with both.

47. On Brim's title, see introduction, note 9. Though there are no statements by Creeks that clearly identify Chigelli, Malatchi, or Togulki as Coweta Mico, a few by Englishmen come close. For example, in 1735 Causton referred to "Chickelly Mico of the Coweta's in the Lower Nation." *CRG*, 21:71.

48. Hahn, *Invention*, 93 ("seven"); James Sutherland to "My Lord," ca. 1730, *SCHM*

68 (1967): 79–84 ("Seaven" at 82). In a controversial article, William S. Willis argues that patrilineal succession for war leaders was more than possible, it was likely. Willis, "Patrilineal Institutions."

49. "Migration Legend" talk, June 11, 1735, *GT*, 54 ("Eldest town"); talks with the Lower Creeks, June 27, 1736, ibid., 69 ("the Chief"); Chigelli's talk to Horton, December 4, 1746, ibid., 132. The talk to Horton is an early example of a written letter sent by a Creek to an English leader. Remarkably, Chigelli closed by complaining that "I have received no Answer" to a previous letter he sent Horton. Ibid., 134. If such correspondence was not already routine, it would become so within a decade.

50. Declaration of Lower Creek headmen, December 14, 1747, ibid., 155; Swanton, "Social Organization," 106; Atkin's talk at Tuckabatchee, July 21, 1759, in Atkin to Lyttelton, November 30, 1759, Lyttelton Papers. See also Hahn, *Invention*, 195–201. Hahn concludes (199) that "Malatchi appears to have served in Coweta as both a civil authority (*mico*) and as head warrior (*opiya mico*)." The civil authority seems doubtful. In the 1749 recognition of Mary as princess, quoted earlier, one of the chiefs listed after Malatchi is a man named Asstuttee: he is identified as "Mico of the Coweta Town." *GT*, 179.

51. Very limited sources make any account of this survey trip somewhat conjectural. The best contemporary sources seem to be the *South Carolina Gazette* for June 30 and July 7, 1733, and the map of "the County of Savannah" published in 1735 (*GT*, illustration 2). The *Gazette* of July 7 reports Oglethorpe's June 12 arrival in Savannah and immediate move to Horse Quarter; the issue of June 30 reports that he returned to Savannah on June 18. For other attempts to reconstruct the trip, see Temple and Coleman, *Georgia Journeys*, 41–44; and Ivers, *British Drums*, 11–23.

52. Louis De Vorsey Jr. "Oglethorpe and the Earliest Maps of Georgia," in Spalding and Jackson, *Oglethorpe in Perspective*, 40–43.

53. Oglethorpe to Trustees, ca. December 1733, *CRG*, 20:40. In 1739 Oglethorpe gave a more realistic estimate of Abercorn's distance above Savannah: "15 Miles." Oglethorpe, "State of Georgia," October 11, 1739, Egmont Papers, 14204, pp. 123–35, quote at 124.

54. Oglethorpe to Trustees, ca. December 1733, *CRG*, 20:40; *GT*, illustration 2. For the Trustees's creation of the county of Savannah (and the abortive county of Frederica), see Egmont, *Diary*, 3:171, 177, 224. Around the end of 1737, Oglethorpe wrote that the county of Savannah lay between the Savannah and Ogeechee rivers, bounded on the west "by the river Ebenezer, and a line drawn from the Ebenezer to the Ogechee." Oglethorpe, "An Account of Carolina and Georgia (1739)," in Oglethorpe, *Publications*, 248. Yet in 1734 Oglethorpe had Fort Argyle built on the south side of Ogeechee River. Thus it appears that both that fort and Ebenezer violated the original boundary; Fort Argyle was beyond the Ogeechee, while Ebenezer was beyond the tidal line.

55. *GT*, 11. Scholars have long estimated the populations of native communities by multiplying the number of "men" by four (some a little more, some a little less). Both Governor Johnson's 1720 estimates (sometimes erroneously called the "1715 census") and the 1725 Charlesworth Glover census give the ratio of Upper to Lower

Creeks (including Yuchis) as about 1.3 to 1. See Johnson to Board of Trade, January 12, 1720, in *The South Carolina Colonial Scene*, ed. H. Roy Merrens (Columbia: University of South Carolina Press, 1977), table at 60; Christian F. Feest, "Creek Towns in 1725," *Ethnologische Zeitschrift* 1 (1974): 161–75, table at 163.

56. *GT*, 18. It is possible to hold (as I did in ibid., 5), that the Upper Creeks and Yuchis came to Savannah because, as Oglethorpe wrote on March 12, "the Creeks and Uchees have referred a Difference to me to determine." Ibid., 11. I now believe that the "Difference" related to the Lower Creeks, not the Upper Creeks, and was mentioned by Gordon on March 7. Tomochichi then complained to Oglethorpe that one of his Yamacraws had "been killed by the Uchis," but said he "would not take revenge without Mr. Oglethorps consent and approbation." Ibid., 9.

57. Ibid., 11, 18. Thus the 1735 Georgia act to regulate the Indian trade, which Oglethorpe mostly copied from the South Carolina act of 1731, retains the earlier statute's requirement that "those taking out Licences to Trade with the Creeks shall first declare whether he will Trade with the Upper or Lower Creeks." *EAID*, 16:368. Cf. ibid., 268.

58. "The [William] Mckenzie Papers, Part II," ed. Albert S. Britt and Lilla M. Hawes, *GHQ* 57 (1973): 93 (quote); *CRG*, 1:133 (August 8), 44 (October 18). For details on the various surviving copies, see *GT*, 365 n. 23.

59. The best of many previous accounts of this visit is in Vaughan, *Transatlantic Encounters*, 150–60.

60. Egmont, *Diary*, 2:122 (quotes). The only contemporary source that provides a complete list of the Indians who visited England is Martyn, "History," 328. Other sources confirm all names on this list except Hinguithi. *CRG*, 32:126, 129, 138; Urlsperger, *Detailed Reports*, 1:20, 23–24. On July 31 Tomochichi's "Cosen," though attended by Sir Hans Sloane, died of smallpox. Egmont, *Diary*, 2:118–19; Egmont, *Journal*, 59. The deceased must have been Hinguithi, for all of the other Indians appear in the records after their return to Savannah on December 28. Oglethorpe described Tomochichi's ranking companions as "the War Captain Hillispilli" and "the Beloved Man Umpechee." *GT*, 61. Referring to Hillispilli, on January 24 John Musgrove reported that Tomochichi had sent "his Brother" to invite the Creeks down for talks. Ibid., 44. Four days earlier Causton wrote that Tomochichi had sent two Yamacraws on this mission, Hillispilli and Santachi. *CRG*, 21:71. As Oglethorpe would confirm (*GT*, 61), the man Musgrove called Tomochichi's brother was Hillispilli, not the youth Santachi. About the same time, Captain George Dunbar, whose ship carried the Indians back to Savannah, referred to "Tooanahowi, his [Tomochichi's] brothers son." Dunbar to Trustees, n.d., quoted in Urlsperger, *Detailed Reports*, 1:23. Thus Hillispilli appears to have been the father of Tooanahowi. Often Tooanahowi was called Tomochichi's "nephew," while Egmont several times said the boy was Tomochichi's "Grand Nephew." Egmont's final and presumably best-informed statement on Tomochichi's relationship to Tooanahowi is this: "His nephew as he calls him, but who is grandson to his wife." Egmont, *Diary*, 2:122. See also *CRG*, 20:198; Egmont, *Diary*, 2:113; Egmont, *Journal*, 57; *GT*, 24. Relying mainly on the statement

by Dunbar and the final one by Egmont, the discordant evidence can most plausibly be untangled as follows: (1) by an earlier husband Senauki had a daughter who became the mother of Tooanahowi; (2) Hillispilli was the husband of Senauki's daughter, and father of Tooanahowi; (3) although Hillispilli was sometimes called Tomochichi's "brother," he was a generation younger and probably related to the older man by common membership in a clan or town; and (4) although Tooanahowi was often called Tomochichi's "nephew" or "grand nephew," he was actually the older man's step-grandson.

61. Jones, *Salzburger Saga*, 14–15; Urlsperger, *Detailed Reports*, 1:199 n. 27. In 1736 the Salzburger minister Johann Boltzius reported that Oglethorpe told him "the entire land from Ebenezer Creek on and further up belongs to the Indians." Jones, "Secret Diary," 83.

62. *CRG*, 1:22, 2:14–15. Each of these grantees also paid the considerable sum of "five Guineas the Consideration Money, mentioned in their Grants." The requisite number of servants was later raised to six, and as high as ten. Ibid., 23; Granger, *Savannah River Plantations*, 171. Gentlemen able to send some servants, but not the requisite number, might receive a proportionate grant. Thus two weeks after Lacy's grant, Henry Pickerton, who said he was able to transport three servants, received a grant of three hundred acres. *CRG*, 2:16. Like many others, Pinkerton soon changed his mind about emigrating, and his grant became a dead letter.

63. His first recorded recommendations, for Jonathan Bryan and six others, were made on June 9, 1733. *CRG*, 20:24.

64. *GT*, 141–42 ("then Husband"); *CRG*, 20:51 ("Gent."). Less than two weeks after the founding of Savannah, Peter Gordon referred to "Musgrave, the Indian traders cow penn" as somewhere upriver. Gordon, *Journal*, 39. The Trustees granted the cowpen area as a five-hundred-acre tract to Dr. Patrick Tailfer on October 18, 1733, but he never settled there. *CRG*, 2:44; Granger, *Savannah River Plantations*, 170–71.

65. Granger, *Savannah River Plantations*, 167–72, 276–79. A hundred-acre lot reserved by the Trustees separated the Musgrove and Watson lands, and a similar reserve separated Watson from Pipemaker's Creek. Oglethorpe asked fellow Trustees to approve a five-hundred-acre grant to Watson on February 26, 1734. *CRG*, 20:51.

66. Causton referred to "the Articles between Musgrove and Watson." *CRG*, 20:174 (see also, *GT*, 43). John's will is lost. Our information about it comes from a 1750 indenture whereby Thomas and Mary Bosomworth conveyed the cowpen to William Francis. *GCCB*, 23. There is no reason to doubt what this document says except the claim that John *specifically* willed the cowpen to his sons. Probably John left each son half of his estate, not half of the cowpen's five hundred acres. The Trustees did not approve a five-hundred-acre grant for Musgrove until October 16, 1734, and the grant was not finalized until September 24, 1735, several months after John's death. *CRG*, 2:75, 124. A memo summarizing the grant is in ibid., 32:186.

67. *GCCB*, 23; Egmont, *Diary*, 2:112–13 ("ninety"). Oglethorpe's estimate of Tomochichi's age was probably high by at least a decade.

68. First meeting of Tomochichi's party with the Trustees, July 3, 1734, *GT*, 20–21;

Martyn to Causton, July 27, 1734, Egmont Papers, 14207, p. 238 ("let them know"); Reese, *Colonial Georgia*, 108.

69. Spalding, *Oglethorpe in America*, 82; *CRG*, 1:180.

70. Egmont, *Diary*, 2:118 ("same foot"), 119 ("sat up").

71. Alured Clarke's account of the royal audience, *GT*, 23 ("mighty gravely"); *Gentleman's Magazine* account, ibid., 21 (other quotes).

72. *Gentleman's Magazine* account, ibid. (king's reply); Egmont's account, ibid., 23–24 ("Stroked" and "He answered" and "War dance"); Alured Clarke's account, ibid., 23 ("finest woman" and "begged pardon"); Moore, "Voyage," 123 ("gold" and Cumberland Island); "The [William] Mackenzie Papers: Part II," *GHQ* 57 (1973): 101. In Georgia a Yamacraw named Estichi later claimed to have been a member of Tomochichi's delegation. In 1742 he killed a trader who had stolen "a gold watch that he brought out of England." Stephens, *Journal*, 1:62; Corkran, *Creek Frontier*, 110. A Thomas Causton letter makes it perfectly clear that Estichi was in Georgia, and in big trouble, during the London visit. Apparently he later somehow acquired Tooanahowi's watch. *GT*, 40–41. One of Georgia's coastal islands was soon named after the second of the king's daughters, Amelia. The strategic town at the falls of the Savannah River was named after Frederick's wife, Augusta.

73. Egmont, *Journal*, 57. In his *Diary* (2:112) Egmont said Tomochichi, "Chief of the Yamacree nation," had come to London "to confirm the peace with that and the eight nations of their Allies last year." Verelst to Eveleigh, August 30, 1735, *CRG*, 29:87–88.

74. Oglethorpe to Newcastle, April 17, 1736, *GT*, 62 (variant copy in C.O.5/365, p. 92); *GT*, 20 (Egmont). When a treaty with the visiting Cherokees was under consideration in 1730, the Board of Trade wrote Newcastle that "words may easily be inserted acknowledging their Dependence upon the Crown of Great Britain." *EAID*, 13:135. After the treaty was signed, the board assured Newcastle that it contained the right words: "there is a full Acknowledgement in this Agreement of their Subjection to his Majesty." Quoted in Crane, *Southern Frontier*, 301–2.

75. *GT*, 23.

76. *CRG*, 1:184–85 (Tomochichi quotes); *GT*, 24–25 ("Rum"); Egmont, *Diary*, 2:124 ("mend"). Egmont reported that "they were for their setting the prices of goods." Ibid., 126.

77. *CRG*, 1:182–83, 2:71, 75, 124, 32:126–27; Egmont, *Journal*, 65.

78. Ettinger, *Oglethorpe*, 146; Egmont, *Diary*, 2:132 ("day of death"); *CRG*, 3:93 ("Left by him").

79. *GT*, 25 ("Great Lyon"); *CRG*, 20:194 ("your picture"); Egmont, *Diary*, 2:406 (Tanner).

Chapter 3. Staking Out the Territory

1. *List of the Early Settlers of Georgia*, ed. E. Merton Coulter and Albert B. Saye (Athens: University of Georgia Press, 1949), 84; Egmont, *Journal*, 346 ("Felony"); Verelst

to Capt. George Dunbar, September 6, 1735, *CRG*, 29:109. Mackay's role in early Georgia is well recounted in Ivers, *British Drums*, chap. 3. For more detail, see Edna Sue Bailes, "The Scottish Colonization of Georgia in America, 1732–1742" (Ph.D. diss., University of Edinburgh, 1977), 86–93, 157–59, 215–16; *CRG*, 2:112; Oglethorpe to Trustees, September 27, 1733, ibid., 20:36–37; Granger, *Savannah River Plantations*, 56–58.

2. *SCCHJ*, 1736–39, p. 122.

3. S.C.S.M.R., Book EE, p. 48, SCDAH (Mackay commission); Egmont, *Journal*, 113 (£8,000); Phinizy Spalding, "South Carolina and Georgia: The Early Days," *SCHM* 69 (1968): 83–96; Ivers, *British Drums*, 33. On April 9, 1734, the South Carolina assembly committed itself to the fort by appropriating £2,320 in currency. According to the conversion rate provided by Samuel Eveleigh a few months later (7¼ to 1), that was equivalent to £320 Sterling. Unless otherwise specified, monetary amounts will henceforth be stated in terms of Sterling. *SCCHJ*, 1734–35, pp. 107, 121.

4. *GT*, 33–35 (instructions to Mackay); Mackay to Trustees, November 20, 1734, *CRG*, 20:109 (complaint). Undaunted, Mackay carried what was apparently the original of his South Carolina commission (along with two from Oglethorpe) into the Creek country, and used it to claim authority over the reluctant Carolina traders. *SCCHJ*, 1736–39, pp. 113, 115, 119, 125.

5. Mackay to Trustees, August 10, 1734, *CRG*, 20:69; Mssrs. Jenys and Baker to Trustees, September 6, 1734, ibid., 79 (flags).

6. Mackay to Causton, March 27, 1735, *GT*, 48; deposition of William Williams, July 4, 1735, ibid., 51.

7. Mackay to Trustees, March 23, 1735, ibid., 46–47. In 1736 Hopoya Hadjo, "King" of the Abeikas, told South Carolina leaders that Mackay "had built a Fort there by his Consent, and had outdone him, but that whoever shall build another Fort on his Land shall be a better Man than he." *South Carolina Gazette*, July 10, 1736. See also Brian M. Wood, "Fort Okfuskee: A British Challenge to Fort Toulouse aux Alibamons," in *Fort Toulouse Studies*, ed. Gregory A. Waselkov, Auburn University Archeological Monograph 9 (Montgomery: Auburn University at Montgomery, 1984).

8. Mackay to Causton, March 27, 1735, *GT*, 48 (emphasis in original); Causton to Mackay, April 10, 1735 (list), ibid., 52–53. Tomochichi's list of invitees included nineteen Lower Creek leaders from nine towns. For the Upper Creeks he specified only eight from four towns and from the others, "each One."

9. Spalding, *Oglethorpe in America*, 54–57; John Pitts Corry, *Indian Affairs in Georgia, 1732–1756* (Philadelphia: G. S. Ferguson, 1936), 55–62. See also George Chalmers, *Opinions of Eminent Lawyers on Various Points of English Jurisprudence, Chiefly concerning the Colonies, Fisheries and Commerce* (London: Reed and Hunter, 1814; 1971 reprint), 298–99.

10. Mackay to Causton, March 27, 1735, *GT*, 48–49; Mackay to Oglethorpe, March 29, 1735, ibid., 49–51; Causton to Trustees, June 20, 1735, ibid., 56–58, and note 27. See also Ivers, *British Drums*, 41–42, 47–48. Earlier I identified Licko with Lika (Lique, Liquor, etc.), Ouseechee mico since 1717, probably in error. See *GT*, 368 n. 21.

11. Egmont, *Journal*, 99 (decision to return), 114 ("notorious"); Martyn to Broughton, January 2, 1735, *CRG*, 29:110–11; Verelst to Mackay, July 18, 1735, ibid., 75; Martyn to Mackay, October 10, 1735, ibid., 110. Mackay later claimed salary due him as Indian agent through February 27, 1736, when Oglethorpe relieved him. The Trustees refused to pay him, arguing rather disingenuously that Oglethorpe had no authority to appoint such an agent prior to the 1735 Indian act. Ibid., 2:414, 456.

12. Mackay to Causton, July 8, 1734, *CRG*, 20:61 ("3 or 4"). Jones's legal wrangle with the elder Robert Parker over this lot indicates that it was an unusually valuable one. Ibid., 64, 122–23, 438.

13. Mackay to Causton, July 8, 1734, ibid., 60–61. The "Taloupouse King" was probably Tickhonaby, the *mico* of Tallassee. On Tickhonaby see Steven C. Hahn, "The Mother of Necessity: Carolina, the Creek Indians, and the Making of a New Order in the American Southeast, 1670–1763," in Ethridge and Hudson, *Transformation of the Southeastern Indians*, 109–14. Chahaway, the "Dog King" (Ifa Mico) of Upper Eufala, had actually gone up with Jones to persuade Choctaws to come. *GT*, 38, 47, 53.

14. Talks with Red Shoes's party of Choctaws, July 1, 1734, *GT*, 36–37.

15. Talks with Choctaws, July 7, 1734, ibid., 37–38; Eveleigh to Oglethorpe, October 19, 1734, *CRG*, 20:86–90. Eveleigh reported (89) that Jones "was in hopes of getting them remove[d] up to the Cohawhabee Hatchee or Petticah Hatchee being forty and Six miles [west] from the Coosah River."

16. *CRG*, 20:60–61, 70, 89, 122; [Thomas Christie], *A Description of Georgia by a Gentleman who has Resided there upwards of Seven Years, and was One of the First Settlers* (London: C. Corbett, 1741), 6. Christie identified the Choctaw spokesman as Red Shoes and provided a version of his July 1 speech that adds a few details, including the preference for Georgia over South Carolina.

17. Richard White, "Red Shoes: Warrior and Diplomat," in *Struggle and Survival in Colonial America*, ed. David G. Sweet and Gary B. Nash (Berkeley: University of California Press, 1981), 49–68; Woods, *French-Indian Relations*, 113, 118–19, 125–26. Following French sources, Wood says the presents came from South Carolina, but they must have been acquired in Georgia. Eveleigh's letter of August 12 from Charles Town indicates that the Choctaws held to their decision not to visit there. *CRG*, 20:70. Red Shoes did lead a Choctaw delegation to Charles Town in 1738, "and made the first solemn Treaty of Peace and Commerce with the Government of So. Carolina." Atkin, *Report*, 72.

18. Christie to Oglethorpe, December 14, 1734, *CRG*, 20:123, 2:124 (Musgrove grant). The path meandered, for it was twice as far by land as by water.

19. Eveleigh to Oglethorpe, November 20, 1734, ibid., 20:106.

20. Egmont, *Journal*, 215, 219, 242 ("poisoned"), 252 ("running naked"); *A True and Historical Narrative*, 57; *CRG*, 20:88 (Eveleigh). On June 9, 1733, Oglethorpe reported that he had named Skee's brother "Captain of the first Militia Company of the Indian allies" and Skee captain of the second company. He added that "their pay is one Bushell of corn per month for each man while we employ them in War or hunting, a Gun at their

first [en]listing and a Blanket per Annum." *GT*, 17. Causton's January 16, 1735, letter to the Trustees is the main source on the imbroglio that followed Skee's death. His brother had died the previous May. Ibid., 39–42.

21. 1733 treaty, *GT*, 16 (Article 5).

22. In 1737 four members of the jury, supported by nearly fifty signers, claimed that the verdict had been "extorted by Menaces from Thomas Causton." Reese, *Clamorous Malcontents*, 320–21; Christie to Oglethorpe, April 6, 1734 (extract), in *South Carolina Gazette*, April 20, 1734; Causton to Trustees, February 19, 1741, Lane, *Oglethorpe's Georgia*, 2:563.

23. Martyn to Savannah magistrates, March 17, 1735, Reese, *Clamorous Malcontents*, 318–20 ("it is Cruel" at 319); Causton to Oglethorpe, March 24, 1735, Lane, *Oglethorpe's Georgia*, 1:141 (accuses Gordon).

24. Trustees to Savannah magistrates, March 17, 1735, *CRG*, 32:112–14 ("Injustice" at 113); Egmont, *Journal*, 78–79 (Watson's license), 104 (Causton promoted); *CRG*, 2:90 ("to pacify"). The gift authorized for Skee's family included "6 guns, 100 flints, 6 Mantles of Blew or striped Duffils, 6 Yards of Strouds, a Pound of Beads, a pint of red Inkle, and some large Needles and blew sewing thread for the Women, 6 Hatchets, 2 Indian brass Kettles, 12 knives and some Whet Stones and also some Paint." Martyn to Causton, March 17, 1735, ibid., 29:48. Causton gave Mary money to buy another Indian slave, which somehow did not happen. In 1739 Oglethorpe gave her a German servant "in lieu of her Indian Servant killed in the Dispute with Mr. Watson." Ibid., 2:327, 20:451–52, and 22, pt. 2:290–91.

25. Fisher, "Mary Musgrove," 72–73; Verelst to Savannah magistrates, May 15, 1735, *CRG*, 29:60 ("sole Licence"); Causton to Oglethorpe, July 7, 1735, ibid., 20:439 ("Millitary manner"); *GCCB*, 23 (Musgrove's will). The 1735 will is paraphrased in a 1750 deed of sale for the property. The Musgrove relocation began shortly after the road being cut by Williams's slaves reached the cowpen in January. On April 2 Causton reported that "Musgrove is wholly at the Cow Penn." *CRG*, 20:165 (road), 306 ("Musgrove"), 452 (storehouse). Recalling the Lower Creek visit to Savannah in early June, Causton refers to the Indians' arrival "at Musgrove's old House." *GT*, 56.

26. Egmont, *Journal*, 109, 308; Tomochichi to the Trustees, February 24, 1735, *GT*, 44; N. Jones to Oglethorpe, July 6, 1735, *CRG*, 20:430 (with text of notice). Boltzius later reported that "I was present in Savannah when Mr. Causton agreed with Mrs. Musgrove to persuade the so-called king, Tomo-Chachi, to exchange his and some other Indian's present residence . . . for other land." Since the Indians simply moved from one end of the Yamacraw tract to the other, there was no "exchange" of land. Urlsperger, *Detailed Reports*, 4:208. In 1737 the blazed trees marked the southern boundary of the tract, but it was now separated from Savannah by "the Rails," a post-and-rail fence. *GT*, 86.

27. Causton to Mackay, April 10, 1735, *GT*, 52–53 (list); "Migration Legend" talk, *CRG*, 20:381–87. The Trustees received the buffalo skin in August. Egmont, *Journal*, 103. See also Steven C. Hahn, "The Cussita Migration Legend: History, Ideology, and the Politics of Mythmaking," in *Light on the Path: The Anthropology and History of*

the Southeastern Indians, ed. Thomas J. Pluckhahn and Robbie Ethridge (Tuscaloosa: University of Alabama Press, 2006), 57–93. Tomochichi's original list not only favored Lower Creeks over Upper Creeks but favored Hitchiti-speakers over Muskogee-speakers. Of the nineteen Lower Creek leaders he named, only five were from Coweta and Cussita; the others were from the non-Muskogee-speaking towns further down the river. He wished to invite two leaders from each town with one exception: Apalachicola, his Hitchiti-speaking hometown, was allotted three. This is one illustration of continuing rivalry between the two language groups among the Lower Creeks. Wright sees the language difference as part of a larger pattern, arguing that by the eighteenth century "a new moiety dualism based largely on ethnic distinctions," especially the divide between Muskogee-speakers and Hitchiti-speakers, had evolved among the Creeks. This seems to go much beyond the evidence. Wright, *Creeks and Seminoles*, 14–18.

28. Causton to Trustees, June 20, 1735, *GT*, 55–58. Christie indicated that he and the other magistrates had required "the Examination of Licka the Indian and Jehu Barton," Mackay's interpreter. He did not report the results. Christie to Trustees, July 6, 1735, *CRG*, 20:432.

29. The three laws are in *CRG*, 1:31–42 (Indians), 44–48 (rum), and 50–52 (black slaves). Ibid., 198 (Trustee approval), 2:73 (royal approval). In general, see Spalding, *Oglethorpe in America*, 48–51.

30. *CRG*, 1:31–42 (Indian act); Egmont, *Journal*, 109 (Oglethorpe's appointments). The South Carolina and Georgia Indian acts are conveniently available for comparison in *EAID*, 16:263–70 and 363–69. Changes include omission in the Georgia act of Articles 17, 18, 21, and 22 of the Carolina act. There was a supplementary Carolina act in 1733 (ibid., 271–72), but this was not reflected in the Georgia act.

31. Egmont, *Journal*, 72, 78 ("he proposes"), 94, 101–2; Egmont, *Diary*, 2:181, 191, 196 ("we named").

32. Trustees' petition to the king in Council, [December 8, 1735], S.C./P.R.O., 17:474; *CRG*, 1:239; Egmont, *Diary*, 2:204 (most quotes); Egmont, *Journal*, 117–18 ("forbid"). The petition was approved by the Board of Trade, but not until November 30, 1736. *JBT*, 7:81, 147–48. See also *APC: Col.*, 3:485–86.

33. Egmont, *Diary*, 2:284 ("orders and instructions"), 168 (£1,000); Newcastle to Broughton, November 19, 1735, S.C./P.R.O., 17:463 ("given Directions"); Egmont, *Journal*, 99 ("guns").

34. Oglethorpe to Broughton, February 15, 1736 (extract), *SCCHJ*, 1736–39, p. 103. When Oglethorpe met with representatives of the Spanish governor the following May, he evidently showed them his 1735 instructions. According to Arredondo, Oglethorpe displayed "orders to settle all the territory yet unsettled." Herbert Bolton and Mary Ross, ed. and trans., *Arredondo's Historical Proof of Spain's Title to Georgia* (Berkeley: University of California Press, 1925), 190. The 1738 instructions are in C.R.G., 35:140–43.

35. "Journal of Benjamin Ingham" (1735–36), in Reese, *Our First Visit*, 175–76. Moore's account is "Voyage," 102–3; Wesley's is in *GT*, 59–60. Oglethorpe presumably knew that encroachment on Yuchi lands was about to take a step forward. The Salzburgers

at Ebenezer had long since become disillusioned about the barrenness of their soil. With Oglethorpe's tacit approval, on February 17 Baron von Reck began a new settlement at Red Bluff, near (but not on) the river a few miles up. The original settlers soon relocated to the new site, dubbed New Ebenezer. Jones, *Salzburger Saga*, 29; Jones, "Secret Diary," esp. 86–92.

36. Oglethorpe to Trustees, March 16, 1736, *GT*, 61 (full text in *CRG*, 21:103–5).

37. Ibid.; Oglethorpe to Newcastle, April 17, 1736, *GT*, 62 ("on the point"); Moore, "Voyage," 121–22 ("in pursuance" and "pretence"). Moore records a speech Tomochichi made to Oglethorpe declaring that "all on this side that river . . . is our ground." Moore indicates that was on April 21; perhaps so, but that speech makes more sense during the reconnaissance a month earlier. Ibid., 124. Moore sprinkles numerous dates throughout his account, but some are clearly mistaken. For example, he says an incident involving an unmarked Spanish vessel occurred on June 8; Oglethorpe described the same incident a month earlier. Cf. ibid., 139; Oglethorpe to Trustees, May 18, 1736, *CRG*, 21:159. Carolinians were sure that early in the century English possession extended down to the St. Johns. In 1734 Eveleigh suggested to Oglethorpe that "his Majesty should build a fort on the North Side of the River St. Jeuan, . . . to Ascertain the Southern Limitts of His American Empire." Oglethorpe doubtless heard from Carolina sources that detachments from the king's independent company "possessed as far as 30 degrees 2 minutes, untill after the year 1720." Eveleigh to Oglethorpe, November 7, 1734, ibid., 101; Oglethorpe, "Memorial, relating to Georgia," August 18, 1737, C.R.G., 35:115.

38. Oglethorpe to Newcastle, April 17, 1736, *GT*, 62–63; same to same, [July 3, 1736], S.C./P.R.O., 18:40–44, quote at 42. The second letter is undated but bears this clerk's notation: "No Date but received with a Letter dated 3 July 1736." Related Oglethorpe statements: to Trustees, March 16, 1736, *GT*, 61; to Broughton, March 28, 1736, *CRG*, 21:121–22.

39. Oglethorpe to Newcastle, April 17, 1736, *GT*, 62–63. The small fort was built on St. Georges Point, a southward projection of St. George Island. On the way back in April, Oglethorpe met the mutinous garrison, which had abandoned the post, and forced them to return. That same month he sent another force led by Captain Christian Hermsdorf "to build another Fort upon Saint George's Point." Instead of building anew, Hermsdorf "chose the old Fort which was erected by Sir Walter Raleigh's first colony when Sir Francis Drake took Augustine" (in 1586). Oglethorpe also wrote Newcastle that "Sir Francis Drake erected Fort Saint George." Oglethorpe to Trustees, May 18, 1736, *CRG*, 21:160 (mutinous garrison and "chose"); same to Newcastle, April 17, 1736, *GT*, 63 ("to build"); same to same, April 2, 1738, C.O.5/654, f. 131v ("Drake erected").

40. Oglethorpe, "Memorial of the King's Title to Georgia," April 1736, *GT*, 63–65. Regarding the 1705 date, Oglethorpe explicitly referred to Creek conquests at the expense of the Spaniards that year, but surely also had a 1705 document in mind. See "THE HUMBLE SUBMISSION OF SEVERAL Kings, Princes, Generals, etc. TO THE Crown of ENGLAND," August 15, 1705, *EAID*, 13:90–91. Better informed about the Cabot voyages later, Oglethorpe credited the earliest English discovery to "Sir John Cabot and Sir Sebastian his Son." Oglethorpe, "Memorial, relating to Georgia," August

18, 1737, C.R.G., 35:115. On the conventional defense of English title, see Juricek, "English Territorial Claims."

41. Recent scholarship on these difficult questions is largely the work of Canadians. On the unchallengeable prerogative, see McNeil, *Common Law Aboriginal Title*, 133. McNeil observes that "the classification of the American colonies is one of the great unresolved questions of American legal history." Ibid., 246 n. 7. The fundamental question is whether American territories were supposed to be acquired by conquest (or cession, typically a surrender under duress) or by settlement. McNeil concludes that "classification as conquered or ceded was probably more likely in earlier times, due to the influence of *Calvin's Case* [1608]." Ibid., 119 n. 48. Stronger Canadian opinions to the same effect: Mark D. Walters, "*Mohegan Indinas* v. *Connecticut* (1705–1773) and the Legal Status of Aboriginal Customary Laws and Government in British North America," *Osgoode Hall Law Journal* 33 (1995): 792–93; and Lester, "Primitivism versus Civilization," 354–59. Similar views by U.S. scholars: Juricek, "English Territorial Claims," 7–8, 16–18; Mary Sarah Bilder, *The Transatlantic Constitution: Colonial Legal Culture and the Empire* (Cambridge: Harvard University Press, 2004), 36–39; and Daniel J. Hulsebosch, *Constituting Empire: New York and the Transformation of Constitutionalism in the Atlantic World, 1664–1830* (Chapel Hill: University of North Carolina Press, 2005), 24–26, 57. An Australian makes the strongest case: Gavin Loughton, "Calvin's Case and the Origins of the Rule Governing 'Conquest' in English Law," *Australian Journal of Legal History* 8 (2004), 143–80.

42. On the New York precedent, see Richard Aquila, *The Iroquois Restoration: Iroquois Diplomacy on the Colonial Frontier, 1701–1754* (Lincoln: University of Nebraska Press, 1997), 66, 106, 113. *APC: Col.*, 4:496 (November 23, 1761; "Dominion but not"); McNeil, *Common Law Aboriginal Title*, 108 ("fundamental distinction").

43. Oglethorpe, "Memorial of the King's Title," *GT*, 64. He made the point more clearly in 1739: "The Trust is in possession in Behalf of his Majesty, from the Garrison of the Okfushees in the upper Creek Nation . . . down to the Gulph of Mexico by the Appelachees, and from thence to Amelia." Oglethorpe, "Introductory Discourse to the State of the Colony of Georgia," October 11, 1739, Egmont Papers, 14204, pp. 123–35, quote at 133.

44. Oglethorpe to Broughton, March 28, 1736, *CRG*, 21:122; Oglethorpe, "Memorial," *GT*, 64.

45. Ivers, *British Drums*, 62, 78, and 56 (map); Oglethorpe to Trustees, May 18, 1736, *CRG*, 21:160; same to Newcastle, April 17, 1736, *GT*, 63 ("to prevent"); John Brownfield to Trustees, April 9, 1736, *CRG*, 21:144 ("directly opposite"); Egmont, *Diary*, 2:286–87 (Brownfield letter), 313 ("had erected"); Egmont, *Journal*, 171 (Brownfield commendation).

46. Egmont, *Journal*, 143–44 ("impossible"); James R. McCain, *Georgia as a Proprietary Province* (Boston: R. G. Badger, 1917), 73–74.

47. Oglethorpe to the Trustees, July 26, 1736, *GT*, 74; Egmont, *Diary*, 2:282.

48. *CRG*, 1:255–57, 21:147–48 (Vernon and Tower); Oglethorpe to Tower, April 17, 1736, *CGHS*, 3:31. The letter to Tower enclosed the memorial on the king's title and

said that a letter to Vernon enclosed the report to Newcastle. The April 1 letter came from Captain Charles Dempsey, Oglethorpe's emissary to St. Augustine, who said he was following Oglethorpe's orders when he told the Spanish governor that Oglethorpe had "a power to draw all the Militia of the Province down upon occasion." It was largely this claim that persuaded the Trustees that Oglethorpe "had received some instructions or powers from his Majesty before going over which were not communicated to us." Egmont, *Diary*, 2:282. The documents are found in Egmont Papers, 14201, p. 365ff., and C.R.G., 35:31ff.

49. Egmont, *Journal*, 169–70 ("strangers" and "concealed"); Newcastle to Oglethorpe, July 2, 1736, C.R.G., 35:56. Newcastle said, not very persuasively, that what "must be meant" by the orders the Trustees complained of was "the Directions" he had sent Broughton the previous October 10 and November 19. Those letters are in S.C./P.R.O., 17:378–80 and 463. Newcastle directed Broughton to (1) respect the Georgia Indian act by requiring Carolina traders operating in Georgia to secure Georgia licenses, (2) consider redeploying the independent company to St. Simons, and (3) consider sending Negroes to Frederica to help build the fort. Newcastle told Oglethorpe that these measures had been "suggested by you" and that "most" were only recommendations.

50. Oglethorpe to Broughton, February 15, 1736 (extract), *SCCHJ*, 1736–39, p. 103; Oglethorpe to Trustees, March 16, 1736, *CRG*, 21:104 ("ninety"); Oglethorpe to Newcastle, April 17, 1736, *GT*, 63; Oglethorpe, "Memorial of the King's Title to Georgia," ibid., 63–65.

51. Egmont, *Journal*, 170 ("because thereby"), 176 ("expressing" and Newcastle letter), 189, 207 ("We confine"); Egmont, *Diary*, 2:284–86 ("we shall" at 286). Carolinians likewise concluded that "the Trustees of Georgia have no Power or Jurisdiction, save only within the Boundaries limited by their Charter." *SCCHJ*, 1736–39, p. 74.

52. Georgia charter, June 9, 1732, *CRG*, 1:18; Egmont, *Journal*, 147 ("Clothogotheo"); Brownfield to Trustees, April 9, 1736, *CRG*, 21:144. The Satilla could easily be mistaken for a branch of the Altamaha, because about twenty miles inland it bends sharply northward. Its northernmost tributary, Little Satilla Creek, arises within five miles of the Altamaha.

53. Oglethorpe, "Introductory Discourse," 123 ("Southernmost mouth"); Oglethorpe to "My Lord" (Newcastle), April 2, 1738, C.O.5/654, f. 131 ("upon that Part"). Ettinger identifies the recipient of the 1738 letter as Newcastle. He also contends (wrongly, it seems) that Oglethorpe deliberately conflated Fort King George and Fort St. George. Ettinger, *Oglethorpe*, 204–5. With the onset of war with Spain, the British had no motive to correct Oglethorpe's error. At least two of the tracts the Trustees published during the war perpetuated it. In 1741 Benjamin Martyn wrote that Amelia Island "is in 30 Deg. 30 Min." Martyn, "Impartial Enquiry," 157. The following year another Trustee tract opens by stating that the mouth of "the most Southern Stream of the Alatamaha . . . is [at] 30½ Deg." "A State of the Province of Georgia" (London, 1742), in Reese, *Clamorous Malcontents*, 3–20, at 3.

54. Lanning, *Diplomatic History of Georgia*, 45–48. Rightly seeing the agreement as a

delaying move by Oglethorpe, the Spanish government promptly repudiated it. Moore to Verelst, September 20, 1736, *CRG*, 21:226 ("the Spaniards"). A copy of the Spanish original of the 1736 agreement (dated October 11) is in C.R.G., 35:62–69; an English translation is in ibid., 57–61.

55. The 1739 treaty, written by Oglethorpe, fully endorses Lower Creek claims; see *GT*, 96 (claims and "Tenants"). See also Oglethorpe, "Introductory Discourse," 133; Dempsey to Oglethorpe, n.d., C.R.G., 35:31–33; Oglethorpe to Dempsey, April 10, 1736, ibid., 37–42; deposition of William Horton, April 13, 1736, ibid., 47; Jones, "Von Reck's Second Report," 327–28. In general, refer to John Tate Lanning, "Colonial International Relations: Oglethorpe and the Theory of Effective Occupation," chap. 13 of *Colonial Hispanic America*, ed. A. Curtis Wilgus (Washington, D.C.: George Washington University Press, 1936).

56. J. H. Parry, *The Spanish Seaborne Empire* (New York: Knopf, 1966), chaps. 7, 9–10.

57. In general, see Anthony Pagden, *Lords of all the World: Ideologies of Empire in Spain, Britain and France c.1500–c.1800* (New Haven: Yale University Press, 1995). Regarding America, Pagden says, "the Spaniards were overwhelmingly concerned with rights over people, the British with rights over things, in this case land" (78).

58. Oglethorpe to Charles Dempsey, April 10, 1736, C.R.G., 35:41 ("only Allies"); Moore, "Voyage," 151 ("subjects"), 111 ("Creek English"); Oglethorpe, "Introductory Discourse," 123 ("their Sovereign"); Oglethorpe to Newcastle, April 2, 1738, C.O.5/654, f. 131 ("Vassals"); same to Trustees, March 16, 1736, *CRG*, 21:104 ("Confederate"). In Europe there was a profound difference between a king's "subjects," who resided on his territory and were subject to his laws, and treaty-bound outsiders who were merely his "allies." Attempts to apply these traditional status terms to Indians led to confusion. On October 6, 1736, the Trustees (minus Oglethorpe) declared that "the Indians are only confederates, not subjects of England." Egmont, *Diary*, 2:300. Two weeks later they reversed themselves: they now avowed that they "had not directed any Settlement to be made but within the Limits of His Majesty's Charter, and if those Indians inhabit within the same, they are his Majesty's Subjects." C.R.G., 35:181. The same year, Carolina legislators disagreed: "They have been treated with as Allies but not as Subjects of the Crown of Great-Britain." Most British officials, including Oglethorpe, would have agreed that more than mere residence on territory claimed by the king of Great Britain was required to make Indians British subjects, but there was no agreement on what exactly was required. Thus on July 26, 1736, Oglethorpe wrote to an unnamed lord that the Chickasaws "submitted themselves to his Majesty King George the first and were declared his Subjects by General Nicholson." (Francis Nicholson was in South Carolina as governor in 1721–24.) *CRG*, 21:196. Oglethorpe's June talk with the Chickasaws begins: "The Chickesaws first produced their Commissions, whereby it appeared they had been declared Subjects to the King of Great Britain by the Governours of Carolina." *GT*, 75. So did Oglethorpe think the Chickasaws became subjects because (1) they had submitted, (2) an English governor declared they had done so, or (3) they accepted

commissions that an English governor issued to them in the king's name? Egmont reflected Oglethorpe's ambiguity: the Chickasaws were both "our allies and his Majesty's subjects." Egmont, *Diary*, 2:312. So did Moore: "The Creek Indians were allies or rather subjects to the crown of Great Britain." Moore, "Voyage," 121. The Mohegan case—resulting in judgments in 1705, 1738, 1743, and 1773—was the great legal case that touched on the status of Indian communities within the colonies. In the end, their status remained ambiguous, neither ordinary subjects nor ordinary allies. Walters, "*Mohegan Indians* v. *Connecticut* (1705–1773)," esp. 793–95, 806, 802 n. 66, and 812.

59. Oglethorpe to the Trustees, July 26, 1736, *GT*, 74.

60. Talks with the Lower Creeks: "First Audience," June 27, 1736, ibid., 68–69 ("the Chiefs" and "who is to succeed"); talks with the Lower and Upper Creeks: "Second Audience," July 3, 1736, ibid., 70–74 ("Coat" and "I was" at 74).

61. Ibid., 74 ("Islands of the Sea").

62. C. Wesley, *Journal*, 65; J. Wesley, *Journal*, 236 (June 27) and 239 (July 1). Although Charles's published journal omits an entry for June 27, he probably took the minutes for that meeting too. The denomination of the meeting as an "audience," a term rarely or never used by anyone but the Wesley brothers to describe an Indian conference, is strong evidence of Charles's hand.

63. *GT*, 74 (July 3 and 26); *CRG*, 3:387 (Martyn). Oglethorpe's March 16 report to the Trustees about dealings with the Yamacraws likewise mentions only islands. *GT*, 61.

64. Oglethorpe to Broughton, March 28, 1736, *CRG*, 21:122; Oglethorpe to Trustees, July 26, 1736, *GT*, 74 ("Islands"); Oglethorpe to "My Lord," July 26, 1736, *CRG*, 21:196 ("Lands"); *GT*, 62 ("in Possession"), 64 ("St. Johns").

65. *GT*, 96 (1739 treaty).

66. *South Carolina Gazette*, July 10, 1736 (Hopoya Hadjo); Oglethorpe to "My Lord," *CRG*, 21:196 ("deny"); Egmont, *Journal*, 214 (Wesley). Presumably the Abeika leader had consented in the treaty of 1717 and/or 1721.

67. Oglethorpe to Trustees, July 26, 1736, *GT*, 74; C. Wesley, *Journal*, 98–99; Egmont, *Diary*, 2:312–13 (December 8), 318 ("papers"). A few weeks later Oglethorpe himself told Trustees that Fort St. George was built "to keep the Spaniards from interrupting his building a Fort at Frederica." Egmont, *Journal*, 226.

68. *CRG*, 4:666, 6:148; Oglethorpe, "Introductory Discourse," 125. Relying largely on a 1715 map, Worth argues that Yuchi cohabitation with the Lower Creeks began earlier. Worth, "The Lower Creeks," 285.

69. Oglethorpe, "Introductory Discourse," 125; *CRG*, 4 (Supp.):86 ("chusing"). See also Neill, "Galphin Trading Post Site," esp. 47–48.

70. Oglethorpe to Trustees, March 16, 1736, *CRG*, 21:104.

71. Oglethorpe to Trustees, May 18, 1736, *GT*, 65–66 (most quotes); same to Causton, March 17, 1736, *CRG*, 21:126 ("dislodged").

72. Baron von Reck's account of Oglethorpe's meeting with the Yuchis, May 11, 1736, *GT*, 65; Oglethorpe to Trustees, early June 1736, ibid., 67 ("to help me"); same to Stephens, September 25, 1741, ibid., 104 ("affectionate Subjects").

73. Martyn to Rev. John Boltzius, June 10, 1736, *CRG*, 29:152; Martyn to Oglethorpe, June 10, 1736, ibid., 137; Oglethorpe, "Introductory Discourse," 125.

74. Egmont, *Journal*, 272–73 (Tanner quotes).

75. Oglethorpe to Trustees, March 8, 1739, *CRG*, 22, pt. 2:109 ("Key").

76. Oglethorpe, "Introductory Discourse," 125 ("was laid out"); Oglethorpe to Trustees, ca. early June 1736, *GT*, 68 ("offer to build"); Stephens, *Journal*, 1:243–44. In June the Trustees received a March 29 letter from Charles Dempsey in St. Augustine, who reported that the Spanish governor "complained that 300 of our white men, with a considerable number of Indians, had entered the Province of the Uches, which belonged to his master, with intention to build a fort there." Egmont, *Diary*, 2:282.

77. Ivers, *British Drums*, 66–67, 75–77; Cashin, *The Story of Augusta*, 9–11. The Carolinians apparently destroyed an earlier outpost, probably the one Yuchis and the Spanish governor had complained about. When Charles Wesley met Oglethorpe in England in January 1737, Oglethorpe told him that the Carolinians "had burned Augusta." C. Wesley, *Journal*, 110.

78. *GT*, 149 (Malatchi, 1747); *DRIA*, II, 67 (Malatchi, 1755); Eveleigh to Verelst, July 20, 1736, *CRG*, 21:179–80. Presumably Oglethorpe decided that the Lower Creeks were the proper parties to approach about Augusta because he supposed that Yuchi land gave way to Creek land below the point where the Creek path crossed the river.

79. Oglethorpe to Trustees, July 26, 1736, *GT*, 74. This rebuff could not have taken Oglethorpe by surprise. Two years earlier Mackay had told the Creeks that "a Castle was to be built on the Alatamaha." They protested that this would be "contrary to Agreements with Carolina," meaning the treaties of 1717 and 1721. Causton to Trustees, January 20, 1735, *CRG*, 21:71. On Oglethorpe's survey up the Altamaha, see Moore to Verelst, September 20, 1736, ibid., 226 ("several days"), and *South Carolina Gazette*, October 9, 1736.

80. *CRG*, 4:675 (Stephens); Martyn, "Impartial Enquiry," 156–57. Martyn's phrase on Okfuskee fort was borrowed from Oglethorpe. See Oglethorpe, "Introductory Discourse," 133.

81. In addition to many prohibitions from the British government, nearly all of the colonies enacted laws forbidding private land purchases from Indians. See Harris, *Origin of the Land Tenure System*, chap. 11.

82. Eveleigh to Oglethorpe, November 20, 1734, *CRG*, 20:106; Martyn to Eveleigh, May 1, 1735, ibid., 29:66.

83. The earliest invocation of "extinguishment" noticed occurred in 1767: New York judges then declared that an alleged Indian title "hath been long since extinguished." Oscar Handlin and Irving Mark, eds., "Chief Daniel Nimham *v.* Roger Morris, Beverly Robinson, and Philip Philipse—An Indian Land Case in Colonial New York, 1765–1767," *Ethnohistory* 11 (1964): 242. Several 1771 examples are cited in Joseph H. Smith, *Appeals to the Privy Council from the American Plantations* (New York: Columbia University Press, 1950), 439 nn. 133 and 134.

84. As time went on the English became less deferential to the Creek notion of

mutual gift giving and more influenced by Scottish ideas. The fraudulent Graham deed of 1751 is the first "official" land cession document that mentions valuable consideration paid to Indians. *GT*, 219. The 1758 Mucklassee deed has the Creeks ceding land "in consideration of the great Love, and Esteem we bear the English Nation, and of the many presents and other favours we have from time to time received from them." Ibid., 277. Not until 1763 did a treaty with the Creeks state that they gave land "in consideration" of something they had received. The Augusta treaty of 1763 has the Creeks ceding land "in consideration of the great marks of clemency and friendship extended to us." *EAID*, 5:297. The last English treaties with the Creeks, those of 1771 and 1773, mention "valuable consideration" for lands. *GFT*, 402 (1771), 119 (1773).

85. *GT*, 74 (Chigelli); Eveleigh to Verelst, October 16, 1736, *CRG*, 21:214.

86. Stephens, *Journal*, 1:92, 219, 249.

87. Talks with the Chickasaws, July 12–13, 1736, *GT*, 75–77; Oglethorpe to "My Lord," July 26, 1736, *CRG*, 21:196 ("have been here"). The presents Oglethorpe gave the Chickasaws came to about £50 (£367 in South Carolina currency), enough for about as much powder and shot as they could carry. Ibid., 2:457–58.

88. Causton, "Humble Petition," November 22, 1739 (excerpt), in Edward J. Cashin, ed., *Setting Out to Begin a New World* (Savannah: Library of Georgia, 1995), 52.

Chapter 4. Faltering Diplomacy with the Creeks and War with Spain

1. Egmont, *Diary*, 2:326 ("his account"), 331; Egmont, *Journal*, 226 ("to keep"). Oglethorpe went public with his claim of an extreme southern boundary in a tract he wrote in late 1737 or early 1738. Implying that the English he referred to were those of Georgia, he declared that "the English now possess the sea-coast, from the river St. John's, in 30 degrees 21 minutes north latitude." Oglethorpe, "A Continuation of the Present State of Carolina" (1739), in Oglethorpe, *Publications*, 246.

2. Ettinger, *Oglethorpe*, 192–200; Egmont, *Journal*, 231 ("National Affair"), 243, 255, 274, 285, 290 (£20,000); Egmont, *Diary*, 2:334 (£30,000 request); Ivers, *British Drums*, 78–79 (regiment). Walpole still hoped to find justification for British territorial claims that was strong enough to dissuade Spain from war. In January 1739 he orally asked the Trustees to provide him with a defense of "his Majestys Title to Georgia." Unwilling to handle this hot potato, they agreed "to make no return to Sir Roberts message either verbal, or in writing, other than that we were unable to say any thing in defence of his Majesties Title to Georgia, having never doubted but it was good, since his Majesty had granted a charter of it to us, and the Parliament confirmed the Grant." *CRG*, 5:107–9.

3. Reese, *Clamorous Malcontents*, 318 ("kept"); Egmont, *Journal*, 242 ("not only drank" and "Watson would").

4. Egmont, *Diary*, 2:368 ("laws of America"); Egmont, *Journal*, 242, 254 ("for allowing"), 274 ("returned"), 362. On June 6 the Trustees altered their instructions and directed that Watson be brought to trial after his release. Ibid., 275. They apparently changed their minds again, for he was never tried. Once free, Watson pressed claims

under the old partnership with John Musgrove against Mary and Jacob Matthews. Before he could bring suit, Jacob Matthews sued him. The action ended with a pale decision that Matthews owed Watson a paltry sum, £10 in currency. *CRG*, 4:22, 30, 94–95.

5. Stephens's journal for 1737 to 1741, all then known to exist, was published early last century in *CRG*, vols. 4 and 4 (Supp.). Its continuation from 1741 to 1745, generally unknown to scholars until 1946, was published in two volumes in 1958 and 1959. See the introduction to these volumes by E. Merton Coulter for information on Stephens.

6. *GCCB*, 23; J. Wesley, *Journal*, 297–98; "Journal of Benjamin Ingham," in Reese, *Our First Visit*, 181; Egmont, *Journal*, 308. See also Fisher, "Mary Musgrove," 80–82; and Dolores Boisfeuillet Floyd, *New Yamacraw and the Indian Mound Irene* (Savannah: Review Printing Co., 1936).

7. *CRG*, 4 (Supp.):218 (Stephens); "Journal of Thomas Causton," in Reese, *Our First Visit*, 254, 263 ("dined with me").

8. Egmont, *Journal*, 277 ("who Shewed"), 291 ("Priests orders"); J. Wesley, *Journal*, 408–9.

9. Egmont, *Diary*, 2:313 ("the Carolinians"), 496 ("more houses"); *CRG*, 22, pt. 1:73–74 (Stephens). In February 1741 Causton told the Trustees that "the present state of the town of Savannah is that the inhabitants are more than half gone, within this two years." Lane, *Oglethorpe's Georgia*, 2:555.

10. Egmont, *Diary*, 2:422–23 (quotes); J. Wesley, *Journal*, 320–21. Ingham left from Savannah on February 26. The Trustees held a two-hour debate on whether to reconsider tail-male tenure on April 12. Egmont supported an amendment to existing law allowing female inheritance "under certain restrictions." He argued that because female inheritance "was the general opinion in England as well as Georgia," the Trustees had already made many exceptions. "That at present we have been very just in taking care of the female successions, by a rule agreed to in our books, . . . but this was not law." If the Trustees had allowed some widows or other women to inherit, but not Mary Musgrove, Mary would surely have protested. Since she did not, it seems safe to assume that the Trustees eventually granted her petition. Interestingly, Oglethorpe vigorously opposed any change in the basic tenure law. He was temporarily successful, but within two weeks the Trustees began to modify tail-male tenure, and by the summer of the following year they had all but abandoned it. Egmont, *Diary*, 2:478–79, Egmont, *Journal*, 345–46; Spalding, *Oglethorpe in America*, 65–66.

11. Mary's memorial to Col. Alexander Heron, August 10, 1747, *GT*, 142–43 ("went to Ruin"); Ivers, *British Drums*, 143. According to Jacob's friends who wrote *A True and Historical Narrative* (147), he had "ten servants." In late 1734 John Musgrove had four. *CRG*, 32:186.

12. *CRG*, 4:49–50 ("to Mrs. Matthews" and "Spot of Land"), 4 (Supp.):218 ("no Good"), 5:590 ("450 acres").

13. Egmont, *Diary*, 2:472–74 ("all branches" and "not thoroughly"); [Oglethorpe and Martyn], *A State of the Province of Georgia*, in Reese, *Clamorous Malcontents*, 15 ("In the beginning"). On March 23 the Trustees also voted to eliminate "the annual certain

allowance made to the Indians under Tomachachi" in favor of a general Indian fund. Egmont, *Diary*, 2:473.

14. Egmont, *Journal*, 354–58 ("relating to" and "wastfull"), 373; *CRG*, 29:278 ("from England only"); ibid., 22, pt. 1:253 ("Northern" and "Southern"); Egmont Papers, 14209, p. 233.

15. *GT*, 87–88 (*Gentleman's Magazine* account). Christie's minutes are in ibid., 88–89, while the deposition Robert Williams gave fifteen years later is in ibid., 90–91.

16. Ibid., 87 (most quotes) and 88 ("his own Towns People").

17. Thomas Christie, Minutes of Oglethorpe's Talks with Headmen of Four Lower Creek Towns, October 13–14, 1738, *GT*, 89 (the forks); Mary's Memorial to Heron, August 10, 1747, ibid., 143 ("at the Request"). Mary added that she spent 1736 and 1737 "on her Lands, at or near Savannah." Storekeeper Thomas Jones provided what seems to be the best evidence on the date Mount Venture was founded, though he had the location wrong. On February 23, 1739, he wrote that Jacob Matthews had "lately gone to live at the Forks." *CRG*, 22, pt. 2:88. Although Mount Venture clearly was their main outpost, several later sources place Jacob or Mary at the forks, suggesting that they may have planted a subordinate outpost there. Ibid., 428; *GT*, 146. For comment by Oglethorpe, see *CRG*, 22, pt. 2:313; for that by Stephens, see ibid., 4:511.

18. *GT*, 87, 89.

19. Christie's minutes, ibid., 89; Egmont, *Diary*, 3:56 (£93).

20. Deposition of Robert Williams, August 17, 1753, *GT*, 90. Recall that the Yamacraw tract was often dubbed "the Indian Land."

21. Fisher concludes that Mary "adopted English customs in many areas of her life and eventually behaved more like a European than an Indian." Also, note her subtitle, "Creek Englishwoman." Most Creek-English mixed-bloods were Creeks with an overlay of English culture. Mary too probably started out this way, but by the time Georgia was founded she was predominantly English. Fisher, "Mary Musgrove," 538.

22. Ellis to Board of Trade, June 27, 1760, *CRG*, 28, pt. 1:254 ("about 4000"). Ellis said that the Savannah government had granted these four thousand acres to individuals "since 1752." Unless every last acre had been granted, four thousand acres probably underestimated the size of the tract.

23. For basic terminology, see *Black's Law Dictionary*, 4th ed. (St. Paul: West Publishing Co., 1951), "investiture," "livery of seisin," and "turf and twig." For an overview see Harris, *Origin of the Land Tenure System*, 43–45. For detailed background see McNeil, *Common Law Aboriginal Title*, chap. 2, "Possession and Title to Land in English Law" ("sufficiently close" at 6). McNeil adds a caution: "As is well known, the legal concept of possession is elusive, and defies precise description." Ibid., 6 n. 1.

24. "Journal of Thomas Causton," in Reese, *Our First Visit*, 248. Legal scholar Kent McNeil notes that "prior to 1845 a feoffee did not acquire a legal interest in the land until he had taken livery of seisin." McNeil, *Common Law Aboriginal Title*, 52. Horton doubtless knew that the Trustees made all of their Georgia land grants "with Livery and Seisin Indorsed," but apparently did not realize that this was some form of written

transfer. For examples of Trustee grants using this formula (including the one to John Musgrove), see *CRG*, 32:185–88.

25. *GT*, 90.

26. Ibid. Williams adds, implausibly, that "the Indians still Persisting to have it done," the magistrates "promissed to Comply therewith but wether the promise was performed or not this Deponent doth not know." It was not done, and Williams almost certainly knew that.

27. Harris, *Origin of the Land Tenure System*, chaps. 1–3, esp. pp. 1–3, 27–28, 43–45; Lester, "Primitivism versus Civilization," esp. 354–57.

28. Harris, *Origin of the Land Tenure System*, chap. 11; Francis Jennings, *The Invasion of America* (Chapel Hill: University of North Carolina Press, 1975), 128–30.

29. Eveleigh to Oglethorpe, November 20, 1734, *CRG*, 20:106; Martyn to Eveleigh, May 1, 1735, ibid., 29:66; Verelst to Eveleigh, August 30, 1735, ibid., 88 ("none can purchase"). See also Verelst to Stephens, December 14, 1741, ibid., 30:226–27.

30. Thomas Bosomworth, "A Narrative in Answer to the Charges . . . ," 1756, ibid., 27:168.

31. Petition to Trustees, December 9, 1738, in Reese, *Clamorous Malcontents*, 247–48. In June the Trustees also dismissed the two magistrates who had signed the December petition, Henry Parker and Robert Gilbert. Parker's signature on that petition was cited as a reason for his dismissal. Likewise, the fact that magistrate John Fallowfield had signed another such petition was given as the reason for his dismissal in February 1742. *CRG*, 30:235. Christie's identification with the Malcontents was only one reason the Trustees decided to replace him. Egmont noted that "Mr. Christie had more than once desired to be dismist [from] his Office of Recorder," and two weeks later the Trustees appointed him third bailiff. After serving less than a year as a magistrate (briefly as first bailiff), Christie was again removed from office. Ibid., 5:177, 192, 327.

32. *CRG*, 4:212 ("nothing passed"), 4 (Supp.):219 ("how far"). According to Williams, the witnesses included Stephens, Horton, "some of the Magistrates and Several other Gentlemen." *GT*, 90.

33. Oglethorpe to Verelst, June 15, 1739, *GT*, 92–93. This letter shows that by "the Creek Nation" he continued in 1739 to mean the Lower Creeks only. The vision of grand conclave was surely a Lower Creek creation, but Oglethorpe also heard about it from another source. In February a delegation of thirty-six Choctaws turned up in Savannah "very urgent" to see "the great Man." By the time Oglethorpe came up to Savannah three weeks later, the visitors had gone. They left a message urging him to prepare for a journey into the backcountry to confer with leaders of the major Southeastern nations. *CRG*, 4:279, 284, 294; ibid., 22, pt. 2:79–80, 87; ibid., 25:168; Corkran, *Creek Frontier*, 100; Spalding, *Oglethorpe in America*, 89.

34. Oglethorpe to Egmont, June 13, 1739, *GT*, 92 (most quotes); same to Newcastle, July 16, 1739, ibid., 93 (French threat); same to Trustees, July 16, 1739, *CRG*, 22, pt. 2:179 ("take Arms"). A year earlier Creek leaders had trekked to St. Marks to confer with a Spanish military officer dispatched from Havana. See Hahn, *Invention*, 177–79.

35. *GT*, 94, 98 ("forty Miles"); *CRG*, 4:552, 4 (Supp.):86; Stephens, *Journal*, 1:105; Mereness, *Travels in the American Colonies*, 221; *SCCHJ*, 1736–39, pp. 92, 118, 138. In March 1735 Mackay recorded a heated exchange with Apalachicola leader Cherokeelichi, a Hispanophile, at Wiggins's house in that town. *GT*, 49–50.

36. "A Ranger's Report on Travels with General Oglethorpe, 1739–1742," in Mereness, *Travels*, 218–22 ("Indian King" at 220); Eyres's account of Oglethorpe's journey, July 8–September 15, 1739, *GT*, 94–95. Eyres says that "Chicola" (Chigelli) was particularly active in the reception.

37. Oglethorpe's second treaty with the Lower Creeks at Coweta, August 11, 1739, *GT*, 95–97; Oglethorpe to Trustees, October 5, 1739, ibid., 99.

38. Treaty of August 11, 1739, ibid., 95. Chigelli was unquestionably the most influential leader of the Lower Creeks; Eyres called him "the Principal man in the Lower Nation." Ibid., 94. As with Brim and Malatchi, however, it is not absolutely clear that he was the *mico* of Coweta. The treaty listing of Lower Creek chiefs begins with "the Mico or Chief King of the Coweta Town Chickely Hiniah Mico of the said Town." Several things suggest that Chigelli was actually second on the list of chiefs, following the Coweta *mico*. First, in addition to the town *mico*, there were lower-ranking *micos* in a Creek Town. If Chegilli was "Hiniah Mico" (which sounds like a title for a "Heniha," a member of town chief's council), it is not likely that he was also the town *mico*. Second, in the remainder of the listing the phrase "of the same town" always follows a reference to several chiefs, not a single chief. Third, there are no commas between any of the named chiefs, so the lack of one before the word "Chickely" does not mean that he and "the Mico or Chief King" are one and the same. Finally, recall that in 1746 Mary introduced Chigelli as "Chickilli Tuskeestonnecah Mico War King or King of the Warriors in the Creek Indian Nation," not as King of Coweta. Ibid., 132.

39. Ibid., 96.

40. Oglethorpe to Verelst, September 5, 1739, ibid., 98. The only eighteenth-century maps that attempt to depict the boundaries of the 1739 cession are inaccurate in that they ignore the coastal strip between the Altamaha and the St. Johns. De Vorsey, *The Indian Boundary*, 172–73.

41. *GT*, 96.

42. Malatchi's speech to Heron, December 7, 1747, *GT*, 150. For Chigelli's similar account, see ibid., 134.

43. *CRG*, 4:422 ("Wall"); Oglethorpe to Trustees, October 5, 1739, *GT*, 98; same to same December 29, 1739, *CRG*, 22, pt. 2:287; Egmont Papers, 14204, p. 141 (October 20 plan).

44. *GT*, 94 ("the General" and "recommended"), 98 ("would probably").

45. Oglethorpe's accounting is not entirely clear, but it appears he paid traders £186.2.7 (nearly half to Wiggins) for presents. He later complained that they charged him twice what they normally charged Indians for the same goods. Additional expenses for the rental of horses and Wiggins's services as interpreter brought the total of direct expenses for the meeting to £234.15.2. The Trustees, having evidently included the cost

of subsequent dealings with the Cherokees, reckoned it at £529.0.9½. Egmont Papers, 14204, pp. 138–39; *CRG*, 2:317, and 22, pt. 2: 244.

46. *GT*, 99 ("above 1000"); *SCCHJ*, 1739–41, p. 176; *CRG*, 5:229; Oglethorpe to Trustees, October 11, 1739, ibid., 22, pt. 2:242 ("as they live"); Egmont Papers, 14204, p. 141 (October 20 plan).

47. Oglethorpe, "Introductory Discourse to the State of the Colony of Georgia," October 11, 1739 (date supplied by Egmont), Egmont Papers, 14204, pp. 123–35, at 123. On October 5 Oglethorpe wrote Verelst that he was about to write this account, which he wished the Trustees "to lay before Parliament." *GT*, 99. The Trustees also arranged to have it published. This Oglethorpe account (minus first-person references and some unfavorable news) constitutes the first half of *A State of the Province of Georgia* (London, 1742), in Reese, *Clamorous Malcontents*, 3–20. The first sentence repeats that the mouth of the Altamaha is in "30½ Deg." Benjamin Martyn (cited as a source on p. 14) probably edited Oglethorpe's contribution and wrote the rest.

48. *GT*, 103 ("to head them"); Ivers, *British Drums*, 147–48.

49. Verelst to Stephens, December 14, 1741, *CRG*, 30:227 ("only to those"); *SCCHJ*, 1739–41, p. 297 (not enslaved); ibid., 1741–42, p. 201 ("refused"); Ivers, *British Drums*, 148.

50. Captain Richard Kent to Oglethorpe, December 31, 1741, *GT*, 105 ("Emperor" and "white Men's King").

51. Mellon, "Christian Priber's Cherokee 'Kingdom of Paradise'"; Rennard Strickland, "Christian Gotelieb Priber: Utopian Precursor of the Cherokee Government," *Chronicles of Oklahoma* 48 (1970–71): 264–79; Verner Crane, "A Lost Utopia of the First American Frontier," *Sewanee Review* 27 (1919): 48–61; *South Carolina Gazette*, August 15, 1743.

52. *GT*, 102 ("main Body" and "if Chigellie").

53. Ibid. ("no Business"); *SCCHJ*, 1741–42, pp. 227 ("Mallachi"), 243 ("obliged"); Corkran, *Creek Frontier*, 106–7.

54. *CRG*, 1:416, 2:367–68 ("the County"), 408 ("the Whole"), 5:494. Oglethorpe had advocated a Savannah county since at least March 1735. Egmont, *Journal*, 78.

55. *CRG*, 5:287 ("totally excluded"), 548 (licenses), 2:371.

56. Lane, *Oglethorpe's Georgia*, 2:539 (£10); *CRG*, 5:437. Verelst's accounts: ibid., 3:86, 116, 145, 169, 192, 211, 227, 241, 255, 268. See also Egmont Papers, 14208, pp. 457, 461.

57. Oglethorpe, "Introductory Discourse," 135 ("will not part"); *CRG*, 4 (Supp.):86 ("ordered him"); *GT*, 104 ("affectionate Subjects" and "not only"); Ivers, *British Drums*, 141. In October 1741 Rev. Boltzius wrote that the Yuchis "have abandoned their old dwelling places and have moved off in the direction of Augusta." Urlsperger, *Detailed Reports*, 8:443. Wiggins died in 1742.

58. *CRG*, 27:68–69 ("standing Order"), 4 (Supp.): 158–60 ("the Wolf"); Stephens, *Journal*, 2:18–19 ("knows how"); *MPAED*, 1:142. Stephens was obeying the Trustees' orders, as Oglethorpe had not, to keep their Savannah storehouse closed to public access. *CRG*, 2:317, 5:421.

59. *CRG*, 4 (Supp.):218 ("grew vain"); *SCCHJ*, 1739–41, p. 161 (Spanish fort).

60. *CRG*, 4 (Supp.):218 ("that Influence"); Stephens, *Journal*, 1:45–46 ("so provoked" and "such manner"). The law prohibiting strong drink was never repealed, but in January 1742 the Trustees decided it caused more trouble than it prevented. In that month they directed Stephens to "wink at the importation of rum and discourage seizures thereof." Reese, *Colonial Georgia*, 51–52. This was good news to the Matthews, but it reached the colony too late to prevent their loss at Frederica.

61. *GT*, 107 (letter burned); *CRG*, 22, pt. 2:434 ("beating").

62. The version published in *A True and Historical Narrative* (88–96) has 117 signers, Matthews not among them. The version published in "An Account Shewing the Progress of the Colony of Georgia . . ." (London, 1741) has 121 signers, including Matthews. See Reese, *Clamorous Malcontents*, 247–49.

63. *CRG*, 4:512, 517–18; ibid., 22, pt. 1:367 ("Negro Plantation" and "Arch Incendiary"); ibid., 23:77 ("Petition . . . at Mr. Mathew's"); Reese, *Clamorous Malcontents*, 342 (Matthews signature); *A True and Historical Narrative*, 73 ("the prospect"), 147 ("great rendevouse"). See also Milton Ready, "The Georgia Trustees and the Malcontents: The Politics of Philanthropy," *GHQ* 60 (1976): 269–81.

64. James A. Henretta, *"Salutary Neglect": Colonial Administration under the Duke of Newcastle* (Princeton: Princeton University Press, 1972), 116–17 (Everard in North Carolina); Thomas Jones to [Verelst], October 23, 1741, *CRG*, 23:123 (quotes). Steven Hahn tells me that one of the sons of Mary's deceased brother was named Richard Everard Griffin.

65. *CRG*, 4:512, 517–19.

66. Stephens to Martyn, September 21, 1741, ibid., 23:109.

67. Verelst to Oglethorpe, February 16, 1742, *GT*, 106 ("to apply" and "necessary"); Verelst to Stephens, June 11, 1742, *CRG*, 30:247 ("is mentioned"); ibid., 2:387 ("and that he").

68. *GT*, 106.

69. Christie minutes, ibid., 89; Verelst to Stephens, June 11, 1742, *CRG*, 30:247 ("Part of").

70. *CRG*, 5:590 ("a grant"), 30:234, 247. On March 2, 1742, Stephens reported that Jacob "was making preparation to build another house on the Land Close adjoyning the Town, granted him by Tomo Chichi." Stephens, *Journal*, 1:48.

71. There is another way to interpret the intent of the 1738 Creek grant to Mary. It seems much less probable, but the evidence is too scanty to rule it out. Instead of holding that the 1738 grant was intended to convey the entire Yamacraw tract, it is possible to argue that it merely aimed to grant the old Yamacraw townsite. Christie's minutes do not say that, but perhaps his words were ill-chosen. There is much evidence that Mary and her third husband used the document to claim the entire Yamacraw tract, but the earliest of it (*GT*, 128) comes from 1745. That makes it possible to argue that the claim to the entire Yamacraw tract was a late afterthought, for which Bosomworth was responsible.

72. *SCCHJ*, 1739–41, p. 161; *South Carolina Gazette*, December 13, 1742; Urlsperger, *Detailed Reports*, 9:238; *CRG*, 6:72 ("the Expence"); ibid., 28, pt. 1: 259 (Bosomworth).

73. *DRIA*, II, 356 (Pepper); Stephens, *Journal*, 1:62 (Estichi); Corkran, *Creek Frontier*, 110–11 (Estichi).

74. Ivers, *British Drums*, chap. 14; *SCCHJ*, 1739–41, p. 161; *South Carolina Gazette*, December 13, 1742; Urlsperger, *Detailed Reports*, 9:238.

Chapter 5. A Wider War and Deeper Discord

1. S.C. Governor James Glen to Ga. President and Assistants, October 1750, *CRG*, 26:63.

2. Ibid., 1:514 (1738).

3. The Savannah authorities even billed Horton, as it had Oglethorpe, for the expense of entertaining Indians on their way to see him in Frederica. Ibid., 25:238–39. C.R.G., 36:172–73 ("good Management").

4. Heron to Verelst, January 2, 1748, *CRG*, 25:250.

5. Stephens, *Journal*, 1:14, 51; T. Bosomworth to James Vernon, March 22, 1743, *CRG*, 24:9 (quotes). In light of his close contacts with South Carolinians over a long period, Thomas was probably related to William Bosomworth "The Joyner." William signed a key anti-proprietary petition in Charles Town in 1717 and remained in South Carolina at least two more years. *SCHM* 62 (1961): 89 (petition); *William Bosomworth* v. *John Grimball*, S.C. Judgement Roll, 1719, SCDAH.

6. *CRG*, 1:403 (secretary), 23:267 ("sprightly Temper"), 24:7–11; Stephens, *Journal*, 1:86 ("studious"), 93, 144, 228 (scandal). Steven Hahn informs me that Bosomworth was born in 1719.

7. *CRG*, 1:415, 421 (appointment), 454, 5:720 ("3 years"); Stephens, *Journal*, 2:65, 86, 116 ("chief place"), 216 ("great Esteem").

8. T. Bosomworth, September 3, 1745, SPG, B12, p. 682 (July 8); Stephens, *Journal*, 2:127 ("Merriment"), 131 (August 5).

9. Although the Trustees had earlier recommended that Watson be granted a new trading license, the Savannah authorities had not complied. A few months after Thomas's complaint they fined Watson £100 "for trading among the Indians without License." *CRG*, 6:110; Stephens, *Journal*, 2:143, 145, 170–71, 174, 191, 195; *CRG*, 27:8 (Oglethorpe).

10. *CRG*, 6:135–36 ("clandestine"); Stephens, *Journal*, 2:222, 223 ("Triumvirates").

11. *CRG*, 1:475–78; T. Bosomworth, September 3, 1745, SPG, B12, pp. 682–84.

12. *CRG*, 1:476–79, and 31:28–31; T. Bosomworth to Verelst, October 12, 1745, ibid., 24:428 ("my Successor"); T. Bosomworth, October 12, 1745, SPG, B12, pp. 686–87.

13. Thomas Bosomworth, Statement of Mrs. Bosomworth's case to Governor Henry Ellis, July 23, 1759, *CRG*, 28, pt. 1:260 (quotes); *GT*, 121.

14. *CRG*, 1:487–88. Robert Williams's success in applying for these bounties no doubt inspired the Bosomworths to follow suit. See ibid., 387, and 5:590–91.

15. Ibid., 1:487 ("a Tract").

16. *GT*, 145 ("in Vain").

17. *CRG*, 25:39 ("thrown aside"), and 28, pt. 1: 260 ("Large Cargoe"); *GT*, 122 (Horton).

18. Memorial of Cousaponakeesa [Mary] to Lords Justice of Council, June 30, 1755, *CRG*, 27:68–69 ("standing Order"), 229; ibid., 28, pt. 1:260 ("Dwelling House"); *GT*, 150 (Malatchi). Horton letters at ibid., 122–23, 129–32, 135–37.

19. Milling, *Red Carolinians*, 187–93 ("Twenty one" at 191); Nairne, *Muskhogean Journals*, 38 ("men of Quality"); S.C.C.J., March 29, 1748 (Dexter).

20. Nairne, *Muskhogean Journals*, 40.

21. Stephens, *Journal*, 1:110 ("half Indian"), 121, 2:239–40 ("which occasioned" and "Convention").

22. Horton to Mary, late March 1746, *GT*, 122–23, 150 (Malatchi). Horton confirmed Malatchi's account of the Kent incident.

23. Ibid., 122 (Horton); S.C.C.J., April 11, 1746 ("to cut" and "old [Chi]Geally"); *CRG*, 27:225 (Galphin).

24. S.C.C.J., May 3, 1748 (quotes). Galphin was another pivotal figure in early Georgia, and what little is known about him makes it clear that he led a fascinating life. The best attempt to outline his early years in the colony is Friedrich Peter Hamer, "Indian Traders, Land and Power: Comparative Study of George Galphin on the Southern Frontier and Three Northern Traders" (M.A. thesis, University of South Carolina, 1982), 13–17, 46–50. See also the special issues on Galphin in *Richmond County History* 13, nos. 1 and 2 (1981).

25. Chigelli's talk to Horton, *GT*, 133 ("Walnut Trees"); T. Bosomworth's 1756 narrative, ibid., 123 ("Very clamorous").

26. Stephens's reply, ibid., 124; Thomas Bosomworth's comment on Stephens's reply, ibid., 124; Chigelli's talk to Horton, ibid., 133 ("their Evidence").

27. Ibid., 133 (Santachi), 123 (Bosomworth).

28. Ibid., 133.

29. Ibid., 132.

30. *DRIA*, I, 170 ("a few"); S.C.C.J., March 29, 1748 ("very Necessary"). The following June, Glen reported that the Squirrel King was a drunkard "despised" by his people. In private, Horton shared Glen's negative view of these Indians. Glen related that in a recent letter Horton described the Lower Chickasaws as "a Pack of Renegades." *SCCHJ*, 1748, p. 401.

31. Horton's account of his talks with the Lower Chickasaws at Augusta, May 15–18, 1746, *GT*, 125–27.

32. Chigelli's talk to Horton, ibid, 134 ("if I" and "call all"); Malatchi's speech to Heron, ibid., 149–50 ("a Paper"). Malatchi also related that shortly after the 1739 treaty conference, Oglethorpe had gone to Charles Town and there met with visiting Creek leaders. "He then gave us a Paper, . . . but did not let us know the Contents of it." Malatchi implied that this document too was later found to be offensive, probably because it was another

copy of the document Galphin translated. The Charles Town meeting must have occurred during Oglethorpe's visit there between March 23 and about April 6, 1740, when a Creek delegation was also in town. *SCCHJ*, 1739–41, pp. 258ff.; Ivers, *British Drums*, 98–99.

33. *GT*, 134 (Chigelli), 150 (Malatchi), 130–31 (Mary); S.C.C.J., May 3, 1748 (Galphin).

34. *GT*, 131 ("uneasy" and "it is possible"), 134 ("about our Lands").

35. Ibid., 123.

36. My guess is that the offending document dealt with a meeting between Oglethorpe and Yamacraw leaders interpreted by Mary. If invited by Oglethorpe to recall the meeting with King George, Tomochichi doubtless would have remembered it positively—and perhaps said something Oglethorpe could interpret as a reaffirmation of submission to the British monarch. That is what Oglethorpe wished the Lower Creek leadership to ratify in 1739.

37. *CRG*, 1:495 (six Negroes), 25:267 ("make good").

38. *GT*, 132.

39. Ibid., 132–34.

40. Ibid., 136 (to Mary) and 137 (to Thomas). This evidently was the basis of the erroneous report by the Savannah magistrates that Horton had agreed to provide Mary with "a handsome annual Salary." *CRG*, 25:414. Thomas later insisted that Horton "never Paid Mrs. Bosomworth Anything." Ibid., 27:188.

41. *CRG*, 6:173, 175.

42. S.C.C.J., November 3, 1746 ("greatest unwillingness"); Glen to President Stephens and Assistants, October 1746, *CRG*, 26:64 ("as long"); *GT*, 147 ("this Scheme").

43. *CRG*, 26:64, 27:13–14 (Cherokee attack); C.R.G., 36:249 (Cherokee attack); "Extract of a Journal from a Person Lately Come from the Creek Nation," April 1747, ibid., 294–95 (all quotes); Corkran, *Creek Frontier*, 121–22.

44. Heron to Mary, July 8, 1747, *GT*, 137–38; *CRG*, 25:414 (magistrates' disgust).

45. Commission to Abraham Bosomworth, C.R.G., 36:485–86; *GT*, 138–39 (July 20), 146 (expected meeting); *CRG*, 26:483 (£300). Abraham's commission called upon traders to render all necessary assistance to him, including translations and provisions. That Heron understood that the traders were not likely to cooperate readily with a Bosomworth is indicated by his threat of maximum legal penalties to any who attempted "to prejudice the Indians against the said Mr. Abraham Bosomworth." After its investigation of the Bosomworth claims, in 1755 the Board of Trade concluded that both Abraham and Thomas went up to Coweta. Shelburne Papers, vol. 49, pp. 29ff.; *APC: Col.*, 4:313.

46. *GT*, 139 (A. Bosomworth); C.R.G., 36:248–51 (traders); *CRG*, 25:414 (magistrates); S.C.C.J., May 3, 1748 (Galphin). Not only did the Bosomworths prevail upon Heron to send a copy of the traders' memorial to Newcastle, but Abraham had another copy recorded in South Carolina. *CRG*, 1:512; S.C.S.M.R., Book GG, p. 241.

47. Mary Bosomworth's memorial to Heron, August 10, 1747, *GT*, 140–46. Other surviving Bosomworth memorials, petitions, etc. include "The Petition of Thomas

Bosomworth" and "The Petition of Mary Bosomworth" to President and Assistants, both March 1, 1751 ("Proceedings of the President and Assistants," *GHQ* 35 [1961]: 341–42); "The Memorial of Thomas Bosomworth . . . in behalf of Mary Bosomworth" to S.C. Governor Glen, May 7, 1754 (*DRIA*, I, 495–98); "Memorial and Representation of Coosaponakeesa . . ." to Board of Trade, fall 1754 (*GT*, 234–36); "Memorial of Mr. Bosomworth in behalf of Himself and Wife . . ." to Board of Trade, fall, 1754 (*CRG*, 26:477–85); Memorial of Abraham Bosomworth to Board of Trade, February 3, 1755 (ibid., 27:31–32); Petition of T. Bosomworth to Lords of the Treasury, February 24, 1755 (ibid., 228–30); Memorial of T. Bosomworth to Board of Trade, April 24, 1755 (ibid., 44–46); "Memorial and Representation of Cousaponakeesa . . ." to the Lords Justices of Council, June 30, 1755 (ibid., 67–70); "The Answer" of T. Bosomworth to two letters, to Georgia Governor John Reynolds, May 12, 1756 (ibid., 237–56); T. Bosomworth, "A Narrative in Answer to the Charges . . . ," to Reynolds, summer 1756 (ibid., 155–93); T. Bosomworth to Governor Ellis, October 31, 1757 (ibid., 28, pt. 1:91–94); and T. Bosomworth, "A Statement of Mrs. Bosomworth's Case . . . to Ellis, July 23, 1759 (ibid., 256–63). In addition, at least seven Bosomworth memorials do not appear to survive. These are Mary's 1745 memorial to the Trustees (see ibid., 1:487–88, and 31: 44); Mary's 1747 "Case" to Oglethorpe (see *GT*, 135); a memorial of December 29, 1748, to the Trustees (see *CRG*, 26:183); a representation by A. Bosomworth to the Secretary of War, early 1748 (see ibid., 1:513); "Memorial of the Rev. Thomas Bosomworth on Behalf of himself and Mary his Wife" to Reynolds, October 3, 1755 (see ibid., 7:269); and the "Case" of Thomas to Reynolds elaborating on previous memorial, October 10, 1755 (see ibid., 272). By far the most important of the lost memorials is the one Thomas mentioned to Ellis in October 1757. Thomas says it was "a Memorial" he and Mary sent to the Board of Trade "setting forth their right and title" to the Yamacraw tract and the three coastal islands. Ibid., 28, pt. 1:92. Note well that this appears to be the *only* document the Bosomworths sent to London or delivered there that discusses their land claims, for none of the surviving documents do so.

48. *GT*, 140–46.

49. Ibid., 140 ("never owed"), 145 (her land claim).

50. Ibid., 145; T. Bosomworth, "Usefull hints," ibid., 236–39, quote at 239.

51. *CRG*, 28, pt. 1:261 ("strip").

52. Ibid., 25:414–15 ("Farce"). A few months later Galphin reported that Thomas was spiteful toward Horton and Captain Richard Kent, pretty clearly because both had resisted the scheme he was developing in Frederica in December 1747 and January 1748. Kent's offense was doubtless his affidavit of January 7, which will be noted shortly. S.C.C.J., May 3, 1748.

53. Malatchi's speech to Heron, December 7, 1747, *GT*, 148–52.

54. Heron's answer to Malatchi, December 7, 1747, ibid., 152–53; Heron to A. Bosomworth, October 4, 1747, *CRG*, 27:262.

55. Heron to Stone, December 8, 1747, C.R.G., 36:312–14, extract in *CRG*, 27:16–17 ("in relation"); same to same, December 8, 1747, *GT*, 154 ("looked upon" and "Annual Support").

56. Declaration of Lower Creek headmen recognizing Malatchi as their "Natural Prince," December 14, 1747, *GT*, 155–56; *CRG*, 27:17–18 (Frederica inhabitants).

57. The three documents are in S.C.S.M.R., Book GG, pp. 239–41. The original of the December 14 document still exists in the Ayer Collection of the Newberry Library, Chicago. It appears to be the only colonial Georgia document signed and sealed by the Creeks that survives in the original manuscript. For the printed text see *GT*, 155–56; for photographic reproduction see ibid., illustration 4. The three documents are among seven Abraham delivered in London. *CRG*, 1:512–13. Writing to Verelst from Charles Town on January 2, Heron related that he had set out ten days earlier. Ibid., 25:250–51.

58. Anonymous friend to Stephens, January 1, 1748 (extract), *GT*, 156. Stephens and the other magistrates later wrote that Horton "could not hear of this idle Farce (for see it He would not) but with the utmost abhorrence." *CRG*, 25:415.

59. Deed from Malatchi to Thomas and Mary Bosomworth for three coastal islands, January 4, 1748, *GT*, 157–59; *CRG*, 27:240 ("the year 1747").

60. *CRG*, 25:236 ("by a Grant"), 27:158 ("most Material"), 271 ("the principal").

61. Deposition of Noble Jones, January 7, 1748, *GT*, 161–62.

62. The two versions of the January 4 deed are in ibid., 157–59 and 159–61.

63. Ibid. The manuscript copies of these deeds that we have were recorded by Thomas Bosomworth in South Carolina four years later. S.C.S.M.R., Book I-I, pp. 426–28 and 520–23. The original was recorded on May 3, 1753, and the revised version on July 27.

64. *GT*, 159. The original has two affidavits attached that are not found on the second. These appear to have been produced on the day the deed itself was signed. The first states that it was on January 4 that "Livery Possession and seizen was had and taken." The second states that the "consideration money" the Bosomworths paid to the Indians for the land was substantial: "10 pieces of Duffils 200 weight of Powder 200 weight of bullets 20 Guns 12 pair of Pistols 100 weight of Vermillion and 30 head of Breeding Cattle." Ibid., 158. Omitting these affidavits, the revised version incorporates similar statements on "livery" and "consideration" into the text of the deed itself.

65. *CRG*, 1:503 (Watson's appointment). Thomas had sailed to England with Watson in 1745, and acknowledged that Watson was "a Friend." Ibid., 27:171.

66. *GT*, 163 ("few hours"), 160 ("forever"). The original deed, unlike the revised version, bears Watson's endorsement that it was "Recorded in my Office." Ibid., 158. It was probably Thomas's concern to preserve this endorsement from Georgia's official record keeper that explains the survival of the original deed. Not only did Thomas in 1753 record the original deed in Charles Town, the following year he gave another copy (not the revised version) to his financial rescuer Isaac Levy. B.C.T., 7–10.

67. *GT*, 156 ("several"); *CRG*, 27:240 ("the main Land"). The Bosomworths recorded a dozen of the more important documents bearing on the case in South Carolina. Three were recorded by Abraham in 1748, and nine others by Thomas in 1753. Those Thomas recorded included both versions of the 1748 deed for the islands and Christie's minutes on the 1738 grant of the Yamacraw tract. A 1748 deed for the Yamacraw tract is not among the documents recorded by either Abraham or Thomas. S.C.S.M.R., Book GG, pp. 239–41, Book I-I, pp. 424–34, 516–29, 544–45. Likewise, on August 2, 1750, the

Bosomworths obtained a confirmation deed from Malatchi and other Creek leaders for the three islands, and another for the Yamacraw tract. The two were treated quite differently. For the islands there is a clear reference to Malatchi's 1748 "Deed of Sale or Conveyance," while the grant of the Yamacraw tract is alluded to in very general terms with no mention of Malatchi. Furthermore, since the critical verbs in the latter are "grant Bargain Sell enfoeff and confirm," it looks more like an original grant than a confirmation. *GT*, 206, 209. Similarly, when Thomas in 1754 made a deal with Isaac Levy to finance his legal effort, he gave Levy as collateral the original 1748 deed for the islands, with no mention of a parallel deed for the Yamacraw tract. B.C.T., 22, 101–2.

68. *GT*, 161–62.

69. *JBT*, 7:182, 190.

70. *GT*, 161 ("already done"); *CRG*, 6:200–201 (Mullryne petition), 207–9; *GT*, 194 ("Good Portion"). The magistrates accused Heron of having often openly declared his support for slavery and having several slaves of his own. Heron clearly hinted at such support in his letter of September 8, 1747, to Stone, and finally avowed it to the Trustees on May 11, 1748. Ibid., 147; *CRG*, 25:294.

71. *GT*, 163 ("he avoided"); *CRG*, 6:205, 27:193 ("holding Lands"). The other two affidavits, which have not survived, were taken from Captain Richard Kent and Isaac Young. Ibid., 26:183, 27:274, 287.

72. *CRG*, 1:512–14.

73. Thomas later reported that letters from England warning him that these threatening documents had arrived reached him in November 1748. Ibid., 27:157.

74. *SCCHJ*, 1749–50, pp. 210–11 ("Colonel Heron"), 264; *CRG*, 27:203. Full texts of Bedford's letters of April 26 and May 28 to Glen are in S.C.C.J., April 21, 1749.

Chapter 6. The Bosomworth Ordeal

1. Ivers, *British Drums*, 213–14; *CRG*, 1:520, 6:214–15 ("Jekyl Island"), 219, 25:353, 395–96 (Cumberland Island), 411–12 ("not above"), 31:199 ("few or no"). Heron's final act regarding the Georgia Indians was an urgent appeal to the South Carolina council that Mary Bosomworth's warnings be heeded and that presents be promptly dispatched to the Creeks. His appeal was rejected. S.C.C.J., February 8 and 11, 1749.

2. *GT*, 195–96.

3. *CRG*, 1:515–16.

4. Instructions to Stephens, July 1, 1748, C.R.G., 33:368–70.

5. *CRG*, 25:415; S.C.C.J., April 21, 1749.

6. *SCCHJ*, 1749–50, pp. 192, 257. The appraisal of the goods fell below £3,000 because various charges had been assessed against them in England, including £267 for Abraham Bosomworth. Ibid., 1750–51, p. 352; S.C./P.R.O., 24:302.

7. S.C.C.J., May 23 and June 1, 1749; *CRG*, 25:379–80 (May 9). Answering a question from the legislature, Graham said "the Indians resident in Georgia are in Number about twelve that live upon St. Catherine's Island." *SCCHJ*, 1749–50, p. 207.

8. *SCCHJ*, 1749–50, p. 259 (May 31); *CRG*, 6:280–83.

9. *CRG*, 6:252.

10. Ibid., 253 ("without previous Orders"); *GT*, 172 ("near Two hundred" and "intended to sap").

11. *CRG*, 6:254 ("publickly"); *GT*, 172–73 (other quotes).

12. T. Bosomworth, "Narrative" (1756), *CRG*, 27:158–61.

13. *GT*, 172 ("acquaints us"); Mary to Stephens, July 27, 1749, ibid., 173–74 ("did not come" and "ordered all"); *CRG*, 6:252–57 (Mary quotes at 253).

14. When John Kenard later that year conducted a group of headmen from Lower Creek country to Savannah, the one-way trip took twenty-eight days. *GT*, 198.

15. *CRG*, 6:269 (Adam); *GT*, 194 ("reported" and "he wrote"), 196 (half); *CRG*, 27:170 ("Prove"), 176.

16. Piercey deposition, September 27, 1751, *GT*, 188–91, quotes at 188–89. Piercey said that Creeks came because "Notice being before sent them" (188) that the presents had arrived.

17. Governor Glen to President Stephens and Assistants, October 1750, *CRG*, 26:64–65.

18. Ibid., 6:269, 27:177.

19. Ibid., 6:254, 256.

20. Mary to Stephens, *GT*, 173–74; *CRG*, 6:257–58 (dinner).

21. *CRG*, 6:269. Captain Allick had a key role in the incorporation of the Yuchis into the Lower Creek confederacy. In 1729 he provoked resentment in Cussita by marrying three Yuchi wives, doubtless sisters. He responded by helping to found Yuchi Town a short distance away, but soon returned to Cussita and apparently became its *mico*. When Governor Glen in 1750 asked three traders to identify the "Head Man" in Cussita, the only one who had an answer replied: "Ellick was—I don't know who is now." *EAID*, 5:289; Benjamin Hawkins, *Letters, Journals and Writings of Benjamin Hawkins*, ed. C. L. Grant, 2 vols. (Savannah: Beehive Press, 1980), 1:313 (3 wives); S.C.C.J., September 5, 1750 ("Ellick was"); Corkran, *Creek Frontier*, 238; Ivers, *British Drums*, 69.

22. *CRG*, 6:258–59 (quotes), 27:219 (salute), 277.

23. Ibid., 6:259–60 (quotes); Presents delivered by Stephens to Creek leaders, 1749, Bevan Papers, nos. 11 (Coweta, August 16), 13 (Cussita, August 16), and 14 (Coweta and Cussita, August 17).

24. *CRG*, 27:175 ("could not understand"), 6:260 ("misled").

25. This and the following paragraphs are mainly drawn from the magistrates' minutes of the conference. See *GT*, 174–79, or *CRG*, 6:260–68. Written in heat, these minutes are more biased than usual. The Bosomworths are invariably cast in a lurid light. Thomas's 1756 narrative (ibid., 27:155–93), often cited herein, contains a paragraph-by-paragraph refutation. When describing the magistrates, Thomas repays their insults with interest. He could only have gained access to the minutes with help from a high-placed friend, in this case Governor John Reynolds.

26. Magistrates' version of August 11–12 events: *CRG*, 6:263–68 ("Tears" at 265). T. Bosomworth's version of August 11–12 events: ibid., 27:171–74 ("spit" at 174).

27. Lower Creek recognition of Mary as Princess, August 12, 1749, *GT*, 179–81.

28. Ibid.; *CRG*, 6:287.

29. *CRG*, 6:266–67 ("soberest" and "Head Ached" and "two Tongues"); Vice-President Parker to Gov. Glen, April 16, 1751, ibid., 26:194–95 ("closely attached").

30. Ibid., 6:267.

31. Ibid., 267–68.

32. This and the following paragraphs are based largely on the magistrates' minutes for events from August 15 to the close of the Creek meeting on August 18. They can be found in *GT*, 181–87, or *CRG*, 6:269–80. Only additional sources are cited in the corresponding notes.

33. Deposition of Adam Bosomworth, April 18, 1752, *CRG*, 27:208–9. In 1756, Kenard, by then a Bosomworth ally, provided unsworn answers to a series of Bosomworth-inspired questions designed to elicit evidence that the magistrates had misrepresented the talks in Savannah in 1749. Although Kenard's replies were generally supportive of the Bosomworth version of events, he stopped short of corroborating Adam's account of the Creek embrace of the August 12 instrument. Ibid., 275–81.

34. Ibid., 180 ("returned the Paper"). Kenard was probably right when he later said that "the Indians were all present at the Time." Ibid., 280. Most of the nine chiefs named were from Coweta and Cussita, but two were not: Nipkee of Ouseechee and Whehannechi of Ocmulgee. Both had subscribed to the 1747 instrument recognizing Malatchi as natural prince. See *GT*, 155–56.

35. *CRG*, 27:181 ("Every Indian").

36. Most of the other Lower Creek towns received their shares by November; the Lower Chickasaws received theirs in July 1750; the Upper Creek town of Tallassee received its share in September 1750; and Patrick Graham delivered shares to other Upper Creek towns in May 1751. Ibid., 6:326–27, 331–33, 26:399; *GT*, 192–93, 198–99.

37. *GT*, 196 ("Poison").

38. After his reassignment to South Carolina, Colonel Heron also blamed his troubles on Oglethorpe. *CRG*, 25:395, 490.

39. Ibid., 27:185 ("extorted" and "to quiet").

40. Ibid., 6:283 ("a Friend"), 27:179, 185; list of presents for Allick and Landlord, August 22, 1749, Bevan Papers, no. 15; *DRIA*, I, 270 (Thomas on Allick), 297–98 (ditto).

41. *CRG*, 26: 183 (Watson), 27:171, 223–24 (Thomas quotes).

42. Stephens and assistants to Martyn, September 8, 1749, *GT*, 193–97, quotes at 195 and 196.

43. In 1750 the South Carolina government protested to London that it was unwise to guarantee annual presents to Indians, arguing that the natives should be rewarded only after a period of good behavior. Stephens and the assistants informed Verelst that they concurred. In November, Bedford accepted the Carolina argument and recalled the presents that had already been supplied for that year. The second and last consignment provided to Georgia during the Trusteeship period was not shipped until March 1751. S.C./P.R.O., 24:141–47; *CRG*, 25:457, 26:449; S.C.C.J., May 28, 1751.

44. Thomas included this quotation in his 1756 narrative. *CRG*, 27:175.

45. Ibid., 6:270 ("His Heart"); *GT*, 203 ("who refused").

46. *CRG*, 27:184; *GT*, 193 ("promised").

47. *CRG*, 6:280–84 (quotes at 280 and 284), 27:227–28. On August 21 Thomas wrote that he was now "under Arrest for upwards of Four Hundred Pounds Sterling for the Cattle and Horses he purchased in Carolina to put upon the Islands of St. Catherine's and Sappala." Ibid., 6:284.

48. A. Bosomworth to Stephens, August 23, 1749, ibid., 6:285–87; *GT*, 195 ("inconsistent").

49. S.C.C.J., September 4, 7, 11, 1749, March 10, 1750; *CRG*, 26:65 ("promised"); Corkran, *Creek Frontier*, 129–30.

50. *CRG*, 6:287.

51. *GT*, 192–93. In this document the Indians are described as being from "Euchitee" town. In editing the document I misidentified this town as Hitchiti town (see also ibid., 378 n. 28). See list of presents delivered to "Stinlapoegee King of the Oseechees," September 8, 1749, Bevan Papers, no. 16. See also C.O.5/389, f. 181.

52. *GT*, 198–99.

53. Ibid., 199 ("the Mouth . . . Lies"); *DRIA*, I, 305 ("to command"); *Bartram on the Southeastern Indians*, 148 ("Chief King"). The presents were distributed to the "Okoanees, Chehaws, Hitchetaws, Swaglaws, Old Swaglaws, Ufallees and Uchee Towns." C.O.5/389, f. 186. The gift list is in Bevan Papers, no. 12. Two months later, one town, apparently Apalachicola, had yet to receive its share. *CRG*, 25:460.

54. Abraham's bride was Susannah Seabrook, "a young Lady endowed with all agreeable Accomplishments, and a Fortune of £15,000." *South Carolina Gazette*, November 6, 1749. *CRG*, 6:302 ("by virtue").

55. *CRG*, 6:305–6.

56. Ibid., 305–7.

57. Ibid., 31:140 (quotes). The Trustees had decided on this approach on May 18; see ibid., 1:557–59.

58. Ibid., 2:493–94 ("to inquire . . . and"). The common council had approved these instructions five days earlier. They state that since the Yamacraws have "long abandoned" their tract, and there were "no longer game" on the islands, "the Trustees are ready to purchase the said Lands and Islands." Instructions to President Parker and Assistants, May 24, 1751, C.R.G., 33:526–30, quotes at 529. See also memorial of Trustees to Board of Trade, June 19, 1752, ibid., 558–60.

59. *CRG*, 31:180.

60. *GT*, 199–200.

61. *CRG*, 31:178–79 ("pleased" and "shall put"), 182–83, 1:540–41; C.R.G., 36:403–6. After the South Carolina assembly refused to pay the £372 bill Abraham submitted for his services as agent, he sailed for England in the spring of 1750, arriving in July. "Peter Manigault's Letters," ed. Mabel L. Webber, *SCHM* 31 (1930): 173. Although Abraham got Bedford to support his claim in 1751, the assembly again spurned it. *SCCHJ*, 1750–51, p. 352, 1751–52, pp. 140–201.

62. *CRG*, 31:193–94.

63. *GT*, 201 ("Impatience"); *CRG*, 26:116 ("doubtless").

64. According to Governor Glen, after the Yuchis had provoked war with the Cherokees in early 1749 they were "called Home" by the Lower Creeks. *DRIA*, I, 170. *SCCHJ*, 1749–50, p. 467; *CRG*, 31:118, 180, 193 (Trustee letters).

65. *GT*, 200.

66. *GCCB*, 15–17, 21–23; *GT*, 201 ("no Means").

67. *GT*, 200–201. On April 14 Malatchi and five hundred Creeks destroyed the Cherokee towns of Echoi and Estatoe. Corkran, *Cherokee Frontier*, 23.

68. *CRG*, 6:331–32. The three confirmation documents are in *GT*, 202–5 ("Princess"), 205–8 (Yamacraw), and 208–10 (three islands).

69. *GT*, 211–12.

70. Ibid., 209.

71. Ibid., 205–8.

72. Ibid., 204–5, 207–8, 210. See also *CRG*, 6:336–37 and 346–47.

73. *CRG*, 6:346–47 ("these Affairs"), 351–52. Three days later Marcer took Adam's deposition relating to his Coweta visit at busk time. *GT*, 211–12. Adam asked Assistant William Spencer to join Marcer in notarizing the affidavits. Spencer, suspecting Marcer "to be concerned with the Bosomworths," refused. *CRG*, 6:336–37. On November 8 the magistrates happily told Marcer that the Trustees had made his suspension as an assistant and magistrate permanent. The following March the Savannah leaders charged that "our Councils have been betrayed" to Thomas Bosomworth by Marcer. C.R.G., 36:183.

74. Anonymous statement recorded by Charles Watson attached to 1750 deed for the Yamacraw tract, *GT*, 208.

75. *CRG*, 6:331–32. The Trustees had appointed Parker vice-president on June 14 and would appoint him president on April 8, 1751. Ibid., 1:547, 555.

76. The affidavit Marcer showed the magistrates was probably the one attached to the 1750 confirmation of Mary as princess. The one Marcer produced (ibid., 6:352–53) is word-for-word the same as the one attached to that document (*GT*, 204–5), though there are differences in spelling and punctuation. Galphin to Parker and Assistants, November 4, 1750, ibid., 213–14.

77. *GT*, 214.

78. *CRG*, 6:346 (October 22).

79. Ibid., 342, 357 (quotes).

80. Instructions to Graham, April 25, 1751, *GT*, 214–15; Parker to Glen, April 16, 1751, *CRG*, 26:194 (quotes)

81. S.C.C.J., September 5, 1750 (quotes); *CRG*, 26:61–66.

82. *GT*, 212–13 ("never behaved better"); *CRG*, 26:193–95.

83. *CRG*, 26:182–84 ("illegal and treasonable" at 182), 27:273–74; *GT*, 238 ("most flaming"). The action branded treasonable was Thomas's procurement of the 1747 deeds, for the assembly evidently based its judgment entirely upon the 1748 affidavits of Jones, Kent, and Young.

84. *CRG*, 1:561, 26:152–55, 31:234 ("seven Persons").

85. "Proceedings of the President and Assistants," *GHQ* 35 (1951): 341–43; *CRG*, 26:182–83.

86. *CRG*, 1:557–59. The final quote is from Martyn's more cogent paraphrase of the Trustees' words; see ibid., 31:231.

87. Instructions to President Parker and assistants, May 24, 1751, C.R.G., 33:526–30 ("he cannot hold" at 528, "King George" at 530).

88. *CRG*, 31:231.

89. *GT*, 214–15. There is a puzzling contradiction in the sources about the deeds Graham carried. His instructions envision two deeds, pretty clearly one for the Yamacraw tract and one for the three islands. The magistrates hoped that both deeds would be signed by both Upper and Lower Creek chiefs. The one Upper Creek deed that Graham actually brought back to Savannah (ibid., 219–21) and the magistrates' commentary on it (see "Proceedings of the President and Assitants," *GHQ* 36 [1952]: 60) tell a different story. These documents indicate that Graham carried two deeds but that they were separate deeds for the Upper Creeks and the Lower Creeks. The signed Upper Creek deed dealt with both the Yamacraw tract and the three islands, and presumably the draft Lower Creek deed "prepared agreable to the Preceding one" did likewise. Evidently this part of the plan changed before Graham set off.

90. *CRG*, 26:192–95; Glen to president and assistants, June 15, 1751, *DRIA*, I, 170–72.

91. "Proceedings of the President and Assistants, 1749–51," *GHQ* 36 (1952): 48–54 ("reputed" at 50, "little Connection" at 54); *DRIA*, I, 120–21, 171–72; S.C.C.J., July 2, 1751. On April 16 Parker observed that neither the Choctaws nor the Cherokees "have visited us in a Body since General Oglethorpe left this Country." *CRG*, 26:193.

92. "Presents Distributed to the Micoes, Chieftains, and Warriours of the Upper Creek Nation, By Patrick Graham . . . ," May 20, 1751, Bevan Papers, no. 30; Graham's talks with Upper Creeks, May 28, 1751, *GT*, 215–17 (quotes).

93. Graham's talks with Lower Creeks, June 3, 1751, *GT*, 217–18. According to Assistant James Habersham, the loan offer had been only "for a Year or two" and the Lower Creeks had "interspersed their Talk with many unjust, publick Reflections." *CRG*, 26:279–80.

94. *GT*, 214 (quotes).

95. Ibid., 218 ("that they knew of"), 227.

96. "Proceedings of the President and Assistants," *GHQ* 36 (1952): 57–60 ("notwithstanding" at 60); *CRG*, 26:279–80.

97. *CRG*, 26:69, 98, 100–101, 115, 311, 319–20, 377–81.

98. C.R.G., 33:559.

99. Atkin, *Report*, 64–66; *GT*, 222–23 ("capable"); *DRIA*, I, 215.

100. *GT*, 222–23.

101. *CRG*, 28, pt. 1:254; C.R.G., 33:559; *GT*, 226 ("by Force"). Nine years passed, however before these grantees could have their grants validated by the royal government, partly because Thomas Bosomworth had entered legal caveats against them.

Thomas charged that the magistrates had begun to issue warrants for this unlawful settlement "about the year 1750." Governor Henry Ellis said it was 1752. *CRG*, 28, pt. 1:92, 254.

102. Piker, *Okfuskee*, 59–60; *DRIA*, I, 224–33 (Acorn Whistler docs.); S.C.C.J., March 31–April 4, April 23, April 28, 1752.

103. *SCCHJ*, 1751–52, pp. 318–19 (May 8), 1752–54, p. 420; S.C.C.J., May 1, 15, 25, 27, 1752.

104. Mary to Glen, June 1, 1752, *DRIA*, I, 264–68; T. Bosomworth to Glen, September 3, 1753, ibid., p. 386 ("to recommend"); S.C.C.J., May 27, June 2, 4, 16, 24, 1752. The best account of the Bosomworths' relations with the South Carolina government during the next two years is in Terry Lipscomb's preface to *SCCHJ*, 1752–54, pp. xix–xxii.

105. Glen's instructions to Thomas, n.d., *DRIA*, I, 343–47, quote at 346; *GT*, 222 (July 28). See also James Habersham's letter of July 7: *CRG*, 26:402–4. Thomas saw Habersham as "Our Most inveterate and Declared Enemy." Ibid., 27:171.

106. Corkran, *Creek Frontier*, 153–59.

107. *DRIA*, I, 289–96; *GT*, 224–26.

108. The nine who signed Graham's deed were "Espogoge" (Ispokogi Mico, better known to the English as Old Bracket), the Oakchoy Captain, the Pucknatalahassee Captain (better known to the English as Duvall's Landlord), the Okfuskee Captain, the Tallassee King, the Fushatchee King, the Otassee King, the Tallapoosa King, and the Notchee King. Upper Creek repudiation of Graham deed and confirmation of Bosomworth deeds, September 23, 1752, *GT*, 224–25. See also affidavit by interpreter Joseph Wright. *CRG*, 27:217.

109. *SCCHJ*, 1752–54, pp. 215–16, 222–23, 341–42 ("concurred . . . Unanimously"); S.C.C.J., October 31, November 15, 1752, March 5, 1753. Thomas submitted a bill of £4,840 currency for expenses and services, but the lower house balked. In March 1754 a committee, reminding members that the house as a body had opposed the mission, questioned "whether the said Mr. Bosomworth ought to be paid for that service." On May 9 the house approved payment to Thomas of £2,200 currency. *SCCHJ*, 1752–54, pp. 420, 513.

110. *GT*, 226–27.

111. Glen to Board of Trade, July 30, 1753, S.C./P.R.O., 25:337–42, quotes at 338. See also *CRG*, 27:217–18.

112. *GT*, 239–40 (Gun Merchant).

113. *DRIA*, I, 405 ("to represent"); S.C./P.R.O., 25:338 ("among Indians"); Glen to Georgia magistrates, October 2, 1753, *DRIA*, I, 462. Glen enclosed a transcript of "what they said with Regard to Georgia."

114. Assistants to Martyn, July 28, 1752, *GT*, 222 ("Patron"); *SCCHJ*, 1752–54, pp. xxi, 218, 257, 259, 298; S.C.C.J., November 15, 1752, February 28, 1753.

115. The 1750 deed for the Yamacraw tract is in S.C.S.M.R., Book I-I, pp. 430–32; that for the islands is in ibid., 428–30; and the document recognizing Mary as princess is in ibid., 516–20. The first two of these (recorded on May 4, 1753) are printed in *GT*, 205–8

and 208–10. The third was recorded on some unstated later date, apparently on July 23, 1753 (the date on the preceding and following documents). It is printed (from a different source) in ibid., 202–5. The Christie minutes and the Williams deposition (recorded on August 2 and August 30, respectively) are in S.C.S.M.R., Book I-I, pp. 527–29 and 544–45. They are printed in *GT*, 88–89 and 90–91.

116. *GT*, 226–27.

117. Georgia charter, *CRG*, 1:22 (500-acre limit).

Chapter 7. Royal Government and Imperial Crisis

1. Reese, *Colonial Georgia*, 21–22; Coleman, *Colonial Georgia*, 180.

2. *CRG*, 7:333, 27:61.

3. *MPAFD*, 5:74 (Vaudreuil), 157–58 (Kerlérec).

4. Ibid., 157 ("ill"); *CRG*, 7:39 ("silly"); McGillivray to Lyttelton, July 14, 1758, f. 1, Lyttelton Papers ("Indians hearts"). According to Kerlérec, the Mobile meeting was essentially a meeting with Choctaws, who made up the bulk of the "more than two thousand" Indians attending. He spent sixty-two days of "the hardest drudgery one might have," listening to Choctaw speeches "from sunrise until after midnight." He mentions that "parties of the Alabamas, Talapoosas, Kawitas, and Abihkas" were present and that he made some progress toward making peace between them and the Choctaws, but says nothing about what he told the Creeks. *MPAFD*, 5:154–59.

5. *CRG*, 7:19 ("prevailed"), 21 ("a Letter"), 24 (Reynolds).

6. Ibid., 40 ("was all"), 27:74.

7. Abbot, *Royal Governors*, chap. 2.

8. Atkin, *Report*, esp. 7–13, 36–40, quotes at 36. Since the French could not match the English for trade goods, they apparently made a virtue of necessity. McGillivray reported that "the French don't trade with the Creeks, because, they know it would create heart burns between them." Thus most of what the Creeks received from the French came as a gift. McGillivray to Lyttelton, July 14, 1758, f. 1v, Lyttelton Papers.

9. Alden, *Stuart*, 68–70.

10. *CRG*, 28, pt. 1:94–98, quote at 96.

11. *GT*, 236–39, quotes at 237 and 239. Before his governorship Glen had been a civil lawyer, trained in Roman law at the University of Leiden. Robinson, *James Glen*, 10. Bosomworth was generally following an argument made in 1751 by Glen in a treatise on the boundaries of South Carolina (S.C./P.R.O., 24:268–94, esp. 278–81). Thomas cited at least one of the maxims from Justinian's *Digest* that Glen had cited: "For what does not belong to anyone by natural law becomes the property of the person who first occupies it" (D. XLI.1.3). See also *GT*, 380 n. 16, and Alex Murdoch, "James Glen and the Indians," in *Military Governors and Imperial Frontiers c. 1600–1799: A Study of Scotland and Empire*, ed. A. Mackillop and Steve Murdoch (Leiden: Brill, 2003), 141–59, esp. 152–55. Glen's acquistion of land from the Cherokees was by deed (not treaty), "in consideration of" valuables. *EAID*, 13: 198–200, 290–91.

12. Jonathan Bryan's Brampton planation was at the extreme upper end of the Yamacraw tract. He bought 250 acres of it in 1765 for £414, and 350 additional acres in 1770 for £500, altogether 600 acres for £914 (prices in Georgia currency, worth almost as much as sterling). Gallay, *Formation of a Planter Elite*, appendix 4, nos. 33 and 59. Thus land within the Yamacraw tract was potentially worth £1.5 per acre, a total of about £6,000.

13. "Memorial and Representation of Coosaponakeesa . . ." to the Board of Trade (fall 1754; *GT*, 234–36); "Memorial of Mr. Bosomworth in behalf of Himself and Wife . . ." to the Board of Trade (fall 1754; *CRG*, 26:477–85); Petition of Thomas Bosomworth to the Lords of the Treasury (February 24, 1755; ibid., 27:228–30); Memorial of Thomas Bosomworth to the Board of Trade (April 24, 1755; ibid., 44–46); "Memorial and Representation of Cousaponakeesa . . ." to the Lords Justices of the Privy Council (June 10, 1755; ibid., 67–70).

14. Thomas described the missing memorial to Governor Ellis on October 31, 1757. *CRG*, 28, pt. 1:92. In 1755 the Board of Trade evidently sent a copy to Reynolds. On October 8 he acknowledged receipt of "Coppies of Two [Bosomworth] Memorials," along with the board's "Resolutions thereon." Ibid., 27:75.

15. "Memorial and Representation of Coosaponakeesa, Rightful and Natural born Princess of the upper and lower Creek Nations . . ." to Board of Trade, fall 1754, *GT*, 234–36 ("being by Marriage" at 235).

16. *CRG*, 26:477–78 ("Indian Extraction"); *GT*, 234 ("Rightful").

17. *GT*, 203 ("full power"), 236 ("all past" and "Audience").

18. *CRG*, 26:479–80. In his 1756 narrative Thomas indicated that the intended deal had been on offer since at least 1749. Referring to the 1749 Savannah document declaring Mary to be Creek princess, he declared: "That paper . . . was Calculated for the Public Emolument; as thereby Mrs. Bosomworth would have been impowered to make further Concessions to the Crown; and Might have been of More Service, in extending the Limits already fixed by the last Treaty, ..." Ibid., 27:180.

19. *JBT*, 10:79–81. *CRG*, 28, pt. 1:92 ("Title Deeds").

20. *JBT*, 10:81–83.

21. "State of the Case relative to the Lands reserved by the Creek Indians in Georgia and of the Claims and Pretensions of the Bosomworths with respect thereto," Shelburne Papers, vol. 49, pp. 27–62, quotes at 30 and 60–62. The 1748 deed is alluded to on pp. 29–31, the 1750 documents on pp. 46–49, and the Graham deed and its repudiation on pp. 52–54.

22. The following paragraphs are based on these resolutions, which are in *JBT*, 10:85–87.

23. *CRG*, 27:46–53.

24. "Oglethorpe's Treaty with the Lower Creek Indians," *GHQ* 4 (1920): 5 (Marriott); 5–9 (1739 treaty) and 12–16 (1733 treaty); *CRG*, 27:249 ("having Countenanced"). See also *GT*, 372 n. 24.

25. *CRG*, 27:67–70 ("Princess . . . God and Nature" at 67–68; "supposed Father" and "forfeits" at 68; "Friendship" at 70).

26. Ibid., 66, 69 ("no Answer"); ibid., 28, pt. 1:92 ("reversion").

27. Ibid., 7:154–67.

28. Ibid., 27:63 (quotes). Reynolds signed the final grant for his 500 Ogeechee acres on October 31, 1755. Ibid., 7:248, 284. Eventually he had grants for 3,810 acres (largely on basis of headrights for fifty Negroes) and three town lots. Ibid., 28, pt. 1:151. A few weeks after Henry Ellis took over from Reynolds, he denounced the headright system but agreed that the capital should be moved to Hardwicke. Ibid., 11, 15.

29. Ibid., 7:93–94.

30. Ibid., 94 ("untill"), 360 (Lambert).

31. Ellis to Lyttelton, March 17, 1758, Lyttelton Papers ("having furnished").

32. The Bosomworths paid for their passage on July 13 at Gravesend. Fisher, "Mary Musgrove," 406 n. 45. On their return (evidently aboard the *Juno*), see *CRG*, 7:269, 27:74–75. For Thomas's renewed effort, see ibid., 7:269 ("a Memorial"), 272 ("Case").

33. *CRG*, 7:275.

34. Ibid., 27:153–54 (Reynolds's letter), 155–93 (the Narrative), 193–237 (49 numbered appendices), and 238–90 (numerous other appendices).

35. Ibid., 7:252–54 (quotes), 262–68. In a sly poke at Reynolds, the September 12 memorial charged that among his faults, Little "frequently misrepresents your Excellency, as having your Promotion in the Navy more at Heart than the Prosperity of the Colony." Ibid., 253. Reynolds also tried to appoint Marcer to the council. Watson and Marcer were Little allies in the lower house. See ibid., 205, 262; Abbott, *Royal Governors*, 49–52.

36. Board of Trade, report to king on Reynolds, July 29, 1756, *GT*, 241–43. Reynolds provided other details. In September 1756 he wrote the board that he had followed its "directions of the 21st of January 1755." These included ordering the Bosomworths to give copies of all the depositions and affidavits they had collected to support their case to surviving members of the Court of President and Assistants; ordering those survivors to answer the charges the Bosomworths brought against them; and ordering Reynolds to report his findings within one year of receiving those directions. *CRG*, 27:153–54; *JBT*, 10:103–4.

37. *CRG*, 27:74; Atkin, *Report*, 10. Similarly, Atkin (29) said "a small Present delivered in any Nation, would be far more acceptable than a very large one fetch'd from Charles Town."

38. *CRG*, 7:294 ("shortly"), 27:105 ("leaving"); *GT*, 242 (November 17). On November 6 the council chose three councillors (Patrick Houstoun, James Habersham, and James Edward Powell) to accompany Reynolds.

39. *CRG*, 27:105 ("a week"); ibid., 28, pt. 1:5 ("Insnaring"); *GT*, 239–41 ("Abstract").

40. "Abstract [of] proceedings at a Conference held at Augusta . . . ," *GT*, 239–41.

41. Ibid., 241.

42. Corkran, *Creek Frontier*, 172–76; Robinson, *James Glen*, 96–97, 103–5; *CRG*, 7:251 (September 12).

43. *GT*, 241–43. The letters from the two councillors who went to Augusta do not survive, but one from another does. On July 7, 1756, Alexander Kellet sent a memorial

to the Board of Trade in which he charged (1) that Reynolds "never in the least consulted the Committee of the Council ordered to attend him at Augusta" and (2) that the Augusta meeting seemed designed solely "to Establish Mrs. Bosomworth's pretended Indian Title, to some Land and Islands, that she is now Prosecuting before the Governor." *CRG*, 27:118. Afterward tireless Thomas collected more depositions from traders that he later submitted as evidence. Ibid., 217–18, 218–21, 225–26.

44. *CRG*, 27:153–54.

45. Abbot, *Royal Governors*, 51–52; *CRG*, 7:450–51; ibid., 28, pt. 1:5 ("Mr. Little"), 32 ("as senior"), 181 ("share").

46. *CRG*, 27:117 ("most of"); ibid., 28, pt. 1:132–55, quotes at 140. Reynolds also implicated Mary as a backer of New Hanover, an illicit settlement on the Satilla River. Ibid., 175–78; *DRIA*, II, 194.

47. *CRG*, 28, pt. 1:140–41. Although the Board of Trade had received the document "transmitted under the public Seal" of the colony, Reynolds denied that it was an official document. It was, he contended, simply one of the many questionable documents the Bosomworths had submitted in their own defense.

48. Ibid., 27:120–21; *JBT*, 10:397.

49. Cashin, *McGillivray*, chap. 7; *CRG*, 7:399 (petition).

50. Reynolds to Tugulki and the Creeks, September 14, 1756, *GT*, 243–44; Reynolds to Lyttelton, September 15, 1756, Lyttelton Papers; *GT*, 248 ("runagates").

51. *GT*, 244–45.

52. Ibid., 245–46.

53. Reynolds's interview with Handsome Fellow, November 16, 1756, ibid., 247–49; *DRIA*, II, 300 (Reynolds's claim).

54. *GT*, 249.

55. Ibid., 251 (quotes); *CRG*, 7:491–94. James Adair, a harsh critic of most governors, praised Ellis's record as "illustrious." Adair, *History*, 272.

56. *CRG*, 7:546–47.

57. For Ellis's statements see *GT*, 254, 261, 265, 280, 310; for Creek statements see ibid., 268, 285.

58. Ibid., 257–58 (July 1757), 281 ("thirteen hundred").

59. *CRG*, 28, pt. 1:45.

60. Ibid., 7:491–92; *GT*, 251 (quotes).

61. *GT*, 253–55.

62. Talk with the Cowkeeper, September 13, 1757, ibid., 259–61 (quotes at 260), 261–69, 273 ("never instigated"); *CRG*, 28, pt. 1:99 ("the french").

63. Corkran, *Creek Frontier*, 186 (Mortar); *CRG*, 7:537 ("reduced"), 539, 541–42 ("in the Woods" and "More Secure"); *GT*, 253.

64. *GT*, 268, 280–81, 285.

65. Ellis to Lyttelton, May 29, 1758, Lyttelton Papers; *CRG*, 28, pt. 1:22–23 ("most mischievous").

66. *CRG*, 28, pt. 1:75 ("I confess"); *GT*, 275.

67. *CRG*, 28, pt. 1:28–29 (presents).

68. Ellis's instructions to Wright, *GT*, 258; Ellis to the Board of Trade, November 25, 1757, ibid., 273 ("each . . . oblige me").

69. Ibid., 98, 262.

70. Ibid., 263.

71. Ibid., 263–64.

72. Ibid., 264 (quotes), 273. On the "Wolf King" or "the Wolf" (variants of a nickname), see *GFT*, 506 n. 4.

73. T. Bosomworth to Ellis, October 31, 1757, *CRG*, 28, pt. 1:91–94, quote at 94; *GT*, 275 ("to obtain").

74. *GT*, 265–66.

75. Ibid., 266–67.

76. Ibid., 267.

77. Ibid., 268–69.

78. Treaty with the Upper and Lower Creeks, November 3, 1757, ibid., 270–72.

79. Ibid., 271.

80. Conference with the Upper and Lower Creeks, October 29–November 3, 1757, ibid., 269 ("deny"); Ellis to Board of Trade, November 25, 1757, ibid., 273 ("own hands").

81. Ibid., 273.

82. Ellis to Pitt, December 10, 1757, C.O.5/18, pp. 513–17, quote at 515.

83. *GT*, 274 (quotes); *CRG*, 7:671.

84. *GT*, 273, 275.

85. Ibid., 276. For the 1758 act see *EAID*, 16:406, or *CRG*, 18:247–49.

86. Creek declaration at Mucklassee, April 22, 1758, *GT*, 277–79.

87. Ibid.; Ellis to Lyttelton, May 29, 1758, Lyttelton Papers; Ellis to Board of Trade, June 28, 1758, *GT*, 282.

88. *GT*, 280–81 (quotes), 285.

89. Ellis to Lyttelton, July 29, 1758, Lyttelton Papers.

90. *GT*, 282–83.

91. Ibid.

92. Board of Trade report on Bosomworth claims, December 6, 1758, C.R.G., 34:325–31, quote at 328; *APC: Col.*, 4:312–16 (Privy Council approval); C.R.G., 34:335–38 (royal instructions); *CRG*, 28, pt. 1:179–80 (order in council), 180 (promotion). See also Ellis's summary of the royal instructions, which he dates at February 9. Ibid., 253–54.

93. *CRG*, 28, pt. 1:210–11.

94. C.R.G., 34:335–36.

95. *CRG*, 7:235 (Evans), 8:84 ("certain Deeds"). The same day Evans received his grant, Christopher Peters received a grant of one hundred acres within the Yamacraw tract. Unlike Evans, Peters and others were deterred by their inability to gain clear

title for these grants. On August 3, 1756, Peters explained that Thomas's caveat has "discouraged" him, so he sought a different grant elsewhere. Ibid., 7:235–36, 374. See also ibid., 28, pt. 1:92–93, 254, 278–79. Other colonists had apparently taken possession of portions of the Yamacraw tract without benefit of grants. Ellis recommended that all those who occupied lands within the tract receive ordinary grants for them. Ibid., 255–56.

96. Ibid., 8:84–85 (most quotes); ibid., 28, pt. 1:254 ("Ordered").

97. Ibid., 8:85 ("had entertained"). Mary account is in ibid., 28, pt. 1:264–65; Thomas's commentary is in ibid., 256–63.

98. C.R.G., 34:331, 337.

99. *CRG*, 8:85–86 (quotes); ibid., 28, pt. 1:254.

100. Ibid., 28, pt. 1:255 (Ellis account), 268–69 ("Articles"), 269–74 (payment to Bosomworths), and 276–77 (sales to Elliott).

101. *GT*, 305. On the removal to Broad River, see John Williams to White Outerbridge, December 11, 1759, in Outerbridge to Lyttelton, December 19, 1759, Lyttelton Papers. See also Alex M. Hitz, "The Earliest Settlements in Wilkes County," *GHQ* 40 (1956): 260–80.

Chapter 8. The Atkin Mission

1. Alden, *Stuart*, 70; Sirmans, *Colonial South Carolina*, 328. Sirmans's account adds details, but it uncritically accepts Atkin's account of his successes. Wilbur Jacobs provides excellent background to Atkin's appointment as superintendent; see Jacobs, introduction to Atkin, *Report*. There are at least four valuable accounts of Atkin's activities as superintendent: Alden, *Stuart*, 68–73, 96–100; Corkran, *Creek Frontier*, chap. 12; Cashin, *McGillivray*, chap. 9; and Hahn, *Invention*, 245–50. These accounts differ in emphases and details but agree that Atkin was not up to the task. All are substantially based on the main source: Atkin's thirty-three-page report to Governor Lyttelton, November 30, 1759, Lyttelton Papers (the pagination is Atkin's own).

2. Alden, *Stuart*, 70–71; Sirmans, *Colonial South Carolina*, 328.

3. Cashin, *Ellis*, 123 (Loudoun); Atkin, *Report*, 19–22 (visits), 71 (Choctaws). Atkin even sneered that Choctaws "eat Creatures and things untasted by other Indians."

4. Hahn, *Invention*, 245–46. When Governor Lyttelton asked McGillivray what it would take to defeat the French at Fort Toulouse and Mobile, McGillivray consulted with James Adair, "an old friend of mine." He replied that "It's our humble opinion that a land Army of Six thousand Men, would be required." Half of them would have to be capable of fighting "after the manner of the Indians." McGillivray and Adair agreed that it would be nearly impossible to raise such an army. McGillivray to Lyttelton, July 14, 1758, f. 2, Lyttelton Papers.

5. Atkin to William Pitt, March 27, 1760, *EAID*, 14:136.

6. McGillivray to Lyttelton, July 14, 1758, f. 1, Lyttelton Papers; Alden, *Stuart*, 96 (not a single ship).

7. Corkran, *Creek Frontier*, 185; *MPAFD*, 5:179, 183; *DRIA*, II, 254 (Pepper); John McGillivray to Ellis, December 2, 1757 (extract), in Ellis to Lyttelton, December 10, 1757, Lyttelton Papers.

8. Alden, *Stuart*, 71–73.

9. Ibid. 78–79; Oliphant, *Anglo-Cherokee Frontier*, 46 (gout); Sirmans, *Colonial South Carolina*, 329–30.

10. Alden, *Stuart*, 97; Sirmans, *Colonial South Carolina*, 329; Cashin, *Ellis*, 50, 52, 125.

11. Alden, *Stuart*, 97; Hahn, *Invention*, 246. Atkin carried large flags for towns and small ones for leaders of war parties, describing both as English flags. The small one he gave Captain Allick was of "St. George's Colours," that is, the venerable Cross of St. George. Why Atkin favored this obsolete emblem over the Union Jack is unclear, but it may be because he thought its clean red-and-white and four-quartered design reflected similar ideas among the Creeks, and therefore would appeal to them. *EAID*, 14:130 (gorgets and flags). On the Indian "handshake," see above, chapter 2, note 16. Bartram, *Bartram on the Southeastern Indians*, 50 ("or rather arms").

12. *CRG*, 7:826–27.

13. Atkin to Horatio Sharpe, June 30, 1757, quoted in Atkin, *Report*, xxiv.

14. Cashin, *Ellis*, 125; Sirmans, *Colonial South Carolina*, 327–28; Corkran, *Creek Frontier*, 199; *CRG*, 28, pt. 1:167 (Ellis); Atkin, *Report*, xxvi ("applications").

15. David Taitt to Stuart, November 8, 1773, C.O.5/75, p. 39 ("our King"); Ellis to Lyttelton, February 5, 1760, Lyttelton Papers ("Cherokee King").

16. Corkran, *Creek Frontier*, 183–86, 197; *MPAFD*, 5:181 (Kerlérec); Atkin's talk with four Tuckabatchee headmen, July 25, 1759, "P.M.," in Atkin to Lyttelton, November 30, 1759, Lyttelton Papers (bullets).

17. Atkin's conference with Captain Allick, February 3, 1760, *EAID*, 14:128; Atkin to Pitt, March 27, 1760, ibid., 135 ("by the Opinion"); Atkin to Lyttelton, November 30, 1759, Lyttelton Papers, p. 3 ("The Scheme").

18. Ellis to Board of Trade, October 25, 1758, *CRG*, 28, pt. 1:167 ("just now"); Atkin, *Report*, xxviii ("cruel"); Cashin, *Ellis*, 125 ("pompous").

19. Corkran, *Creek Frontier*, 198 (proclamation); Ellis to Lyttelton, February 24, 1759, Lyttelton Papers. Ellis reported that "I have many complaints from the Traders, on account of their being delayed unaccountably." Ellis to Lyttelton, February 12, 1759, ibid.

20. *CRG*, 28, pt. 1:212.

21. Adair, *History*, 268. Very likely the individual the traders wanted to go in Atkin's stead was one of the two most influential traders to the Creeks: partners Lachlan McGillivray among the Upper Creeks and George Galphin among the Lower Creeks. As Cashin cogently argues, either of these two, but especially McGillivray, would have been a better choice for superintendent than Atkin. Cashin, *Ellis*, 123. Adair, who dedicated his book to these fellow traders (along with George Croghan), surely would have agreed. Adair, *History*, xxxiii.

22. G.C.J., March 8, 1759, *CRG*, 8:5 (Atkin quotes); Sirmans, *Colonial South Carolina*, 327 (Dobbs).

23. G.C.J., March 8, 1759, *CRG*, 8:5–8. Nevertheless, Ellis reported that on March 10 he tried to gratify the superintendent as much as Georgia law allowed (perhaps offering to give immediate attention to any Atkin request for revocation of a trading license). Ellis to Lyttelton, April 25, 1759, Lyttelton Papers.

24. Corkran, *Creek Frontier*, 194, 197; *CRG*, 28, pt. 1:163 ("well affected"), 167 ("Security"), 209 ("uncommonly favorable"); *GT*, 285 (Sempoyaffi). Ellis first acknowledged that a Creek-Cherokee conspiracy was a real possibility in his letter of August 27, 1759, to Lyttelton. Lyttelton Papers.

25. Ellis's talk with Sempoyaffi and other headmen from Coweta and Cussita, October 10, 1759, *GT*, 301. Sempoyaffi's Spanish commission states that he was "Malatchi's brother." Hahn, *Invention*, 248. Malatchi was often said to be Brim's son. Had Sempoyaffi actually been Malatchi's brother, someone would have said he was Brim's son, but no one did. Furthermore, Sempoyaffi had two identifiable brothers (Escotchaby and Ufylegey), who likewise were never linked to Brim.

26. *GT*, 301 (Sempoyaffi); Atkin's speech at Tuckabatchee, July 9, 1759, *EAID*, 14:70 (Choctaws); Atkin to Pitt, March 25, 1760, ibid., 135 ("Interview"); Cashin, *Ellis*, 125 (Choctaw proclamation).

27. *EAID*, 14:65 (Atkin); *GT*, 301–2 (Sempoyaffi). Although Sempoyaffi criticized Atkin both for keeping the Creeks waiting many months "in Expectation of his Arrival" and for not informing them of his intention to visit, this was not necessarily a contradiction. In Augusta six months, Atkin apparently told Lower Creeks he would visit long before he showed up unexpectedly.

28. *GT*, 284–85 (Wright), 309 (Allick); *EAID*, 14:80 (spokesman), 127 (Allick); Atkin's conference with Tuckabatchee Mico, July 24, 1759, in Atkin to Lyttelton, November 30, 1759, Lyttelton Papers.

29. Atkin to Ellis, January 25, 1760, *GT*, 308 ("overrules all"); Atkin to Lyttelton, June 17, 1759, Lyttelton Papers ("in his Absence"). Atkin does not identify the fourth brother. Stumpe, often referred to as Tugulki's uncle, may have been that brother. Since none of the three identified brothers were ever called Tugulki's uncle, more likely Stumpe was a fifth senior kinsman.

30. Corkran, *Creek Frontier*, 199–200; *MPAFD*, 5:201 (Kerlérec); Atkin's talk with Tuckabatchee Mico, July 24, 1759, in Atkin to Lyttelton, November 30, 1759, Lyttelton Papers (Escotchaby in Mobile); *GT*, 308 ("not coming once").

31. Atkin's talk with Tuckabatchee Mico, July 24, 1759, in Atkin to Lyttelton, November 30, 1759, Lyttelton Papers; *GT*, 302 (Sempoyaffi).

32. Corkran, *Creek Frontier*, 200. In his letter of January 25, 1760, to Ellis, Atkin says he is about to provide a review of his actions "with respect to stopping the Trade of any place." He then mentions five such stoppages (Alabama towns, Oakchoy, Yuchi Town, Apalachicola, and Coweta), clearly not in chronological order. *GT*, 307–8. The

halt of trade to Yuchi Town probably came first, while Atkin was among the Lower Creeks; he seems to have issued the other bans later while among the Upper Creeks. On September 7, 1759, "by an Injunction served upon the Traders," Atkin cut off trade with the Alabama towns. *EAID*, 14:136; Atkin to licensed Upper Creek Traders, September 7, 1759, C.O.5/64, pp. 343–45. Either this ban, the only one presently datable, or the one for Oakchoy appears to have come last.

33. Atkin's talk with Tuckabatchee Mico, July 24, 1759, in Atkin to Lyttelton, November 30, 1759, Lyttelton Papers. Atkin added that "when the French found that it was discovered, what was in Ufylegey's Commission, and did not want the Creek Nation to know it, then they denied first, that there was any such thing in it." The commander at Fort Toulouse then began to replace these hot documents with less provocative ones. For photos of two French commissions, dated 1760 and 1762, see Patricia Galloway, *Practicing Ethnohistory* (Lincoln: University of Nebraska Press, 2006), 300–301. For similar language in the 1757 treaty see *GT*, 271.

34. *EAID*, 14:135–36, 71; *GT*, 302 (Sempoyaffi); *CRG*, 28, pt. 1:209 (thirty or so; Wolf King).

35. Atkin to Pitt, March 27, 1760, *EAID*, 14:135 ("two Parties"); *DRIA*, II, 298 (Wolf King).

36. Atkin to Ellis, January 25, 1760, *GT*, 309 ("natural Jealousy"); Atkin to Lyttelton, November 30, 1759, Lyttelton Papers, p. 3 ("the Plot").

37. *EAID*, 14:136.

38. Ibid., 62–63 (spare welcome); Atkin to Lyttelton, June 17, 1759, Lyttelton Papers (Allick and Abraham).

39. Atkin to Ellis, January 25, 1760, *GT*, 306.

40. *EAID*, 14:64–66.

41. Ibid., 66–71.

42. Ibid., 71–73 (Choctaw treaty).

43. Ibid., 72 ("read"), 95, 136 (to Pitt). Years later one Choctaw chief, Cholko Holacta, was reported to have "received from the Superintendent Mr. Atkin a pair of colours for his Village." *GFT*, 334.

44. Atkin to Lyttelton, August 18, 1759, *EAID*, 14:76 (August 9); Atkin to Ellis, January 25, 1760, *GT*, 306 ("in the woods" and "ruin it"); G.C.J., November 9, 1759, *CRG*, 8:187–88.

45. *CRG*, 8:187–88 ("Ebitapogola-Mingo"); Atkin to Ellis, January 25, 1760, *GT*, 306 ("impudent falsehood"). Spencer's Choctaw leader appears to be the same one the Red Captain called "my elder Brother the Great King of Betapoucolou," Atkin called "the Betapoucoulou Mingo, the first Man in the Nation," and Stuart called "Mingo Emitta" of "Boukloukoulouchito." *EAID*, 14:93 (Red Captain), 137 (Atkin); *GFT*, 278 (Stuart). Had this great chief (a French great medal chief) been in Upper Creek country in 1759, some Englishman should have mentioned it. Evidently no one did, which tends to support Atkin's claim that the message was fraudulent.

46. *EAID*, 14:76 ("first Cargo"); Lyttelton to Board of Trade, September 1, 1759 (extract), C.O.5/386, f. 113 ("Sixty horse Loads"); Ellis to Lyttelton, August 27, 1759, Lyttelton Papers. On Johnston see *CRG*, 28, pt. 1:79.

47. *EAID*, 14:77 ("monstrous"); Atkin to Lyttelton, November 30, 1759, Lyttelton Papers, p. 2 ("2 Nations").

48. Archibald and John McGillivray, Lachlan's older kinsmen, were leading Carolina merchants to the Creeks who had launched Lachlan on his trading career in 1741. Evidently one or the other had established the family base at Little Tallassee. Cashin, *McGillivray*, 34–36; Atkin to Lyttelton, November 30, 1759, Lyttelton Papers, p. 2 ("more infamous" and "450 Albahma Indians"), p. 31 ("illegal Dealings"), and p. 32 ("Infamous Trade" and "first Disregard"). Atkin added that Spencer at first supported the embargo to the Alabamas because he thought it would bring "those who used to deal at Little Talsey Store, to his own Store." Ibid., p. 7.

49. *GT*, 322 (Mad Dog); Atkin, *Report*, 7–13 (French methods).

50. *Nairne's Muskhogean Journals*, 40–41. Patricia Galloway (in her foreword to this volume) immediately recognized that the calumet ceremony was a component of this institution. The following year she argued persuasively that a modified version of the institution shaped diplomatic relations between the French and the Choctaws. See Galloway, "'The Chief Who Is Your Father.'" More recently, Joshua Piker has argued that the institution was crucial to the diplomatic connection between Charles Town and Okfuskee. See Piker, *Okfuskee*, chaps. 1–2.

51. Stuart to Board of Trade, March 9, 1764, C.O.323/17, ff. 240–71, quotes at 259v and 262. Alexander Cameron reported that "Tuckassie, the Creek King or Kemitah of Seneca" headed a Cherokee party carrying a message to the Creeks. Cameron to Stuart, March 1, 1774, *DAR*, 8:56. Similarly, the Long Second Man (Neathluko Chupko) of Wiwoka, an Upper Creek town, was "a great King among the Chactaws." Daniel Pepper to Lyttelton, March 30, 1757, *DRIA*, II, 354.

52. Stuart to Board of Trade, March 9, 1764, C.O.323/17, ff. 264–65.

53. Ibid.; Galloway, *Practicing Ethnohistory*, 361 (by 1732).

54. Atkin's talk with four Tuckabatchee headmen, July 25, 1759, and his speech in Tuckabatchee Square, same day, both in Atkin to Lyttelton, November 30, 1759, Lyttelton Papers. Atkin evidently took his first step in this direction a month earlier at Cussita. He reported that before taking leave of the Cussitas, he gave "the particular care and charge of the Trader to two of them, being the chief Warriour and his Second, binding the covenant with proper Presents." He identified the Cussita chief warrior as "the Scotchman," apparently another mixed-blood. Atkin to Lyttelton, June 17, 1759, ibid.

55. Atkin's talk with four Tuckabatchee headmen, July 25, 1759, in Atkin to Lyttelton, November 30, 1759, ibid.; Atkin, "Great Talk," *EAID*, 14:83; Atkin "to the Licensed Traders in the Lower and Upper Creek Towns," February 5, 1760, in Atkin to Lyttelton, February 13, 1760, Lyttelton Papers; *EAID*, 14:130 (Allick).

56. Atkin's talk with four Tuckabatchee headmen, July 25, 1759, "P.M.," in Atkin to Lyttelton, November 30, 1759, Lyttelton Papers.

57. *EAID*, 14:77–81; Atkin's talk with Tuckabatchee Mico, July 24, 1759, in Atkin to Lyttelton, November 30, 1759, Lyttelton Papers. The minutes of the general meeting were taken by Atkin's secretary George Mackenzie, with additions by Atkin himself. The careful attention to Creek identities in this document makes it perhaps the single most important document for the study of the Creek social structure during the colonial era. Citing Spanish documents, Hahn (*Invention*, 248) calls attention to the Tuckabatchee colony, probably one of the numerous Creek fragments beginning to coalesce as Seminoles.

58. Atkin's Talk with the Gun Merchant, November 10, 1759 (extract), in Atkin to Lyttelton, November 30, 1759, Lyttelton Papers; *EAID*, 14:66.

59. *EAID*, 14:77–81; *GT*, 300–305.

60. Atkin to Lyttelton, November 30, 1759, Lyttelton Papers, p. 8 ("decisive point") and p. 27 (long quote). There are many examples of Creek leaders saying something to the effect that it was too late for them to do without trade goods from the English. Earlier in the same document (p. 6), Atkin quotes the Mortar as telling the French commandant in 1759 that blocking the English trade with the Choctaws was no longer possible: "That might have been done before; but it is now too late." Similarly, in 1772 the Second Man of Little Tallassee observed that it was now "too late" for the Creeks to make war upon the English. Affidavit of Joseph Dawes, August 4, 1772, *DAR*, 5:162.

61. Atkin's speech at Tuckabatchee, July 9, 1759, *EAID*, 14: 69.

62. Atkin, "Great Talk," ibid., 81–83.

63. Ibid., 82–84, 136; Atkin to Licensed Upper Creek Traders, September 7, 1759, in Atkin to Pitt, March 27, 1760, C.O.5/64, pp. 343–45.

64. Atkin, "Great Talk," *EAID*, 14:84–85; Atkin to Lyttelton, November 30, 1759, Lyttelton Papers, p. 9 ("on my Skull").

65. Atkin to Pitt, March 27, 1760., *EAID*, 14:137 ("the Signal"); Atkin to the Creeks, February 5, 1760, ibid., 132 ("not to spoil"); Adair, *History*, 269–72.

66. Ellis to Lyttelton, October 16, 1759, Lyttelton Papers. Six days earlier Sempoyaffi had publicly denied this to Ellis. *GT*, 301.

67. *GT*, 304 ("served him so"), 322 ("intollerable").

68. Atkin, "Great Talk," *EAID*, 14:85.

69. Ibid., 86. Emphasis in original.

70. Ibid., 86–87.

71. Ibid., 87.

72. Ibid. ("*no Answer*"); Atkin to Lyttelton, November 30, 1759, Lyttelton Papers ("some Alterations"); Atkin's talk with the Gun Merchant, November 10, 1759 (extract), in Atkin to Lyttelton, November 30, 1759, ibid. With mock concern the Gun Merchant added that "he never knew the time when no Answer was made to a Talk." When the superintendent asked if he could explain it, the Oakchoy leader could only suppose it was because the Creeks "had never been used to hear such Talks before . . . and did not know what Answer to make."

73. *EAID*, 14:88 (treaty), 136 ("on my own Terms").

74. Ibid., 88–90.

75. *GT*, 306 ("helped greatly"); *EAID*, 14:118 (message from Atkin).

76. *EAID*, 14:137. Atkin gave the brother an armband (ibid., 96). For a sketch of the Red Captain, see *GFT*, 533–34 n. 36.

77. Atkin's conference with the Choctaws at Okfuskee, October 25–November 1, 1759, *EAID*, 14:90–91.

78. Ibid., 91–97. The following paragraphs are also based upon this significant document. Atkin later reported that in October "the Betapoucolou Mingo went in Person in the Chicasaw Towns with many of his Headmen, . . . and confirmed the Peace . . . , since which their People have hunted together." Ibid., 137 (also, "turn the Tables").

79. Alden, *Stuart*, 99 (December 23); Atkin to Lyttelton, November 30, 1759, Lyttelton Papers, p. 1 ("Happy") and p. 30 ("Satisfactory Answer"). In the second paragraph (ibid., p. 1), Atkin tells Lyttelton that he is reporting on "my Transactions since I came to these Upper Creeks." The document says nothing about his earlier visit to the Lower Creeks, nor is there a corresponding report on that visit. These circumstances, along with his comment about Ellis's responsibility for the Lower Creeks, indicate that Atkin had been ordered to concentrate his mission upon the Upper Creeks. Such an order would have had to come from the British commander in chief, doubtless predicated on the fact that the Upper Creeks could hurt the French far more than the Lower Creeks could.

80. Ibid., p. 29 ("I have closed"), p. 8 ("lost Credit"), p. 3 ("as good a Friend"), pp. 2–3 (the Mortar), and p. 5 ("greatest Opponents"); Atkin to Ellis, January 25, 1760, *GT*, 306.

81. *GT*, 309 (forty head); *EAID*, 14:95, 138 ("Before I left"). Meeting Captain Allick in Augusta in February, Atkin gave him "a small St. George's Colours . . . such as he commonly has given to Indian War Parties." By this time Atkin was focused on the Cherokees, and Captain Allick was clearly reluctant to go to war. Ibid., 130. In January 1760 Atkin solicited Ellis's support for his plan to root Allick in Cussita, noting that Lyttelton had already agreed. Ellis promised thirty head, but in 1766 Allick complained that they had never been delivered. *GT*, 309–10; *CRG*, 17:247.

82. Atkin to Lyttelton, November 30, 1759, Lyttelton Papers, p. 24 ("would be contradictory").

83. Atkin to the Creeks, February 5, 1760, *EAID*, 14:131–32; Atkin to Licensed Traders in the Lower and Upper Creek Towns, February 5, 1760, in Atkin to Lyttelton, February 13, 1760, Lyttelton Papers.

84. *EAID*, 14:134–35. The Pucknatallahassee captain was Duvall's Landlord (Hoithlepoya Hadjo), who was also *mico* of that town. *GT*, 220; *DRIA*, I, 292.

85. *GT*, 303 (came close), 322 ("Imprudence").

86. Ellis to Lyttelton, October 11, 1759, Lyttelton Papers; *CRG*, 28, pt. 1:226–27 ("Philosopher").

87. Ellis's reply (oral, June 30, 1760) to Creek talks of May 26 and June 7, *GT*, 327.

88. Atkin to Lyttelton, November 30, 1759, Lyttelton Papers, p. 24 ("constantly inveighed") and p. 27 (Glen).

89. Akin to Pitt, March 27, 1760, *EAID*, 14:138.

Chapter 9. The Cherokee War and Imperial Triumph

1. Ellis to Lyttelton, September 25, 1759, Lyttelton Papers.

2. Ellis to Lyttelton, August 25, 1757 ("principal Negotiator"), September 25, 1759 ("Licences"), ibid.; Atkin to Lyttelton, August 18, 1759, *EAID*, 14:76; Cashin, *Ellis*, 85.

3. *DRIA*, II, 356.

4. Ibid., 371, 475–76; *GT*, 286–90, quotes at 286 and 288; *EAID*, 14:147 ("Exchange"); Cashin, *McGillivray*, 182–83 (Cashin's interpretation differs). In January 1758 Glen had advised Lyttelton that McGillivray was the man to consult on Indian affairs: "he is a man of sense and substance and may be trusted and he knows ten times more of their affairs than any other trader." Quoted in Cashin, *McGillivray*, 169. The Lower Chickasaws apparently told Pepper that they had moved across the river because of encroachments on their land (*DRIA*, II, 371), but they told both William Bull and Edmond Atkin that they moved out of fear of enemies (ibid., 476; *GT*, 286).

5. *DRIA*, II, 45, 52. In the second message to Lyttelton, on April 29, Grant reported that the Cherokees had solicited Lower Creek participation in a joint assault upon traders. Other such proposals followed. On August 9, 1756, Lower Creek headmen assured Lyttelton that they "have agreed to throw all the Cherockees bad Talks away." Ibid., 154.

6. Oliphant, *Anglo-Cherokee Frontier*, 32–33, 41–42, and map 3; *EAID*, 13: 199; *DRIA*, II, 410–11.

7. Milling, *Red Carolinians*, 291–94; Oliphant, *Anglo-Cherokee Frontier*, 54–55. Sworn depositions by Virginians involved in these incidents are in *DRIA*, II, 467–70.

8. Oliphant, *Anglo-Cherokee Frontier*, 84–88; Paul Demere to Lyttelton, May 12, 1759, *DRIA*, II, 488; Wawatchee to Lyttelton, May 11, 1759, ibid., 491–92.

9. Oliphant, *Anglo-Cherokee Frontier*, 78–79.

10. Ibid., 88–89. An "extract" of Cotymore's August 3 letter is in C.O.5/386, ff. 127–31. Purporting to convey his informant's account exactly, Cotymore encloses most of it (excepting the alleged threat to Fort Prince George) within quotation marks. The quoted portion includes the alleged statements by the Creek and Cherokee spokesmen.

11. Ellis to Lyttelton, August 10, 1759, Lyttelton Papers; Ellis to Board of Trade, September 6, 1759, *CRG*, 28, pt. 1:216–17.

12. Ellis to Lyttelton, August 27, 1759, Lyttelton Papers. The account of Wawatchee's talk is Lyttelton's summary, which he sent to the Board of Trade on September 1. C.O.5/386, ff. 111v–113.

13. Oliphant, *Anglo-Cherokee Frontier*, 90–91.

14. Ibid., 93–95.

15. Ibid., 93; S.C.C.J., August 28, 1759. The South Carolina reply is in C.O.5/474, f. 10; Ellis's comment is in *CRG*, 28, pt. 1:217. Since Lyttelton had a copy of the Wawatchee

letter only a day or two after Ellis received the original, Vann had probably sent a copy to Lyttelton.

16. *GT*, 298–99 (reports), 300 (Mary). Ellis may have withheld McGillivray's name so that it would not devalue intelligence he wanted Lyttelton to take very seriously. McGillivray and Atkin were rivals. Atkin the Carolinian had good relations with Lyttelton; McGillivray the Georgian did not. Atkin had exposed McGillivray's role in relocating the Lower Chickasaws to Georgia, and repeatedly disparaged him. In 1758 McGillivray had crossed Lyttelton by pointing out that his grandiose scheme for an overland attack on Mobile was almost certain to fail. When they learned of plans for Atkin's mission, "the Augusta traders thought that Atkin should have let Lachlan McGillivray go in his place." Cashin, *McGillivray*, 169–72, 175, 182–84 (quote at 183), 188.

17. *GT*, 298–99. The second letter is undated. On September 11 Sempoyaffi had given Outerbridge an account of the Creek-Cherokee meeting similar to Stumpe's. Corkran, *Creek Frontier*, 203.

18. *GT*, 298 (quotes), 308.

19. Grant's account seems to confirm both Cherokee initiative and particulars of Wawatchee's alleged scheme. He reported that Cherokees of "the Lower Towns, Kewohee especially, had sent into the Cawetae's to have their Traders killed, that the Creeks should first strike the Blow, and that these were ready to follow." Ludovic Grant to Glen, April 29, 1755, *DRIA*, II, 52.

20. *GT*, 307; *EAID*, 14:78–81; *South Carolina Gazette*, May 24, 1760 (Mortar's brother). One of Atkin's Upper Creek sources was the Okfuskee Captain, an influential friend of the English. In early January 1760 he flattered Atkin that, but for his diplomacy, the Lower Creeks "would have" joined the Cherokees. *GT*, 305.

21. *GT*, 298–99.

22. Oliphant, *Anglo-Cherokee Frontier*, 88–89.

23. *GT*, 300–305, 308 ("overrules"); Ellis to Lyttelton, February 5, 1760, Lyttelton Papers ("worst person").

24. *GT*, 300–302.

25. Ibid., 300–301; Ellis to Lyttelton, October 16, 1759, Lyttelton Papers.

26. *GT*, 301–3.

27. Ibid., 303. In June 1757 Pepper had reported that the Ogeechee settlement had been "abandoned by the Virginia People," but evidently they had returned. The previous November he had noted that the Creeks too had some "Riffle Guns," purchased at "monstrouw [monstrous] Price." *DRIA*, II, 296 and 353 (rifles), 389 (Ogeechee).

28. *GT*, 304, 315 (Tupahutke).

29. Ibid., 304, 352 (Handsome Fellow).

30. Ibid., 304–5; Ellis to Lyttelton, October 16, 1759, Lyttelton Papers.

31. Oliphant, *Anglo-Cherokee Frontier*, 98–99.

32. Ibid., 100–104; Hatley, *Dividing Paths*, 114.

33. Oliphant, *Anglo-Cherokee Frontier*, 104–5; Hatley, *Dividing Paths*, 121–23. Lyttelton did not learn from an earlier incident of Carolina hostage taking. In 1753

Governor Glen incarcerated six Shawnees who thought they had been invited to meet him. Their leader died in prison. Ian Steele argues persuasively that this incident turned the Shawnees into inveterate enemies: "this bungled hostage-taking triggered anti-English violence that began six decades of intermittent war." Ian Steele, "Shawnee Origins of Their Seven Years' War," *Ethnohistory* 53 (2006): 657–87, quote at 671.

34. *CRG*, 8:191–92; Ellis to Lyttelton, December 7, 1759, Lyttelton Papers; Cashin, "The Business of the Backcountry," in Cashin, *Colonial Augusta*, 46. Afterward, Ellis repeatedly complained that Lieutenant Outerbridge and his replacement, Lieutenant Lachlan Shaw, had refused to recognize his authority, and that Lyttelton lacked authority to appoint these Carolinians to command at Augusta. Ellis to Lyttelton, January 10, February 4, 16, 27, 1760, Lyttelton Papers.

35. Hatley, *Dividing Paths*, 123–24; Oliphant, *Anglo-Cherokee Frontier*, 108–10.

36. Oliphant, *Anglo-Cherokee Frontier*, 106–10. The treaty is in *EAID*, 14:120–22.

37. Oliphant, *Anglo-Cherokee Frontier*, 110–12; John Pearson to Lyttelton, February 8, 1760, *DRIA*, II, 495–96; Alexander Miln to Lyttelton, February 24, 1760, ibid., 497–99; Hatley, *Dividing Paths*, 127 (Calhoun).

38. Oliphant, *Anglo-Cherokee Frontier*, 113–16, 123; Cashin, *McGillivray*, 194; Cashin, "The Business of the Backcountry," 46–47.

39. *CRG*, 8:228, 248. Milledge was still in command at Augusta in May. Corkran, *Creek Frontier*, 217–18.

40. Cashin, *McGillivray*, 194–96; John Williams to White Outerbridge, December 11, 1759, in Outerbridge to Lyttelton, December 19, 1759, Lyttelton Papers (Broad River).

41. Cashin, *McGillivray*, 197–98; *CRG*, 28, pt. 1:230 (Ellis).

42. *GT*, 310–12.

43. *South Carolina Gazette*, April 7, 1760, cited in Corkran, *Creek Frontier*, 214. See ibid. regarding Tallapoosa and Abeika guards (217, 224, 226) and Fort Toulouse meeting (215).

44. *South Carolina Gazette*, May 24, 1760, excerpt in *GT*, 312. Since the Gun Merchant was attempting to excuse Creek inaction he probably exaggerated the "irresolution" of Englishmen in Creek country.

45. *CRG*, 28, pt. 1:231, 246; *GT*, 313, 315; Ellis to Lyttelton, February 27, 1760 ("Mrs. Bosomworth"), Lyttelton Papers; Corkran, *Creek Frontier*, 212 (Sempoyaffi).

46. *CRG*, 28, pt. 1:250; *South Carolina Gazette*, May 24, 1760.

47. *GT*, 313–14. On May 2 Ellis held a similar reception for a Yuchi party that brought in one Cherokee scalp. The Yuchi spokesman said they had not been recruited, but "came and offered their Service" to Ellis, who had "fitted them out in a proper manner." Ellis promised them presents a day or two later. *CRG*, 8:295–97.

48. *GT*, 314–16.

49. Ibid., 316. Silver armbands engraved "The gift of his Excellency Henry Ellis Esq. 1760" were recently unearthed in an Alabama burial. These almost certainly were those given to Tupahutke. See *GFT*, frontispiece. English silver was soon in demand. *GT*, 343; *CRG*, 8:539.

50. *CRG*, 8:312.

51. *GT*, 316 ("Stump-finger"), 318 (Mortar's brother). The sudden concern of Stumpe's party for English prisoners and scalps may have been due to a recent embarrassment at Coweta. Based on April reports from Creek country, the *Gazette* said this: "2 more Cherokees had very lately arrived in the Coweta town, with a bloody hatchet, scalps, etc., on whose arrival the Lieutenant [Escotchaby] was exerting himself in their favour, but met with great opposition from the Young Twin [Tugulki] and a head man called half-breed Abram." *South Carolina Gazette*, May 24, 1760.

52. Corkran, *Creek Frontier*, 200, 213–14; *GT*, 316 (Stumpe). Atkin repeatedly urged Ellis to punish Spencer, beginning with a revocation of his trading license, because of his illicit trading outside of Mucklassee and dubious dealings with the Choctaws. Ellis evidently at first agreed, for his attorney general had begun legal action against Spencer's license. In February, however, Ellis and his council decided it was "Expedient for the public Service" to allow the shady Spencer to return for two or three months for "the Purpose of setting the Creeks to War against the Cherokees." Ibid., 305–6; *CRG*, 8:253. The English later had reason to be more charitable toward both Spencer and the Gun Merchant. On May 24, 1760, the *South Carolina Gazette* reported that the Cherokees had delivered "the two English prisoners to the Gun Merchant, who gave them up to Mr. John Spencer, but first stipulated with him, that he should pay 50 lb. of leather for their redemption, to the two Cherokees who saved them from being burnt."

53. *GT*, 316–17; *South Carolina Gazette*, May 24, 1760 ("they offer").

54. *South Carolina Gazette*, May 24, 1760.

55. Oliphant, *Anglo-Cherokee Frontier*, 113–17.

56. Piker, *Okfuskee*, 52, 135; Adair, *History*, 278; Oliphant, *Anglo-Cherokee Frontier*, 133.

57. Piker reviews earlier interpretations and their shortcomings in *Okfuskee*, 53–54.

58. *CRG*, 8:314–16; Adair, *History*, 279.

59. *GT*, 321–22.

60. Piker, *Okfuskee*, 58–59 (Ross and McIntosh quotes); *CRG*, 28, pt. 1:286–87 (Ellis); Adair, *History*, 280.

61. Piker, *Okfuskee*, 54. Historians have generally followed Adair (*History*, 278) in blaming the Mortar for inciting the attacks. The Mortar undoubtedly was largely responsible for the hostile atmosphere surrounding the attacks, but there seems to be no evidence that he was directly involved.

62. Hahn, *Invention*, 264, citing Atkin to Lyttelton, September 21 and November 30, 1759.

63. In his generally excellent recent book, *Okfuskee*, Joshua Piker offers a novel interpretation of the motivation behind the attack. In his view, the attack "was a manifestation of the Creek clan system in action. More specifically, the events of May 16, 1760, exemplified the punishment meted out by a clan uncle to an offending member of his clan" (56). The "correction" decided upon was "interclan capital punishment" (52, 59). Piker's effort to explain and support this remarkable conclusion requires an

argument too long and intricate to be summarized here (see 21–24, 52–63, 135–37). Briefly, it is a bold extension from the Southeastern Indians' practice of establishing "protector" chiefs in each others' towns, discussed above in chapter 8.

Pointing out that Charles Town and Okfuskee were often said to be of "one fire," Piker argues that the special relationship between the towns implies that each had a "Fanni Mico" responsible for protecting people of the other. In Charles Town it was the South Carolina governor; in Okfuskee it was the *mico*. Piker contends that this partnership was on display in 1732, when the Red Coat King came to Charles Town for a treaty conference. He signed as "Fannemiche King of the Oakfuskeys" (21). His mark on the treaty is "the strongest argument for an Okfuskee becoming a Fanni Mico for the British" (24). As such he was a kind of "clan uncle" responsible not only for protection of the English, but punishment of those who misbehaved. Hence the extreme punishment in 1760 for those guilty of extreme misbehavior.

The argument is ingenious but far from persuasive. There is no evidence that South Carolina governors saw themselves playing the role Piker says Okfuskees assigned to them. There is no evidence that a Carolina governor or agent appointed the Red Coat King Fanni Mico, but every likelihood that the chief received the title from the another Indian group. The most probable donors were the Chickasaws resident in Upper Creek territory. Nor is there much evidence that a native protector's responsibility extended to punishment.

64. *GT*, 320–21.

65. Ibid., 323–24 (Lower Creeks), 324 (Wolf King).

66. Ibid., 319–20.

67. Ibid., 328 and n. 44 (Salechi). On June 5 Mad Dog told Ellis that on his way down to Savannah he had met Salechi on the path. He identified him as "the Chehaw King," a transposition perhaps due to the close association of Ouseechee and Chehaw as "point towns." Ibid., 323.

68. Ibid., 322–23 (Mad Dog), 325–26 ("not less"). On June 2 a joint address from both houses of the Georgia assembly urged Ellis "to suffer Justice to give Way to Prudence" in his dealings with the Creeks. *CRG*, 16:499.

69. Oliphant, *Anglo-Cherokee Frontier*, 123–34, esp. 132, and 140.

70. *GT*, 325–27.

71. *CRG*, 28, pt. 1:280–85.

72. *GT*, 329–30.

73. Ibid., 330–31.

74. Ellis to Board of Trade, October 20, 1760, *CRG*, 28, pt. 1:288–90; James Wright to Upper and Lower Creeks, November 7, 1760, *GT*, 334–35. Wright identified the Lower Creek intermediaries as "Wehanny the Cusseta Mico, Toopa-Hatkee [Tupahutke], and Ocoatly [Occothli]," the last two from Chehaw.

75. *CRG*, 28, pt. 1:288–89; *GT*, 332–34 (quotes).

76. *CRG*, 28, pt. 1:288–89 (most quotes); *GT*, 333–34 ("made straight" and "large Supplies").

77. *CRG*, 28, pt. 1:288–90.

78. Oliphant, *Anglo-Cherokee Frontier*, 136–39.

79. Ibid., 140–43 ("bluntness" at 143), 152.

80. *GT*, 334–37.

81. *CRG*, 8:423–24.

82. *GT*, 337–40.

83. Ibid., 341–42; *CRG*, 28, pt. 1:309 ("Mohawks").

84. Wright to Board of Trade, February 20, 1761, *CRG*, 28, pt. 1:301–4, quotes at 303; same to same, May 16, 1761, ibid., 332–35, quote at 334. For Wright's tally, see ibid., 293, 302, 309, 334.

85. Oliphant, *Anglo-Cherokee Frontier*, 140–47.

86. *GT*, 342–43.

87. Ibid., 343.

88. On Little Tallassee see *GFT*, 506–7 n. 6; Saunt, *A New Order of Things*, 70 and fig. 4. A later writer described the townsite as "the old Bob Cornells place, known by some as Little Tallasse—named after Bob's wife, who was a tallasse." Thomas S. Woodward, *Woodward's Reminiscences of the Creek, or Muscogee Indians* (1859; Tuscaloosa: Alabama Book Store, 1939), 107.

89. *GT*, 344. Here the spokesman is erroneously identified as the Wolf King. Wright said the talk came from the Okfuskee Captain and Handsome Fellow. *CRG*, 8:542. Since the spokesman said he was "now grown old," he was probably the former.

90. *CRG*, 8:512 ("written Talk"); *GT*, 345 ("bad Accident"), 346 ("never spilt"). In June a Lower Creek delegation headed by Abraham and Tugulki met with Bull in Charles Town. (In 1756 "half breed Abraham" had been "King of the Covetaws." Ibid., 245.) Abraham told Bull that the talk sent to Wright "contains every thing we have to say to you," which was essentially that "we have resolved never to depart from the English." Tugulki added that the talk "may be relied upon as genuine and sincere." *EAID*, 14:162–63.

91. *GT*, 346–47.

92. *CRG*, 8:468 ("short Time"); ibid., 28, pt. 1:294 ("hemmed in" and "Indian Claim"), 348 ("Release"). Another example of Wright's policy to appease the Creeks came in July. In response to a request from the Mortar, the council (presumably with Wright's support) decided to send him "a Silver Gorget and Arm Plates." Ibid., 8:539.

93. Oliphant, *Anglo-Cherokee Frontier*, 120–21 (1760 terms), 140–46, 149, 180; Bull to Grant, April 14, 1761, S.C.C.H.J., September 15, 1761, C.O.5/479, ff. 112v–113v. The following paragraphs are based mainly on Oliphant's chapters 5 and 6.

94. Henry Laurens to John Ettwein, July 11, 1761, in *Papers of Henry Laurens*, ed. Philip M. Hamer and George C. Rogers, vol. 3 (Columbia: University of South Carolina Press for the South Carolina Historical Society, 1972), 75 (crops), 279, 286, 339.

95. Attakullakulla's answer to Grant, August 31, 1761, C.O.5/479, f. 120; *Pennsylvania Gazette*, October 22, 1761, quoting *South Carolina Gazette*, September 12, 1761 (which does not survive).

96. Grant to Bull, September 2, 1761, in S.C.C.H.J., September 15, 1761, C.O.5/479, ff. 113v–115; Laurens, *Papers*, 3:286. The preliminary and final texts of the treaty are in *EAID*, 14:167–68 and 181–83.

97. Johnstone to Henry Conway, secretary of state, June 23, 1766, *MPAED*, 1:510.

98. *CRG*, 8:777.

99. *GT*, 348–49.

100. Ibid., 350.

101. Ibid., 351.

102. Ibid., 352.

103. Hahn, *Invention*, 258–70, quote at 263.

Bibliography

Primary Sources

MANUSCRIPT COLLECTIONS

Georgia Department of Archives and History, Morrow
Georgia (Colony), Governor and Council Minutes. Record Group 49, Series 15.
Great Britain, Public Record Office [National Archives], London and Kew
Colonial Office Papers. Series 5 and 323.
Society for the Propagation of the Gospel in Foreign Parts, London
American Material in the Archives of the Society for the Propagation of the Gospel. Series A and B (microfilm).
South Carolina Department of Archives and History, Columbia
South Carolina (Colony), Council, Council Journal.
South Carolina (Colony), Secretary, Miscellaneous Records.
South Carolina (Colony), Upper House, Upper House Journal.
University of Georgia Libraries, Athens
The Phillipps Collection of Egmont Manuscripts.
William L. Clements Library, University of Michigan, Ann Arbor
Sir Jeffrey Amherst Papers.
General Thomas Gage Papers
Sir William Lyttelton Papers.
Earl of Shelburne Papers.

TRANSCRIPTS OF MANUSCRIPTS

Georgia Department of Archives and History, Morrow
"The Colonial Records of the State of Georgia." Typescripts of unpublished vols. 33–39.
Georgia Historical Society, Savannah
The Joseph V. Bevan Papers.

Library of Congress, Washington, D.C.

"The Bosomworth Controversy Transcripts," in "The Peter Force Transcripts," Series VII-E, Item 11 (Joseph V. Bevan Collection).

Transcripts of Documents from C.O.5, Public Record Office, London.

South Carolina Department of Archives and History, Columbia

"Records in the British Public Record Office Relating to South Carolina, 1663–1782" (the Sainsbury Transcripts). 36 vols.

University of Georgia Libraries, Athens

Oglethorpe, James Edward. "Introductory Discourse to the State of the Colony of Georgia," October 11, 1739. Egmont Papers, 14204, 123–35.

The Phillipps Collection of Egmont Manuscripts (typescripts).

PUBLISHED PRIMARY SOURCES

Adair, James. *History of the American Indians* [London, 1775]. Ed. Samuel Cole Williams. Johnson City, Tenn.: National Society of Colonial Dames of America, in Tennessee, 1930. Reprint, New York: Promontory Press, 1986.

Atkin, Edmond. *The Appalachian Indian Frontier: The Edmond Atkin Report and Plan of 1755*. Ed. Wilbur R. Jacobs. Columbia: University of South Carolina Press, 1954. Reprint, Lincoln: University of Nebraska Press, 1967.

Bartram, William. *William Bartram on the Southeastern Indians*. Ed. Gregory A. Waselkov and Kathryn E. Holland Braund. Lincoln: University of Nebraska Press, 1995.

Beverley, Robert. *The History and Present State of Virginia* [London, 1705]. Ed. Louis B. Wright. Chapel Hill: University of North Carolina Press, 1947.

The Colonial Records of the State of Georgia. Vols. 1–19, 21–26, ed. Allen D. Candler et al. Atlanta: Franklin Printing and Publishing Co., 1904–16. Vols. 20, 27–32 to date, ed. Kenneth Coleman and Milton Ready. Athens: University of Georgia Press, 1976–89.

Early American Indian Documents: Treaties and Laws, 1607–1789. Gen. ed. Alden T. Vaughan. 20 vols. Bethesda, Md.: University Publications of America, 1979–2004. Vol. 5, *Virginia Treaties, 1723–1775*, ed. W. Stitt Robinson. Vol. 11, *Georgia Treaties, 1733–1763*, ed. John T. Juricek. Vol. 12, *Georgia and Florida Treaties, 1763–1776*, ed. John T. Juricek. Vol. 13, *North and South Carolina Treaties, 1654–1756*, ed. W. Stitt Robinson. Vol. 14, *North and South Carolina Treaties,1756–1775*, ed. W. Stitt Robinson. Vol. 16, *Carolina and Georgia Laws*, ed. Alden T. Vaughan and Deborah A. Rosen.

Egmont, John Percival, First Earl of. *Diary of Viscount Percival, Afterwards First Earl of Egmont*. Ed. R. A. Roberts. 3 vols. London: Historical Manuscripts Commission, 1920–23.

———. *The Journal of the Earl of Egmont: Abstract of the Trustees Proceedings for Establishing the Colony of Georgia, 1732–1738*. Ed. Robert C. McPherson. Athens: University of Georgia Press, 1962.

Georgia (Colony), Register of Records Office. *Abstracts of Georgia Colonial Conveyance*

Book C-1, 1750–1761. Comp. Frances Howell Beckemeyer. Atlanta: R. J. Taylor, Jr., Foundation, 1975.

Gordon, Peter. *The Journal of Peter Gordon, 1732–1735*. Ed. E. Merton Coulter. Athens: University of Georgia Press, 1963.

Jones, George Fenwick, ed. "The Secret Diary of Johann Martin Boltzius." *Georgia Historical Quarterly* 53 (1969): 78–110.

———, ed. "Von Reck's Second Report from Georgia." *William and Mary Quarterly*, 3rd ser., 22 (1965): 319–33.

Lane, Mills, ed. *General Oglethorpe's Georgia: Colonial Letters, 1733–1743*. 2 vols. Savannah: Beehive Press, 1975.

[Martyn, Benjamin]. "History of the Rise, Progress, and Present State of the Colony of Georgia." In *Navigantium atque Itinerantium Biblioteca, or A Complete Collection of Voyages and Travels*, comp. John Harris et al., 2:323–47. London, 1744–48.

Martyn, Benjamin. "An Impartial Enquiry into the State and Utility of the Province of Georgia" (London, 1741). In *The Clamorous Malcontents: Criticisms and Defenses of the Colony of Georgia, 1741–1743*, ed. Trevor R. Reese, 125–78. Savannah: Beehive Press, 1973.

McDowell, William L., Jr., ed. *Documents Relating to Indian Affairs, May 21, 1750–August 7, 1754*. Columbia: South Carolina Archives Department, 1958.

———, ed. *Documents Relating to Indian Affairs, 1754–1765*. Columbia: South Carolina Department of Archives and History, 1970.

———, ed. *Journal of the Commissioners of the Indian Trade, September 20, 1710–August 29, 1718*. Columbia: South Carolina Archives Department, 1955.

Mereness, Newton D., ed. *Travels in the American Colonies*. New York: Macmillan, 1916.

Mississippi Provincial Archives: English Dominion. Vol. 1 (all published). Ed. Dunbar Rowland. Nashville: Brandon Printing Co., 1911.

Mississippi Provincial Archives: French Dominion. Vols. 4 and 5. Ed. Patricia Galloway. Baton Rouge: Mississippi Department of Archives and History, 1984.

Moore, Francis. "A Voyage to Georgia Begun in the Year 1735" [London, 1744]. *Collections of the Georgia Historical Society* 1 (1840): 79–152.

Nairne, Thomas. *Muskhogean Journals: The 1708 Expedition to the Mississippi River*. Ed. Alexander Moore. Jackson: University Press of Mississippi, 1988.

Oglethorpe, James Edward. *The Publications of James Edward Oglethorpe*. Ed. Rodney M. Baine. Athens: University of Georgia Press, 1994.

"Proceedings of the President and Assistants in Council of Georgia, 1749–51." Ed. Lilla M. Hawes. *Georgia Historical Quarterly* 35 (1951): 323–50 and 36 (1952): 46–70.

Reese, Trevor R., ed. *The Clamorous Malcontents: Criticisms and Defenses of the Colony of Georgia, 1741–1743*. Savannah: Beehive Press, 1973.

———, ed. *Our First Visit in America: Early Reports from the Colony of Georgia, 1732–1740*. Savannah: Beehive Press, 1974.

South Carolina (Colony), Commons House of Assembly. *The Journal of the Commons House of Assembly*. Ed. J. H. Easterly et al. 14 vols. to date [covering 1736–56]. Columbia: South Carolina Department of Archives and History, 1951–.

Stephens, William. *The Journal of William Stephens, 1741–1743*. Ed. E. Merton Coulter. 2 vols. Athens: University of Georgia Press, 1958–59.

A True and Historical Narrative of the Colony of Georgia, by Pat. Tailfer and Others, with Comments by the Earl of Egmont. Ed. Clarence L. Ver Steeg. Athens: University of Georgia Press, 1960.

Urlsperger, Samuel. *Detailed Reports on the Salzburger Emigrants Who Settled in America*. Ed. George Fenwick Jones. 17 vols. Athens: University of Georgia Press, 1968–93.

Von Reck, Philip Georg Friedrich. *Von Reck's Voyage: Drawings and Journal of Philip Georg Friedrich von Reck*. Ed. Kristian Hvidt. Savannah: Beehive Press, 1980.

Wesley, Charles. *The Journal of the Rev. Charles Wesley, M.A., Sometime Student of Christ Church, Oxford: The Early Journal, 1736–1739*. Ed. John Telford. London: R. Culley, 1909.

Wesley, John. *The Journal of the Rev. John Wesley, A.M., Sometime Fellow of Lincoln College, Oxford*. Ed. Nehemiah Curnock. Vol. 1. London: R. Culley, 1909.

CONTEMPORARY PERIODICALS

Gentleman's Magazine. London

South Carolina Gazette. Charles Town

Secondary Sources

Abbot, W. W. *The Royal Governors of Georgia, 1754–1775*. Chapel Hill: University of North Carolina Press, 1959.

Alden, John R. *John Stuart and the Southern Colonial Frontier*. Ann Arbor: University of Michigan Press, 1944.

Axtell, James. *The Indians' New South: Cultural Change in the Colonial Southeast*. Baton Rouge: Louisiana State University Press, 1997.

———. "Making Do: Trade in the Eighteenth-Century Southeast." Chapter 5 of Axtell, *Natives and Newcomers*. New York: Oxford University Press, 2001.

Barker, Eirlys. "'Much Blood and Treasure': South Carolina's Indian Traders, 1670–1755." Ph.D. diss., College of William and Mary, 1993.

Braund, Kathryn E. Holland. *Deerskins and Duffels: The Creek Indian Trade with Anglo-America, 1685–1815*. Lincoln: University of Nebraska Press, 1993.

Cashin, Edward J., ed. *Colonial Augusta: "Key of the Indian Country."* Macon: Mercer University Press, 1986.

———. *Governor Henry Ellis and the Transformation of British North America*. Athens: University of Georgia Press, 1994.

———. *Lachlan McGillivray, Indian Trader*. Athens: University of Georgia Press, 1992.

———. *The Story of Augusta*. Augusta: Richmond County Board of Education, 1980.

Coleman, Kenneth. *Colonial Georgia: A History*. New York: KTO Press, 1976.

Corkran, David H. *The Cherokee Frontier: Conflict and Survival, 1740–62*. Norman: University of Oklahoma Press, 1962.

———. *The Creek Frontier, 1540–1783*. Norman: University of Oklahoma Press, 1967.

Crane, Verner W. *The Southern Frontier, 1670–1732*. Durham: Duke University Press, 1928.

Cumming, William P. *The Southeast in Early Maps*. 3rd ed., revised and enlarged by Louis De Vorsey Jr. Chapel Hill: University of North Carolina Press, 1998.

De Vorsey, Louis, Jr. "Indian Boundaries in Colonial Georgia." *Georgia Historical Quarterly* 54 (1970): 63–78.

———. *The Indian Boundary in the Southern Colonies, 1763–1775*. Chapel Hill: University of North Carolina Press, 1966.

———. "Maps in Colonial Promotion: James Edward Oglethorpe's Use of Maps in 'Selling' the Georgia Scheme." *Imago Mundi* 38 (1986): 35–45.

Driver, Harold. *Indians of North America*. Chicago: University of Chicago Press, 1961.

Ethridge, Robbie. *Creek Country: The Creek Indians and their World*. Chapel Hill: University of North Carolina Press, 2003.

Ethridge, Robbie, and Charles Hudson, eds. *The Transformation of the Southeastern Indians, 1540–1760*. Jackson: University Press of Mississippi, 2002.

Ettinger, Amos A. *James Edward Oglethorpe: Imperial Idealist*. Oxford: Clarendon Press, 1936.

Fabel, Robin F. A. "St. Marks, Apalachee, and the Creeks." *Gulf Coast Historical Review* 1 (1986): 4–22.

Fisher, Doris. "Mary Musgrove: Creek Englishwoman." Ph.D. diss., Emory University, 1990.

Forbes, Jack D. *Africans and Native Americans: The Language of Race and the Evolution of Red-Black Peoples*. 2nd ed. Urbana: University of Illinois Press, 1993.

Gallay, Alan. *The Formation of a Planter Elite: Jonathan Bryan and the Southern Colonial Frontier*. Athens: University of Georgia Press, 1989.

———. *The Indian Slave Trade: The Rise of English Empire in the American South, 1670–1717*. New Haven: Yale University Press, 2002.

Galloway, Patricia. "'The Chief Who Is Your Father': Choctaw and French Views of the Diplomatic Relation." In *Powhatan's Mantle: Indians in the Colonial Southeast*, ed. Peter H. Wood, Gregory A. Waselkov, and M. Thomas Hatley, 254–78. Lincoln: University of Nebraska Press, 1989.

———. "Choctaw Factionalism and Civil War, 1746–1750." In *The Choctaw before Removal*, ed. Carolyn Keller Reeves, 120–56. Jackson: University Press of Mississippi, 1985.

———. *Choctaw Genesis*. Lincoln: University of Nebraska Press, 1995.

Goff, John H. "Of Warriors and Chiefs." *Emory University Quarterly* 9 (1953): 95–110.

———. "The Path to Oakfuskee." *Georgia Historical Quarterly* 39 (1955): 1–36, 152–71.

———. *Placenames of Georgia*. Ed. Francis Lee Utley and Marion R. Hemperley. Athens: University of Georgia Press, 1975.

Granger, Mary, ed. *Savannah River Plantations*. Savannah: Georgia Historical Society, 1947.

Green, Michael. "Mary Musgrove: Creating a New World." In *Sifters: Native American Women's Lives*, ed. Theda Perdue, 29–47. New York: Oxford University Press, 2001.

Hahn, Steven C. "The Invention of the Creek Nation." Ph.D. diss., Emory University, 2000.

———. *The Invention of the Creek Nation, 1670–1763*. Lincoln: University of Nebraska Press, 2004.

Hann, John H. *Apalachee: The Land between the Rivers*. Gainesville: University Press of Florida, 1988.

Harris, Marshall. *Origin of the Land Tenure System in the United States*. Ames: Iowa State College Press, 1953.

Hatley, Tom. *The Dividing Paths: Cherokees and South Carolinians through the Era of Revolution*. New York: Oxford University Press, 1993.

Hudson, Charles. *The Southeastern Indians*. Knoxville: University of Tennessee Press, 1976.

Ivers, Larry E. *British Drums on the Southern Frontier: The Military Colonization of Georgia, 1733–1749*. Chapel Hill: University of North Carolina Press, 1974.

Jones, George Fenwick. "Portrait of an Irish Entrepreneur in Colonial Augusta: John Rae 1708–1772." *Georgia Historical Quarterly* 83 (1999): 427–47.

———. *The Salzburger Saga*. Athens: University of Georgia Press, 1984.

Juricek, John T. "English Territorial Claims in North America under Elizabeth and the Early Stuarts." *Terrae Incognitae* 7 (1975): 7–22.

Lanning, John Tate. *The Diplomatic History of Georgia*. Chapel Hill: University of North Carolina Press, 1936.

Lester, Geoffrey. "Primitivism versus Civilization: A Basic Question in the Law of Aboriginal Rights to Land." In *Our Footprints are Everywhere*, ed. Carol Brice-Bennett, 351–74. Ottawa: Labrador Inuit Association, 1977.

MacMillan, Ken. *Sovereignty and Possession in the English New World: The Legal Foundations of Empire, 1576–1640*. New York: Cambridge University Press, 2006.

McNeil, Kent. *Common Law Aboriginal Title*. Oxford: Clarendon Press, 1989.

Mellon, Knox, Jr. "Christian Priber's Cherokee 'Kingdom of Paradise.'" *Georgia Historical Quarterly* 57 (1973): 319–46.

Meriwether, Robert L. *The Expansion of South Carolina, 1729–1765*. Kingsport, Tenn.: Southern Publishers, 1940.

Merrell, James H. *The Indians' New World: Catawbas and Their Neighbors from European Contact through the Era of Removal*. Chapel Hill: University of North Carolina Press, 1989.

Milling, Chapman J. *Red Carolinians*. 2nd ed. Columbia: University of South Carolina Press, 1969.

Moore, John H. "Mvskoke Personal Names." *Names* 43 (1995): 187–212.

Neill, Wilfred T. "The Galphin Trading Post Site at Silver Bluff, South Carolina." *Florida Anthropologist* 21 (1968): 42–54.

Nelson, Paul David. *General James Grant: Scottish Soldier and Royal Governor of East Florida*. Gainesville: University Press of Florida, 1993.

Oatis, Steven J. *A Colonial Complex: South Carolina's Frontiers in the Era of the Yamasee War, 1680–1730*. Lincoln: University of Nebraska Press, 2004.

Oliphant, John. *Peace and War on the Anglo-Cherokee Frontier, 1756–63*. Baton Rouge: Louisiana State University Press, 2001.

Perdue, Theda. *Mixed Blood Indians: Racial Construction in the Early South*. Athens: University of Georgia Press, 2003.

Piker, Joshua A. *Okfuskee: A Creek Indian Town in Colonial America*. Cambridge: Harvard University Press, 2004.

Ramsey, William L. *The Yamasee War: A Study of Culture, Economy, and Conflict in the Colonial South*. Lincoln: University of Nebraska Press, 2008.

Reese, Trevor R. *Colonial Georgia: A Study in British Imperial Policy in the Eighteenth Century*. Athens: University of Georgia Press, 1963.

Reid, John Philip. *A Better Kind of Hatchet: Law, Trade, and Diplomacy in the Cherokee Nation during the Early Years of European Contact*. University Park: Pennsylvania State University Press, 1976.

Robinson, W. Stitt. *James Glen: From Scottish Provost to Royal Governor of South Carolina*. Westport, Conn.: Greenwood Press, 1996.

Saunt, Claudio. *A New Order of Things: Property, Power, and the Transformation of the Creek Indians, 1733–1816*. New York: Cambridge University Press, 1999.

Shoemaker, Nancy. *A Strange Likeness: Becoming Red and White in Eighteenth-Century North America*. New York: Oxford University Press, 2004.

Sirmans, M. Eugene. *Colonial South Carolina: A Political History, 1663–1763*. Chapel Hill: University of North Carolina Press, 1966.

Spalding, Phinizy. *Oglethorpe in America*. Chicago: University of Chicago Press, 1977.

Spalding, Phinizy, and Harvey H. Jackson, eds. *Oglethorpe in Perspective: Georgia's Founder after Two Hundred Years*. Tuscaloosa: University of Alabama Press, 1989.

Sturtevant, William C. "Creek into Seminole." In *North American Indians in Historical Perspective*, ed. Eleanor Burke Leacock and Nancy Oestreich Lurie, 92–128. New York: Random House, 1971.

———, ed. *A Creek Sourcebook*. New York: Garland, 1987.

Swanton, John R. *Early History of the Creek Indians and Their Neighbors*. U.S. Bureau of American Ethnology, Bulletin 73. Washington, D.C.: Government Printing Office, 1922.

———. "Social Organization and Social Usages of the Indians of the Creek Confederacy." In *Forty-second Annual Report of the Bureau of American Ethnology*, 23–472. Washington, D.C.: Government Printing Office, 1928.

Sweet, Julie Anne. *Negotiating for Georgia: British-Creek Relations in the Trustee Era, 1733–1752*. Athens: University of Georgia Press, 2005.

Temple, Sarah B. Gober, and Kenneth Coleman. *Georgia Journeys*. Athens: University of Georgia Press, 1961.

Thomas, David H. "Fort Toulouse: The French Outpost at the Alibamos on the Coosa." *Alabama Historical Quarterly* 22 (1960): 139–230.

Usner, Daniel H. *Indians, Settlers, and Slaves in a Frontier Exchange Economy: The Lower Mississippi Valley before 1783*. Chapel Hill: University of North Carolina Press, 1992.

Vaughan, Alden T. *Transatlantic Encounters: American Indians in Britain, 1500–1776*. New York: Cambridge University Press, 2006.

Waselkov, Gregory A. "Indian Maps of the Colonial Southeast." In *Powhatan's Mantle*, ed. Peter H. Wood, Gregory A. Waselkov, and M. Thomas Hatley, 292–343. Lincoln: University of Nebraska Press, 1989.

Waselkov, Gregory A., and Marvin T. Smith. "Upper Creek Archeology." In *Indians of the Greater Southeast: Historical Archeology and Ethnohistory*, ed. Bonnie G. McEwan, 242–64. Gainesville: University Press of Florida, 2000.

White, Richard. *The Roots of Dependency: Subsistence, Environment, and Social Change among the Choctaws, Pawnees, and Navajos*. Lincoln: University of Nebraska Press, 1983.

Willis, William S. "Patrilineal Institutions in Southeastern North America." *Ethnohistory* 10 (1963): 250–69.

Wood, Peter, Gregory A. Waselkov, and M. Thomas Hatley, eds. *Powhatan's Mantle: Indians in the Colonial Southeast*. Lincoln: University of Nebraska Press, 1989.

Woods, Patricia Dillon. *French-Indian Relations on the Southern Frontier, 1699–1762*. Ann Arbor: UMI Research Press, 1980.

Worth, John E. "The Lower Creeks: Origins and Early History." In *Indians of the Greater Southeast: Historical Archeology and Ethnohistory*, ed. Bonnie G. McEwan, 265–98. Gainesville: University Press of Florida, 2000.

———. *Struggle for the Georgia Coast: An Eighteenth-Century Retrospective on Guale and Mocama*. Athens: University of Georgia Press, 1995.

Wright, J. Leitch. *Creeks and Seminoles*. Lincoln: University of Nebraska Press, 1986.

Index

John T. Juricek is professor of history at Emory University. He is the editor of volumes 11 (*Georgia Treaties, 1733–1763*) and 12 (*Georgia and Florida Treaties, 1763–1776*) of *Early American Indians Documents: Treaties and Laws* (20 vols.; University Publications of America, 1979–2004).